IRISH STAMP DUTY LAW

IRISH STAMP DUTY LAW

Fourth Edition

by

David Donegan
BCL (NUI), AITI,
Solicitor, Henry PF Donegan & Son Solicitors, Cork

&

Raymond J Friel
BCL (NUI), LLM, (Exon),
BL (Kings Inn),
School of Law, University of Limerick

Edited by

Amanda-Jayne Comyn
BBLS, BL, AITI, TEP

Tottel
publishing

Tottel Publishing, Maxwelton House, 41–43 Boltro Road, Haywards Heath, West Sussex, RH16 1BJ

A CIP Catalogue record for this book is available from the British Library.

ISBN 10: 1 84592 069 4
ISBN 13: 978 1 84592 069 2

Typeset by Marlex Editorial Services Ltd, Dublin, Ireland
Printed and bound in Great Britain by William Clowes Limited, Beccles, Suffolk

Preface

Since the book's original publication in 1995, and the publication of the subsequent editions, stamp duty rates on commercial properties have been increased substantially, while no allowance has been made for the increase in property prices in the intervening period.

Due to the financial pressure on first time buyers/owner occupiers, and the increase in property prices in Ireland due to the Celtic Tiger, the Government was forced to amend the rates applying to first-time buyers/owner occupiers to reduce the stamp duty burden placed on them in purchasing properties.

This did result in a lower rate of stamp duty for prospective purchasers, but the effect of lowering the stamp duty rate is that it increased the amount charged by the vendor so that there is no real saving to the house buyers.

As a method of fiscal control, stamp duty is not appropriate and in practice does not work.

The Stamp Duty Consolidation Act 1999 resulted in the consolidation of all prior legislation, which commenced with The Stamp Duty Act 1891, and has been tampered with by the legislature over a period of 108 years, resulting in complex stamp duty provisions.

Consolidation did assist in the interpretation of stamp duty, but the legislature should have used this as an opportunity to consolidate and codify the legislation to ensure it was more rational and coherent in its structure.

We, as authors, have advocated such amendment to the legislation since the publication of the first edition in 1995. The onus of collecting stamp duty is placed on the purchasers' solicitors, as each document is subsequently presented to the Stamp Office for stamping. Solicitors are charged with the responsibility of advising correctly in respect of the stamp duty implications of any such Instrument executed by their client and the full review of the legislation to simplify matters would be of great assistance to all parties concerned including the Stamps Office.

We felt it important to review the approach taken in completing this new edition and Amanda undertook responsibility of revising and editing the book which has resulted, we hope, in a new user-friendly fourth edition.

This approach resulted in the expansion of some chapters and the insertion of further chapters and examples, while maintaining the original ethos of the book.

We would like to thank all of those who assisted us, namely David and Raymond's spouses Majella and Rena, and Amanda's family who suffered most during the production of this fourth edition.

We would like to thank Grant Thornton, Chartered Accountants and Tax Advisers, Amanda's employers, who facilitated her work in the project, and all our friends for their support and assistance.

David and Raymond wish to acknowledge the substantial amount of work done by Amanda in this edition of the book, and for her new approach and input, which resulted in a more indepth study of the stamp duty legislation.

We would like to thank Totttel Publishing and in particular Amy Hayes, Sandra Mulvey and Marian Sullivan for all their assistance.

The responsibility for this work is ours, and ours alone, and we have endeavoured to state the law as we believe it to be as of the first day of July 2006.

David P Donegan

Raymond J Friel

Amanda-Jayne Comyn, Editor

Cork, 1 July 2006.

Contents

Chapter 6 Leasehold Interests

Table of Cases

A

B

I

J

K

L

M

N

O

S

T

U

Table of Statutes

Ireland

Stamp Duties Consolidation Act 1999 (contd)

Stamp Duties Consolidation Act 1999 (contd)

Stamp Duties Consolidation Act 1999 (contd)

Statutory Instruments

European Council Directives

European Legislation

Chapter 1

Introduction to Stamp Duty

Common law

[1.01] There are two principal legal systems in the western world, both of which originated in Europe. The civil law system operates in mainland Europe. In Ireland and most English-speaking nations, the common law system operates. This system emerged from the Norman conquest of England in 1066. When the Norman duke declared himself King of England, he confiscated all of the land and began to divide it amongst his followers as payment for their support. They in turn would use the land as payment for their followers, and so on. This sequence of events had two consequences. Firstly, from the King's point of view it ensured loyalty from his followers as otherwise they would forfeit their land which would revert to the King. Secondly, as they now had tenancy of this land they would have to complete the process of being subjugated if it were to yield an income from them.

[1.02] Disputes which arose would be resolved by the King. He delegated this particular role to the judges of the King's Bench and they travelled the length and breadth of the country dispensing the King's justice. Such justice was common to all and it was from this that the term the common law arises. When resolving private disputes, judges could not be seen to be making rules and regulations, for that was exclusively in the province of the King. Instead they based their authority on the ability to declare law that had existed since time immemorial but which had not been written down. By using this fiction they did not blur the lines of decision in making within society. The King, or whatever body replaced him, had the exclusive power to make laws or change them, the judges merely told them what the existing law was. Until recent times the extent of such power in the judiciary was immense, given the fact that legislation was relatively rare. Today the body of legislation in existence has become increasingly large and important particularly in light of EU legislation. Nonetheless, the role of the judiciary remains paramount in the common law, but is restricted in regard to EU legislation.

[1.03] It is useful to clearly enumerate a number of characteristics that flow from the historical evolution of the common law. The role of judges is pre-eminent for they declare the law, but more than that, until the law is so declared, it is effectively unknown. No matter how interesting a point may appear, or how desirable from everybody's point of view that a definitive ruling should be made, no such declaration will be made by a judge until such time as a real dispute arises before the courts. The common law, unlike the civil law, is only defined to the extent necessary to resolve an existing dispute: there is no theoretical or abstract law. Moreover, the law is merely declared, not made by the judges. The natural consequence of such an ideology is that once declared the judges have no option but to apply it – any change is the function of the Sovereign, that is the King or parliament. Each decision is important not merely because it declares law which had previously been unknown but also because it acts as a precedent by which all future cases of a similar nature must be decided. The precedent, being a declaration of existing law, must be followed by all courts, no matter how absurd such an application may be. We shall see later that a rigid application of such a declaratory doctrine gave rise to a rival legal system – equity. The undesirability of such a concept has in modern times been abrogated by judicial techniques and pronouncement, which effectively recognise the true law-making nature of the judges. Every single decision of every court does not constitute a precedent. The ability to declare law was confined to the upper echelons of the judiciary, the Supreme Court. Finally the common law is an ad hoc development. The Declaration of Law comes from actual disputes and in many ways justice is sought in individual cases without regard to the future. Yet the decision binds future courts.

Equity

[1.04] The advantages of certainty in a legal system which uses the doctrine of precedent can be outweighed by the danger of growing irrelevancy as the declared laws are not changed by the legislature quickly enough to meet changing circumstances. The common law nearly became obsolete by its insistence on following previously decided cases, even when this resulted in the court refusing jurisdiction over certain types of disputes and deciding cases against the interests of justice. By the fifteenth and sixteenth centuries the doctrine of precedent had become so rigid that many litigants felt unhappy with the common law courts. Such litigants began to appeal directly to the King. These cases were delegated to the Chancellor for resolution of the dispute and the Chancellor began to dispense justice rather than administer the law.

[1.05] The common law courts reformed to face the competition. They implemented a more refined use of the doctrine of precedent, increased jurisdiction and a desire to compete with the Chancellor and his court of equity. Equity never overruled the common law. The concept of remedies at common law consisted of damages, that is monetary compensation, but this was extended by the equitable remedies of injunctions, specific performance, etc. Equity created new causes of action and gave ancillary relief where the law did not. Competition between the two courts grew. Some common law lawyers began to be appointed to the courts of equity and they formed an administrative system modelled on the common law and introduced the doctrine of precedent into the decisions of equity. By the early nineteenth century, the common law and equity had come to dominate the legal scene – a far from satisfactory a situation. A litigant might commence action in the common law court only to find that he would not get judgment in that court but would have in the court of equity. The long process would then have to begin all over again. There were many other abuses which were eventually resolved by the reform Acts of the mid-nineteenth century. The Judicature Act 1877 fused the two courts into a unified court which would administer both equity and the common law. Where the two differed, equity was to prevail. It is important to remember that the legal systems were not fused, only the courts of application. Equity and the common law as two legal systems still exist today.

Legal title and trusts

[1.06] Real property is land or anything attached to land. An item attached to land may constitute real property depending on the degree of the permanence of the attachment. If it can be removed without damage to either the land or to itself, then it is normally regarded as personal property. But if the removal would destroy the item or damage the land then it is considered real property. A difficulty arises where a freehold interest is not attached directly to the land but is suspended in air, for example a second floor flat. These are known as "flying freeholds". Since at common law it is only land in its natural state that is entitled to support from its neighbours, theoretically it is possible to destroy the ground floor apartment, causing the flying freehold to disappear. To overcome these difficulties, most apartments are sold by way of a leasehold interest and a covenant for support and shelter is included in the terms of the lease (for an Australian approach, see New South Wales Strata Titles Act 1976). However, for the purposes of this text, these apartments are sufficiently attached to the land to be considered real property.

The common law recognised the following legal titles to real property:

Freehold

[1.07]

(a) *Fee simple*: This estate is the largest possible estate in land but it is not absolute. It has the potential to last forever. However, at some point in the future it may come to an end, for example where the current owner of the fee simple interest dies without benefit of a will and there are no ascertainable relatives who are entitled to the estate under the intestate provisions of the Succession Act 1965. Where no person is entitled to the estate, the land will revert back to the State by virtue of the Succession Act 1965, s 73 as ultimate intestate successor. This is a legacy of English law where ultimately the King held all land in an allodial system of land holding. A fee simple is alienable and inheritable. Alienable means that the property is capable of being disposed of, that is the property can be transferred by way of sale or gift. Inheritable means that the property can be passed on the death of the owner either by way of a will, or under the laws of intestacy;

(b) *Fee tail*: This estate is of lesser extent than a fee simple. It is limited to the direct lineal descendants of a particular person and is of indefinite duration. It will come to an end at some stage and the land will then revert back to the holder of the fee simple. A fee tail is alienable by virtue of the Settled Land Acts and is descendible. Descendible means the interest in the land passes on the death of the owner by way of family relationship. It cannot pass by way of a will;

(c) *A life estate*: This estate lasts for as long as the life upon which the estate is dependant. The tenant for life is limited in the enjoyment of the land and the interest, whilst alienable, is neither inheritable nor descendible. A life estate may depend upon the life of stranger to the land, that is, the property could be held by A for the life of the local bishop for example. This is called a life estate *pur autre vie*. Some of these life estates *pur autre vie* were made renewable forever, so that when the local bishop died, his name could be replaced on the payment of a 'fine' to the superior owner of the land. In many instances this life estate was made renewable forever. Thus the nature of the holding was freehold but subject to the payment of fines. Such interests created after 1849 are now deemed to operate as a fee farm grant, pursuant to the Renewable Leasehold Conversion Act 1849. Such interests created prior to 1849 which were not converted under the above Act into fee farm grants, now take effect as a fee simple (Landlord and Tenant (Amendment) Act 1980, s 74);

(d) *Fee farm grant*: This is a hybrid freehold estate being a fee simple subject to the payment of a rent. It is found virtually only in Ireland;

(e) *A base fee*: This is an estate less than a fee simple and arises where a fee tail has not been enlarged into a fee simple, for example, the incorrect execution of a disentailing assurance.

[1.08] More than one freehold interest can exist over land at any one time. For example Blackacre might be held in fee simple by Harry, subject to the fee tail of Dick subject to the life estate of Tom. Tom may also grant a leasehold interest to Miriam for 3 years. A multiplicity of owners is quite possible. Given that each of these people in turn reflect only the legal title to Blackacre, there could be as many, if not more equitable owners of each of these estates. The legal owner of property is the person in whose name the property is recorded. The legal owner may be required to exercise the benefit of ownership in favour of another. The person who is to receive this benefit is known as the equitable or beneficial owner of the property.[1]

Example 1.08.1

By conveyance dated 12 October 2003, Mary, who owns the fee simple, grants Joseph a fee tail over Whiteacre. By conveyance dated 23 October 2003, Joseph granted Simon a life estate. Simon gives a lease for 9 months to Fiona on 1 January 2004.

Freehold interests in the property:

Mary: fee simple reversion.

Joseph: fee tail

Simon: life estate

Leasehold interests in the property:

Fiona: lease for term certain (9 months)

Leasehold

[1.09]

(a) *Term certain*: This is a temporary interest in property limited to a specific length of time – for example a 900-year lease;

(b) *Periodic tenancy*: This is a temporary interest in property and on a continuing renewal basis. The parties anticipate that at the end of the term the tenancy will be renewed for the same period, though it may be terminated on notice. For example, a weekly letting of a flat;

(c) *Tenancy at will/sufferance*: These tenancies arise in special situations – for example overholding by a tenant at the expiry of a term certain.

---

1 See para **[1.04]**.

[1.10] Real property means land, or anything attached to land, or estate or interest therein. All other property is classified as personal property.[2] For personal property, legal title is a matter of public regulation or private agreement. Certain personal property (cars, ships, etc, for example) must be registered by a State authority and will be issued with a certificate of legal ownership. For other property not registered by the State, the legal title is that identified by the contract of sale or that which arises by operation of law. Legal ownership of personal property lasts for as long as the property exists.

[1.11] The legal title to property, real or personal, does not necessarily mean the true ownership. The legal title could be held on trust for someone else. The trust originated in the time of the Crusades. During the Crusades, English landowners would leave England to fight in the Holy Land. The common law was based on feudal notions and prohibited women from holding land in their own right and the right of ownership to land was based on presence. Propertied men would transfer the legal ownership of the land to a relative or friend on the basis that they would tend to the obligations of land ownership during the owner's absence and later would return the legal title to the owner. If the owner was married, the relative or friend would ensure that the family was looked after.

[1.12] The dangers in such a transaction are obvious. The owner's absence for a year or two, the high mortality rates in the times of the Crusades and the poor communication network encouraged the relative or friend to believe that he was the owner of the land which had been given to him as a custodian. Very often the owner's family would be thrown out. The land itself might be sold since the custodian had the legal title to the property and full power of disposition over it. Upon return, the true owner would seek redress through the common law courts. There would be no resolution there since it had all been legally achieved.

[1.13] The owner would then appeal to the King for justice. This appeal would be dealt with by the Chancellor and his courts of equity. Equity would honour the law: the custodian was the legal owner but his rights of ownership would be exercised in favour of the true owner. This avoided a direct confrontation with the common law yet still achieved justice. The legal owner had to exercise the privileges of legal ownership in favour of the real owner or the equitable owner of the land. Land could now be owned in two ways: legally by the common law courts or beneficially by the courts of equity, and this concept of ownership became known as a trust. This division of ownership would prove useful in all sorts of arrangements, and became a vehicle for tax planning.

[1.14] A trust is defined as:

> an equitable obligation, binding a person (who is called a trustee) to deal with property over which he has control (which is called the trust property) for the benefit of persons (who are called the beneficiaries) of whom he himself may be one, and any of whom may enforce the trust.[3]

---

2 See para **[1.06]**.

3 Underhill, *Law of Trusts and Trustees* (15th edn, 1995).

to which has been added:

> or for a charitable purpose, which may be enforced at the instance of the Attorney General, or for some other purpose permitted by law though unenforceable.[4]

A trust is the responsibility the legal owner of property owes to another person or persons in respect of that property, arising either by express creation or operation of law and which does not offend public policy.

[1.15] A trust can protect an interest in property which the beneficiary of the trust may not be in a position to legally hold, because they are, for example, a minor, incapacitated person, etc. A trust may be created to disguise ownership, to reduce a tax liability, to ensure a course of action is maintained in one's absence or to pass wealth to others. There will be three parties involved: the settlor, the person who vests the legal title in another person, the trustee/trustees, the person or persons in whom the legal title is vested, and the beneficiary/beneficiaries, the person or persons for whom the benefit of the property is to be exercised. There are in general no restrictions on who may be appointed a trustee. A trustee of property may be the settlor or beneficiary, though care should be taken with the appointment of minors, mentally disturbed persons, corporate bodies and statutory bodies. Whilst it is possible for a trustee to also be a beneficiary, this would not be so where there is complete unity as to the identity of the trustees and the beneficiaries, since if the legal and beneficial title are the same there is no trust.

[1.16] Almost anyone can be a trustee, the one exception being a corporation prohibited from being a trustee by its articles or memorandum of association. A trustee is expected to perform to a certain standard, not merely in the interests of preserving the trust, but to avoid legal liability for shortfalls. Trusteeship may involve exposure to personal liability. The settlor must have the utmost faith in the trustees since they have absolute power to deal with the trust. More often than not lawyers or accountants are appointed as trustees. The procedure for creating a trust will depend on the nature of the trust property involved, but something will normally be put in writing. Equitable principles apply to trusts. Equity looks to the substance and not the form and it may be that a trust has been created despite failure of formalities at law.

Express trust

[1.17] A classification of trusts has evolved. Express trusts are most common of all trusts. In such trusts, the settlor expressly creates the trust by writing or word of mouth but the intention is clear. In order that a trust may be created, the subject matter must be certain, the objects of the trust must be certain and the words relied on in creating the trust must have been used in an imperative sense so as to show that the settlor intended to create an obligation.

[1.18] Express trusts must have the three certainties – object, property and creation. The object of a trust is normally the beneficiary. The law does not recognise the so called purpose object, such as a trust to encourage fidelity in marriage or sobriety in driving. George Bernard Shaw's legacy to establish a trust to develop a new language on

---

4 Pettit, *Equity and the Law of Trusts* (10th edn, OUP, 2005).

scientific grounds failed. A vague provision such as this has the potential to defeat bone findes purpose trusts however, there are noted exceptions, for example where the purpose is charitable. There is a growing tendency for the courts to be more lenient with respect to purpose trusts. The property of an express trust tends to be certain and few difficulties arise in determining the extent of the trust property. Finally, the intention must be imperative as opposed to being precatory. Phrases like 'in fullest confidence', or 'my desire' have been held to be insufficient.

Resulting trust

[1.19] In a resulting trust, the benefit of the trust reverts back to the settlor because it has failed to be created expressly; for example, there is a failure of one of the certainties. The legal title is in the trustee but the beneficial title has now resulted back to the original settlor. A resulting trust is an express trust gone wrong and the law in refusing to honour the wishes of the settlor, defeats it.

[1.20] Joint bank accounts have caused some difficulties in this area. The traditional view in *Owens v Greene*[5] that joint accounts automatically went to the survivor was overturned in *Lynch v Burke and AIB plc*[6]. The Supreme Court held that a resulting trust would not be applied to a joint bank account where the weight of the surrounding evidence indicated a contractual intention to benefit the surviving account holder. In the absence of such a contractual intention to benefit, a resulting trust arises and the asset remains with the estate.

Implied trust

[1.21] An implied trust occurs where the settlor has failed to create the trust expressly but has acted sufficiently that the court will imply that such a trust has come into existence. The court is giving effect to the settlor's wishes and curing the defect. It may be impossible to tell what the settlor's intentions are and the court may impose its own view of what the settlor's intentions are.

Constructive trust

[1.22] This trust is imposed upon the parties concerned irrespective of their desires. It is designed to prevent the unjust or fraudulent enrichment of one person at the expense of another. For example, one who is in a fiduciary relationship may find a constructive trust imposed upon them with respect to any profit, advantage or gain arising personally to them. A stranger who interferes with trust property becomes, by virtue of the law, a constructive trustee, provided that he is not a bona fide purchaser for value and without notice. Finally, the vendor of property becomes a constructive trustee until such time as the consideration and possession of the property is exchanged. Under the principles of contract law, an agreement for sale passes the ownership of the property to the purchaser. It is not dependent upon the receipt of the consideration. However, case law in Ireland has indicated that beneficial ownership only passes to the extent that consideration has been discharged on foot of the contract. Once the agreement has been completed, the

5 *Owens v Greene* [1932] IR 225.

6 *Lynch v Burke and AIB plc* V ITR 391.

equitable ownership of the item in question transfers to the purchaser and the vendor is a constructive trustee, since he still holds the legal title. This is a constructive trust because it is imposed by the law and not by intent. The scope of this constructive trust is far from clear; it applies only to the property in question and not anything which is substituted for it, such as the proceeds of an insurance policy.[7] This concept has been criticised and there are alternative remedies available to the parties to such a contract, which do not require the imposition of such a trust. It should be noted that contracts for the sale of property undertaken in accordance with the *Law Society General Conditions of Sale* (2001 Edition) hold the vendor liable for any loss or damage between the date of the contract for sale and the date of closing, effectively reversing the position with respect to these contracts, including any chattels purchased.

Discretionary trust

[1.23] A discretionary trust is an express trust that leaves the payment of the trust fund at the discretion of the trustees. No beneficiary has a right to any of the trust property. The advantage of this type of trust is twofold: it prevents the payment of trust funds to those beneficiaries who are incapable of managing their own affairs and it may be used to reduce or defer a tax liability.

Protective trust

[1.24] A protective trust aims to protect certain interests in the event of the bankruptcy of a particular person. For example, suppose property is given to a daughter by her father on her marriage. In order to prevent the property being available for distribution on the daughter being declared a bankrupt, she would be given a determinable life interest which would determine, on the declaration of bankruptcy, at which point the property would be held on trust for the benefit of the daughter, her spouse and children. This form of trust would be appropriate to protect an underwriter in a Lloyd's syndicate. This trust must be expressly created and it cannot be created in favour of the settlor.

Beneficial ownership

[1.25] The concept of beneficial ownership is crucial to the trust. It is also of general importance in the area of tax mitigation. For example, relief from stamp duty may only be available if the taxpayer has the beneficial ownership of the property. In most situations both legal and equitable title subsist within the one individual. Thus:

> It is a mistake to assume that the law always requires the separate existence of two different kinds of ownership ... Equity in fact calls into existence and protects equitable rights and interests in property only where their recognition has been found to be required in order to give effect to its doctrines.[8]

This was approved in *In the Matter of Roche & Mohan* [1990] No 785, Sp-11/2/91.

---

[7] *Simmons v Pennington & Son* [1955] 1 WLR 183.

[8] *Stamp Duties Commissioners (Queensland) v Livingston* [1965] AC 694.

[1.26] The law will normally require that in cases of dispute as to the beneficial ownership of property, if the beneficial ownership is not with the legal owner then it must be with someone else, so that:

> ... if anyone says that (he or she) has lost part of its beneficial interest, that proposition can only be established if it can be shown that it has gone somewhere.[9]

For example, where a deposit account is given as security for a loan and the borrower is not able to withdraw the funds from this account, then the interest arising on the account belongs beneficially to the borrower, even though his or her freedom to deal with the account is limited.[10] No one else has a right to deal with the interest or indeed the account, until the borrower defaults.[11]

[1.27] In *Wood Preservation Ltd v Prior*[12] two definite viewpoints emerge as to beneficial ownership. Firstly, the crucial element was whether or not an order of specific performance could be made; if so, the beneficial ownership would be that of the person who would be entitled to such order. The order for specific performance compels a party, against whom it is made, to comply with an agreement that had been reached. Secondly, the Court of Appeal looked at the problem from the viewpoint of the legal owner and his rights or limitations in dealing with the property. The divergence in these viewpoints is not academic, as it suggests that if the Court of Appeal's reasoning is correct, there might be situations where no one has beneficial ownership. It is necessary to determine who exactly is the beneficial owner. This approach was adopted for stamp duty cases. In *J Sainsbury plc v O'Connor*,[13] the exercise of a call option over shares did not effect the beneficial ownership of those shares prior to its exercise. The legal owner was able to enjoy the benefits of ownership. The call option fettered the rights of disposal but did not sufficiently interfere with the benefits of ownership to impact on the equitable title to the shares. The decisions of the courts have distinguished cases between charging and relieving provisions. A charging provision normally places more emphasis on determining the beneficial ownership. A relief is of lesser significance and the courts infer that the beneficial title is in suspense. This is difficult to justify as the non-availability of a relief to duty can be as detrimental as a charge to liability and the distinction has not been fully explained on a logical basis.

[1.28] The decision in *The English Sewing Cotton Co v CIR*[14] has not been entirely superseded. The dissenting judgment of Widgery LJ in *Wood Preservation Ltd v Prior*[15] is worthy of mention:

> I have found it difficult to accept a proposition that on a contract of sale of this kind the beneficial ownership can leave the vendor without simultaneously arriving in the purchaser. I appreciate that there are many other circumstances in which there may be no

---

9 *The English Sewing Cotton Co v CIR* [1947] 1 All ER 679, per Greene MR.

10 *Pearcha v Miley* [1989] STC 76.

11 However, see *McPherson v Bond* [1985] STC 678.

12 *Wood Preservation Ltd v Prior* [1969] 1 All ER 364.

13 *J Sainsbury plc v O'Connor* [1991] STC 318.

14 *The English Sewing Cotton Co v CIR* [1947] 1 All ER 679.

15 *Wood Preservation Ltd v Prior* [1969] 1 All ER 364.

> identifiable beneficial owner of property, but I would have thought that where an unquestioned beneficial owner enters into a contract for sale he should be regarded as remaining a beneficial owner until the interest has passed to the purchaser.

In this case, the difference between the beneficial ownership being in suspense or with the purchaser had little impact since it was not with the vendor. In *J Sainsbury plc v O'Connor*[16] the judgment of the Court of Appeal navigated a fine line between reversing the decision in *Wood Preservation Ltd v Prior* and simply refusing to apply it. Lloyd J stated in that case:

> ... it is difficult at any rate in the case of a contract, to see how the equitable ownership could have been severed from the legal ownership unless it has passed to somebody else. There are of course special circumstances in which a person may be deprived of the beneficial ownership of his assets even though it is not yet possible to identify his successors in title. The best known example would be property held by a trustee in bankruptcy or the property of a company in liquidation. But in all these cases the legal owner is deprived of his beneficial ownership by operation of the law as a consequence of supervening events. I would be reluctant to extend the same context to the case of an ordinary commercial transaction inter partes ...

And Nourse LJ went on:

> ... in the absence of authority to the contrary I am unable to grasp the concept of the beneficial ownership being suspended somewhere between the vendor and the purchaser. I think that it must be vested in one or in the other and, if it has not passed to the purchaser, that it must remain in the vendor.

[1.29] A more cogent argument has been advanced that the characteristics of beneficial ownership will vary depending upon the asset involved. The limiting of one's ability to deal with an asset is not sufficient to transfer the beneficial ownership or put it in suspense. The one exception is where the asset in question has only one attribute of ownership.

> **Example 1.29.1**
>
> Tom has a pre-emptive option to buy shares from Fred for which he paid £10,000.
>
> Tom agrees with Harry not to exercise the option without his consent to enable Harry acquire further shares in Fred's company.
>
> Tom no longer has the beneficial ownership of the option.

To hold shares which are the subject of such an option does not transfer the beneficial interest or put it into suspense since there are many other attributes of ownership to the holding of shares, such as the right to dividends, to vote, etc.

[1.30] A person is the beneficial owner of property if he exercises control over a substantial element of the attributes of ownership of the property. It is not necessary that the claimant should be able to get an order for specific performance. This is where *Wood Preservation Ltd v Prior*[17] is in error and it also explains the dilemma facing the court in *J Sainsbury plc v O'Connor*.[18] The difference between beneficial ownership and legal

---

16 *J Sainsbury plc v O'Connor* [1991] STC 318.

17 *Wood Preservation Ltd v Prior* [1969] 1 All ER 364.

18 *J Sainsbury plc v O'Connor* [1991] STC 318.

ownership has become a very important distinction for the purposes of stamp duty planning and is examined further in **Chapters 5** and **9**.

[1.31] In this jurisdiction, the case of *Tempany v Hynes*[19] gives rise to some concern over the issue of beneficial ownership. The case involved land that was registered in the Land Registry. It was being sold by the plaintiff as a receiver for the asset of the company that owned the land. The plaintiff struck a deal with the purchaser, the defendant in this action, for the sale of the property for the sum of £30,500, and a contract for sale was signed, with a deposit of £7,625 being paid as part of the purchase price. The title to the property proved problematic and the date of closing of the sale passed whilst various matters were being resolved. Finally, the only problem that remained on foot of the title was the existence of two judgment mortgages which had been registered on the folio of the property in question after the contract for sale had been signed, but before the sale had been closed. Both the plaintiff's and defendant's solicitors were of different opinions as to the effect of these judgments on the title. The plaintiff's solicitor believed that the property could be conveyed without discharging the judgments and that once the defendant became the registered owner of the land, the judgments would cease to exist. This would have satisfied the special condition of the contract that stated:

> The vendor shall discharge all charges registered against the said folio on or before closing and shall pay all land registry fees for the cancellation of such charges.

The defendant's solicitor did not accept this view and required that the plaintiff discharge the judgments and convey the land free from the encumbrance. A compromise was reached whereby £4,500, a sum sufficient to discharge the judgments, would be retained from the purchase price and held on deposit for six weeks, during which time an application to register the purchaser as owner would be lodged with the Land Registry. If the Registrar registered the property free from the judgments, as the plaintiff's solicitor believed, the retained money would be released. If the registration occurred subject to the judgments, then the money would be used to discharge same and remove the burden from the folio.

[1.32] Both solicitors agreed on this compromise which seemed to adequately protect both parties. The defendant, against the advice of his solicitor, refused to complete the sale on this basis and sought to have the money retained solely by the defendant. When this proved unacceptable to the plaintiff, the defendant refused to close the sale. The plaintiff sought an action for specific performance which was refused in the High Court and the issue fell to the Supreme Court on appeal. The High Court's refusal arose from the belief that the property could not be conveyed free of the judgments and accordingly the discretion to grant specific performance was not to be exercised.

[1.33] In the Supreme Court, Henchy and Kenny JJ disagreed in their decision of whether to allow the appeal and grant the plaintiff an order of specific performance. However, O'Higgins CJ concurred with the judgment of Kenny J allowing the appeal, thus making the majority decision of the case. Whilst both judgments came to the same conclusion, the route taken differed considerably. The minority decision of Henchy J

---

19 *Tempany v Hynes* [1976] IR 101.

adheres to what we discussed earlier at para **[1.29]** concerning the effect of a contract for sale on the beneficial ownership of property. He states:

> When a binding contract for the sale of land has been made, whether the purchase money has been paid or not, the law (at least in cases where the parties proceed to the stage of conveyance) treats the beneficial ownership as having passed to the purchaser from the time the contract was made.[20]

However, the vendor still retains some beneficial interest in the property, for the vendor of property subject to a contract for sale may:

> remain in possession until the purchase money is paid and as such possessor he has a common law lien on the property for the purchase money; even if he parts with possession of the property he has an equitable lien on the property for the unpaid purchase money; and he is entitled to take and keep for his own use the rents and profits up to the date fixed for completion. It is clear therefore that *between contract and completion the vendor has a beneficial interest in the property which is capable of being charged by a judgment mortgage* ... (Authors' emphasis added).

[1.34] Thus, the registration of the judgment mortgages affected the transient beneficial interest of the vendor where they were registered after an enforceable contract came into existence. On completion of the sale the registered judgment mortgages would not transfer to the new owner, since they only affected whatever transient beneficial interest the vendor had between the contract for sale and completion. Since the burdens could not survive the closing of the sale, the plaintiff had discharged the onus of producing good title under the contract for sale. Specific performance would issue.

[1.35] It is with Kenny J that the argument becomes more difficult to reconcile and, given that it is this judgment, and not Henchy J's judgment, that O'Higgins CJ concurs with, its importance should not be dismissed. Kenny J views the issue in a radically different manner when he states:

> A vendor who signs a contract with a purchaser for the sale of land becomes a trustee in the sense that he is bound to take reasonable care of the property until the sale is completed, but he becomes a trustee of the beneficial interest to the extent only to which the purchase price is paid. He is not a trustee of the beneficial interest merely because he signs a contract.

In doing so he dismisses the generally received wisdom that a purchaser is the owner of the entire beneficial interest in the land, irrespective of whether any payment has been made. He asserts that the beneficial interest passes only to the extent that the purchase price has been paid. In doing so he relates the strong arguments in its support of this view when he goes on:

> Thus in *Shaw v Foster* [1872] LR 5 HL 321 Lord Cairns said of the report ... there cannot be the slightest doubt of the relation subsisting in the eye of a Court of Equity between the vendor and the purchaser. the vendor was the trustee of the property for the purchaser; the purchaser was the real beneficial owner in the eye of a Court of Equity, subject only to this observation, that the vendor...was not a mere dormant trustee, he was a trustee having personal and substantial interest in the property.

---

[20] *Gordon Hill Trusts Ltd v Segall* [1941] 2 All ER 379.

> ... In *Lysaght v Edwards* [1876] 2 Ch D 499 Jessel MR said of the report: "the moment you have a valid contract for sale ... the beneficial ownership passes to the purchaser ..." Both these statements ... are, I believe, incorrect. When a contract for sale has been signed, the vendor becomes the trustee of the beneficial interest to the extent that the purchase money has been paid.

[1.36] Kenny J cited *Rose v Watson*[21] and the following dictum from Lord Cranworth as being the correct view on the issue:

> There can be no doubt, I apprehend, that when a purchaser has paid his purchase money, though he has got no conveyance, the vendor becomes a trustee for him of the legal estate, and he is in Equity considered the owner of the estate. When instead of paying the whole of his purchase money, he pays a part of it, it would seem to follow, as a necessary corollary, that, to the extent to which he has paid his purchase money, to that extent the vendor is a trustee for him ...

The cumulative effect of the reasoning of Kenny J is that, as far as the broad issue of beneficial ownership is concerned this is not transferred on a contract for the sale of property except to the extent that the purchase money has been paid. It is this proposition which requires examination.

[1.37] A number of points need to be made with respect to this case. Firstly, the ratio of the case revolves around the effect of registration of a burden on registered land before the completion of the sale. It had long been held that registration of a burden on registered land after the sale had been completed but before the transfer had been registered, would not transfer to the purchaser, see *Re Strong*[22]. *Tempany v Hynes*[23] is a clear authority indicating that the same is true for burdens so registered after the contract for sale had been signed, but before the closing of the sale. The discussion on beneficial ownership is therefore *obiter*, that is, not binding on future courts. Secondly, it is clear from the facts that the defendant had decided, shortly after signing the contract for sale, to do all in his power to avoid the consequences of the contract. He had admitted to the court that he was no longer interested in pursuing the contract, not because of the difficulties over title but because his personal circumstances had substantially altered and he was no longer able to move his family as he had earlier hoped to do. He had admitted that he had seized on the issue at hand to avoid the contract. There can be little doubt that it was this which swayed the court as to its decision to grant specific performance. Finally, the real difficulty in the case had to do with the priority of interests over the property; that is the priority of registered over unregistered interests. If the land had been unregistered it is submitted that a different approach would have been taken.

[1.38] The question that falls for discussion for the purposes of this discourse is whether or not the judgment of Kenny J with respect to beneficial ownership under a contract for sale represents sound principle. It has not been the perceived wisdom of the common law, nor that of its leading authorities. As Kenny J himself admits, most of the leading writers adopt the approach that the beneficial ownership passes on signing of the

---

21 *Rose v Watson* [1864] 10 HL Case 672.

22 *Re Strong* [1940] IR 382.

23 *Tempany v Hynes* [1976] IR 101.

contract irrespective of the payment of the purchase price. There is considerable case law to a similar affect on this issue. In practice, the legal and real estate professions believe this to be the case.

[1.39] Kenny J has rested his argument on two cases only. Despite this, it remains a strong *obiter* statement from the current Supreme Court. To what extent has this novel approach in *Tempany*[24] been followed by subsequent Supreme Courts? In *Coffey v Brunel Construction*[25], Griffin J said:

> Whilst different views have been expressed as to the time when, and the extent to which, the beneficial interest passes to the purchaser before the entire purchase money has been paid, there has at all times been unanimity that, where the purchase money has been paid in full, the entire beneficial interest is vested in the purchaser.

[1.40] Moreover, the case has been applied in *Murnaghan Brothers v O'Maoldaomhnaigh*[26] and *Viek Investments.*[27] In both cases Murphy J accepted without question the view of Kenny J. It should also be noted that these cases were from the High Court, which would not have been in a position to question the superior court decision of *Tempany.* What would be the impact if Kenny J was correct? The judgment does not explain what interest, if any, a purchaser who has signed a contract for sale has in the property which is the subject matter of the contract. Why has it been accepted for some time that a purchaser must insure property for which he or she has signed a contract for sale? It should be noted that the recent standard conditions of sale issued by the Law Society now provide that the vendor insure, the property until the sale is completed, but the practice of advising the purchaser to insure as and from the date of the contract of sale remains. Under General Condition 43 of the *Law Society General Conditions of Sale* (2001 edition), the risk remains with the vendor from the date of sale to the actual date of completion limited to the extent of the purchase price. General condition 45 specifically provides for the purchaser's right to effect his or her own insurance on the property or any part thereof or on the chattels purchased without in any way affecting his rights under Condition 43, see para **[1.04]**. If the purchaser is not the beneficial owner of the property, then it could not be made the subject of an order for specific performance if the subject matter was destroyed prior to transfer. Under what principle would the purchaser have the right to compel specific performance where he or she has only a limited interest therein?

[1.41] If *Tempany v Hynes*[28] represents good law, then it leaves open as many questions as it answers. Further, it stands against the weight of numerous authorities and does not represent the position in practice. It remains, however, an unchallenged decision of the Supreme Court. Further elucidation from that court on this issue would be welcomed. The Law Reform Commission[29] concluded that the approach of Henchy J in *Tempany*

---

24 *Tempany v Hynes* [1976] IR 101.

25 *Coffey v Brunel Construction* [1983] IR 36.

26 *Murnaghan Brothers v O'Maoldaomhnaigh* IV ITR 304, [1991] IR 455.

27 *Viek Investments* IV ITR 367.

28 *Tempany v Hynes* [1976] IR 101.

29 In a report entitled 'Report on interests of Vendor and Purchaser in Land during the period between a contract and completion.' (LRC 49–1995).

was the "only means by which the purchaser's interests prior to completion could be adequately protected" and recommended statutory provisions to be put in place to provide that beneficial ownership passes at contract stage.

For stamp duty implications on beneficial ownership, see **Chapter 5**.

The Irish legal system

[1.42] Under the provisions of the Free State Constitution, the existing legal system was carried over into the new State. English law, both its legislation and its *modus operandi*, was adopted by the State. There had been a long Irish legal tradition which continued with the adoption of a new Constitution in 1937, Bunreacht na hÉireann, where this law was carried over by Article 50. Judges swore a new loyalty to the State, rather than the Crown, but the law they applied and the manner in which they applied it was Crown law. In the mid-1960s the courts began to question this automatic acceptance of English law and encouraged the development of local precedents using influences from the United States and elsewhere and, with regard to taxation, New Zealand. In a landmark case[30] the court held that cases decided prior to the Courts (Establishment and Constitution) Act 1961 could not be binding on the current Supreme Court, but were of persuasive value only. Cases decided from 1961 were binding on future courts but the Supreme Court was free to depart from such decisions if there were compelling reasons to do so. This had a number of effects. Firstly, it greatly reduced the amount of precedence as precedent started from 1961. Secondly, precedence could be challenged if the litigant could show good reasons for the law to be changed. Thirdly, since English cases were now of persuasive authority only technically, they were no more or less persuasive than decisions from other jurisdictions. Decisions from these jurisdictions which operated written constitutions were of more relevance. However, since Irish legislation is closely modelled, in most cases, on English statutes, it follows that the interpretation of the English courts with respect to these statutes and their provisions would have significant impact on our own courts.

[1.43] In practice the Irish courts have not embraced the theoretical freedom given by the Supreme Court. Generally, English precedents are followed particularly, as our laws take the same approach as English law. Very seldom has the Supreme Court reversed its own precedent and the citing of cases other than English cases remains rare. Most textbooks reflect this fact, with the English decisions being seen as the parent case and the Irish judgment as an application of that ruling in a local context. There has been no development of a local jurisprudence in its own right. Where Irish cases are cited, they are done so artificially.

[1.44] There are good reasons why the two jurisdictions are no longer able to share an established stream of jurisprudence. Reference has already been made to the written constitution, a corresponding version of which does not exist in the United Kingdom. This Constitution gives certain rights which must be protected. Tax laws must be in conformity with constitutional provisions. The Supreme Court has held that legislation enacted after the coming into effect of the constitution has a presumption of

---

[30] *AG v Ryan Care Hire Ltd* [1965] IR 642.

constitutionality. This presumption does not operate in favour of legislation enacted prior to the constitution. The Stamp Act 1891 therefore had no presumption of constitutionality, except as re-enacted or amended after 1961. Since the legislative provisions have now been consolidated into the Stamp Duty Consolidation Act 1999 (SDCA 1999), the presumption of constitutionality now applies to all stamp duty provisions, thus placing a higher burden on the taxpayer to establish unconstitutionality. In addition, tax law tends to be locally enacted and, where a provision is based on a comparable provision from the United Kingdom, slight differences in terminology can make a dramatic difference. Stamp duty legislation in the United Kingdom remains voluntary in nature and case law on the legislation reflects this. In contrast, since 1991 liability to stamp duty in Ireland has become mandatory and care must be taken in using English case law in this context. Finally, the approach has tended to be more European focused. The adoption of European laws, an increasing phenomena, has had a far greater impact on the approach taken by the judiciary here.

European issues

[1.45] As a member of the European Union since 1973, Ireland's integration into the Union has been quite extensive. As well as the minor laws and regulations that form part of our legal system, crucial legislation is based on European initiatives, particularly in company law.[31] European law is found in the constitutional documents of the Union, principally the Treaty of Rome, the Single European Act and the Treaty on European Union. These give the Union the power of legislation for all Member States. This legislation can take two forms: regulations and directives. Regulations are promulgated in Europe and become part of our domestic legal system. They require no implementing legislation from the State; indeed any such legislation is inconsistent with Union membership. Directives are general guidelines which must be enacted by the individual Member State. Until such enactment occurs, these directives do not form part of our legal system. A Member State which fails to enact the directive by a given date is open to proceedings for failure to honour its obligations. Except in rare circumstances, these directives do not give rise to individual rights that can be vindicated in a court of law. Once a law from the Union has become part of our legal system, its enforcement falls to the government and the judiciary.

[1.46] European Union law has two principle characteristics. First, it prevails over any conflict with national law. This is referred to as the principle of supremacy. This supremacy applies even to constitutional provisions of a Member State. Article 29 of our Constitution expressly grants constitutional immunity to Union law which arises from our obligations of membership, but this is now redundant since the legal basis for supremacy is the ruling of the Union. Even if the relevant section of Article 29 of Bunreacht na hÉireann were to be repealed, the supremacy issue would remain. Second, much national law is based on Union directives. To understand national law requires an understanding of Union law since the Irish courts have held that in interpreting domestic law based on these directives, it is legitimate to have recourse not merely to the directive but the *travaux preparatoires* (ie the preparation papers relating to the formation of the

---

31 See **Chapter 7** with respect to capital duty.

directive). The Interpretation Act 2005 (IA 2005) has followed the principles of the interpretation of European legislation.[32]

[1.47] Since our law must yield to Union law, the validity of stamp duty law remains threatened both by a constitutional attack and by the doctrine of supremacy. Article 33 of the Sixth VAT Directive does not preclude the introduction or maintenance of, inter alia, stamp duty, provided it is not in reality a disguised VAT or turnover tax. In *Beaulande v Directeur des Services Fiscaux de Nantes*[33] stamp duty on a land transaction was held not to be equivalent to either value added tax or a turnover tax. This follows the reasoning in a number of cases like *Dansk Denkavit Aps & Ors v Skatteministeriet*.[34] The key issue remains that where a stamp duty imposition becomes a turnover tax, it is invalid under Union law. A turnover tax has the effect of compromising the functioning of the common system of VAT throughout the Union by levying a charge on the movement of goods and services and on commercial transactions. In *Denkavit* the court held that there were three principal criteria in determining if it were a turnover tax. Firstly, the tax would have to be a general tax; secondly, the tax would have to be charged at each stage and; thirdly, the tax would have to be levied on the added value to the goods or services between transactions.

[1.48] When interpretating tax laws derived from European legislation, the Irish courts must take cognisance of the underlying rationale of the European legislation and interpretations of the national law must be in accordance with that rationale.

Finally, all issues of our domestic law may give rise to applications to the judicial body of the Union, the European Court of Justice (ECJ). It is this body which is the final definitive judge on the correct application and interpretation of laws which have a Union aspect.

Legal terminology explained

[1.49] The practice of law involves the use of terms which are peculiar to that discipline and which have a very definite meaning. These meanings are not always clear from the word itself, and, on occasion, such words can be radically different from that which the layman might understand. For example, a conveyance on sale is a specific head of charge within the meaning of the Stamp Act, yet the phrase might be misunderstood by the lay person. What follows is a brief attempt to explain some of the more common legal expressions which might cause some difficulty. The listing is not exhaustive and should be read in conjunction with major legal dictionaries.[35] Furthermore, throughout the text, other specific terms are fully explained where appropriate.

---

32 See **Chapter 3**.

33 *Beaulande v Directeur des Services Fiscaux de Nantes* [1993] 1 CMLR 765.

34 *Dansk Denkavit Aps & Ors v Skatteministeriet* Case 200/90, 31 March 1992.

35 Such as *Murdoch's Dictionary of Irish Law* (4th edn, Lexis Nexis, 2004), *Osborne, Legal Dictionary* (9th edn, Sweet and Maxwell, 2001).

Contract

[1.50] A contract is a legally enforceable agreement between two or more individuals who undertake a particular course of action. To be enforceable, the agreement must be supported by *consideration,* that is the agreement must be an exchange of money or something that is capable of being valued in money. For example, if A agrees to paint B's house, this is a gift, not a contract, for there is no exchange of money or money's worth. If A agrees to paint B's house for €500, then this is enforceable as a contract since there is an exchange of consideration; A gets the €500 and B gets his house painted (which is something that can be valued in money). If A agreed to paint B's house because B is his friend, the agreement is not enforceable since one cannot place a monetary value on love and affection. Neither would the agreement be enforceable if A agreed to paint B's house because last year, B gave him €50 as a gift. There is no current exchange of consideration, the consideration is said to be past.[36]

[1.51] Most contracts need not be written, but can be oral, written or a mixture of both. As an exception pursuant to the Statute of Frauds (Ireland) Act 1695, contracts for the sale of land must be evidenced in writing signed by the person against whom it is sought to enforce the agreement, or his agent lawfully authorised in writing. The entire contract need not be in writing and all that is required is that its existence be evidenced in writing. It can be evidenced by way of written communications between the parties, cheques, etc.[37]

Contracts under seal

[1.52] If the parties wish to make an agreement enforceable without consideration, then the contract should be executed under seal. Contracts executed under seal are enforceable without consideration. A contract under seal is a written contract which has been signed and a small seal attached. Traditionally, a seal was a blob of red sealing wax which had been impressed with a ring or thumbnail. In modern times, a red adhesive sticker is often used in place of the sealing wax.[38] Indeed, a more recent development has been the use of *Locus Sigilli* – LS – in place of seal.

Conveyance

[1.53] The term *conveyance* refers to the formal transfer of ownership of property from one person to another. The conveyance normally follows a contract for the sale of property, but a conveyance can also be required where the property is being gifted over to another individual. It is usual in the case of land to execute the conveyance by way of a deed, which is a written record of the conveyance which the parties have signed and sealed. In the case of property other than land, a deed of conveyance is seldom used; the conveyance of personal property normally occurs by transfer and delivery of the property. It should be clear that where two individuals decide to transfer property between themselves, there are two distinct elements to the transaction. Firstly, the

---

36 Friel, *Law of Contract in Ireland* (2nd edn, Thompson Roundhall, 2000).

37 Wylie and Woods, *Irish Conveyancing Law* (3rd edn, Tottel Publishing, 2005).

38 Friel, *Law of Contract in Ireland* (2nd edn, Thompson Roundhall, 2000).

decision to transfer the property, whether by contract or gift or otherwise, and secondly, the execution of that decision by way of conveyance.

Assignment

[1.54] The term *assignment* is used to indicate the transfer of a right or interest in property from one person to another. An assignment has the effect of a conveyance. By custom and usage, the term assignment now applies to the transfer of such right or interest in certain types of property only, notably choses in action and leasehold rights. A *chose in action* is the right to sue an individual for some legal infringement. For example, if A owes B €1,000, B has a chose in action, that is the right to sue A for €1,000, which he might assign to C; that is transfer the right to sue B to C. It is usual to execute an assignment by way of a deed.

Disposition inter vivos

[1.55] A disposition *inter vivos* is the transfer of property which occurs during the lifetime of the person making the conveyance, that is the seller or, in the case of real property, the vendor. A disposition includes the transfer of property occurring not only by the act of the parties but by operation of law. Thus a conveyance is a disposition but it is a disposition that normally arises from the acts of the parties. In some cases, a disposition is referred to as a *voluntary disposition*; that is, it is a transfer of property for which no money, or to use the legal term, *consideration*, has passed between the parties. By statute, a voluntary disposition also arises where the consideration is insufficient in that it does not reflect the market value of the item.[39]

Effectively, a conveyance is a subset of the concept of disposition. *Inter vivos* is merely the Latin term for "whilst alive". It is to be distinguished from the next concept: a testamentary disposition.

Testamentary disposition

[1.56] This is the transfer of property from one person to another arising from the death of the original owner under the terms of his or her will.[40] A *will* is a document which satisfies the formal requirements of the Succession Act 1965 and sets out the deceased person's intention as to how his or her estate should be distributed. A will speaks from the date of death, not the date of execution of the will.

Intestate succession

[1.57] Where an individual dies without benefit of a will, he or she is said to die *intestate* and the distribution of his or her *estate*, that is the entire property held by that person at the time of his or her death, will be governed by the rules of intestate succession.[41] Where there is no ascertainable relative under the provisions of the Act, then the estate will revert to the State as *ultimate intestate successor.*

---

39 For further details, see **Chapter 11**.

40 Succession Act 1965, s 101.

41 See Succession Act 1965, Pt VI.

Ad valorem *duty*

[1.58] This is the term used to describe a rate of stamp duty which is proportionate to the value of the transaction involved. For example, if a house is sold for between €150,000 and €190,000, then the rate of duty under the conveyance on sale head is 3 per cent of the sale price. It is not a *fixed rate of duty* as might apply say with respect to credit card accounts where the duty levied is €40 irrespective of the credit limit of the card. Such a fixed duty is not related to value. *Ad valorem* is a Latin term meaning "by value".

Vesting of property

[1.59] Property is said to vest when the owner of the property has a present right to either current or future enjoyment of land, it is an absolute, unconditional and indefeasible interest. Where it is not specified that the vesting occurs in the future, it is assumed that the term relates to a current right to the present enjoyment of land.

Company

[1.60] A *company* is an association of people who have formed a group through which they undertake a common business venture. In many instances the company will be incorporated, that is it will be created in accordance with the Companies Act 1963 as amended. In doing so, it will benefit from the concept of *limited liability.* Limited liability means that the liability of the shareholders of the company is limited to the extent that they have not fully paid for their shares in the company. Thus if A owns 100,000 shares at €1 each in Acme Ltd, the maximum extent of A's liability will be €100,000 which he may discharge by paying the full value on the shares once they have been allotted to A, or he may defer the liability by not paying for the shares, either in full or in part, until called upon to do so. The word "share" signifies the division of ownership, the right to participate in the profits (called a dividend), the right to participate in the decision-making process in a company and the right to participate in the assets on the winding up of a company. Shares can be divided into *ordinary shares* and *preference shares*. Ordinary shares normally give a right to vote at company meetings but the return on the investment is variable in that it is linked with the profits of the company. Preference shares may deny the shareholder the right to vote at company meetings in exchange for a definite dividend that is not linked to the amount of the profits made. The preference shares may be redeemable, that is the company may have to buy them back after a period of time has elapsed, or they may be convertible into ordinary shares.

[1.61] The capital of a company will be divided into the above mentioned class of shares amongst others. The total amount of shares that the company can have is limited and is referred to as the authorised or nominal share capital. Of this authorised share capital, only some may be issued to shareholders in a process known as allotment of shares. These *issued* shares may be either fully or partly paid up. For example where 100,000 shares at €1 each are issued but the shareholder has to pay only 15 cent on each share, the company will have received €15,000 paid up in respect of the issued share capital. The company can call up the balance at any stage, either in full or in part, and on the termination of the company's existence the full amount outstanding will be called up. In limited situations, shares which were issued by the company can be purchased back and these shares are then known as treasury shares.

[1.62] If the company offers these shares for sale to the general public, then it will be classified as a public limited company and must use the letters "plc" after its name. If the company restricts the sale of shares to a limited number of people, it is referred to as a private company and must bear the legend "Ltd" after its name, unless exempted by the Minister of Enterprise, Trade and Employment.

A subsidiary of a company is defined in the Companies Act 1963. A company is a subsidiary when another company is a member of it and controls the composition of the board of directors, or it holds more than one half of the equity share capital, or it holds more than half the value of the shares carrying voting rights. A subsidiary of a subsidiary is the subsidiary of the parent company.[42]

Equity of redemption

[1.63] The equity of redemption is the right of the mortgagor to redeem the mortgage on payment of principal and interest even where the date for redemption of the mortgage as specified in the agreement has passed. [43]

Partnerships

[1.64] When two or more people agree to pursue a common business venture they may decide not to form a company for one reason or another (for example, taxation, publicity or the formalities of company formation). They will, therefore, organise themselves as a partnership. A *partnership* has no separate legal identity from its owners and property will be held in the names of all the partners. The partners are liable to the full extent of any debts or losses incurred by the partnership. In certain cases, it may be possible to retain the advantages of the partnership organisation of the business whilst also gaining limited liability. This is possible under the Limited Partnership Act 1907 which permits a person who invests in a partnership, but takes no active part in the running of the business, to limit his or her liability to the amount invested in the partnership. Such partners are referred to as limited partners.

In 1994, the Investment Limited Partnership Act was passed establishing a broader-based limited partnership scheme for collective investment to encourage growth in the financial services sector.

Precedent, ratio decidendi and obiter dicta

[1.65] *Precedent* is the term given to decisions of a superior court, such as the Supreme Court, which operate to bind inferior courts, such as the High, Circuit and District Courts. Precedent also operates to bind future courts and cannot be departed from unless there are sound and compelling reasons to do so. Not every element of the judgment will bind another court. Only the *ratio decidendi,* that is the reason for the decision, must be followed by subsequent courts. Other statements made by the court in the course of delivering judgment will be regarded as *obiter dicta* and will have persuasive authority

---

[42] CA 1963, s 155.

[43] See **Chapter 9**.

only. This means that a subsequent court is not obliged to follow a statement which is obiter, but such a statement must be carefully considered by such a court.

Escrow

[1.66] Escrow is the process of placing a document, signed by both parties to the agreement, in the hands of an independent third party who will only release the document on the happening of a specified event.[44]

44 For further discussion see **Chapter 3** (for an example of a certificate of escrow – see **Appendix 4**.

Chapter 2

Jurisdiction and Territoriality

Introduction

[2.01] Two issues arise with respect to disputes concerning stamp duty: they are jurisdiction and territoriality. Jurisdiction is the concept whereby a court, or other administrative body may bring a defendant before it to pursue a matter for adjudication. Whilst specific concerns arise with respect to stamp duty, the question of jurisdiction is a general question of practice and procedure that operates in most legal spheres.

[2.02] Territoriality, on the other hand, concerns the physical scope of the application of a law, in this case the Stamp Duty Act. If the instrument covers property outside the State, or if it is executed outside the State, or if it is entered into by non-residents of the State, does it come within the territoriality of the Act? The issue of territoriality is used by a practitioner to determine whether or not a proposed instrument is obliged to be stamped. Jurisdiction is of concern to the authorities in their enforcement of the Act. Questions of jurisdiction always involve resolution of the territoriality aspect of the Act, whereas territoriality issues can arise without recourse to jurisdictional concerns.

Example 2.02.1

Joe Bloggs conveys a property in Ireland valued at €4 million to Fred Flintstone, and both parties are resident in the United States. The duty on the instrument is €360,000.

Prior to 1991, the duty was voluntary and the parties could elect not to stamp the instrument until they needed to enforce the transaction in this jurisdiction.

Since 1991, the duty has become now mandatory. The Revenue Commissioners are empowered to raise an assessment on the accountable person, Fred Flinstone. This would involve seeking to serve process to bring Fred within the jurisdiction of the courts.

Example 2.02.2

Fred Flintstone and Joe Bloggs convey property situate in America. Both parties are resident here but the instrument is executed in America.

No duty arises since both the instrument and the property are excluded from the territoriality of the Act.

To apply the provisions of the Act the instrument must come within its territoriality. If it does, it is liable to duty.

Jurisdiction

[2.03] The Revenue Commissioners are empowered to recover any unpaid stamp duty from the accountable person. Such duty shall be deemed to be a debt due by the accountable person to the Minister for Finance for the benefit of the Central Fund and shall be payable to the Commissioners and may be sued for and recovered by action or other appropriate proceedings ... in any court of competent jurisdiction.[1] The liability as an accountable person will vary according to the nature of the instrument.[2]

[2.04] If the accountable person is not present within the jurisdiction, he may still have process served on him, pursuant to Order 68 of the Rules of the Superior Court, where the Revenue are seeking to enforce the liability. Order 68 entitles the Revenue Commissioners, on application to the High Court, to enforce the recovery of taxes and/ or fines, even where this involves service outside the jurisdiction. Such service shall be granted on the production of an affidavit or other evidence showing that the deponent believes that the plaintiff has a good cause of action, and setting out the location of the defendant and whether he is an Irish citizen or not. Such order for service outside the jurisdiction shall be granted at the court's discretion.

Territoriality

[2.05] Any instrument specified in First Schedule of SDCA 1999[3] which is executed in the State,[4] or, wheresoever executed, relates to any property situate in the State or any matter or thing done or to be done in the State, is chargeable to duty.[5]

Instruments executed within the State

Example 2.05.1

Amount met out of assets of Rintoul Ltd to redeem unsecured loan stock	€
– market value of €67,700 9.5% Exchequer Stock at 15/9/05	60,000
Part of 9.25% unsecured loan stock issued otherwise than for new consideration (1/2/99)	36,000
Value of 9.25% unsecured loan stock when issued (1/2/99)	50,000
Amount treated by TCA 1997, s 130(2)(c) as distribution on 15/9/05:	
€60,000 x 36/50	43,200

[2.06] Any instrument executed within the State, regardless of the location of the property to which it relates is liable to duty.

Example 2.06.1

Tom owns a holiday home in Florida. Harry agrees to buy the property for €200,000. The conveyance is drawn up and executed in Cork.

Duty payable €8,000 (4% *ad valorem*)

SDCA 1999, s 98 provides that the following instruments executed within the State are no longer chargeable to duty:

(a) conveyance or transfer of any kind not hereinbefore described in the First Schedule; and

(b) deed of any kind whatsoever not described in the First Schedule;

---

1 SDCA 1999, s 2(4).

2 See **Appendix 7**.

3 See **Appendix 9**.

4 For exceptions, see paras **[2.06]** et seq.

5 SDCA 1999, s 2(1).

unless they relate to Irish immovable property, any right or interest therein, or stocks or marketable securities of a company having a register in this State.

The following instruments executed within the State are also no longer chargeable to duty:

(a) lease of any kind whatsoever not hereinbefore described in the First Schedule;

(b) mortgage, bond, covenant or debenture which is a charge or encumbrance on property situate in the State, other than shares in stocks or funds of the Government or Oireachtas; and

(c) release or renunciation of any property or of any right or interest in any property;

unless they relate to Irish immovable property, any right or interest therein.

[2.07] Policies of insurance executed in the State are chargeable to duty in the following situations only:

(a) where there is a conveyance or transfer on sale of any policy of insurance or life insurance where the risk to which the property relates is located within the State;

(b) not exceeding two years, where the risk to which the policy relates is located in the State;

(c) on a policy of life insurance and non-life insurance policies where the risk to which the policy relates in both cases is located in the State.[6]

The location of the risk of a policy of insurance for the purposes of these provisions will depend on the nature of the items insured. The location of a building and its contents (where they are covered by the same insurance policy) is its physical location.[7] A vehicle is located in the state in which it is registered.[8] Travel insurance taken out within the State, and which operates for four months or less, is located within the State.[9]

[2.08] In all other cases, the risk is located within the State if the policy holder is habitually resident within the State, or if the policyholder is a legal person, other than an individual, whose establishment is situated within the State.[10] The concept of establishment is that defined within European Communities (Non Life Insurance) (Amendment) (No 2) Regulations 1991.[11] Habitual residence is a term used by the European legislature and the European Court of Justice and is not one found in Irish legislation. The Jurisdiction of Courts and Enforcement of Judgments (European Communities) Act 1988 specifically uses the phrase 'ordinarily resident'. There is little difference between the two and both are based on factual residence and not the intention of the party.

---

6 SDCA 1999, Sch 1.

7 SDCA 1999, s 61(2)(a).

8 SDCA 1999, s 61(2)(b).

9 SDCA 1999, s 61(2)(c).

10 SDCA 1999, s 61(2)(d).

11 SI 142/1991.

[2.09] Pursuant to FA 1994, s 151, the concepts of residence and ordinary residence are now statutorily defined from fiscal year 1994/1995 onwards.[12] The concept of residence prior to this fiscal year was that of the English courts and was adopted in this jurisdiction as a matter of practice. An individual was resident within the jurisdiction if he or she spent more that 183 days in each fiscal tax year within the State. In the alternative, they were also considered to be resident if over a period of four consecutive years, the average of their stay within the State amounted to 91 days or more. Finally, residency status also arose where the individual had accommodation within the State and visited the State during any fiscal tax year, the exception being a person whose domicile was Irish but who was employed with a full-time occupation abroad. A person was ordinarily resident if he or she qualified as resident year after year; that is continuity of the link became important.

[2.10] With the passing of the 1994 Act, the new rules are as follows. Residence will be proven if the individual has spent:

(a) more than 183 days in the State in any given fiscal tax year; or

(b) the individual is present for more than 280 days over a two-year tax period (where the individual is present for less than 30 days in one fiscal tax year, then the individual may elect to be treated as resident, but failing such an election, he will not be so treated).

[2.11] An individual will now be regarded as being ordinarily resident where that individual has satisfied the terms of the residency for three continuous tax years. The individual becomes ordinarily resident on the fourth fiscal tax year. Ordinary residence is not lost until the individual has been a non-resident for three fiscal tax years.

Example 2.11.1

Pre-1994/95

Harry visited Ireland for the following number of days in the given tax years:

1985/86	39 days
1986/87	180 days
1987/88	90 days
1988/89	72 days

Average duration of stay over 4 consecutive fiscal tax years = 381/4 = 95. Since this exceeds 91 days, Harry is a resident.

Example 2.11.2

1994/95 onwards

Assuming the same facts as per Example **2.11.1**, residency is determined on presence within the State for more than 280 days over a two year fiscal tax period.

Total stay over any two-year period does not exceed 280 days, therefore Harry is not resident.

---

12 The Revenue Commissioners have issued an explanatory leaflet entitled 'Explanatory Leaflet on the legislative provisions relating to the residence in Ireland, Res 1'.

Example 2.11.3

Harry spent the following time in the State:

1994/95	103 days
1995/96	180 days
1996/97	170 days
1997/98	130 days

Over the two-year period 1994-96 total stay exceeded 280 days so Harry was resident in 1995/96.

Over 1995-97 total stay exceeded 280 days so Harry was resident in 1996-97.

Over the two-year period 1996-98 total stay exceeded 280 days so Harry was resident in 1997-98.

Since Harry has been resident for three continuous tax years, he will become ordinarily resident in fiscal tax year 1998-99.

[2.12] The Revenue Commissioners have issued an explanatory leaflet entitled 'Explanatory Leaflet on the legislative provisions relating to the residence in Ireland, Res 1'.

Where any risk is located within the State, the policy insuring the risk is liable to duty.

Example 2.12.1

Joe Bloggs owns a holiday home in Florida valued at $1,200,000. A policy of insurance is executed in Gortnaclune, Ireland to cover the risk. The duty payable on the policy of insurance is nil as the risk covered is physically located outside the State.

An instrument effecting a conveyance, transfer, lease or assignment executed within the State which relates exclusively to foreign immovable property shall not be chargeable with duty.[13]

Example 2.12.2

Tom owns a holiday home in California. Harry agrees to buy the property for €100,000. The conveyance is drawn up and executed in Cork. The duty payable is nil.

Further exemptions are set out in **Chapter 13**.

Instruments relating to property situate in the State

[2.13] An instrument, wherever it has been executed, which relates to property situate in the State is liable for duty.

Example 2.13.1

Tom and Jerry both live in New Jersey. Tom sells his farm in Ireland to Jerry for $110,000. The conveyance is drawn up and executed in New Jersey.

Assuming €1 = $1.10

Duty payable (€100,000 at 6%) €6,000

[13] SDCA 1999, s 98.

Instruments relating to any matter or thing to be done in the State

[2.14] Where the document relates to anything done or to be done within the State, it is chargeable to duty. In *IRC v Maples & Co (Paris)*[14] the transaction concerned land situated within France which was to be transferred by way of a document executed within France. The consideration for this was shares in a United Kingdom registered company. The document was liable to duty since it involved something to be done with respect to the document within the State, namely the issue of shares. M'Naghten LJ stated:

> The Act speaks of the 'instrument'. The provision is not confined to the operative part of the instrument. It speaks of the instrument as 'relating to' certain subjects. There is no expression more general or far-reaching than this. This instrument relates to the capital of the new company out of which it was agreed that a specified number of shares should be appropriated and allotted to the old company. The share capital of the new company, if it was situate anywhere, was situate in England. In my opinion this instrument does relate to property situate in England. Be that as it may, it certainly relates to something to be done in England. It relates to the registration in the name of the old company of shares which were to be allotted in an English company as the consideration for the purchase of the French property.

[2.15] In *Faber v IRC*[15] a covenant was executed in Canada for consideration of shares in a Canadian company. The amount was in proportion to the earnings of the covenanter from his profession carried out in England. It was held to be liable to duty. The case is interesting as the only connection with England was that the party earned a portion of his living in that jurisdiction.

[2.16] An instrument executed between two parties outside the jurisdiction will be liable to duty if it has a connection with the State that requires some active participation. It will not be liable where there is a reference to an Irish standard which is used in the abstract; for example, an agreement fixing the return on property to the consumer price index published by the Government.

[2.17] The liability to duty covers not merely those parts of the instrument that require something further to be done, but includes all of the instrument. An instrument for which the rate of return is proportionate to the income earned by one of the parties in the State becomes liable in total to duty, even for elements of the instrument that take place exclusively outside the State. This could have consequences where a company with worldwide holdings, including property situate in Ireland, were to sell itself as a complete going concern. Since some of the property is situate within the State, all of the document becomes liable to duty, no matter where it is situate. The exposure to duty is to be calculated on the entire assets of the company. The same would be true of a transfer of worldwide intellectual property rights which included the intellectual property rights within the State.

---

14 *IRC v Maples & Co (Paris)* [1908] AC 22.

15 *Faber v IRC* [1936] 155 LT 228.

Example 2.17.1

Acme Industrial Inc, an American conglomerate, has a production facility in Kinsale, Co Cork. The Kinsale facility is valued at €100,000 comprising of a commercial premises only. Acme Industrial, including the Kinsale facility, is worth $11,000,000. Assuming €1 = $1.10.

If the company is transferred then the duty would be payable on €10,000,000.

Duty payable 9%	€900,000

[2.18] There are a number of options available to reduce the potential liability. The Irish portion of the transaction may be separated and dealt with independently; for example, by conveying the property situate within the State in one instrument and then conveying the worldwide interests, excluding Ireland, in another instrument.

Example 2.18.1

Assume the facts as given in Example **2.17.1** with respect to Acme International Inc, except that a separate instrument is executed in favour of the purchaser with regard to the Kinsale facility.

Duty payable (€100,000 at 6%)	€6,000

The Revenue has stated in SP-SD/1/91 para 4.2[16] that the transaction would have to substantially relate to the State. Essentially the view of the Revenue Commissioners in relation to this criterion is that the instrument and/or the underlying transaction should relate to, or involve, a substantive action or obligation to be carried out or undertaken in the State. It is stated in the Revenue Commissioners Notes for Guidance on the SDCA 1999 that:

> An illustration of this view would be where an instrument is executed abroad relating to foreign property where the only connection with the State is that one of the parties is Irish resident. The Revenue Commissioners' view in that in such a case the instrument would not be liable to duty.

In this case it is quite likely that, since €100,000 is only a small part of the amount involved the Revenue would not seek to charge the duty as set out above, but the instrument would be liable to duty on €100,000 (ie. 6% or €6,000).

Example 2.18.2

Let us assume that in the Example **2.17.1**, the total value of Acme including the Kinsale property is $220,000. The Revenue would be more likely to charge the duty on €200,000 (i.e. $220,000 where €1 = $1.10)

Duty at 9%	€18,000

[2.19] However, in such a case, each conveyance must be a distinct matter within the meaning of SDCA 1999, s 147, otherwise it will be charged as a composite transaction.[17] A transfer of shares in a company to several residuary legatees was liable to a separate stamp in respect of each part of the transfer, see *Freeman v IRC*.[18] What constitutes a

---

16 Collection and Enforcement Of Stamp Duty Finance Act 1991(SP-SD/1/91).

17 See **Chapter 3**.

18 *Freeman v IRC* [1871] LR 6 ExCh 101.

distinct matter under this provision is far from clear. In *Ansell v IRC*,[19] it was stated by Rowlatt J that:

> If one turns to SA 1891, s 4 the distinct matters there must be distinct matters for the purposes of the Stamp Act. If two different classes of property are being transferred by the same words of assignment in the same document and these two different classes of property in the same document are different from the point of view of the Stamp Act and taxation, it seems to me in common sense that they are distinct matters.

This could render the document partly liable to duty and partly exempt.

[2.20] *Monroe and Nock on The Law of Stamp Duties*[20] argue that local and foreign property constitute different classes of property and it might be that these constitute distinct matters. In talking of different classes of property, Rowlatt J was referring to the distinction between real and personal property, tangible and intangible and so on. The location of the property itself cannot be sufficient to hold that it is of a different class. Rowlatt J contemplated a different treatment of properties under the Stamp Act rather than differentiation by reference to the location of the property.

Location of subject matter

[2.21] The location of the subject matter of the document will pose few problems. Land is clearly located where it is physically situated, and includes any leasehold interest in land. For the purposes of the Stamp Act, the State means the 26 counties of Ireland. Where land straddles the border it must be that part of the land situate within the State that falls to be charged with duty. However, any instrument relating to such lands will normally be stamped since it will require registration within the State. The double taxation agreement discussed below[21] governs such situations.

[2.22] Capital moneys held under the provisions of the Settled Land Act 1882 are treated as land and located accordingly. In *Re Staughton*[22] the deceased had converted some Irish land into capital moneys under the Settled Land Acts and had used the proceeds to purchase certain English securities. On her death, the liability of the estate to Irish death duties came before the court. The court held that the situs of the capital moneys, although in the form of English securities, was Ireland since it was to represent the land so situated before benefit of the conversion under the Settled Land Act. The case has been criticised but appears to represent a valid statement of the law. A mortgagee's interest is treated as movable property, if the decision of *Lawson v CIR*[23] is correct. Though there is case law in other jurisdictions which would suggest that such an interest is in fact immovable property.[24] and thus located where the land is situated, the judgment of Palles CB in *Lawson v CIR* seems to be definitive.

---

19 *Ansell v IRC* [1929] 1 KB 608.

20 Sweet and Maxwell, 1989.

21 See para **[2.28]**.

22 *Re Staughton* [1941] IR 166.

23 *Lawson v CIR* [1896] 2 IR 418.

24 See *In re Hoyles, Row v Jagg* [1911] 1 Ch 179, expressly dismissing the *Lawson* case.

[2.23] The only matter of law for determination is whether, according to our law, a debt secured by a mortgage of land in a foreign country is movable or immovable property, and we determine this the moment we determine whether the property is in character a debt with an accessory right to resort to land for payment, or is in character an estate in land, measured by the amount of the debt. Now this cannot depend upon the locality of the land upon which the debt is charged. The character must be the same, whether the land is situate in a foreign country or here. Movable property, that is goods, are located where they are physically situate at the relevant time. Merchant ships and aircraft are, however, deemed to be located in the State where they are registered.

[2.24] Contract debts and speciality debts are located where the debtor resides. A speciality debt is one which arises from a document under seal and is distinguished from a contract debt. Since the speciality debt arises from a document executed under seal, it might be argued that the location of such a debt should be the place of execution of the said document. In the alternative, the location of the debt might be where the deed itself is located. In *Re Deane (Deceased)*[25] the location of a speciality debt was where the document was located at the relevant time. Thus, in the case at hand, an Irish domiciled person had taken out a policy of life insurance with a Scottish company and the question arose as to the location of the debt. The court found in favour of the location of the document as the governing principle. It cited, with approval, from *AG v Bouwens*[26] the following statement:

> it was established as law, that judgement debts were assets, for the purposes of jurisdiction, where the judgement is recorded; leases, where the land lies; speciality debts, where the instrument happens to be; and simple contract debts, where the debtor resides at the time of the testator's death ... (Lord Abinger CB, at page 1398).

Following this reasoning a mortgage debt, since it is attached to land and thereby creates an interest in land, is located where the land is situated though the position is far from clear.[27]

[2.25] Bills of exchange are located in the State where they are to be found from time to time.[28]. Shares are located where the Register of Shareholders is kept in accordance with law.[29] This rule applies irrespective of whether the legal and beneficial ownership are in the one person or not. The sale of a company involves determining its location with respect to where its central management and control is located.[30] In most instances the central control of a company is to be determined from the residence of the directors of the company, since they will control the company.[31] At all times it is a question of fact to be ascertained, and may be determined by looking at all relevant facts.

---

25 *Re Deane (Deceased)* [1936] IR 556.

26 *AG v Bouwens* 150 ER 1390.

27 See **Chapter 5**.

28 *Re Duddy* [1925] 1 IR 196.

29 *Re Ferguson, Deceased* [1935] IR 21.

30 *De Beers Consolidated Mines Ltd v Howe* [1906] AC 455.

31 *Hood (John) & Co v Magee* [1918] 2 IR 34.

Execution of a document

[2.26] Liability to duty arises if the document is executed within the State. Executed means that which is done or completed and the execution of a deed is accomplished by the sealing and delivery of it by the parties as their own act and deed in the presence of witnesses. Signing is not a strict requirement for execution of a document,[32] but the practice is for both parties to sign the document. It would be usual for the purchaser to execute the deed even though there may be no legal requirement for him to do so, as he will be giving a financial certificate for stamp duty purposes. Under SDCA 1999, s 1(1) the term 'executed' is enlarged to include documents not under seal but merely signed. A signature can include an illiterate's mark, initials, a rubber stamp or headed notepaper.[33] It must 'authenticate the whole document of which it forms part', as *per* Kenny J in *McQuaid v Lynam.*[34]

[2.27] It shall be seen later (**Chapter 5**) that liability to duty may arise even though no enforceable transaction has been achieved. The liability occurs once the document is completed. Completion occurs when the *last* minimum act required has been implemented. A contract is executed when all the parties have signed the document, even if the contract is unenforceable. It is on the execution of the document that liability arises and the time of implementation of the transaction is irrelevant. The transaction may be completed in one jurisdiction whilst the document formalising that transaction is executed in another. For example, a contract comes into effect in the jurisdiction where the offer is accepted, but the document may be signed in another jurisdiction. The law governing the contract is that of the jurisdiction where the acceptance is received but its liability to duty is governed by the jurisdiction where the document was executed.

Example 2.27.1

Two parties are negotiating the sale of property in the United States, Jack lives in Dublin and Jill in Peru. Whilst both parties are on holiday in the United States Jack makes an offer to sell the property to Jill, which is immediately accepted by Jill. Jill sends Jack the instrument effecting the sale, duly executed by her, for execution.

The instrument receives the final signature by Jack in Dublin.

In this example the contract was concluded in the United States and is governed by United States law but the instrument itself is executed in Ireland and would have been liable to duty prior to FA 1992.

Double taxation arrangements

[2.28] An instrument may be liable to duty both in Ireland and in another State. There is, in general, no relief from such double taxation. However, a bilateral arrangement with the United Kingdom has been put into place. An instrument which is liable to duty in both Ireland and the United Kingdom and which has been stamped in one of the two countries is deemed to be stamped in the other country to the extent of the duty so stamped upon the instrument. If the liability to duty is higher in one country then the

---

32 *Blennerhassett v Day* [1813] Beat 468.

33 *Hucklesby v Hook* [1900] 82 LT 117.

34 *McQuaid v Lynam* [1965] IR 564 at 569.

excess must be paid.[35] A composite agreement which is exempt from duty in one country is deemed to be duly stamped and the instrument is denoted with a stamp reflecting the duty that would have been paid were it not for the relief. The relief applies to instruments executed after 1 April 1923. For the purposes of this provision, the term United Kingdom includes Northern Ireland until such time as the Government of Northern Ireland chooses to withdraw the relief. No decision was taken prior to the proroguing of the Government of Northern Ireland. Since 1974, the administration of Stamp duties in Northern Ireland has been taken over by the Commissioners for Inland Revenue and accordingly Northern Ireland is no longer a separate state with regard to Stamp Duty. The rules which apply are therefore the same as those which apply to any other part of the United Kingdom as described above.

Example 2.28.1

An instrument is liable to stamp duty in the United Kingdom for £1,000 and in Ireland for €1,500.

Assume €1=stg£0.90

UK duty paid	€1,100 (i.e. stamped with stg£1,000)
Ireland duty owing	€1,500
Excess to be stamped in Ireland	€400

Prior to 1991, the instrument would only need to be stamped with €400 excess duty when the instrument was brought into the State.

Since 1991, the excess duty payable on the instrument has to be paid within 30 days of execution.

If the instrument were stamped in Ireland for €1,500, no excess is payable in the United Kingdom and the instrument will be deemed stamped by the United Kingdom Revenue Authorities.

Example 2.28.2

An instrument is liable to duty in Ireland for €1,000 and in Massachusetts, USA for $2,000. The duty payable is €1,000 in Ireland and $2,000 payable in the USA. No relief is available.

---

35 Double Taxation (Relief) Order (No 1) 1923.

Chapter 3

History and Principles of Stamp Duty

History

[3.01] Stamp duty has been in existence as a tax for 300 years and constitutes one of the oldest forms of taxation to survive into modern times. When one compares this with income tax, which only became permanently established as a revenue source in England in 1842, it is clear that the usefulness and inherent ease of such a source of revenue becomes obvious. Introduced, like most forms of taxation, as a temporary measure during the reign of William and Mary under SA 1694, the tax has developed so that by 1984 it raised the sum of £1,000 million in the United Kingdom, supplying the equivalent of one penny in the pound at the standard rate of income tax to the Crown's coffers.

[3.02] In Ireland, at the time of writing the first edition of this book[1], the yield from stamp duty was £240 million per annum. In the Revenue Commissioners' Annual Report of 1996, the yield had risen to £332 million per annum. The phenomenal growth in the property market in Ireland since the first edition of this book, the changing of stamp duty from a voluntary tax to a mandatory tax and the increasing rates of stamp duty explain the difference in the stamp duty yields over the years. It is clear that whilst the duty itself would not be sufficient to fund the State to any great extent, its loss would be difficult to sustain, and it is highly likely that it will continue to be a valuable source of revenue for many years to come. As this tax is effectively self-enforcing, it is a relatively inexpensive tax to collect. Stamp duty, in general, is a tax on instruments and not transactions or income. Currently stamp duty is the fastest growing tax. Moreover it is the one tax which is beating the estimate yield set the preceding year. While all other tax yields are below expectations, stamp duty yield exceeded expectation.

[3.03] Stamp duty law is the result of a long and tortuous legislative history that has left us with a far from satisfactory or coherent form of taxation today. There had been consolidating statutes in SA 1804, SA 1870 and SA 1891 which formed the core legislation on the matter. Operating in tandem with the SA 1891 was the Stamp Duties Management Act 1891 (SDMA 1891) which governed the administration of this duty. The result was a plethora of anomalous incidents of duty which were no longer viable in many respects and a labyrinth of technical details and statutory sections which formed an almost impenetrable barrier for those who are most closely concerned with the enforcement of the tax. Stamp duty law has been heavily amended by subsequent legislation, resulting in the Stamp Duties Consolidation Act 1999 (SDCA 1999), which places the responsibility on professional advisers who have a further professional duty

---

[1] 1995.

of care to the Revenue Commissioners for failure to provide the relevant information on the imposition of the stamp duty liability.

[3.04] Since the foundation of the State, the legislature, as is the case with other taxes, has not taken the opportunity to fundamentally re-examine the whole issue of stamp duty in pursuit of coherent and rational taxation. It is true to say that stamp duty is not likely to bring people onto the streets in protest, but it has a major impact on ordinary lives. Certainly no one may object to paying a notional duty on certain instruments as the failure to pay it may negate an entire transaction worth thousands of euro. Likewise, the relief from stamp duty for new houses qualifying for a floor area certificate tilts the balance of purchasing a house away from the used market, and in real terms it means that those who select to purchase a pre-owned property must discharge the stamp duty liability. The extent of the disparity was reduced in 1998 with a general reduction in the rates of stamp duty payable on secondhand houses. The stamp duty rates applicable to the purchase of residential property for first-time buyers have again been revised. The first-time buyers' grant of £3,000 which had been available has been abolished and replaced with reduced stamp duty rates on second hand residential property. First-time buyers who are owner-occupiers of new houses with a certified floor area under 125 square metres are exempt from stamp duty. Partial relief for first-time buyers of new houses with a floor area over 125 square metres is available at the same reduced rates as for secondhand property. On commercial properties, the stamp duty payable can be quite a large overhead in the acquisition of corporate assets or the conduct of certain business.

[3.05] In 1983, the then Chancellor of the Exchequer in the United Kingdom indicated in his budget speech that he intended to reform the maze of stamp duties and a consultative document was published shortly thereafter. The aim, inter alia, was to remove low yield stamp duties and to bring the appeals procedure and late fines into line with other taxes. This was attempted in 1985 when large swathes of stamp duties were abolished reducing by nearly one half the number of documents which had to be stamped. The aim at that time of budget surpluses was to remove elements from the taxation net and to concentrate on forms of high revenue yields. The reverses suffered in UK fiscal policy and the return to an increasing need for revenue in budget deficit times has halted any further progress in this sphere. However, in 1991 the United Kingdom for the first time used stamp duty as an instrument of economic planning by temporarily suspending the level of duty payable on private houses under £250,000 in an effort to revive a failing property market and to stimulate growth in that sector. It is not clear how this affected investments in capital securities which did not benefit from this relief, nor indeed if such measures have anything more than short-term impacts. In 1998 in Ireland, in a similar use of stamp duty as a tool of economic regulation, stamp duty rates were significantly reduced in an effort to slow down an overactive property market which had led to large increases in the cost of housing. This was done on the recommendation of a house price study by Peter Bacon and Associates, economic consultants, with a view to restoring order to the housing market. In the view of the authors, a reduction in stamp duty rates tends to increase house prices as vendors take the view that purchasers total cost has been reduced. This was clearly the motivation behind the British decision to stimulate the market, a decision which proved successful and restored market value to a depressed housing market. It has to be said, of course, that the Irish reduction in rates was coupled with other measures designed to remove the investor from the residential property section. These measures resulted in a slow down in the investor market for about 12 months. In addition to these measures there was to be a rental property levy which was subsequently abolished. The result of these measures is that they have not been, perhaps, as effective as was envisioned on their introduction, with the housing market in Ireland reaching new levels both in the investor and owner-occupier market.

[3.06] Finally in the United Kingdom a new stamp duty reserve tax was introduced in 1986 which was designed to be a tax on transactions. As a result of the emerging technology in the financial services sector, many transactions would no longer require a document that would be liable to stamp duty. Whether this is the first step on the road to a general transaction tax is unclear but it remains a possibility. Similar provisions with respect to the CREST[2] system of electronic settlement were enacted in Ireland in FA 1996. Where an electronic transfer of shares occurs under the CREST system, liability to stamp duty arises under s 69, despite the absence of an instrument. Amending company law provisions had to be enacted to enable the registrar of a company to update the company register on receipt of a valid message from CREST Ltd.

[3.07] The major changes in this jurisdiction occurred in FA 1991 when the voluntary nature of the duty was replaced by a mandatory nature and the imposition of liability on persons connected with the document, and FA 1994 where the appeal procedures in respect of stamp duty were brought in line with other taxes. In 1992 a limited amnesty was introduced along similar lines to other tax amnesties.[3] Any instrument executed before 1 November 1991, which was not stamped or was insufficiently stamped on 30 January 1992, could be presented for stamping on or before 30 June 1992 without payment of fines, penalties or interest thereon. Where said instrument was not presented until 30 September 1992, the interest was to be calculated as and from 30 June 1992.[4] A further general amnesty for tax liabilities was introduced in the Waiver of Certain Tax, Interest and Penalties Act 1993. Under this Act, a general amnesty enabled those in arrears of tax up to 5 April 1991 to pay the amount of tax outstanding in full and avoid any interest or penalty that might have arisen, provided that the tax was paid in full. Stamp duty came within the ambit of the general amnesty.

[3.08] In the authors' view, the time has come to rewrite and reform the legislation into a more coherent and rational system of tax. Currently the collection of stamp duty rest with the solicitors who interpret the provisions and then lodge the document and duty with the Revenue for stamping. If no effort is made to reduce the arcane complexity fi the tax, such practitioners should in the interests of the suty of care now owed by them pass this collection over to the Revenue Commissioners and request the Revenue to assess the duty arising on each document. In the words of Vinelott J:

> In the field of stamp duty... the presumption that the legislature intended to create a rational and coherent system of taxation is at least weaker than in other fiscal fields.[5]

---

2 CREST is the name of an electronic system which settles transfers of shares that are dealt with on the Irish and UK Stock Exchanges.

3 FA 1992, s 201.

4 Amnesty for Stamp Duties (SP-SD/1/92).

5 *Blandett v IRC* [1983] STC 17.

Consolidation of the legislation in 1999 resulted in the enactment of the SDCA 1999. The purpose of this Act was to remove some of the impenetrability of the legislative provisions governing the imposition of stamp duty as was the case under the Stamp Act 1891. It did so by consolidating into a single legislative enactment that which was previously to be found in a bewildering array of locations. The opportunity was not taken to simplify or streamline these legislative provisions in the SDCA and this is to be regretted. This Act has not dealt with the difficult nature and potential minefield of the law of stamp duty. With property prices escalating at an alarming rate and international transactions playing an increasingly important role in our economy, the repercussions for incorrectly assessing stamp duty are far greater than they ever were. Yet, it remains a tax which is difficult to understand and open to interpretation. With interpretation come mistakes, and it would appear far more so than with any of the other legislated taxes and often with greater financial cost.

General principles of stamp duty

General rules of interpreting tax statutes

[3.09] Because stamp duty is a tax, it falls within the general rubric of construction placed upon taxing Acts. Ambiguities in the Stamp Act, and related provisions, were to be construed in favour of the taxpayer prior to the passing of the Interpretation Act 2005 (IA 2005). Thus, in *JF O'Sullivan v Revenue Commissioners*,[6] the Revenue contended that a premium on the creation of a lease was stampable under the conveyance or transfer of sale head. Maguire CJ stated:

> Even if such a construction be one of the two constructions reasonably open the contention of the Revenue Commissioners must fail in view of the principle... that if the legislature intends to impose a tax upon the citizen, it must do so in clear language.

The legislature subsequently amended the Stamp Act to impose a liability to duty in these circumstances.[7]

[3.10] In *McGrath v McDermott*,[8] the Chief Justice stated that the interpretation of taxing statutes is strictly confined to the true meaning and in the case of doubt, the purpose of the statute may be determined by reference to other provisions of the Act or other relevant legislation. Carroll J in *Waterford Glass v The Revenue Commissioners*,[9] ruled that form should give way to substance in transactions designed to avoid tax. The traditional approach to the interpretation of taxing statutes was to be found in the decision of the House of Lords in *Duke of Westminster v IRC*.[10] In essence, it is the argument of substance over form and the result of the judgment is that form is to triumph. As Lord Tomlin said:

> Every man is entitled if he can to order his affairs so that the tax attaching under the appropriate Acts is less than it would otherwise be; if he succeeds in ordering them so as

6 *JF O'Sullivan v Revenue Commissioners* V ITR 570.

7 SDCA 1999, s 54.

8 *McGrath v McDermott* III ITR 683.

9 *Waterford Glass v The Revenue Commissioners* IV ITR 187.

10 *Duke of Westminster v IRC* [1936] AC 1.

> to secure this result then, however unappreciative the Commissioners of Inland Revenue or his fellow taxpayers may be of his ingenuity, he cannot be compelled to pay an increased tax. This so called doctrine of the substance seems to me to be nothing more than an attempt to make a man pay notwithstanding that he has ordered his affairs that the amount of tax sought from him is not legally claimable.

It followed in the interpretation of taxing acts, that they were to be construed strictly and without any preference given to the Revenue. This judgment encapsulated the earlier case law on the issue. In *Cape Brandy Syndicate v IRC*,[11] Rowlett J stated:

> In a taxing Act one has to look at what is clearly said. There is no room for any intendment. There is no equity about a tax. There is no presumption as to a tax. There is nothing to be read in, nothing to be implied. One can only look fairly at the language used.

And in *Re Micklethwaite*,[12] Parke B propounded:

> It is well established rule that the subject is not to be taxed without the clear words for that purpose; and also that every Act of Parliament must be read according to the natural construction of its words.

[3.11] It is clear, therefore, that in the application of a taxing Act, the court had very little discretion as to the consequences of the wording. A double-edged sword that affected both the Revenue and the taxpayer, it clearly operated in favour of the taxpayer who could plan to minimise tax liability by careful navigation through the precise wording of the language used. For the Revenue authorities their role was reduced to, in essence, closing the stable door after the horse had bolted. The Revenue closed loopholes in the next tax year but could not pre-emptively close them. In addition, in *Inspector of Taxes v Kiernan*,[13] Henchy J said:

> if a word or expression is used in a statute creating a penal or taxation liability, and there is looseness or ambiguity attaching to it, the words should be construed strictly so as to prevent a fresh imposition of liability from being created unfairly by the use of oblique or slack language ...

[3.12] Therefore, not only was the statute to be construed strictly, but where the meaning of the statute was ambiguous it was to be resolved in favour of the taxpayer. Note, however, that in the case of a relief or an exemption from a tax liability, this presumption would not apply as these provisions are to be construed strictly. In *IRC v Doorley*[14] the taxpayer left a bequest from which the income was to be paid to his wife for so long as she should live and thereafter to the Catholic Bishop of Elphin and another. A question arose as to whether legacy and succession duties were payable on the estate which passed to the Bishop as a charitable bequest. The Supreme Court held that the tax exemption covering charitable bequests was limited to such expenditure incurred within the jurisdiction.

---

11 *Cape Brandy Syndicate v IRC* [1921] 1 KB 64.

12 *Re Micklethwaite* [1855] 11 Ex 452.

13 *Inspector of Taxes v Kiernan* III ITR 19.

14 *IRC v Doorley* [1933] IR 750.

[3.13] It is the authors' opinion that it is the duty of the court to reject a priori line of reasoning and to examine the text of the taxing act in question and determine whether the tax in question is thereby imposed expressly and in clear and unambiguous terms, on the alleged subject of taxation, for no person or property is to be subject to taxation unless brought within the letter of the taxing statute ...[15].

[3.14] In this jurisdiction, the *Duke of Westminster* principle was accepted and approved in *O'Sullivan v P Ltd.*[16] This was re-affirmed by Keane J in *Revenue Commissioners v Henry Young.*[17] The idea that form is to be preferred over substance is somewhat misleading. In the *O'Sullivan* case the court rightly rejected the argument that a payment of money should be deemed to be the payment of a premium on a lease, merely because that was how the parties themselves labelled the document. On looking at the transaction, it was clearly a pre-payment of rent, whatever the instrument purported to call itself. The argument of form over substance applies in a situation where, for example, one wishes to convey property to another and, rather than execute an ordinary conveyance, one executes a series of different transactions which lead to a similar result but whereas the straightforward transaction would have been liable to tax, the series of transactions would not be so liable. There, even though the substance of the transaction is the same in both, the form prevails and the taxpayer, according to the principles we have been discussing, is under no tax liability. One caveat needs to be entered however, and that is that the transactions must be real transactions not sham transactions which are meant to be legally worthless. A sham transaction is a fraudulent transaction and no court will uphold such a transaction.[18]

[3.15] As time passed, the nature of society changed radically from the era of the decisions we have been discussing. The State's need for tax revenues became immense, and the skill and expertise of tax planners grew so that by the 1980s the favourable treatment of the taxpayer may have seemed difficult to justify.

[3.16] In two landmark decisions, the whole principle of the *Duke of Westminster v IRC*[19] case appeared to have been overturned. In *Ramsay v IRC*[20] the court effectively, albeit not expressly, rejected the basis of form over substance in taxing statutes and talked of how the entire transaction designed to avoid tax could not be successful where it relied on form to achieve this avoidance but where the substance of the transaction was taxable. This line of argument reached a zenith in *Furniss v Dawson*[21] where it was referred to as a pre-ordained series of transactions, or in the words of Brightman LJ:

> First there must be a pre-ordained series of transactions or, if one likes, one single composite transaction. this composite transaction may or may not include the achievement of a legitimate commercial end ... Secondly there must be steps inserted which have no

---

[15] *IRC v Doorley* [1933] IR 750, per Kennedy CJ.

[16] *O'Sullivan v P Ltd* II ITR 464.

[17] *Revenue Commissioners v Henry Young* V ITR 294.

[18] See *Revenue Commissioners v Moroney* [1982] IR 372.

[19] *Duke of Westminster v IRC* [1936] AC 1.

[20] *Ramsay v IRC* [1980] STC 174.

[21] *Furniss v Dawson* [1984] STC 153.

> commercial purpose apart from the avoidance of a liability to tax ... If these two ingredients exist, the inserted steps are to be disregarded for fiscal purposes. The court must then look at the end result. Precisely how the end result will be taxed will depend on the terms of the taxing statute sought to be applied.

[3.17] The radical nature of this decision caused unease in tax planners as to the new approach that would be taken by the courts. Construed at its broadest it would render many transactions which carried a substantial element of tax avoidance, worthless. In essence, an individual would no longer be able to order his or her affairs in a manner so as to minimise the liability to tax. In *Ingrams v IRC*[22] it was held that in assessing the liability to stamp duty the court must ascertain the substance of the transaction, not merely the instruments involved. The court was entitled to disregard transactions which had no business purpose and were part of a pre-ordained series of transactions and treat all the transactions as one transaction, taxing the end result. Later this approach was overturned in England, in particular in the case of *Shephert v Lyntress*[23] where Vinelott J stated:

> The [Revenue] Commissioners cannot characterise a series of steps as a single composite transaction unless they have first found facts sufficient to support that inference...It is not enough to say that [the shares] were transferred with a view to a sale and in order that the gains should be realised ... That would be to make the fiscal motive alone a sufficient ground for imposing tax.

It is clear, therefore, that the courts have decided to give a narrow application to the rule in *Furniss* and *Ramsay* but are unwilling to abrogate the new approach in its entirety.

[3.18] The approach was not particular to the United Kingdom and there are numerous decisions of the courts of the United States which have effectively tilted the balance in favour of the Revenue authority and away from the well-advised taxpayer. In America, much difficulty has centred around transactions that come within the strict wording of a tax-relieving statute, where the transaction has no purpose other than to avail of the relief. That is, it is not a commercial transaction in the real sense. In *Gregory v Helvering*[24] the US Supreme Court held that such transactions could not benefit from the relevant statutory provision as the legislation had not so intended them to benefit. In *CIR v National Carbide*,[25] Learned Hand J put it in the following manner:

> It is not the presence of an accompanying motive to escape taxation that is ever decisive but the absence of any motive which brings the transaction within those which the statute normally includes ...

This concept is very much in accordance with the principles espoused in *Furniss* and *Ramsey*. Doubtless in many commercial transactions tax minimisation is an important part of the process, but it cannot be the sole purpose of the transaction. Tax transactions apply to real transactions that would have occurred in any event, not to transactions

22 *Ingrams v IRC* [1985] STC 835.

23 *Shephert v Lyntress* [1989] STC 617.

24 *Gregory v Helvering* [1934] 293 US 465.

25 *CIR v National Carbide* [1948] 167 Fed 2, 304.

whose sole existence derives from the tax acts themselves. To do otherwise would be to permit fraud through statutory protection and few courts are willing to do this.[26]

[3.19] The entire issue was revisited in this jurisdiction in *McGrath v McDermott*[27] by the Supreme Court. In that case, the Revenue Commissioners placed considerable emphasis on the decisions in the United States and in *Furniss* and *Ramsey* in the United Kingdom. Both the High Court and the Supreme Court roundly rejected the principles so proposed to them. They re-affirmed the decisions in *O'Sullivan v P Ltd*[28] and *Duke of Westminster v IRC.*[29] Form was to triumph again over substance. In the words of Finlay CJ:

> The function of the courts in interpreting a statute of the Oireachtas is, however, strictly confined to ascertaining the true meaning of each statutory provision, resorting in cases of doubt or ambiguity to a consideration of the purpose and intention of the legislature to be inferred from other provisions of the statute involved, or even of other statutes expressed to be construed with it. The courts have not got a function to add to or delete from express statutory provisions so as to achieve objectives which to the courts appear desirable. In rare and limited circumstances words or phrases may be implied into statutory provisions solely for the purposes of making them effective to achieve their expressly avowed objective. What is urged upon the court by the Revenue in this case is no more and no less than the implication into the provisions of either CGTA 1975 ss 12 or 33 of a new sub-clause or sub-section providing that a condition precedent to the computing of an allowable loss pursuant to the provisions of s 33(5) is the proof by the taxpayer of an actual loss, presumably at least co-extensive with the artificial loss to be computed in accordance with the sub-section. I must reject this contention.

[3.20] Since this judgment was approved unanimously by the Supreme Court, the issue should have been put to rest in this jurisdiction with a straightforward re-affirmation of the traditional principles. However, by virtue of FA 1989, s 86,[30] a catch-all anti-avoidance measure was introduced into law whereby the Revenue Commissioners were given the power to cast an opinion that a transaction was designed primarily to avoid tax liability. Effectively, the Revenue could now look to the purpose of the transaction and if the transaction was designed to avoid a tax liability or in corollary, benefit from a tax relief, then it could be ignored. The section applies to almost all taxes, including stamp duty. An appeal lies to the Appeal Commissioners and the Circuit Court where a taxpayer is aggrieved at the determination of the Revenue. In coming to a decision, the Revenue can look at three things only: the result of the transaction, the methodology of the transaction and the scope of alternative methods aimed at achieving the same result. The section is relatively long and complex and it would be inappropriate to deal with it in considerable detail in a text of this nature; suffice it to say it is a far-reaching power of the Revenue, though judicial decisions may raise the need for substantial amendments if it is to remain effective. It is clear that s 86 could arguably be regarded as investing the

---

26 *Nestor v Murphy* [1979] IR 326.

27 *McGrath v McDermott* III ITR 683.

28 *O'Sullivan v P Ltd* II ITR 464.

29 *Duke of Westminster v IRC* [1936] AC 1.

30 Now consolidated in TCA 1997, s 811.

Revenue Commissioners with a judicial role in the assessment to liability, thus breaching the separation of powers principle enshrined between the organs of state. It may also arguably be an unjustified attack on the constitutional right to own property. It is in the light of this that we briefly look at the decision in *Waterford Glass*[31] from Carroll J in the High Court.

[3.21] In essence the decision preferred substance over form and did not follow the *McGrath v McDermott*[32] decision but appeared to be adopting the *Furniss* and *Ramsey* decisions. In this regard it is to be regretted and, failing further elucidation from the Supreme Court, to be treated with a degree of caution. What is even more curious about the decision of Carroll J in *Waterford* is that it was in direct contrast to her decision in the High Court in *McGrath v McDermott* rejecting the Ramsay approach, which was upheld by the Supreme Court. Neither can it be said that Carroll J relied on s 86[33] in reaching her decision. That particular section is not referred to, and indeed was not applicable to a transaction carried out before 25 January 1989. Carroll J's new approach was also followed in *Viek Investments v IRC*[34] shortly after. Whether it points to a new departure for the Irish courts remains to be seen. While these cases would indicate that the approach of the courts to a stamp duty avoidance scheme will be difficult to predict, it is the view of the authors that they do not signal a movement to the substance over form approach. In England, *IRC v McGuckian*[35] upholding *Ramsay*, appears, however, to signal a more forceful approach to the principal that the new development was not based on the linguistic analysis of the particular words of a statute. It was founded on the broad purposive interpretation giving effect to the intention of Parliament (per Steyn LJ).

> As stated earlier, whether such cases should be followed in this jurisdiction with a tax which is mandatory as distinct from voluntary and in a legal framework of a written constitution remains to be seen.

[3.22] The approach of Steyn LJ in *IRC v McGuckian* has since 1 January 2006 been given statutory authority in this State with the passing of the IA 2005[36]. Section 5 broadly states that ambiguous or obscure provisions should be given a construction that reflects the plain intention of the Oireachtas or relevant parliament where the intention can be ascertained from the Act as a whole. In addition to this it states that, where the literal interpretation would be absurd, then the provision should be given a construction that reflects the intention of the maker of an instrument. Section 6 relates to construing provisions in changing circumstances and states that the courts are entitled, in interpreting the legislation, to make allowances for any changes in the law, social conditions, technology, the meaning of words used in the Act or the making of that statutory instrument. This right of the courts is restricted in so far as they may only make allowances as far as the legislation's text, purpose and context permit.

---

31 *Waterford Glass* IV ITR 187.

32 *McGrath v McDermott* III ITR 683.

33 Now TCA 1997, s 811.

34 *Viek Investments v IRC* IV ITR 367.

35 *IRC v McGuckian* [1997] STC 908.

36 See IA 2005, ss 5 and 6.

[3.23] In essence these provisions mean that from the date of enactment of IA 2005 (ie 1 January 2006), any ambiguous legislation will now be read in favour of the intention of the legislator. Prior to this date, ambiguous legislation was read in favour of the taxpayer as decided in the case of *Inspector of Taxes v Kiernan*.[37] In the author's view the limitations of these provisions lie, firstly, in the fact that the intention of the legislator is not necessarily directly comparable to that of the Revenue Commissioners, and, secondly, proving the intention of the legislator may be impossible in the absence of any direct commentary on the reasoning behind the enactment of certain legislation.

[3.24] In addition to the enactment of the IA 2005, the Finance Act 2006 at s 126 has introduced s 811A which further extends TCA 1997 the scope of s 811. This section provides that where the opinion of the Revenue Commissioners that a transaction is a tax avoidance transaction becomes final, interest and a 10 per cent surcharge will be payable on the tax that the taxpayer unsuccessfully attempted to avoid paying. The section also provides that, by making a protective notification to Revenue in respect of a transaction within 90 days of beginning a transaction, the taxpayer can, on a wholly non-prejudicial basis, obtain protection from the possibility of such interest or surcharge arising, in the event of Revenue successfully challenging the transaction. The combination of the new provisions and legislation together with the existing provisions of TCA 1997, s 811 has potentially huge ramifications for tax planning and tax practitioners.

[3.25] Kevin Kenny in his paper[38] commented on the difficulties of the practical application of TCA 1997, s 811. In this paper he summarised the limitations of the section as follows:

1. Administrative Burden – the starting point for a Revenue opinion in relation to this section requires that the Revenue must take the initiative in forming an opinion and that the sheer administrative burden of this would deter the Revenue from using the section on a wide basis;
2. Defences to TCA 1997, s 811 – transactions can still be entered into for tax avoidance purposes and still not be caught within the remit of the section particularly due to the lack of any official reports or memoranda in the spirit and purpose of the tax legislation;
3. Tax Avoidance Transaction – the section requires that the transaction be entered into primarily for a tax avoidance purpose which is a stringent test for the Revenue to meet. There are very few transactions without a commercial purpose and in some cases the transaction may be structured to comply with other legal requirements such as company law;
4. Quantification of Tax Consequences – the tax consequences of transactions are difficult to quantify as there is rarely one tax consequence in a complex

[37] *Inspector of Taxes v Kiernan*

[38] 'The Evolution of General Anti-Avoidance Legislation including the Analysis of Legislation in the US, Canada and Australia' given in March 1990.

situation. There are several possible combinations all with substantially different tax effects.

[3.26] It is the view of the authors that the enactment of FA 2006, s 126 will put to rest most, if not all of these limitations of TCA 1997, s 811. The administrative burden has been shifted to the taxpayer. In addition to this, and probably the single most important effect of this section, the decision as to whether a transaction could potentially be classified as a tax avoidance transaction has been shifted to the taxpayer. While the defences to TCA 1997, s 811 and the commercial reality of transactions still exist, the obligations and responsibilities under the section have been firmly moved to the taxpayer's court. There is no Revenue guidance or any case law dealing with the definition of a tax avoidance transaction. In light of this, to expect the tax payer to be the one to make the decisions as to what constitutes tax avoidance seems unfair and inequitable especially as the Revenue appeared to fail to do so when it was their responsibility.

[3.27] It is impossible at this point to comment on the long-lasting effects of these new provisions, but certainly it can be said that a new climate of tax planning will have to evolve. In applying the provisions to any particular circumstances, it may be worth reviewing the court's interpretation of European legislation as it will look at the preparation papers relating to the formation of the Directive and apply them if they are assistance. This may provide precedents for the application of the IA 2005.

Tax on instruments

[3.28] Stamp duty applies, in general, to instruments and not transactions, unlike value added tax, capital gains tax, capital acquisitions tax and corporation tax which rely on transactions and not on instruments.[39] An instrument includes every written document.[40] In the absence of an instrument there would be the practical difficulty of the placement of any such stamp. It is interesting to realise that the greatest limitation on this form of taxation arises almost exclusively from practical concerns.

[3.29] As Lord Esher points out:

> ... the thing which is made liable to duty is an 'instrument'. If a contract of purchase and sale... can be or is carried out without an instrument the case is not within the section, and no tax is imposed. It is not the transaction of purchase and sale which is struck at; it is the instrument whereby the purchase and sale are effected which is struck at.[41]

This resulted in the Revenue Authorities requiring the existence of a written instrument where ordinarily one was not required, such as the transfer of shares or debentures in order to ensure continued revenue flows from that source. Specific provisions have been introduced concerning electronic share dealing, discussed earlier.[42] It has been further

---

39 See *Royal Liver Friendly Society v IRC* [1870] LR 5 Ex 78.

40 SDCA 1999, s 1(1).

41 *IRC v Angus* [1889] 23 QB 579, 589.

42 See para **[3.06]**.

eroded by the imposition of company capital duty which reflects European input on fiscal legislation.

Stamp duty also involves a dispute concerning substance over form. Traditionally in taxing statutes the principle of form over substance as enunciated by the *Westminster* case has predominated, but the extent of this doctrine was curtailed in the *Ramsay* case by the forceful judgment of Lord Wilberforce:

> ... (the) well known principle of *IRC v Duke of Westminster* [1936] AC 1 ... is a cardinal principle but it must not be overstated or over extended ... it does not compel the court to look at a document or transaction in blinkers, isolated from any context to which it properly belongs.[43]

[3.30] To what extent may the court look behind the instrument and attach liability to the transaction? If it is possible for a court to do this, then it would strike at the very heart of tax planning for stamp duty purposes. It may well be that, as currently framed, the legislation imposing stamp duty cannot be the subject of the *Ramsay* principle, yet since stamp duty is viewed as a tax it is difficult to see how it can be avoided. This was certainly the view in the English case of *IRC v Ingrams*[44] where the court held that it was entitled to ascertain the substance of the transaction in order to determine whether the instrument was chargeable. This difficulty has been evidenced in the judgments of Irish courts in cases such as *Waterford Glass v The Revenue Commissioners, Viek Investments* and *McGrath v McDermott* even though the principles as enunciated in the latter have been somewhat eroded. What remains important at this point is that the duty attaches only to an instrument that comes into existence in an effort to achieve a stated aim. If the stated aim can be achieved in the absence of such an instrument, there seems little reason to deny the efficacy of such a transaction and subject it to duty.[45]

The memorandum rule

[3.31] The cardinal rule is that an instrument is chargeable to duty only to the extent of that which is achieved by the instrument. The question is what is achieved by the instrument? For example, does the instrument affect a sale? The more important question is whether or not an instrument that records the existence of a previous transaction, that is a receipt falls liable to duty.

[3.32] Clearly where a transaction is effected orally and no instrument comes into being, there is no stamp duty liability. It is in situations where a transaction is effected partly orally and partly in writing that difficulties can arise. Where there has been an oral agreement and a document subsequently comes into existence evidencing this oral agreement, it is possible that this document may fall to be stampable on the basis that the oral agreement, together with the written evidence of this agreement, were one and the same transaction. The case of *Cohen & Moore v IRC*[46] led to the 'memorandum rule' which essentially indicates that a later written memorandum of a transaction carried out

---

43 *Ramsay v IRC* [1982] AC 300, 323.

44 *IRC v Ingrams* [1985] STC 835.

45 See **Chapter 4** for a further discussion on this issue.

46 *Cohen & Moore v IRC* [1933] 2 KB 126.

orally may be stampable as if it effected the transaction. There are four limitations to the scope of the doctrine:

(a) The principle shall not apply where the instrument is brought into existence for some other purpose, which could be said to the primary purpose. (Therefore there is authority that the recording of a transaction in board minutes would not render the minute book a dutiable memorandum);
(b) The instrument must be intended to be an effective record. It would seem that a signature of necessary authentication by at least one of the parties or a duly authorised agent is necessary (this should be the vendor or person transferring the title). A record signed by the purchaser would seem to be ineffective for this purpose as this would not be sufficient to transfer the property;
(c) The principle cannot be used to alter the substance of an instrument;
(d) The principle does not permit the duty to be shifted from one instrument to another nor to charge stamp duty upon one document in respect of another part of the same transaction.

[3.33] What we are talking of here is documentary evidence of a completed transaction. The instrument serves an evidentiary function only and unless made expressly liable by the Acts, does not fall within any head of charge. In *International Power v IRC*[47] an instrument in the United Kingdom evidenced an instrument of a conveyance of foreign property. It was held that the United Kingdom instrument which evidenced the foreign conveyance of a property, even though same was not stamped or produced in evidence, was not stampable as a conveyance.

[3.34] This rather large gap in the legislation has been somewhat remedied by judicial interventionism. A receipt has been held to be stampable per Channell J in *Garnett v IRC*.[48] In that case, a receipt of the share on the dissolution of partnership was held liable to duty. This has been followed in *Cohen & Moore v IRC*[49] where it is more readily identified that it is not the receipt which attracts the duty but that the receipt forms part of a single transaction. In this case, the parties had orally supplemented the funds of a settlement and some five weeks later executed an appointment of new trustees detailing the additional funds. In holding the instrument liable to duty, Finlay J stated:[50]

> I think the transaction was really all one transaction, and being one transaction, the whole was recorded in the document.

This sort of reasoning was well in accord with the dicta of Channell J in *Garnett v IRC*,[51] who went further by pointing out that 'If there was a clearly independent transaction then it would stand on a different footing'. These decisions remain open to question but the practice has been to treat them as a correct statement of the law. The Revenue must prove that the instrument in question is part of a single transaction. This was easier to

47 *International Power v IRC* [1933] 12 ATC 413.
48 *Garnett v IRC* [1899] 81 LT 633.
49 *Cohen & Moore v IRC* [1933] 2 KB 126.
50 [1933] 2 KB 126 at 137.
51 [1899] 81 LT 633 at 638.

prove in *Cohen & Moore* where there was evidence that the instrument had been provisionally prepared when the oral transaction was effected. It would appear that some reasonable method of avoidance might involve having the recording instrument prepared for some other purpose, such as the minutes of a meeting or perhaps a recital referring to a prior transaction. The reasoning behind why board minutes may circumvent the memorandum rule is on the basis that they fall into the first limitation of the rule in that the primary purpose of board minutes is to record the minutes of a director's meeting and is a requirement of company law and in addition give effect to a commercial purpose.

[3.35] It might be arguable that if the instrument comes into existence prior to the transaction it may not be liable to duty since the relevant date for liability to duty arises at the date of the execution of the document and at such time no transaction has occurred. The facts and decision in an Irish case[52] are illuminating in this regard. The facts were that by a contract for sale dated 4 March 1987 the Donaghmede Shopping Centre, Co Dublin was to be sold subject to, but with the benefit of, numerous leases. The consideration was set out in clause 7 as follows:

> ... the consideration for the agreement herein shall be satisfied by:
>
> (a) the issue by the purchaser to the vendor of 1,281,000 ordinary shares in the purchaser on 12 March 1987; and
>
> (b) the payment of the sum of £46,000 in cash by the purchaser to the vendor on 13 April 1987.
>
> On the issue of the said shares to the satisfaction of the vendor in accordance with Clause 8 hereof, the purchaser shall be entitled to the possession of the property sold hereby and shall be entitled to the receipt of the rents and the profits thereof and will be liable for all outgoings thereof.

The shares were duly transferred on 12 March 1987 in accordance with the conditions of the contract. By a further contract on the same date the purchaser under the first contract purported to sell to Viek Investments Ltd the same premises subject to the consideration of £46,000.

The Revenue Commissioners assessed the stamp duty payable, being *ad valorem* duty on the full consideration in the first contract.

[3.36] Viek Investments Ltd counter-argued that they were not a party to the first contract and the consideration passing was £46,000. It was held that it was all one transaction and the Revenue Commissioners' view prevailed. Any potential ability to argue that they are two separate transactions would be somewhat limited.

[3.37] The instrument which it is sought to charge must be signed by the effecting party; for example, by the vendor who aims to transfer title. An instrument that is not signed, or otherwise authenticated, would presumably not be chargeable. Finally, any such instrument must have come into existence as a result of the transaction alone and it is not possible to use this doctrine to combine instruments, or to shift duty from one instrument to another. It cannot be used to change the nature of the instrument and make it

52 *Viek Investments Ltd v IRC* IV ITR 367.

chargeable with more duty than the purpose the instrument gives effect to; that is, a mortgage cannot be changed into a conveyance.

[3.38] The liability to stamp duty on an instrument depends on the facts and circumstances present at the time of execution of the instrument. This principle was extensively used for avoidance techniques and it resulted in considerable anti-avoidance legislation. The principal difficulty is determining the date of execution of the instrument. It is accepted that the date the instrument is first executed is the date the instrument first becomes effected. In *Byrne v IRC*[53] there was a sale of a premises and the deed was signed and sealed but not delivered in January 1932. It took three to four months to rectify the title which was complete in May 1932. At that stage the deed was delivered. In March 1934 the parties noticed that the deed was wrongly stamped and immediately applied for a refund. Under SDMA 1891, s 10 the parties were entitled to make an application for a refund, provided it was made within two years from the date of execution of the instrument. The question at issue was whether the instrument was executed in January 1932 and outside the time limit, or in May 1932 and within the time limit for which the taxpayer would be entitled to a refund. The court held the date of delivery was the date of execution and the taxpayer was entitled to a refund. It has been held that an escrow is not executed on the date of the fulfilment of a condition but on the date of delivery.[54]

Composite documents

[3.39] There are two distinct possibilities here. Either an instrument may effect more than one purpose or it may be capable of classification under more than one heading and we turn to deal with both of these issues.

Primary purpose

[3.40] There is no better established rule as regards stamp duty than that all that is required is that the instrument should be stamped for its leading and principal object and that this stamp covers everything accessory to this object.[55]

[3.41] An instrument is liable only for its primary purpose and not for every single issue raised.[56] Liability will attach to the primary object of the instrument and will 'hide' liability for subsidiary matters, but it will not do so where there are two or more distinct matters contained within one instrument and liability may fall under more than one heading.

[3.42] Under SDCA 1999, s 7(a), an instrument relating to several distinct matters is to be separately charged with duty as if it were a separate instrument in respect of each of the matters, except where express provisions are made to the contrary by legislation. For example, in *Hadgett v IRC*[57] on the creation of a trust, an order appointing new trustees

53 *Byrne v IRC* [1935] IR 664.

54 See *Re Duke of Devonshire Settlement* [1952] 31 ATC 399.

55 *R v Ridgewell* [1827] 6 Bx C 665.

56 *Wills v Bridge* [1849] 4 Exch 193.

57 *Hadgett v IRC* [1877] 3 Ex D 46.

was held liable for duty, both as a conveyance of the property, since the property was vested in the trustees by the order, and as the appointment of trustees. By contrast, only one stamp is required for the surrender of a lease in consideration for the grant of a new lease.[58]

[3.43] Whether there is more than one distinct matter in the instrument will be determined by the question set down by Lord President Dunedin in *General Accident Assurance v IRC*[59] where he said:

> I cannot think of any better test than to take the second so called contract and see if it would stand alone; and that is to say, to use the current expression, whether it would stand on its own feet.

The question of the interpretation of the term 'matter' in this section causes some difficulty. In *Reversionary Interest Society v IRC*[60] the court stated that the term 'matter' must refer to matters falling within the various heads of charge. In *Ansell v IRC*[61] Rowlatt J stated that:

> If two different classes of property are being transferred by the same words of assignment in the same document and those two different classes of property in this same document are different from the point of view of the Stamp Act and taxation, it seems to me in common sense that they must be two distinct matters.

> For example in a lease with a rent review clause the rent review clause is chargeable separately and liability attaches to the rent under the lease head. A further example is the Bank of Ireland mortgage which may contain the assignment of the endowment policy within the mortgage deed and is stampable as:
>
> (i) a mortgage, and
>
> (ii) collateral assignment of an endowment or life policy.
>
> Other forms of mortgages effect the assignment by way of separate documents. Bank of Ireland now appear to use separate instruments.

[3.44] Any alteration to an instrument that has already been stamped creates a new instrument which falls liable to duty.[62] If the alteration is to the quantum of consideration only, then the *ad valorem* duty will be paid on the increase of the quantum. For example, if the rent review clause is exercised in a lease, stamp duty should be paid under the lease head on the increase of the rent only and this would be inserted by way of memorandum into the lease so as to ensure the landlord would be able to effectively recover the rent outstanding, together with the increased rent, in a court of law.[63] This is subject to limitations.[64] Indeed it may be that there is no alteration in the consideration and, provided the alteration to the instrument does not create a new

58 *Doe D Phillips v Phillips* [1840] 11 Ad&El 796.

59 *General Accident Assurance v IRC*[1906] 8F (Ct of Sess) 477).

60 *Reversionary Interest Society v IRC* [1906] 22 TLR 740.

61 *Ansell v IRC* [1929] 1 KB 608.

62 *London & Brighton Poly v Fairclough* [1841] 2 M&G 674.

63 *Limmer Asphalte Paving Co Ltd v IRC* [1872] LR 7 Exch 211.

64 See **Chapter 6**.

transaction, no additional liability will be incurred. One interesting feature of this rule is that if the primary object of the instrument is exempt from liability, so too will a secondary aim of the instrument be even if that secondary aim by itself would be liable to the duty. The corollary is also true that a secondary aim of the instrument which would be exempt from duty will suffer if the primary object of the instrument is liable to duty. For example, a lease attracts only one charge to duty, even if the lease should contain a clause giving an option for renewal, which would normally attract two stamp duty liabilities if this option was contained in different instruments. Finally, SDCA 1999, s 7(b) concerns an instrument which contains two or more considerations and under this section the instrument shall be chargeable to duty for each of the considerations involved; for example a lease of property at a rent of €5,000 and 10 per cent of turnover. Duty would be payable on both considerations, that is the €5,000 and the 10 per cent.[65]

Instruments falling under more than one head of charge

[3.45] Notwithstanding the provisions of SDCA 1999, s 7 as described above, despite the fact that an instrument may contain several distinct matters, the Revenue may treat the primary purpose as being that which attracts the largest amount of duty.[66] If the primary object is liable to charge and the secondary object is within an exemption, the instrument shall still be chargeable.[67]

Example 3.45.1

The voluntary transfer of property with a market valuation of €90,000, subject to a mortgage of €40,000 could be charged under the following heads:

(a) SDCA 1999, s 41 on the debt €40,000;

(b) on the equity of redemption on €50,000;

(c) SDCA 1999, s 30(4) at market value less the mortgage liability which equals of €50,000.

[3.46] The Revenue Notes for Guidance[68] indicate that where a voluntary disposition *inter vivos* is subject to a mortgage, the Revenue Commissioners will, as a matter of practice, deduct the mortgage liability in arriving at the value of the benefit passing. This gives effect to the actual value of what is passing.

[3.47] Where there is a gift and a debt assumed by the donee, the value of the debt is subtracted from the market value to arrive at the net value of the gift. Duty is assessed on the net value of the gift, ie the equity of redemption or the debt, whichever is the greater. The rule of the equity of redemption states that a mortgagee must always be entitled to redeem the charge on their property. The relevant phrase in respect of the equity of redemption is 'no clog or fetter on the equity of redemption'. In the above example,

---

65 Note: As the 10 per cent turnover consideration is unascertainable, specific rules would apply, see **Chapter 6**.

66 *Speyer Brothers v IRC* [1908] AC 92.

67 *Deddingtons SS Co Ltd v IRC* [1911] 2 KB 1001, CA.

68 Guidance Notes on SDCA 1999, at p 41.

while the Revenue Commissioners would be entitled to charge tax on the largest amount, in practice, they would charge tax on the equity of redemption, that is €50,000.

[3.48] Once the Revenue has selected the primary purpose, no liability arises for secondary purposes according to the principles outlined above. If an instrument is chargeable by way of statutory provision to a specific head of charge, it is not possible for the Revenue to seek to have it charged under a general head of charge, even if the duty so payable is greater than that to be levied under the specific head of charge. For example, an increase in rent could have been chargeable under the general mortgage bond head but the legislation specifically provides that the increase in rent under the lease should be chargeable as an additional rent only under the lease head.[69]

Presumption of proper stamping

[3.49] There is a rebuttable presumption that all documents are properly stamped. This does not apply to instruments relating to foreign law which do not come within the ambit of the Stamp Act.[70]

Foreign stamp duty

[3.50] In general, no account of foreign stamp duties will be taken by the courts. A foreign document that is not stamped by the source country, even though it should be, and does not fall within the charging section of this jurisdiction, is nonetheless admissible in evidence. The corollary is also true that the presence of a foreign stamp on an instrument carries no significance. There is one exception to this, where the instrument in question is the subject of foreign stamp duty laws which render the document void if not stamped. The courts will take notice of such legislation and if the instrument is not stamped, then it will be treated as void by the court.[71]This also applies where the instrument is void for insufficient stamp duty.

Incidents of stamp duty liability

Introduction

[3.51] Prior to the passing of FA 1991, there was no compulsion on the party to an instrument, which came within the charging sections of SA 1891, to stamp the instrument. In *IRC v Maple and Co (Paris) Ltd*[72] Lord M'Naghten said:

> I think that it is clear that there is nothing criminal in a purchaser omitting to stamp his conveyance. By such an omission he commits no breach of duty. He does nothing wrong.

The sanctions for not stamping the instrument were negative in fashion as stamp duty was a voluntary tax. In *Henty and Constable (Breweries) Ltd v IRC*[73] Donovan LJ stated:

> … there was however no legal obligation on Henty to stamp the transfer; there was simply the prospect of future disabilities and disadvantages if they did not.

---

[69] SDCA 1999, s 52(4) and *Gambit Construction Co v IRC* [1968] 2 All ER 968.

[70] *Henty & Constable (Breweries) Ltd v IRC* [1961] 3 All ER 1146.

[71] *Republica de Guatamala v Nunez* [1927] 1 KB 669.

[72] *IRC v Maple and Co (Paris) Ltd* [1907] 77 LJ KB 55.

[73] *Henty and Constable (Breweries) Ltd v IRC* [1961] 1 WLR 1504.

FA 1991 made stamp duty a compulsory tax. The parties to an instrument which comes within the charging sections of SDCA 1999 are compelled to discharge the stamp duty liability, and in certain circumstances both parties to the deed may be liable for the duty.

[3.52] Under SA 1891, s 1,[74] stamp duty was to be charged on the several instruments specified in Sch 1 to the Act. Prior to FA 1991, there was no compulsion to discharge the duty arising on the deed, but there were exceptions to this rule. The following provisions encouraged the parties to stamp an instrument.

SA 1891, s 14 (now SDCA 1999, s 127)

[3.53] This imposed a duty on judges, arbitrators and referees to inspect any instrument produced as evidence in any court of civil judicature to ensure that the instrument was properly stamped.[75] This duty exists even where the parties do not dispute the fact that the deed is properly stamped and even when they consent to admitting same in evidence.[76] If an instrument is required to be used in evidence, the payment of the duty becomes mandatory. However, it has become the practice of judges to accept an undertaking by solicitors to stamp the instrument and to produce it so stamped and the order is made subject to the production of the stamped instrument. Judges accept these undertakings as solicitors are officers of the court.[77]

Once a judge makes a ruling as to the stamp duty liability on an instrument, either that it is sufficiently stamped or is not liable to stamp duty, his decision is deemed to be final.[78] If a judge rejects a document as insufficiently stamped the duty must be tendered immediately and the tendering noted so that the parties have a right to appeal.[79]

[3.54] In a case where the instrument cannot be produced in evidence since it is missing, it is normally presumed to have been properly stamped.[80] This presumption is rebuttable but the presumption may be revived by proving facts confirming that the document was properly stamped. If a notice to produce is served and the party upon which it is served fails to furnish the deed, the opposite party can call evidence proving a copy of the original deed and such copy may be read without being stamped, since the copy deed was used in evidence merely to refresh the witness's memory.[81] If it is known that the original deed was unstamped, and a copy is produced in evidence, this copy would also be inadmissible. However, the production of a stamped copy covering the duty and penalty may be admissible in court.[82] This arises from the decision in *London & County Banking Co v Ratcliffe*[83] where Lord Blackburn admitted such a stamped copy. Both

74 Now SDCA 1999, s 2(1).

75 SDCA 1999, s 127(1).

76 *Bower v Williamson* [1889] 5 TLR 382 and *Nixon v Albion Marine Insurance Co* [1867] LR 2 Exch 338.

77 *Re Coolgardie Goldfields Ltd* [1900] 1 Ch 475 and *Parkfield Trust v Dent* [1931] 2 KB 579.

78 *Blewitt v Tritton* [1892] 2 QB 327.

79 *Campbell v Loader* [1865] 34 LJ Ex 50.

80 *Henty & Constable (Breweries) Ltd v IRC* [1961] 1 WLR 1504.

81 *Braythwayt v Hitchcock* [1842] 10 M&W 494.

82 *Nally v Nally* [1953] IR 19 and SDCA 1999, s 127(1).

83 *London & County Banking Co v Ratcliffe* [1881] 6 AC 722.

decisions failed to cite the contrary judgment in *Connor v Cronin*.[84] It is inappropriate for counsel to raise a defect in stamping of an instrument unless such defect invalidates the instrument.[85]

[3.55] Where the stamp duty and penalty are paid to an officer, arbitrator or referee, a receipt shall be given for same, and a full return of all the relevant details should be made to the Revenue Commissioners.[86] Once the documentation has been furnished to the Revenue Commissioners together with the receipt, the instrument should be denoted accordingly.[87]

SDCA 1999, s 127(4)

[3.56] Any instrument executed in any part of the State or relating to any property so situate or to any manner or thing done or to be done in any part of the State shall not be given in evidence unless it is duly stamped, except in criminal proceedings[88] where proceedings for recovery of a penalty were held to be of a criminal nature). This section has a very wide ambit. In *IRC v Maple & Co (Paris) Ltd*[89] an 'acte d'apport' was executed in France where one English company transferred property situate in France to another English company. Shares in the latter company were used as consideration for the property and were to be issued and delivered to the former company in England. The court held that the agreement was liable to *ad valorem* duty as a conveyance on sale and was caught within the ambit of SA 1891, s 14(4). The limitations of this obligation were outlined in *Parin v (Hatfield) v IRC*[90] which held that these words were not an absolute prohibition and referred only to the fact that one person cannot compel another to produce an unstamped document but that, for example, the Revenue Commissioners were not prevented from looking at the instrument to assess the amount of duty payable.

[3.57] A deed, when produced in evidence, has to be duly stamped in accordance with the law in force at the time when it was first executed. In *Clarke v Roche*[91] a deed was produced in evidence which appeared to be sufficiently stamped, as it was stamped according to the law in force at the date appearing on the deed. However, the deed was executed some years previously when the duty was different and the court held that the deed could not be produced in evidence. In *AIB v Bolger*[92] the defendants appealed an order from the High Court granting possession of their property to AIB Bank. They argued that the date of execution on the mortgage was in reality significantly earlier than that stated on the instrument. An issue arose as to the admissibility of the instrument under the provisions of SA 1870, s 17, as amended by SA 1891, s 14(4), as same may

[84] *Connor v Cronin* [1858] 7 ICLR 450.

[85] See *Collenette v Ryan* (1933) ILT 33.

[86] SDCA 1999, s 127(2).

[87] SDCA 1999, s 127(3).

[88] See *R v Lee* [1882] 9 QB 394.

[89] *IRC v Maple & Co (Paris) Ltd* [1908] AC 22.

[90] *Parin v (Hatfield) v IRC* [1996] STC 933.

[91] *Clarke v Roche* [1877] 3 QBD 170.

[92] *AIB v Bolger* V ITR 1.

not have been properly stamped. In the Supreme Court, Finlay CJ held that the issue of liability between the defendants and AIB was the matter at hand, the issue of the date of the instrument was an issue of fact and the High Court judge had discretion as to whether it was necessary to make a determination or not. The issue of the date of execution of the instrument went to a matter of penalty payments owed to the Revenue Commissioners and did not impact on the liability *inter partes*.

[3.58] In *Kelly v Revenue Commissioners, Goodman and Gemon Ltd*[93] Costello J held that it was not open to an applicant to seek judicial review of an adjudication by the Revenue Commissioners of the duty payable on an instrument by another party. In the case at hand an instrument had been adjudicated by the Revenue Commissioners and was held liable to a fixed duty of €12.50. The applicant, a notice party who had been joined to the action, contested this and claimed that it was, in fact, a promissory note and liable to duty of some £3 million. Costello J stated in discussing SA 1891, s 14:

> this section confers certain statutory rights on a defendant in an action, namely a right to object to the admission in evidence of certain instruments on the grounds that they have not been duly stamped, and it confers on the court certain powers when such an objection is taken (or on its own motion) to investigate and adjudicate upon an issue whether an instrument should be stamped or on the adequacy of the stamp duty actually paid. Whilst the section does not confer on a defendant an 'interest' entitling him to raise a question as to the duty payable on an instrument sought to be put into evidence, the interest only arises in proceedings in which it is sought to put in evidence the instrument in question and not otherwise.

See **Chapter 16** for further discussion on judicial adjudication of instruments.

[3.59] If the signing of an instrument conditional upon the happening of an event, the instrument shall be stampable on the date upon which the condition is satisfied.[94] Where an instrument is delivered in escrow, the instrument does not attract duty until the condition subject to which it was delivered has been performed.[95] However, in *Allen Estates Ltd v WG Stores Ltd*[96] Denning MR argued that the date the escrow took effect was the date the deed was delivered, though this seems incorrect. In modern practice where the vendor 'signs, seals and delivers' the deed in the presence of his solicitor prior to the completion of a sale, this places the deed in escrow pending receipt of the consideration moneys.[97]

[3.60] There have in the past been some views expressed to the contrary; for example, in *Byrne v Revenue Commissioners*[98] it was held that the date on which an escrow came into operative force was the date on which the deed was first executed. In *Re Duke of*

---

93 *Kelly v Revenue Commissioners, Goodman and Gemon Ltd* V ITR 363.

94 *Crane Fruehauf Ltd v IRC* [1974] 1 All ER 811.

95 *Terrapin v IRC* [1976] 2 All ER 461.

96 *Allen Estates Ltd v WG Stores Ltd* [1981] 3 WLR 892.

97 *Glessing v Green* [1975] 2 All ER 696.

98 *Byrne v Revenue Commissioners* [1935] IR 644.

Devonshire Settlement[99] it had been held that the escrow should be dated on the date of delivery and not the date of satisfaction of the condition.

[3.61] If the deed has been dated but left in escrow, a certificate as to escrow duly executed by a solicitor has to be produced to the Revenue Commissioners.[100] While the primary rule is that an unstamped instrument cannot be admitted in evidence to prove matters or collateral matters,[101] the instrument may be produced to a witness for the purpose of refreshing his memory.[102] In *McDermott's Application*[103] the applicant argued that the provisions of the Act merely prevented the actual unstamped instrument from being put into evidence but that this did not prevent secondary evidence of the existence, effect and signature by both parties from being admitted. The court held that there is no rule admitting secondary evidence of an unstamped instrument. Even though the instrument may appear to be sufficiently stamped at face value, if it does not reflect the true or actual consideration, then it is not deemed to be duly stamped and not admissible as evidence pursuant to SDCA 1999, s 127.[104]

Proof of title

[3.62] The vendor must produce good title proving undisputed ownership of the property ending in the document which vested the property in the vendor. There is also a duty to produce a properly stamped instrument for the purchaser. A purchaser may refuse to close the sale if the vendor fails to produce properly stamped instruments,[105] but the purchaser can only refuse in the case where the document is necessary to prove the vendor's title.[106] In *Tyrrell v Imperial Tobacco Co Ltd*,[107] Kennedy CJ said that:

> It is well settled that a purchaser is entitled to have all instruments and documents which constitute the muniments of title to the property sold, and which are liable to stamp duty properly stamped at the vendor's expenses ...

However, it remains the obligation of the purchaser to prove that the documents are insufficiently stamped.[108]

[3.63] The practical way around this problem is for the vendor to produce, by way of closed contract, a root of title which is at least 20 years old.

Example 3.63.1

A agrees to sell to B a house for €130,000 and the title consists of as follows:

(a) conveyance dated 12 April 1945 duly stamped;

(b) conveyance dated 14 April 1952 unstamped;

---

[99] *Re Duke of Devonshire Settlement* [1952] 31 ATC 399.

[100] See **Appendix 4**.

[101] *Fengl v Fengl* [1914] 112 LT 173 and *Sun Alliance Insurance v IRC* [1972] Ch 133.

[102] *Birchall v Bullough* [1896] 1 QB 325.

[103] *McDermott's Application* [1996] STC 483.

[104] *Lap Shun Textiles Industries Co Ltd v Collector of Stamp Revenue* [1976] 1 All ER 833.

[105] *Whiting v Loames* [1881] 17 Ch D 10.

[106] *Ex parte Birkbeck Freehold Land Society* [1883] 24 Ch D 119.

[107] *Tyrrell v Imperial Tobacco Co Ltd* [1926] IR 285.

[108] *Re Weir & Pitt's Contract* [1911] 55 Sol J 536.

(c) conveyance dated 1 March 1970 unstamped;

(d) conveyance dated 10 October 1971 duly stamped.

By a special condition in the contract a vendor can commence the title with the deed of conveyance dated 12 April 1945 and then pass to deed of conveyance dated 10 October 1971 excluding all intermediate title.

This would be deemed to be a good root of title under present conveyancing practice. The excluded deeds could be handed over on closing and while being unstamped would not be necessary to prove the vendor's title.

[3.64] The special condition of the contract limiting the root of title must not be phrased to exclude liability to stamp duty as such condition would be deemed to be void. An indemnity by the vendor to the purchaser against any such liability to stamp duty shall be void.[109]

This conveyancing practice may be departed from as and from 1 November 2011, the twentieth anniversary upon which stamp duty became mandatory by nature and the parties to the deed were made accountable. The Revenue Commissioners power to recover stamp duty is now limited to four years from the date of the instrument (subject to statutory exceptions) and this may result in a change in conveyancing practice.

Penalties for stamping instruments after execution

[3.65] Pre-1991, any unstamped or insufficiently stamped instrument could be stamped after execution on the payment of the unpaid duty and a penalty of £10 together with the payment of the interest on such duty at a rate of 5 per cent per annum. Interest was calculated from the date on which the instrument was first executed up to the time of stamping, but the interest could not exceed the unpaid duty.[110]

This practice has been greatly changed since the passing of SDCA 1999, s 14.[111]

Conveyancing law/practice

[3.66] As stated previously the purchaser may refuse to complete a purchase of a property on the grounds that the instrument necessary to prove title is unstamped. The rationale behind this is that in proving title in a court of law, documents would have to be properly stamped to be produced in evidence. If the documents of title were unstamped or insufficiently stamped, they could not be produced in a court of law until stamp duty, penalties and interest had been discharged in full. A duty has been imposed on the Registrar of Titles to ensure stamp duties are paid and prior to registering a purchaser as either first-registered owner of lands or as owner under a transfer of registered land, the Registrar shall ensure that all stamp duties have been properly satisfied as if the lands to be transferred or conveyed had been unregistered property (Register of Titles Act 1964, s 104). The Land Registration Rules 1972, r 59(2) provides for the presentation of a properly stamped deed to the Registrar of Titles when presenting a dealing for registration.

---

[109] SDCA 1999, s 131 – for further discussion see para **3.15**.

[110] SA 1891, s 15.

[111] See **Chapter 13**.

[3.67] The Registrar can also insist on the transfer being adjudicated as being properly stamped where he has doubts as to the amount of stamp duty payable on the instrument. The solicitor for the applicant can arrange to have the deed duly adjudicated upon and, provided the instrument is relodged within the time limits fixed, the registration shall be completed as of the date of the original application. However, in the event of the deed not being lodged in time or in compliance with the undertaking given by the applicant's solicitor to the Registrar of Titles, then the entry of the instrument for the purpose of registration applied for shall be cancelled.[112] It should be noted that it is now the practice of the Revenue Commissioners to inspect documents in the Land Registry to ensure that documents have been correctly stamped. They attend at the Land Registry and review certain dealings to ensure that the transfers were correctly stamped. This practice is extremely unusual as there is a statutory obligation of the Registrar of Titles to ensure that documents are properly stamped. This can only take place in the Land Registry as the original deeds in the Registry of Deeds are retained by the legal owner to prove their root of title.

SDCA 1999, s 131

[3.68] As the onus for ensuring that an instrument is properly stamped rests on the purchaser, it could be possible to frame the contract in such a way that the vendor would not be obliged to produce properly stamped instruments. SDCA 1999, s 131 provides that:

> (a) any contract for sale framed with a view of precluding objection or requisition upon the grounds of absence or insufficiency of stamp on instruments executed after 16 May 1888; and
>
> (b) every contract, arrangement or undertaking for assuming the liability on account of the absence or insufficiency of duty upon any such instrument or indemnifying against any such liability, absence or insufficiency shall be void.

This section clearly prohibits any agreement whereby a vendor undertakes to indemnify against any penalty or interest charges arising from a failure to stamp an instrument at the date of execution, but it is unclear whether it also applies to an indemnity by the vendor with respect to the payment of the actual duty itself. A suggested route to circumventing the provisions of this section is to provide a form of trigger event which results in sufficient funds being made available for any potential liability to stamp duty or any other tax. Sergeant and Simms on Stamp Duties appear to suggest that an indemnity as to the amount of duty payable is lawful and enforceable and that the section applies only to penalty and interest provisions, see also *Abbott v Stratton*.[113] There is considerable merit in this interpretation as the section refers to 'liability *on account of*' (author's emphasis added).

[3.69] Until such time as this section is interpreted by the Irish courts, the more advisable approach is to regard an undertaking or indemnity by a vendor in respect of stamp duty to a purchaser as unenforceable.

---

112 Land Registration Rules 1972, r 66.

113 *Abbott v Stratton* (1856) 3 Jo & Lat 603.

A practice has developed whereby solicitors acting on behalf of builders dispose of the property by way of sub-sale to mitigate their clients' stamp duty liability. The consideration for the land will have been discharged in full on the first contract and the builder will be in full occupation and have begun development of same. They then insert a condition in the contract insisting that no inquiry is made in respect of stamp duty and this condition may be void. The writer, in practice, will advise his client to sign the contract as is and once received from the vendor's solicitor's offices will request that the documents be stamped as the condition is void.

Fines

[3.70] Fines are imposed by the SDCA 1999. These fines are recoverable in the High Court in the name of the Attorney General.[114]

CA 1963, s 58

[3.71] Where a company makes an allotment for shares in return for a contract for sale, for services or for other consideration, and whether or not the contract was reduced to writing, the company has a duty, within one month after the allotment, to deliver to the Registrar of Companies for registration particulars of the contract, stamped with the same duty as would have been payable if the contract had been reduced to writing. This return shall be deemed to be an instrument within the meaning of SDCA 1999. The Registrar has the power to require that the stamp duty payable thereon be adjudicated under SDCA 1999, s 20.[115] For rules relating to transfer of shares, see **Chapter 7**.

Post-FA 1991

[3.72] FA 1991 radically altered the obligation on taxpayers to pay stamp duty. No new stamp duties were created; however, a mandatory obligation was imposed on the relevant parties to a transaction, depending on the nature of the transaction. The new mandatory obligations are in addition to the existing enforcement provisions which were in effect prior to 1 November 1991. The new regime can be summarised as follows:

(a) the payment of stamp duty (and any interest and penalties) is mandatory and must take place within certain time limits, by the accountable person(s);

(b) stamp duty (and any interest and penalties) is a debt due to the Minister for Finance, which is recoverable by legal action or other appropriate proceedings;

(c) new penalties for fraud and negligence in the preparation of instruments and in their presentation for stamp duty are in place (this has been further extended to encompass valuations of residential property by FA 1997);

(d) the Revenue Commissioners have the power to raise assessments as to the stamp duty liability on their own initiative;

(e) the penalties for late payment of duty have been substantially revised and increased;

---

[114] SDCA 1999, s 138(1).

[115] See **Chapter 15**.

(f) understatements of market value in the context of gifts and in relation to incorrect apportionments of consideration in conveyances or leases of mixed residential/non-residential property may give rise to a surcharge as well as other liabilities;

(g) the Revenue Commissioners have further powers to enable them to inspect documents and in respect of the enforcement of stamp duty.

Each of these aspects will now be discussed in turn.

Payment of stamp duty is mandatory

[3.73] These new provisions apply to instruments executed after 1 November 1991.[116] The legislation provides that any instrument which is:

(a) specified in the Schedule 1; and

(b) is executed in the State or wheresoever executed, relates to any property situate in the State or any matter or thing done or to be done in the State shall be chargeable with stamp duty.

Under the earlier provisions, the sanctions for the non-payment of stamp duty were that the document could not be produced in evidence in a civil court of law. It had been possible to avoid or defer a liability to stamp duty by retaining the documents abroad, since they did not have to be stamped until they were brought into the State and then could be stamped within 30 days of importation without penalty or interest.[117] The traditional loophole of executing mortgages in the Isle of Man, repatriating them only in the event of enforcement becoming necessary and stamping them at that stage is no longer possible due to the mandatory nature of stamp duty.

[3.74] New provisions render all documents wheresoever executed relating to property situate in this State liable to stamp duty within 30 days of execution regardless of the place of execution.[118] An instrument shall now be stamped with proper duty within 30 days after its first execution unless it has been referred for adjudication within the said period of 30 days. In the case of adjudication, the instrument shall be stampable in accordance with the assessment of the Commissioners within 14 days after the notice of assessment issues.[119] In practice difficulties have been encountered due to the strict enforcement of these provisions by the Revenue Commissioners as they are imposing penalties together with interest once the 14 days from the date of issue of the notice of assessment has elapsed. This has been found by solicitors or tax advisers to be a rather restrictive time limit to impose. With the introduction of a new computer system by the Revenue commissioners in 1998, this period may be further extended. In practice the Revenue allows 44 days before imposing penalties or interest.

---

[116] SDCA 1999, s 2(1).

[117] SA 1891, s 15 now repealed by FA 1991, s 100.

[118] SDCA 1999, s 2.

[119] SDCA 1999, s 2(3)(b).

[3.75] If the instrument is not stamped or is insufficiently stamped, the Revenue Commissioners can recover the stamp duty through the courts from the accountable person or where there is more than one accountable person they are jointly and severally liable. The accountable person shall be liable for the stamp duty and any penalty relating to any such duty. The definition for accountable person under SDCA 1999, s 1(1) amends the original definition section of the Stamp Act which depended on the nature of the instrument, details of which are set out in **Appendix 8**.

Table of accountable persons

[3.76]

	Instrument	*Accountable person*
1.	Bond, covenant or instrument of any kind	The obligee, covenantor or other person taking the benefit
2.	Conveyance or transfer on sale of any stock or marketable securities	Vendee or transferee
3.	Conveyance or transfer on sale of any property other than stock or marketable securities	Vendee or transferee
4.	Lease	Lessee
5.	Mortgage, bond, debenture or covenant (except a marketable security) and warrant of attorney to confess and enter up judgment	The mortgagee, the obligee, in the case of a transfer the transferee
6.	Settlement	The settlor
7.	Duplicate or counter part of any instrument chargeable	Any of the persons specified in this column as appropriate
8.	Voluntary disposition or instrument deemed to operate as such	Parties to the instrument
9.	Any other instrument not set out above	Parties to the instrument
10	A transfer of shares by way of CREST	Transferee

[3.77] Where the provisions of SDCA 1999, s 45(2), as inserted by SDCA 1999, s 16(2), apply, there is a duty imposed on both parties to sign a statement concerning the financial structure of the consideration. If there is a shortfall, the purchaser is liable and can recover same from the vendor in certain circumstances. In effect, this makes the vendor accountable for the surcharge. See **Chapter 4** for further discussion. These provisions render the recipient of the property or interest therein primarily liable for the duty. For example, in the case of a mortgage, the mortgagee is liable for this duty. The exception to this rule is that the settlor is liable for the duty on an instrument of settlement. The accountable person is also liable for the duty on a counterpart or duplicate.

[3.78] Where an instrument operates or is deemed to operate as a voluntary disposition *inter vivos* in accordance with the provisions of SDCA 1999, s 30, all parties to such instrument shall be liable for stamp duty. If the recipient of the property by way of gift has discharged the liability, it is arguable that this liability can be deducted from the market value of the gift in calculating the taxable value of the gift for capital acquisitions tax purposes (according to CATCA 2003). In all other cases every party to the instrument is an accountable person. In the event of the accountable person being dead, his or her personal representatives shall be liable to the stamp duty together with penalties.

[3.79] Since the tax is now mandatory at the date of execution of the instrument, the Revenue Commissioners should now provide a service of advance ruling to the parties of the instrument. This is particularly important in light of the fact that the valuation office may dispute the valuation submitted by the parties to an instrument in the case of a voluntary disposition *inter vivos* which may render the parties liable to a larger liability. Prior to the passing of FA 1991, if this occurred the parties could withdraw the instrument and not proceed with the transaction. Now it would appear that as the liability to stamp duty is absolute once executed it cannot be resiled from. In the absence of advance rulings by the Revenue Commissioners, the procurement of professional advice is important. Failure by the Revenue Commissioners to provide a service of advance ruling reflects seriously on the creation of any form of tax equity in this country, particularly in light of the Revenue Commissioners stance on enforcement provisions on all taxes.

New penalties for fraud and negligence

[3.80] Prior to FA 1991, any person who executed any instrument or who was employed or concerned in or about the preparation of any instrument which did not set forth truly and fully all the facts and circumstances surrounding the instrument with intent to defraud the State ,was liable to a fine of £10.[120] This still applies to all instruments executed on or before 1 November 1991. SDCA 1999, s 8 imposed a presumption of negligence. SDCA 1999, s 8(4) provides that where an instrument was executed by a person and at that time there was no fraud or negligence and subsequently it comes to the notice of the one of the parties (or should have come to his attention applying the 'reasonable man' test) that the instrument or accompanying statement did not present all the facts in a true and full manner as required by SDCA 1999, s 8(2), then, unless the Revenue Commissioners are informed of the error without reasonable delay, the person will be presumed to have acted negligently for the purposes of SDCA 1999, s 8(3). This imposes an ex-post facto form of negligence which applies to the parties of the deeds only and not to the professional adviser.

Fraud

[3.81] Stephens points out:

> ... fraud involves ... the idea of injury wilfully effected or intended to be effected either by deceit or secrecy. It is essential to the fraud that the fraudulent persons' conduct should not be merely wrongful, but should be intentionally and knowingly wrongful ...[121].

120 SDCA 1999, s 8.

121 *History of the Criminal Law of England*, Vol 3, p 124.

Traditionally it is notoriously difficult to prove fraud in civil cases; more so in relation to taxing statutes as they must be construed more narrowly. These provisions obviously are mitigated by the introduction of the negligence concept. In most cases fraud must be proved, but the onus of proof has shifted to the taxpayer who has to prove that fraud does not exist.[122]

Negligence

[3.82] The concept of negligence revolves around the test of the reasonable man. The reasonable man has often been described as an ordinary man on the Clapham Omnibus. For the professional the standard is much higher, being defined as:

> ... the degree and knowledge of care to be expected is thus seen to be that degree possessed by the notional duly qualified person practising that profession. The test is, therefore, if I may put it that way, an objective test referable to the notional member of the profession and not a subjective test referable to the particular man employed.[123]

SDCA 1999, s 8(3) imposes a liability upon a person who:

> fraudulently or negligently executes any instrument, or
>
> (b) is employed or concerned in or about the preparation of any instrument fraudulently or negligently prepares any such instrument.

Such person is liable to a fine of €1,265 and, in the case of negligence, the amount of duty payable is the difference between the amount actually paid and the amount that would have been payable if all the facts had been fully and truly set forth in the instrument or statement and, in the case of fraud, twice that amount.[124]

[3.83] The parties have two duties:

(a) They have a duty of care to the Revenue Commissioners and can be liable for a substantial fine together with the stamp duty payable and negligence. The duty of care will vary depending on the nature of the professional adviser involved. It is imperative that such professional adviser confines himself to advice in his given field of expertise. For example, in a voluntary transfer of property the valuation of the property submitted should be given by an auctioneer and not by a solicitor. Solicitors are not expected to be experts in property valuations. They must advise their clients of these provisions, and advise them to employ competent and qualified valuers. The solicitor is entitled to accept that the valuation is done properly, subject to the proviso that in his view the valuation is realistic.[125] The development of multi-disciplinary practices may limit the benefit of this guidance from the Revenue Commissioners.

---

[122] SDCA 1999, s 8.

[123] Graham J in *Andrew Master Homes Ltd v Cruikshank & Fairweather* [1980] RPC 16.

[124] SDCA 1999, s 8(3).

[125] Notice from the Revenue Commissioners Law Society Gazette April 1993, Vol 87, No 3.

(b) If they have any doubt or question in relation to the transaction, they should bring it to the attention of the Revenue Commissioners and, where they fail to do so, they may be liable under the above provisions.[126]

[3.84] Traditionally, the duty to disclose applied only to disclosure that could be evidenced in the instrument. Under the current legislation, where it is not practicable to set out the relevant facts and circumstances in an instrument, they should be fully and truly set forth in a statement that provides such additional facts and circumstances which:

(a) affect the liability of the instrument to duty;

(b) affect the amount of the duty with which such instrument is chargeable; or

(c) may be required from time to time by the Revenue Commissioners.

The form of this statement can be prescribed by the Revenue Commissioners. An example of this is an SD4 which the Revenue require to be completed for both 'over the counter' stamping and where the share transfers have been submitted for adjudication in relation to the stamping of shares in private companies.

[3.85] Such statements should be delivered to the Revenue Commissioners together with the instrument for stamping. The Revenue Commissioners have indicated that the intention behind this is that the deed should be drafted under the normal drafting conventions and practice. Where information is not covered by using these conventions they should be set out in an accompanying statement[127] practically in the form of a letter.

[3.86] This section raises certain questions as to privilege and confidentiality. Privilege applies only in relation to legal advice, and not purely financial advice. In *Smurfit Paribas Bank Ltd v AAB Export Finance Ltd*[128] Finlay J points out that lawyer and client privilege is absolute in connection with communications which are made for the purposes only of obtaining legal advice or the conduct of litigation, but not with respect to legal assistance. In the case at hand, an instruction to draft mortgages was deemed to be 'legal assistance' and the correspondence was not privileged.

[3.87] With respect to the mandatory stamp duty provisions, the legal assistance given is not privileged, whereas legal advice is. Note McCarthy J in *Smurfit Paribas Bank Ltd v AAB Export Finance Ltd* indicated that 'litigation arising out of assistance given could in fact constitute legal advice and therefore be protected'. In *Re Bula Ltd, in liquidation*[129] the court followed *Murphy v Kirwan*[130] in approving Paribas. The only exception to this privilege arises in cases of moral turpitude, such as fraud. This opinion on advice and

126 See **Chapter 5**.

127 SP-SD 1/91 para 6.2.

128 *Smurfit Paribas Bank Ltd v AAB Export Finance Ltd* [1991] IR 469.

129 *Re Bula Ltd, in liquidation* [1994] 1 ILRM 495.

130 *Murphy v Kirwan* [1994] ILRM 293.

assistance is contradicted in Commission Consultative Des Barreau de la Communaute Europeenne where it is stated that:

> ... the purpose of the law is not to protect the individual lawyer or his individual client. The purpose is, first, to protect every person who requires the advice and assistance of a lawyer in order to vindicate his rights and liberty and, second, to ensure the fair and proper administration of justice. This cannot be achieved unless the relationship between the lawyer and his client is a relationship of confidence. The right duties and privileges given to a lawyer are therefore an essential element in the protection of individual liberty in the free society. They exist for public interest; they have not been created by lawyers for their private benefit. It must however be remembered that the privilege rule can always be waived by the client.

This section applies to 'any person employed or concerned in or about the preparation of any instrument'. This definition is quite wide as it applies to all persons 'concerned' and would include any other person who would be interested in the preparation of the instrument. Taking it at its widest interpretation it could potentially apply to all persons employed in a firm, or partners in a partnership, the purchasers and vendors and all parties with any interest whatsoever in the instrument.

[3.88] Where a person doubts matters contained in the instrument, he may bring those matters to the attention of the Revenue Commissioners when submitting the instrument for stamping. He would be deemed to have made a full and true disclosure with regard to the matter in doubt[131] provided that the doubt is genuine and not a tactic to evade stamp duty.[132]

[3.89] In addition to the above a party to an instrument will be presumed negligent in two specific situations. This shifts the onus of proof onto the party, or parties, who fail to comply with the relevant provisions. Firstly, under the provisions of the SDCA 1999, s 16(2), there is a duty imposed on the parties to deliver a statement of their estimates of the amount or aggregate consideration where the provisions of SDCA 1999, s 45(2)(a) or SDCA 1999, s 52(5)(a) apply. Where the estimates give rise to a surcharge, then any person who executes an instrument effecting the sale or lease is presumed to have acted negligently until the contrary is proven.[133]

Secondly, in the case of an instrument which comprises a gift or a transfer of property at an undervalue and comes within the provisions of SDCA 1999, s 30 or SDCA 1999, s 54(1), the parties have a duty to bring this to the attention of the Revenue Commissioners. A statement should be delivered to them setting out all the information as required under SDCA 1999, s 8, together with a full statement as to the value of the property. If these provisions are not complied with, all parties to the instrument shall be presumed to have acted negligently until the contrary is proven.[134] The Revenue Commissioners have indicated that the questions of valuations by competent valuers are not matters of doubt within this context.

---

131 SDCA 1999, s 8(6).

132 SDCA 1999, s 8(7).

133 SDCA 1999, s 8(3).

134 SDCA 1999, s 8(5).

Example 3.88.1

X buys a house in December 1991 for €200,000 and sells it to Y in December 1993 for €150,000. In January 1994 Y sells the property to Z for €250,000.

In a subsequent transaction of sale for €250,000 by Y the solicitor has a duty to his client to advise his client of the difference in value and the client should in turn inform the Revenue Commissioners. As it would appear that the December 1993 transaction by Y may be deemed to operate as a voluntary disposition *inter vivos*, as it is a transfer at an undervalue, the parties to the deed have a duty to bring the sale at an undervalue to the notice of the Revenue Commissioners.

This may not apply where property prices are increasing significantly as they did during the late 1990s.

If a professional advisor has doubts as to whether or not the instrument is voluntary by nature, he should bring the matter to the notice of the Revenue Commissioners.[135] Failure to do so may render him liable for the penalties.

[3.90] In *Lap Shun Textiles Industrial Co v The Collector of Revenue*[136] the property was sold at an undervalue due to pressure by the vendor to obtain finance and discharge liabilities. The instrument was stampable on the full market value and not on the consideration passing between the parties, as there was a transfer at an 'undervalue'. A solicitor who is instructed to sell a property below the value of an identical property in which he was acting within the recent past may also have a duty to disclose this undervalue to the Revenue Commissioners. All the facts must be fully and truly set forth in the instrument and failure to comply with the words 'fully' and 'truly' may give rise to a liability.

[3.91] It has been held by Latham CJ that:

> ... where the word 'disclosure' is used with reference to information to be provided it should, in my opinion be understood as acquiring a statement of the relevant information which is in the possession of the person who is required to make the disclosure for a particular purpose or to bring himself within some particular statutory or other provision. In other words, a person cannot be said to fail to disclose something which he never knew.[137]

He further stated that:

> There is a difference between 'disclosing' a fact and stating a fact. Disclosure consists in the statement of a fact by way of disclosure so as to reveal or make apparent that which (so far as the 'discloser' knows was previously unknown to the person to whom the statement was made.[138]

---

135 SDCA 1999, s 8(6).

136 *Lap Shun Textiles Industrial Co v The Collector of Revenue* [1976] AC 53.

137 *FCT v Westgarth* [1950] 81 CLR 396 at page 407.

138 *Foster v FCT* [1951] 82 CLR 605 at page 614).

Finally, Fullanger J stated:

> I would think that even a merely inadvertent omission of a material fact may be enough to enable the Commissioners to maintain that the full and true disclosure required had not been made.[139]

The duty however is only to disclose facts and circumstances to the Revenue Commissioners.

The Revenue Commissioners' power to raise an assessment of stamp duty[140]

[3.92] The Revenue Commissioners are empowered to adjudicate over the liability of stamp duty on instruments.[141] The Revenue Commissioners can make an assessment as to the amount of stamp duty payable to the best of their knowledge, information and belief which they felt ought to be charged, levied and paid thereon and the 'accountable person' shall be liable for the payment of stamp duty so assessed, unless the Revenue Commissioners make another assessment upon delivery of the instrument to them.[142] Where a transaction occurs under the CREST trading system, the Revenue are similarly empowered to raise an assessment as to what they consider the appropriate duty payable to be.[143] The provisions under SDCA 1999, ss 20(10) and 20(11) relating to the power of varying assessments already made are also applicable. It should be noted that the time limit in respect of the Revenue Commissioners making enquiries and assessments has been reduced to four years from the date of the stamping of the instrument by the Revenue Commissioners or the date the type of instruction is under s 76 (CREST provisions) and time limit is under SDCA 1999, s 159C.

Penalties for late payment of stamp duty

[3.93] Prior to 1 November 1991 the penalty for late payment of stamp duty was £10 plus an interest rate of 5 per cent per annum.[144] SDCA 1999, s 14 provides for the following penalties (which are in addition to the duty payable) where instruments are not stamped within the relevant time limits:

(a) a presentation penalty of €25; and

(b) where the unpaid duty exceeds €30, simple interest on the duty at the rate of 0.0273 per cent per day (or part thereof) from the date of first execution to the date of payment. The rate of 0.0273 per cent per day (or part thereof) applies with effect from 1 April 2005. The applicable rate of interest prior to 1 April 2005 was 0.0332 per cent per day (or part thereof);

(c) in respect of instruments stampable under Schedule 1, further penalties calculated as follows:

---

139 *Australian Jam Co & Property Ltd v FCT* [1953] AITR 566 at page 573.

140 The duty imposed on auditors will be dealt with in Ch 13.

141 SDCA 1999, s 20.

142 SDCA 1999, s 20(2) as amended by SDCA 1999, s 71(f).

143 SDCA 1999, s 71.

144 SA 1891, s 15.

(i) 10 per cent of the unpaid duty where the instrument is stamped not later than 6 months after it was first executed;

(ii) 20 per cent of the unpaid duty where the instrument is stamped more than 6 months, and not later than 12 months, after is was first executed;

(iii) 30 per cent of the unpaid duty where the instrument is stamped more than 12 months after it was first executed.

The above penalties are chargeable and recoverable in the same manner as if they were part of the duty on the relevant instrument[145] and any penalty paid is denoted on the instrument by a particular stamp ('P' or 'PM' where the penalty is mitigate).[146]

Surcharge provisions

[3.94] Surcharge provisions were introduced in FA 1991, s 103 to apply to transfers by way of gifts where the duty was chargeable not on the consideration paid, but on the value of the property.[147]

Table of Surcharge

Instruments executed after 1 November 1991 but on or before 23 May 1994:

Value in property	*Surcharge*
Greater than value submitted by 10% but less than 30% subject to the proviso that difference in value is less than €6,350	50% of stamp duty
Greater than value submitted by 30% but less than 50% subject	100% of stamp duty
Greater than value submitted by 50% or more	200% of stamp duty

Instruments executed after 23 May 1994:

Value in property	*Surcharge*
Greater than value submitted by 15% but less than 30% subject to the proviso that difference in value is less than €6,350	25% of stamp duty
Greater than value submitted by 30% but less than 50% subject	50% of stamp duty
Greater than value submitted by 50% or more	100% of stamp duty

145 SDCA 1999, s 14(5).

146 SDCA 1999, s 14(4).

147 F(1909-10)A 1910, s 74, FA 1949, s 24.

[3.95] In the case of residential property where the provision of SDCA 1999, s 16(3) applies and the purchaser's estimate of the residential value is less than that of the Revenue Commissioners, a surcharge shall be payable as follows:

Submitted value	*Surcharge*
Where the submitted value is less than the assessed value and the difference is less than 10%	Nil
Where the submitted value is less than the assessed value which is greater than 10% but not greater than 30%	50% of the difference between the duty chargeable and that chargeable on the submitted value
Where the submitted value is less than the assessed value which is greater than 30%	100% of the difference between the duty chargeable and that chargeable on the submitted value

This is the case provided that notwithstanding any provisions of the Act, the vendee shall be entitled to recover from the vendor one half of the relevant surcharge, subject to the proviso that the amount the vendee shall be entitled to recover shall not exceed one half of the surcharge that would have applied if the vendor's estimate[148] had been the submitted value where the vendor's estimate is higher than that of the vendee. See **Chapter 11** for further details.

The Revenue Commissioners' powers to inspect documents

[3.96] Any person who is a party to an instrument, or has documents in their custody or control which might reveal any outstanding liability to stamp duty or fraud, negligence or omission in relation to any duty, shall furnish such information to the Revenue and permit inspection of any documents by the Revenue following a written notice from them to that effect.[149] The documents are defined so as to include material maintained, stored or preserved by electronic or mechanical means.[150]

[3.97] Compliance with these provisions must be undertaken within 14 days of receipt of the written notice. Refusal to comply with these provisions renders the person liable to punishment pursuant to TCA 1997, s 1078(2)(g)(iv). If the person still refuses to comply with these provisions after being convicted under the above provision, then they are liable to a fine not exceeding €125 for each day of such refusal.

It shall be a good defence to show that the person is entitled by law to refuse the request of the Revenue for compliance with these provisions.[151] Accordingly, since the communications between a lawyer and client are privileged, then a lawyer has a good defence to any request for compliance by the Revenue. However, other professional relationships, for example, accountant and client, may not be so privileged and compliance with the provisions is mandatory.

148 SDCA 1999, s 16(4).

149 SDCA 1999, s 128(2).

150 SDCA 1999, s 128(1).

151 SDCA 1999, s 128(3).

[3.98] There remain, however, serious issues concerning these provisions. If they are to be read as absolute, then it appears that the Revenue may order compliance simply on a belief that a person may have evidence likely to lead to the exposure of any unpaid liability to duty. Abusively used, this could empower the Revenue to seek to inspect records simply in the hope that such inspection may yield unpaid liability. It is suggested that the power conferred upon the Revenue is not absolute but must be exercised within the limits of administrative law. Accordingly, in issuing a written notification under these provisions, the Revenue must act in accordance with the principles of natural and constitutional justice. There must be reasonable grounds for the Revenue to believe that such a notice is likely to lead to the uncovering of unpaid liability. The exercise of the power must not be arbitrary. The exact limits of the scope of such powers, and their compatibility in implementation with fundamental human rights and constitutional provisions, remain a matter for judicial determination in future case law.

Responsibilities of tax advisers, advisers and auditors

[3.99] TCA 1997, s 1079[152] requires auditors and tax advisers to take certain steps on discovering tax irregularities in the affairs of a company for which they act. The adviser is required to notify the company of the relevant offence and to request that the company rectify the matter within 6 months. If the company fails to do so, the adviser is required to retire from acting for the company for a period of three years (or until the matter is rectified), and in the case of an auditor, he must return the details of his resignation to the Revenue Commissioners. This section does not operate to prevent an advisor engaging in the preparation for, or conduct of, legal proceedings.

In addition, an adviser may be guilty of a Revenue offence under TCA 1997, s 1078 if the adviser knowingly aids, abets, assists, incites or induces a person to make knowingly or wilfully an incorrect return leading to the fraudulent evasion of tax. The word 'wilfully' has been held to mean intentionally or deliberately in *IRC (ex-parte) Chisholm.*[153]

[152] Formerly FA 1995, s 172.

[153] *IRC (ex-parte) Chisholm* [1981] STC 253.

Chapter 4

Conveyance or Transfer on Sale Head

Introduction

[4.01] The principal incidence of stamp duty arises on instruments which convey or transfer property. The Act states that a conveyance on sale:

> includes every instrument, and every decree or order (including a decree or order for, or having effect of an order for, foreclosure) of any court or of any commissioners, whereby any property, or any estate or interest in any property, on the sale or compulsory acquisition of that property or that estate or that interest is transferred to or vested in a purchaser, or any other person on such purchaser's behalf or by such purchaser's direction.[1]

The expression "conveyance on sale" has an extremely broad remit. It is designed to encompass as many documents as possible. The courts have chosen to interpret the term very widely. Wilberforce LJ states in *Fitch Lovell Ltd v IRC*[2]:

> Those words "conveyance or transfer on sale" have been given a wide extension. It is sufficient for a document to amount to a conveyance or transfer on sale, if it is the instrument chosen the parties to complete the sale in such a way as to show that they did not intend an other document to be executed.

SDCA 1999, ss 30–38 deem other transactions to be conveyances on sale.

[4.02] It is important to distinguish between a conveyance on sale and another transaction, including a contract for sale of land that is to be subsequently conveyed. This is not only so that the correct amount of duty can be applied, but also so that the correct reliefs and exemptions are applied. A transaction on sale can be divided into two elements. Firstly, there is the agreement to sell; secondly there is the conveyance of the property from the seller to the purchaser. The difference in time between these two elements may vary from being very short to being very long depending upon the nature of the property being sold. When A sells a book to B, the agreement to sell is quickly followed by the conveyance of the book in question, unless A does not at that moment have possession of the book. If the book is elsewhere there will be a longer gap between agreement and effecting the conveyance or, more accurately in the case of personal property, the transfer. Compare this to the situation of the sale of a house. In such a case, the agreement to sell often occurs six to eight weeks before the conveyance is effected. In some cases, the gap can last for many years, but by virtue of SDCA 1999, s 2, the instrument which effects the conveyance of the property is chargeable, not the agreement itself.

---

1 SDCA 1999, s 1.

2 *Fitch Lovell Ltd v IRC* [1962] 3 All ER 685.

Example 4.02.1

A and B enter into a written agreement for the sale of Blackacre on 1 January 2004. The conveyance is completed by instrument executed on 1 March 2004. The section charges the instrument executed on 1 March 2004.

Example 4.02.2

Assume the facts are as above but that the parties are unable to complete the written agreement of January 1 because the title to the property is unsatisfactory.

The section does not operate as there is no conveyance of the property and no liability to duty.

[4.03] By virtue of SDCA 1999, s 2 the charge to duty arises on an instrument which gives effect to an agreement to convey, not on a mere agreement to convey itself. This could be so even if the purchaser was in possession and control of the property. Despite the Revenue's broad interpretation of the word 'conveyance', not all documents are covered. For example, a document agreeing to the transfer of property is not caught under, s 2. In order to be a conveyance on sale the document must be a document *whereby* property is transferred to another person. The transfer of the property must be made by the document itself. If something more than the instrument is required to carry through the transfer, then the document is not a conveyance. However, SDCA 1999, s 31 was introduced to combat this distinction between documents actually transferring and documents agreeing to transfer property. This section treats certain agreements or contracts to transfer property as conveyances.

[4.04] SDCA 1999, s 1 principally charges conveyances of land rather than personal property, as a conveyance of property other than land can be effected by delivery and no written documents are normally necessary. At most, registration of ownership might be required, but the conveyance, that is the transfer of property from one to another, occurs by delivery, that is the passing of possession and control with intent to transfer ownership. In the case of land, however, pursuant to the Statute of Frauds (Ireland) 1695, s 2, to be enforceable, any conveyance of land must be evidenced in writing and signed by the party against whom it is to be enforced, or by his agent, lawfully authorised in writing. The aim of the Statute was to reduce the level of fraud that had arisen in dealings over land as a result of oral agreements. It follows that to be enforceable, all agreements concerning the sale of land must be in writing and, therefore, there is an instrument which will fall liable to the duty. For personal property, an oral agreement is sufficient to make it binding and few parties to such a transaction will convey property by way of a written instrument, and where they do it will give rise to a charge to stamp duty. It follows that the legislature sought primarily to charge conveyances of real property since they would normally be executed by way of a written instrument to be enforceable.

[4.05] There is nothing, however, to prevent a taxpayer from executing a conveyance of land, other than by way of a written instrument subject to the Real Property Act 1845. The Conveyancing Act of 1881 offered a modern alternative mode of conveyance, namely the deed, but it did not prohibit the older forms of conveyance, such as livery of seisin (the transfer of land by symbolic act). While, in theory, this is possible it does not occur; as in practice it would render the agreement unenforceable and run the risk that the vendor might deny the agreement. More importantly, if the taxpayer can devise a method whereby his interest in the property is secured without the aid of a written instrument, then he or she can still avoid the duty whilst ensuring that the conveyance is valid and enforceable. The use of the equitable doctrine of part performance, whereby an unwritten agreement for the conveyance of land which is not enforceable at common law can be enforced in equity if the parties have undertaken sufficient acts so as to indicate to the court that it would be unjust not to uphold the agreement, could prove useful in this regard.

Example 4.05.1

A agrees orally to sell a plot of land to B. There is no written instrument. B moves into possession and builds a house on the property with A's full knowledge and consent.

A now sues B for the recovery of his property since the oral agreement is unenforceable under the Statute of Frauds 1695 since there is no written evidence.

The court exercises its equitable jurisdiction and decrees that sufficient acts of part performance have occurred to vest the property in B.

Such a transfer is caught under this head of charge.

[4.06] There are seven principal elements to the statutory definition under this head of charge:

(a) every instrument;

(b) every decree or order of any court or of any commissioners;

(c) any property;

(d) any estate or interest in property;

(e) the sale thereof;

(f) transferral to or vesting in a purchaser;

(g) transferral to or vesting in any other person.

The application of this section should be viewed in its entirety and recourse should be made to the factual results of the transaction rather than to the means by which it has been carried out. The decision of Carroll J in *Waterford Glass (Group Services) Ltd v Revenue Commissioners*[3] is illuminating. The result of that decision is that the reality of the dealings is more important than the form through which they are brought about. It involved the transfer of property for £3.9 million, of which £3.899 million was to be paid as deposit and the transfer was to take place in return for £1,000 consideration. The argument that no duty was payable under this section was rejected by the court which imposed the full *ad valorem* duty on the transaction. The consideration chargeable to duty was £3.9 million.

> The court is entitled to look at the reality of what has been done. Just because the parties put a particular label on a transaction the court is not obliged to accept that label blindly. The court will look at the legal affect and the legal rights of the parties resulting from the transaction.

[4.07] This judgment appears to be in line with a general trend amongst both the courts and the legislature which are endeavouring to tax the transaction based on its result,

3 *Waterford Glass (Group Services) Ltd v Revenue Commissioners* IV ITR 187.

rather than allowing form to take precedence.[4] Moreover, TCA 1997, s 811,[5] which empowers the Revenue Commissioners to deem certain transactions to be carried out for no other purpose than the avoidance of tax, has yet to be judicially tested in relation to stamp duty. In practice, regarding most stamp duty cases, the courts have not had to rely on substance over form arguments because the wide intrepretation of "conveyance" allowed the courts to decide cases instead of having to look to s 811. The IA 2005 may impact on this as it gives a legislative basis to the provisions of, s 811. The full effect of the IA 2005 will remain to be seen as it came into force on 1 January 2006. The Revenue Commissioners have the power to raise assessments of stamp duty and the power to inspect documents, which obviates much of the need to resort to the provisions of TCA 1997, s 811.[6]

Every instrument

[4.08] An instrument, according to SDCA 1999, s 1 includes any written document and, therefore, includes documents whether under seal or not.[7] This broad definition means that transactions that do not conform with the formal requirements of the Statute of Frauds 1695 will still be liable for duty, even though the transaction itself remains unenforceable. There is provision for the repayment of duty paid on foot of an instrument which is void from the beginning or for other specified reasons.[8]

[4.09] A further question arises as to what constitutes "writing". The database of a computer or a disk for a computer may contain much information but do they in fact constitute writing? Certainly they can be reduced to writing, but what if they are not? Would a transaction occurring solely by way of computer disks avoid the incidence of stamp duty? Moreover, the ability to transform the contents of a database to writing does not turn it into writing, since this would mean that audio tapes would similarly constitute writing. There have been few cases on this point.[9] In *Derby v Weldon (No 9)*,[10] it was held that a computer database was a document within the meaning of the Rules of the Superior Court, Order 24. The dicta of McInerney J in *Beneficial Finance Corp v Conway*[11] that it would not constitute writing unless it could be visually inspected was disapproved of, whilst that of *Grant v South Western & County Properties* was followed.

[4.10] The principal difficulty with the stamping of non-written instruments such as computer disks would appear to be administrative in nature, as there is no place upon which to impress any stamp. Where the information is reduced to writing, then many of

4 *Viek Investments Ltd* IV ITR 367 contrary to the Supreme Court decision in *McGrath v McDermot* and also contrary to the views expressed by Carroll J in the High Court.

5 Formerly FA 1989, s 86.

6 SDCA 1999, s 128, SDCA 1999, s 20, see para **3.25**.

7 *National Telephone Co v IRC* [1900] AC 1.

8 SDCA 1999, s 151 – see **Chapter 13**.

9 *Grant v South Western & County Properties* [1975] Ch 185 and *R v Whyte* [1983] 76 Cr App Rep 149.

10 *Derby v Weldon* (No 9) [1991] 1 All ER 901.

11 *Beneficial Finance Corp v Conway* [1970] VR 321.

the problems disappear. Under SDCA 1999, s 6, all instruments that are to be stamped must be written in such a manner so that the stamp may "appear on the face of the instrument and cannot be used for or applied to any other instrument written upon the same piece of material". Therefore a computer disk cannot be stamped in accordance with the administrative procedures. Further, s 6 may impose a positive obligation to reduce computer records, or other electronic records, into written instruments. Given that new legislation was enacted to deal with the computerised transfer of shares under the CREST system[12] to be effectively deeming such computer records an executed instrument, this suggests that such records are not chargeable unless expressly covered by specific legislation.

[4.11] One further possibility is that the question of whether such communications constitute writing need not be settled with respect to their liability for duty. The requirement is of an instrument, the definition of which 'includes written documents'. But is the phrase 'includes written documents' to be seen as enlarging the scope of instruments from merely formal documents or documents under seal, or is it to be viewed to include non-written instruments. The concept of inclusion carried with it the corollary of exclusion; that is to say that if instruments include written documents, there must be other items that qualify as instruments that are not written documents. 'Instrument' is given a statutory definition that includes and therefore does not limit the possible meaning but rather assists it. Clearly oral communications are not covered by the section for they are not instruments and such transactions will in fact be excluded from liability; for example, an equitable deposit of title deeds with a bank by way of an oral declaration only. 'Instrument' implies a degree of physical tangibility that is unlike an oral transaction and for which computer generations seem ideally suited.

[4.12] These problems aside, typical examples of instruments for which duty is payable would normally take the form of leases, transfers, conveyances, declarations of trust and assents. The instrument must bring into effect the transaction which it purports to achieve.[13] In *Carlill v Carbolic Smokeball Co*[14] the instrument came into existence prior to the transaction and did not therefore give effect to it. This means it would not be liable to duty.[15]

Every decree or order of any court or commissioners

General

[4.13] A court order or decree may have the effect of transferring property from one person to another. In this case, such a decree or order will be deemed to be a conveyance on sale. More often that not, the court authorises something to happen and a document effecting the transaction will come into existence by virtue of this. Alternatively, the court can order or direct the parties to take a certain course of action, the effect of which

---

[12] SDCA 1999, s 69.

[13] *International Power & Paper Co of Newfoundland Ltd v IRC* [1961] Ch 597.

[14] *Carlill v Carbolic Smokeball Co* [1893] 1 QB 256.

[15] See **Chapter 3**.

is the creation of a document. In *IRC v Angus & Co*[16] it can be seen that an order for specific performance of a contract does not have the effect of transferring the property; the parties have to create a stampable document to transfer the property.

[4.14] The concept of a decree appears on the surface to be somewhat of a redundancy given the more detailed inclusion of the phrase "... or order of any court ...". Since a decree is defined as an order of a court pronounced on the hearing of a suit[17] and would form (an) "order of any court ..." it is not clear why this phrase was inserted into the definition. Presumably, it was designed to cover not only final court orders, but interim orders as well. It includes an order of the court which is drawn up, passed and entered.[18] The term 'commissioners' is confined to those commissioners who are capable of issuing decrees or orders that have an almost equal status with that of a law court decree or order. It is doubtful if they must be styled commissioners, but they must have statutory conferred powers with respect to the determination of facts or disputes or entitlements – for example, the Irish Land Commission.

Foreclosure

[4.15] Foreclosure orders are specifically included[19] but it should be noted that the *ad valorem* rate should not exceed the duty on a sum equal to the value of the property,[20] such value stated on the order to be conclusive. A subsequent conveyance of property that has been the subject of such order, and where the duty has been paid, is exempt from liability under this.[21] This shifts the obligation of payment of duty onto the person exercising the right of foreclosure.

Example 4.15.1

A advances €80,000 to B, which is equal to the value of B's land. This advance is secured by way of mortgage over B's land. B "defaults" and A seeks foreclosure. The property vests in A. Prior to this amendment, duty would have been chargeable on the mortgage and not the foreclosure.

Stamp duty payable on mortgage of €80,000	€80

If A re-sold the property, liability to duty on conveyance would arise. This foreclosure mechanism could be used to effect a conveyance at a lower rate of duty.
Now A is liable to pay duty on the foreclosure order but is exempt from it upon the first resale thereafter.

	€
Stamp duty payable on mortgage of €80,000	80
Stamp duty payable on foreclosure of €80,000 (5%)	4,000
Total payable on these transactions	4,080

16 *IRC v Angus & Co* [1889] 23 QB 579.

17 *Murdoch's A Dictionary of Irish Law* (4th edn, LexisNexis, 2004).

18 *Sun Alliance Insurance Ltd v IRC* [1972] Ch 133.

19 SDCA 1999, s 1.

20 SDCA 1999, s 39(1).

21 SDCA 1999, s 39(2).

[4.16] The quantum of duty payable relates to the value of the property and not the amount owing by the debtor to the creditor. Such value is that value accepted by the court and it is not open to the Revenue Commissioners to impose any other such value.[22]

It is more common for a mortgagee to proceed by way of a mortgage sale when repossessing a property and pass the liability to duty on to the new purchaser, since the property never falls into the hands of the mortgagee. In practice, the incidence of foreclosure remains small and it must be borne in mind that the Act states that it applies, not merely to decrees or orders for foreclosure, but, to decrees or orders having the effect of a foreclosure.[23] It might be that the redemption of any mortgage, including a judgment mortgage and a mortgage sale, operate with like effect as an order or decree for foreclosure and are covered by the foregoing provisions, something that is not currently the practice. Perhaps the real distinction is that the property does not vest in the mortgagee in a mortgage sale.

Property

[4.17] Property is that which is capable of being owned and includes both real and personal property and intangibles.[24] Real property consists of land or that which is attached to land, the degree of its attachment being crucial. Thus a house is real property, whereas a mobile home is probably not. Personal property consists of all non-real property that has a physical attribute with respect to its substance, for example an automobile, painting, leaseholds, etc. Intangible property is that category of property that has no physical attribute to its substance, but may be represented by a physical symbol, such as a patent or a chose in action.

[4.18] Distinguishing the different forms of property is important in terms of stamp duty, as different forms of property require different methods to effect their transfer, which by their nature requires different documentation to give effect to the transfer of the property. Bell points out that property is that over which property rights accrue.[25] In *Potter v IRC*[26] [1854] 10 Exch 147 property was defined as that 'which belonged to a person exclusive of others, and which could be the subject of a bargain and sale to another'. The concept of property is flexible, so flexible that at one stage it was thought that property rights could accrue over individuals in the form of slavery . Today that right is no longer recognised but it does illustrate the range of possibilities as regards what constitutes property and that the notion of property will vary from time to time. In *Waterford Glass*,[27] Carroll J stated:

> The word "property" is not defined and must take its meaning from the sense in which it is used ...

22 SDCA 1999, s 39(1).

23 SDCA 1999, s 39(1).

24 See paras **[1.06]** and **[1.09]**.

25 Bell *Modern Law of Personal Property in England and Ireland* (Butterworths, 1989), p 3.

26 *Potter v IRC* [1854] 10 Exch 147.

27 *Waterford Glass* IV ITR 187.

[4.19] It should be noted that the Constitution specifically protects the right to private property, subject to the public good.[28] Revenue in their Notes for Guidance pp 152 have described property as anything which can be bought and sold which, and considering the preceeding paragraph, in the view of the authors is overly simplified.

[4.20] One of the important features of a property right is that it operates so as to bind third parties, often expressed as the fact that personal rights operate against individuals whereas property rights operate against the whole world. Of course, this is not strictly true as such rights are only enforced against a party who is joined to the action. Although the rights may be valid as against the whole world, they must be continually asserted against each party who would seek to violate them and in this way resemble rights valid only between the parties and not *erga omnes* (against the world at large). In *National Provincial Bank v Ainsworth*[29] a wife who had been deserted by her husband remained in the former family home, which was mortgaged by her husband and on which he subsequently defaulted. The House of Lords ruled that the wife's interest was not a property right that would bind third parties like the bank, but a personal right only. Lord Wilberforce pointed out that a property right must be:

> ... definable, identifiable by third parties, capable in its nature of assumption by third parties and having some degree of permanence or stability (at page 494).

[4.21] In this jurisdiction, a party to a marriage is protected under the Family Home Protection Act 1976, which requires the consent of a spouse in writing before any sale or mortgage of the family home is enforceable.[30] The final criterion of permanence and stability must surely be open to question, if not given an extremely liberal and vague definition (decaying fruit, property which is sinking like Venice, almost all perishables). On the other hand, the concept that a property right must be capable of assumption by third parties is relevant. If a right is assignable, then it is probably a property right for by making the interest assignable ('assignable' in this context means not only between parties, but also the creation of subsidiary rights over property), the law effectively converts it into a property right. The ability to assign a contractual debt creates property with respect to the debt because whilst it is not operative against the whole world, it is now capable of being used by a third party and, therefore, must be more than a personal right. In *Western Abyssinian Mining Syndicate Ltd v IRC*[31] it was held that the benefit of a contract was property; the assignment of such benefit is therefore chargeable to duty under the conveyance on sale head. In relation to taxing statutes, the courts take an even wider view of what constitutes property. In *Zim Properties v Proctor (Inspector of Taxes)*[32] an employee's rights under a contract of employment were held to be taxable

---

28 Article 40.3.2°.

29 *National Provincial Bank v Ainsworth* [1965] 2 All ER 472.

30 *Nestor v Murphy* [1979] IR 326; see also the Judicial Separation and Family Law Reform Act 1989, Family Law Act 1995, Family Law (Divorce) Act 1996 – parties to an agreement to marry are protected under the provisions of the Family Law Act 1981.

31 *Western Abyssinian Mining Syndicate Ltd v IRC* [1935] 14 ATC 286.

32 *Zim Properties v Proctor (Inspector of Taxes)* [1985] STC 90.

assets despite the fact that they did not conform to the concept laid down by Lord Wilberforce.

[4.22] Some typical examples of property coming within the stamp duty charge include:

(a) Land;

(b) Goodwill;

(c) Copyright and trademarks;

(d) Patents, licences, etc;

(e) Options;

(f) Annuities;

(g) Chattels;

(h) Right to sue;

(i) Shares;

(j) Tenant's fixtures;

(k) Cash and bank accounts;

This list is illustrative, not exhaustive. In *Macklin & McDonald v Gracen & Co Ltd*[33] the court held:

> that a liquor licence could not be sold independent of the premises to which it was attached. Therefore a licence to sell liquor does not constitute property of itself. To sell such a licence separate from the premises, the legal interest to which the licence attaches must be "destroyed' in the legal sense, extinguishing the licence and allowing it to be revived for an alternative premises under the provisions of the Act.

Land

[4.23] The words 'all lands' are to be taken literally and include land comprising the sea bed.[34] Land includes anything attached to land, including buildings or other structures, provided that the structures are permanently attached to the land. A first floor apartment, or higher, is also considered to be land, though it is attached to the apartment below it rather than the land itself. The difficulties of these 'flying freeholds' has been discussed earlier.[35]

Goodwill

[4.24] This is an intangible right to the advantage of the business, in particular the reputation built up by the business over a period of time.[36] For a further discussion, see para **[5.10]** and **[7.11]** below.

---

[33] *Macklin & McDonald v Gracen & Co Ltd* [1982] ILRM 182.

[34] See *Trustees of Kinsale Yacht Club v Commissioners of Valuation* [1993] ILRM 393.

[35] See para **[1.06]**.

[36] *Eastern National Omnibus Co Ltd v IRC* [1939] 1 KB 161.

Copyright and trademarks

[4.25] Copyright and trademarks are examples of intellectual property. Intellectual property rights consist of the right to exploit creation. For example, if A writes a book, A exploits the fruits of his initiative by controlling the sale of the book through copyright. No one else may reproduce the work without permission. The same is true of trademarks, which protect a name or brand identification. They should be treated as property per se, that is, property in its own right. A trademark is intangible property since it is an intellectual property right but a trademark may also include an amount of goodwill, for example, the use of a particular name on a product can ensure that that product sells at a premium and has a ready acceptance in the marketplace in terms of repeat and new customers. The 'Sony' brand on electrical equipment means that these products command a higher price than lesser known brands of an equivalent nature. On the sale of the trademark, a proportion of the price will cover the right to reap the financial rewards, but a substantial element will cover the goodwill attaching to a particular trademark.

Goodwill attaching to a trademark is located where the trademark is registered.[37]

Patents, licences, etc

[4.26] Patents, licences, etc, are regarded as a form of property. A patent is the legal choice for the right to protect know how. For example, an inventor who builds a better mousetrap can exploit this invention by obtaining the patent for it and then granting a licence to others who wish to use the know how in return for payment. Know how which is not patented does not constitute property and is not subject to stamp duty liability. As Lord Tomlin indicated in *Handley Page v Butterworth*[38]:

> ... it may be only the documents, and drawings containing the secret knowledge or processes and the right to restrain any disclosure (which) constitute property.

[4.27] In certain circumstances they are liable to *ad valorem* stamp duty. If there is a grant of an exclusive licence to use the patent for so long as that patent continues in return for consideration, then this licence is chargeable to *ad valorem* stamp duty. On the other hand, a non-exclusive licence or a licence containing a revocation clause is not liable to *ad valorem* duty, although it may give rise to a fixed duty liability. The reason for this is that, where the licence is both exclusive and does not contain a clause enabling the grantor to revoke the said licence, then there is a transfer of the interest in the property and, therefore, it falls under the relevant head of charge to duty.[39] However, where the licence is non-exclusive or can be revoked, then this is not a transfer of property. The non-exclusivity and the fact that it can be revoked lead to the conclusion that the interest in the licence has not been transferred but is now operated almost on an agency basis. Such a construction would render the relevant licence outside the scope of the charging provision for *ad valorem* duty. However, since the licence would normally

---

37 *Brooke & Co v IRC* [1896] 2 QB 536.

38 *Handley Page v Butterworth* [1935] 19 TC 328 at p 372.

39 SDCA 1999, s 31.

take effect through a written document, then it may fall to be liable under the fixed head of charge.

Options

[4.28] An option is a right created by a contract giving a person a right to buy or not to buy a specific asset at a specific price within a specified time limit and is property in its own right. An option to purchase property at some time in the future is a property right that can be conveyed.[40] A pre-emptive right, however, is not an interest in land.[41] Options in practice come in two forms, namely a put option and a call option. A call option is the right of the purchaser to call on the owner of the property to dispose of the property under the terms of the option agreement. A put option is the right of the owner of the property to call upon the purchaser to purchase the property under the terms of the option agreement. Most option agreements contain put and call clauses which in effect bind both parties. If the vendor is bound to sell under the option agreement but has no right to call on the purchaser then no contract exists and no disposal has taken place, as the vendor has no right to dispose of the property.

Annuities

[4.29] An annuity is a yearly right to income, whether payable quarterly or such other period being less than yearly, and constitutes property.[42]

Chattels

[4.30] Generally chattels may be passed by delivery. This means that their legal title can pass by delivering the assets according to the terms of the contract. No further documentation is required to make the contract or physical passing enforecable. However, it is imperative to include a clause clearly stating that the title to this assets is passing by delivery. In the case of chattels that cannot be physically handed over, a written document may be created to hand over title to the property. This document will be liable to stamp duty as a conveyance on sale.

Right to sue

[4.31] While this is not a tangible asset, it has been decided by case law that it constitutes property.[43]

Shares

[4.32] Shares in unlisted companies are transferred by a stock transfer form and this is a stampable document. Shares in listed companies may be transferred by means of the CREST system, whereby the operator's instruction is deemed to be the stampable document. Where a company allots shares in return for assets other than cash, Companies Act 1963[44] requires that the written particulars of the contract or the contract

---

40 *Wimpey & Co v IRC* [1975] 1 WLR 995.

41 *Pritchard v Briggs* [1980] 1 All ER 299.

42 *Hennell v IRC* [1933] 1 KB 415.

43 *Zim Properties v Proctor (Inspector of Taxes)* [1985] STC 90.

44 Companies Act 1963, 58,

itself returned to the registrar of companies. There was a requirement, prior to the FA 2006, that the contract or written particulars should have been duly stamped with the appropriate duty for such a contract.

Tenant's fixtures

[4.33] The general legal rule is that which is attached to land is land. There are two major factors taken into consideration as to whether a chattel attached to land has become a fixture. These are the degree of annexation to the land and the purpose or object of the annexation. Tenant's fixtures[45] are chattels which have been attached to land (those that have to be physically detatched from the land). While they are not land, they are also not chattels that can pass by delivery. Where there is a written agreement to transfer a leasehold with the tenant's fixtures, the element of the contract relating to the fixtures will be stampable at contract stage under the operation of SDCA 1999, s 31.

Cash and bank accounts

[4.34] Cash is property that can be passed by delivery. A distinction is made between cash on deposit and current accounts. Current accounts are a means of money management and are therefore not strictly debts. Cash on deposit is a debt due on the bank to the account holder. It should be noted that this distinction is not automatic; the transactions on the current account should demonstrate continual use of the account for the purposes of the trade. Revenue will seek to stamp an instrument transferring cash on deposit account, whereas an instrument transferring cash on current account may not be stampable.[46]

Any interest or estate in any property

[4.35] An 'estate' refers exclusively to a particular type of interest in land and includes[47]:

Freehold estates

(i) *fee simple*: to A in fee simple (statutory wording), to A and his heirs (common law wording);

(ii) *fee tail*: to A in tail (statutory wording), to A and his issue or heirs of his flesh (common law);

(iii) *fee farm grant*: a fee simple subject to a perpetual rent reserved to the grantor (Landlord and Tenant (Amendment) Act 1860 (Deasy's Act), Renewable Leasehold Conversion Act 1849);

(iv) *base fee*: the failure to enlarge a fee tail into a fee simple by not barring the entail or failing to gain the consent of the protector of the settlement; and

(v) *life estate*: to A for life (statutory wording), any transaction that fails to create a larger estate.

---

45 See further paras **[5.13]** and **[7.15]**.

46 See para **[5.19]** and **[7.12]**.

47 See para **[1.07]**ff.

Leasehold estates

(i) *periodic tenancy*: a tenancy that lasts for a given period of time with the presumption that it will be renewed for the same period at the expiration of the period for example a weekly rental of a bedsit;

(ii) *term certain*: a tenancy that is agreed to last for a given period of time and there is no presumption that the agreement will be renewed; for example, a lease for two years; and

(iii) a tenancy at will and at sufferance.

[4.36] Property is capable of being divided in various ways which can result in the division of interests or the creation of rights over the property. It is not possible to have an estate in goods, though it is possible to have interests in land, which are not estates but lesser rights and obligations, such as easements (a right enjoyed by the owner of land over the lands of another, for example a right-of-way), *profit a prendre* (a right to take the harvest or soil from another's land, for example hunting and fishing rights, quarries and trapper, the right to take turf[48] etc.

[4.37] An interest is the situation where a person has rights, titles, advantages, duties, liabilities over, in this case, property, whether present or future, ascertained or potential, provided they are not too remote. This covers an extremely wide range of possibilities. The most common of which is the option contract, whereby an offeror binds himself to keeping open a particular offer to the offeree for a given period of time. This is clearly an interest in property and must contain consideration to be enforceable.[49] It is liable to stamp duty, subject to the provisions of para **[4.06]**.[50]

[4.38] SDCA 1999 does not differentiate between legal and equitable ownership and it would seem that either will suffice. It is important to be clear that property can be owned in two distinct ways. Legal ownership is for all external purposes being regarded as the owner of the property, the owner on record where that is possible, or one who has the legal obligation to assign the property or its profits by the direction of the equitable owner. Equitable ownership means having the benefit of the exercise of the legal ownership (a equitable owner is empowered to call upon the legal owner to transfer the property or its profits by his direction). Equitable ownership is often referred to as 'beneficial ownership' and this term is perhaps more illustrative of what occurs.[51] Legal ownership is governed by the common law and is to be found from the form of one's rights to the property; for example, whether the property is registered in one's name. If so, then one has the legal title to it, which may well be subject to another person's interest and that person's right will be recognised under the law of equity.[52] Equity will not defeat the common law and so will uphold the legal ownership, but demand that it be

48 *Convey v Regan* [1952] IR 56.

49 *Walker v Glass* [1979] NI 129.

50 See also **Chapter 5**.

51 See **Chapter 1**.

52 See **Chapter 1**.

exercised for the benefit of the equitable owner.[53] This is also commonly referred to as a trust; for example, upon the signing of a contract by both parties for the purchase of a property, the beneficial ownership passes to the purchaser whilst the legal ownership remains vested in the vendor.[54] The purchaser can then call upon the vendor for a conveyance or transfer of the legal title. In the interim period, the vendor is entitled to the rents and profits of the property until the time for completion is present, per Henchy J in *Tempany v Hynes*.[55] If no date for completion is fixed by the parties, the date is when the vendor first makes out a good title to the property, *Monro v Taylor*[56] are 51. If completion does not take place on the completion date, the vendor is trustee of the rents and profits for the purchaser and is obliged to account for them. Of course he is also at a certain degree of risk and reference should be made to a discussion of the purchaser's assumption of the risk, particularly with respect to land sales and the Law Reform Commission report thereon.[57] Note that under the Incorporated Law Society general conditions of the standard contract of sale, the risk is now retained by the vendor until such time as the sale is completed.

[4.39] This beneficial ownership may arise in a number of ways. It may arise expressly, for example where a solicitor is required to purchase property in trust for his client who has supplied the purchase price. Implied trusts are those of a similar nature but which do not take the form of express trusts. For instance, where the conduct of the parties is such that despite the absence of an express agreement to so create a trust, it must have been implied.

Example 4.39.1

An engaged couple contribute jointly to the purchase of a house but it is conveyed into the name of one of the parties only. An implied trust arises with respect to the other party.[58]

A resulting trust arises where an attempt to create a trust has failed, except where it fails due to the lack of intention to create a trust, it "results" back to the settlor, see *Lynch v Burke & AIB plc.*[59]

Example 4.39.2

The settlor attempts to create a trust but fails to do so because it lacks one of the three certainties.

[4.40] The three certainties are the subject matter of the trust, object of the trust and the words of the trust. For a trust to be enforceable, it should be possible to readily and accurately identify the property which will be held in trust (that is the subject matter),

53 Judicature (Ireland) Act 1877.

54 But see *Tempany v Hynes* [1976] IR 101 – **Chapter 1**.

55 *Tempany v Hynes* [1976] IR 101.

56 *Monro v Taylor* [1848] 8 Hare 51.

57 See **Chapter 1**

58 See also Family Law Act 1981.

59 *Lynch v Burke & AIB plc* V ITR 391.

the aims of the trust (that is the objects) and that a trust was intended to be created (that is the words).[60]

Example 4.40.1

Tom leaves his house to Dick in trust for Harry. Tom has two houses but it is unclear which house is to be held in trust for Harry. Tom has a resulting trust since the subject matter of the trust is uncertain.

Example 4.40.2

Tom leaves Blackacre to Dick in trust for those who knew him. Identification of the beneficiaries is too uncertain. The express trust fails. Tom has a resulting trust in Blackacre.

Example 4.40.3

Tom leaves Blackacre to Dick in the hope that Dick will look after Harry. There are insufficient words to create a trust in favour of Harry.

Dick will take the property absolutely. There is no resulting trust but a full conveyance of Tom's interest to Dick.

[4.41] A constructive trust is one imposed by the courts in order to prevent an unjust enrichment and this is done despite the wishes of the parties but because the court feels it is the equitable solution.

Example 4.41.1

Money given to an accountant for investment is appropriated for the accountant's personal use to purchase a plot of land. This means the accountant is the legal owner of the property but a constructive trust may be imposed upon him.

The use of the constructive trust is the most radical and has been the subject of considerable alteration and controversy.[61] In the United States, for example, the constructive trust is viewed as a remedy much like an award of damages.[62] Liability to duty cannot be avoided by transferring the equitable interest in property and likewise a transfer of the legal ownership only will result in liability.

Example 4.41.2

A transfers his legal title to X, for the benefit of A.

The transaction is liable to stamp duty.

[4.42] By operation of law the equitable ownership in property passes to the purchaser on the signing of the contract for sale and will be subsequently followed by the parties transferring the legal ownership. This should not expose the parties to double duty on the transfer of both interests because in reality there is only one transaction, which by virtue of law is broken into two distinct events. However, if goodwill attaches to the property such contract would be stampable in respect of goodwill and the subsequent conveyance or transfer would be stampable in respect of the legal ownership passing.[63]

---

60 See para **[1.17]**.

61 *W v W* [1981] ILRM 202; Martland J, diss, in *Pettkus v Becker* [1980] 2 SCR 834.

62 Restatement of Restitution generally; *Beatly v Guggenheim Exploration Co* 225 NY 380.

63 SDCA 1999, s 31.

[4.43] The sale of either the legal or equitable ownership in property gives rise to liability to duty. Where the transfer of the two interests is part of one continuous transaction, but by operation of law the two interests are transferred at different times, only a single charge to duty arises. In *Peter Bone Ltd v IRC*[64] the vendor and purchaser executed an agreement whereby the vendor remained a bare trustee of property for the benefit of the purchaser and for which the vendor was the nominee of the purchaser. Unlike a traditional conveyance on sale, the vendor was not entitled to call for the purchaser to complete the conveyance as this was entirely in the hands of the purchaser. A question arose whether this was chargeable under s 2 of the SDCA 1999 as a conveyance on sale or s 31 as an agreement for sale of an equitable interest in property. On appeal the court held that it constituted a conveyance on sale and was liable to *ad valorem* duty under s 2.

> In the case of an agreement for the sale of a legal estate in land the agreement is said to merge with the conveyance of the land, although of course some contractual obligations may remain …[in this case the vendors did] not have the right, which a vendor under an uncompleted contract has, to require the purchaser to take a conveyance and so relieve him of a potentially burdensome legal title. I think that, strictly, the agreement operated as a transfer of the equitable estate in the freehold property, and not as an agreement for the sale of the equitable estate. (per Vinelott J)

Vinelott J also states that a contract ceases to be executory when the parties have performed their obligations under the contract. There was no longer any contractual obligation which remained to be performed. As such, the distinguishing factor in this case was that all the conditions of the contract had been fulfilled, and there was nothing further to be done after the exchange of the contracts. The agreement operated to transfer the equitable interest (not an agreement for the transfer of an equitable interest) and as such the agreement was considered to to be a conveyance in all but name.

[4.44] In the case of *Prudential Assurance Co Ltd v IRC*[65] the judge noted that:

> A given commercial result can often be reached by more than one route. If the parties have genuinely chosen that route, rather than a different route having different legal incidents and consequences, for better or for for worse stamp duty will be assessable accordingly…

On the basis of this, provided there are no terms in the contract for sale which would allow the document to be interpreted as a conveyance, such a contract should never be liable to stamp duty.

[4.45] In *Chesterfield Brewery Co v IRC*[66] a declaration of a trust by the vendor in favour of the purchaser constituted a conveyance on sale. Again in this decision, the court found that the real intention of the parties was that the written agreement should be the purchaser's only title to the property. No further obligations were required to complete the contract. The intention of the parties from the outset was that the declaration of trust should be the purchaser's only title. This is in accord with the *Bone*

---

64 *Peter Bone Ltd v IRC* [1995] STC 921.

65 *Prudential Assurance Co Ltd v IRC* (1993) 1 WLR 211.

66 *Chesterfield Brewery Co v IRC* [1899] 2 QB 7.

decision since what was being attempted was a splitting of the ownership and a transfer of one part only. The failure to transfer the remainder did not absolve it from duty.

The sale

[4.46] A 'sale' is defined as the transfer of a property right from the seller to the buyer in return for a monetary consideration, usually referred to as the price. The term sale relates specifically to the assignment for value of a property right. The concept of a sale is critical in discovering the nature of transactions that are covered by this section. As indicated at para **[3.30]**, the decision of Carroll J in the *Waterford Glass (Group Services) Ltd v Revenue Commissioners*[67] case suggests that the definition concerns not the form of the transaction but the underlying reality of it.

[4.47] A sale may only be entered into by parties who have both the capacity and intent to so do. Any transaction where the parties lack either capacity or intent does not constitute a sale. Capacity is governed by the usual rules in the law of contract. Few adults will be excluded from making a contract for sale and the principal area of difficulty arises from the capacity of corporations which are confined by their articles and memorandum. The articles concern the governance of the company and are usually found to consist of those offered by CA 1963, Table A. The memorandum governs the objects of the company and though offered by CA 1963, Table B it is usual that they are purpose designed. There is a difference between powers and objects. Powers may only be exercised in furtherance of the objects of association. A contract made outside of these provisions is ultra vires and not enforceable.[68]

[4.48] Capacity attacks the enforceability of a contract and normally gives the party who lacks the required capacity the opportunity to avoid or to ratify the contract. The lack of capacity will not remove liability to duty where a sale has occurred, even if the sale is not enforceable.

Example 4.48.1

A contract for the sale of land may be unenforceable because it does not conform with the Statute of Frauds, but if the land is actually transferred or conveyed, it is liable to duty despite the formal flaw.

The timing for liability arises at the execution of the document and there must be some argument as to whether or not any transfer is actually required before a liability arises. A sale made to a company or a minor, which is void or voidable for lack of capacity will be liable to duty as if an enforceable contract had come into existence. Where one of the parties sets the agreement aside for the lack of capacity, no effective sale has occurred.

[4.49] Where the parties have the requisite capacity, it may be that their intention was not to proceed by way of sale. Alternatively, it may be that one of the parties is forced into a sale by external pressures. In the case of *Ridge Nominees v IRC*[69] the applicant was a

---

[67] *Waterford Glass (Group Services) Ltd v Revenue Commissioners* IV ITR 187.

[68] Keane *Company Law in Ireland* (3rd edn, LexisNexis, 2000) Courtney *Law of Private Companies* (2nd edn, Lexis Nexis Butterworths, 2002) for a fuller discussion.

[69] *Ridge Nominees v IRC* [1961] 3 All ER 1108.

minority shareholder in a company which was the subject of a takeover. The overwhelming majority of shareholders (more than nine-tenths) wished to accept the offer, which brought the compulsory sale provisions of company law into effect which required that the applicant sell her shares to the bidder. This was against the wishes of the applicant and an exemption from duty was sought on the basis that a sale could not take place without either intent to sell or assent to sell and that the applicant was being forced to transfer her shares by operation of law. The application was rejected, the effect of which must be that the concept of sale under the Act differs from the normal contractual context of assent and intent and instead refers to the result of a transaction and not its cause or method. Once the effect of the transaction has resulted in the transfer of the property rights for value, a sale has occurred under the Act and liability to stamp duty arises. In *Great Western Railway v IRC*[70] it was held that, where the undertaking of two railway companies were amalgamated to form part of a third company by statute and the amalgamated companies were dissolved, this transaction was a sale and liable to *ad valorem* duty. A forced transfer without compensation, as far as such a transaction would be permissible under constitutional law, would not be a sale because no consideration was made. Compulsory acquisition with compensation is liable to stamp duty, unless the transfer on foot of a compulsory purchase order to a statutory authority is exempt from stamp duty.

[4.50] The concept of a sale as outlined by SDCA 1999 means the transfer or conveyance of property rights from one party to another in return for consideration[71]. Problems of capacity and intent are, therefore, somewhat spurious. If the transfer is valid, even though it may not be enforceable, neither the intent nor capacity of the parties is relevant. In certain circumstances, the requirement that such transfer be for value has been removed by statutory provisions, particularly transfers by gift.[72] For stamp duty purposes a "conveyance" is an instrument whereby any property is transferred from one person to another and includes both formal instruments of conveyance and other instruments that achieve the same result. Attempts to avoid stamp duty by using some other instrument other than a conveyance of sale instrument usually fail.

[4.51] Typical types of sale that are chargeable under the conveyance of sale head include the following:

(a) Transfers that give effect to an agreement for sale where the property coincides. In *Henty & Constable (Breweries) v IRC*,[73] Lord Evershed said:

> I do not at all question the validity of the proposition that an instrument may be liable to *ad valorem* duty as a conveyance on sale where it operates as the completion of a pre-existing bargain although the property transferred by the instrument is not the same property as that which was the subject of the earlier bargain provided that the former does in truth and reality "represent" the latter.

70 *Great Western Railway v IRC* (1894) 1 QB 507 (CA).

71 Where the vendor takes part of the consideration by way of property in satisfaction of the purchase price, this still constitutes a sale, see *Simpson v Connolly* [1953] 2 All ER 474.

72 SDCA 1999, s 30.

73 *Henty & Constable (Breweries) v IRC* [1961] 3 All ER 1146.

(b) Declaration of trust by the vendor in favour of the purchaser.[74] "The real intention of the parties was that this agreement should be the new company's only document of title, and that it should not be followed by a legal transfer of the shares in the old company" per Wills J in *Chesterfield v IRC*[75]. There was no doubt that this agreement was a conveyance on sale under s 1.

(c) Transfers which appear to be incomplete; for example, where the name of the transferee and the consideration is left blank. It is sufficient for a document to amount to a conveyance or transfer on sale if it is the instrument chosen by the parties to complete the sale in such a way as to show that they did not intend any other document to be executed.[76]

(d) Receipt or acknowledgment can be a sale and chargeable if it can be shown that the intention of the parties was that the property should pass and it, in fact, did so. However, it should be pointed out that the authority for this proposition is partially based on the judgments of Hanworth MR and Romer LJ in *Fleetwood-Hesketh v IRC* who held the receipt to be an agreement for sale.[77]

(e) An agreement for sale of a residual interest which had been preceded by an agreement for sale granting immediate possession

> "the court is entitled to look at the reality of what has been done. Just because the parties put a particular label on a transaction, the court is not obliged to accept that label blindly. The courts will look at the legal effect and the rights of the parties arising from the transaction",

See Carroll J in *Waterford Glass*.

(f) A deed of release of an option in a series of transactions held to be a conveyance on sale and as such liable to *ad valorem* duty under the conveyance on sale head.[78]

[4.52] Other examples include *Horsfall v Hey*[79] where a document stating the fact that the property had been conveyed in the terms 'Mr Thomas Hey has sold to G Hey all the goods, stock and trade ... for 90 pounds' was held to be a conveyance and chargeable. However, in a case in Scotland a similar document detailing the existence of an oral agreement and a statement that the property had in fact been handed over was held not be a conveyance on sale. The division of partnership property on the retirement of one of the partners has had mixed treatment. The majority view treats such documents as conveyances on sale, at least with respect to deeds executed pursuant to an agreement to dissolve the partnership.[80] An order to pay an amount outstanding by the person to whom it is owed, to one other than to whom it is owed, may constitute a conveyance on

---

74 *Chesterfield v IRC* [1899] 2 QB 7.

75 *Chesterfield v IRC* [1899] 2 QB7 at 12.

76 *Fitch & Lovell v IRC* [1962] 3 All ER 685, *Cohen & Moore v IRC* [1933] 2 KB 126.

77 *Fleetwood-Hesketh v IRC* [1936] 1 KB 351.

78 See *Cherry Court v Revenue Commissioners* V ITR 180.

79 *Horsfall v Hey* [1848] 2 Exch 778.

80 *Garnett v IRC* [1899] 81 LT 633, *Christie v IRC* [1866] LR 2 Exch 46, *Cf Macleod v IRC* [1885] 22 SLR 674.

sale as an equitable assignment of a debt.[81] In *Vandervell v IRC*[82] an order made by the person who was entitled to the allotment of shares, to allot those shares to a person other than to one who was entitled to them was held to be a conveyance. In *Danson v IRC*[83] a conveyance of property by the executors of a will in satisfaction of a pecuniary legacy was held to be a conveyance.

[4.53] The concept of "upon the sale thereof" has also been enlarged to include "in contemplation of a sale",[84] or more accurately the so-called "conveyance option contracts". In *Cory v IRC*[85] it was held that a conveyance subject to an option to purchase the shares in a company was not a sale and therefore not liable to duty. This was specifically amended in 1978. The provision states that:

> any instrument whereby property is conveyed or transferred to any person in contemplation of a sale of that property shall be treated for the purposes of SA 1891, as a conveyance or transfer on sale of that property for a consideration equal to the value of that property.

The duty is payable on the value of the property and not the value of the conveyance option contract.

Example 4.53.1

The shares of a company are conveyed subject to an option to purchase the shares within six months at €1 million. The cost of the option €10,000. The duty is charged based on the value of the property passing €1 million.

Where the option contract, whether conveyance or otherwise, is assignable, and can be the subject matter of a sale, any such sale is liable to duty on the value of the option. This is in addition to the duty payable on the value of the property in a conveyance option contract where such conveyance occurs, if at all.

[4.54] The duty payable under this provision is refundable in full or part upon claim to the Revenue Commissioners within six years of its creation, provided that the property was reconveyed to the original owner or his assignees on death or bankruptcy.[86] Where the actual price paid was less than the amount upon which the duty was levied, the overpayment is refundable[87] provided that the provisions of the SDCA 1999 with respect to avoidance measures in the disposition of property with inadequate consideration have not been infringed.[88] Any such instrument must be adjudicated upon by the Revenue prior to stamping.[89] Finally, liability under these provisions applies whether or not the

---

[81] *Brice v Bannister* [1878] 3 QBD 569.
[82] *Vandervell v IRC* [1965] 2 All ER 37.
[83] *Danson v IRC* [1905] 2 IR 69.
[84] SDCA 1999, s 33(1).
[85] *Cory v IRC* [1965] 1 All ER 917.
[86] SDCA 1999, s 33(2)(a).
[87] SDCA 1999, s 33(2)(b).
[88] SDCA 1999, s 33(3).
[89] SDCA 1999, s 33(4).

instrument would be liable to separate duty for the transfer of other property contained within the instrument.[90]

[4.55] Does the option contract, constituting an interest in property, incur the incidence of stamp duty without a sale being necessary? The creation of such an interest involves a sale of that right for value and consequently falls within this provision of SDCA 1999 and is liable to *ad valorem* duty on the quantum paid for such a right. In *Escoigne v IRC*[91] it was held that a contract for transfer or conveyance can bring the sale into existence. This important point is often overlooked with respect to rent review clauses where in a commercial lease it is treated as an option to increase rent and accordingly is stampable with the €12.50 duty in addition to the other duty. The Act specifically requires that the sale of an annuity or right not previously in existence, that is only secured by, amongst others, contract is deemed to be a conveyance on sale.[92] In *George Wimpey v IRC*[93] the owner of property received £15,000 as consideration for granting an option to the company to purchase the land. It was held that the option constituted property, the grant of which for consideration, was a sale.

[4.56] The requirement for a sale imposes, unless otherwise provided, the transfer, or promise of transfer, of consideration as discussed earlier. In *Littlewoods Mail Order Store v IRC*[94] the House of Lords held that the Act confined consideration for contracts of sale to cash, securities or discharge of a debt. In the transfer of freehold property in exchange for leasehold property there was no conveyance on sale for what was being effected was not a sale but an exchange for which SDCA 1999 did not impose liability, at least under this head of charge. This restrictive view of what constitutes a sale excludes contracts where the consideration is of any kind other than the three outlined earlier. The courts view the overriding impact of these provisions to charge the transfer of money as distinct from the transaction itself. Stamp duty under this charge is approached from the point of view of a sales tax, attaching effectively to cash transactions only.

[4.57] Certain transactions will not be deemed conveyances on sale. These include:

(a) partition;

(b) ineffective conveyance;

(c) impossability;

(d) family arrangements.

Partition

[4.58] Partition is the division of land owned by persons jointly among the owners in severalty according to the quantum of their interest. Where property is owned jointly by

---

[90] SDCA 1999, s 33(5).

[91] *Escoigne v IRC* [1958] AC 549.

[92] SDCA 1999, s 32, *Great Northern Railway Co v IRC* [1901] 1 KB 415.

[93] *George Wimpey v IRC* [1975] 2 All ER 45.

[94] *Littlewoods Mail Order Store v IRC* [1962] 2 All ER 279.

two or more persons, those persons may decide to split the property between them.[95] This is done by a deed of partition. A partition of property is not on sale and therefore cannot be charged to stamp duty under the conveyance on sale head of charge.

[4.59] If the property division is unequal, equalisation money may be paid by the benefitting party or, where there is no equalisation moneys paid, the benefitting party may be deemed to be receiving a gift of the difference in the value of the property received. Where equalisation moneys are paid and they exceed €130, the instrument will be chargeable to stamp duty under the conveyance on sale head of charge on an amount equal to the equalisation moneys paid.[96] Where no equalisation moneys are paid and the division is unequal, the difference in the value may be deemed to be a voluntary disposition *inter vivos*[97] which will also bring it under the conveyance on sale head of charge but with more implications for the parties to the deed.

Ineffective conveyance

[4.60] In *R v Ridgewell Inhabitants*[98] an instrument purported to be a conveyance of land which, not being a deed, could not convey the property and was held not to be a conveyance. The instrument contained a clause which stipulated that the party to take the premises not be disturbed. This indicated that the transaction was not a conveyance.

Impossibility

[4.61] In *Limmer Asphalte Paving Co v IRC*[99] the parties attempted to convey that which was neither in existence nor that which they could create, namely the exclusive right to asphalt within Lancaster and Chester. This resulted in the document not being stampable as no conveyance had occurred.

Family arrangements

[4.62] These receive mixed treatment. In general, they are not liable to duty so that a conveyance made to a son by his father in consideration of natural love and affection and for which the son promised augmentation of the fortunes of his sisters was held not to be a conveyance.[100] An arrangement between one person and his heir whereby the heir promised to assume the mortgage of certain properties and in consideration of that those properties were conveyed to the heir subject to the encumbrances, with the stipulation that it could be cancelled or altered at any time ,were held to be a conveyance on sale.[101]

Transferral to or vesting in a purchaser

[4.63] It has been suggested that the wording of this section aims to attach to land transactions because the concept of vesting is particular to land transactions. This is not

95 Revenue Notes for Guidance p 47.

96 SDCA 1999, s 38.

97 Revenue Notes for Guidance p 47.

98 *R v Ridgewell Inhabitants* [1827] 6 B&C 665.

99 *Limmer Asphalte Paving Co v IRC* [1872] LR 7 Exch 211.

100 *Denn D Manifold v Diamond* [1825] 4 B&C 243.

101 *Marquess of Bristol v IRC* [1901] 2 KB 336.

so, for the definition of property is not restricted to real property only. If the legislature had intended this, it is doubtful that they would have gone to such subtle lengths to achieve that which could have been achieved more readily by direct wording. It is intended to cover those situations where real property is not transferred but is vested in an individual to avoid the provisions of SDCA 1999. Recently, some practitioners had proposed a scheme for large property transactions where at closing the parties would agree the format of the deed and the vendor would execute the power of attorney enabling the purchaser to execute the deed at some later date. These practitioners were of the view that as no instrument existed, there was no liability to duty. At a later date, the purchaser could execute the deed under the power of attorney when the need arose. However, the correct view is that the power of attorney has the effect of conveying the property to the purchaser and accordingly should be stampable as a conveyance on sale. Where a power of attorney is granted under which the purchaser (directly or indirectly) may complete a transaction, it may be deemed to be a conveyance on sale. This is because any notice by which the power of attorney is exercised will operate as a memorandum of the contract which incorporates a power of attorney in favour of the purchaser. Such a contract could be held to be a conveyance on sale. The Revenue Commissioners are currently challenging a power of attorney transaction in the High Court on the basis that the power of attorney is tantamount to a conveyance on sale.

[4.64] Vesting refers to the distinction between vesting in interest and vesting in possession. Vesting in interest is not the immediate transfer of property but a current right to future enjoyment in it. Without this inclusion, SDCA 1999 would only cover a current right to present enjoyment that is vested in possession. This interpretation is sought to be specifically excluded. A sale of a remainder which is vested in interest could be caught by the Act. A contingent interest because it is not vested, either in possession or interest, is not caught within the charging section of the Act and escapes liability to duty. A contingent interest is that which may or may not occur and care should be taken to distinguish it from a vested interest subject to divesting (ie a vested interest that may be taken away). A vested interest carries liability irrespective of the possibility of divesting. A contingent interest carries no liability on creation but if it subsequently vests, it is liable to stamp duty. The value upon which the duty is levied is that at the time of the execution of the document with respect to a vested right, even if it should not vest in possession for many years to come. A contingent interest is subject to liability on the vesting of it, whether in interest or possession, and the value is adjudged accordingly.

Example 4.64.1

To A in fee simple

A's right to the property is vested in possession, that is a present right to current enjoyment of the land.

To A for life, remainder to B in fee simple

This creates a life estate vested in possession for A, and a fee simple vested in interest in B; that is, a present right to future enjoyment in land. Both A and B's rights are vested and therefore liable to duty.

To A for life if he marries

This creates a contingent life estate in A. His interest being contingent is not liable to duty on creation, despite the fact that it is alienable. If it were to be so alienated it would be liable to duty as the transfer of an estate or interest in land as described earlier???. If the contingency is satisfied then the life estate will vest and, upon vesting, liability to duty will arise.

Finally, a transaction that appears to create a contingent interest may be construed as being vested, subject to divesting on the principle of law which favours vesting of property over contingent interests.

Example 4.64.2

To A for life but if he marries B, then to C for life

This will be construed as a vested life estate in A subject to divesting, liability in that situation arising on creation. C's interest is contingent (on A marrying B) and is not liable at this stage to duty.

This has been taken to extremes in the case of wills, and though subject to much criticism, appears to represent good law.

Example 4.64.3

To A provided that he attains 25 years of age

If this is a devise in a will, it has been held to be a vested gift subject to divesting if A fails to attain that age.

It is not required that the vendor be the person to effect the vesting of the property in the purchaser. It is sufficient that the vendor can direct that the purchaser become vested with the property.[102]

Transferral to or vesting in any other person

[4.65] Liability attaches even should the purpose of the sale not involve a formal transfer between the vendor and purchaser and include a subsale situation. The concept of any person "on his behalf or by his direction" is broad and goes beyond a trustee or agent and includes any individual so nominated by the purchaser. No formal contract or agreement need exist between the parties. Conduct may suffice but both the supplier of the consideration and the beneficiary of the sale must be clear that such an arrangement exists.[103]

Charges and rates of duty

[4.66] The rate of duty under the conveyance of sale head of charge remained, for the most part, static for a long number of years. However, during the late 1990s, the rapid increase in property while the economy was buoyant, led to the use of stamp duty rates as an instrument of economic management by the government. To slow down this enormous increase in property values, the government first increased the rates of stamp duty on properties over a certain value in the FA 1997. Fifteen months later, pursuing the same policy, the government decided to lower these stamp duty rates in the Finance

---

[102] *AG v Brown* [1849] 3 Ex 66.

[103] *Jophins v IRC* (1940) 2 KB 282, see also *Waterford* and *Viek*.

(No 2) Act 1998 and have continued to do so. The constantly changing stamp duty regime is leading to complexity both in the enforcement of the regulations and in the conveyancing process, resulting in increased costs. Government policy, reacting in kneejerk fashion to the latest sound-bite, cannot be a substitute for the complete review of the law of stamp duty. To further aggravate the issue, a third round of changes was introduced again in a vain attempt to use stamp duty as a tool of market regulation. It had the twin-track approach of trying to deter investors from the property market and lessen the burden on owner-occupiers and first-time purchasers in particular. The net effect was less than moderate on house prices but caused considerable increases in rental rates in the private sector. The stamp duty rates were again addressed in the FA 2005. This Act brought about increases in the rate bands for first-time buyers. It is arguable that the increase in the bands is causing a parallel increase in the house prices, cancelling any benefits for any first-time purchasers.

Rates of stamp duty up to 22 January 1997

[4.67] Where an instrument operated as a conveyance or transfer on sale of any property, other than marketable securities, duty was charged on the consideration passing at a rate relative to the amount of the consideration as set out in the table below:

Amount or value	*Rate of duty*
Not exceeding £5,000	*Exempt*
Exceeding £5,000 but not £10,000	£1 for every £100 or part thereof (1 %)
Exceeding £10,000 but not £15,000	£2 for every £ 100 or part thereof (2%)
Exceeding £15,000 but not £25,000	£3 for every £100 or part thereof (3%)
Exceeding £25,000 but not £50,000	£4 for every £100 or part thereof (4%)
Exceeding £50,000 but not £60,000	£5 for every £100 or part thereof (5%)
Exceeding £60,000	£6 for every £100 or part thereof (6%)

To qualify for any of the lower rates of duty or for the deed to not be liable to duty, the instrument had to contain a statement certifying that the transaction did not form part of a larger transaction or series of transactions in respect of which the amount or value or aggregate amount or value of the consideration exceeded the band involved. If this was not inserted, the higher rate applied. Finance certificates are discussed in more detail below.

Rates of stamp duty from 23 January 1997 to 22 April 1998

[4.68] Where an instrument operated as a conveyance or transfer on sale of any property other than marketable securities, duty was charged on the consideration passing at a rate relative to the amount of the consideration as set out in the table below:

Amount or value	*Rate of duty*
Not exceeding £5,000.	Exempt
Exceeding £5,000 but not £10,000	£1 for every £100 or part thereof (1%)
Exceeding £10,000 but not £15,000	£2 for every £100 or part thereof (2%)
Exceeding £15,000 but not £25,000	£3 for every £100 or part thereof (3%)
Exceeding £25,000 but not £50,000	£4 for every £100 or part thereof (4%)

Exceeding £50,000 but not £60,000	£5 for every £100 or part thereof (5%)
Exceeding £60,000	£6 for every £100 or part thereof (6%)

The highest rate applicable to non-residential properties was 6%, irrespective of the consideration. However, where the property was a residential property, the consideration for which was in excess of £150,000, higher rates of duty applied, on a sliding scale, up to a maximum of 9%.

Increased rates for residential property

[4.69]

Amount or value	*Rate of duty*
Exceeding £150,000 but not £160,000	£7 for every £100 or part thereof (7%)
Exceeding £160,000 but not £170,000	£8 for every £100 or part thereof (8%)
Exceeding £170,000	£9 for every £100 or part thereof (9%)

A residential property is defined as:

(a) a building or part of a building which, at the date of the instrument of conveyance or lease:

  (i) was used or was suitable for use as a dwelling, or

  (ii) was in the course of being constructed or adapted for use as a dwelling, or

  (iii) had been constructed or adapted for use as a dwelling and had not since such construction or adaptation been adapted for any other use, and

(b) the curtilage of the residential property up to an area (exclusive of the site of the residential property) of one acre: provided that

  (i) where in the year ending on the 31st day of December immediately prior to the date of that instrument of conveyance or lease;

   – a rate was made by a rating authority as regards any hereditament to which the provisions of section 3 of the Act of 1978 did not apply, or

   – a rate was made by a rating authority, and an allowance made under that section of that Act, as regards any hereditament which was at the time the rate was made a mixed hereditament, secondary school or community hall, or

   – a hereditament was described as exempt, or partially exempt, from rating in the valuation lists, then the whole or an appropriate part of that hereditament as is referable to ordinary use other than as a dwelling at the date of that instrument of conveyance or lease or, where appropriate, when last ordinarily used, shall not be residential property in relation to that sale or lease,

  (ii) where the area of the curtilage (exclusive of the site of the residential property) exceeds one acre, then the part which shall be residential property shall be taken to be the part which, if the remainder were separately occupied, would be most suitable for occupation and enjoyment with the residential property.[104]

[4.70] Simply put, the higher rates of duty applied to any property which, at the time of the execution of the instrument, was suitable for use as a dwelling. A key factor appears to be whether the local authority had commercially rated the property. If the property was commercially rated, the maximum rate of duty applicable was 6 per cent. For example, a registered bed and breakfast will have had a commercial rateable valuation by the local authority and attracted a maximum of 6 per cent duty once the consideration exceeded £60,000 and the non-rated area did not exceed £150,000. However, if an unregistered bed and breakfast did not have a commercial rateable valuation and the consideration exceeded £150,000, it fell liable to duty at a rate of up to a maximum of 9 per cent. These rates became effective for conveyances executed on or after 23 January 1997.[105] If a binding contract was entered into prior to 23 January 1997, the higher rates of duty did not apply where the instrument effecting the conveyance or lease was executed before 1 May 1997.[106]

[4.71] Where a property was derelict, and was incapable of being used as a dwelling as where, for example, it had no roof, it would not be classified as a residential property and so attracted a maximum level of duty of 6%. Even though a derelict property probably falls within the ambit of s 1, the issue is moot given that, in general, such a derelict property would not come within s 3 of the 1978 Act referred to in s 122(b)(i)(I).

[4.72] Where a property was mixed, that is to say partly used for residential purposes and partly used for non-residential purposes, the higher rates of duty applied to that portion of the value of the property which was attributable to residential purposes. The apportionment was to be made on a just and reasonable basis.[107] This apportionment was not limited to that which the parties themselves specified in the transaction but was one which had to be objectively justifiable. When presenting the instrument for stamping, details of the apportionment had to be disclosed to the Revenue Commissioners. Apportionment details had to include both the vendor's and the purchaser's objective estimate of the consideration of the portion attributable to the residential element of the property. In practice, the contract as executed between the parties was lodged with the instrument for stamping. This will normally be determined by the percentage amount of the rateable valuation remaining after it has been reduced by the domestic rates allowance.

[4.73] To qualify for any of the lower rates of duty or for the deed to be exempt, the instrument had to contain a statement certifying that the transaction did not form part of a larger transaction or series of transactions in respect of which the amount or aggregrate amount of the consideration exceeds the band involved. Further, once the consideration

[104] SDCA 1999, s 1.
[105] FA 1997, s 116.
[106] FA 1997, s 116.
[107] SDCA 1999, s 45(2).

for the transaction exceeded £150,000, the instrument also had to contain a certificate as to the nature of the property. For fuller treatment of finance certificates, see below.

Rates of stamp duty between 23 April 1998 and 14 June 2000

[4.74] Where an instrument operated as a conveyance or transfer on sale of a non residential property other than marketable securities, duty was charged on the consideration passing at a rate relative to the amount of the consideration.

Amount or value	*Rate of duty*
Not exceeding £5,000	Exempt
Exceeding £5,000 but not £10,000	£1 for every £100 or part thereof (1%)
Exceeding £10,000 but not £15,000	£2 for every £100 or part thereof (2%)
Exceeding £15,000 but not £25,000	£3 for every £100 or part thereof (3%)
Exceeding £25,000 but not £50,000	£4 for every £100 or part thereof (4%)
Exceeding £50,000 but not £60,000	£5 for every £100 or part thereof (5%)
Exceeding £60,000	£6 for every £100 or part thereof (6%)

[4.75] Where an instrument operated as a conveyance or transfer on sale of any residential property, or property a portion of which comprises residential property, other than marketable securities, duty was charged on the consideration passing at a rate relative to the amount of the consideration.

Amount or value	*Rate of duty*
Not exceeding £60,000	Exempt
Exceeding £60,000 but not £100,000	£3 for every £100 or part thereof (3%)
Exceeding £100,000 but not £170,000	£4 for every £100 or part thereof (4%)
Exceeding £170,000 but not £250,000	£5 for every £100 or part thereof (5%)
Exceeding £250,000 but not £500,000	£7 for every £100 or part thereof (7%)
Exceeding £500,000	£9 for every £100 or part thereof (9%)

The term 'residential property' is given the same definition as that in the FA 1997, as detailed above. However, in the case of mixed properties, that is property which contains both residential and non-residential sections, aggregation no longer occurs and each section is assessed as a separate property. Apportionment details must be submitted to the Revenue Commissioners on Form SD5 which is available from the Revenue, see **Appendix 8**.

[4.76] The highest rate of duty (9%) will apply in the absence of any certificate in the deed. The insertion of a certificate in the deed certifying that the property is non-residential will reduce the rate of duty applicable to 6% (the highest rate on non-residential property). To avail of any lower rate for either residential or non-residential property, the appropriate finance certificate must be inserted. Further, the exemption from stamp duty liability available on new houses coming within a certain floor area size is retained, but this exemption is restricted. It is only available to a purchaser who will occupy the new dwellinghouse as their only or principal residence. A relevant certificate must be inserted in the deed if the exemption is to be claimed. The exemption will be clawed back if the property is let within a period of five years from the date of the deed.

A sale of the property to a bona fide purchaser during this five-year period brings the original purchaser's liability under these clawback provisions, to an end. Investors will be liable to duty at the relevant residential property rates.

[4.77] The rates and reliefs applied to all conveyances executed on or after 23 April 1998. Transitional arrangements applied for contracts to purchase/lease by investors where there was evidence in writing that the contract was entered into prior to 23 April 1998 and the conveyance took place before I January 1999. The Revenue's view was that the contract must comply with the Statute of Frauds in all respects; however, the contract did not need to be executed by the vendor. A certificate to this effect was put in the deed in order to claim the benefit of the transitional relief.

Rates of stamp duty between 15 June 2000 and 6 December 2001

[4.78] Once again, stamp duty was used as an instrument of policy in an attempt to control market forces with respect to property. There were a number of objectives on the part of the government. Principal among them have been (a) to make house purchasing more affordable with respect to a principal private residence and (b) to cool the demand for property with a consequential steadying of prices. Alterations have been made to the rate of stamp duty in an attempt, firstly, to provide for exemptions or relief from the full effect of the *ad valorem* rate of duty for private purchasers of their principal private residence and, secondly, to deter the investor from the housing market. Stamp duty on property transfers is an efficient revenue source from the point of view of the State. Its affect on market supply and demand is limited. Nonetheless, the new regime has, in a rather cumbersome way, re-introduced some concept of equity that was missing when the bands were left unchanged. Since 15 June 2000, the *ad valorem* rate under the conveyance on sale head of charge depended on the nature of the property being conveyed.[108]

Residential property

[4.79] With respect to the transfer of property, the appropriate rate of duty is 9 per cent on that part of the consideration that is attributable to residential property. The duty is rounded up to the nearest euro. To qualify for this *ad valorem* rate, the instrument should contain a statement certifying that either the whole or part of the consideration relates to residential property. The usual aggregation rules apply.

There are some special cases:

(a) where the property being purchased was a new property for which a relevant floor area certificate has been issued, then the instrument was exempt from duty;

(b) where the property being purchased was a new property which exceeded the floor area for exemption purposes, then the duty was levied on 25% of the consideration payable;

[108] SDCA 1999, Sch 1.

(c) where the purchaser used the property (whether that property was new or pre-owned) as his principal private residence and the instrument contained a statement to that effect, then the duty payable was calculated as follows:

Amount or value of consideration relating wholly to residential property	*Fraction of duty that would otherwise be payable*
Not exceeding £100,000	Nil
Exceeding £100,000 but not £150,000	Three-ninths (3/9)
Exceeding £150,000 but not £200,000	Four-ninths (4/9)
Exceeding £200,000 but not £250,000	Five-ninths (5/9)
Exceeding £250,000 but not £300,000	Six-ninths (6/9)
Exceeding £300,000 but not £500,000	Seven-and-half-ninths (7½/9)

for the purposes of calculating the band into which the value or consideration should fall, the value of any contents transferring should be included, although the duty was only payable on the actual consideration relating to the residential property;

(d) where the purchaser was a first-time purchaser (whether or a new or pre-owned house) and a statement to that effect was inserted into the instrument then the amount of duty payable was calculated as follows:

Amount or value of consideration relating wholly to residential property	*Fraction of duty that would otherwise be payable*
Not exceeding £100,000	Nil
Exceeding £100,000 but not £150,000	Nil
Exceeding £150,000 but not £200,000	Three-ninths (3/9)
Exceeding £200,000 but not £250,000	
Exceeding £250,000 but not £300,000	Three-and-3/4-ninths (3¾ /9)
Exceeding £300,000 but not £500,000	Four-and-1/2-ninths (4½ /9)

For the purposes of calculating the band into which the value or consideration should fall, the value of any contents transferring was included although the duty was only payable on the actual consideration relating to the residential property.

Investment property

[4.80] In February 2001, the Minister for Finance announced his plans to alter the stamp duty rate applicable to purchases of property by investors. Originally, this had been planned to be 9 per cent irrespective of the type of property involved. However, in the period between announcing his intention to impose this rate on investment property and the finalisation of the Finance Act, the matter had been reviewed. Rates were as follows:

Second hand homes purchased other than by owner-occupier: 9%

New homes purchased other than by owner-occupier:

Amount of consideration	*Rate of duty payable*
Up to £150,000	3%
Up to £200,000	4%
Up to £250,000	5%
Up to £300,000	6%
Up to £500,000	7.5%
In excess of £500,000	9%

The aim of the amendment was to encourage investment purchases of new properties, thereby continuing to stimulate the construction industry.

Non-residential property

[4.81] Where the property was not residential, then the duty was calculated on that amount of the consideration which related to non-residential property, as set out below. The amount of duty payable was rounded up to the nearest whole pound. The usual rules of aggregation applied.

Amount or value of consideration not relating to residential property	*Duty payable*
Not exceeding £5,000	Exempt
Exceeding £5,000 but not £10,000	1%
Exceeding £10,000 but not £15,000	2%
Exceeding £15,000 but not £25,000	3%
Exceeding £25,000 but not £50,000	4%
Exceeding £50,000 but not £60,000	5%
Exceeding £60,000	6%
In all other cases	9%

Current rates of stamp duty – with effect from 6 December 2001 (as amended on the 2 December 2004)

A. Residential property

(1) First-time residential property purchasers

[4.82] A purchaser who is an owner-occupier of the property being purchased and who has never previously built or purchased a previous house either in Ireland or abroad is subject to the following rates of duty:

Amount of value of consideration	*First-time (new & s/h)*
	On or after 2/12/2004
0 to 127,000	0%
127,001 to 190,500	0%
190,501 to 254,000	0%
254,001 to 317,500	0%

317,501 to 381,000	3%
381,001 to 635,000	6%
635,001 to upwards	9%

In order to qualify, the purchaser must not rent the property within five years of purchase, save as allowed under the rent-a-room scheme. If the failure to honour this will result in a clawback.[109]

(2) New house purchasers

[4.83] The purchaser and owner-occupier of a new house for which a floor certificate is in existence is exempt from stamp duty. In all cases where a new house has not been issued with a floor certificate, then the duty is levied in accordance with the rates outlined but only on the value of the site or 25% of the total value of the house whichever is the greater.

(3) All other residential property

[4.84]

Amount of value of consideration	*Owner-occupiers & investors*
0 to 127,000	0%
127,001 to 190,500	3%
190,501 to 254,000	4%
254,001 to 317,500	5%
317,501 to 381,000	6%
381,001 to 635,000	7.5%
635,001 to upwards	9%

These rates apply to transactions executed after 2 December 2004. These rates also apply if there is in existence a binding contract before 2 December 2004, provided it has been executed before June 2004.

B. Non-residential property

[4.85] The following rates of duty apply to all non-residential property:

Amount of value of consideration	*Rate of duty*
Less than €10,000	*Exempt*
Between €10,001 and €20,000	1%
Between €20,001 and €30,000	2%
Between €30,001 and €40,000	3%
Between €40,001 and €70,000	4%
Between €70,001 and €80,000	5%
Between €80,001 and €100,000	6%

[109] Full details are to be found in **Chapter 11**.

Between €100,001 and €120,000	7%
Between €120,001 and€150,000	8%
In excess of €150,000	9%

Some worked examples

[4.86] Some examples will clearly demonstrate the application of the new rates and bands.

Example 4.86.1

Mary purchases a small retail outlet for €95,000.

Calculation of duty	€
Consideration	95,000
Duty at 6%	5,700
Duty payable	5,700

Example 4.86.2

Fiona purchases a fish and chip shop for €48,523.

Calculation of duty	€
Consideration	48,523
Duty at 4%	1,940.92
Duty payable	1,941.00

Example 4.86.3

Jacintha purchases a new house for which there is a floor area certificate. The price is set at €157,250. Exempt from duty.

Example 4.86.4

Michael purchases a large newly built executive-style house that does not have the relevant floor area certificate. The consideration is €450,000.

Calculation of duty	€
Consideration	450,000
25% of the consideration	112,500
Duty at 7.5%	8,437.50

Example 4.86.5

Biddy and Miley purchase their first home together, a pre-owned property, the consideration for which is €110,000.

Calculation of duty	€
Consideration	110,000
	(exempt under the first-time purchaser provisions)

Example 4.86.6

Billy purchases a house and pub for €400,000. €100,000 is attributable to the residential portion of the property. The instrument contains the relevant statements.

Calculation of duty	€
Consideration attributable to residential property	100,000
Consideration attributable to non-residential property	300,000
Duty at 9% (on commercial only)	27,000
Total Duty Payable	27,000

Note that Billy cannot claim any relief, such as owner-occupier relief, with respect to the residential portion of the property as the relief only applies where the instrument refer wholly to residential property.

For a more detailed analysis of the various exemptions and reliefs, please refer to **Chapter 13**.

Certificates

[4.87] In order to avail of the lower rates of duty, or exemptions from liability to duty, relevant certificates need to be included in the deed. The new provisions now require considerable care and attention in determining the relevant certificate or certificates appropriate in every case. Please see **Appendix 8** for the Revenue guidance on wording of certificates to be used in conveyances and leases.

Non-residential property certificate

[4.88] To avail of the lower rates of duty for non-residential property, the appropriate certificate must be amended to read as follows:

> It is hereby certified that the consideration (other than rent) for the sale/lease is wholly attributable to property which is not residential property and that the transaction effected by this instrument does not form part of a larger transaction or of a series of transactions in respect of which the amount or value, or the aggregate amount or value of the consideration (other than rent) which is attributable to property which is not residential property exceeds ____________ (insert relevant amount).

The responsibility for this certificate, since it forms part of a deed executed by both parties, lies with both the purchaser and the vendor. It should be noted that knowingly furnishing an incorrect certificate is a Revenue offence.

Residential property certificates

[4.89] In the absence of any certificate, the highest rate of 9% applies. Where the property is residential property, in order to avail of the reduced rates, the appropriate certificate must be inserted as follows:

> It is hereby certified that the consideration (other than rent) for the sale/lease is wholly attributable to residential property and that the transaction effected by this instrument does not form part of a larger transaction or of a series of transactions in respect of which the amount or value, or the aggregate amount or value of the consideration (other than rent) which is attributable to residential property, or which would be so attributable if the

contents of the residential property were considered to be residential property, exceeds ____________ (insert relevant amount).

Residential/commercial property

[4.90] Where the property is partly residential and partly commercial, then the duty is charged as if they were separate and distinct properties at the relevant rate. The Revenue Commissioners will put two separate markings on the deed for classification purposes. Accordingly, a finance certificate in the following form must be inserted:

> It is hereby certified (a) that the consideration (other than rent) for the sale/ lease is partly attributable to residential property and (b) that the transaction effected by this instrument does not form part of a larger transaction or of a series of transactions in respect of which the amount or value, or the aggregate amount or value, of the consideration (other than rent) which is attributable to residential property or which would be so attributable if the contents of the residential property were considered to be residential property, exceeds ____________ (insert relevant amount) and
>
> (c) that the transaction effected by this instrument does not form part of a larger transaction or of a series of transactions in respect of which the amount or value, or the aggregate amount or value of the consideration (other than rent) which is attributable to property which is not residential property exceeds ____________ (insert relevant amount).

Transitional certificates

[4.91] For investors and other persons relying upon the transitional arrangements set out above, the Finance (No 2) Act 1998 provides that a certificate must be inserted in the deed as set out below:

> It is hereby certified that this instrument was executed in pursuance of a contract which was evidenced in writing prior to the 23 April 1998.

Certificate content

[4.92] We turn now to look at the certificates in more detail. The term "transaction" carries a relatively wide meaning; it is certainly broader than the term contract. A transaction is an act, agreement or several acts or agreements between or among parties whereby a cause of action or alteration of legal rights occurs. These acts or agreements must be connected with each other to form the transaction or series of transactions. The term transaction must be read in conjunction with the conveyance on sale head of charge. The term conveyance on sale has been previously defined.[110]

[4.93] *Cherry Court v Revenue Commissioners*[111] is illustrative. A number of agreements were executed between the parties in July of 1990, one of which was an option agreement. In 1992, the taxpayer executed a release with respect to the option agreement, and it was his contention that the release was executed to remove an impediment to the sale of certain property and not to effect a transfer or sale in itself. Accordingly, he claimed that it should be liable to a fixed duty of £10 only. The Revenue

---

[110] See para **[4.01]**.

[111] *Cherry Court v Revenue Commissioners* V ITR 180.

Commissioners assessed the release as a transfer or sale and subjected it to an *ad valorem* rate, rendering it liable to £48,000 in duty. The taxpayer appealed this determination. McCracken J held that the wording of the release was only open to the interpretation that there was a transfer of the option which gave rise to *ad valorem* duty under the conveyance on sale head. The taxpayer's intention differed from the manner of execution: the taxpayer may have only intended to remove the impediment on sale, but in reality he had executed a conveyance of the option. In doing this, McCracken J followed the approach of Carroll J in *Waterford Glass (Group Services) Ltd v Revenue Commissioners*[112] holding that the court was bound to look at the nature of the transaction and was not obliged to follow the label assigned by the parties themselves.

If the transaction has taken place and is recorded in an instrument, the Revenue Commissioners are empowered to raise assessments in respect of such instruments.[113]

[4.94] The certificate applies to a "series of transactions". It is the total consideration passing as a result of the series of transactions that is used in ascertaining the rate of *ad valorem* duty applicable to the instrument. The instrument may only be required to effect the delivery of a portion of the assets passing. For example, real property must be passed by way of an instrument, whereas personal property, such as the contents of a house, can pass by way of delivery without an instrument being necessary. There should be no contractual linkage between these contracts in accordance with the decision of *AG v Cohen.*[114] In that case, six individual lots were purchased at an auction. The court held that this did not constitute a series of transactions as each lot purchased was an independent transaction. However, the particular facts of the case should be treated with a degree of caution as the six lots were purchased in an auction situation. In *Prudential Assurance Company*[115] the court separated what appeared to be a single transaction into two separate transactions. In practice, such transactions are best submitted for adjudication clearly and fully setting forth all the relevant facts.

Example 4.94.1

Fred negotiates the purchase of two sites for the sum of €19,000 from AV Investments Ltd. They are conveyed by two separate instruments so that Fred holds two separate titles to the property. These form part of a series of transactions for which the consideration does not exceed €40,000. Stamp duty is payable on €38,000 at 3% for a total of €1,140 or €570 on each deed.

Example 4.94.2

Blue Eyes Ltd agreed to purchase from Mafiosa Ltd a site for €150,000 on 1 January. On February 16, they purchased a second site for €165,000.

Blue Eyes Ltd purchases two further sites from Mafiosa Ltd for €110,000 each on June 1 following a successful sale of the original sites. All four transfers were completed on July 1 and presented for stamping to the Revenue Commissioners. The first two sites should be

[112] *Waterford Glass (Group Services) Ltd v Revenue Commissioners* IV ITR 187 (1989) – see para **[4.06]**

[113] SDCA 1999, s 20 – see para **[15.05]**.

[114] *AG v Cohen* [1937] 1 KB 478.

[115] *Prudential Assurance Company* (1993) 1 WLR 212.

stamped individually if it can be shown to the Revenue Commissioners that the transactions were distinct and separate; the latter two sites should be as a series of transactions.

Example 4.94.3

Bill purchases two sites, one from Tony and one from Bertie, neither of whom are connected in any way, for €250,000 each. These are separate and distinct transactions and do not form part of a series of transactions. Where such contracts are conditional upon one another, they would still not form part of a series of transactions.

Example 4.94.4

Bill and his wife Hilary purchased two sites from Gerry for €250,000 and are conveyed into their own individual names, separately.

It could be argued by the Revenue Commissioners that this constitutes a series of transactions and should be stamped accordingly.

[4.95] The term "amount or value or aggregate amount or value of the consideration" refers to the full consideration payable under the transaction or series of transactions, whether in the form of cash or not. In certain situations where the consideration payable is not in the form of cash, or is not discharged immediately, there are statutory rules for ascertaining the amount of consideration payable.[116] If contents are capable of passing by delivery they may not be in the deed and therefore not liable to duty.[117] In *Prudential Assurance v IRC*[118] Nicholls VC stated that "no stamp duty is payable by reference to the consideration payable for chattels even though the contract for sale of the land and chattels was one single and indivisable contract by any test ..." In practice, the contract will state the contents are passing by delivery with an attributable value which must be realistic. However, they are included in quantifying the total rate of duty payable on the instrument. There were serious doubts about this practice as contents passing by delivery should not be chargeable to duty. However the FA 1998 gave legislative authority for this practice when the contents passing by delivery relate to residential property.

Example 4.95.1

Bertie purchases a house from Charlie to help him out of financial difficulties. The house is purchased for €260,000 which includes some art and antiques valued at €25,000. The contents pass by delivery and a finance certificate is inserted in the deed stating that the consideration does not exceed €317,500. Stamp duty is payable on €235,000 at 5% in the amount of €11,750.

If the contents pass by the instrument, stamp duty will be payable on the total consideration, that is €260,000 at 5% in the amount of €13,000.

The contents must be capable of passing by delivery. Fixtures are not capable of passing by delivery as they automatically pass by way of the instrument. Where no certificate is included, the highest rate of *ad valorem* duty – 9 per cent – automatically applies. For both residential and commercial properties, in order to qualify for a rate of duty less than 9 per cent a relevant certificate stating that the total consideration does not exceed the band involved must be included.

---

[116] See **Chapter 13** generally.

[117] See *Horsfell v Hey* [1848] 2 Ex 778.

[118] *Prudential Assurance v IRC* [1993] WLR 212 at 215.

Chapter 5

Stampable Contracts

Introduction

[5.01] The original definition of conveyance on sale head as enacted in the charging section of SA 1891 was restrictive and any dealings with interests in property, exclusively passing by way of contract, were not chargeable.

[5.02] The effect of the contract for sale is to give the purchaser an equitable interest in the property and once all conditions have been satisfied the purchaser can call upon the vendor to convey the property to him.[1] In *IRC v Angus & Co*[2] the parties had entered into a contract for sale of the goodwill of a tannery business. The Revenue Commissioners contended that this agreement for sale of the goodwill fell within the charging section of 'conveyance on sale', as a beneficial interest passed under the agreement. The Court of Appeal held against the Revenue Commissioners that the instrument was a contract. Its nature or substance could not be charged due to its equitable nature. Lord Eshmer held:

> ... it would be a contradiction in terms to say that that which requires a decree for specific performance is in itself 'a conveyance' which has conveyed the property to the purchaser. If there had been a 'conveyance' of the property, you do not require specific performance?[3]

Lord Escher went onto say:

> But any conveyancer – any lawyer – would see in a moment that this is not a conveyance at all. It is an agreement, which is a totally different thing. Lord Cottenham pointed out long ago in *Tasker v Small* that although if a person agrees to buy land and the agreement is one of which a court of Equity will decree specific performance, the purchaser becomes thereby in equity the owner in a certain sense, and acquires rights and interests which he can devise or sell, and which will pass to his heirs by inheritance, still it is an entire mistake to suppose that an agreement is equivalent to a conveyance.

As a consequence of this potential for avoidance, SDCA 1999, s 31 was enacted to ensure a charge to liability on the passing of an equitable interest in property by way of contract. The section was introduced to bring within the charge to stamp duty certain contracts or agreements on sale which the parties would normally be satisfied with the passing of the property in equity and therefore not need a conveyance.

---

1 *West London Syndicate v IRC* [1898] 2 KB 507.

2 *IRC v Angus & Co* [1889] 23 QB 579.

3 *IRC v Angus & Co* [1889] 23 QB 579.

Stampable contracts

[5.03] SDCA 1999, s 31(1) (originally SA 1891, s 59) charges stamp duty on any contract or agreement for sale of:

(a) any equitable interest in any property; or

(b) *any estate* or interest in any property except the following:

 (i) immovable property situate in the State,

 (ii) property locally situate out of the State,

 (iii) goods, wares or merchandise,

 (iv) stock or marketable securities, not including share warrants issued under CA 1963, s 88,

 (v) any ship or vessel or aircraft or any part interest in such property.

Any such contract shall be charged with *ad valorem* duty as if it was an actual conveyance on sale of the interest in the property contracted to be sold.

[5.04] The charge to duty under (a) applies to the equitable interest only. It is important to note that the charge to duty under (b) refers to the legal title of property. The exceptions to the charge under (b) are inserted to prevent a double charge to duty arising.

[5.05] There is no difference between the word 'contract' or 'agreement' and no distinction is drawn between them in the Act. In *Cory v IRC*[4] Reid LJ said:

> ... it was argued that the two words, 'contract' and 'agreement', would not have been used if both had been intended to mean the same thing and that here there was an agreement to sell because the shareholders had bound themselves to sell if the option was exercised. I am satisfied that no such inference can be drawn from the fact that this section includes both the word 'contract' and the word 'agreement'.

The effect of SDCA 1999, s 31 is that all equitable interests in property, including book debts, goodwill, licences, etc, now come within the charge of stamp duty. This section only applies to 'conveyance on sale' and has no application in respect of agreements for a lease. However, legislation has been enacted to overcome this and shall be discussed later in this chapter.

SDCA 1999, s 31(1)(a) – first limb

Equitable estate or interest in property

[5.06] This charge applies to a contract for the sale of an equitable interest in property. In *George Wimpey & Co Ltd v IRC*[5] it was held that a contract for the sale of an option to purchase a legal interest in property was deemed to be a contract of sale of an equitable interest in property and came within the ambit of SA 1891, s 59. A transfer of any equitable interest must be evidenced in writing.[6]

4 *Cory v IRC* [1965] 2 WLR 924.

5 *George Wimpey & Co Ltd v IRC* [1975] 2 All ER 45.

6 Statute of Frauds (Ireland) 1695, s 4.

[5.07] In *Chesterfield Brewery Co v IRC*[7] it was held that a written agreement to execute a declaration of trust in favour of the purchaser would be an agreement for the sale of an equitable interest coming within the ambit of SA 1891, s 59 and was chargeable under either SA 1891, s 54 (conveyance on sale head) or under SA 1891, s 59. The facts were that the shareholders of company A, which was being voluntarily wound up, entered into an agreement in writing with company B providing that the shareholders of company A would exchange their shares for shares in company B. Once the shares in company B were allotted to the shareholders of company A, the shareholders of company A would hold all their shares in company A in trust for Company B.[8] An acknowledgment of purchase moneys by way of receipt by a reversioner for the reversionary interest under a will has been held to be an agreement for sale of an equitable interest.[9]

[5.08] A contract for the sale of financial options is exempt from stamp duty if it satisfies the terms of SDCA 1999, s 90. A contract to transfer either a debt factoring agreement, swap agreement, forward agreement, financial futures agreement, an option agreement or any combination of the above shall not be chargeable to stamp duty. If the instrument is liable to stamp duty in respect of any other provision it contains under any heading in SDCA 1999, Sch 1, the instrument shall be chargeable under that heading. This prohibits any potential abuse of measures aimed to assist the development of the financial services industry in Ireland.[10]

Property

[5.09] 'Property'[11] is defined in *Potter v IRC*[12] as:

> that which belonged to a person exclusive of others, and which could be the subject of a bargain and sale to another.

SDCA 1999, s 31 charges all property excluding the exceptions as set out previously and charges contracts for the sale of intangible goods, which include the following:

(a) Goodwill;

(b) Tenants' fixtures;

(c) book debts; and

(d) cash on deposit.

Goodwill

[5.10] Goodwill is intangible property.[13] It is intangible because it has no physical form yet it is property because it can be the subject of a bargain and sale. Goodwill is only one example of intangible property. Any legally protected right which has no physical form

---

7 *Chesterfield Brewery Co v IRC* [1899] 2 QB 7.

8 See also *Bone v IRC*, para **[4.43]**.

9 *Fleetwood-Hesketh v IRC* [1936] 1 KB 351.

10 SDCA 1999, s 90 – see para **[14.34]**.

11 See paras **[1.06]**, **[1.09]** and **[4.17]**ff.

12 *Potter v IRC* [1854] 10 Exch 149 at 156.

13 See para **[4.24]**ff and **[7.11]**.

but which can be sold is intangible property, for example, patents and trademarks are intangible property, as are choses in action. A chose in action is the right to sue someone for some legal right. If A owes B €1 million, B may be in no mood to wait to sue A for this amount, but might require an immediate payment. C on the other hand might be willing to invest in a gamble and might pay B €750,000 in return for B's assignment of A's debt. B's right to sue A for this money is a chose in action – intangible because it has no physical form, yet property because it can be sold. Such practice is common in invoice and debt factoring agreements.

[5.11] Goodwill is the financial value that attaches to a place or a name or a product by virtue of its reputation amongst existing and potential customers. The existence of goodwill ensures that the product might command a higher price, that the company will attract more customers, etc. Typical examples include the goodwill that attaches to a restaurant that has carefully built up a reputation and thereby continues to attract customers. The owner who has built this reputation is entitled to a return on this effort. Thus the restaurant premises might only be worth €300,000 but, because of the goodwill, a purchaser can expect a certain level of customer interest which would make it economically viable to pay €450,000 for the premises. The difference, €150,000, is the goodwill of the business.

The nature of goodwill was described in *Tergo v Hunt*[14] as being:

> ... the whole advantage, whether it may be, of the reputation and connection of the firm, which may have been built up by years of honest work or gained by lavish expenditure of money.

[5.12] Goodwill may attach to a premises or to a particular business.

Example 5.12.1

A restaurant premises with a thriving clientele is valued at €400,000 as a going concern. It is estimated that the premises alone is valued at €300,000 and the goodwill of the business at €100,000.

Is this goodwill attributable to the actual building or the business, in other words is it chargeable at the contract stage or the conveyance on sale stage? If it is attached to the building, it is stampable at conveyance stage. If it is attached to the business it is an equitable interest and stampable at contract stage. In *West London Syndicate Ltd v IRC*[15] the vendor had agreed to sell a hotel business and the lease of the hotel in which the business was carried on together with further property. The court held that the goodwill was capable of being sold independently and was not merely the enhancement value of the property. The agreement, in so far as it related to the goodwill, was liable to *ad valorem* duty at the contract stage. A contract for goodwill attaching to property and an agreement for sale of such equitable interest is liable to *ad valorem* duty.[16] Goodwill is situated where the item to which it is attached is registered or situated. An agreement which restricts the ability to carry on trade in a particular area in consideration of a

14 *Tergo v Hunt* [1896] AC 7 at 24.

15 *West London Syndicate Ltd v IRC* [1898] 2 QB 507.

16 *Benjamin Brooke Co v IRC* [1896] 2 QB 356.

money payment does constitute an agreement for sale of a goodwill.[17] Such agreements may fall foul of the provisions of the Competition Act 1991 but the unenforcibility of such an agreement does not remove the liability to duty.

Tenants' fixtures

[5.13] Fixtures form part of the property and are deemed to attach to the premises. Once they are attached to freehold property, they come within the ambit of SDCA 1999, s 1 and are specifically excluded in SDCA 1999, s 31(1). In *Lee v Gaskell*[18] it was held that as an agreement for the sale of the tenant's fixtures[19] did not constitute an agreement for the sale of land nor for the sale of goods, it was chargeable under SA 1891, s 59. The total price had to be apportioned; the amount apportionable to the tenant's fixtures was chargeable at contract stage. The difference in essence appears to revolve around the degree of attachment to the premises.

[5.14] If the item can be removed without causing substantial damage either to the land or the item itself, then it is a fitting; if not, it is a fixture. The intention of the person affixing the articles would appear to be important at common law,[20] and it is unclear as to how this has been effected since the issue is now governed by Deasy's Act, s 17. It would appear that under any test, removal of a fixture by its destruction is not permissible. In *Lombard & Ulster Banking Ltd v Kennedy*[21] it was held that an automatic car wash installed on a garage premises had become a fixture and therefore could not be removed. In *Maye v Revenue Commissioners*,[22] following *Whelan v Madigan*,[23] it was held that a television ariel was a fixture. Further, the removal must take place whilst the tenant is in possession or if the tenancy has terminated by virtue of an uncertain event, then within two calendar months of the termination occurring.[24]

Intellectual property

[5.15] Instruments executed on or after 1 April 2004 effecting a sale, transfer or disposition or contract for the sale, transfer or disposition of intellectual property within the meaning of SDCA 1999, s 101(1) are exempt from stamp duty under all heads of charge. Prior to this exemption coming into effect, instruments transferring intellectual property could be chargeable to *ad valorem* stamp duty. The definition of intellectual property under SDCA 1999, s 101(1) is very broad but does not specifically cover intelletual property, such as brand names and know how. (It should be noted that know how that is not patented does not constitute property and is not subject to stamp duty liability.)[25] However, Revenue has indicated that this list under SDCA 1999, s 101 is

17 *Eastern National Omnibus Co v IRC* [1939] 1 KB 161.

18 *Lee v Gaskell* [1876] 1 QBD 700.

19 See para **[7.15]**.

20 *Leigh v Taylor* [1902] AC 157.

21 *Lombard & Ulster Banking Ltd v Kennedy* [1974] NI 20.

22 *Maye v Revenue Commissioners* III ITR 332.

23 *Whelan v Madigan* [1978] ILRM 136.

24 For a fuller discussion, see Wylie *Irish Land Law* (3rd edn, Butterworths, 1997).

non-exhaustive. The goodwill attaching to this intellectual property is also exempted under the section. The exemption covers all forms of transfer of intellectual property, including licences and contracts for sale of intellectual property. While the exemption is a much awaited change in legislation, difficulties will arise where there is a business being sold that includes intellectual property. This is because the transfer of the intellectual property itself and the goodwill attaching to same is exempt; the goodwill attaching to the business is not. In addition, the part of the consideration attributable to intellectual property is disregarded in determining the rate of duty on the other chargeable property.[26] The value of the goodwill attaching to the intellectual property and that to the business will be difficult to ascertain and separate and Revenue has not, to date, given any guidance on how this apportionment is to be effected.

Book debts

[5.16] Book debts[27] are those debts owed to a business during the ordinary course of trading and the term derives from the practice of maintaining records of such debtors in ledgers or books, hence the term book debts. An agreement for the sale of an undertaking by a company which includes book debts is chargeable at contract stage. In *Measures Bros v IRC*[28] the agreement had been entered into for the sale of an undertaking. Book debts were the amount due and owing to the vendor company at the end of the preceding year of the contract. When the agreement was signed, only a small proportion of the debts were still due and owing. It was held that *ad valorem* duty was payable on the amount of book debts at the end of the preceding year. The converse would also be true, that if the book debts at the time of the sale were larger, duty should be payable on the previous end of year smaller figure. However, doubts must be cast on, the validity of the decision. SDCA 1999, s 8 requires that the full and true facts either be set forth in the instrument or in an accompanying statement. Also the *Waterford Glass*[29] case which gives precedence to the factual reality over the form followed in *VIEK Investments.*[30]

[5.17] To be charged, the property has to be locally situated within the State. A simple contract debt is deemed to be located in the country where the debtor resides. A debt factoring agreement shall not be chargeable to stamp duty, and is defined in SDCA 1999, s 90(1) to mean:

> ... an agreement for sale, or a transfer on sale, of a debt or part of a debt where the sale occurs in the ordinary course of the business of the vendor or the purchaser.

---

25 See para **[4.26]**.

26 SDCA 1999 s.101(4).

27 See para **[7.14]** for further discussion of book debts.

28 *Measures Bros v IRC* [1900] 82 LT 689.

29 *Waterford Glass* IV ITR 187.

30 *VIEK Investments* IV ITR 367.

However, if the debt factoring agreement contains some other provision which deems it to be liable to stamp duty under another heading in SDCA 1999, Sch 1, the instrument shall be chargeable with the latter's stamp duty.[31]

[5.18] In *Dragges Ltd v IRC*[32] it was held that where goods are sold with the benefit of a hire purchase agreement they are not liable to duty where the purchaser will receive the goods, but will be liable to duty if the purchaser receives only the financial benefit of the agreements.

Cash on deposit

[5.19] Cash placed on deposit with a bank is a debt owing by the bank to its customer as a chose in action; that is, a thing of which a person has not the present enjoyment but merely a right to recover it (if withheld) by action.[33] Consideration paid for a deposit account shall be chargeable with *ad valorem* duty under SDCA 1999, s 31. However, cash in a current account is not chargeable in practice by the Revenue Commissioners. Current accounts are not strictly speaking debts but a procedural mechanism for money management.[34] This exception is justifiable only as a matter of practice by the Revenue Commissioners. If a bank goes into liquidation the money held in the current account is treated no differently from money on deposit. Both are debts which the customer may not recover other than as an unsecured creditor. This practice is open to withdrawal by the Revenue Commissioners.

[5.20] A contract usually contains a mixture of properties, some coming within the ambit of s 31. Apportionment of the market values of the property comprised in the contract as necessary and the contract is stamped *ad valorem* on s 31 properties.

SDCA 1999, s 31(1) – second limb

[5.21] A contract or agreement for the sale of any estate or interest in any property is chargeable with duty under SDCA 1999, s 31 except the following:

(i) immovable property situate in the State (see note 1);

(ii) property locally situate out of the State (see note 2);

(iii) goods, wares or merchandise;

(iv) stock or marketable securities; and

(v) any ship or vessel or aircraft or any part interest in such property (see **Chapter 13** for general exemptions).

The words of exception refer to the second limb of s 31(1), namely 'the sale of any estate or interest in any property' as per *Farmer and Co v IRC*.[35].

---

[31] SDCA 1999, s 90(4).

[32] *Dragges Ltd v IRC* [1927] 6 ATC 727.

[33] *Foley v Hill* [1843-1860] All ER 16.

[34] See para **[4.34]** and **[7.12]**.

[35] *Farmer and Co v IRC* (1898) 2 QB 141.

Immovable property situate within the State

[5.22] Immovable property is real property and this is discussed in **Chapter 4**. Effectively these transactions are caught under the conveyance on sale head, of the SDCA 1999, s 1 and this provision is to avoid a double charge to duty.

Property situate outside the State

[5.23] According to SDCA 1999, s 31(1). an agreement for the sale of an equitable interest in foreign property is treated 'as if it were an actual conveyance on sale of an estate, interest, or property contracted or agreed to be sold' and contracts for the sale of such interest come within the ambit of SDCA 1999, s 1, provided the agreement is executed in the State. However, a conveyance or transfer, assignment, lease or licence of immovable property situate outside the State shall not be chargeable to stamp duty.[36]

[5.24] This poses some difficulty in terms of reconciling the differing provisions and it is unfortunate that the consolidating Act did not take the opportunity to resolve the inherent contradiction. A reading of SDCA 1999, s 31 in isolation leads to the conclusion that a contract for the sale of the equitable interest in foreign immovable property is liable to duty. The wording however is quite specific – it states that the instrument is chargeable to duty in *like manner as if it were an actual conveyance*. It does not state that the instrument is chargeable to *ad valorem* duty *simpliciter*. The distinction is crucial. If the wording of s 31 had simply rendered the agreement liable to *ad valorem* duty, the matter would be closed. However, under the actual wording used, an argument could be made that the relevant agreement should be treated the same as an actual conveyance of foreign immovable property, and therefore exempt from duty under the provisions of SDCA 1999, s 98.

[5.25] It is unclear whether SDCA 1999, s 98 should apply to a deemed conveyance on sale. If it does not, then SDCA 1999, s 31 will apply in full to a contract or agreement for the sale of foreign immovable property. SDCA 1999, s 31 states that such contracts or agreements are to be stamped as if they were a conveyance on sale. This implies that such contracts are not a conveyance on sale. Since SDCA 1999, s 98 exempts any instrument which is a conveyance, does the section cover contracts which do not fall within s 1 but are treated in like manner by virtue of s 31? The matter requires a judicial pronouncement before it can be fully resolved.

[5.26] In summary, the following appears to be an accurate synopsis of the possible permutations involved in these provisions:

(i) a contract or agreement for sale of any legal interest in foreign movable property is exempt;[37]

(ii) a contract or agreement for sale of any legal interest in foreign immovable property is exempt;[38]

[36] SDCA 1999, s 98.

[37] SDCA 1999, s 31(1)(b).

[38] SDCA 1999, s 98.

(iii) a contract or agreement for sale of any equitable interest in foreign movable property is liable to duty;[39] and

(iv) a contract or agreement for sale of any equitable interest in foreign immovable property may or may not be liable to duty depending on a judicial or legislative reconciliation of ss 98 and 31.

[5.27] The House of Lords in *English, Scottish & Australian Bank Ltd v IRC*[40] held that an agreement for the sale of a simple contract debt owing from debtors resident outside the United Kingdom fell within the exemption as it was property locally situate outside the United Kingdom. The situs position of the asset or right is a matter of private international law. Normally the situs rule accepted under these headings is accepted for stamp duty liability.

[5.28] It must be noted that if a debt is connected with a branch or agency, even though the branch or agency may not be technically resident within the State for fiscal purposes, this may constitute official presence for the purpose of being sued and any agreement for the sale of the said debt may be chargeable in that jurisdiction (see **Chapter 2**).

Goods, wares and merchandises

[5.29] This exception clearly covers personal property. Again the distinction between a fixture and a fitting is of relevance, see above for a fuller discussion, see paras **[5.13]** and **[5.14]**.

Stocks or marketable securities

[5.30] Stocks or marketable securities are exempt from this head of charge. However, the SDCA 1999, s 31(1) excludes share warrants issued under CA 1963, s 88 from the definition of stocks or marketable securities, thus rendering the contract for the sale of share warrants liable under s 31. This applies to contracts entered into on or after 4 March 1998. Revenue's view is that a contract for the sale of bearer shares is exposed to duty under this section. This new provision will not apply where the title to the share warrant is passed by delivery or where the contract for the share warrant relates to bearer shares of a company incorporated outside the state. See **Chapter 7** for a detailed discussion of stocks and marketable securities.

Any ship of vessel or aircraft or any part interest in such property

[5.31] See **Chapter 14** for general exemptions.

Stamping of such contracts/instruments

[5.32] Where a purchaser has paid *ad valorem* duty and then enters into a contract or agreement for sale of the acquired beneficial interest before having obtained a conveyance or transfer of the property and the consideration for the sale is in excess of the consideration for the purchase, the stamp duty is paid at the *ad valorem* rate on the

---

39 SDCA 1999, s 31(1)(a).

40 *English, Scottish & Australian Bank Ltd v IRC* [1932] AC 238.

excess consideration.[41] If the consideration is not in excess of the original consideration, then it is charged with a fixed duty.

[5.33] Where *ad valorem* stamp duty has been paid at contract stage and a conveyance or transfer is then made to the purchaser or subpurchaser, the conveyance or transfer shall not be chargeable with any duty and, upon application to the Revenue Commissioners, they can either:

(a) denote the payment of *ad valorem* duty upon the conveyance or transfer; or

(b) transfer the *ad valorem* duty to the conveyance or transfer upon the production of the original contract or agreement duly stamped.[42]

[5.34] If a contract is stamped with a fixed rate of duty and the conveyance or transfer of the subject matter of the contract is presented to the Revenue Commissioners for stamping with *ad valorem* duty during a period of six months after the execution of the contract (or such extension of same as the Revenue Commissioners may deem reasonable in the circumstances), the conveyance or transfer shall be stampable and the contract or agreement shall be deemed to have been duly stamped.[43]

In practice, the Revenue Commissioners will not stamp the contract with the fixed duty. If the contract is lodged with them, they will return the contract requesting further information and if this contract and the request is subsequently lodged with the conveyance for stamping, they will charge stamp duty on the conveyance only.

[5.35] If the agreement or contract upon which duty has been paid is afterwards rescinded or annulled or not substantially performed or carried into effect, the duty will be refunded.[44]

Accountable persons

[5.36] The accountable person for duty under these provisions is the purchaser.[45]

Apportionment

[5.37] A contract or agreement for the sale of a number of assets in consideration of a single payment may have to be apportioned amongst the various assets for stamp duty purposes. This apportionment, if done, must be a bona fide apportionment.[46]

[5.38] Where the contract for the sale of a property contains deliberate misstatements, ,the contract may be rendered inadmissible in evidence due to the unlawful purpose to be achieved.[47] In addition, the duty to set out fully and truly all the facts in the instrument or in an accompanying statement further reinforces this requirement.[48]

41 SDCA 1999, s 31(2).
42 SDCA 1999, s 31(3).
43 SDCA 1999, s 31(3).
44 SDCA 1999, s 31(4).
45 SDCA 1999, s 31(4).
46 *West London Syndicate v IRC* [1898] 2 QB 507.
47 *Saunders v Edwards* [1987] 2 All ER 651.
48 SDCA 1999, s 8 as amended by FA 1991, s 97.

In *Saunders v Edwards* it was held that:

> ... where a contract for sale of property contains deliberate misstatements regarding the apportionment of the purchase price between the property sold and chattels sold with it, in order to facilitate the fraudulent evasion of stamp duty, a party to the contract who subsequently seeks to enforce the contract may find that the court will treat the contract as being unenforceable because of the unlawful purposes sought to be achieved. Furthermore a solicitor involved in such a false apportionment may be guilty of professional misconduct, and he and the parties to the transaction may be committing a criminal offence.

[5.39] The facts of the case were that a defendant sold the lease of a flat to the plaintiff which he misrepresented to include a roof terrace. The purchase price for the property was £45,000 including chattels, and the price was apportioned as to £40,000 for the flat and £5,000 for the chattels with a view to reducing the stamp duty payable on the conveyance, even though the parties both knew the chattels were worth less. The plaintiff, after discovering the flat did not include the roof terrace, brought an action against the defendant for fraudulent misrepresentation and for inconvenience and disappointment. In the High Court, the Honourable Judge Rubin awarded the plaintiff damages for fraudulent misrepresentation and a further sum of £500 for inconvenience and disappointment and interest from the date of the writ. The defendant appealed on the grounds that:

(a) the plaintiff's claim required them to rely on their own illegal conduct in making a false apportionment in the contract of sale to reduce stamp duty; and

(b) that an award for inconvenience and disappointment should not have carried interest.

It was held:

(a) where a plaintiff's claim in tort against the defendant arose out of a fraudulent contract between parties, their conduct and relative moral culpability could be relevant in determining whether as a matter of public policy the court would take notice of the illegality. However, on the facts of the case, the court disregarded the illegality because:
    (i) there was an unanswerable claim against the defendant for fraudulent misrepresentation,
    (ii) the defendant's own moral culpability greatly outweighed that of the plaintiff's and he should not be allowed to keep the fruits of his fraud, and
    (iii) the illegal apportionment of the contract was wholly unconnected to the plaintiffs cause of action and the plaintiff would have suffered a loss as a result of fraudulent misrepresentation regardless of whether the contract contained the illegal apportionment;

(b) an award for damages for inconvenience and disappointment ought usually to be a global sum covering inconvenience and disappointment suffered up to the date of trial and in the future, but where such a global sum is awarded then it is a matter of principle that interest should not be added to the award. In Ireland,

Courts Act 1981, s 22 requires that damages should be specified and not global.

The stamping branch of the Revenue Commissioners provide a form (ADJN 14) upon which apportionment should be carried out.[49] In this jurisdiction the solicitor would be deemed to be liable to the Revenue Commissioners for fraud and/or negligence.[50]

Means of reducing stamp duty on the purchase of a business

[5.40] All these steps have to be carried out pre-contract as the liability to stamp duty arises at the contract stage.

The following steps can be carried out to reduce stamp duty liability:

(a) *bank accounts*: transfer all cash held in deposit accounts to the current account, as an agreement or contract which has the effect of transferring cash in a current account is not by concession stamped by the Revenue Commissioners;

(b) *book debts*: the vendor, if possible, should retain the debts due to the business and should also discharge the creditors;

(c) *movable property*: movable property (that is fittings) is capable of passing by delivery and if they can so pass and are not included in the conveyance of the property, no stamp duty will be paid on their delivery; fixtures are attached to the land and pass by way of conveyance, they are not capable of passing by delivery;

(d) *apportionment*: the consideration should be apportioned between the assets that are stampable at contract stage (s 31 assets) and those stampable at conveyance stage. Apportionment must be carried out on a bona fide basis, see **[5.37]**.

Example 5.40.1

Company A enters into an agreement for the sale of its undertaking to company B. The undertaking and assets are as follows:

Creditors	€	*Assets*	€
Trade creditors	45,000	Leasehold premises	42,000
Secure creditors		Goodwill	80,000
Bank mortgage	61,000	Stock	120,000
		Tenants' fixtures	22,000
		Plant and machinery	112,500
		Book debts	38,800
		Bank account deposit	30,000
		Current account	20,000
	106,000		465,300

[49] See **Appendix 2**.

[50] SDCA 1999, s 8 as amended by FA 1991, s 97.

Company B is taking over responsibility for the trade creditors and bank mortgage and is paying a purchase price of €404,300, being the net value of the undertaking. The following assets shall be chargeable to stamp duty at contract stage:

	€
Goodwill	80,000
Book debts	38,800
Tenants' fixtures	22,000
Deposit account bank deposit	30,000
Total	170,800

The stamp duty rate is based on the total consideration passing and, as the debts and liabilities have been taken over by company B, these are added to the total consideration to ascertain the rate of stamp duty. When the amount of money in the current account is deducted, the total consideration passing is €445,300.

		€
Stamp duty – contract stage	170,800 at 9%	15,372
Stamp duty on subsequent conveyance in sale:		
Leasehold premises (including mortgage)	42,000 at 9%	3,780
Plant and machinery and stock being conveyed:	232,500 at 9%	20,925
Total stamp duty liability on foot of this agreement		40,077

Steps to be taken to mitigate stamp duty liability

(a) the plant, machinery and stock should pass by delivery;

(b) the sum of €30,000 in the deposit account should be transferred to the current account prior to entering into the agreement; and

(c) company A retains the book debts of €38,800 and it retains liability to all the creditors of €106,000.

The purchase price is now €415,300. Stamp duty is as follows:
Contract stage – s 31 contract

	€
(a) Goodwill	80,000
(b) Tenants' fixtures	22,000
	102,000
Total stamp duty @ 7%	7,140

Conveyance stage

	€
€42,000 at 7%	2,940
Contract stage	7,140
Total stamp duty liability	10,080

By taking these steps, the stamp duty liability has been reduced from €40,077 to €10,080 – a total saving of €29,997. The stock, plant and machinery now pass by delivery.

Example 5.40.2

Jack agrees to purchase Peter's business. The business assets are as follows:

Creditors	€	*Assets*	€
Trade creditors	17,500	Freehold	380,000
Bank loan	20,000	Goodwill	40,000
		Stock	50,000
		Fixtures	15,000
		Plant and machinery	50,437
		Book debts	55,000
		Current account	9,000
	37,500		734,437

Jack is taking over the creditors, but not the bank loan, as he requires an unencumbered freehold to provide his bank with security as part of his loan facility.

Purchase price: €716,937 which is the value of the company after the deduction of the creditors. The following assets will be chargeable at contract stage:

	€
Goodwill	40,000
Book debts	55,000
	95,000

The stamp duty is based on the total consideration, including trade creditors, less the current account: €707,937

		€
Stamp duty – contract stage	€95,000 at 9%	8,550
Plant, machinery and stock (being conveyed)	€100,437 at 9%	9,039.32
Freehold property (including fixtures)	€395,000 at 9%	35,550
Total stamp duty payable on foot of agreement		53,139.32

As the fixtures form part of the freehold property, they come within the ambit of SDCA 1999, s 1 and are chargeable at conveyance stage.

Steps to be taken to mitigate stamp duty liability:

(a) plant, machinery and stock should now pass by delivery; and

(b) Peter should retain the book debts of €55,000 and retain its liabilities to all the creditors of €17,500.

The purchase price is now €679,437. Stamp duty is payable at a rate of 9%.

		€
Stamp duty payable – contract stage	€40,000 at 9%	3,600
Freehold property including fixtures	€395,000 at 9%	35,550
Total Duty payable		39,150

Checklist for agreements for the purchase of a business or undertaking

(a) Stock, plant and machinery should pass by delivery provided they are capable of doing so.

(b) The vendor should retain book debts and the liability for creditors or the purchaser should collect the book debts as agent of the vendor only.

(c) Transfer all moneys held in the deposit account into the current account of the undertaking, or the vendor may retain the deposit account.

(d) Ensure that the consideration of the contract is apportioned on the basis of the value of the assets.

(e) Investigate the possibility of purchasing the company outright by purchase of the shares of that company. Stamp duty on the transfer of shares is payable at a rate of 1 per cent. However, such a transaction may have far-reaching commercial implications due to the previous trading of the company, which may have given rise to an exposure to liability that will not be readily apparent.

(f) Other tax liabilities arising as a result of the re-structuring shall be considered.

Pre-FA 1991

[5.41] Prior to FA 1991, agreements or contracts for the purchase of an equitable interest in property were not always presented for the payment of stamp duty. This was consistent with the then voluntary nature of the duty. The main reasons they would have been presented for stamping prior to FA 1991 were:

(a) A document could not be produced in civil proceedings or given in evidence or be available for any purposes whatsoever in court proceedings unless it was duly stamped in accordance with the law at the time it was first executed.[51] There is an obligation imposed upon a judge, arbitrator or referee to ensure that any document chargeable with stamp duty produced as evidence in a civil matter is properly stamped;[52]

(b) The agreement may be needed for some official purposes. The company has a duty, when it acquires assets in consideration of issuing shares in the company, to return the contract in writing which constitutes the allottees entitlement to the allotment together with any contract for sale duly stamped to the Registrar of Companies, within one month of the allotment of shares.[53]

[5.42] If there was no written contract in existence the companies office Form 52 should have been returned to the Registrar of Companies duly stamped. This ensures that the company cannot complete the agreement by way of oral contract and the stamp duty will have to be paid on Form 52.

This section also extends to the takeover of an undertaking by a company where a trader decides to incorporate his or her business.

---

51 SA 1891, s 14(4).

52 SA 1891, s 14(1).

53 CA 1963, s 58(1)(b).

Post-FA 1991

[5.43] These instruments are now compulsorily stampable and once executed have to be stamped forthwith.[54]

Agreements concerning the sale of leasehold interest (SDCA 1999, s 36)

Position prior to FA 1978

[5.44] An assignment of a leasehold interest in a property is chargeable under the conveyance on sale head. Prior to the passing of FA 1978, it was possible to avoid stamp duty on the purchase of a leasehold interest in a property by using the following scheme:

(a) the purchaser enters into a contract with the vendor for the purchase of a long leasehold interest in a property;

(b) the purchaser would then purchase the reversionary interest in the property subject to, but with the benefit of, the vendor's leasehold interest at its nominal value;

(c) the purchaser, rather than taking an assignment of the vendor's interest in the property, would then direct the vendor to surrender the leasehold interest to him orally.

A statutory declaration would be sworn by a witness to the verbal surrender of this property, recording both the verbal agreement by the parties and the formal act of handing over the title documentation and the purchase moneys, which would enable the purchaser to prove title. This declaration would not constitute a chargeable instrument.

[5.45] Deasy's Act, s 7 provided that no tenant shall surrender his interest in a lease otherwise than by deed executed or note in writing or by act and operation of law. Act and operation of law can include an oral notice to the landlord, or be inferred from acts such as handing over the keys or vacating the premises. Partial surrender can be effective according to Brady CB in *Lynch v Lynch*[55] where he states:

> ... a surrender by act and operation of law I think may properly be stated to be a surrender effected by the construction put by the courts on the acts of the parties, in order to give those acts the effect substantially intended by them.

Typical examples of the construction of the parties, acts would include delivery and acceptance of possession, new tenancy granted to tenant, new tenancy granted to a third party, and continued occupation inconsistent with tenancy and disclaimer.

[5.46] In practice, it is felt that a joint declaration sworn by both the landlord and tenant clearly establishing the facts, whereby a surrender may be implied, is sufficient. Such statutory declaration could also be given by an independent witness which would still be accepted as conclusive evidence that a surrender was effected, and, therefore, satisfy the purchaser's requirements as to title. As there was no formal deed or instrument of

---

54 See **Chapter 3**.

55 *Lynch v Lynch* [1843] 6 Ir LR 131.

surrender, there was no chargeable instrument and duty was avoided under the conveyance on sale head.

SDCA 1999, s 36

[5.47] This section is an anti-avoidance provision which provides that a contract or agreement for sale of any leasehold interest in any immovable property is to be stamped with *ad valorem* duty as if it was an actual transfer on sale of the leasehold interest contracted or agreed to be sold if:

(a) the purchaser enters into possession of the property before having obtained a transfer, duly stamped of such interest; and

(b) a transfer of such interest made in pursuance to the contract or agreement is not duly stamped by the parties within the period of nine months from the first execution of the contract or agreement or such longer period as the Revenue Commissioners may specify in writing, being a period which they consider reasonable in all the circumstances of the case.[56]

The contract or agreement for the sale of the leasehold interest in the above example is now caught by this anti- avoidance section.

[5.48] Where the contract or agreement has been charged with *ad valorem* duty, a subsequent transfer or assignment shall not be chargeable to any duty.[57] The Revenue Commissioners can, upon application, either denote the payment of the duty upon the transfer, or can transfer the stamp duty onto the subsequent deed upon the production of the contract or agreement duly stamped.[58] Upon proving to the satisfaction of the Revenue Commissioners that the contract was rescinded or annulled, stamp duty will be refunded.[59] The net effect of these anti-avoidance provisions is to ensure that once the contract or agreement entered into between the parties has been stamped, no subsequent liability arises upon completion of the contract. This avoids a double taxation liability.

[5.49] This section does not go any further in defining contract or agreement than discussed earlier in this chapter. However, to qualify for a contract or agreement, it would have to satisfy the requirements set down by the Statute of Frauds. The view that there appears to be an inconsistency between SDCA 1999, s 36 and SDCA 1999, s 14 as amended has been expressed, which poses an obligation to pay stamp duty within 30 days after the first execution of the instrument. This may not be fully supportable. SDCA 1999, s 14 as amended by FA 1991 expressly states '... save where other express provision is in this Act made' and this is in accordance with the maxim that *lex generalibus non derogat lex specialibus* (general law shall not supersede specific law).

[5.50] SDCA 1999, s 36 states the contract or agreement for the sale of the leasehold interest in immovable property is stampable where the purchaser has entered into possession of the property and the transfer of such interest pursuant to the contract is not

[56] SDCA 1999, s 36(2).

[57] SDCA 1999, s 36(2)(i).

[58] SDCA 1999, s 36(2)(ii).

[59] SDCA 1999, s 36(2)(iii).

stamped within nine months from the date of execution of the contract. The contract is then treated as an actual conveyance from that date onwards, subject to the provisions of SDCA 1999, s 14, and time runs from the expiration of the date pursuant to SDCA 1999, s 36.

[5.51] However, it is worth noting that an examination of the wording of SDCA 1999, s 36 shows that it would appear to be confined to contracts for the sale of a leasehold interest. As such, an agreement for the grant of a lease would appear to fall outside the scope of the section. This can, in circumstances where an agreement for the grant of a lease is commercially viable, be an effective stamp duty planning tool.

Example 5.51.1

Roger enters into a contract for the purchase of leasehold property from Harold on 8 June 2001 and immediately enters into possession of the property without having obtained a transfer. This contract shall be stampable as if it were an actual conveyance on 8 March 2002, provided that a transfer of the property had not previously been made.

Stamp duty must be paid within 30 days of 8 March 2002.

Avoidance under SDCA 1999, s 36

[5.52] It is obvious from the provisions of SDCA 1999, s 36 that once there is no agreement or contract that satisfies the Statute of Frauds, stamp duty could still have been avoided. However, under CGTA 1975 a vendor may be required to produce a certificate pursuant to Sch 4, para 5 and even in the absence of a written contract or agreement, this certificate could constitute a memorandum in writing and would be stampable. The following scheme could have been used to avoid the ambit of SDCA 1999, s 36:

(a) the purchaser would have agreed orally with the vendor for the purchase of a long leasehold interest in the property, which the vendor would surrender by operation of law;

(b) the purchaser would purchase the landlord's reversionary interest in the property at a nominal value; and

(c) the vendor at a formal ceremony of the property would surrender his lease by operation of law and this would be recorded by an independent third-party witness by way of statutory declaration, as set out above.

As there is no agreement or contract or any written instrument of surrender, there is no chargeable instrument.

SDCA 1999, s 67

[5.53] Further anti-avoidance legislation was enacted by SI 151/1985[60] with effect from 11 June 1985, which was subsequently enacted in SDCA 1999, s 67. This amended the First Schedule by extending the conveyance on sale head to include any instrument bearing witness to or acknowledging:

---

60 The Imposition of Duties (No 277) (Stamp Duty on Certain Instruments).

(a) the surrender, by parole or otherwise, of a leasehold interest in immovable property;[61] or

(b) the merger of such interests in a superior interest, shall be chargeable with stamp duty as if it was a surrender of that leasehold interest.[62]

[5.54] The statutory declaration sworn by the independent witness, as set out above, would be chargeable under the conveyance on sale head with stamp duty. Any other document entered into by the vendor or lessee which records the surrender of the leasehold interest is now stampable as a document under the conveyance on sale head. The declaration or certificate is stampable once it has been executed after 11 June 1985, even though it may relate to a surrender or merger of the property which took place prior to that date.

[5.55] It appears from a strict reading of the section that there is also a charge on instruments where the inferior leasehold interest is merged.

Example 5.55.1

A holds a property under a long lease subject to a nominal rent. He purchases the superior or freehold interest of his landlord in the property.

The conveyance to the leaseholder contains a declaration of merger.

On a strict interpretation, a merger of such leasehold interest in the superior interest shall be chargeable to duty as if it was a surrender of the leasehold interest. The effect of this is that the declaration of merger in the deed would be deemed to be stampable as if it was a conveyance on sale of both the freehold and leasehold interest. In practice, the Revenue Commissioners do not charge stamp duty on such mergers where the leasehold has been held for a long period.

Example 5.55.2

A holds a property under a lease for a considerable number of years.

A subsequently acquires the freehold with a view to enlarging his title.

The merger contained in the deed will not be stampable but duty will be payable on the conveyance of the freehold interest based on the consideration passing.

[5.56] To avoid coming within SDCA 1999, s 67, the lessee should take a conveyance or assignment of his superior lessor's interest in the property without such declaration of merger. In modern jurisprudence a merger cannot occur without intention.[63] For example, a lessee holding under a lease who subsequently acquires the lessor's interest and then purports to assign the lease to a third party can do so. At common law it is felt that a merger can only take place when all of the lands held under the lease became vested in the person who is entitled to the fee simple in the entire property and in all other cases certain doubts have arisen as to the effectiveness of a merger.[64] In practice, it is recommended that where a leasehold and a superior leasehold interest are acquired by way of the same deed, they should be acquired separately and not merged to ensure the

---

61 SDCA 1999, s 67(a).

62 SDCA 1999, s 67(b).

63 *McIlvenny v McKeever* [1931] NI 161.

64 Law Reform Commission Report on *Land Law and Conveyancing Law*, at p 5.

effective passing of both interests. This is done with a view to perfecting title, rather than avoiding tax. When disposing of the property where a conveyance and assignment of the property are required, there is a possibility of apportioning the consideration for capital gains tax purposes between the two interests, provided they have some value.

SDCA 1999, s 35

[5.57] The Conveyancing Act 1881, s 65 provides that where a lease is for more than 300 years' duration and there is not less than 200 years to run, the leasehold interest can be enlarged into a freehold interest. No rent should be payable, or if it is, it must merely be a peppercorn rent or a rent of no money value, or be a rent which has been released or barred by the lapse of time or ceased in any other way to be payable.[65]

[5.58] SDCA 1999, s 35 was employed to counteract a saving on stamp duty effected as follows:

(a) A agreed to purchase a non-residential freehold property for £2,000,000 from B;

(b) A and B entered into an agreement whereby B was going to grant a lease to A for a term of 800 years at a premium of £2,000,000 subject to a peppercorn rent;

(c) A then paid the premium and took possession of the property but did not yet call for a lease. A was the beneficial owner of the leasehold interest;

(d) A could execute a deed of enlargement and obtain the freehold interest in the property which was chargeable with a nominal stamp duty. A potential liability was, therefore, avoided of £120,000.

[5.59] Since 11 June 1985, the declaration of enlargement by way of deed, provided the interest it enlarges was created within six years of the date of execution of the deed of enlargement, shall be chargeable to stamp duty as a conveyance or transfer on sale of that land. The consideration shall be deemed to be equal to the value of the land, that value being determined without regard to the leasehold interest created.[66] This provision will not apply to deeds or instruments covered by SDCA 1999, s 82, which exempts from stamp duty any instrument transferring land for charitable purposes. The deed of enlargement as set out in the Example **5.55.2** gives rise to a stamp duty liability of £120,000. If such a declaration by deed pursuant to the Conveyancing Acts is to be used to enlarge a freehold interest, it should be executed after a period of six years has expired from the date of the original instrument creating the term.

Consideration allocation

[5.60] SDCA 1999, s 34 was introduced to counteract avoidance schemes that allocated the bulk of the consideration from the conveyance on sale head to that of a non-chargeable head, that is an agreement for lease exceeding 35 years. Prior to the enactment of SDCA 1999, s 34 the following scheme could be used:

---

[65] But see *Atkins v Atkins* (30 March 1976, unreported) HC, Kenny J.

[66] SDCA 1999, s 35(1).

(a) Mr Smith who owns a freehold interest in non-residential property has agreed to sell same to Mr Jones for €95,000. If this property was conveyed the stamp duty liability would amount to €5,700, that is €95,000 at 6 per cent.

(b) Mr Smith and Mr Jones abhor the payment of tax and they entered into an agreement for a grant of a lease by Mr Smith to Mr Jones for a term exceeding 50 years.

Stamp duty: the term has to exceed 35 years to avoid stamp duty at the *ad valorem* rate chargeable under SDCA 1999, s 50.

Income tax: the term has to exceed 50 years to avoid the charge to income tax (ITA 1967, s 83(1)).

Capital gains tax: as the consideration is under the relevant amount, no capital gains tax clearance certificate will be required under TCA 1997, s 980.

Consideration for the lease would be €92,000.

(c) Mr Jones and Mr Smith further agree the sale or purchase of the freehold interest in the property after execution of the lease for the sum of €3,000 and that both interests shall merge so that Mr Jones will have acquired the fee simple interest in the property in totality.

As the consideration of the conveyance on sale is under €10,000, stamp duty is nil and as the agreement for lease is over 35 years, it is not liable for stamp duty.

[5.61] It was felt that individuals who took both agreements for the leasehold and freehold interests as in the preceding example were taking a risk as these transactions could have been regarded by the Revenue Commissioners as being linked together and would fall within the *Ramsay*[67] principle. This English case appeared to suggest that the courts should look at substance over form and that steps inserted into a transaction merely to reduce tax liability could be ignored if they were deemed to be a fiscal nullity. In light of the Supreme Court decision in *McGrath v McDermott*,[68] this belief was unfounded. However, the decision in *Waterford Glass*[69] and *Viek*[70] IV ITR 367 gives some cause for concern as the court in both these cases ruled that form should give way to substance in a transaction designed to avoid this. For a fuller discussion see **Chapter 3**.

[5.62] The Statute now states:

> where in connection with or in contemplation of, a sale of property, the vendor enters into:
>
> (a) an agreement for the grant of a lease of the property for a term exceeding 35 years; or
>
> (b) an agreement (other than a contract for the sale of property) under which the vendor grants any other rights in relation to property;

[67] *Ramsay* [1980] STC 174.

[68] *McGrath v McDermott* III ITR 683.

[69] *Waterford Glass* IV ITR 187.

[70] *Viek* IV ITR 367.

> any conveyance or transfer, subject to the agreement, of the property by the vendor shall be chargeable to stamp duty as a conveyance or transfer on sale of the property for a consideration equal to the value of the property and the value shall be determined without regard to the agreement".[71]

The subsequent conveyance of the property is regarded as a conveyance of the property for the full consideration involved in both agreements.

[71] SDCA 1999, s 34.

Chapter 6

Leasehold Interests

Introduction

[6.01] The charge to duty under the lease head arises on the creation of a lease and, in certain circumstances, on executing an agreement for the creation of a lease, of lands, tenements or heritable subjects. The duty is charged on the rent payable under the lease, and any premium payable and the rate of duty is ascertained by reference to the term created by the lease.

Chargeable instruments

[6.02] The instrument must be a lease or an agreement for a lease of lands, tenements or heritable subjects.

Leases

[6.03] SDCA 1999 does not provide a statutory definition of a lease, which must be given its general legal meaning. A lease is defined as an agreement whereby one party (called the landlord or lessor) relinquishes his right to immediate possession of property, while retaining ultimate legal ownership (title). A lease constitutes the grant by one party to another of lands, tenements or heritable subjects, in consideration of any rent. A tenement at early common law meant anything that could be held by tenure; all land was a tenement. However, the term 'tenement' here relates to the statutory definition given for the purposes of landlord and tenant relationships. For these purposes, a tenement means premises consisting or defined thereof, of a building, or of land covered either wholly or partly by buildings, provided that that part of the land which is not covered by buildings is subsidiary and ancillary to the buildings.[1] Agricultural lands are not tenements but a residential house, an apartment block, factory, etc would be tenements. Heritable subjects are those interests which are capable of being passed on by inheritance, that is, by way of a will or by the rules of intestate succession. There are two kinds of hereditaments: corporeal and incorporeal. The former generally refers to tangible things. The latter refers to rights growing out of or connected to any property including such items as an easement and rent. They should be distinguished both from those interests which cannot be passed on by way of inheritance – a life estate, for example, cannot be passed on by way of a will or by rules of intestacy since the estate comes to an end when the holder of the life estate dies and those interests which cannot pass by way of a will but are descendible and so they can be passed on according to certain rules of succession – for example, a possibility of reverter after a fee simple determinable. The best known heritable subjects would be incorporeal hereditaments and such as easements, rights of way, profits a prendre.[2] The original party may retain a

1 Landlord and Tenant (Amendment) Act 1980, s 5.

reversion, or have a right to a reversion in the event of a breach of any of the terms of the lease, but such reversion is not necessary.[3]

[6.04] The courts have encountered difficulties in setting down a distinct and final criteria as to the nature of the landlord and tenant relationship and the criteria are still evolving. The courts look at the agreement between the parties, the intention of the parties, the right to occupation of the property, the rent payable if any and finally at the relationship that has been created. The mere fact that the parties have labelled the agreement under one heading will not deem it to be such an agreement though it may be taken into account. Griffin J stated in *Gatien Motor Co Ltd v Continental Oil Co of Ireland Ltd*[4]:

> To find whether it was intended to create a relationship of landlord and tenant, one must look at the transaction as a whole and at any indications that are to be found in the terms of the contract between the two parties ...

The right to exclusive occupation is not conclusive as to the existence of a tenancy, but it bears a considerable importance for the courts. In *Street v Mountford*[5] the court held that '... residential accommodation offered and accepted with exclusive possession for a term at a rent, the result is a tenancy'.

[6.05] While it is likely that this approach will be followed in this jurisdiction, Griffin J in *Bellew v Bellew*[6] doubted whether the issue of exclusive possession needed to be determined in resolving the nature of the interest, a tenancy being found without reference to possession. This caution is understandable given the problematic nature of 'possession', which has to be established on the facts of each individual case. This is more in accord with the peculiar nature of Deasy's Act, which founds the tenancy relationship on the intention of the parties and renders English precedent of marginal benefit. If the parties did not intend to create a tenancy, then they will have created a licence which is not chargeable to duty under this head of charge. Finally, to create a relationship of landlord and tenant within the definition of Deasy's Act, s 3 rent has to be payable. The Supreme Court has taken the view that where no rent is payable no tenancy exists but this may be rebutted depending on the circumstances.[7] The instrument must be executed creating a new leasehold interest in property to be chargeable under this head. If the instrument has the effect of leasing two properties subject to separate rents and remedies to one or more lessees, then the instrument should be chargeable as two (or more) leases. The agreement or instrument may not create a leasehold interest, but may be stampable as such. For example, an unconditional notice to quit may be served under the terms of the lease. Subsequently, agreement may be reached between the parties that the notice to quit would be withdrawn and is effected by way of agreement or instrument, which would be chargeable to stamp duty as it now creates a new leasehold

---

2 **Chapter 1**.

3 Landlord and Tenant Law (Amendment) Act 1860 also referred to as Deasy's Act 1860, s 3.

4 *Gatien Motor Co Ltd v Continental Oil Co of Ireland Ltd* [1979] IR 406.

5 *Street v Mountford* [1985] AC 809.

6 *Bellew v Bellew* [1982] IR 447.

7 For a further discussion see Wylie, *Irish Landlord and Tenant Law* (2edn, Butterworths, 1998.

interest.[8] Note, however, that the Irish Court of Appeal has taken a different approach to this issue and the matter will be dealt with more fully in the following paragraphs.

Agreement for lease

[6.06] An agreement for a lease is a contract to enter into a lease and, as specific performance is available for such contract in equity, the parties are regarded as being in the same position as if a lease was executed.[9] In the Revenue Notes for Guidance, p 45 it is stated that this provision was enacted to prevent a situation where a purchaser contracts to acquire the leasehold interest in a property and, instead of taking an assignment of the leasehold property, the purchaser acquires the reversionary interest for nominal value, followed by an oral surrender of the leasehold. The legislature, when enacting SA 1891, acknowledged this case and any agreement for a lease or with respect to a letting for a term not exceeding 35 years or for any indefinite term is chargeable as if it were a lease, subject to the same terms and conditions as the agreement.[10] Where subsequently an instrument is executed giving effect to the terms of the agreement which has already been duly stamped and both are produced to the Revenue Commissioners and the Revenue Commissioners can then note the lease as duly stamped, such instrument shall be chargeable with the duty of €12.50 (Lease SDCA 1999). Duty can also be transferred from the original agreements to the lease. If the agreement is not completed or is rescinded, there is no provision for the repayment of the duty. The provisions of the Act are more extensive than the rule set out in *Walsh v Lonsdale*. Further, the rule in *Walsh v Lonsdale* is an equitable remedy and is, therefore, discretionary and specific performance may be refused.

[6.07] The agreement must be for a lease for a term not exceeding 35 years or for an indefinite term to be chargeable under this head.[11] Where the agreement is for a term in excess of 35 years and is for a definite term, it shall not attract duty under this head, but may:

(a) attract duty as an agreement for a lease made in contemplation of a sale;[12] or

(b) if it is not made in contemplation of a sale and is executed under seal, attract nominal stamp duty.

Example 6.07.1

Construct Ltd, a well known development construction company, purchased an old building in the centre of a town with a view to converting it into a shopping mall. To ensure success with the venture, they enter into an agreement for a lease for a term of 36 years, which is executed under seal.

This agreement will not attract stamp duty under this head of charge as it is an agreement for a lease for a definite term of years exceeding 35 years, but will give rise to a nominal duty of €12.50 as the agreement is executed under seal. When the lease is subsequently executed, it shall be chargeable to duty.

---

8 *Freeman v Evans* [1922] 1 Ch 36.

9 *Walsh v Lonsdale* [1882] 21 Ch D 9.

10 SDCA 1999, s 50.

11 SDCA 1999, s 50.

12 SDCA 1999, s 34.

Example 6.07.2

The facts are as above, except the agreement entered into is a lease for a term of 12 years, subject to a rent of €15,000 per annum. Duty is charged at a rate of 1%. The stamp duty liability is €150. The development is subsequently completed and a formal lease is entered into. The lease and the original agreement (duly stamped) are presented to the Revenue Commissioners. The lease is denoted as being properly stamped and is chargeable with duty of €12.50.

Agreement for lease made in contemplation of a sale without executing a lease

[6.08] Where a purchaser enters into a contract or agreement for the purchase of a leasehold interest in property and enters into possession of the property prior to obtaining a transfer duly stamped and the transfer is not duly stamped within a period of nine months from the date of the contract or agreement, the contract or agreement shall be charged with *ad valorem* stamp duty as if it were an actual transfer on sale. The Revenue Commissioners may extend the period of nine months as they feel appropriate in the circumstances. Such a contract or agreement is not stampable under the lease head, but rather under the 'conveyance on sale head'.[13]

Land, tenements or heritable subjects

[6.09] This head of charge applies to leases or agreements for leases of any lands, tenement, or heritable subjects or leases relating to immovable property situate in the State or to any right over, or interest in, such property. If the lease does not come within the ambit of the heads of charge numbers one to five of the lease head,[14] it is not liable to duty. Leases or hiring arrangements which are concerned with movable property or personal property do not come within this head of charge; for example, leases of machinery or cars.[15] A lease has to be of immovable property or the lease of an interest in immovable property; for example, sporting rights.[16]

[6.10] Movable goods may, by way of annexation and attachment to land, be rendered fixtures which are deemed to form part of the land. This may also have consequences for a hirer under a lease agreement which could be to the benefit of a mortgagee or landlord. In *Lombard & Ulster Banking Ltd v Kennedy*,[17] the tenant of a garage entered into a hiring agreement with the bank for an automatic car wash which included the right to termination by serving one month's notice. The tenant served the notice prior to disappearing. The landlord repossessed the premises, and retained possession of the car wash as it was 'a fixture and addition' to the garage. The court agreed that the car wash had become a fixture. It became the property of the landlord and the bank lost its interest in it.

---

13 SDCA 1999, s 36 – see **Chapter 5**.

14 As set out in the SA 1891, Sch 1.

15 *Jones v IRC, Sweetmeat Automatic Deliveries Co v IRC* [1895] 1 QB 484.

16 *Bird v Higginson* 6A & E 824.

17 *Lombard & Ulster Banking Ltd v Kennedy* [1974] NI 20.

[6.11] In *Re Galway Concrete Ltd*[18] two cement silos and two screw conveyors were installed in the premises and were deemed to be two tenants' fixtures. When the company went into liquidation the court was asked to decide whether or not the silo and screw conveyors could be removed. Keane J held they could, taking the view that otherwise the prior agreement would be totally confused. This case and *Lombard & Ulster Banking Ltd v Kennedy* are not immediately reconcilable. Keane J appeared to place considerable emphasis on not frustrating the contractual agreement between the parties as distinct from the attachment of the item to the land in question. In truth, the choice is one of policy, as to whether the courts prefer to safeguard the rights of a lender or the rights of the land-owner. It would appear that the approach in *Galway Concrete Ltd* is to be preferred if credit facilities are to continue to be available. It is for the landlord and the tenant to deal with the issue of liability for damage to the land.

[6.12] The mere fact that a third party may acquire certain rights in respect of the movable property by virtue of its attachment as a fixture to land, rendering it immovable, would not appear to change the nature of the lease of that equipment and is not chargeable under the lease head.

Creation of a leasehold interest

[6.13] The creation of a lease or an instrument which has the effect of creating a leasehold interest in lands, tenements or heritable subjects, or is deemed to be such an instrument, is stampable under this head of charge. The term of a lease commences from the date of execution of a lease and cannot be earlier, as a lease cannot take effect retrospectively.[19]

[6.14] An instrument, while not being a lease itself but creating a leasehold interest, shall be stampable. A lease which is for a term certain with the benefit of an option to renew in favour of the tenant, will be stampable as a lease for a fixed term. When the option is exercised by way of instrument, the instrument shall be stampable as a lease as it has the effect of creating a leasehold interest. In England, where an unconditional notice to quit is served on a tenant which is subsequently waived, abandoned or withdrawn, any instrument giving such effect shall be stampable with duty. The English courts take the view that this has the effect of creating a new tenancy.[20] This must be contrasted with the view expressed by the old Irish Court of Appeal in *Lord Inchiquin v Lyon*[21] where the court took the opposite view and felt that as such waiver, withdrawal or abandonment must be done by agreement between the parties, the old tenancy therefore continues, albeit under new terms. Such waiver, withdrawal or abandonment of a notice to quit in Ireland, because it does not create a new leasehold interest in property but is a continuation of the old tenancy, is not stampable.

[6.15] SDCA 1999 also deems certain instruments to be stampable under this head. There are two distinct situations. The first concerns a deed of variation or document

18 *Re Galway Concrete Ltd* [1983] ILRM 402.

19 *Bradshaw v Pauley* [1979] 3 All ER 273.

20 *Tayleur v Wildin* [1868] LR 3 Exch 303, approved by *Freeman v Evans* [1922] 1 Ch 36.

21 *Lord Inchiquin v Lyon* [1887] 20 LR IR 474.

which has the effect of increasing the rent reserved. The second concerns a memorandum which records an increase in rent allowed by virtue of the document originally creating the leasehold interest. In considering the liability under the English legislation for an instrument having the effect of increasing the rent, Goff J held that the instrument itself will be chargeable under the 'bond covenant' head but SDCA 1999, s 52 provided a relief and charged such an instrument under the lease head.[22] Similarly, if the duty chargeable under the bond, covenant or instrument of any kind head was less than that chargeable under the lease head, then the relieving provision would not apply. Furthermore, to support this argument, the English legislator when abolishing the 'bond of any kind whatsoever' head specifically excluded instruments increasing the rent reserved by other instruments.[23] Therefore, the bond, covenant or instrument of any kind head continues to exist in England in respect of such instruments subject to the relieving provision of s 52. In Ireland, the head of charge bond covenant or instrument of any kind whatsoever has been abolished in full with no exception and an instrument recording an increase in such rent shall not be chargeable any further.[24] In practice, since the first edition of this book, the Revenue Commissioners have changed their view and expressly stated in their Guidelines that no additional stamp duty is payable on the review provided the increase was provided for in the lease, thereby following the decision of *Gable Construction & Co Ltd.*

[6.16] This decision *held* that an instrument which has the effect of increasing rent shall not be liable to stamp duty as the head of charge has been abolished and this relieving provision has no effect. This view of the Revenue can be found in their Revenue Notes for Guidance p 58 on the provision detailing how the stamping of documents increasing rents is a relieving provision rather than a charging provision. They have also stated that since the provision from which it provides relief is now abolished, it is now redundant.[25] On this basis, an instrument providing for an increase in rent under another provision should not be stampable. This view is at odds with the view in the Revenue Commissioners Stamp Duty Work Manual which indicates that where a subsequent instrument is drawn up increasing the rent, the additional rent is chargeable to duty. It should be noted that the Revenue Notes for Guidance are more up to date that the Manual and, in this respect, may be relied on as the current Revenue practice.

[6.17] Under SDCA 1999, s 52(4) any instrument that amends the rent reserved by another instrument is liable to duty as if it were a lease, the consideration for which is the increase in the rent payable, and for no other duty. To qualify for this provision, the original instrument must itself not only be chargeable to duty, but the instrument must be duly stamped. Accordingly, an instrument increasing the rent payable is liable to *ad valorem* duty on the amount of the increased rent, but is not liable to any fixed duty. To qualify, however, the original lease instrument must be correctly stamped. It remains

---

22 *Gable Construction Co Ltd v IRC* [1968] 2 All ER 968 as approved in *Jenkins R Lewis & Son Ltd v Kerman* [1971] CH 477.

23 FA 1971 (UK), s 64.

24 SDCA 1999, Sch 1.

25 Revenue Notes for Guidance p 59.

unclear whether an alteration to an existing lease, marked on the existing lease, would itself create a new lease which would then render the entire lease liable to duty again.

[6.18] As already stated at para **[6.16]** the instrument has to have the effect of increasing the rent. In a 35-year lease with a standard rent review clause, it is the original lease which is the instrument by which the increase is effected. Any memorandum recording the agreement between the parties as to the increase of the rent under the review clause shall not be stampable under this head, as it does not increase the rent but records an increase in the rent. Such instrument should not be executed under seal, but if executed under seal, should be stamped as a collateral document to the original instrument.

[6.19] The question arises as to whether an alteration which would reduce the rent payable under the agreement, should fall liable to duty. The difficulty would be the amount on which such duty should be levied, since it reduces the rent payable. One possible argument is that a reduction in rent of an existing lease would create a new tenancy and thus duty would be levied on the entire amount of the reduced rent. If this were so, a reduction in rent would, normally, incur a higher charge to duty since all of the rent would be used to calculate that duty, whereas an increase in rent is liable to duty only to the extent of the increase.

Example 6.19.1

Bulldog rents land from Paddy at €500 per month. Bulldog finds the land is very profitable and so agrees to execute an instrument increasing the rent to €600.

No duty is chargeable according to current Revenue practice €0

Example 6.19.2

Assume the same facts as above but that the land is not profitable. Bulldog and Paddy execute an instrument reducing the rent to €400. Duty is payable on the entire rent of €400 since it would be regarded as a new tenancy. The duty payable on the average annual rent is:

Duty on €4,800 x 1% = €48

This would appear to be inequitable, not with respect to the taxing statute, but with respect to the interpretation of a transaction, and would tend to suggest that a reduction in rent should not be viewed as the creation of a new tenancy.

Example 6.19.3

Fashion Ltd take a lease in a shopping centre for a term of 35 years from 1 May 1982, subject to a rent of €10,000 per annum with no rent review clause.

In 1994 the landlord and tenant decide that the rent is too low and agree to increase the rent to €20,000 per annum. The instrument recording the increase in rent shall be chargeable under the lease head and shall be chargeable on the increase in rent only.

Stamp duty liability (€10,000 at 1%) €100

(According to current Revenue practice

Example 6.19.4

Fashion Ltd has had the lease of a premises since 1 May 1994, subject to a rent of €10,000 per annum for the first five years, reviewable on the fifth anniversary and reviewable every five years for the remainder of the term. Stamp duty is chargeable is as follows:

	€
On the creation of the lease (€10,000 at 1%)	100.00
The rent review clause chargeable under para 5 of head of charge	12.50
Total stamp duty	112.50

Due to difficult trading conditions in the shopping centre in 1999, the landlord decides not to carry out a rent review.

In 2002 the landlord arranges a letting to a large anchor tenant which draws considerable business to the shopping centre resulting in a substantial increase in trading.

In 2004 the rent review notice is served and, after referring the matter to arbitration, the rent is increased to the sum of €25,000 per annum by way of arbitrator's award. As this instrument does not have the effect of increasing the rent but merely records the increase of rent under a rent review clause, no stamp duty should be payable.

If completed under seal, the document should be stamped collaterally with €12.50 duty.

In practice, in Example **6.19.4** an original and counterpart lease would be executed by both parties, both firstly being executed by the tenant and returned to the landlord's solicitor with the stamp duty payable thereon. Once the landlord executes the lease and counterpart, they are then stamped with the original lease being returned to the tenant. When completing the memoranda recording the increase in rent the same practice, is adhered to but the landlord's solicitor should also obtain the original lease from the tenant to enable him to stamp the memoranda as collateral to the original lease (if executed under seal). The Revenue Commissioners require the original lease to be produced to ensure that the rent review clause was stamped with the €12.50 duty.

Charge to duty

[6.20] On the creation of a new leasehold interest in property, stamp duty is charged on both the premium payable on the creation of the lease and also on the annual rent reserved by the lease. The rate of stamp duty on the annual rent is calculated by reference to the term created by the lease.

Duty on premiums

[6.21] On the creation of a lease, a capital sum may be paid to the landlord as part of the consideration for the granting of the lease, which may be by way of fine or premium. Premiums are not defined by stamp duty legislation. According to *Regent Oil Co Ltd v Strick*[26] a premium is a lump sum paid by a tenant as consideration for the grant of a lease. Generally, if the rent is chargeable at market rates, a premium will not be charged. Rent paid up front is not chargeable as a premium but is chargeable as rent as indicated by the Revenue. Prior to the Landlord and Tenant (Ground Rent) Act 1978 it was common to grant a lease subject to a covenant to erect a premises, the consideration

26 *Regent Oil Co Ltd v Strick* [1965] 3 All ER 74.

comprising the payment of a premium and subject to a ground rent. The creation of new ground rents for residences, has now been abolished, except for flats.

[6.22] The rate of stamp duty applicable to the premium is calculated by reference to the consideration passing and not to the term of the lease, whether definite or indefinite. Any consideration (other than the rent) consisting of money, stock or security moving either to the lessor or to any other person is chargeable to duty as set out in **Chapter 4**. The rate of duty is the same as payable under the 'conveyance on sale head'.

[6.23] Where a premium is exempt from stamp duty or entitled to a low rate of duty due to the consideration passing, the finance certificates as set out in **Chapter 4** must be inserted in the lease.

> IT IS HEREBY CERTIFIED that the transaction hereby effected does not form part of a larger transaction or of a series of transactions in respect of which the amount or value, or the aggregate amount or value, of the consideration other than the rent exceeds € (the appropriate figure to be inserted herein).

If the finance certificate is not inserted in the lease the highest rate of duty applies.

Example 6.23.1

Mico grants a lease of a commercial premises to Paco for a term of 99 years subject to a rent of one peppercorn per annum, and a premium which is paid on the execution of the lease of €35,000. No finance certificate is inserted in the lease.

Stamp duty payable on the premium at 9%	€3,150

But a certificate setting out the nature of the property is inserted in the lease.
If the finance certificate had been inserted in the lease stating that the consideration did not exceed €40,000, liability would be as follows:

Stamp duty liability (€35,000 at 3%)	€1,050

The premium passing must consist of any money, stock or security.[27] Money includes all sums, whether expressed in Irish or foreign currency. Stock includes any share in any stock or fund, defined in SDCA 1999, s 1. When the consideration does not come within that definition, it is not chargeable under the premium head.

Example 6.23.2

A grant of a lease in consideration of a surrender of a previous lease, shall not be chargeable under this head.[28]

As previously stated, the rate of duty on premiums is the same as charged under the conveyance on sale head and the rule applicable on these for ascertaining the consideration passing also applies to premiums chargeable.[29]

[6.24] Where the consideration for the grant of the lease comprises stock, duty is chargeable based on the value of the stock or where it is granted in satisfaction of a debt

---

27 SDCA 1999, Sch 1.

28 *Littlewoods Mail Order Stores Ltd v IRC* [1961] Ch 597.

29 *Blendett v IRC* and *Quietlece v IRC* [1984] STC 95.

or security, duty is chargeable on the amount of the debt or the value of that security.[30] In *Jinjell v Purkins*[31] the court held that, as the lease was granted in satisfaction of a debt, the lease was deemed to be granted at a premium equivalent to the debt. Where a premium is subject to a contingency and therefore unascertainable, the Revenue may calculate the duty payable on the premium as if the contingency had taken place on the date of the execution of the agreement, see *LM Tenancies plc v IRC*.[32]

[6.25] Previously, where value added tax was chargeable on the creation of the lease, the Revenue Commissioners deemed it to be part of the consideration and, accordingly, it was chargeable with duty. In *Glenrothes Development Corp v IRC*[33] the court held that, since the purchaser had to pay value added tax in order to secure implementation of the contract, then the value added tax so payable was part of the consideration of the contract and liable to duty.

[6.26] However, duty is no longer chargeable on any value added tax arising on the creation of a lease by way of instrument executed on or after 11 April 1994.[34] All documents which were stamped prior to 11 April 1994, even though duty may not have been chargeable on the value added tax payable on the creation of such lease, shall be deemed to have been properly stamped. The Revenue Guidance Notes, p 63 state that the Revenue assume that the rent and premium set out in a lease is the VAT exclusive consideration unless informed otherwise.

Duty on rent

[6.27] The rate of duty payable on the rent is ascertained by reference to the term of years granted or deemed to be granted by the lease. Stamp duty is charged on the average annual rent payable under the lease. Prior to discussing the relevant charge, the following points should be considered.

Rent

[6.28] Rent is not defined in SDCA 1999, s 1. A lease is defined in the Landlord and Tenant (Amendment) Act 1980 as meaning:

> ... an instrument in writing, whether under or not under seal, containing a contract of tenancy in respect of any land in consideration of a rent or return and includes a fee farm grant (s 3(i)).

Rent has been defined to include:

> any sum or return in the nature of rent, payable or given by way of compensation, for the holding of any land.[35]

---

30 SDCA 1999, s 40(1).

31 *Jinjell v Purkins* [1854] Exch 720.

32 *LM Tenancies plc v IRC* [1996] STC 880.

33 *lenrothes Development Corp v IRC* [1993] STC 74.

34 SDCA 1999, s 56.

35 Deasy's Act, s 1.

[6.29] The Feudal Rule was that rent could only issue out of land and payments not reserved out of land could not constitute rent.[36] The definition of rent in Deasy's Act was considered by the Supreme Court which defines rent as being 'compensation for the holding of any lands', but it made an exception in that case so that what was described by way of rent in the lease would be apportioned into the rent payable in respect of the lands and also into the payments made by way of contract in respect of chattels, provided the owners of the lands and chattels were separate and distinct, *Munster & Leinster Bank Ltd v Hollinshead.*[37] The mere description of the payment as rent is not conclusive.[38] Even though the payment may be described as a premium this is not conclusive where the payment retains a characteristic of a rent.[39] In *The Duke of Westminster v Store Properties Ltd*[40] the payment to a landlord being described as rent and charged over the land so demised was not, in fact, rent, as it was made in consideration of a licence to convert the premises. Where the person receiving an amount equivalent to the rent is not authorised to receive it, then the payment shall not constitute rent.[41] Lord Fraser in *United Scientific Holdings v Burnly Borough Council,*[42] cites the statement in *Foa's General Law of Landlord and Tenant*[43] that 'prima facie rent is the monetary compensation payable by the tenant in consideration for the grant however it is described or allocated'. In *Irish Shell & BP Ltd v Costello Ltd*[44] the court had to consider whether an agreement for the use of petrol pumps, machinery and other items supplied on a petrol station in return for the payment for hire was a lease or not. Griffin J stated:

> whilst it is correct to say that the agreement did not provide for the payment of any 'rent' as such for the premises, when the true nature of the agreement is considered the reality of the position is that the periodic payments made by the defendants were in fact rent, although cloaked under the guise or under the label of payment for hire of the equipment.

Once the payment, or part thereof, is made for the holding of any lands it is chargeable to stamp duty as rent, whether or not it is described as such.

Quantification of rent

[6.30] Stamp duty is charged on the average annual rent.[45] The word 'average' was inserted in the Act to charge situations involving rent variation over the term.

---

36 *Hill v Booth* [1930] 1 KB 381.

37 [1930] IR 187. Note Kennedy CJ, *diss*, who believed that Deasy's Act had made the feudal notion of rent obsolete and would therefore allow for apportionment between chattels and lands.

38 *Donnellan v Read* [1832] 3 B & Ad 899.

39 *Samuel v Salmon & Gluckstein Ltd* [1946] Ch 8.

40 *The Duke of Westminster v Store Properties Ltd* [1944] Ch 129.

41 *Freeman v AG* [1949] Ir Jur Rep 61.

42 *United Scientific Holdings v Burnly Borough Council* [1977] 2 All ER 6.

43 (8th edn, 1957).

44 *Irish Shell & BP Ltd v Costello Ltd* [1981] ILRM 66.

45 SA 1891, Sch 1.

Example 6.30.1

A Ltd leases a factory to B Ltd for a term of five years with the rent payable as follows:

	€
Year 1	10,000
Year 2	12,000
Year 3	13,000
Year 4	14,000
Year 5	15,000
Total rent	64,000
Average annual rent = €12,800	
Stamp duty at 1%	128

The lease, which reflects the agreement between the parties, usually clearly sets out the rent payable under the lease. In certain cases the rent may be subject to a contingency, or be unascertainable, or may consist of produce, which has to be valued.

Penal rent

[6.31] Revenue Guidance Notes, p 57 state that SDCA 1999, s 52 places limits on the amount of duty chargeable on certain leases or agreements to lease. A penal rent is any additional rent provided for in the lease in the event that the tenant breaches a covenant. Penal rents are not subject to stamp duty.

Rent subject to contingency

[6.32] The grant of the lease may be subject to a contingency. For example, a lease granted for a term of 21 years subject to a rent of €10,000 per annum plus 4 per cent of profits is subject to a maximum extra payment of €5,000 per annum. In this case, the average rate would be calculated by reference to the maximum amount payable under the lease so that the stamp duty would be charged on the rent of €10,000 per annum plus the maximum sum payable under the lease of €5,000 per annum totalling at €15,000 per annum.

[6.33] In *Coventry City Council v IRC*[46] the grant of a lease was subject to a formulated contingency, and the upper limit of the contingency ascertainable under the formula was £105,846. As this was the maximum rent that might become payable over the release period of the lease, the court held that the Revenue Commissioners were correct in ascertaining *ad valorem* duty by reference to the sum of £105,846.

[6.34] In our example in para **[6.30]** stamp duty is chargeable on the rent of up to €15,000 per annum even though the company may never make a profit. SDCA 1999, s 55 (as amended) enacted a rule in respect of unascertainable rent[47] which now empowers the Revenue Commissioners to charge *ad valorem* duty on the market value of the property. Where the rent is unascertainable, even where the maximum amount is

46 *Coventry City Council v IRC* [1978] 1 All ER 1107.

47 Discussed at **[6.35]** below.

ascertainable by reference to the contingency rule, the Revenue Commissioners are obliged to charge duty under the unascertainable consideration rule. This would appear to limit the contingency principle to cases where the rent payable under the contingency is fixed and determinate. In the above example, the duty is no longer payable on the €15,000 (the upper limit of the contingency) but is now charged on the market value. In our above example, if the contingency was a fixed sum per annum, for example €1,000 extra rent per annum, every year that 100,000 customers used the shopping centre, then duty would be charged under the contingency principle. The matter has not been conclusively determined by the courts at this point.

Unascertainable consideration

[6.35] Unascertainable consideration became chargeable to stamp duty in respect of leases with effect from 29 May 1991. The original section as enacted charged duty on the amount or value of the consideration other than the rent (premium) that would have been obtained from a tenant, disregarding any premium or rent payable under the lease. This had the affect of charging duty on the open market value premiums. Since duty could also be assessed on any rent payable, this could give rise to a double charge to duty. This section applies to leases executed between 29 May 1991 and 27 May 1992.

[6.36] With effect from 27 May 1992 the following rules apply:

(a) where the average rent or consideration is unascertainable at the date of execution of the lease, but if ascertainable would be chargeable to *ad valorem* duty, then the duty shall be charged on the amount or value of the consideration or rent that would have been obtained from a purchaser or tenant paying full consideration or rent for such sale or lease, in other words on the open market premium or rent;[48] and

(b) where both the rent and the consideration other than the rent payable (the premium) are unascertainable, but if ascertainable would be charged to duty, then duty should be charged on the amount or value of the consideration other than rent (the premium) as would be paid by a tenant paying full consideration for such a lease subject to a nil rent reserved by the lease.[49]

[6.37] The effect of these provisions are threefold.

(a) *Both the premium and the rent are unascertainable*: duty is charged on the open market premium for such a lease on the basis that the rent reserved by the lease is a nil amount.

Example 6.37.1

Develo Ltd agrees to grant a lease in a new shopping centre to Conman Ltd for a term of 35 years, subject to a premium of 4% of turnover in the first 12 months and subject to a rent of 1% turnover per annum. The market value premium at a nil rent of the premises is €73,000.

---

48 SDCA 1999, s 55(1).

49 SDCA 1999, s 55(2).

The Revenue Commissioners will charge duty on the market value premium (€73,000) on the basis that the rent payable in respect of the property is nil.

Stamp duty premium (€73,000 at 5%)	€3,650

(b) *The rent is unascertainable but the premium is ascertainable*: duty is chargeable on the open market rent for such a lease subject to the premium payable and duty shall also be charged on the premium payable.

Example 6.37.2

Develo Ltd grants a lease to Conman Ltd in a new shopping centre for a term of 35 years, subject to a premium of €25,000, subject to a rent of 1% of turnover. The necessary finance certificate is inserted in the lease. The open market rent for the premises, subject to a premium of €25,000, would be €8,000 per annum. Stamp duty is as follows:

	€
Premium (€25,000 at 2%)	500
Annual rent (€8,000 at 1%)	80
Total duty	580

(c) *The rent is ascertainable but the premium is unascertainable*: duty is charged on the open market premium of such a lease, subject to the same terms, conditions and rent payable.

Example 6.37.3

Develo Ltd grants a lease in a new shopping centre for a term of 35 years to Conman Ltd, subject to a rent of €2,000 per annum, subject to a premium based on 50% of the first year's profits. The open market value premium, subject to the same terms and conditions and subject to the rent of €2,000 per annum would be €80,000. Stamp duty is as follows:

	€
Premium (€80,000 at 5%)	4,000
Rent (€2,000 at 1%)	20
Total duty	4,020

Where both the premium and rent, or the premium itself, are unascertainable, it would be advisable to obtain an open market valuation of the premium payable so that the necessary finance certificate could be inserted in the lease to obtain a reduced rate of stamp duty. If the necessary finance certificate is not inserted in the lease and the deemed premium is less than €150,000 in commercial property, then stamp duty shall be payable at a rate of 9 per cent.

[6.38] The provisions applying to the consideration consisting of periodic payments, where the payments exceed a period of 20 years,[50] shall not apply where the rules under

[50] SDCA 1999, s 42.

SDCA 1999, s 55(1) as set out above are applicable to the instrument.[51] These provisions do not apply to a lease relating to the transfer of building lands where the consideration cannot be ascertained, and the instrument is stampable under SDCA 1999, s 53.

Lease in consideration of produce

[6.39] Where the consideration (or any part thereof) consists of produce or other goods, the deemed consideration passing is the value of the produce or the goods, and the lease is chargeable with *ad valorem* stamp duty.[52] Where the value of the produce or goods is to amount at least to, or not to exceed a given sum, then the value of produce or goods is estimated at that given sum or according to the permanent rate of conversion, if applicable, and is charged to *ad valorem* duty.[53] Where the consideration (or part thereof) comprises of produce or goods and a statement is contained to the value thereof, then the lease is stamped in accordance with that statement and shall be deemed duly stamped unless it is shown that the said statement is incorrect.[54]

Term of lease

[6.40] The rate of stamp duty chargeable on the creation of a lease is ascertained by reference to the term of years granted by the lease. The date of creation of the lease may differ from the commencement date. If the date of creation of the lease is subsequent to the commencement date, then the expired period of the lease is taken into account in calculating the term, and the stamp duty is chargeable on the lease as of the date of creation. Duty is chargeable under three terms:

(a) where the term does not exceed 35 years or is indefinite;

(b) if the term exceeds 35 years but does not exceed 100 years; and

(c) if the term exceeds 100 years.

If a lease is granted for a fixed term with the benefit of an option to renew, that is regarded as a lease for the fixed term only, and an instrument exercising the option to renew will be liable to duty as a new lease.[55] The view has been expressed that the reference to a lease which 'is indefinite' refers to a periodic tenancy, since otherwise such a lease would be invalid. This view is based on the finding of the English courts that a lease has to be for a fixed duration, as this is inherent to the grant of the lease.[56] In light of Deasy's Act, ss 3 and 4 this view is incorrect in its application to Ireland. The relationship of landlord and tenant can be created for an indefinite or an uncertain period; all that is required is the intention to create the relationship. Where it can be shown that the tenancy was for an indefinite period, it could be stampable under this head.

[51] See **Chapter 13** with regard to period payments.

[52] SDCA 1999, s 51(1)).

[53] SDCA 1999, s 51(2).

[54] SDCA 1999, s 51(3).

[55] *Baker v Merckel* [1960] 1 QB 657.

[56] *Lace v Chantler* [1944] KB 368.

[6.41] The lease may be granted for a definite period, subject to an option to terminate or a right of determination. The option to terminate may be a right to surrender the premises after a rent review has been carried out, or a right to terminate the lease after a specified period, for example, a 35-year lease with an option to terminate in favour of the tenant exercisable on the third anniversary of the lease. The right to determination may occur upon the change of use of the premises by the tenant and in both these cases the lease is deemed to be a full term as stated in the lease.[57] A lease for a period certain which contains a clause bringing the lease to an end in the event of the death of the tenant or tenants, is not a lease for an indefinite period.[58]

Charges and rates of duty

[6.42] The rates of duty applying where the consideration (or part thereof) is any rent, whether reserved as a yearly rent or otherwise are as follows:

(a) for any indefinite term or any term not exceeding 35 years of any dwellinghouse (or part thereof) or apartment where the rent does not exceed €19,050 per annum: exempt;

(b) for a definite term less than a year of any lands, tenements, hereditaments or subjects: the same duty as a lease for a year at a rent reserved for a definite term;

(c) where the consideration (or part thereof) is any rent, in respect of such consideration where the rent, whether reserved as a yearly rent or otherwise:

(i) if the term does not exceed 35 years or is indefinite: €1 for every €100 (or part thereof) of the average annual rent (1%):

Example 6.41.1

Mrs Greene lets a shop to Conman Ltd for a term of 35 years at a rent of €25,000 per annum subject to review every five years. Stamp duty liability is as follows:

	€
€25,000 at 1%	250.00
Rent review clause	12.50
Total liability	262.50

(ii) where the term exceeds 35 years but does not exceed 100 years: €6 for every €100 (or part thereof) of the average annual rent (6%):

Example 6.41.2

Mrs Greene lets a shop to Conman Ltd for a term of 50 years at a rent of €25,000 per annum subject to a five year review. The lease is chargeable as follows:

	€
€25,000 at 6%	1,500.00

---

57 *Cummins Engine Co Ltd v IRC* [1981] STC 604 and *Kushner v Law Society* [1952] 1 KB 264.

58 *Earl Mount Edgcumbe v IRC* [1911] 2 KB 24.

Rent review clause	12.50
Total	1512.50

(iii) where the term exceeds 100 years: €12 for every €100 (or part thereof) of the average annual rent (12%)

Example 6.41.3

Mrs Greene lets a shop premises to Conman Ltd for a term of 150 years at a rent of €25,000 per annum subject to a five year review. The duty on the instrument is as follows:

	€
€25,000 at 12 %	3,000.00
Rent review clause	12.50
Total	3012.50

(d) a lease made subsequent to, and in conformity with the agreement duly stamped with the provisions of SDCA 1999, s 50: €12.50;

(e) any other instrument not already charged under this head of charge which relates to immovable property situate in this State or any right over or interest in such property: €12.50.

Apportionment

[6.43] Where the property to be leased consists partly of an interest in residential property, then the consideration, other than the rent, shall be apportioned in a manner which is just and reasonable between the interest in the residential property and the other interests so created.[59]

Particulars delivered stamp

[6.44] On the grant of any lease for a term exceeding 14 years, the lessee is under a duty to present to the Commissioners the instrument or reasonable particulars thereof.[60] The instrument is deemed not properly stamp unless it is stamped confirming that all particulars have been delivered to the Commissioners.[61] The provisions regarding PD (particulars delivered) stamping have been amended by SDCA 1999, s 12.[62] Effectively the Act now requires that on the transfer of any fee simple, or any lease of lands for a term exceeding 14 years, certain information must be furnished to the Revenue Commissioners. The information is to be of such content and in such form as the Revenue Commissioners have laid down by SI 144/1995.[63] The Statutory Instrument extended the term for a lease of lands to be impressed with a PD stamp thereon to thirty years. Unless such information is presented as laid down by regulation, and a stamp verifying that particulars of the lease has been delivered to the Revenue Commissioners,

59 SDCA 1999, s 52(5).

60 SDCA 1999, s 12.

61 SDCA 1999, s 12(3).

62 As amended by FA 1995, s 149.

63 Stamp Duty (Particulars to be Delivered) Regulations 1995 (SI 144/1995).

the instrument shall not be deemed to be duly stamped.[64] Failure to conform with this provision renders the transferee or lessee liable to a fine not exceeding €635 on summary conviction.[65] These provisions will apply to any instrument executed after 31 August 1995 and SDCA 1999, s 12 shall have no effect as to instruments executed after this date.[66] Further details on the regulations for PD stamping are to be found in **Chapter 13** (see **Appendix 3** for SI 144/1995 and **Appendix 2** for relevant PD Form).

Creation of leaseholds in practice

[6.45] The grant of a lease creates an interest in land which is subject to an interest (albeit sometimes notional) reserved in favour of the lessor. As the lessor retains an interest in the land, the lease usually contains covenants by the lessee to ensure that this interest is protected. If the lessee breaches one of these covenants, or fails to discharge the rent or breaches any other term of the lease, the landlord has to be in a position to enforce the lease in a court of law. The landlord can produce a counterpart in court which will be regarded as equivalent proof of the original lease. If no counterpart existed, or it has been lost, destroyed or mislaid, a copy of the original lease or counterpart is sufficient evidence of the contents of the lease and proceedings against the lessee or his assignee.[67] Where a formal lease has to be entered into between the parties, it is usually executed in duplicate and first executed by the lessee. Both instruments are stampable, the original lease with the *ad valorem* duty payable on it and the counterpart with €12.50 and impressed with a counterpart dye, the original lease being retained by the lessee and the counterpart being retained by the lessor.[68]

Accountable person

[6.46] On the grant of a lease, the lessee is the accountable person for the duty payable on the lease and duplicate or counterpart. Where a person would have been accountable if alive, their personal representative shall be deemed to be the accountable person.[69] If the instrument operates or is deemed to operate as a voluntary disposition *inter vivos* under the provisions of SDCA 1999, s 54, both parties to such instrument are accountable persons.[70]

Duty in particular cases

[6.47]

(a) *Service charges*: the premises which are the subject of the lease may form part of a development, larger building or other area which has services or common areas shared with other tenants. The landlord will usually take on the

64 SDCA 1999, s 12.

65 SDCA 1999, s 12.

66 SDCA 1999, s 12.

67 Deasy's Act, s 23.

68 For further discussion on this topic see Wylie *Irish Landlord and Tenant Law* (2edn, Butterworths, 1998.

69 SA 1891, s 122, as amended SDCA 1999, s 1(1)(d).

70 SDCA 1999, s 1.

responsibility of maintaining such common areas, repairing and cleaning the building as a whole and insuring the premises, and, in turn, will recover his costs by way of service charges levied on the tenant under the terms of the lease. The service charges may sometimes be included in the reddendum (the clause in a lease which charges the rent payable and the time the rent is payable) and be recoverable as if they were rent, which previously rendered them liable to duty.[71] In *Property Holding Co v Clark*,[72] Evershed LJ in holding that payments for the use of services and furniture were rent stated:

> the question in each case is to determine what in substance is the subject matter of the tenancy granted to the tenant by contract. Prima facie rent is monetary compensation payable by the tenant in consideration of the grant, howsoever it be described or allocated.

Differentiating between rents and service charges it was stated '.... in that no element of the premise's rent is attributable to the cost of providing such services'.[73]

Accordingly, once the rent and service charges can be clearly differentiated only the rent is liable to *ad valorem* duty. However, where a single sum is payable on foot of a lease covering both rent and service charges, the total sum shall be chargeable under the lease head;

(b) *Penal rent or a lease in consideration of surrender of a lease*: An additional rent may be reserved in favour of the lessor which is incurred by the lessee in the event of a breach of any of the lessee's covenants. This is known as a penal rent. For example, in *Pollitt v Forest*[74] it was held that a penal rent was reserved if the tenant sold hay or manure off the property in breach of the lease. The parties to a lease may agree that in consideration of the surrender of an original lease, a new lease in the same property shall be granted; for example, the tenant may be willing to surrender the original lease in consideration of a grant of a new lease for a longer duration. Where a lease reserves or agrees to be reserved or make payable any penal rent or increase in rent of a penal nature, or is made in consideration of the surrender or abandonment of an existing lease, relating to the same subject matter, then the penal rent or the consideration for the surrender shall not be chargeable to duty.[75]

Consanguinity relief

[6.48] Duty charged under the lease head on premiums is charged at the equivalent rate as under the conveyance on sale head. No consanguinity relief is available under the lease head on premiums, so that the full rate of duty is payable on such premiums even though the parties may be related.

---

71 *Cox v Harper* [1910] 1 Ch 480.

72 *Property Holding Co v Clark* [1948] 1 KB 630.

73 Law Society/RICS Working Party.

74 *Pollitt v Forest* (1848) 11 QB 962.

75 SDCA 1999, s 52(1).

Lease stampable more than once

[6.49] A lease may demise several properties to different lessees and as such would be liable to separate duties.[76] If the lease contains an option for the tenant to purchase the property, then it should only be stampable in respect of the lease.[77] However, if the option contained in the lease refers to other properties, this may be stampable.[78]

Guarantee of rent

[6.50] A guarantee for a payment of rent reserved under a lease is not stampable, see *Price v Thomas.*[79]

Leases delivered as escrow

[6.51] A lease and counterpart may be placed in escrow. Exposure to stamp duty arises at the time of execution of an instrument. The date of execution is the date the deed becomes effective. Delivery of a deed into escrow means that there is a condition outstanding on the deed and delivery is incomplete. Delivery of an instrument in escrow means that the deed is ineffective and therefore not fully executed. The leases are deemed to commence on the date the escrow takes effect, that is the date the conditions of the escrow are satisfied, and no other date.[80] Denning MR stated in *Wm Cory and Sons Ltd v IRC*[81] 'it only becomes a deed when the conditions are fulfilled.'

The grant of a lease in conjunction or in connection with the contract for the building of a dwellinghouse or apartment

[6.52] The grant of a lease as part of an arrangement involving a dwellinghouse or apartment which has been built or is being built or is to be built on the lands, where they do not qualify for a floor area certificate, is liable to stamp duty.[82] SDCA 1999, s 53 applies stamp duty to transactions where there is a site purchase combined with a building agreement. The site purchase and the building agreement must be connected in some way. Revenue has indicated that this will be a question of fact depending on the circumstances of each case. Factors taken into consideration are the relationship between the vendor and the builder and also whether the building works were started prior to the execution of the lease.

[6.53] SDCA 1999, s 53(3) provides that where the construction has commenced prior to the execution of the lease, the two contracts will be deemed to be connected. However, Revenue Commissioners Stamp Duty Work Manual and Practices, p 17 indicates that if it can be shown that there is no connection between the lease of the land and the employment of the builder, then stamp duty will be charged on the cost of the site plus

---

76 *Doe D Copley v Day* [1811] 13 East 241.

77 *Worthington v Warrington* [1848] 5 CB 635.

78 *Lovelock v Franklyn* [1846] 8 QB 371.

79 *Price v Thomas* (1831) 2 Bead 218.

80 *Alan Estates Ltd v WG Stores Ltd* [1981] 3 All ER 48.

81 *Wm Cory and Sons Ltd v IRC* [1964] 3 All ER 66 at 74.

82 SDCA 1999, s 53 – see para **[13.55]**.

any works completed at the date of the execution of the lease. If the building has not commenced for two years after the stamping of the instrument, the stamp duty on the construction portion of the transaction can be refunded. There is a time limit of three years from the date of stamping of the instrument to make a claim for repayment. If the site cost and construction cost is unascertainable, Revenue may stamp the instrument using a multiple of between 5 and 10 times the open market value of the site. If stamp duty has been overcharged by the application of this valuation, stamp duty may be reclaimed within three years of the stamping of the instrument.

Covenants by the lessee for improvements or additions

[6.54] Unless provided in the provisions set out in the last paragraph, a lease granted where the consideration is chargeable with *ad valorem* duty, and further consideration consists of:

(a) the lessee having previously made or covenanting to make any substantial improvement or addition to the property demised to him; or

(b) to any covenant relating to the matter of the lease;

then the lease shall not be chargeable in respect of such further consideration.[83] This exemption does not apply where such a covenant would be chargeable to *ad valorem* duty if contained in a separate deed. The lease containing such a covenant shall be charged to duty in respect of the further consideration.[84]

***Lease operating or deemed to operate as a voluntary disposition* inter vivos**

[6.55] Where a lease has the effect of conferring a substantial benefit on the lessees, whether it be a voluntary disposition *inter vivos* or be deemed as such, the lease is chargeable to duty on the rent (if any) chargeable under the lease, together with a premium that would have been paid if the lease had not operated as a voluntary disposition *inter vivos*. Stamp duty is assessed on the capital value of the 'substantial benefit' conferred on the lessee.

[6.56] Any lease which is not executed in good faith and for valuable consideration shall be deemed to operate as a voluntary disposition *inter vivos*. Where the Revenue Commissioners are of the opinion that, due to the inadequacy of the consideration or other circumstances, the lease confers a substantial benefit on the lessee, then the consideration passing shall be deemed not to be valuable consideration. When a lease is deemed to operate as a voluntary disposition *inter vivos*, duty is charged on a notional capital payment (premium) equal to the minimum amount or value (given the rent payable under the lease) that would be paid if the lease would not operate as a voluntary disposition *inter vivos*.[85]

---

[83] SDCA 1999, s 51(2).

[84] SDCA 1999, s 52(3).

[85] SDCA 1999, s 54.

Example 6.55.1

Mrs Greene lets her shop premises to her brother, Mr Browne, for a term of 35 years subject to a rent of €1,000 per annum.

The market value rental of the premises is €4,900 and the premium payable on the open market based on the rent of €1,000 passing is €32,000. Stamp duty liability is as follows:

	€
Rental (€1,000 at 1%)	10
Premium (€32,000 at 3%)	960
Total liability	970

[6.57] No consanguinity relief is available as this does not apply under the lease head. It is arguable that, as no finance certificate has been inserted in the lease, stamp duty could be charged at 9 per cent, rather than 3 per cent. Where a lease operates, or is deemed to operate, as a voluntary disposition *inter vivos*, such facts surrounding the execution of the instrument, including a statement of value as to the minimum amount of value necessary so that the lease would not operate as a voluntary disposition *inter vivos*, should be brought to the attention of the Revenue Commissioners in a statement delivered pursuant to SDCA 1999, s 8(2). Any person who executes such an instrument and fails to comply with these requirements shall, for the purposes of s 3, be presumed to have acted negligently, until the contrary is proven.[86] To be duly stamped, the lease must be adjudicated upon by the Revenue Commissioners, in the same manner as applicable to a conveyance or transfer operating as a voluntary disposition *inter vivos*.[87]

Deeds of enlargement

[6.58] A lessee may have a right under statute to enlarge their leasehold interest into a freehold. The lease when created must have been for more than 300 years in duration, with not less than 200 years to run, where no rent was originally reserved, or is of no monetary value, or, if substantial, was either waived by agreement between the parties or ceased to be payable by lapse of time.[88]

[6.59] The deed of enlargement could be used as an effective means of minimising the liability to stamp duty by creating a lease and subsequently enlarging it into a freehold avoiding stamp duty under the conveyance on sale head. The enlargement of an interest in land pursuant to the Conveyancing Act 1881, s 65(2) is chargeable to duty as a conveyance or transfer of land where the consideration is equal to the value of the land passing without regard to the leasehold interest created, provided that the deed of declaration giving effect to the enlargement is executed within six years of the original deed creating the instrument.[89] If such a declaration by deed pursuant to the Conveyancing Act 1881 is to be used to enlarge a freehold interest, it should be executed

---

[86] SDCA 1999, s 8(5).

[87] SDCA 1999, s 54(3) – see **Chapter 13**.

[88] Conveyancing Act 1881, s 65, for further discussion see Wylie, *Irish Landlord and Tenant Law* (2nd edn, Butterworths, 1998).

[89] SDCA 1999, s 35(1).

after a period of six years has expired from the date of the original instrument creating the term.

Surrender of leases

[6.60] A deed of surrender, not being an instrument chargeable under the conveyance on sale head, is chargeable with a fixed duty of €12.50. Even if there is consideration passing on the surrender, once the instrument operates as a surrender of the premises only, stamp duty is chargeable with €12.50 and not the *ad valorem* rate.

Exemptions under the lease head

[6.61] The lease of any apartment or dwellinghouse (or part thereof) for any indefinite term or a term not exceeding 35 years where the rent does not exceed €19,050 per annum is exempt.

Example 6.60.1

Mrs Greene lets her property in Dublin by way of letting agreement for a term of 12 months certain at a rent of €15,000 per annum. No stamp duty is payable on this letting due to the rent payable. If the rent payable under the lease was €25,000 per annum, stamp duty would be payable as follows:

	€
Original letting agreement	250
Counterpart thereof	12.50
Total	262.50

[6.62] *Premium on leases*: Where the amount payable by premium on a commercial premises does not exceed €10,000 or €127,000 on a residential property and the lease contains the necessary certificates, the premium is exempt from stamp duty. If the necessary finance certificate is not inserted in the lease, then the premium passing shall be subject to stamp duty at a rate of 9 per cent.

[6.63] *The grant of lease in consideration of a surrender or abandonment of any existing lease*: Where a lease or agreement for lease is created in consideration of the surrender or abandonment of any existing lease, tack or agreement relating to the same property, duty is not chargeable on the consideration attributable to the surrender.[90]

[6.64] *Foreign immovable property*: Stamp duty is not chargeable on a lease of any immovable property situate outside this State. If the lease, however, does relate to immovable property, or any right over or interest in such property situate in this State or any stock or marketable security of a company having registered in this State, then such instruments shall be chargeable to duty.[91]

[6.65] *Commercial woodlands*: There is an exemption for the lease of commercial woodlands provided the instrument contains a certificate stating that there are trees growing on a substantial part of the lands. Trees in this regard are 'woodlands managed

---

[90] SDCA 1999, s 52(1).

[91] SDCA 1999, s 98.

on a commercial basis and with a view to the realisation of profits'. Exemption from stamp duty applies in respect of part of the consideration for the lease which represents the value of the trees growing on the land.[92]

[6.66] *Duty payable solely out of Oireachtas funds*: Where the duty chargeable on the instrument would be payable solely out of Oireachtas funds, then no duty shall be chargeable on such instruments.[93]

[6.67] *Exemptions for certain dwellings*: No stamp duty is payable on any deed, agreement or instrument which creates a tenancy for a month or a period of less than a month of a dwelling mentioned in the Housing Act 1966, s 58(3).[94]

[6.68] *Licence – Petroleum and Other Mineral Development Act 1960*: Stamp duty is not chargeable on a licence granted under the Petroleum and Other Mineral Development Act 1960 ss 8, 9 or 19, nor on a lease granted under, s 13 or sale or lease of any right therein.[95]

[6.69] *Leases to charities*: Stamp duty shall not be charged on any lease of land made or agreed to be made for charitable purposes in this State or Northern Ireland to a body or persons established for charitable purposes only or to the trustee or trust so established.

[6.70] *Leases to Courts Services*: The FA 2006 inserted s 99A into the SDCA 1999. The purpose of this new section is to exempt from stamp duty any instrument under which any land, easement, way-leave, etc, is acquired by the Courts Service.

Reliefs applying to instruments chargeable under the lease head

[6.71] *New houses and flats*: The stamp duty exemption granted to owner-occupiers on new smaller properties under SDCA 1999, s 91A also applies to premiums under the lease head.[96]

[6.72] *Lease of a house by a local authority*: A lease of a house by a local authority pursuant to the Housing Act 1966, or a lease of a house by a society registered under the Industrial and Providential Society Acts 1893–1966 made in accordance with a scheme for the provision of houses for its members, to a member or to such member and the spouse of the member, shall be exempt from stamp duty.[97] To qualify, the instrument has to be adjudicated upon by the Revenue Commissioners.[98]

[6.73] *Shared ownership leases*: Stamp duty is not chargeable under share-ownership lease or on an instrument by the lessee of a share-ownership lease exercising the right to purchase the interest of the lessor of the demised house under the Housing (Miscellaneous Provisions) Act 1992, s 2(1)(c).[99]

---

92 SDCA 1999, s 95.

93 SDCA 1999, s 111.

94 Housing Act 1966, s 50.

95 SDCA 1999, s 104.

96 For a further discussion on this see **Chapter 11**.

97 SDCA 1999, s 93.

98 For a further discussion on this see **Chapter 11**.

99 SDCA 1999, s 103.

[6.74] *Miscellaneous*: SA 1891, s 77(3) originally limited the duty payable on a lease for lives (with no more than three lives, or a lease for a term certain determinable with lives not exceeding three) or a lease for a term absolute where the period did not exceed twenty-one years granted by an ecclesiastical corporation or sole, to one pound and seventy five pence only. SA 1891, s 77(4) further limited the duty payable on a lease for a definite term exceeding 35 years by Trinity College (Dublin) Leasing and Perpetuity Act 1851, to that of a lease for a definite term not exceeding 35 years. Both of these provisions were repealed by FA 1998, s 125, Sch 8.

Chapter 7

Transactions by Capital Companies

Introduction

[7.01] Shares in listed companies are transferred using the Crest system. Transfers of shares in private companies are effected by a stock transfer form (Form SD4) as prescribed in the Stock Transfer Act 1963 (STA 1963). The stock transfer form is the instrument of transfer in respect of the sale of shares and thus is the stampable document. The STA 1963 provides that where shares in private companies are transferred, a standard stock transfer form can be executed by the seller only, whereas the transfers of shares of an unlimited company must be executed by the seller and buyer. Typically the transfer of shares in private companies is effected by means of a share purchase agreement and stock transfer form. A share purchase agreement transfers the beneficial interest in the shares to the purchaser with the benefit of warranties and indemnities. The buyer's title to the shares will be complete once the stock transfer form is executed and the buyer's name is entered into the register of the members of the company.

Charge to stamp duty

[7.02] The sale of shares in an Irish registered company for cash consideration is chargeable under the Conveyance or Transfer on sale of any stocks or marketable securities head of charge and will be liable to duty at a rate of 1 per cent. Marketable securities are securities which are capable of being sold on any stock market in the state.[1] Shares of a private company fall within the definition of stock, which is defined under SDCA 1999, s 1(1) as including any share in any stock or funds transferable at the Bank of England or at the Bank of Ireland and any share in the stock or funds of any foreign state or government, or in any capital stock or funded debt of any county council, corporation, company or society in the State, or of any foreign corporation, company or society.

[7.03] The acquisition of any stock or marketable securities of a company which is registered outside the State is exempt from stamp duty under SDCA 1999, s 88 unless it relates to:

(i) any immovable property situated in Ireland or any right or interest in such property; or

(ii) any stocks or marketable securities of a company which is registered in Ireland (except a company which is an investment undertaking within the meaning of TCA 1997, s 739B).

---

1 SDCA 1999 s1(1).

[7.04] The 'accountable person' in relation to the transfer of stocks or securities under SDCA 1999, s 2(4) is the buyer or transferee. As discussed in para **[7.01]** above, the chargeable instrument in relation to the transfer of shares is the stock transfer form. In the case of *Chesterfield Brewery Company v IRC*[2] the vendors agreed to sell their shares under a written agreement. No stock transfer form was executed; instead, the vendors executed a declaration of trust in favour of the purchasers. The courts found the declaration of trust to be a conveyance on sale as the intention of the parties was that the declaration of trust be the purchaser's only title to the shares. Under SDCA 1999, s 129 the registrar or person who maintains the register of members of a company is liable to a fine of €630 for registering a transfer that is not duly stamped. In addition to this the need to enter the buyer's name in the register of members of the target company in order to perfect title results in buyers insisting on a stock transfers on completion.

Alternative consideration

[7.05] Where a share-for-share exchange takes place, stamp duty is assessed on the market value of the shares issued as consideration under SDCA 1999, s 40(1). Alternatively, a share-for-share exchange that forms part of a reconstruction or amalgamation may qualify for relief under SDCA 1999, s 80. In the event that the acquiring party agrees to assume or discharge debts of the target company, stamp duty is charged on the amount of debts assumed or discharged under SDCA 1999, s 41. If the consideration provided for the transfer is less than the market value of the shares issued, the transfer will operate as a voluntary conveyance and will be chargeable under SDCA 1999, s 30.

[7.06] Earn outs are common practice in the purchase of shares. For stamp duty purposes (this differs from the treatment capital gains tax purposes), SDCA 1999, s 44 requires that, where the consideration for a transfer cannot be ascertained on the date of execution of the instrument, the transfer should be stamped at a fair value of the asset transferred. The general view is that, where an earn-out consideration is to be paid in an acquisition, it is necessary for the purchaser to have a professional valuation conducted in relation to the transferred property for stamping purposes and to pay stamp duty on that notional valuation. In contrast to the principal for capital gains tax purposes as established in *Marren v Ingles*[3] which requires a valuation of the earn out, SDCA 1999, s 44 requires a valuation of the transferred assets.

Sale of a business

[7.07] A business will either be sold as a company or the sale will be effected by way of a straight sale of assets. In respect of both methods, there are various commercial and tax reasons for structuring the purchase of a business as a share sale or an asset sale. The benefits of a share sale are as follows:

(a) avoidance of double taxation of the shareholders of the company on the extraction of the profits of an asset sale;

(b) avoidance of the costs of the liquidation of a company post-asset sale;

---

2 *Chesterfield Brewery Company v IRC* [1899] 2 QB 7.

3 *Marren v Ingles* [1980] STC 500.

(c) employees move with the company and any redundancy arrangements are avoided;

(d) lower transaction costs for the seller;

(e) stamp duty at a rate of 1 per cent of the market value of the shares; and

(f) base cost in the shares for the purchaser for a future sale of the company.

The benefits of an asset sale are as follows:

(a) opportunity for the seller to retain valuable assets;

(b) avoidance of hidden liabilities in the company for the purchaser;

(c) opportunity for selective acquisition of assets by the purchaser; and, finally

(d) the vendor gives limited warranties and indemnities, as the vendor retains the company.

In all situations, the decision to buy the company or the assets will depend on the facts of the case and, in particular, the nature of the business being purchased.

[7.08] SDCA 1999, s 31 was introduced to charge to stamp duty contracts transferring certain types of property. While this section operates to bring within the remit of stamp duty the transfer of a number of assets on the sale of a business, there are methods that can be employed to mitigate the charge to stamp duty on the sale of a business.

[7.09] SDCA 1999, s 31(1)(a) makes a contract of agreement for the sale of any equitable estate or interest in any property liable to the same *ad valorem* duty as if it were an actual conveyance on sale. SDCA 1999, 31(1)(b) makes an estate or interest in any property liable to the same *ad valorem* duty as if it were an actual conveyance of that property. The exceptions under this second leg are as follows:

(a) foreign immovable property;

(b) property situate in the State;

(c) goods, wares or merchandise;

(d) stock or marketable securities; and

(e) ships, vessels or aircraft.

The net effect of this section in relation to the sale of a business is that intangible property such as goodwill, cash in bank, benefits of contracts and book debts are brought within the charge to stamp duty.

Procedure for stamping

[7.10] When presenting an asset purchase agreement for stamping, it is necessary to also submit form ADJN 14, which apportions the sales proceeds to each category of asset. If this is not filed, the Revenue Commissioners will assess duty on the full purchase price. Such an agreement must be presented for stamping 30 days (in practice the Revenue Commissioners allow 44 days to pass before imposing interest and penalties) after its execution.

Goodwill

[7.11] Goodwill is a form of property that is capable of existing independently of a physical asset.[4] If goodwill is attached to property it will be transferred with that property unless specified otherwise. The exemption for the transfers of intellectual property under SDCA 1999, s 101 mentions goodwill, but this is restricted to the goodwill associated to the intellectual property. A contract for the sale of goodwill will be chargeable to stamp duty at *ad valorem* rates under SDCA 1999, s 31. The value of the goodwill is usually the difference between the net assets and the sale proceeds in respect of the sale of the business.

Cash in bank

[7.12] The Revenue Commissioners do not consider moneys to be held in a current account to be chargeable under SDCA 1999, s 31; moneys held on deposit account that are the subject of a contract for sale are so chargeable. Therefore, before the sale of a business, any moneys held on deposit should be transferred to a current account. See for more detail, paras **[4.34]** and **[5.19]**.

Benefit on contracts

[7.13] By virtue of the decision in *Western Abyssinian Mining Syndicate Ltd v IRC*[5] the assignment of the benefit of a contract for consideration on the sale of a business is liable to stamp duty under SDCA 1999, s 31. The possibility of novating the contract should be examined.[6]

Book debts

[7.14] A contract for the sale of book debts[7] is chargeable to stamp duty under SDCA 1999, s 31. Normally, a contract for the sale of a business provides that the book debts remain with the seller, but the purchaser shall act as the agent of the seller in the collection of these debts and use the proceeds to discharge the preclosing trade creditors and remit any surplus to the seller. By virtue of such a provision, the trade creditors and book debts remain with the seller hence reducing the consideration liable to stamp duty.

Tenant's fixtures

[7.15] Generally, fixtures are chattels which are attached to land and, as such, may be regarded as land and are stampable as if they were land. In contrast, chattels are capable of passing by delivery. Tenant's fixtures are classified as neither. Under *Lee v Gaskell*[8] tenant's fixtures are not considered land or chattels but choses in action. Where tenant's fixtures are affixed to property in a permanent manner (ie cannot be removed without causing substantial damage), a contract for the sale of same is chargeable to stamp duty under SDCA 1999, s 31.

---

4 See paras **[4.24]** and **[5.10]** ff.

5 *Western Abyssinian Mining Syndicate Ltd v IRC* [1898] 2 QB 507.

6 See paras **[4.33]** and **[5.13]**.

7 See paras **[5.16]**.

8 *Lee v Gaskell* [1876] 1 QB 700.

Intellectual property

[7.16] Transfers of intellectual property are no longer chargeable to stamp duty under SDCA 1999, s 101. The definition of intellectual property is very wide and incorporates, inter alia, patents, trademarks, designs, rights over designs and any goodwill associated with the intellectual property being transferred. It has been indicated that this definition under s 101 is not exhaustive.

Know how

[7.17] Know how is the specialised knowledge of a person or persons and under *Musker v English Electric Company Ltd*[9] and *John & E Sturge v Hessel*[10] is not considered to be property. These cases did not relate to stamp duty but the principles applied are widely viewed to apply to stamp duty. In applying this principle the agreements for the transfer of know how are not chargeable to stamp duty.

Chattels or assets

[7.18] The title of some assets and chattels can be passed by delivery as the ownership of the title to these is determined by who is physically in possession of the asset or chattel. As such, when selling a business, any assets or chattels that are capable of passing by delivery should be passed by delivery and the business transfer agreement should be drafted in such a manner as to ensure that it does not transfer the title to same. This can be done by ensuring that the agreement specifically states that the title of any assets that are capable of passing by delivery, are passed by delivery. Examples of assets that this can apply to are plant and machinery, stock or equipment.

Incorporation of a business

[7.19] Stamp duty is chargeable at *ad valorem* rates on the transfer of property to a company on the incorporation of a business. The same principles should be applied to mitigate the charge to stamp duty as dealt with above on the sale of a business. Where shares in the company are issued as consideration for the property, stamp duty will be chargeable on the transfer of the assets based on the market value of the shares issued by the company.[11] The Revenue Commissioners will determine the value of the shares by reference to the value of the property transferring.

[7.20] A company is required under company law to file a written agreement or, where there is no written agreement, a written memorandum of the terms of the agreement relating to the issue of shares for non-cash consideration. CA 1963, s 58(3) specifically deems any such contract or memorandum to be an instrument for the purposes of stamp duty. Therefore, the mitigating principles set out above, can only be used to a limited extent. Capital duty on the issue of shares has been abolished on transactions effected on or after 7 December 2005 and, as such, there will be no charge to capital duty in respect of the issue of shares on the incorporation of a business.

---

9 *Musker v English Electric Company Ltd* 41 TC 556.

10 *John & E Sturge v Hessel* [1975] STC 573.

11 SDCA 1999, s 40.

Share buy-backs

[7.21] CA 1990, Part XI allows Irish registered companies limited by guarantee or by shares to purchase their own shares out of the company's profits available for distribution. It is required, in the case of private companies, that the terms of the purchase set out in a written contract or, if there is no written agreement, a written memorandum setting out the terms, are passed by a special resolution of the members of the company. Section 209 of the Act sets out that once the shares are purchased by the company, they must be cancelled or held as treasury shares capable of being reissued within specific periods at certain prices. The company must file a return with the Companies Registration Office within 28 days of the purchase. The Revenue Commissioners do not deem this return to be a stampable instrument. The ability of a company to issue redeemable shares and to redeem such shares has been extended by Part XI of the CA 1990.

[7.22] The Revenue Commissioners Stamp Duty Work Manual and Practices states at page 41:

> The shares can be bought back on foot of a contract or share purchase agreement. If the shareholder and the company enter into an agreement and the shareholder simply hands over the share certificates to the company there is no need for a stock transfer form and no duty can be charged. The share purchase agreement is not chargeable to duty as it falls outside the scope to of, s 31, Stamp Duties Consolidation Act 1999.

If, however, a stock transfer form is executed, stamp duty will be charged on this instrument of transfer.

[7.23] The position is not the same in the UK where legislation has been introduced to deem the statutory return to the companies office a stampable instrument. In practice, the shareholders hand their share certificates back to the company and this is sufficient to ensure that no-one other than the company can claim title to the shares. Clearly, this is not an absolute method of transferring the legal title in the shares to the company but it appears to be sufficient especially in the case of shares that are cancelled post purchase.

[7.24] In the case of a subsidiary company purchasing shares in its holding company, it is insufficient to allow the transfer of the shares to rest on contract. A contract for the transfer of the shares only transfers the beneficial interest in the shares to the holding company. It is necessary under the CA 1963, s 81 to register the transfer of shares in a company by a written instrument. Where a subsidiary is purchasing shares in its holding company, it must be registered as the owner of the shares, thereby requiring a written instrument of transfer which will attract *ad valorem* stamp duty.

[7.25] It is also possible for a company to purchase and cancel its own shares to reduce its share capital. The procedure for this type of transaction is a the passing of a special resolution by the members of a company together with a High Court Order pursuant to the CA 1963, s 73. Under the CA 1963, s 205, the High Court may make 'such order as it sees fit', including the purchase by a company of shares belonging to one or more parties to the proceedings, or the transfer of shares of one party to the proceedings to another party to the proceedings. In the case where a company buys back its own shares, and a cancellation of these shares follows, no stamp duty will arise based on the reasoning above. However, where the High Court orders that one party purchase the shares of another, such an order will be liable to stamp duty under the decision in the case of *Sun Alliance Insurance Ltd v IRC.*[12]

Raising finance

[7.26] The issue of shares in a company, in the case of transactions effected on or after 7 December 2005, is no longer liable to capital duty. In the case of transactions made prior to this date, the issue of shares by a capital company that had its effective centre of management and control or its registered office in the State, gave rise to a charge to capital duty at a rate of 0.05 per cent on the value of the amount contributed in money or of the value of assets contributed.

[7.27] 'Loan capital' is defined under SDCA 1999, s 85(1) as any debenture stock, bonds or funded debt, by whatever name known, or any capital raised which is borrowed or has the character of borrowed money, whether in the form of stock or in any other form. SDCA 1999, s 85(2) exempts from stamp duty the transfer of loan capital meeting certain conditions. These conditions are as follows:

(a) it does not carry any rights on conversion into stocks or marketable securities (other than loan capital) of a company having its register in the State, or into loan capital carrying such rights;

(b) it does not carry rights of the same kind as shares in the capital of the company, including rights such as voting rights, a share in the profits or a share in the surplus on liquidation;

(c) it is redeemable within 30 years of the date of issue and not thereafter;

(d) it is issued for a price which is not less than 90 per cent of its nominal value; and

(e) it does not carry a right in respect of the repayment or interest related to certain movements in an index or indices specified in any instrument or other document relating to the loan capital.

Capital contributions are another common method of raising finance for companies. Such a contribution will not be liable to capital duty where the person making the capital contribution does not receive any rights over shares, right to repayment, or any other rights associated with the ownership of shares, such as voting rights, rights to dividends or assets on a winding up.

Distributions by companies

[7.28] There are two main methods by which a company makes distributions to its shareholders – in cash by way of dividends and by distributions *in specie* (ie distributions of the assets of the company to its shareholders). Distributions of cash by way of dividend are not liable to stamp duty.

---

12 *Sun Alliance Insurance Ltd v IRC* [1972] Ch 133.

[7.29] A distribution of assets by a company to a shareholder, where the company is not in liquidation and there is no consideration provided by the shareholders, is treated as a voluntary disposition and as such is chargeable to *ad valorem* stamp duty under SDCA 1999, s 30. Where the transfer of assets is made in satisfaction of a cash dividend the distribution will be chargeable as a satisfaction of a debt under SDCA 1999, s 41 or as a voluntary disposition under SDCA 1999, s 30. The position is different where a company is in voluntary or compulsory liquidation. In either of these types of liquidation the company is no longer the beneficial owner of the assets of the company. In each of *Re Oriental Inland Steam Company, ex-parte Schinde Railway Company*[13] and *Ayerst v C & K (Construction) Ltd*[14] [1975] 2 All ER 537 the legal title to the assets remains with the company but the assets are held for the benefit of the creditors of the company as a whole. The decision in *Re Strathblaine Estates Ltd*[15] provides that, once the liabilities to creditors of the company have been discharged, the beneficial interest in the remaining assets vests in the shareholders. As such, any distribution to the shareholders by the liquidator is not chargeable to stamp duty. The Revenue Commissioners state in the Stamp Duty Work Manual and Practices that:

> … a transfer by the liquidator of a company of property which forms part of the assets of the company to the persons who were the shareholders in satisfaction of their rights on a winding-up is not a transfer on sale or a transfer operating as a voluntary disposition. As the transfer is not on a sale or does not operate as a voluntary disposition, it is not liable for PD stamping.

[7.30] In the case of transfers of immovable property in the State or of stocks or marketable securities of a company having its register in the State, a certificate should be included in the instrument of transfer certifying that the instrument is a conveyance or transfer on any occasion not being a sale or mortgage. In the event that this certificate is not included in the instrument of transfer, the instrument will be liable to a fixed duty of €12.50. There are situations in which a distribution *in specie* will give rise to a charge to stamp duty and the charge is under SDCA 1999, s 41. These situations are: where the assets being distributed are subject to a mortgage or charge; where the shareholders assume a debt of the company to a third party; or where the shareholders forgive a debt of the company owed to them in consideration of the distribution.

[7.31] It is worth noting that the availability of relief under SDCA 1999, s 79 can be affected where a subsidiary has gone into liquidation. Where a company holds shares in another company, it ceases to be the beneficial owner of these shares on the commencement of a winding-up. This can interrupt the 90 per cent relationship between a transferor and transferee as is the requirement for relief under SDCA 1999, s 79.

---

13 *Re Oriental Inland Steam Company, ex-parte Schinde Railway Company* [1874] 9 Ch App 557.

14 *Ayerst v C & K (Construction) Ltd* [1975] 2 All ER 537.

15 *Re Strathblaine Estates Ltd* [1948] 1 All ER 162.

Companies' capital duty

Introduction

[7.32] FA 2006 has abolished the charge to capital duty in respect of transactions effected on or after 7 December 2005. Capital duty is still covered in this text as transactions effected before 7 December 2005 were still liable to capital duty.

The charge to capital duty that was imposed was as a direct result of Ireland's membership of the EC and was the first step taken in the harmonisation of taxes relating to companies in the community. Pursuant to Council Directives 69/335/EEC, 73/79/EEC and 73/80/EEC, which were subsequently enacted in Ireland in FA 1973 the object of the measure was to ensure that the indirect taxes charged on the raising of capital in each Member State of the EEC would be imposed at the same rate, in order to ensure the free movement of capital. Prior to its enactment in Ireland, stamp duty was charged on the nominal share capital value as opposed to the amount actually being subscribed. The implementation of the directive in Ireland resulted in capital duty being charged on the actual contribution made to the capital of the company.

Pre-1973

[7.33] Stamp duty was charged based on the value of the nominal capital of a limited company on incorporation, or on any increase in the nominal value of that share capital at the same rate.[16] Duty was also charged in respect of the amounts contributed by a limited partner to limited partnerships.[17] The stamp duty was charged at a rate of 25p per £100 or part thereof, that is .25 per cent on the nominal capital value, or on the assets contributed in the case of a partnership. This stamp duty was abolished with effect from 1 January 1973; the new regime came into effect on 4 August 1973. Transitional provisions were provided for, for the intervening period and prior to the enactment of FA 2006, and these are discussed more fully below.

Post-1973

[7.34] In this context, stamp duty payable was commonly referred to as capital duty and will be referred to as such in this text. Capital duty was charged on the value of the consideration, or on the assets, contributed to a capital company in return for the issue of shares either on the incorporation of the company, or on the further increase of issued share capital in the company.

[7.35] A 'capital company' as defined in SDCA 1999, s 114 is:

(a) a company incorporated with limited liability, or a limited partnership formed under the law of the State or a company or partnership which is incorporated or formed in any other Member State and which, under the law of that State, corresponds to any such company or partnership; or

(b) any other company, firm, association or legal person the shares in whose capital or assets can be dealt in on a stock exchange; or

---

16 SA 1891, ss 112-113.

17 Limited Partnership Act 1907, s 11.

(c) any other company, firm, association or legal person operating for profit whose members have a right to dispose of their shares to third parties without prior authorisation and are responsible for the debts of the company, firm, association or legal person only to the extent of their shares.

This definition of a capital company includes both public and private limited liability companies, limited partnerships or any other corresponding company or partnership as formed under Member State law. It includes companies whose shares can be dealt in any stock exchange and is not restricted to a stock exchange in a Member State. It therefore does not cover non-EU unquoted companies. It was a question for the national authorities as to whether an entity came within the definition of capital company under the European legislation.[18]

[7.36] The term 'Member State' means: 'a Member State of the European Community'.[19] Currently the following countries qualify as Member States: United Kingdom, France, Belgium, Denmark, Germany, Holland, Italy, Luxembourg, the Republic of Ireland, Greece, Spain, Austria, Portugal, Sweden, Finland, Slovenia, Poland, Cyprus, Hungary, Slovakia, Latvia, Estonia, Lithuania and the Czech Republic. The following territories do not qualify as Member States: the Isle of Man, the Channel Islands and Gibraltar.

[7.37] Subparagraph B covers those entities whose shares can be dealt with on the stock exchange. The liability of the company involved will depend greatly on the rules of the relevant stock exchange. In Ireland or the United Kingdom an unlimited liability company cannot be traded on the Stock Exchange. However, the Irish legislation does not restrict this definition to a stock exchange being situate in a Member State.

[7.38] Subparagraph C extends the definition of capital company to a legal entity operating for profits whose members' liability is limited to the extent of their shares, and who have a right to dispose of the shares to third parties without prior authorisation. This includes an ordinary private limited company and a company limited by guarantee, whether having share capital or not. There is no definition or explanation given for the words 'without prior authorisation' in the legislation nor in Directive 69/335/EEC. This term may have been relevant in determining whether a third country limited liability company which intended to move its effective centre of management to Ireland would constitute a capital company. It would appear, however, that the words should have been interpreted literally. The crucial requirement was to determine that the shares could have been transferred subject to verification or verification had to be obtained prior to the transfer of shares.

[7.39] The question arose as to whether pre-emption rights constituted prior authorisation. Pre-emption rights occur where, on the disposal of existing shares by one member, these shares must first be offered to the other shareholders and it is only in the event that none of the other shareholders wish to subscribe that the shares may be sold to

---

18 *Amro Aaneden Fonds v Inspecteur der Registratie en Successie* [1989] 1 CMLR 789, [1987] ECR 4453.

19 SDCA 1999, s 114.

outsiders. Where pre-emption rights existed, whether by contractual agreement or otherwise, an argument might have run that this constituted prior authorisation and, therefore, such entities would fall outside the scope of the provision. It is submitted that the better view is that pre-emption rights did not constitute prior authorisation since all that happens is the sale must follow a certain procedure as to who should first be offered the shares for sale, but at no stage is the consent of the other members required in order to effect the transfer. It is thought that the words 'without prior authorisation' refer to restrictions in the articles of association or constitutional documents of a company rather than mere contractual restrictions.

[7.40] If the former, the company would have qualified as a capital company.[20] For example, a member of a company may have had a right to transfer the shares without prior consent but the directors may have had an absolute discretion as to whether they should register any such transfer of shares (provision similar to CA 1963, Reg 3, Pt 2 Table A). If the latter, then this did not qualify as a capital company. Thus, in the case of a non-EU limited liability company, where the transfer, as distinct from the registration, of such transfer requires prior board approval, then it would appear not to have qualified as a capital company. This raised an interesting point in respect of pre-emption rights. While ordinarily pre-emption rights by their nature would not have come within 'without prior authorisation', in certain circumstances the directors may have had an unfettered discretion as to whether or not they would consent to the proposed transfer as it may have been 'detrimental' to the interest of the company at large. These provisions would be more usual in the case of an agreement between the parties to the company or firm or association and may be incorporated in its constitution. These could have had the affect of deeming the entity to be a non-capital company.

Charge of capital duty

[7.41] SDCA 1999 defined particulars of transactions which gave rise to a charge to capital duty on the contribution of assets to a company in return for the issued shares in that company. The details details of these transactions are set out in paras **[7.42]**–**[7.55]**.

SDCA 1999, s 116(1)(a)

[7.42] SDCA 1999, s 116(1)(a) pertains to the formation of a capital company. This charged all companies incorporated with limited liability pursuant to CAs 1963–1994, or the registration of a limited partnership pursuant to the Limited Partnership Act 1907. The capital duty had to be discharged before a certificate of incorporation would issue.

SDCA 1999, s 116(1)(b)

[7.43] The conversion into a capital company of a company, firm, association or legal person which is not a capital company is dealt with in SDCA 1999, s 116(1)(b). An unlimited company can be converted into a company limited by shares or guarantee or both.[21] Where such conversion takes place, this constitutes the formation of a capital company and capital duty would have been payable. The alteration of the status of a

20 SDCA 1999, s 114(1).

21 CA 1963, s 20, amended by CA 1983, s 53.

capital company was not chargeable since capital duty would have already been paid on the original formation. For example, a company limited by guarantee converting into a company limited by shares was not chargeable on conversion. Neither would a limited company becoming an unlimited company have been chargeable, since the unlimited company was not a capital company.

SDCA 1999, s 116(1)(c)

[7.44] SDCA 1999, s 116(1)(c) dealt with the increase in the capital of a capital company by the contributions of assets of any kind other than an increase of capital through capitalisation of profits or of reserves, whether temporary or permanent reserves, but including the conversion of loan stock of a capital company into share capital. The term 'increase' was considered in *Cambridge Petroleum Royalties Ltd v IRC*[22] by Nourse J. It means the addition of something to, and not the substitution of something for something else. In this case, shares had been allotted in a company, and were partly paid up. A further call was made on those shares after the enactment of the capital duty legislation and the question arose as to whether this is further chargeable with capital duty as a contribution of further assets to the capital company. The court held against this contention by the Inland Revenue Commissioners in finding that the call was merely the substitution of one form of capital for another; ie cash for the right to make the call.

[7.45] Chargeable increase concerns the issued share capital of a company and not the nominal share capital of the company. Excluded from this subsection was the increase in capital through the capitalisation of profits or reserves, for example, bonus issues. The issue of bonus shares allows a company to distribute profits by increasing the nominal amount of the issued share capital, but does not involve the raising of further funds, or the contribution of assets from outside the company, and therefore does not come within the charge to capital duty.

[7.46] A rights issues does involve the further contribution of assets to a company as the rights issue raises further funds. The shares are usually offered to the existing shareholders in the company on more favourable terms than if offered to the public so that a certain portion of the rights issue could be deemed to be a bonus issue. Accordingly a bonus portion of the rights issue would not have been liable to capital duty. Returns as to allotments must be made to the Registrar of Companies in respect of all issues of share capital, whether they are bonus issues, rights issues or ordinary issues.[23]

[7.47] The issue of loan stock, debenture stock, and convertible loan stock did not give rise to a charge to capital duty, as this was not the contribution of assets which increased the capital. The charge to capital duty only arose when the loan stock was converted into share capital. The loan may not necessarily need to be repaid. The stockholder may have had a right to elect to take shares on maturity of the loan stock rather than the repayment of the loan, or be entitled to participate in surplus assets on winding up or liquidation.

---

[22] *Cambridge Petroleum Royalties Ltd v IRC* [1982] STC 325.

[23] CA 1963, s 58 amended by CA 1982, s 19.

The charge to capital duty arose once the loan ceased to be repayable. The issuing of an interest-free loan to a company was an increase in the assets of that company and the amount of the interest saved was chargeable to duty.[24]

[7.48] Doubts were expressed as to whether or not the issue of shares in a capital company in satisfaction of a debt owed by the company could have constituted a chargeable transaction. The argument was that the repayment of the debt by the issue of share capital of the company did not, in effect, contribute to any further assets of the company. It is clear, however, that this argument was untenable. The transaction effectively transfered an asset, namely that of the debt itself, to the company. Accordingly, the UK legislative provisions were repealed to avoid any doubt, and in this jurisdiction in practice the Revenue Commissioners charged such a transaction. In *Deltakabel BV v Staatssecretaris Van Financien*[25] the court held that where a shareholder waives a debt owed to him by the company, this constitutes an increase in the capital of the company and is chargeable to duty since it helps strengthen the economic potential of the company. And in *Waldrick Siegen Werkzeugmaschinen Gmbh v Finanzamt (tax office) Hagen*[26] an agreement whereby the shareholder took over the losses of a company in exchange for the future profits of that company was held to be an increase in the capital of the company and liable to duty.

SDCA 1999, s 116(1)(d)

[7.49] SDCA 1999, s 116(1)(d) deals with an increase in the assets of a capital company by the contribution of assets of any kind in consideration, not of shares in the capital or assets of the company, but of rights of the same kind as those of the member of the company, such as voting rights, a share in the profits or a share in the surplus upon liquidation.

[7.50] As we have already seen, limited partnerships constitute capital companies. Under limited liability partnership law, partners may play either an active or inactive role in the partnership.[27] The contribution by a limited partner of assets into a limited partnership may have been liable to capital duty. This means that, for example, an 'investor' partner in a limited partnership may have contributed capital in return for a percentage in voting rights or a share of profits in the partnership. which would be liable to capital duty.

SDCA 1999, s 116(1)(e)

[7.51] The transfer from a third country to the State of the effective centre of management of a capital company whose registered office is in the third country is covered in SDCA 1999, s 116(1)(e). Foreign companies are attracted to Ireland due to the availability here of tax incentives and concessions such as our low corporation tax

24 *Trave Schiffahrts-Gesellschaft GmbH & Co KG v Finanzamt Kiel* [1992] 3 CMLR 777 as followed in *A/S Richard Frederiksen v Skatteministeriet* [1996] 3 CMLR 784.

25 *Deltakabel BV v Staatssecretaris Van Financien* [1993] 1 CMLR 116.

26 *Waldrick Siegen Werkzeugmaschinen Gmbh v Finanzamt (tax office) Hagen* [1991] 2 CMLR 84.

27 Limited Partnership Act 1907.

rate, but to qualify the company must either be resident or incorporated in Ireland. To avail of these concessions, the third country capital company had to transfer its effective centre of management to Ireland and in doing so would have been liable to stamp duty on the net value of the assets of the company. This provision had the effect of foreign multinationals incorporating Irish subsidiary companies to avail of the tax incentives and concessions available, rather than transferring the effective centre of management, which would have given rise to a far more substantial charge to capital duty. The question arises as to what constitutes the effective centre of management of a capital company. The term itself is not defined in the SDCA 1999 and, in practice, no distinction is drawn between this phrase and the residence test of 'central management and control'. Its place of incorporation is of some influence but is in no way conclusive. The overriding factor would appear to be the location of the exercise of control plus, for example, the location of board meetings, annual general meetings, and the location of official company documentation, including the seal amongst other items.

[7.52] Lord Loreburns, in discussing the residence of a company, felt that the courts should examine all the evidence and should attempt to ascertain 'where the central management and control actually abides'.[28] The difficulty, of course, is that a company may have two or more effective centres of control.[29] Control is where the real decision in directing authority effecting the company is taken and not merely where the directors hold their meetings.[30] When examining the company, the courts look at the factors governing the management and control of the company, which must be present in the jurisdiction to prove residence,[31] but it can be possible that a company may be resident in two countries.[32] In *John Hood & Co Ltd v Magee*[33] the company was held to be controlled by the shareholders in general meeting. The fact that a company's constitution contains a stipulation that the company is managed only from a specific jurisdiction is not conclusive evidence as to its residence.[34] A question arises as to the relationship between parent and subsidiary companies. In *Untelrab Ltd v McGregor*[35] a subsidiary incorporated in the Channel Islands took 'instruction' from its parent company in London, to the extent that resolutions for the subsidiary were, in fact, drafted in London and forwarded to the Channel Islands for action. A question arose as to where the effective centre of management of the subsidiary was located. The Special Commissioners held that the subsidiary was effectively located in the Channel Islands, despite the actions of the parent company. The case appears specific to the constitutional relationship between the United Kingdom and the Channel Islands (and presumably other offshore locations for the United Kingdom) and seems dubious in terms of an Irish court.[36]

---

28 *De Beers Consolidated Mines v Howe* [1906] AC 455, 5 TC 198.

29 *Union Corporation v CIR* [1953] AC 482, *Swedish Central Railway Co v Thompson* 9 TC 342.

30 *The American Thread Co v Joyce* 6 ITC 163, *Calcutta Jute Co Ltd v Nicholson* ITC 83.

31 *Union Corporation v CIR* [1953] AC 482.

32 *Swedish Central Railway Co v Thompson* 9 TC 342.

33 *John Hood & Co Ltd v Magee* [1918] 2 IR 34.

34 *Unit Construction Ltd v Bullock* [1960] AC 351.

35 *Untelrab Ltd v McGregor* [1996] STC (SCD) 1.

36 For further discussion see Feeney *Taxation of Companies 2006* (Tottel Publishing, 2006).

The Revenue Commissioners in their Companies Capital Duty Manual state:

> The effective centre of management is generally located where the day to day management of the company takes place. This usually coincides with the tax residence of the company.

SDCA 1999, s 116(1)(f)

[7.53] SDCA 1999, s 116(1)(f) relates to the transfer from a third country to the State of a registered office of a capital company whose effective centre of management is in a third country. This provision would appear to have little effect. Few, if any, countries will permit the incorporation of a company whose registered office lies outside the jurisdiction of incorporation. Certainly under Irish law it is not possible to transfer the registered office of that company to another state.[37] Where an overseas company operated by way of a registered agent, the Revenue Commissioners took the view that there was no difference between a registered agent and a registered office.

SDCA 1999, s 116(1)(g)

[7.54] The transfer from a Member State to the State of the effective centre of management of a capital company which is not considered to be a capital company in the other Member State is covered by SDCA 1999, s 116(1)(g). This charged the intercommunity transfer of the effective centre of management of a company into a State where it was deemed to be a capital company, and did not constitute a capital company in the other Member State. If the complete harmonisation of company law had taken place in the EU, this section would have been obsolete.

SDCA 1999, s 116(1)(h)

[7.55] SDCA 1999, s 116(1)(h) deals with the transfer from a Member State to the State of the registered office of a capital company whose effective centre of management is in a third country and which is not considered to be a capital company in the Member State from which the registered office has been transferred. It provided for the intercommunity transfer of a registered office of a company into a Member State where, as a result of the transfer of its registered office there, it would have been deemed to be a capital company, where it was not previously considered to be a capital company in the original Member State. However, at present it is not feasible to have a registered office outside the Member State of incorporation. For example, under the Irish companies legislation, a company is required to maintain a registered office in this State. The most common transactions that gave rise to a charge to capital duty are those referred to in paragraphs (a) to (c) of SDCA 1999, s 116.

Rate of duty

[7.56] From 1 December 2004 to 7 December 2005 capital duty was charged at the rate of one half percent (0.5%) of the amount chargeable in accordance with SDCA 1999, s 118, rounded down to the nearest euro,[38] subject on the formation of a company to a

[37] CA 1963, s 113 substituted by C(A)A 1982, s 4.

[38] SDCA 1999, s 117(1).

minimum of €1.[39] Prior to 1 December 2004 the rate was one per cent (1%). FA 2006 has abolished the charge to capital duty in respect of transactions effected on or after 7 December 2005.

Amount on which capital duty was chargeable

[7.57] Previously stamp duty was charged on the nominal value of the company's share capital. However, in the cases of the transactions specified in paras **[7.42]**, **[7.43]**, **[7.44]** which concern the formation of a capital company, the increase in capital by the contributions of assets and an increase in the assets of a capital company by the contribution of assets, capital duty was chargeable on the amount of the 'actual value' of the assets of any kinds contributed by the members to the capital company at the date of the transaction. This was subject to the proviso that the amount on which the duty was chargeable shall not have been less than the nominal value of the shares (if any) allotted to the members of the capital company in connection with the transaction or belonging to the members of a capital company immediately after the transaction.[40] Therefore capital duty was chargeable on the greater of:

(a) the nominal value of the issued share capital; or

(b) the assets contributed at the date of the chargeable transaction.

[7.58] In calculating the actual value of the assets contributed or to be contributed the following are deducted:

(a) the liability attaching to such assets and assumed by the capital company; and

(b) expenses incurred by the capital company in connection with the transaction.[41]

There was no definition of the words 'the actual value' in the legislation or the directive but presumably it was taken to mean the market value of the assets.

[7.59] The European Court of Justice, in considering the Danish legislation on capital duty, held that the charge to capital duty had to be based on a uniform and objective criteria which applied throughout the community. In Case No 171/78 *Advokatradet [Bar Council] as representative of P Conradsen A/S v Minister for Fiscal Affairs*,[42] it was found that under Danish law the assets were taken on their book value and no account was taken of potential tax liabilities chargeable under Danish law on the profits of the company. The court held that:

(a) these deductions were not permissible and that 'the actual value', meaning market value in this context, should be substituted for the value of the assets contributed to the company by the Danish shareholders at the time of the transaction; and

---

39 SDCA 1999, s 117(2)(a).

40 SDCA 1999, s 118.

41 SDCA 1999, s 118(1)(a).

42 Case No 171/78 *Advokatradet [Bar Council] as representative of P Conradsen A/S v Minister for Fiscal Affairs* [1979] ECR 2221.

(b) the liabilities and expenses (which must exist at the date of the transaction) are deductible from 'the actual value', and must exist on the date of the transaction, the amount of which is certain.

The formation of a capital company

[7.60]

Example 7.60.1

Jack and Jim incorporate a limited liability company named JJ Ltd with a nominal share capital of €1,000,000 divided into 1,000,000 ordinary shares of €1 each. Ten thousand and four shares are to be issued on incorporation. Prior to the FA 2006, capital duty of €50 would have been due (10,004 x 0.005 being 0.5%) prior to the incorporation of the company. However, since FA 2006, if the transaction was effected on or after 7 December 2005, there would be no charge to capital duty on the issuing of the shares in the company.

Increase in capital of a capital company by a contribution of assets

[7.61]

Example 7.61.1

Jack conveyed to JJ Ltd a factory premises together with plant and machinery that pass by conveyance, valued at €3.2 million, in return for which he received the following consideration:

(a) €700,000 cash; and

(b) 996 ordinary shares of €1 each.

The expenses and liabilities incurred by JJ Ltd were as follows:

	€
Stamp duty (3.2 million at 9%)	288,000
Accountants' fees, valuers fees, legal fees	32,000
Cash consideration	700,000
Total	1,020,000

Value of assets passing €3.2 million, less liabilities and expenses incurred = €1,020,000.

	€
'Actual value' of shares	2,180,000
Value per share	2,188.70
Capital duty	10,900

The 'actual value' of the assets exceeded the nominal value of the shares.

If this was reversed, so that JJ Ltd had a nominal share capital of €10,000,000 divided into 10,000,000 ordinary shares of €1 each and, in consideration of the conveyance of the factory, Jack received the consideration of €700,000, together with 3.2 million ordinary shares of €1 each, the capital duty would be increased as follows:

	€
Actual value of shares	2,180,000
Nominal value of shares	3,200,000

Capital duty was chargeable on the greater of the nominal value of the issued share capital or the value of the contributed assets. Therefore in this example the capital duty is levied on €3.2 million at 0.05% = €1,600.

Unlimited liability shareholders and members

[7.62] When calculating the actual value of the amount on which capital duty was chargeable, no account was taken of any assets contributed to the capital company by a member with unlimited liability or the share of such member in the assets of a company.[43] Where assets were contributed by unlimited liability partners to a company, then as a general rule no charge to stamp duty arose. However, in the case of limited partners, a charge to capital duty will have arisen. Where transactions were effected involving both limited and unlimited partners the transaction should have been chargeable to capital duty in so far as it related to the limited partners only.

[7.63] In the case of other transactions, mentioned at paras **[7.49]**, **[7.51]**, **[7.53]** and **[7.54]** which relate to the conversion of an entity into a capital company, the transfer of the effective centre of management of a capital company from a third country to this State, the transfer of the registered office of a capital company from a third country to this State whose effective centre of management remains in the third country, the transfer from the Member State to this State of the effective centre of management which resulted in the company becoming a capital company, the transfer of a non-capital company in a Member State of its registered office to Ireland while retaining its effective centre of management in the third country, capital duty is chargeable on:

(a) the amount of the 'actual value' of the assets of the capital company on the date of the transaction after the deduction of its liabilities and expenses incurred in the transaction; or

(b) the nominal value of shares allotted to the members of the capital company in connection with the transaction or belonging to the Members of the capital company immediately after the transaction.[44]

Example 7.63.1

Rhino Ltd is a Zimbabwean limited liability company with its registered office at Harare, Zimbabwe. It decided to move its effective centre of management to Ireland to avail of the tax incentives and concessions available here. The value of the company at the date of the transfer of its effective centre of management was €1.2 million. It incurred expenses of €10,000.

Capital duty was chargeable on the value of the assets less the expenses incurred, ie €1,200,000-€10,000 = €1,190,000.

Capital duty was charged on €1,190,000 at 0.05% €595

43 SDCA 1999, s 118.

44 SDCA 1999, s 118.

Exemptions

[7.64] The exemptions, except as set out above, were introduced on the passing of FA 1973. SDCA 1999, s 115 provides that Part 8 of SDCA 1999, does not apply to:

UCITS

[7.65] As a result of the European objective for the free movement of capital and the harmonisation of laws and taxes, the European Council Directive 85/611/EEC of 20 December 1985 was introduced to ensure the co-ordination of law, regulations and administrative provisions pertaining to Undertakings for Collective Investments and Transfer of Securities (UCITS). This was given legal effect in Ireland on 18 April 1989 under the European (Undertaking for Collective Investments and Transferable Securities (UCITS) Regulations 1989.[45] The UCITS to which Council Directive 85/601/EEC[46] applied and any directive amending the Council Directive, are deemed to be exempt from capital duty.[47]

[7.66] FA 1989 introduced new provisions for taxing UCITS on capital raised from the public operating on the basis of risk spreading, and whose units are redeemable at the request of the unit holders. Previously such UCITS had been liable to income tax at the standard rate and to capital gains tax at half the applicable rate; the unit holders bore no liability. This has now been altered;[48] the unit holders now become liable to tax for the income or capital arising.[49] Further measures were introduced for the enforcement of the provisions including additional accountability by the imposition of a withholding tax on the UCITS,[50] and by requiring disclosure of information from intermediaries regarding the UCITS at the request of the Revenue.[51]

Authorised investment companies under the UCITS regulations

[7.67] Authorised investment companies under the UCITS regulations were exempt from capital duty (see **7.20**). However, subsequent legislation enabled variable capital investment companies to be established which did not comply with the UCITS regulations[52] and which therefore did not qualify for the relevant exemption. Subsequently these companies were made exempt from capital duty.[53] This provision does not have retrospective effect.

---

45 SI/78/1989.

46 OJ L375 of 31/12/1985.

47 FA 1990, s 115.

48 Council Directive 85/661/EEC.

49 FA 1989, s 18.

50 FA 1989, s 18.

51 FA 1989, s 19.

52 C(A)A 1990, Pt XIII.

53 SDCA 1999, s 115 amended by FA 1991, s 110.

Imposed levy on UCITS

[7.68] A duty of 3 per cent was imposed on all investments in units of collective investment undertakings or other similar investments.[54] This is dealt with in detail in **Chapter 10**. Under the Investment Limited Partnership Act 1994, recognition was given to a new entity for collective investment in Ireland, modelled on a United States version, and designed to encourage investment in the financial services industry in Ireland. Such investment limited partnerships were the subject of capital duty as if they were a limited company. However, as an investment limited partnership is similar to a UCITS, investment limited partnerships are exempted from capital duty on or after 12 April 1995.[55]

Reliefs

Relief in respect of certain payments of capital duty

[7.69] Relieving provisions applied in respect of the payment of capital duty in certain circumstances, subject to conditions; for example, where there was a replacement of capital, where capital duty was already paid in respect of the company, the reconstruction or amalgamation of a company, or where a company was formed for charitable purposes. Reliefs may have been withdrawn if the conditions of the relief were breached.

Increase in capital following a reduction in issued capital as a result of losses

[7.70] An increase in capital of a capital company by the contribution of assets of any kind, including the conversion of loan stock of the capital company into share capital, was liable to capital duty.[56] Where, within a period of four years immediately before the date of the transaction and after the operative date, which is 4 August 1973, there was a reduction in the issued capital of the company as a result of losses sustained by the company, capital duty was charged at a rate of 0 per cent in respect of either:

(a) the greater of the actual amount of the assets contributed to the company; or

(b) the nominal value of the shares allotted, to the extent that it corresponds with the reduction of issued capital.

Where this relieving provision was already used, further relief was only available to the extent of the reduction of issued capital to which the rate of 0 per cent had not been applied in respect of the earlier transaction or transactions.[57]

[7.71] In effect, the transaction was deemed exempt to the extent that the increase of capital replaced the previously reduced capital, provided the increase was carried out within four years and the relief was not applied in respect of any transaction occurring since the reduction in capital. Where the increase in the capital exceeded the previous

54 FA 1990, s 109.

55 SDCA 1999, s 115(c).

56 SDCA 1999, s 116(1)(c).

57 FA 1973, s 71(6).

reduction, capital duty was charged on the excess of the increase in capital over the previous reduction in capital due to losses.

[7.72] The whole ethos behind company law legislation is to ensure the maintenance by a company of its capital.[58] However, in certain circumstances and subject to court confirmation, a company may, if authorised by its articles, reduce its share capital, or cancel its share capital by means of a special resolution.[59]

Example 7.71.1

Panut Ltd was incorporated in December 1980 with a nominal share capital of £1,000,000 divided into 1,000,000 ordinary shares of £1 each and an issued share capital of 50,000 ordinary shares of £1 on incorporation. The company, pursuant to CA 1963, s 72, reduced its capital by cancelling 45,000 of its shares on 1 July 1986 on account of losses incurred by the company.

Capital duty on incorporation December 1980
1% of issued share capital

	£
1% of £50,000	500
Capital duty payable	500

Possibility 1

On 1 June 1990 the company issued 40,000 ordinary shares of £1 each. Capital duty was charged as follows:

	£
Issued share capital	50,000
Reduction in capital on 1 July 1986	45,000
Capital reduced to	5,000
Increase in capital on 1 July 1990 = 40,000 at 0%	Nil
Capital duty payable	Nil

Possibility 2

On 1 June 1990 the company issued 100,000 ordinary shares of £1 each. Duty was payable as follows:

£45,000 at 0%	0
£55,000 at 1%	£550
Capital duty payable	£550

Reconstructions or amalgamations of capital companies

[7.73] In the case of reconstructions or amalgamations of capital companies which satisfied certain conditions, capital duty was to be charged at a rate of 0 per cent on the issue of shares.[60] See **Chapter 8** for a full discussion of the relief.

58 CA 1963, s 72(1).

59 For a further discussion on this matter see Keane *Company Law* (3rd edn, LexisNexis, 2000), Ch 16; Courtney *The Law of Private Companies* (2nd edn, Lexis Nexis, 2002).

60 SDCA 1999, s 119.

Relief from capital duty on the issue of shares where duty was already paid on the nominal value of shares prior to 4 August 1973

[7.74] Credit was allowed for stamp duty paid on the nominal value of shares prior to 1 August 1973 against any future liability to capital duty as a result of a further issue of shares in the company. Credit was allowed for stamp duty paid on the nominal share capital, or increase of nominal share capital under SA 1891, ss 112-113 where the nominal share capital exceeded the total issued share capital in the company. In effect, relief was given for the stamp duty paid on the nominal share capital of the company in direct proportion to the further issue of shares in the company to ensure double taxation did not arise.[61] The following formula was used to calculate the relief:

$$A = \frac{(B \times C)}{D}$$

where

A = stamp duty already paid on shares being issued. (This is the credit to be applied);

B = stamp duty already paid on nominal capital pre -1973;

C = increase in issued share capital post-1973;

D = total nominal share capital on which old duty was paid.

Example 7.73.1

Brandon Ltd was incorporated on 1 January 1970 with a nominal share capital of £2,500,000 divided into 2,500,000 ordinary shares of £1 each. On 1 August 1973 the company had an issued share capital of 150,000 ordinary shares of £1 each. On 1 June 1990 the company issued a further 1,000,000 ordinary shares of £1 each.

Using the formula above, stamp duty is calculated as follows:

A = to be calculated;

B = old stamp duty rate 0.25p per £100 or part thereof:

2,500,000 x 0.25% = £6,250;

C = the increase in share capital £1,000,000; and

D = the total nominal value of the old share capital on which stamp duty has already been paid £2,500,000.

Credit	2,500
Capital duty liability (£1,000,000 at 1%)	10,000
Less credit	2,500
Capital duty payable	7,500

As can be seen from this example the aim was to give relief for that proportion of the capital duty that was already paid in the form of stamp duty on the nominal share capital of company prior to 1 August 1973.

---

61 FA 1973, s 71(4).

[7.75] Where there was a reduction of nominal share capital by way of relief under SDCA 1999, s 80 (concerning reconstruction or amalgamations of companies and discussed more fully in **Chapter 8**), for the purpose of this provision, the reduction shall be ignored and relief granted on the original amount of duty paid.[62]

Where on 4 August 1973 there was included in the share capital of the company referred to in FA 1973, s 71(4) shares not fully paid up, the amount unpaid on those shares should be treated as nominal share capital which was not issued at that date.[63]

> Suppose X Co Ltd has a nominal share capital as at 1 January 1971 of £1,000,000 and issued capital of £100,000 of which only £5,000 is fully paid up. The stamp duty liability would be £2,500. In January 1975 the company calls up the balance owing on the issued share capital (£95,000). Capital duty applies to the full amount so called up, £950 less the relevant credit of £237.50 as calculated using the formula para **[7.74]**.

Exemption for certain companies

[7.76] Transactions effected by certain capital companies were not liable to capital duty, provided the capital company involved was either:

(a) a capital company which is formed for the purposes of and carries on exclusively the business of supplying a public service, such as public transport, port facilities, or the supplying of water, gas or electricity, and not less than 50 per cent of the issued share capital is owned by the state or a local authority; or

(b) a capital company whose objects are exclusively cultural, charitable or educational.[64]

It is quite clear from (a) of the above definition which the capital companies qualifed for the relief, but definition (b) is somewhat ambiguous. The objects of a company are to be found in its memorandum of association and they limit the sort of activities that may be pursued by the company. The problem is in the use of the word 'exclusive' in the section.

[7.77] Ordinarily, the objects of a company are given broad definition by the framers of the memorandum, even though the courts have tended to view each independent object of the company as being the powers given to the company to achieve its main object. Even though a company may have many independent objects, it will be bound in the use of such objects to achieve its primary object.

[7.78] In an application for charitable status for the purposes of the Income Tax and Corporation Tax Acts, the Revenue Commissioners in practice insist that the memorandum of association includes the following points:

(a) the main object must be clearly stated;

(b) all other objects must be stated to be secondary to the attainment exclusively of the main object;

---

[62] FA 1973, s 71(4).

[63] FA 1973, s 75(5).

[64] SDCA 1999, s 120(b).

(c) the members must not have an entitlement in any way to share in the profits or capital of the company;

(d) on a winding up, all funds must be reinvested in a company of a similar nature;

(e) the Revenue Commissioners shall approve all further alterations to the memorandum and articles of association; and

(f) accounts must be made available to the Revenue Commissioners.

It is submitted that (a) and (b) are the relevant parts in determining for the purposes of this section what the 'exclusive object' of the company is.

[7.79] Once the main object of the company has been so identified, it must according to the Act, be either cultural, charitable or educational. A charity has been defined by M'Naghten LJ in *Commissioners for Income Tax v Pemsel*[65] as being that whose objects are aimed at furthering the advancement of education, religion or the relief of poverty or some other purpose beneficial to the community.

[7.80] Charity in its legal sense comprises four principle divisions: trusts for the relief of poverty; trusts for the advancement of education; trusts for the advancement of religion; and trusts for other purposes beneficial to the community not falling under any of the other preceding heads. The trusts last referred to are not any less charitable in the eye of the law, because incidentally they benefit the rich as well as the poor, as indeed, every charity must do either directly or indirectly.

[7.81] The determination of what is a charitable organisation is well classified, but since it includes the advancement of education, to what extent is the Act a tautology? It is submitted that it is not and the inclusion of companies whose exclusive objective is cultural or educational would extend this relief to those companies who pursue these objectives even in a commercial sense; for example, a private school or college, an art gallery etc. The statement to be delivered pursuant to SDCA 1999, s 117, detailing the transaction had to be adjudicated upon (under the provision of SDCA 1999, s 20) to claim the relief before the statement was deemed duly stamped.

Redeemable preference shares issued in replacement of other redeemable preference shares

[7.82] A company, limited by shares, may issue preference shares which are redeemable, or at the option of the company, liable to be redeemed.[66] Redemption of the shares, which have to be fully paid up, has to be carried out in compliance with the stringent conditions set out in the legislation.

[7.83] Relief from stamp duty was provided for in CA 1963, s 64(4), which empowered companies to issue replacement shares up to the nominal amount of the shares redeemed without giving rise to a charge to stamp duty. As seen previously, FA 1973 gave effect to the EEC directive on capital duty, giving rise to new charge to duty based on the

65 *Commissioners for Income Tax v Pemsel* [1891] AC 531 at 583.

66 CA 1963, s 64 now repealed by CA 1990, s 220 but still applicable to shares issued before Part XI of the Act came into operation.

actual value of the shares issued, rather than the nominal value. However, the relief provided for under CA 1963, s 64(4) granted relief based on the nominal value of the shares, rather than the actual value, so that capital duty could be avoided.

Example 7.83.1

Company A previously issued 9,800 redeemable preference shares of €1 each.

The company opts to redeem these shares for €50 per share and to pay for the redemption issues a further 9,800 redeemable preference shares of €1 each at €100 a share. The consideration consists of a share of €1 and a share premium of €99. As the nominal value of the shares remains the same, there is no capital duty payable.

[7.84] FA 1990, s 119 amended CA 1963, s 64(4) and provided that capital duty shall be payable on the difference between the actual value of the shares issued and the actual value of the preference shares redeemed at the date of their redemption. Where there was an excess, the stamp duty was chargeable on the difference between the duty which would have been chargeable on these shares and the value of the shares redeemed.

Example 7.84.1

Taking the facts of the above example, stamp duty would in effect now be chargeable on the premium on each share of €99 each. Capital duty is chargeable on 9,800 shares at €100 each = €980,000.

	€
Capital duty which would have been chargeable	4,900
Less capital duty on shares redeemed	2,450
Capital duty	2,450

In the event of the new shares being issued prior to the redemption of the old shares, redemption must take place within one month after the issue to obtain capital duty relief.[67]

The cancellation of issued share capital followed by the issue of new share capital

[7.85] Maintenance of capital in a company is vital, protecting both the interests of the creditors and the shareholders, and it has resulted in the rule that a company could not acquire its own shares.[68] A company has also been prohibited from financing the purchase of its own shares except in certain circumstances.[69] However, these provisions were seen as rather restrictive, particularly in the case of a private company limited by shares as it may result in the lack of funds for investors, or rendering those shares unmarketable.

Redeemable shares

[7.86] C(A))A 1990, Pt XI somewhat relieves these restrictive provisions as it enables the company to purchase its own shares or shares in its holding company. A company

---

67 CA 1963, s 64(5).

68 *Trevor v Whitworth* [1887] 12 AC 409.

69 CA 1963, s 60 – for further discussion on this topic see Keane *Company Law* (3rd edn, LexisNexis, 2000) and Courtney *The Law of Private Companies* (2nd edn, Lexis Nexis, 2002).

limited by shares, and now a company limited by guarantee having a share capital, where so authorised by its articles of association, can issue redeemable shares which are redeemable subject to certain conditions.[70]

[7.87] Shares so redeemed may be cancelled upon redemption.[71] These shares can be redeemed out of profits available for distribution or redeemed wholly or partly out of the proceeds of a fresh issue of shares. Where shares have been redeemed and cancelled, or are about to be redeemed and cancelled, the company can issue further shares without giving rise to a charge to capital duty unless the actual value of the shares issued exceeds the actual value of the shares redeemed at the date of the redemption. Where there was an excess in the value, capital duty was chargeable on the difference between the amount of capital duty payable which would have been charged on the shares issued, and the value of the shares redeemed at the date of redemption.[72] Where the issue of new shares takes place before the redemption, the old shares must have been redeemed within one month of the issue of new shares to qualify for this relief.[73]

Treasury shares

[7.88] The company now has an option of holding the shares as 'treasury shares' rather than cancelling them on their redemption. Where treasury shares are held by a company, they cannot exceed 10 per cent of the nominal value of the share capital of the company and the company is not entitled to exercise any voting rights in respect of the shares nor receive any dividend in respect of the shares.[74]

Conversion of shares

[7.89] The company is now empowered to convert shares into redeemable shares subject to certain restrictions to ensure the protection of the shareholders and creditors.[75] These shares can subsequently be redeemed under C(A)A 1990, Pt XI. Where shares are redeemed subject to C(A)A 1990, ss 207 and 208, capital duty was not payable.

[7.90] If the shares were purchased and cancelled under any other empowering provisions of C(A)A 1990, the Revenue Commissioners will charge duty at a rate of 1 per cent. Certain doubts exist as to the validity of the Revenue Commissioners' stance.[76] Where the shares are held as treasury shares, this may have given rise to a charge of capital duty, but on the reissue, the company is deemed not to have increased its issued share capital for any purpose including stamp duty; therefore, no capital duty was payable.[77]

---

70 C(A)A 1990, s 207.

71 C(A)A 1990, s 208.

72 C(A)A 1990, s 208(c).

73 C(A)A 1990, s 208(d).

74 C(A)A 1990, s 209.

75 C(A)A 1990, s 210.

76 For further discussion on this subject see Brennan, *A Company Purchasing Its Own Shares* (1991 Britton Publications in assoc with Oak Tree Press), Ch 3.

77 C(A)A 1990, s 209(5).

Obligation to pay stamp duty

[7.91] As already discussed in this chapter, certain transactions concerning capital companies formerly gave rise to a charge to capital duty. Capital duty was charged on the actual value of the transaction concerned, provided always that the actual value was not less than the nominal value of the shares. Where such transactions took place, a statement of all the assets, contributions, liabilities and expenses involved in ascertaining the actual value were to be delivered to the registrar of companies prior to the incorporation or registration of the capital company. The registrar could not incorporate the capital company under CA 1963 or register a capital company formed under the Limited Partnership Act 1907 until the statement relating to the capital company had been stamped (in compliance with SDCA 1999, ss 117(1)).

[7.92] Where an increase in the capital of the company occured after incorporation or registration, a statement of the assets, liabilities and expenses had to be delivered to the registrar within 30 days of the transaction.[78] Capital duty was charged at a rate of 0.0 per cent of the amount calculated in accordance with SDCA 1999, s 118, provided always the minimum amount of duty was €1.

Example 7.92.1

Fred and Barney decide to incorporate and call their company Yabahdabah Ltd. Fred contributes a premises valued at €55,000 and Barney contributes €45,000 in cash. The proposed nominal share capital of the company is €1,000,000 divided into 1,000,000 ordinary shares of €1 each, and 100,000 shares are to be issued on incorporation in proportion to the assets contributed.

Before incorporation can occur, a statement must be delivered to the registrar concerning the contribution of assets and issue of shares. Stamp duty payable on incorporation was €50 (€100,000 at 0.05%).

Example 7.92.2

Assume the facts stated above, but that a year later on 1 January, to enable expansion, Wilma contributed €35,000 cash to Yabahdabah Ltd and received 17,500 ordinary shares of €1 each.

A statement had to be delivered to the registrar to this effect and stamp duty payable on this transaction would be €17.50. Stamp duty was charged at a rate of 0.05% calculated on the actual value of the transaction.

Example 7.92.3

Suppose the above given facts in Example **7.92.2**, but there is a failure to make a return to the registrar and only on completion the accounts at the end of the year the matter is brought to the attention of the company secretary by the auditor. They immediately arrange to deliver the statement to the registrar on 15 July, some seven-and-a-half months after the transaction.

---

[78] SDCA 1999, s 117(1).

	€
Duty payable (0.05% of €35,000)	17.50
Interest on penalty at 0.273% per day from the date of the original transaction (195 days)	93.00
Total duty payable	268.00

This example ignores any other penalty provisions that may be applicable and only concerns the main capital duty together with the interest payable.

[7.93] Where the statement was delivered to the registrar on the formation of a capital company and there was a difficulty in calculating the amount on which stamp duty was chargeable (pursuant to SDCA 1999, s 118(1)), the statement was charged in the first instance with the amount the Revenue Commissioners considered appropriate and if afterwards:

(a) it was established that too little duty had been paid, the additional duty was payable and was treated as duty in arrear,[79] and

(b) it was established that too much duty has been paid, the excess was repaid by the Revenue Commissioners with interest at a rate of 0.0161 per cent per day or part of a day.[80]

Where too little duty was paid under SDCA 1999, s 117(2)(b)(ii), additional duty was payable and interest was charged on the additional duty at a rate of 0.273% per day or part of a day from the date of the original chargeable transaction until such time as the additional duty had been discharged.[81]

[7.94] Where there was a failure to deliver the statement so required to the registrar within 30 days after the date of the transaction, simple interest was payable by way of penalty. The interest was charged on the amount of stamp duty which remained unpaid more than one month from the date of the transaction. The interest rate was 0.273 per cent per day or part thereof during which the duty remained unpaid, and was chargeable and recoverable as if it were duty.[82] Surcharge provisions also apply, see **Chapter 15**.

Relief in certain situations

[7.95] Where within a period of 4 years immediately before the date of the transaction, there was a reduction in the issued capital of the company as a result of losses accrued, then any statement delivered pursuant to the company capital duty provisions was levied at 0 per cent on the amount which was equal to the reduction in capital.[83] This provision applied to transactions executed on or after 15 December 1999. Effectively it exempted from duty any reduction in capital where, and only where, the reduction arose from losses arising from the company's business.

79 SDCA 1999, s 117(2)(b)(i).

80 SDCA 1999, s 117(2)(b)(ii).

81 SDCA 1999, s 117(4).

82 SDCA 1999, s 117(3) substituted by FA 1979, s 53.

83 SDCA 1999, s 120A.

Appeals

[7.96] There were rights of appeal against the amount of capital duty that was deemed payable by the Revenue Commissioners. Where the actual value of the assets was in dispute between the Revenue Commissioners and the taxpayer, then an appeal went to the Appeals Commissioners[84] where the assets being valued consisted of stocks, shares or other securities not dealt with on the stock exchange. All shares on the stock exchange would have had their value set by the market. In the case of land, an appeal to the Commissioner of Valuations (Reference Committee) could have been made (in the manner prescribed by SDCA 1999, s 121(a)).

Recovery of capital duty and furnishing information

[7.97] Capital duty together with any interest was recoverable from the capital company concerned. Where the capital company was not a body corporate, it was recovered from the members of the capital company jointly and severally.[85] The statement to be furnished was in the form and contained such particulars as were required by the Revenue Commissioners. Every person that was accountable for capital duty should, if they were called upon, have verified such particulars and delivered such evidence as was required in relation to any transaction or to any company concerned in any such transaction.[86]

[7.98] On incorporation Form A1[87] included a company capital duties statement pursuant to SDCA 1999, s 117. Since November 1993, Form B5[88] should have been completed in respect of the return of allotments which included a statement required under SDCA 1999, ss 114–122. The Revenue Commissioners assessed capital duty payable on such an instrument.

Duty payable on the transfer of shares

[7.99] The transfer of shares in a company attracts *ad valorem* duty under the conveyance on sale head of charge of the SDCA 1999, see **Chapter 4**. The rate of duty is 1 per cent (€1 for every €100 or part thereof). However, the valuation of the shares transferred is subject to special rules. In general, the rules for valuation provided for in the CATA 1976, s 15 apply,[89] with suitable modification where necessary. Under s 15 the market value is that which, in the opinion of the Commissioners, the property would fetch if placed for sale on the open market and subject to such conditions as might be reasonably applied to obtain the best price for the vendor. In determining such price, the Commissioners are entitled to assume that there is available all information which a prospective purchaser might reasonably require if the sale were to occur by private treaty at arms length. No account is to be taken on any reduction which might occur if the

84 SDCA 1999, s 121(b).

85 SDCA 1999, s 122(1).

86 SDCA 1999, s 122(2).

87 See **Appendix 2**.

88 See **Appendix 2**.

89 See FA 1991, s 105.

entire of the shares were placed on the market at the one time. It is immaterial whether the shares can actually be sold, see *IRC v Crossman*.[90] However, the existence of a special purchaser willing to pay more than the market value of the shares can be taken into account, see *IRC v Clay, IRC v Buchanan*,[91] but note that a special purchaser needs only to bid one euro higher than the surrounding market offers.[92]

[7.100] The Revenue Form SD4, introduced in November 1997, sets out the requirements and documentation to accompany the stock transfer forms when lodged with the Revenue Commissioners. It is suggested that the form would be signed by the accountants acting on behalf of the company as they are in a position to certify the true value of the shares. Provided that the valuation appears reasonable, this protects the solicitor under the negligence provisions.

[7.101] In Ireland a practice has developed when dealing with the repurchase of its own shares by a private company, of entering a contract for the sale and purchase of the shares by the company and avoiding a stock trasnfer form or other instrument that transfers the legal title in the shares. If the contract does not itself operate as a conveyance, then it is not stampable. This practice has been recognised by the Revenue Commissioners in their Stamp Duty Work Manual and Practices[93] where it is stated:

> The shares can be bought back on foot of a contract or share purchase agreement. If the shareholder and the company enter into an agreement and the shareholder simply hands over the share certificates to the company there is no need for a stock transfer form and no duty can be charged. The share purchase agreement is not chargeable to duty as it falls outside the scope of SDCA 1999, s 31 (stamp duty on contracts).

This practice leaves some legal uncertainty as to the transfer of the legal title in the absence of an instrument of transfer. Some private companies will insist on a share transfer form to ensure that the shareholder retains no title to the shares thus incurring a charge to stamp duty on the transfer. Other private companies may be willing to rely on the share purchase contract. Public listed companies will rarely rely on the practice outlined above when effecting a repurchase of their own shares.

[7.102] CREST transactions are subject to the same *ad valorem* rate of duty, despite the absence of a written instrument upon which to impress a stamp, FA 1996.[94] See **Chapters 3, 7** and **15** for further discussion.

---

90 *IRC v Crossman* [1937] AC 26.

91 *IRC v Clay, IRC v Buchanan* [1914] 3 KB 466.

92 For a further discussion see Bohan and McCarthy *Capital Acquisitions Tax* (2nd edn, Lexis Nexis, 2004). See also Revenue Form SD4 in **Appendix 8**.

93 Stamp Duty Work Manual and Practices at p 41.

94 SDCA 1999, s 69.

Chapter 8

Reliefs Available to Capital and Non-Capital Companies

Transfer of assets between associated companies

Introduction

[8.01] There are situations where it is necessary to transfer property within a group of associated companies which could give rise to a charge to *ad valorem* stamp duty. This could make the proposition quite expensive and impractical.

> **Example 8.01.1**
>
> Company A has purchased a freehold property for €1,000,000 from which to conduct a high-profit, upmarket retail outlet. Unfortunately it has not been successful. It decides to trade under a more down market name and set up a subsidiary company, B. Any transfer of the property would be stampable as a conveyance on sale for which a market value would be assessed by the Revenue Commissioners. If, at the time of the intended transfer, the market value is €1,300,000, Company A will have paid 9% *ad valorem* duty (€117,000) on the initial purchase, amounting to stamp duty of €90,000. On the transfer to its subsidiary, it will have to pay a further 9% on €117,000.

Accordingly, relief measures are available which will eliminate the amount of duty payable in such instances.[1] The relief is modelled on the English legislation.

[8.02] Originally, transfers of shares, either by conveyance on sale or voluntary disposition, were excluded from relief. Prior to FA 1995, such relief would be of no benefit in any event since the charge to stamp duty for shares was 1 per cent which was less than the relief under these provisions. Shares consist of stocks and marketable securities. The relieving provisions have been extensively amended since their introduction in 1952.

[8.03] Since 8 February 1995, the conveyance or transfer on sale of any shares, between connected companies, is now fully exempt from the payment of stamp duty.[2] The same also applies to the conveyance or transfer on sale of any policy of insurance or life insurance where the risk is located within the state. For the purposes of clarity, the use of the word 'property' herein, shall mean the conveyance and transfer on sale of property, insurance policies, stocks and marketable securities, unless otherwise stated.

Conditions for relief

[8.04] The relieving provisions have been extensively amended. The relief applies to any instrument chargeable under either the conveyance on sale head, the conveyance or

1 SDCA 1999, s 79.

2 SDCA 1999, s 79.

transfer on sale of stocks or marketable securities or the conveyance or transfer on sale of a policy of insurance, or life insurance, where the risk is located in the state, which transfers the beneficial interest in property between associated companies. The relief reduces the *ad valorem* stamp duty to 0 per cent on the instrument for instruments exempted after 8 February 1995.[3] Prior to this, the reduced rate was 2 per cent. In order to qualify for relief, the following three conditions must be satisfied:

(a) the instrument must be chargeable under either the conveyance on sale head, the conveyance or transfer on sale of stocks or marketable securities or the conveyance or transfer on sale of a policy of insurance, or life insurance, where the risk is located in the state;

(b) the beneficial interest must be transferred; and

(c) the transfer must take place between associated companies.

Associated companies

[8.05] 'Associated' for the purposes of this section, means that, at the time of the execution of the instrument, the transferor and transferee must be associated to each other to the extent that:

(a) one body corporate was the beneficial owner of not less than 90% of the ordinary share capital of the other body corporate, or a third body corporate was the beneficial owner of not less than 90% of the ordinary share capital of both the transferor and the transferee; and

(b) one body corporate is beneficially entitled to not less than *90% of any profits available for distribution* (being profits available for distribution as defined in TCA 1997, s 414) to the shareholders of the other body corporate, or a third body corporate is beneficially entitled to not less than 90% of any profits available for distribution to the shareholders of the transferor and the transferee, and

(c) one body corporate is beneficially entitled to not less than *90% of any assets of the other body corporate available for distribution* (being assets available for distribution as defined in TCA 1997, s 415) to its shareholders on a winding-up, or a third body corporate is beneficially entitled to not less than 90% of any assets available for distribution to the shareholders of the transferor and the transferee on a winding-up.

[8.06] Originally, the relief was not available for transfers between a parent company and a sub-subsidiary, even if there was the required 90 per cent shareholding.[4] It is not clear why such cases were excluded since it has always been recognised that transfers between subsidiaries of a common parent company will qualify for the relief and this is inconsistent with any theory of direct shareholding.

---

3 SDCA 1999, s 79.

4 *Rodwell Securities v IRC* [1968] 1 All ER 257.

Example 8.06.1

Company A owns 100% of both Company B and Company C. Company D is owned 100% by Company C. Transfers between Company A and Company B or Company C all qualify for relief yet, under the original legislation, a transfer between Company A and Company D would not. In practice, two transfers would occur in order to avail of the reliefs. This position is now changed so that such transfers will in fact qualify for the relief, provided that a direct or indirect relationship of 90% can be proven. Care should be taken in calculating the 90% shareholding in the sub-subsidiary. If Company A owns 90% of company C, which owns 90% of company D, then the relationship between Company A and Company D is only 81% and, therefore, any transfer will not qualify for the relief.

The connecting relationship will often arise through more complex pyramid-style structures in groups of companies and, in such cases ,the relief will apply if the indirect relationship of 90 per cent can be proven. CTA, s 156 should be utilised here with the necessary substitution 'body corporate' for 'company'.

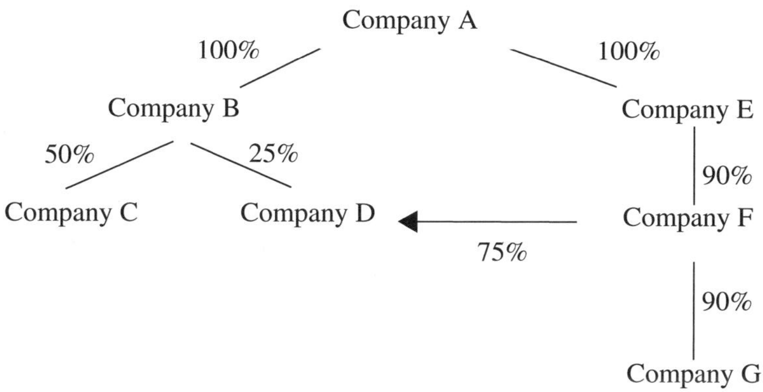

Company A owns 100% of Company B which in turn owns 50% of Company C and 25% of Company D. Company A owns 100% of Company E which in turn owns 90% of Company F. Company F owns 75% of Company D. The following connections will qualify for relief:

(i) Company A to Company B (100%)

(ii) Company A to Company E (100%)

(iii) Company A to Company F (90%)

(iv) Company A to Company D (92.5%)

(v) Company B to Company E (100%)

(vi) Company B to Company F (90%)

(vii) Company B to Company D (92.5%)

(viii) Company D to Company F (92.5%)

(ix) Company D to Company E (92.5%)

(x) Company E to Company F (90%)

(xi) Company F to Company G (90%)

Companies A, B, D, E and F are all interrelated. Company G is related to Company F only. Company C is not related to any other company.

[8.07] The next point to be considered is 'ordinary share capital'. The term was introduced with respect to instruments executed on or after 6 February 2003. It means 'all the issued share capital (by whatever name called) of the body corporate, other than capital the holders of which have a right to dividend at a fixed rate, but have no other right to share in the profits of the body corporate'.[5] Prior to 6 February 2003 the section referred to the concept of 'issued share capital'. The concept of share capital includes ordinary, preference or redeemable share capital. The only requirement is that they be issued. A question then arises as to the difference between allotted and issued. The new test (ordinary share capital) now ignores fixed rate preference shares but otherwise the requirement remains that the relevant shares must be issued which means the shares must be registered in the register of members of the relevant body corporate. See *National Westminster Bank plc v IRC*.[6]

[8.08] Harman J stated in *Holmleigh (Holdings) v IRC*[7] that mere allotment would be insufficient until the allottee's name had been registered with the company. The validity of this statement must be questioned in light of the judgment in *Shop & Store v IRC*[8] where renouncible letters of allotment were used to create a variation of the 'dummy bridge corporation' (ie a company used to effect a transaction rather than a trading entity). Traditionally, what had been attempted was to form a subsidiary with a nominal ordinary shareholding, say 100 ordinary shares issued to Company A. Company B would then subscribe to, say, 900 non-voting shares. Company B would then transfer the property in question to the shell company and claim the relief to duty by virtue of its 90 per cent shareholding. But, in reality, Company A would have acquired the property since it controlled all the voting shares. A transfer would have taken place outside the necessary relationship and yet still have been entitled to the relief. This is no longer possible.

[8.09] In the above example, the shelf company would have to finance the purchase through an independent source of finance. Company A could not supply the consideration to the transaction or it would fall foul of the requirement for the consideration to be supplied by a connected person (See below). Anti-avoidance legislation was introduced to curb this sort of activity and we shall discuss this case more fully at para **[8.14]**. The meaning of the issue of shares was dealt with in the House of Lords in *National Westminster Bank plc v IRC*[9] where Lord Flynn stated:

> I accept that the word 'issue' has been seen to have different meanings in different contexts ... I do not consider that the shares in the present case were 'issued' on allotment. They were not issued until registration took place.

This appears to extend the concept of issue of shares to arise only on registration. However, the decision was split and there was no consensus between the judiciary as to the meaning of the term 'issue'.

---

5 SDCA 1999, s 79(3A).

6 *National Westminster Bank plc v IRC* [1994] 3 All ER 1.

7 *Holmleigh (Holdings) v IRC* [1958] 46 TC 435.

8 *Shop & Store v IRC* [1967] 1 All ER 42.

9 *National Westminster Bank plc v IRC* [1994] 3 All ER 1.

[8.10] In *Canada Safeway Ltd v IRC*[10] it was held that the percentage shareholding refers to the nominal value of the shares and not their real value. In that case, the shares of a Canadian company were divided into two classes, ordinary and preference. The nominal value of the ordinary shares was CAN$2.8 million, while the value of the preference shares was CAN$6.2 million. In reality, the market value of the ordinary shares was CAN$195 million and the market value of the preference shares was CAN$7 million. Despite this, the calculation was based solely on the nominal value and the relief denied accordingly. This is more a matter of convenience, since it is easier to calculate the relationship by reference to a fixed value, rather than to a floating value.

[8.11] SDCA 1999, s 80(4) requires that the 90 per cent shareholding rule be amended so as to make it a requirement that the body corporate is beneficially entitled to a 90 per cent share of the available profits for distribution and to a 90 per cent share of the surplus funds of the company on a liquidation, imposing for the first time a definition that requires the issued shares to be of value in terms of profits and entitlement to share in profits on a liquidation. The percentage is calculated whether the beneficial interest arises, either directly or indirectly, through other bodies corporate or a mixture thereof.[11] This means that the *Safeway* case is redundant since the 90 per cent relationship now depends on the type of share involved, the dividend payout entitlements in a winding up, etc. By imposing this definition of the issued shares the Revenue has curtailed the abuse of reclassifying corporate share structures in order to avail of the relief.

Body corporate

[8.12] The term 'body corporate' is not defined by legislation, but would appear to include both limited and unlimited companies under the Irish Companies Acts and bodies such as building societies and industrial and provident societies. It also includes many foreign companies. Because the test of association, as outlined above, relies on the ownership of share capital, this leaves a difficulty where the shareholding test falls to be traced through a body corporate whose capital structure in not based on share capital. Issues do not arise where the foreign company without a share capital structure is the direct parent, but rather where the foreign body corporate is a subsidiary and the test of ownership is sought to be applied to the ownership by reference to the issued share capital of the subsidiary.

[8.13] SDCA 1999, s 79(9) was introduced by FA 2003, s 136 with effect from 6 February 2003 and it provides that a foreign body corporate that corresponds under the laws of its own jurisdiction to a body corporate, which has an 'ordinary share capital' within the meaning of SDCA 1999, s 79(3A), can avail of the relief. This gave a legislative confirmation for already existing practices. The Irish Revenue Commissioners in their most recent Guidance Notes, p 80 stated:

> While 'body corporate' is not defined it would include limited and unlimited companies, foreign companies, industrial and provident societies and incorporated associations... Relief will be granted to foreign bodies corporate which do not have a capital structure

10 *Canada Safeway Ltd v IRC* [1972] 1 All ER 666.

11 SDCA 1999, s 80(4).

based on share capital provided that they have a capital structure which is equivalent to a share capital which is equivalent to a share capital structure and also comply with all other conditions of the relief.

[8.14] Whilst the primary object of the relief is to prevent a penal tax where there is no real substantive alteration in the true beneficial ownership of property, tax planners have not been slow in identifying a number of tactics that can make use of such relief in situations that it was not really designed to cover. This has resulted in a complex series of anti-avoidance amendments designed to counteract such transactions. One of the loopholes in the original legislation is best explained in the case of *Escoigne Properties v IRC*[12] and the so called dummy bridge company. In this case a shelf £100 company was formed and owned 100 per cent by Company A which then proceeded to transfer property held by Company A to the shelf or bridge company. The transaction was left incomplete, in that no money was paid and there was no liability to duty under the relief on transfers between associated companies provisions. Company A would then sell the shares of the bridge company to Company B for £100 and pay the stamp duty on that figure. Company B would transfer the property from the bridge company to itself and discharge the amount owing to Company A. Since Company B and the bridge company were connected no liability to duty arose. Transfers of many hundreds of thousands of pounds could take place between unconnected persons for the payment of a notional stamp duty. It was clear that this could not continue and amending legislation was introduced to close this and similar loopholes while retaining the benefits accruing to genuine cases.

Instruments

[8.15] The instrument must satisfy two conditions. Firstly, the relief is only available where the document would have been liable to duty under either the conveyance on sale head, the conveyance or transfer on sale of stocks or marketable securities, or the conveyance or transfer on sale of a policy of insurance, or life insurance, where the risk is located in the state. Secondly that the instrument transfers the beneficial interest in the property. If the document is not so chargeable to duty, then the relief outlined will not apply. Since 1979, relief has also been available for voluntary dispositions.

[8.16] It is unclear whether this relief applies to contracts chargeable under SDCA 1999, s 31. These contracts are 'charged with *ad valorem* duty as if they were conveyances of the estate, interest or property contracted or agreed to be sold'. This section was enacted, primarily, to charge the transfer of an equitable interest in property.[13] Thus a contract for the sale of an interest chargeable under s 31 is not a conveyance. It is a separate head of charge and the contract is liable to duty as if it were a conveyance on sale under SDCA 1999, s 1.

[8.17] On a strict interpretation of the legislation, such contracts would not qualify for the relief between associated companies, since according to *Tempany v Hynes*,[14] they do

12 *Escoigne Properties v IRC* [1958] 1 All ER 406.

13 See **Chapter 5**.

14 *Tempany v Hynes* [1976] IR 101.

not have the effect of conveying or transferring 'a beneficial interest in property...'. To overcome this difficulty, the contract could be stamped with a fixed duty and the instrument could be presented to the Revenue Commissioners for stamping within six months or such longer period as the Revenue Commissioners may think reasonable.[15] If the contract is stamped with a fixed duty, the document that becomes chargeable with *ad valorem* duty is the conveyance or transfer on sale, rather than the contract itself. At that stage the s 59 transaction is liable to be stamped with the full *ad valorem* duty on the conveyance or transfer. This subsequent conveyance or transfer would come within the instruments eligible for relief between associated companies, provided the other conditions are met.

Example 8.17.1

Company A agrees to dispose to its holding company (associated within the meaning of this section) a business comprising a building of €100,000 and goodwill of €200,000.
The contract for the sale of the business will be chargeable to duty:

Under, s 59 in respect of the goodwill	€200,000 @ 9% = €18,000
And the conveyance of building	Exempt (FA 1952, s 19)
Total duty payable	€18,000

However, under SDCA 1999, s 79, the liability to duty could be minimised if the following steps were taken:
Under, s 59(5) the original contract for goodwill could be stamped with a fixed duty of €12.50.
The charge to duty would be as follows:

Contract fixed rate, s 59(5)	€12.50
Subsequent conveyance (within six months)	Exempt (FA 1952, s 19)

These steps will only qualify for this relief provided the entire subsequent conveyance comes within the conveyance on sale head.
Between associated companies, it would be recommended that no contract would be executed, but rather that the property would pass by a straightforward conveyance on sale, so that no contract would brought into existence within the meaning of, s 31.

[8.18] In *Littlewoods Mail Order v IRC*[16] it was held that, despite the fact that a premium payable in respect of a lease is charged to duty as if it were a conveyance on sale, this does not alter the fact that such transaction was chargeable in reality as a lease and the relief for transfers between associated companies does not apply. There appears to be no reason why the relief should not be extended to include transactions chargeable under the leasehold head of duty. In England the relief was extended to encompass leases or agreement for leases.[17] Secondly, the instrument must effect a transfer of the beneficial ownership, not merely the legal ownership. This is discussed fully below in para **[8.20]**ff. There is a certain amount of doubt as to whether the relief applies where the effect of the document is not exclusively that of transferring the beneficial interest.

15 SDCA 1999, s 31(5). For a further discussion see **Chapter 5**.

16 *Littlewoods Mail Order v IRC* [1961] Ch 597.

17 FA 1995 (UK), s 151.

[8.19] In *Escoigne Properties v IRC*,[18] the court expressed a divergence of views. In that case a transaction purported not merely to transfer the beneficial interest from a purchaser to a subpurchaser, but also to complete a sale agreed upon many years before between the purchaser and vendor. The issue, however, was obiter to the decision.

Beneficial ownership requirement

[8.20] One of the conditions required before the relief is available is that the conveyance transfers the beneficial ownership of the property. In order for this to occur, the transferor must hold the beneficial title to the property.

> **Example 8.20.1**
>
> Company A has agreed to sell a property to Company B on 4 January. The beneficial ownership will pass to Company B on that date under the ordinary rules of law. The document giving effect to the transaction, which is the document that will be sent for stamping, will transfer the legal title only. It will not qualify for the relief (*Tempany v Hynes*[19] took the view that beneficial ownership passed only to the extent that the purchase price had been paid).

Ordinarily this would not pose a problem as the instrument would be stamped by reference to the value of the beneficial interest previously passed between the companies, *per* Somervell LJ, *Escoigne Properties v IRC* and therefore it would not qualify. A number of difficulties do, however, arise in determining at what point the beneficial ownership has changed hands, because if it has been transferred prior to the conveyance of the asset then no relief applies. If the relief was available, the clawback provisions would need to be addressed.

> **Example 8.20.2**
>
> Company A wishes to buy Company B, a wholly owned subsidiary of Company C. Company C wishes to retain a building owned by Company B. As part of the agreement for the sale of the shares in Company B to Company A, Company B will transfer the building to Company C. This transfer between Company B and Company C should qualify for the relief available as a transfer between connected companies, but if the transfer occurs after Company C and company A have arrived at a binding agreement for sale, Company C is no longer the beneficial owner of Company B. The relief is, therefore, not available.

This would not be unusual since under common law, contracts come into existence even though no formal record of them is made. There are many instances where courts have held that the parties have concluded a binding contract even though that might not have been their understanding of the situation. The agreement to sell Company B in the above example may have become legally binding during oral negotiations and long before the asset in question is transferred. The property should be transferred between connected companies prior to any such agreement and the relief will still apply even where the transfer is undertaken with a view to the prospective sale to an unconnected person.

[8.21] *Sergeant* and *Simms* postulate that beneficial ownership exists whenever someone other than the legal owner of the asset could secure a court order mandating transfer of

18 *Escoigne Properties v IRC* [1958] 1 All ER 406.

19 *Tempany v Hynes* [1976] IR 10.

the asset at their direction. For example, if the court were to find that a binding contract for sale had come into existence, it could order that the asset be transferred to the purchaser and in such a case the vendor would cease to be the beneficial owner. Such transfer of beneficial ownership occurs only where a purchaser takes sufficient steps to entitle them to apply to the courts for equitable relief, such as an order for specific performance, or a mandatory injunction. Equitable remedies such as specific performance or injunctions are not available where a common law remedy, such as damages, would be more appropriate and accordingly, except in the case of land, a binding agreement for the sale of property, and for which no further steps have been taken, would be most appropriately dealt with by an order for damages if the vendor were to refuse to proceed with the transaction. This is a question of remedy rather than of the interest in the property. The limits of the remedy available could not impact upon the interest of the purchaser or vendor. An award for damages in the above instance is compensation for the loss of the purchaser's interest. This is why land is an exception since, unlike personal property, it is impossible to find an exact alternative to the property in question.

[8.22] The basis for the *Sergeant and Simms*' approach comes from a number of cases, commencing with *Leigh Spinners v IRC*.[20] In *Homleigh (Holdings) v IRC*[21] (following *Puddephatt v Leigh*[22]), it was claimed that the company was not a party to the transaction to sell the shares of its subsidiaries, but Harman J held that the directors of the company could have had an order made against them compelling them to honour their undertakings to procure a transfer of the company. These cases prove that where such an award can be made, it is clear that the beneficial ownership has transferred and the relief is not available.

[8.23] The fact that beneficial ownership is transferred does not prevent the parties from claiming the required relief, even if the correct remedy was damages for breach of agreement. This is supported by a number of cases concerning contracts with conditions attached to them. In *Parway Estates v IRC*[23] the long held rule that once a contract for sale is executed the purchaser becomes the beneficial owner of the property and this is not altered by the imposition of certain obligations on the vendor to be completed prior to or on the completion date, was affirmed. In *Wood Preservation v Prior*[24] it was held that the transfer of beneficial title occurred even in a conditional contract for sale where the conditions could be waived by the purchaser or where the purchaser is prevented from waiving the conditions but where the vendor has acted in a manner so as to deprive himself of the right to sell or otherwise dispose of the property. In *Baytrust Holdings v IRC*[25] two subscribers' shares which were issued on the formation of a new company were held by the parent company, F Ltd. F Ltd was not free to deal with these shares

[20] *Leigh Spinners v IRC* [1956] 46 TC 425.

[21] *Homleigh (Holdings) v IRC* [1958] 46 TC 535.

[22] *Puddephatt v Leigh* [1916] 1 Ch 200.

[23] *Parway Estates v IRC* [1957] 45 TC 135.

[24] *Wood Preservation v Prior* [1968] 2 All ER 849, [1969] 1 All ER 364.

[25] *Baytrust Holdings v IRC* [1971] 3 All ER 76.

since it was committed to a scheme of arrangement where the shares had to be available for transfer as part of the consideration for the entire transaction. It was held that F Ltd was not the beneficial owner of these shares. In contesting this case the parties wrongly assumed that the company could be the beneficial owner of shares which it was not free to deal with. At any stage subsequent to the contract for sale but prior to performance of the conditions, a purchaser could obtain an injunction preventing a vendor from disposing of the interest.[26] The relief is not available from that point in time when the beneficial ownership has passed to the purchaser, even where the appropriate remedy for breach of completion of the contract would not be an order for specific performance. In *Sainsbury plc v O'Connor (Inspector of Taxes)*[27] the Revenue contended, inter alia, that a call option held by a third party over shares in a subsidiary owned by a parent company involved the transfer of the beneficial ownership, since the parent company was not free to deal with the shares as they saw fit. Millet J held that an unfettered freedom of disposition was not crucial to the existence of the beneficial ownership. On appeal it was confirmed that a call option was an irrevocable offer which does not affect beneficial ownership or the rights attaching thereto. Further reference should be made to **Chapter 1**, concerning the concept of beneficial ownership within our legal system; in particular, the decision of *Tempany v Hynes*,[28] should be referred to.

Beneficial ownership on liquidation

[8.24] A legal owner does not always hold the beneficial title on trust or for himself as per Vinelott J in *Conservative & Unionist Central Office v Burrell (Inspector of Taxes)*.[29] This is the case, for example, when a company goes into liquidation. In *Re Albert Life Assurance Co, The Deli Bank* case,[30] Cairns LC stated that, as the assets of the company in liquidation were held for the benefit of the creditors of the company, the beneficial ownership of the assets was no longer held by the company. This does not mean that the beneficial ownership vests in any one creditor, or in the collective body of creditors and/or shareholders. The beneficial interest in the assets of that company is held in suspense.[31] If a subsidiary goes into liquidation and the parent company desired to purchase some of the assets of the subsidiary company, it would not qualify for the relief available under these provisions since the subsidiary would not have a beneficial interest to dispose of, but would merely have the legal title.[32]

[8.25] *Sergeant* and *Simms* suggest that in the case of a wholly owned subsidiary in liquidation, the balance remaining after paying off creditors, and the associated costs of the liquidation are beneficially held by the parent company and any transfer is entitled to the relief. Because this would not be a normal occurrence, this point is debatable. At the end of the liquidation any surplus assets are distributed to the shareholders, in this case

---

26 24 *Halsbury's Laws of England* (4th edn) para 1005.

27 *Sainsbury plc v O'Connor (Inspector of Taxes)* [1991] STC 318.

28 *Tempany v Hynes* [1976] IR 101.

29 *Conservative & Unionist Central Office v Burrell (Inspector of Taxes)* [1980] 3 All ER 42.

30 *Re Albert Life Assurance Co, The Deli Bank* case [1871] 15 Sol J 923.

31 *Ayerst v C & K (Construction) Ltd* [1975] 2 All ER 537.

32 *IRC v Olive Mills Spinners* [1963] 2 All ER 130.

the parent company, and it can be argued that the beneficial interest in the surplus assets remains in suspense until such time as they are distributed and not before. The relief would not, therefore, be available.

[8.26] In practice, the Revenue Commissioners have allowed the association test to apply where the ownership of the asset remains in the same group. For example, a holding company and two 100 per cent subsidiaries agree to carry out a reconstruction within the group and the subsidiary which effected the transfer of the property is liquidated within the two-year period. The Revenue Commissioners by concession accept that the association is not broken, as the beneficial ownership in the subsidiary has not changed (ie the holding company is the beneficial owner of the asset at all times).

[8.27] The transfer of shares by a liquidator in satisfaction of the rights of the shareholders of the company being liquidated is deemed to be a mere conveyance and is liable to a fixed rate of duty of €12.50, by a note issued by the Revenue Commissioners. This extends to other property transferred in satisfaction of the rights of the shareholders, provided that the assets conveyed or transferred do not exceed the entitlement of the beneficiaries shares, see **Chapter 14**.

Beneficial ownership on receivership

[8.28] In *English Sewing Cotton Co v IRC*[33] it was suggested that the appointment of a receiver never affects the beneficial ownership of the shares of the company in question. There have been no further judicial statements on the issue. The appointment of a receiver seeks to realise a secured asset for a mortgagee and nothing further. Once the asset has been realised, the receivership will theoretically come to an end. The assets which are the subject matter of the receivership are vested in the receiver, any transfer of assets between the receiver and the company does not qualify for relief. The beneficial ownership of property which is not subject to receivership remains with the company and any such transfer could avail of the relief.

Consideration for the transfer

[8.29] The relief is not available where the consideration for the conveyance or transfer is provided either directly or indirectly by an outsider, that is, one unconnected with the company, or where the beneficial ownership in the property had been previously conveyed or transferred by an outsider SDCA 1999, s 79(5)(a). In *Curzon Offices v IRC*[34], M'Naghten J was of the opinion that provision of part of the consideration involved would bring the transaction outside the scope of the relief. In this case, property was transferred to a subsidiary partly by way of an advance given to the subsidiary by a bank and partly by way of a mortgage secured over the property in question. The subsidiary company became the owner of the property and the parent company was owed the balance outstanding that had not been paid by way of the bank loan. This transaction would be exempt from liability to duty, being eligible for the relief between associated companies. However, the parent company had arranged for a third party to

---

33 *English Sewing Cotton Co v IRC* [1947] 1 All ER 679.

34 *Curzon Offices v IRC* [1944] 1 All ER 163.

purchase the entire issued share capital of the subsidiary the next day. The payment for the property was effectively being made by the third party and not eligible for the relief. On appeal to the Court of Appeal [1944] 1 All ER 606 no dissent to this proposition emerged. However, in *Times Newspapers v IRC*[35] this case was distinguished but statutory anti-avoidance provisions have effectively reduced *The Times* case to an historical footnote.

[8.30] A true avoidance scheme was that used in *Shop & Store Developments v IRC*.[36] The facts are relatively complex but, in synopsis, there were two companies owned by one family: a property company and a clothing company. The aim was to redistribute the assets between the two companies and to take the property company public. In doing this they made an arrangement with an issuing house and underwent a series of transactions in the space of a few hours. Basically, the clothing company purchased the bulk of the ordinary shares in the property company for £269,700 and then proceeded to sell property and assets to the property company for the issue of 2.9 million ordinary shares. At this point, the clothing company sold its shares in the property company to the issuing house for £385,000. The property company appealed a decision of the Revenue Commissioners to charge *ad valorem* duty on the transfer of the assets. The Court of Appeal held that the term 'consideration' was not confined to the technical definition given under the law of contract, neither was the concept limited to the consideration listed under the document of transfer. Instead, the court held that it was to be defined in accordance with the words surrounding it so that if it was found that a substantial benefit was to be provided not by a connected person but by an outsider, then the relief would not apply. On appeal to the House of Lords, this ruling was reversed. It was held (with Lord's Reid and Guest dissenting) that the term 'consideration' meant that which was taken by the transferor under the transfer alone and not to any 'quid pro quo'.

[8.31] FA 1980, s 85 inserted SDCA 1999, s 79(5)(a) which contains anti-avoidance measures to prevent this sort of abuse. Effectively, this section extends the concept of the outsider and outlaws the sort of activity that occurred in *Shop & Store*. The onus is on the claimant to prove to the satisfaction of the Revenue that the transaction comes within the scope for relief. The section also introduces a time requirement for the connection to exist after the transaction has occurred and if the connection between the bodies corporate is dissolved during that period, the Revenue can impose the full liability to duty. This shall be discussed in this chapter.

[8.32] Consideration for the transfer which is provided at arm's length by way of an ordinary financial loan will not render the transaction outside the relief. A sale or transfer of an asset to a subsidiary to be financed by a loan taken by the subsidiary from, for example, a bank does not fall outside the provisions as being consideration provided by an unconnected person. The Guidance Notes[37] issued by the Irish Revenue Commissioners state:

---

35 *Times Newspapers v IRC* [1971] 3 All ER 98.

36 *Shop & Store Developments v IRC* [1967] 1 All ER 42.

37 See www.revenue.ie and the Institute of Tax publication of SDCA 1999.

However, in practice, the relief will not be denied where the consideration (or any part of it)is borrowed from a financial institution as part of an independent commercial transaction.

Cessation of association

[8.33] If the companies cease to be associated within two years of the transaction, then the instrument becomes chargeable to the full rate of duty without any exemption and the liability to pay such duty rests both jointly with the transferor and the transferee.[38] This means that, on cessation of association within two years, the liability to duty would be the *ad valorem* rate on the instrument, as if SDCA 1999, s 79(1) had not been enacted. Previously, the exemption was:

> deemed not to have been allowed and an amount equal to the duty remitted shall forthwith be a debt due from the transferee and transferor jointly and severally to the Minister for Finance ... as if the duty was the stamp duty referred to in that subsection and the date of the conveyance was a date one month after the date of the transaction referred to in that subsection, with any other necessary modifications.

[8.34] This was open to a number of possible interpretations. Firstly, on cessation of association, both transferor and transferee become liable to *ad valorem* duty on the instrument. Secondly, on cessation of association, there is a double charge to duty as duty and penalty are payable one month from the date of the deed.

Example 8.34.1

Tracy Ltd is an associated company with Chapman Ltd.

Tracy Ltd transfers a commercial property worth €100,000 to Chapman Ltd and the duty is relieved.

Some months later the companies cease to be associated.

Liability to Duty

If the section is interpreted to charge duty as a single charge only, then the liability is as follows:

Duty €6,000 (6% of €100,000) plus penalty plus interest payable one month after the date of the deed.

If the section is interpreted to charge duty as a double charge, then the liability is as follows:

(a) Duty €6,000 (6% of €100,000) previously relieved,

(b) Duty €6,000 (6% of €100,000) plus penalty plus interest payable one month after the date of the deed.

While a strict reading of the section might appear to give rise to a double charge to duty, principles of statutory interpretation would have favoured an interpretation giving rise to a single charge only (before the enactment of the IA 2005). SDCA 1999, s 79(7) now provides that the duty is levied as if the relieving provision had not been enacted together with interest on the duty at a rate of 0.273% per day, or part thereof, from the date on which the parties ceased to be associated. Thus the transaction falls within the ordinary *ad valorem* liability to duty with the appropriate accountable person in accordance with SDCA 1999, s 1.

---

[38] SDCA 1999, s 79(7)(b).

[8.35] Further, these provisions also apply where it is found that any evidence or certificates furnished with respect to the transaction are untrue in any particular material and interest runs from the date of the transfer or conveyance. It does not matter why the qualifying relationship was dissolved, a liquidation of the transferor or transferee company within two years of the transaction is sufficient to render it liable to the full duty. The removal of the exemption does not render the document inadmissible as evidence, given that it was correctly stamped at the time of execution and had been adjudicated upon.[39]

Procedure to avail of the relief

[8.36] Adjudication is compulsory in order to claim the relief under SDCA 1999, s 79(2). The claim for relief must be accompanied by a statutory declaration[40] and the whole instrument must then be adjudicated upon. In claiming for the relief, the following questions should be asked:

(a) Are the companies associated companies under the relevant provisions? If not, the relief is not available.

(b) Has any of the consideration been provided by an outsider? If yes, then the relief is not available.

(c) Can a statutory declaration containing the following elements be signed by a solicitor or officer of the associated companies:

 (i) full details of the types of companies involved, their names, registered offices, details of share capital, date of incorporation, company registered number, etc;

 (ii) that the effect of the instruments is in accordance with that of SDCA 1999, s 79;

 (iii) the purpose of the transaction;

 (iv) certify that the transferor was the beneficial owner of the property and that, as a result of the transaction, the transferee became the beneficial owner;

 (v) the relationship between the two companies and its compliance with the legislative provisions;

 (vi) that the relationship is intended to be maintained between the two companies and that the transferee intends to continue to hold the beneficial interest in the property;

 (vii) the instrument is not part of an arrangement in breach of SDCA 1999, s 79(5).[41]

---

[39] SDCA 1999, s 20 states that once an adjudication stamp appears on a document such instrument shall be admissible in evidence notwithstanding any difficulty over the amount of duty, see **Chapter 15**.

[40] SDCA 1999, s 79(6).

[41] Full details are to be found in **Appendix 5**.

If the preceding issues can be satisfied, the relevant instruments, together with the declaration, should be forwarded for adjudication. From a practical point of view, it may be possible to get insurance to cover this potential risk of clawback of the relief.

Relief on reconstruction or amalgamation of companies (stamp duty)

Transfer of assets

[8.37] The transfer of assets in the course of a reconstruction or amalgamation of any company or companies may attract a liability to *ad valorem* stamp duty. Provided that the reconstruction or amalgamation satisfies the requirements of the relieving provision[42] the transaction is exempt from stamp duty under the heading conveyance or transfer on sale as set out in SDCA 1999, Sch 1. To qualify, the transaction must be either a 'reconstruction' or an 'amalgamation'. While these words are not defined in the legislation, they have been interpreted judicially.

Reconstruction

[8.38] Definitions of both amalgamation and reconstruction are given a rather wide meaning. Provided the scheme comes within one of those definitions and within the relieving provision, the transfer of the undertaking or assets will be relieved from *ad valorem* duty under the conveyance on sale head.

[8.39] Reconstruction usually involves the transfer of the undertaking or part of an undertaking to a new company which has substantially the same ownership as the original company. The original English legislation was contained in FA 1927, s 55 and was subsequently repealed by FA 1986, s 65 which imposed stricter rules in the United Kingdom. The Irish legislation is, however, still based on the original UK legislation. Considering the word 'reconstruction' in 1904, Buckley J stated in *Re South African Supply & Cold Storage Co Ltd, Wilde v Sale*[43] 'it involves, I think, that substantially the same business may be carried on and substantially the same person shall carry it on'.

[8.40] In an application under FA 1927, s 55(i) in England, Lord Hanworth MR held the exemption was allowed:

> ... because the old company is really represented or replaced by the new company, and the shareholders in the new company are to be in substance the shareholders of the old company.[44]

The word reconstruction was considered further by Pennycuick J who stated:

> in ordinary speech the word 'reconstruction' is, I think, used to describe the refashioning of any object in such a way as to leave the basic character of the object unchanged. In relation to the companies, the word 'reconstruction' had a fairly precise meaning which corresponds, insofar as the subject matter allows, to its meaning in ordinary speech. It denotes the transfer of the undertaking or part of the undertaking of an existing company to a new company with substantially the same persons as were members of the old company.[45]

---

42 SDCA 1999, s 80.

43 *Re South African Supply & Cold Storage Co Ltd, Wilde v Sale* [1904] 2 Ch 268.

44 *Oswald Tillotson Ltd v IRC* [1933] 1 KB 134 at 155.

45 *Brooklands Selangor Holdings Ltd v IRC* [1970] 2 All ER 76.

[8.41] This interpretation only covers a reconstruction that consists of a transfer of an undertaking or part of an undertaking from one company to the other but does not allow a share-for-share swap reconstruction. Plowman J stated that:

> ... a reconstruction normally involves the transfer of a company's undertaking (or part of it) to a new company which is going to carry on substantially the same business as the business transferred to it.[46]

This interpretation of reconstruction by Plowman J envisaged that there might be other transactions that would come within the definition of reconstruction.

[8.42] The following examples set out situations where relief from *ad valorem* stamp duty can be sought.

Example 8.42.1

A, B and C are the shareholders in Squigy Ltd, a company that both manufactures and installs refrigeration units.

Due to this diversity in trade, it was decided by the three shareholders that two separate companies should be set up to run separate businesses, and that Squigy Ltd would be the holding company.

The two companies then incorporated were Manu Ltd and Frigi Ltd. The installation business was transferred to Frigi Ltd in exchange for shares and the manufacturing business was transferred to Manu Ltd in exchange for shares.

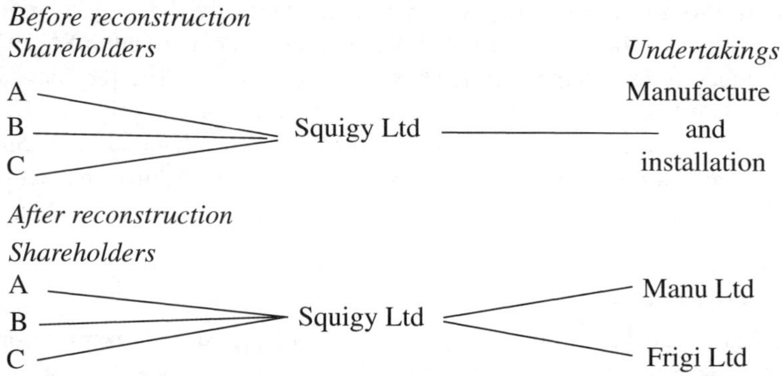

Example 8.42.2

Undertaking transferred in consideration of shares. The target company agrees to transfer the undertaking to the acquiring company in consideraton of shares.

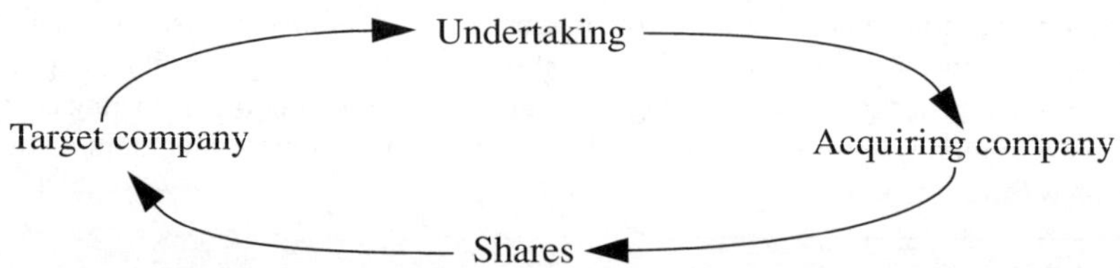

[46] *Baytrust Holdings Ltd v IRC* [1971] 1 WLR 1333.

Consequences

Example 8.42.3

Company A transfers its undertaking of furniture manufacturing to Company B, the acquiring company, which, in consideration for the transfer of the undertaking, transfers shares to the shareholders of Company A.

The shareholders in Company A now own the shares in Company B which operates the undertaking.

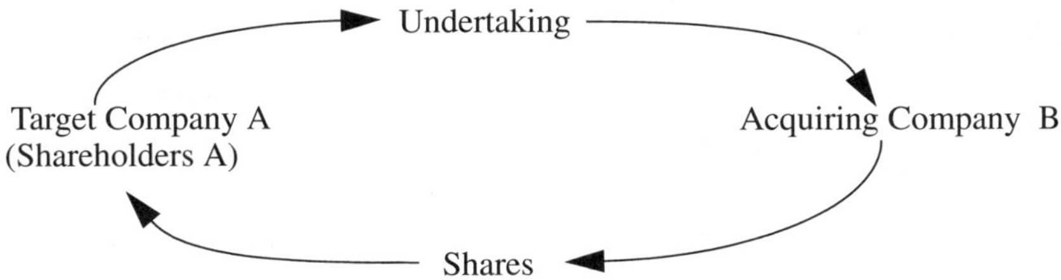

Consequences

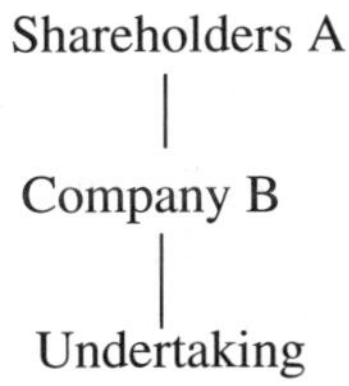

Example 8.42.4

The shareholders in Company A transfer their shares to Company B in consideration for an issue of shares in Company B to them.

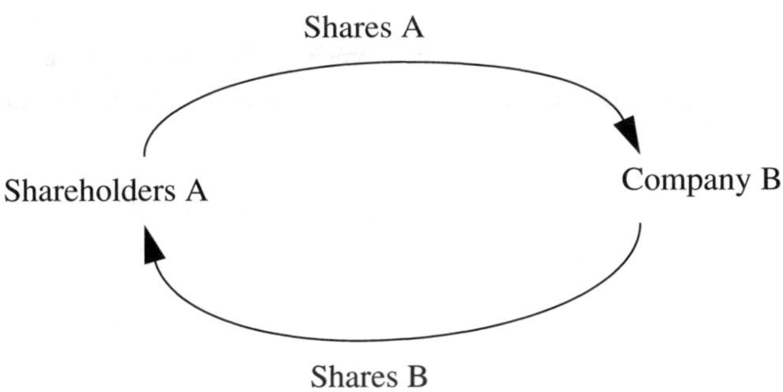

Consequences

Shareholder A
|
Company B
|
Company A

Amalgamation

[8.43] Amalgamation is not defined in the legislation. It was considered judicially by Romer LJ in considering the Trustee Act 1925 in England where he held that amalgamation:

> ... contemplates a state of things under which two companies are so joined as to form a third entity, or one company is absorbed and blended with another company.[47]

'A scheme for the amalgamation of any companies ...' was considered in *Crane Freuhauf Ltd v IRC*.[48] The court held that an amalgamation in effect is the joining of two or more companies so that they are in substance owned by the same person. It has also been held that in its ordinary meaning amalgamation consists of the blending of two concerns into one.[49] Romer LJ indicated that an amalgamation can be effected in the following ways:

(a) the undertaking of the target company is acquired by the acquiring company in consideration of the issue of shares in the acquiring company to the target company (a two-party, share-for-undertaking swap); or

(b) the undertaking of the target company is acquired by the acquiring company in exchange for the issue of shares in the acquiring company to the shareholders of the target company (a three-party, share-for-undertaking swap);

(c) the shares of the target company are acquired by the acquiring company in return for the issue of shares in the acquiring company to the shareholders of the target company (a share-for-share swap).

Example 8.43.1

Company A wishes to amalgamate with Company B. It acquires the shares of Company B by the issue of shares in Company A to the shareholders of Company B.

A (Shareholders) | B (Shareholders)
| |
A Ltd | B Ltd

47 *Re Walker's Settlement* [1935] Ch 567 at 583.

48 *Crane Freuhauf Ltd v IRC* [1975] 1 All ER 429.

49 *Swithland Investments Ltd v IRC* [1990] STC 448.

The result is that now both shareholders A and B hold all the shares in Company A, which in turn holds all the shares in Company B (the undertaking).

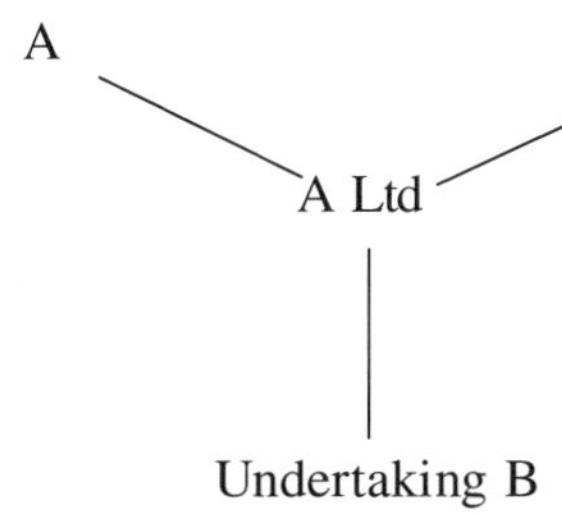

Example 8.43.2

Assume the facts are the same as those in Example **8.43.1**, except this time the shares in the acquiring Company A shall be issued directly to B Ltd.

The result is that the shareholders in Company B still retain the shares in B Ltd, which in turn holds shares in A Ltd, together with the shareholders in A Ltd.

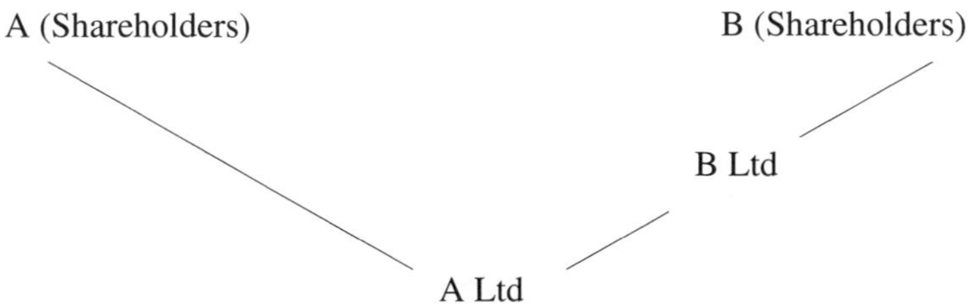

Example 8.43.3

Assume the facts are the same as those in Example **8.43.1** except that A Ltd acquires the undertaking of B Ltd in return for the issue of shares in A Ltd to the shareholders of B Ltd.

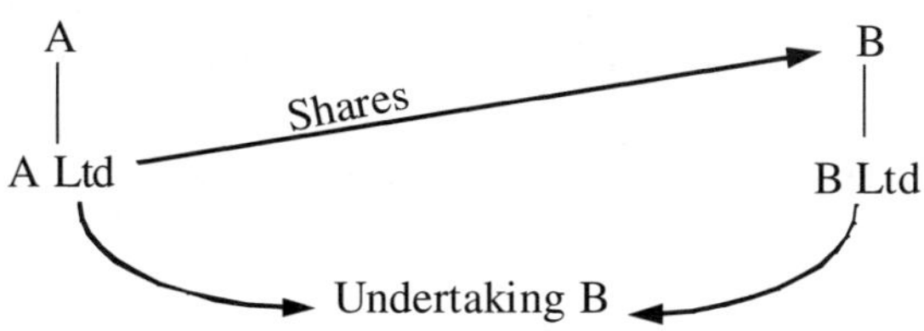

Qualifying conditions for relief

Scheme for reconstruction or amalgamation

[8.44] To qualify, the following conditions have to be satisfied. The Revenue Commissioners have to be satisfied that the scheme is a bona fide reconstruction of any company or companies or an amalgamation of any companies which qualifies with certain other conditions.[50] The Revenue Commissioners must now also be satisfied that the scheme of reconstruction or amalgamation is undertaken for bona fide commercial reasons and not a scheme or arrangement whose main purpose is to avoid a tax liability.[51] Whether the main purpose of an arrangement is to avoid a tax liability is one of fact. In *IRC v Brebner*[52] Lord Upjohn observed:

> The question of whether in fact one of the main objects was to avoid tax is one for the Special Commissioners to decide on a consideration of all the relevant evidence before them and the proper inferences to be drawn from that evidence.

Lord Upjohn also stated that just because there were two ways to effect a transaction, one of which involved paying tax and the other resulting in no tax being payable, it could not be concluded that the taxpayer in chosing the latter route had the main object of avoiding tax.

[8.45] A scheme for reconstruction has been interpreted to mean the transfer of an undertaking or part of an undertaking of an existing company to a new company where the new company comprises substantially the same members as the old company, and the new company carries on substantially the same business as the old company.[53] It has been held that an amalgamation comprises the coming together of businesses in the manner which would ensure that there is no substantial change in real ownership.

[8.46] *Crane Freuhauf Ltd v IRC*[54] involved a scheme of amalgamation consisting of an acquisition of shares in exchange for shares plus cash. The shares obtained by the vendor shareholders were subject to an option arrangement where one-third of the shares acquired by them could be purchased by a third party. The Revenue Commissioners argued that, as there was such an option, this prevented the amalgamation from being a scheme of amalgamation.

[8.47] The facts of the case were as follows. Crane Freuhauf Ltd entered into an agreement with Boden Traders Ltd and its shareholders to acquire the whole of the ordinary share capital in Boden Traders Ltd. In return for every 49 shares held in Boden Traders Ltd, the shareholders were allotted 18 fully paid up ordinary shares of two shillings each in Crane Freuhauf Ltd, together with one pound cash, the full consideration being 1.8 million ordinary shares and £100,000 cash. The new shares were

---

50 SDCA 1999, s 80(2).

51 SDCA 1999, s 80(4).

52 *IRC v Brebner* [1967] 1 All ER 779.

53 *Brooklands Selangor Holdings Ltd v IRC* [1970] All ER 76.

54 *Crane Freuhauf Ltd v IRC* [1975] 1 All ER 429.

subject to an option in favour of Freuhauf International Limited by the board and shareholders to sell to it one-third of the consideration shares in Crane Freuhauf Ltd.

[8.48] The option over the 600,000 shares was exercised prior to the allotment of the 1,800,000 shares in Crane Freuhauf Ltd. When the 1,800,000 shares were registered and issued to the Boden shareholders, 600,000 shares immediately vested in Freuhauf International Ltd who became the registered owners. The company claimed capital duty relief and the Revenue Commissioners argued they were not entitled to the relief as:

(a) it was not a scheme of amalgamation due to the option agreement; and

(b) the cash consideration exceeded the amount allowed by statute, that is 10 per cent.

Templeman J in the Chancery division[55] stated that it was a scheme for amalgamation notwithstanding the proposed option but, as more than 10 per cent of the consideration for the acquisition consisted of cash or a right to cash, the scheme failed. This decision was confirmed in the Court of Appeal.[56]

[8.49] The effect of this decision is that a scheme for reconstruction or amalgamation ends when the consideration shares, that is the shares in the acquiring company, are registered. An option to be exercised by a third party later which results in the onward transmission of shares was to be ignored. Distinguishing this case in *IRC v Kent Process Ltd*[57] the court extended its interpretation of the scheme of reconstruction or amalgamation. The subsequent transaction transferring the consideration shares was deemed to be part of the original transaction. This case would more accurately reflect the current Irish courts' approach to taxing statutes. *Swithland Investments Ltd v IRC*[58] involved a group of companies. The company (Estates Ltd) operated a licensed premises with three shareholders: A, A's wife and B. They had received an offer from Whitbread to acquire their licensed premises. Although the shareholders were in agreement as to the offer, they wished to reinvest the moneys in different ways. They incorporated three companies, namely Newco, Investment, and Leisure. The companies carried out the following steps:

(a) Newco acquired the licensed premises from Estates Ltd and the shares in Newco were then transferred to Whitbread;

(b) A and his wife transferred their share in Estates Ltd, which previously owned the licensed premises, to Investments Ltd in consideration for shares in Investments Ltd; A and his wife owned 100 per cent of Investments Ltd which in turn owned 90 per cent of Estates Ltd;

(c) B transferred his interest in Estates Ltd to Leisure Ltd in consideration of shares in Leisure Ltd plus a cash consideration of £100,000;

---

55 *Crane Freuhauf Ltd v IRC* [1974] 1 All ER 811.

56 *Crane Freuhauf Ltd v IRC* [1975] 1 All ER 427.

57 *IRC v Kent Process Ltd* [1989] STC 245.

58 *Swithland Investments Ltd v IRC* [1990] STC 448.

(d) Investments Ltd transferred to Leisure Ltd part of its shareholding in Estates Ltd in consideration of shares in Leisure Ltd;

(e) Leisure Ltd transferred to Investments Ltd shares in Estates Ltd in consideration of £2 million;

(f) A transferred to Investments Ltd one share in Leisure Ltd in consideration of £1.

[8.50] Relief was claimed in respect of transfers under step (b) and also the transfer occurring in step (d). It was held by the court that, as the present transaction consisted of nothing more than a mere partition of purchase shares, it did not qualify as a scheme for either reconstruction or amalgamation. Ferris J stated:

> ... it does not seem to me to be correct to try to separate the Newco part of the transaction from the rest when letter (f) makes clear all the steps are planned and carried through as a composite whole. I cannot regard the Newco part of the transaction as a preliminary to the rest of the transaction. It was both the reason why the transaction as a whole was devised and an integral part of it. Viewed in this way I consider that the transaction was not a reconstruction in the sense in which the word is used in, s 55. Like the transaction in *Brooklands Selangor* it was, in effect, a partition of assets previously belonging to a single company, in this case Estates Ltd.

[8.51] The courts in both the *Kent* case and this case limited the interpretation given to reconstructions and amalgamations by the *Crane Freuhauf* case. This approach has been severely criticised in the United Kingdom[59] where they are considered odd decisions and have not found a wider application. The Irish provisions contain the phrase 'bona fide reconstruction of any company or companies or the amalgamation of any company or companies'. This is not found in the equivalent UK legislation. This empowers the Revenue Commissioners to look at the overall transaction or scheme to satisfy themselves that there does exist a scheme for the bona fide reconstruction of a company or companies or the amalgamation of any companies prior to granting the relief.

[8.52] Prior to FA 1995, the reconstruction or amalgamation must not have been part of a transaction which was carried out exclusively for the purpose of avoiding tax as this may have fallen foul of the general anti-avoidance provisions.[60] If the reconstruction or amalgamation was carried out for the purposes of obtaining any relief, allowance or other abatement provided for in the legislation, it was not effected by the anti-avoidance provisions.[61]

[8.53] These general anti-avoidance provisions have been replaced by SDCA 1999, s 80(4) by setting down a further qualifying condition, namely that the scheme is effected for bona fide commercial reasons and is not part of a larger scheme or overall transaction for the purposes of avoiding liability to tax. Since *lex generalibus non derogat lex specialibus* (general law does not alter special law) applies, the general anti-avoidance provisions do not apply to reconstructions and amalgamations after the

[59] *Nock* [1990] BTR 269.

[60] TCA 1997, s 811.

[61] TCA 1997, s 811(3)(b).

passing of this section, and the procedures under these general provisions no longer apply. This seems undesirable as they place the onus on the taxpayer to prove that the scheme is for bona fide commercial purposes. In completing the declaration to avail of the relief, the solicitor should bear in mind the negligence provisions, particularly with regard to the amount of disclosure of information required.

Qualifying company

[8.54] To qualify for relief, a company with limited liability must be registered (meaning incorporated) or (since 30 July 1965) the company must be established by an Act of the Oireachtas or its nominal share capital must have been increased.[62] The Revenue Commissioners, when granting this original relief, gave a restrictive interpretation to the word 'company' to mean a company incorporated under Irish law. This was based on their interpretation of the English case of *Nestle v IRC*.[63] As a result of Ireland's membership of the EU, this interpretation was contrary to the provisions of the Treaty of Rome (Article 7), as it discriminated between a company registered under Irish law and a company incorporated in an EU Member State.

[8.55] Amending legislation was enacted which applied, subject to the provisions of SDCA 1999, s 80, where it was shown that:

(a) the transferee company was duly registered in another member state of the EU; and

(b) acquired all the issued share capital of a particular existing company and the consideration consisted wholly of the issue of shares in the transferee company to the holders of shares in the existing company in exchange of shares held by them in the existing company; and

(c) it was shown to the satisfaction of the Revenue Commissioners that both the existing company and the transferee company were wholly owned subsidiaries of the same holding company.

If these conditions were met, then *ad valorem* stamp duty would not be chargeable on any instrument made for the purposes of or in connection with the transfer of shares which were executed on or after 20 December 1988.[64]

[8.56] Both the holding company and subsidiary in this case are given the same meaning as they have in CA 1963. A company is deemed to be the subsidiary of another company if:

(a) the other company (ie the parent company) is a member of it and controls the composition of its board of directors; or

(b) the parent company holds more than half of the nominal value of its equity share capital; or

---

62 SDCA 1999, s 80(2)(a).

63 *Nestle v IRC* [1953] 1 All ER 877.

64 FA 1989, s 70.

(c) the parent company holds more than half in nominal value of the shares carrying voting rights; or

(d) the company is a subsidiary of a third company which is also a subsidiary of another company.

[8.57] The equity share capital in this regard is deemed to be the issued share capital of a company excluding any part which does not have the right (in so far as dividends or capital are concerned) to participate beyond a specified amount in the distribution.[65]

[8.58] This extension of the relief, while allowing the transferee company to be registered in another member State of the EU, required the existing company to be an Irish registered company. This relief was further extended to apply to a scheme satisfying the provisions of FA 1965, s 31[66] where:

(a) the existing company was registered in another member State of the EU; and

(b) the transferee company, which was an Irish registered company, acquired the undertaking or part of an undertaking situate in the State of the existing company; and

(c) relief was claimed in respect of instruments executed on or after 20 April 1990.

[8.59] In this case *ad valorem* duty was not chargeable.[67] Relief then applied to the following:

(a) reconstructions and amalgamations involving Irish registered companies;

(b) a share-for-share swap, where the transferee company was registered in a member State of the EU and acquired all the issued share capital in the existing Irish registered company and the consideration consisted wholly of the issue of shares in the transferee company to the holders of shares in the existing company in exchange of their shares in the existing company; and

(c) where an existing company was registered in a member State of the EU and the transferee company (Irish registered) acquired the undertaking or part of the undertaking situate in the State of the existing company and all other conditions were met.

[8.60] Amending legislation was passed in FA 1995 that repelead FA 1989, s 70 and FA 1990, s 117.[68] Further, SDCA 1999, s 80 is now to be applied in any situation where the relevant companies are incorporated within any Member State of the European Union and which meets the requirements of, s 31.[69] The impetus for these extensions came from a number of decisions of the European Court of Justice rendering direct discrimination for other EU-registered companies unlawful. In 1994 the ECJ decided in *Halliburton Services BV v Saatssecretaris Van Financien*[70] that Article 52 of the EEC

---

65 CA 1963, s 155.

66 As amended by FA 1989, s 70.

67 FA 1990, s 117.

68 FA 1995, s 144(3).

69 FA 1995, s 144(2)(a).

70 *Halliburton Services BV v Saatssecretaris Van Financien* [1994] STC 655.

Treaty prohibited indirect discrimination on the grounds of nationality. SDCA 1999, s 80(6) thereby extended the concept of qualifying company to include acquiring companies registered in other EU member states and target companies wherever registered, provided such companies corresponded with the law of the state where they were incorporated, and subject to such modifications for Irish companies which would qualify for relief, as may be necessary. In summary the acquiring company must be a company with limited liability[71] and may be incorporated in Ireland or in any other member state of the European Union, provided that, in the latter case, the acquiring company corresponds under the law of its state of incorporation to an Irish acquiring company. The Revenue Commissioners consider that the liability of all members must be limited in order to qualify for the relief.

The transferee company

[8.61] A transferee company must be one of the following:

(a) A limited liability company incorporated with a view to carrying out the reconstruction or amalgamation, which must be reflected in the objects of the memorandum of association of the company.[72]

(b) A limited liability company that has increased its capital with a view to carrying out the reconstruction or amalgamation which must be effected by way of resolution of the company stating the purpose of the increase.[73] The increase in the share capital relates to an increase in the nominal share capital or the issue of the unissued share capital.

(c) A company established by Act of the Oireachtas which is effected by Act or other authority, or a company established by Act of the Oireachtas after 1965 which has an increase in its capital with the view to acquiring the undertaking or shares of an existing company, for the purposes of reconstruction or amalgamation.

The reconstruction and amalgamation carried out under paras (a) to (c) above must result in the acquisition of either:

(i) the undertaking of an existing company; or

(ii) not less than 90 per cent of the issued share capital of an existing company.

The object to be included in the memorandum of association must state that the company intends to acquire not less than 90 per cent of the issued share capital of the existing company. It has been held that where the company was incorporated with a view to acquiring less than 90 per cent of the issued share capital but which subsequently acquired 90 per cent of the share capital it did not qualify for relief: *Lever Brothers Ltd v IRC*.[74] If the decision in *IRC v Kent Process Ltd*[75] applies in this jurisdiction then the

[71] SDCA 1999, s 80(1)(b).

[72] SDCA 1999, s 80(6).

[73] SDCA 1999, s 80(6)).

[74] *Lever Brothers Ltd v IRC* [1938] 2 KB 518.

[75] *IRC v Kent Process Ltd* [1989] STC 245.

value of *Lever Bros v IRC* decision must be open to question. Further statutory provision alters the need to acquire 90 per cent of the shareholding where the 90 per cent shareholding is acquired within six months of the transaction.[76]

Where the transferee owns in excess of 10 per cent of the issued share capital of the existing company the condition cannot be met and the exemption will not be obtained, see *Lever Bros Ltd v IRC*.

Existing company

[8.62] In *Chelsea Land Investments v IRC*[77] the term 'existing company' was held to include unlimited companies. Fox J had held, agreeing with the Revenue Commissioners that the term 'existing company' had to refer to a company on which capital duty would have been payable, but this was rejected on appeal. The ordinary meaning and not a specialist meaning of existing company was to apply. An amendment in the legislation to require that the existing company must be a limited liability company, however, only applied in the transferee company.[78]

Consideration for the acquisition

[8.63] Consideration for the acquisition, discounting any transfer to or discharged by the transferee company of liabilities of the existing company, cannot be less than 90 per cent of the issue of shares in the transferee company where:

(a) an undertaking has to be acquired if shares are to be issued to the existing company or to the holders of shares in the existing company; or

(b) shares are to be issued to the holders of shares in the existing company in exchange for the shares held by them in the existing company.[79]

The transfer of any debt in the target company to the acquiring company or the discharge of such debt by the acquiring company is ignored for the purposes of calculating the 90 per cent requirement.

[8.64] The acquiring company must be the company to move the consideration. Any inducements may be considered to form part of the consideration unless they are a truly independent inducement from an independent source, not being part of the scheme of reconstruction or amalgamation. When these requirements are met, subject to certain provisions and clawbacks, relief is granted. Previously, to qulaify for the relief, both companies had to be Irish registered companies, or an Irish company acquiring the undertaking or part thereof situate in the State of a company registered in another member State of the EU.[80]

[8.65] Prior to the passing of FA 1995, no charge to duty arose under the conveyance on sale head, where the transferee company was registered in a Member State of the EU and

76 SDCA 1999, s 80(9)(a).

77 *Chelsea Land Investments v IRC* [1978] 2 All ER 113.

78 SDCA 1999, s 80(7)(a).

79 SDCA 1999, s 80(2)(c)(i) and (ii).

80 SDCA 1999, s 80.

acquired 100 per cent of the issued share capital of an existing company, and the consideration for the acquisition consisted wholly of the issue of shares in the transferee company to holders of shares in the existing company in exchange of shares held by them in the existing company, and the existing company and the transferee company were shown to the satisfaction of the Revenue Commissioners to be wholly owned subsidiaries of the same holding company.[81] Similar relief was formerly available in England and was subject to much judicial interpretation. This relief was available under FA 1927, s 55, which has now been replaced by FA 1985, ss 78, 79 and 80, which a far more stringent relieving provision.

Requirements for the transaction

Consideration defined

[8.66] The words 'the consideration for the acquisition' were, according to the House of Lords in *Central & District Properties Ltd v IRC*,[82] to be given their natural meaning and the consideration should be provided by the acquiring company. A consideration provided by a third party could be ignored provided it was not part of an overall scheme instigated by the transferee company.

The facts of this case were as follows:

(a) Central and District Properties Ltd (CD) which was a subsidiary of U Ltd had a stock exchange quotation;

(b) 98 per cent of the ordinary share capital in U Ltd was held by two directors and the company was not quoted on the stock exchange;

(c) the two directors then arranged for CD to acquire U Ltd's shares so as to effect a merger;

(d) CD could not, pursuant to CA 1963, buy its holding company's shares. U Limited thus sold the shares it held in CD to L Ltd (an unconnected issuing house);

(e) the preference shareholders of U Ltd were offered preference shares in CD Ltd together with an attractive option over the ordinary shares in CD Ltd which were offered directly to them by L Ltd, provided the offer became unconditional. The offer was by way of negotiable letters of entitlement under which rights could be sold.

[8.67] If the options were deemed to be part of the consideration, the consideration passing in the form of shares would be less than 90 per cent and the relief would not apply. The Revenue Commissioners assessed stamp duty on this basis. The majority in the Court of Appeal and the House of Lords took the view that CD was legally responsible for ensuring that L Ltd would carry out the option offers. Consequently, as this formed part of the consideration for the acquisition, the relief could not apply. Where 'the consideration for the acquisition' comprised the issue of shares to the shareholders in the existing company and these shares were subject to an option

---

81 FA 1989, s 70, FA 1995, s 144(2).

82 *Central & District Properties Ltd v IRC* [1966] 2 All ER 433.

agreement in favour of a third party, then, in the event that the option is exercised, the consideration would consist of those shares retained plus any proceeds from the sale of the shares under the option.[83]

[8.68] In *IRC v Kent Process Control Ltd*[84] two subsidiaries, Introl Ltd and BBK Investments Ltd, which were wholly owned subsidiaries of a holding company agreed to transfer their undertakings, property and assets to Kent Process Control Ltd in return for the issue to them of shares in Kent Process Control Ltd, based on a net asset value of their undertakings.

[8.69] In July 1980 Kent Process Control Ltd increased its share capital and allotted shares to Introl Ltd and BBK Investments Ltd. BBK Investments Ltd and Introl Ltd on 15 December 1980 transferred their shares to their holding company for monetary considerations. Part of the Revenue Commissioners' contention was that the consideration of the acquisition did not consist of 90 per cent in the issue of shares as the further sale to the holding company involved substantial monetary consideration. The court held that as the payment from their holding company did not emanate from Kent Process Control Ltd it was not part of 'the consideration for the acquisition' and, as the consideration for the acquisition consisted of 90 per cent of the issue of shares, the conditions had been satisfied.

[8.70] Any cash payment together with any payment made by a third party procured by the transferee company is taken into account in ascertaining whether the consideration for the acquisition comprises not less than 90 per cent of the issue of shares in the transferee company to the existing company or holders of shares in the existing company.

Issue of shares

[8.71] The transferee company must issue shares:

(a) where an undertaking is to be acquired, to the existing company or the holders of shares in the existing company; or

(b) where the shares are to be acquired, to the holders of the shares in the existing company.

The issue of any authorised unissued share capital of the transferee company is to be treated as an increase in nominal capital of that company.

[8.72] It has been held that to come within the meaning of the issue of shares, the shares have to be registered in the name of the allottee. In *Crane Freuhauf Ltd v IRC*[85] the Revenue Commissioners argued that, because the vendor shareholders had a further obligation in respect of the new shares and never enjoyed full ownership, the shares were not issued to them.

---

[83] *Crane Freuhauf Ltd v IRC* [1975] 1 All ER 429, discussed further at para **8.43**.

[84] *IRC v Kent Process Control Ltd* [1989] STC 245.

[85] *Crane Freuhauf Ltd v IRC* [1975] 1 All ER 429.

[8.73] Templeman J in the Chancery Division held that the shares had been issued. The issue of shares meant the registration only of the names of the shareholders on the register and the issue of share certificates in their name. Stamp LJ in the Court of Appeal went further, stating that the issue of shares must be construed as reference to a condition that the shares are issued to those holders beneficially and not as nominees (at page 435). In *Murex v IRC*[86] it was held that if the shares to be issued to the shareholders in the existing company were issued to their nominees would this not qualify as the issue of shares to the shareholders. The issue of letters of allotment with forms of renunciation does not qualify as an issue of shares.[87] Romer LJ stated in interpreting FA 1927, s 55(1)(c):

> I cannot read this section without seeing that, whatever the word 'issue' may mean in other connotations, here it is the equivalent to the creation of a registered shareholder.

[8.74] In *Holmleigh Holdings Ltd v IRC*[88] it was held that share capital was unissued until it was placed in the register of members, for a mere allotment did not constitute an issue of shares until such time as the allottees' names were put on the register of members.[89]

[8.75] In *IRC v Kent Process Control Ltd*[90] as part of an internal re-organisation, certain shares were issued to two subsidiary companies: Introl Ltd and BBK Investments Ltd. These shares were then held by the companies until the holding company (Kent Process Control Ltd) ordered that they be transferred to Kent Process Control Ltd. The Revenue Commissioners argued that, as Introl Ltd and BBK Investments Ltd transferred the shares to their holding company, they could have at any time been compelled to transfer these shares by that holding company. Introl and BBK were never in a position to deal with the shares and, accordingly, were not the beneficial owners of them. The court held that the holding company, Kent Process Control Ltd, would have had to place a limitation on dealing with these shares as part of the consideration for the acquisition of the undertaking, even though by virtue of its shareholding, the holding company could force Introl Ltd and BBK Investments Ltd to transfer the shares to it. This obligation was not part of the consideration imposed on it by Kent Process Control Ltd and the shares had been issued within the meaning of FA 1927, s 55(1)(c)(i) and the tax payer was entitled to the relief.

Valuation of consideration

[8.76] When establishing whether the consideration for the acquisition consisted of not less than 90 per cent of the issue of shares, the nominal value of the issued share capital is taken into account rather than its market value.[91]

86 *Murex v IRC* [1933] 1 KB 173.
87 *Oswald Tillotson Ltd v IRC* [1933] 1 KB 134.
88 *Holmleigh Holdings Ltd v IRC* [1958] 46 TC 435 and 453.
89 *National Westminster Bank* [1994] 3 All ER 1.
90 *IRC v Kent Process Control Ltd* [1989] STC 24.
91 *Canada Safeway Ltd v IRC* [1972] 1 All ER 666.

Liabilities

[8.77] When calculating the consideration, the liabilities of the existing company that are transferred to or discharged by the transferee company are excluded.[92] This enables the transferee company to take over the debts and liabilities of the existing company where they have been incurred more than two years before the proper time for making a claim for the exemption. Where the debts were incurred by the company less than two years before the proper time for making the claim for exemption, such debts and liabilities must be debts due to banks or to trade creditors only.[93]

Example 8.77.1

Fred and Mable own all the shares in Bark Ltd, which has a nominal share capital of €1 million (one million ordinary shares of €1 each), of which 28,000 ordinary €1 shares are issued and fully paid up.

Albo Ltd, makes Fred and Mable an offer for all their shareholdings in Bark Ltd. The consideration is as follows:

(a) the issue of 28,000 ordinary shares of €1 each in Albo Ltd credited as fully paid up to Fred and Mable equally;

(b) a payment to Fred and Mable of €1,250 each.

$$\frac{\text{Share capital}}{\text{Total consideration}} \qquad \frac{€28{,}000}{€30{,}500} \times \frac{100}{1} = 91.8\%$$

As at least 90% of the total consideration of €30,500 comprises of shares, the transaction will qualify for relief from stamp duty.

Example 8.77.2

The facts are the same as above except for the following:

(a) the consideration comprises the issue of 28,000 ordinary shares of €1 each credited as fully paid up to Fred and Mable equally; and

(b) Fred and Mable are paid 30 cent cash for each ordinary share in Bark Ltd, bringing the total consideration to €36,400.

$$\frac{\text{Share capital}}{\text{Total consideration}} \qquad \frac{€28{,}000}{€36{,}400} \times \frac{100}{1} = 76.92\%$$

The total consideration is €36,400 of which only 76.92% consists of shares and the relief will not be available.

Example 8.77.3

The exact same facts as above except for the following:

(a) the consideration comprises the issue of 28,000 ordinary shares of €1 each credited as fully paid up to Fred and Mable equally; and

---

92 SDCA 1999, s 80(2)(c).

93 SDCA 1999, s 80.

(b) Albo Ltd also assumes the liabilities of the trade creditors and bank facilities (at present amounting to €50,000) and a director's loan from Fred of €18,000 which he lent to the company four years previously.

This transaction will qualify for the relief as the director's loan was incurred more than two years before the proper time for making a claim for an exemption.

Example 8.77.4

The exact same facts apply as in Example **8.77.1** except the director's loan was given by Fred to Bark Ltd three months prior to this transaction. In this case, the debt would be deemed to be part of the total consideration as the debt was incurred less than two years earlier.

$$\frac{\text{Share capital}}{\text{Total consideration}} \qquad \frac{€28{,}000}{€46{,}000} \times \frac{100}{1} = 60.43\%$$

The total consideration is deemed to be €46,000 of which 60.34% comprises the issue of shares and the transfer of the undertaking and the assignment of the debt would not qualify for the relief.

Notes

1 Director's loan of €18,000 + Shares of €28,000 = Total Consideration of €46,000.

Recipient of the shares

[8.78] As previously discussed at **8.16** the consideration for the acquisition must consist of 90 per cent of the issue of shares in the transferee company. Shares are issued as follows.

Where an undertaking is to be acquired

[8.79] Shares are to be issued:

(a) to an existing company; or

(b) to the holders of shares in the existing company.

As already seen, as per Buckley J, in *Re South African Supply & Cold Storage Co Ltd, Wilde v Sale*,[94] substantially the same business must be carried on as a result of the reconstruction by substantially the same person or persons. It must not constitute a sale to a third party.

[8.80] In *Brooklands Selangor Holdings Ltd v IRC*[95] Pennycuick J put forward the proposal that preference shareholders should not be taken into account in calculating the consideration requirements in certain circumstances; that is, their entitlement as shareholders or in conjunction with other shareholders in the company might not amount to 90 per cent of the real value of the company. There has been no further judicial debate on this issue to date and the position remains unclear.

---

94 *Re South African Supply & Cold Storage Co Ltd, Wilde v Sale* [1904] 2 Ch 268.

95 *Brooklands Selangor Holdings Ltd v IRC* [1970] 2 All ER 76.

Where shares are to be acquired

[8.81] Shares are issued by the transferee company to the holders of shares in the existing company in return for their shares. The shares must be issued to the holders of shares in the existing company in exchange for the shares held by them on a proportionate basis. The equivalent English provisions are far more stringent in their requirements.[96]

An EU transferee company

[8.82] Prior to the passing of FA 1995, if the transferee company was duly registered in a Member State of the EU and it acquired 100 per cent of the issued share capital of an existing Irish company, then the consideration consisted wholly of the issue of shares in the transferee company to holders of shares in the existing company in exchange of the shares held by them, and both companies were wholly owned subsidiaries of the same holding company.[97] This distinction has now been abolished.[98]

Where an Irish undertaking of an EU company is being acquired

[8.83] Prior to the passing of FA 1995, if the existing company was registered in the EU and an Irish-registered company acquired its undertaking or part of its undertaking situate in this State, the shares had to be issued to:

(a) the existing company; or

(b) the shareholders in the existing company,

so that substantially the same business was carried on by substantially the same shareholders in the acquiring company.[99] This has now been repealed by FA 1995, s 144(2).

Meaning of undertaking

[8.84] An undertaking may be acquired by the transferee company as part of the qualifying transaction. The term undertaking is not defined in the SDCA 1999. In this context, an undertaking of an existing company includes reference to part of an undertaking of an existing company.[100] When interpreting an undertaking in the context of the English section, it was held that the term 'undertaking' was the value of the undertaking excluding liabilities, so that it is the gross value that is taken into account, not the net value.[101]

[8.85] 'Undertaking' has been interpreted by the court to mean the business or enterprise undertaken by the company including all its assets, goodwill and other tangible rights. The disposal of assets is not necessarily a disposal of an undertaking.[102] If the scheme for

---

96 FA 1986, ss 75 and 76.

97 FA 1989, s 70.

98 FA 1995, s 144(2).

99 FA 1990, s 117.

100 SDCA 1999, s 80(1)(c).

101 *E Gomme Ltd v IRC* [1964] 3 All ER 497.

102 *Baytrust Holdings Ltd v IRC* [1971] 3 All ER 76.

reconstruction or amalgamation involves only part of an undertaking, that part of the undertaking must constitute a separate business. Even the disposal of trading assets by a trading company would be unlikely to be considered a disposal of an undertaking unless those assets were capable of constituting a business in their own right. In *Swithland Investments Ltd v IRC*[103] the court held that the scheme as carried out was nothing more than a partition of assets and did not constitute a scheme of reconstruction or amalgamation of undertakings and any relief was not available. Each case will depend on its own facts. In *Muii Bouwgroep BV v Staat Secretaris Van Financien*[104] the European Court, in considering the meaning of Council Directive 69/335/EEC 17 July 1969, Art 7(1)(b), as amended, held that the transfer by a company of 100 per cent of the share capital it held in a second company was not a transfer of part of the business of the first company. In *Thomas Firth & John Brown v IRC*[105] it was held that the acquisition of investments held by the existing company does not constitute part of the undertaking of that company.

The mere purchase of an undertaking will not qualify for relief, as the acquisition of the undertaking or part of the undertaking must be carried out in a scheme for reconstruction or amalgamation.

The relieving provision

[8.86] Once the scheme for reconstruction or amalgamation qualifies for exemption under SDCA 1999, s 80:

(a) stamp duty under the heading 'conveyance or transfer of sale' will not be charged on the instrument effecting the transfer of undertaking or shares nor on the instrument assigning the debts secured or unsecured of the existing company; and

(b) where a company is established by way of an Act of the Oireachtas no stamp duty is chargeable on any copy of the Act of the Oireachtas or on the instrument vesting or relating to the vesting of the undertaking or shares in the transferee company.[106]

Stamping of instrument

[8.87] An instrument must either be stamped with the full *ad valorem* duty or be adjudicated upon and stamped with a denoting stamp stating that it is not chargeable to stamp duty or that it is duly stamped.[107] The power of adjudication vested in the Revenue Commissioners is in addition to the powers already conferred upon them under SDCA 1999, s 20. An application should be made in accordance with the form ADJN7 (see **Appendix 2**).

---

103 *Swithland Investments Ltd v IRC* [1990] STC 448.

104 *Muii Bouwgroep BV v Staat Secretaris Van Financien* [1992] 2 CMLR 129.

105 *Thomas Firth & John Brown v IRC* [1971] 3 All ER 76.

106 FA 1895, s 12, FA 1965, s 31(1)(b).

107 SDCA 1999, s 80(3).

Time limits for the execution of instruments

[8.88] Relief can only be obtained for *ad valorem* duty where the instrument giving effect to the scheme for reconstruction is:

(a) executed within a period 12 months from the date of registration of the transferee company; or

(b) executed within a period of 12 months from the date of resolution for the increase of the nominal share capital of the transferee company, (or issue of unissued share capital[108] whichever is appropriate, or alternatively;

(c) where the agreement or particulars have been filed with the Registrar of Companies within the period of 12 months as required for (a) and (b) above, and the instrument is executed for the purposes of giving effect to this agreement.

On an allotment of shares by the transferee company, a return to the Companies Office must, within one month, be delivered to the Registrar of Companies setting out full details of the allotment. This can be extended in certain circumstances by the court.[109]

Statutory declaration

[8.89] The Revenue Commissioners are empowered to require the delivery of a statutory declaration setting out the details of the transaction. This must be sworn by an Irish solicitor of the courts. At present the Revenue Commissioners in practice do require a statutory declaration to be furnished.[110]

Group reconstruction/amalgamations

[8.90] Where a reconstruction or amalgamation is carried out within a group, the transaction may only be commercially viable as a result of the availability of these reliefs or exemptions. To protect the parties concerned, such contracts or agreements could be made conditional on the granting of the relief or exemption, so that, if the exemption was denied the transaction would not be stampable, subject to the proviso that the main purpose of the transaction was commercial, and not the avoidance of tax.

Clawback of relief

[8.91] The exemption from *ad valorem* duty may be withdrawn and stamp duty becomes payable on the instrument. The exemption may be withdrawn if any of the following occur:

(a) the exemption was allowed as a result of a declaration furnished or other evidence which is subsequently found to be untrue or the reconstruction or amalgamation as carried out does not comply with SDCA 1999, s 80(8)(a); or

---

[108] SDCA 1999, s 80(3)(b)(i).

[109] CA 1963, s 58 as amended – see Courtney *Law of Private Companies* (2nd edn, LexisNexis, 2002), Keane *Company Law* (4th edn, Tottel Publishing, 2006) ch 9.

[110] SDCA 1999, s 80(7)(a) – alternatively a declaration can be supplied by Revenue draft form ADJN6.

(b) any of the conditions specified in SDCA 1999, s 80(2) are not fulfilled in the reconstruction or amalgamation as actually carried out; or

(c) the existing company, within a period of two years from;

 (i) the date of registration or establishment of the transferee company; or,

 (ii) the date of the authority for the increase of capital of the transferee company,

 ceases to be the beneficial owner of the shares issued to it except where another reconstruction, amalgamation or liquidation is carried out;[111] or

(d) where the transferee company within a period of two years from;

 (i) the date of its registration or establishment, or

 (ii) the date of the resolution authorising it to increase its capital,

 ceases to be beneficial owner of the shares acquired by it in the existing company, except where another reconstruction, amalgamation or liquidation is carried out.

[8.92] In respect of paras (b) and (c) in para **[8.91]**, the clawback only applies and stamp duty becomes payable by the transferee company where:

(a) the shares are issued in the transferee company to the existing company and the existing company ceases to be the beneficial owner of the shares so issued; or

(b) where the transferee company ceases to be the beneficial owner of the shares so acquired,

provided this occurs within two years of the transaction.

[8.93] The existing company and the transferee company must not for a period of two years lose the beneficial ownership of the shares, whether issued to them or acquired by them. If either company ceases to be the beneficial owner of the shares the exemption is lost even though the company may still be the legal owner of the shares.

Example 8.93.1

The shares are made subject to a charge in favour of a lending institution within two years of the date of the transaction and the charge contains a clause stating that the equity of redemption is held in trust for the bank pending discharge. It could be argued that the beneficial ownership passed to the mortgagee and the exemption would be deemed to have not been allowed and *ad valorem* duty would be payable on the transfer of the assets or undertaking.

[8.94] If the company enters into an unconditional contract to sell the shares, then it would cease to be the beneficial owner of those shares.[112] In *Homleigh (Holdings) Ltd v IRC*[113] it was argued that since the company itself had not been a party to a rather complex arrangement for the sale of its shares to its subsidiary, which had been reached by the directors and shareholders without the involvement of the company, it had not lost

---

[111] SDCA 1999, s 80(8)(b). The second reconstruction or amalgamation need not be a qualifying amalgamation or reconstruction under s 80, see *Kent Process Control v IRC* [1989] STC 245.

[112] *Parway Estates Ltd v IRC* [1958] 45 TC 135.

[113] *Homleigh (Holdings) Ltd v IRC* [1958] 46 TC 435.

its beneficial ownership. Harman J, rejecting this, held that an order could have been granted against the directors to carry out the transaction to transfer the shares and the beneficial ownership had passed. In *IRC v Ufitec Group Ltd*[114] a company had entered into an agreement to sell shares, which had previously availed of this relief less than two years before, subject to the following conditions:

(a) that the consent of the Bank of England under the Exchange Control Acts be obtained; and

(b) the approval of the vendor's company shareholders be obtained.

[8.95] These were to be obtained within two months from the date of the agreement and if they weren't obtained, the agreement was null and void between the parties. The contract had been signed within the two-year time limit but the company argued that as these conditions would be satisfied outside the two-year time limit, beneficial ownership had not passed and, accordingly, relief on the original transaction was available. May J held that the conditions were:

> ... merely a condition precedent to liability to complete the operation provisions of the agreement ... and was not a condition precedent to the formation of any legally enforceable relationship between the parties at all ... In my opinion, therefore, the taxpayer company became liable on (the date of the agreement) to sell the shares... subject to the fulfilment of the conditions precedent to performance in Clause 1. To this extent it was then and thereafter legally bound.

As the company was not free to deal with the share capital, it ceased to be the beneficial owner. Doubts about this case have been expressed in light of the decision of *J Sainsbury plc v O'Connor (Inspector of Taxes)*[115] with respect to the concept of beneficial ownership.[116]

[8.96] The two-year rule clawback provision does not apply to the holders of shares in the existing company and the shareholders would be entitled to dispose of their new shares in the transferee company within the two-year period. If it is envisaged that the shares to be issued in the transferee company may be disposed of within the two-year period, it would be more appropriate to issue these shares to the shareholders of the existing company rather than to the existing company itself. However, it is imperative that the subsequent sale by the shareholders is totally independent of the original transaction and is not connected in any way, as per *Crane Freuhauf Ltd v IRC*[117] and *IRC v Kent Process Control Ltd.*[118]

[8.97] If any of the conditions set out at paras (a), (b) and (c) above occur, the exemption is deemed to have not been allowed and the transferee company will be liable for the

---

[114] *IRC v Ufitec Group Ltd* [1977] 3 All ER 924.

[115] *J Sainsbury plc v O'Connor (Inspector of Taxes)* [1991] STC 318.

[116] This is more fully discussed in **Chapter 1**.

[117] *Crane Freuhauf Ltd v IRC* [1975] 1 All ER 429.

[118] *IRC v Kent Process Control Ltd* [1989] STC 245.

duty which should have been payable on the instrument if the exemption had not been allowed in the first instance, together with interest. Interest runs from:

(a) the date of registration or establishment or the date of the resolution of the transferee company; or

(b) the date, if this exemption had not applied, that the duty would have been chargeable under FA 1998, s 125;

whichever is applicable in the circumstances.

The granting of exemption where stamp duty has already been paid

[8.98] Where a scheme for reconstruction or amalgamation is carried out and complies with all the conditions of SDCA 1999, s 80(2), except that the transferee company has not acquired 90 per cent or more of the issued share capital in the existing company and stamp duty has been paid on the instrument transferring the undertaking assets or assigning the debts and liabilities, the Revenue Commissioners have powers to repay the stamp duty.

[8.99] Where the transferee company subsequently acquires 90 per cent or more of the issued share capital under the scheme for reconstruction or amalgamation within a period of six months from either:[119]

(a) the last period of one month after the first allotment of shares made for the purpose of acquisition; or

(b) the date on which the invitation was issued to the shareholders of the existing company to accept the shares in the transferee company, whichever is the earlier;

the Revenue Commissioners may remit the duty provided it was paid and would have been exempted if the conditions had been met originally.

The time limits are the earlier of seven months from the date of the first allotment of shares made for the purpose of the acquisition or six months from the date on which the invitation was issued to the shareholders of the existing company to accept the shares. All the other necessary conditions have to be satisfied at 'the proper time for making the claim for exemption from stamp duty'.[120]

[8.100] The proper time for stamping an instrument generally or lodging for adjudication is 30 days from the date of its first execution.[121] This would apply to all recent schemes for reconstructions or amalgamations involving companies which were not created by Act of the Oireachtas. Where the transferee company has been incorporated by Act of the Oireachtas any instrument relating to the vesting or the printed copy of the Act shall be stampable within the latter of:

(a) three months after the passing of the Act; or

---

[119] SDCA 1999, s 80(9).

[120] SDCA 1999, s 80(9).

[121] SDCA 1999, s 2(3).

(b) three months after the vesting of the property or completion of the purchase as the case may be.[122]

Recent anti-avoidance measures

[8.101] Specific anti-avoidance measures were introduced by s 68 of the FA 2004. These measures were introduced to counteract schemes where target companies were acquired which held the benefits of executory contracts for the purchase of land with the contracts being completed upon completion of the acquisition of the target companies' shares. The measures provide that where a target company is being acquired and the target company has not taken a conveyance of property prior to the date of execution of the instrument effecting the transfer of the target company's undertaking, then relief under SDCA 1999, s 80(2) will not be available.[123] The provisions apply to instruments to be executed on or after 20 February 2004 and apply in respect of a conveyance for the transfer on sale of any property except marketable securities or a policy of life insurance.

[8.102] The Revenue Commissioners have clarified in their most recent version of their Guidance Notes that:

> Where the undertaking of a target company comprises a leasehold interest in property, the target company will be treated by the Revenue Commissioners, for the purposes of this subsection, as having obtained a conveyance of the property where the leasehold interest has been directly acquired by the target company by virtue of the grant of a lease from the lessor and such lease has been duly stamped. In addition, relief under this section will not be denied in circumstances where an undertaking of a target company comprises goodwill which has been acquired by the trading company over a long number of years. This treatment will only be granted where the Revenue Commissioners are satisfied with the bona fides claim for relief under this section and that the reconstruction or amalgamation does not involve the avoidance of stamp duty or any other tax or duty.

Reorganisation of undertakings for collective investments

[8.103] Stamp duty will not be chargeable on any transfer of assets which does not give rise to a chargeable gain under TCA 1997, s 739A.[124]

Reconstruction and amalgamation (capital duty)

Capital duty relief

[8.104] The reconstruction or amalgamation of a capital company may involve transactions which are chargeable for capital duty, but if the transaction qualifies for capital duty relief, the statement delivered to the Revenue Commissioners pursuant to SDCA 1999, s 117 will be charged at a rate of 0 per cent. The relief from stamp duty under the head conveyance on sale as discussed previously, is substantially different from the capital duty relief which was introduced in Ireland as a result of membership of the EEC.

---

[122] FA 1998, s 125.

[123] SDCA 1999, s 80(2A)(2).

[124] SDCA 1999, s 88A.

[8.105] FA 2006 abolished the charge to stamp duty on the issuing of shares in respect of transactions effected on or after 7 December 2005. As such, the relief is redundant in respect of transactions effected on or after 7 December 2005. It is unclear at this stage whether the Revenue Commissioners expect claims for the relief to continue to be submitted. It is the view of the authors that this cannot be the case as the relief operated to relieve a charging provision which has now been abolished. However, the Finance Act removes the charge to capital duty altogether on the issuing of shares which means that effectively there is no chargeable transaction to be relieved. The relief under SDCA, s 119 applies to the following transactions effected before 7 December 2005:

Share-for-share transaction

[8.106] This arose where Company A issued shares to the shareholders of Company B in exchange for the shares they held in Company B. In transactions of this kind, company A was known as the transferee, whereas Company B was termed the transferor company.

Example 8.106.1

Company A purchases shares of Company B from the shareholders in consideration of the issue of shares in Company A.

Shareholders B
Shares
Company B

Company A
Shares
Company A

Consequences

The shareholders, previously of Company B, are now shareholders of Company A. Company A now holds shares in Company B.

Shareholders
Company A
Company B

Transfer of undertaking

[8.107] The undertaking was transferred for shares. This could have occured in a number of ways and the two most common methods are dealt with below.

Example 8.107.1

Company B transfers its undertaking to Company A in consideration for the issue of shares in company A to the shareholders in Company B.

Consequences

The shareholders still hold shares in Company B and Company A, who presently operate the undertaking.

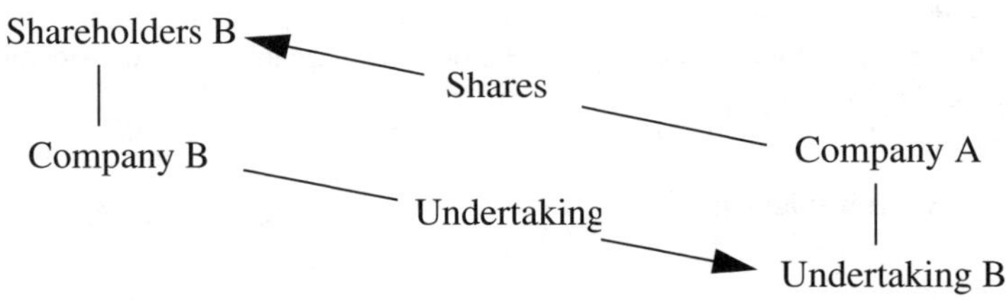

Example 8.107.2

Company B transfers the undertaking to company A in consideration of the issue of shares in Company A directly to Company B.

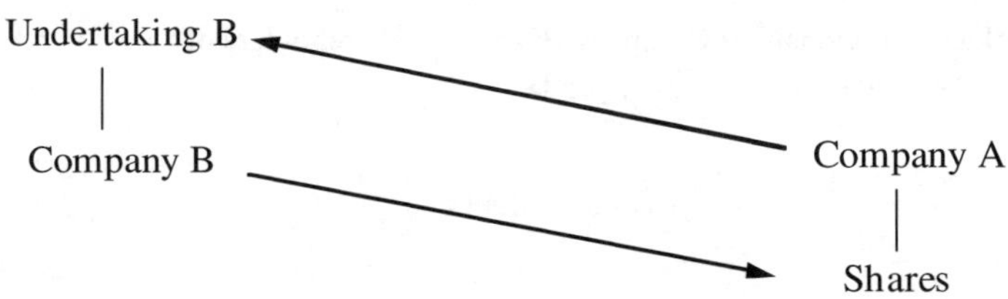

Consequences

Company B now holds shares in Company A which is now operating the undertaking. The shareholders are not directly involved in the transaction.

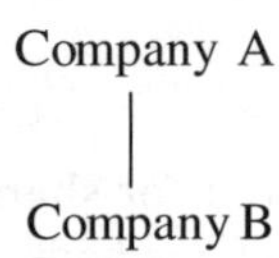

Qualifying conditions for relief

[8.108] To qualify for the zero rate of duty, the reconstruction or amalgamation has to comply with the conditions set out below.

Transferee company

[8.109] The transferee company which is issuing the shares as part of the consideration for the acquisition must be either:

(a) a capital company; or

(b) a capital company which is in the process of being formed.[125]

Acquired shareholding

[8.110] In the case of a share-for-share transaction the transferee company must, after the transaction has been completed, hold at least 75 per cent of the issued share capital of the transferor company.[126] This percentage of ownership can have been achieved as a result of more than one transaction. The relief is only available for the transaction which results in the transferee company holding at least the 75 per cent shareholding, or any subsequent transactions which are in excess of the required shareholding.

Example 8.110.1

A (40%), B (20%), C (20%), D (20%) are the shareholders in NicCongail Knitwear Ltd. A and C accept an offer from Gaggi Ltd for their shares in NicCongail Knitwear Ltd (60% of the share capital) in exchange for which they obtain shares in Gaggi Ltd. The result is that this transaction would be a chargeable transaction so that the issued shares in Gaggi Ltd would be chargeable to capital duty at a rate of 0.05%.

Example 8.110.2

B agrees to enter into a swap-for-swap arrangement for the issue of shares in Gaggi Ltd. This transaction qualifies for the relief as Gaggi Ltd now owns 80% of the shares in NicCongail Knitwear Ltd.

Example 8.110.3

Six years after the transfer by C to Gaggi Ltd, Gaggi Ltd disposes of 35% of its share capital in NicCongail Ltd. Two weeks later D agrees to enter into a swap for swap arrangement, for the issue of shares in Gaggi Ltd in return for its shares (20%) in NicCongail Ltd.

The issue of shares to D is liable to capital duty as the total shareholding of Gaggi Ltd in NicCongail Ltd after this transaction amounts to 65 per cent of the share capital. Therefore duty is payable at a rate of 0.05 per cent.

Under Irish law, after the transaction the transferee company has to own at least 75 per cent of the issued capital of the transferor company. Under English law, which implemented the same directive dealing with reconstructions and amalgamations, the concept of ownership in shares was extended to include beneficial ownership. This is more onerous.

[8.111] The qualifying percentage of ownership must continue to exist after the transaction. This is discussed further in *R v IRC, ex parte J Rothschild Holdings plc*[127] where the applicant made two allotments of shares in exchange for shares. The first allotment took place on 19 December 1983, and the subsequent allotment on 6 January 1984. Both allotments were returned to the Revenue Commissioners on one form. A

---

[125] SDCA 1999, s 119(1) – for further discussion on the meaning of 'capital company' see **Chapter 7**.

[126] SDCA 1999, s 119(1)(b).

[127] *R v IRC, ex parte J Rothschild Holdings plc* [1986] STC 410.

claim was made that these allotments constituted a single transaction and were exempt from capital duty pursuant to the English legislation. This claim was rejected and the allotments did not constitute a single transaction. As the shares acquired on the date of the first allotment were less than the 75 per cent of the nominal value of the total shareholding, the transaction was held not to be exempt. The decision rests primarily on the interpretation of the English legislation and the court believed that, as that legislation was sufficiently clear, it was unnecessary to revert to the directive for clarification on this issue. In this jurisdiction the courts have evidenced a far more liberal approach, even to the extent of preferring to interpret domestic legislation exclusively on the basis of its European counterpart where the legislation derives substantially from the obligations of membership of the Union.

Transferor company

[8.112] The transferor company's effective centre of management or the registered office of the transferor company involved in the transaction must have been in a Member State.[128] For the purposes of these provisions the definition of a capital transferor company was extended to include:

> ... a company, partnership, firm, association or legal person that meets the criteria of a capital company in another member State even though it may not be considered a capital company in this jurisdiction.[129]

The transfer of an undertaking in consideration of shares

[8.113] The transferee company must have acquired the undertaking or part of an undertaking of another capital company. The acquisition must be of part or all of the undertaking of the company, not just a distribution of assets. The undertaking, or part of the undertaking could be transferred as a going concern and carried on in the same manner. Part of an undertaking for the purposes of this relief had to comprise a separate independently trading business or an independent branch of the main business.[130] There was no definition of an 'undertaking' contained in the legislation. In this case Plowman J stated that:

> ... a reconstruction normally involves the transfer of a company's undertaking (or part of it) to a new company which is going to carry on substantially the same business as the business transferred to it.

[8.114] An undertaking would include all the assets, including goodwill and other intangible assets of the business. It is possible that an investment could constitute an undertaking within the meaning of the provisions, provided the investment constitutes a business of the company.[131] A fuller discussion of an undertaking is to be found in the section on reconstruction and amalgamations, relief from stamp duty.

---

[128] SDCA 1999, s 119(7).
[129] SDCA 1999, s 119(8) inserted by FA 1979, s 52.
[130] *Baytrust Holdings Ltd v IRC* [1971] 3 All ER 76.
[131] *IRC v Tyre Investments* [1924] 12 TC 646.

The consideration

[8.115] The consideration for the acquisition has to consist of:

(a) the issue of shares in the transferee company to the transferor company (or its shareholders), where it involves the transfer of an undertaking or part thereof; or

(b) the issue of shares in the transferee company to the holders of the shares in the transferor company in exchange for their shares, where shares in the transferor company are acquired.

Where cash was involved the payment could not exceed 10 per cent of the nominal value of the shares issued in the transferee company as part of the consideration.[132] In calculating the consideration no account is taken of such part thereof as consists of the transfer to or discharge by the transferee company of the liabilities of the transferor company.

Example 8.115.1

BK Ltd, an Irish-registered company with a nominal share capital of 1,000,000 shares divided into 1,000,000 ordinary shares at €1 each, of which only 50,000 had been issued to Brandon and Kelly equally. The market valuation of these shares at 1st November 2005 was €2.50 each. FF Ltd, a company registered in France, wished to take over BK Ltd and made an offer to each shareholder in BK Ltd of 25,000 ordinary shares at €1 each in FF Ltd plus 15 cent per share a total cash consideration of €7,500. The computation is as follows:

	€
Nominal value of shareholding	50,000
Cash consideration	7,500
$\frac{7{,}500}{50{,}000} \times \frac{100}{1}$	15%

This transaction does not come within the relieving provisions, and capital duty was payable as follows:

	€
50,000 ordinary shares at €1 each (market value €2.50 each)	
Total market value	125,000
Less cash consideration	7,500
Total contribution to FF Ltd	117,500
Capital duty 0.5%	588

If the cash consideration set out above was 9 cent per share, the cash consideration passing would amount to €4,500 and no capital duty would be payable as the consideration not consisting of shares did not exceed 10% of the total consideration.

132 SDCA 1999, s 119(3).

Example 8.115.2

FF Ltd acquired the undertaking of BK Ltd including a bank loan of €80,000. FF Ltd transfered 50,000 ordinary shares at €1 each to the shareholders of BK Ltd, namely Brandon and Kelly.

As the liabilities were not taken into account in calculating the consideration, and the consideration consisted entirely of the transfer of 50,000 ordinary shares at €1 each in FF Ltd to Brandon and Kelly, the issue of shares in FF Ltd would not have incurred a capital duty liability.

The consideration had to consist of 'issue of shares'. Capital duty relief applied where there was an issue of shares in the transferee company in return for which the transferee company acquired the undertaking or part of undertaking of the transferor company, or the share capital of the transferor company. The transferor company, or its shareholders, had to be registered as holders of the shares forming part of the consideration.[133] Shares issued on a mere allotment letter which were renouncible were not deemed to be an issue of shares qualifying for this relieving provision.[134] It was also been held that the issue of shares to nominees is not sufficient.[135]

Clawback of relief

[8.116] The transferee company has to retain, for a period of five years from the date of the chargeable transaction, at least 75 per cent of the issued share capital of the other company and all the shares which it holds following the transaction.[136] The transaction which qualifies for the reduced rate of stamp duty, is charged under SDCA 1999, s 117, where within a period of five years of the date of the transaction, the transferee company:

(a) ceases to retain at least 75 per cent of the issued share capital of the transferor company concerned; or

(b) disposes of any of the shares of the transferor company which it held after this transaction and to which the reduced rate applied.

The withdrawal of the relief is subject to the proviso that the reduced rate will continue to apply provided the second transfer of shares is:

(a) part of a further qualifying transaction which would qualify for the relief; or

(b) a transfer in the course of liquidation of the transferee company.

The latter proviso in respect of a transfer in the course of a liquidation arose from a declaration by the EEC Council which adopted Directive 73/79.[137] The Council adopted this Directive on the understanding that the provisions of the Declaration would apply.

[8.117] Where the relief is lost, the statement as delivered to the Registrar of Companies setting out full details of the transaction becomes chargeable as if it was chargeable on the date it took place. The date of the transaction for the purpose of paying the duty and

---

[133] *Oswald Tillotson Ltd v IRC* [1933] 1 KB 134.

[134] *Brotex Cellulose Fibres v IRC* [1933] 1 KB 158.

[135] *Murex v IRC* [1933] 1 KB 173.

[136] SDCA 1999, s 119(4).

[137] OJ 1973 12, 1173 p 1.

the date on which interest will run from is the date upon which the relief was lost. The statement must be delivered within 30 days of this date together with the duty payable.

Applying these rules to the relevant transaction the result would be as set out in the following paragraphs.

Share-for-share transaction

[8.118] Where the transferee company fails to retain 75 per cent of the issued share capital of the company or disposes of any of the shares held in the company after the transaction upon which the relief was obtainable, there is a clawback for relief, except where the subsequent transfer of shares occurs in the course of liquidation of the transferee company.

Transfer of undertaking

[8.119] The relief will still applied if:

(a) the transferee company disposed of the undertaking it acquired in return for shares; or

(b) the original shareholders of the transferor company disposed of the shares in the transferee company.

Case study 1

[8.120] X and Y are the registered owners of the share capital in an Irish registered company XY Ltd. The nominal share capital of the company is €1,000,000 divided into 1,000,00 ordinary shares of €1, each of which 36,000 shares are issued, owned equally by X and Y. The shares are valued at €2.50 each.

X and Y made an offer on 1 October 2005 for their shareholdings by Value Ltd, an Irish-registered company the consideration of which is as follows:

(a) the issue of 18,000 ordinary shares of €1, each which are fully paid up in Value Ltd in return for their shareholdings in XY Ltd;

(b) a cash payment of €1,600 each; and

(c) Value Ltd automatically assumes the liabilities of XY Ltd which is a director's loan for the sum of €10,000 which was entered into six months before this takeover took place.

The stamp duty liabilities were as follows:

Stamp duty

[8.121] Not less than 90 per cent of the consideration must comprise the issue of shares in the transfree company SDCA 1999, s 80(2). In calculating the value of the consideration passing, the nominal value of the shares is taken.[138] The liability and expenses are excluded in calculating the consideration except where they are incurred less than two years before the claim for relief, and not due to banks or trade creditors.[139]

---

[138] *Canada Safeway Ltd v IRC* [1972] 2 WLR 443.

[139] SDCA 1999, s 80.

[8.122] The relevant consideration paid is as follows:

	€
Issue of shares – nominal value	36,000
Cash payment	3,200
Director's loan	10,000
Total	49,200

$$\frac{€36,000}{€49,200} \times \frac{100}{1} = 73.17\%$$

As the issue of shares only comprises 73.17 per cent of the total consideration, the following shall be liable to stamp duty:

(a) the transfer of shares by XY Ltd to Value Ltd; and

(b) the assignment of the director's loan to the sum of €10,000.

Company capital duty

[8.123] The director's loan in this case is not taken into account as there is no restriction on excluding liabilities in company capital duty, but it does not form part of the consideration.

The consideration comprises:

(a) cash payment of €3,200; and

(b) issue of shares to the value of €36,000.

As the cash consideration is less than 10 per cent of the nominal value of the shares in Value Ltd, the relief would have applied and no capital duty would have been payable on the issue of shares in Value Ltd to X and Y.

Case study 2

[8.124] A and B Ltd are the registered owners of all the share capital in Compo Ltd. The nominal share capital of the company is 100,000 ordinary shares of €1 each and the issued share capital comprises 100,000 ordinary shares of €1 each, fully paid up, valued at €50 each, of which 20,000 are held by A and the remainder by B.

Insurer Ltd decides it wishes to take over and control Compo Ltd and makes an offer to the shareholders as follows:

(a) to issue 20,000 ordinary shares of €1 each credited as fully paid up in Insurer Ltd to A;

(b) to issue 80,000 ordinary shares of €1 each credited as fully paid up in Insurer Ltd to B;

(c) cash consideration of €2,200 payable to A and €8,800 payable to B;

(d) assumption by Insurer Ltd of all trade debts and liabilities amounting to €10,000 incurred six months before the transaction.

Stamp duty

[8.125] In calculating the consideration attributable to the shares, the nominal value of the shares is taken.[140] The debts and liabilities assumed by Insurer Ltd here are not taken into account as they comprise bank or trade debts.

The consideration is comprises:

	€
Issue of shares	100,000
Cash consideration	11,000
Total	111,000

$$\frac{€100{,}000}{€110{,}000} \times \frac{100}{1} = 90.9\%$$

As the consideration passing comprises 90.9 per cent of the issue of shares in Insurer Ltd, this transaction is exempt from stamp duty and there is no stamp duty payable on the transfer of the shares by A and B Ltd to Insurer Ltd.

Capital duty

[8.126] Relief from capital duty is subject to the proviso that the cash consideration must not exceed 10 per cent of the nominal value of the shares in Insurer Ltd.

The calculation is as follows:

Cash consideration

Total consideration $\frac{€11{,}000}{€100{,}000} \times \frac{100}{1} = 11\%$

As the cash element of the consideration exceeded 10 per cent of the nominal value of the shares, company capital duty was payable on the issue of shares by Insurer Ltd, which would have been calculated as follows:

Market value of the shares is €50 each

	€
Total consideration	5,000,000
Less cash element	11,000

Total consideration €4.989 million at 0.05% = €2,494.50.

[8.127] For relief for securities given by a subsidiary company to a holding company, see para **9.46**.

140 *Canada Safeway Ltd v IRC* [1972] 1 All ER 666.

Relief from stamp duty and capital duty compared for transactions effected on or before 7 December 2005

[8.128]

	Stamp duty relief (SDCA 1999, s 80)	Capital duty relief (SDCA 1999, s 119) (transactions before 7 December 2005)
(a)	The scheme must be a bona fide reconstruction or amalgamation.	Not necessary.
(b)	The scheme must be for a bona fide commercial reason and not for the avoidance of a liability to stamp duty, income tax, corporation tax, capital gains tax or capital acquisitions tax.	General anti-avoidance provisions only.
(c)	The transferee company must be established for the purpose of carrying out the acquisition of another company or its undertaking or, where there is an increase in capital, it must be authorised by way of resolution for the purpose of acquiring an undertaking or the existing company.	Not necessary.
(d)	Exemption is available to an EU incorporated acquiring company in accordance with the terms of this section.	Relief applies to capital companies, and the company being acquired has to have its effective centre of management and registered office within the Member State.
(e)	The reconstruction or amalgamation must result in the acquisition of either: the undertaking or part thereof; or not less than 90% of the issued share capital of the existing company.	As a result of this transaction the capital company must hold not less than 75% of the issued capital of another company.
(f)	The consideration for the acquisition must consist of (at least 90%) of the issue of shares in the transferee company and the cash consideration must not exceed 10% of the consideration (excluding the discharge of any debts or liabilities owed by the existing company, subject to certain restrictions).	The consideration consists of the issue of shares in the transferee company and any cash payment must not exceed 10% of the nominal value of the shares issued by the acquiring company.

(g)	Under a share for share swap, the transferee company and the target company must both retain beneficial ownership of the shares for a period of two years from the date on which the relief was granted.	The existing company shares are obtained by the transferee company and the transferee company may retain all the shares so acquired after the transaction and retain beneficial ownership of 75% of the shares in the company for a period of five years from the date of the transaction. The existing company is not required to hold the shares of the acquiring company for any period.
(h)	A statutory declaration by a solicitor is required.	No such restriction.
(i)	Prior to the transaction, the transferee company cannot hold more than 10% of the issued share capital of the existing company.	No such restriction.
(j)	Where the target company ceases to be the beneficial owner of the shares within two years, the relief is lost. Exemption is preserved if the connection is broken through another reconstruction or amalgamation or liquidation.	Exemption is preserved if the connection is broken through another transaction which would qualify for relief or through the liquidation of the transferee company.

Chapter 9

Mortgage Bond – Promissory Notes

Introduction

[9.01] Mortgages, bonds, debentures and covenants are normally created by instruments which in general provide security for the payment or repayment of moneys that are secured or charged on property situated in Ireland. Promissory notes, bills of exchange and cheques are negotiable instruments which grant an entitlement to payment of money. All these instruments must be stamped in accordance with the relevant stamping requirements to be enforceable in a court of law and ensure the effective payment or repayment of moneys. The instruments are stampable under the following headings:

(a) mortgage, bond, debenture, covenant (except a marketable security);

(b) bond covenant or instrument of any kind whatsoever;

(c) promissory notes and bills of exchange.

Mortgage, bond, debenture, covenant

Mortgage

[9.02] A mortgage which is security for the payment or repayment of money charged or encumbered on property situate in the State, other than shares in stock or funds of the Government or the Oireachtas is chargeable to duty.[1] This is referred to as the mortgage head of charge. A mortgage is defined as:

> ... a security by means of mortgage for the payment of any definite and certain sum of money advanced or lent at the time, and previously due and owing, or forborne to be paid, being payable or for the repayment of money to be thereafter lent, advanced, or paid or which may become due upon an account current, together with any other sums already advanced or due or without, as the case may be; and includes:
>
> (a) ...further charge, and heritable bond, disposition, assignation, or tack in security, and of or affecting any lands, estate or property, real or personal, heritable or movable, whatsoever.[2] This definition as enacted commenced with the words 'conditional surrender by way of mortgage' which was deleted by FA 1970, Sch 2, s 60 from 4 August 1970.
>
> (b) any conveyance of any lands, estate, or property whatsoever in trust to be sold or otherwise converted into money, intended only as a security and redeemable before the sale or other disposal thereof, either by express stipulation or otherwise, except where the conveyance is made to the benefit of creditors, generally, or for the benefit of creditors specified who accept the provisions made

1 SDCA 1999, s 1.

2 SA 1891, s 86(1)(a).

to the payment of their debts, in full satisfaction thereof, or who exceed five in number;[3]

(c) any defeasance, letter of reversion, back bond, declaration or other deed or writing for defeating or making redeemable or explaining or qualifying any conveyance, transfer, disposition, assignation, or tack of any lands, estate or property whatsoever, apparently absolute, but intended only as a security;[4] and

(d) any agreement (other than an agreement chargeable with duty as an equitable mortgage), contract, or bond accompanied with the deposit of title deeds, for making a mortgage, wadset or other security or conveyance as aforesaid of any lands, estate or property comprised in the title deeds, or for pledging or charging the same as security;[5] and

(e) any deed operating as a mortgage of any stock or marketable security.[6]

[9.03] The definition of mortgage as set out in the Stamp Act is extremely broad and would include any instrument which offers security for the payment or repayment of money which is secured over property by an instrument. The list set out above is not exhaustive. In considering a mortgage from the legal point of view, Fisher and Lightwood in *Law of Mortgage*[7] defined a mortgage as:

> ... a form of security created by contract, conferring an interest in property defeasible (that is annullable) upon performing the conditions of paying a given sum of money, with or without interest or of performing some other condition.

For a fuller discussion on mortgages see *Banking & Security Law in Ireland.*[8]

[9.04] In *City of London Brewery Co v IRC*,[9] SA 1891, s 86 was used to provide clarity regarding the nature of instruments coming within the charging provision. It has been held that an agreement executed under seal which agreed to execute on demand a mortgage as security for moneys lent, was chargeable as a mortgage under a mortgage bond, etc head.[10]

[9.05] A legal agreement which is executed under seal could be stampable. The majority of lending institutions issue letters of loan offer to prospective mortgagors which set out in detail conditions of the proposed advance. As these are executed under hand only and not under seal,[11] they are not stampable under this head.[12] In *IRC v Henry Ansbacher & Co* the full security documentation comprised an instrument which was not executed under seal. It was held not to be chargeable under the mortgage head, except where the title documentation is lodged by way of equitable mortgage.

---

3 SDCA 1999, s 1.

4 SDCA 1999, s 1.

5 SDCA 1999, s 1.

6 SDCA 1999, s 1.

7 Fisher and Lightwood, *Law of Mortgage* (11th edn, LexisNexis, 2001).

8 Johnston *Banking & Security Law in Ireland*, (Butterworths, 1998), Ch 10

9 *City of London Brewery Co v IRC* [1899] 1 QB 121.

10 *United Kingdom Realisation Co v IRC* [1899] 1 QB 361.

11 See **Chapter 2** para **2.26**.

12 *IRC v Henry Ansbacher & Co* [1963] AC 191.

A mortgage offers security by way of instrument. Wright J stated in *Jones v IRC* that:

> ... security does not mean (as in popular language) some obligation which is auxiliary to some other obligation, but means any obligation created by any instrument.[13]

The security offers the mortgagee a form of protection for moneys advanced.

[9.06] The mortgage provides security for the payment of any definite and certain sum of money advanced or lent which relates to the capital portion only and not interest, and stamp duty is chargeable on the capital sum advanced only. Stamp duty is not chargeable on the interest even though the interest is secured by means of the instrument. If the capital sum secured by the mortgage also includes interest which has been capitalised, or moneys advanced on foot of an insurance policy covering the property or the life involved, then these moneys are deemed to be part of the moneys advanced or lent and are chargeable to duty.

[9.07] A question arises with respect to fixed rate mortgages, which are mortgages where the interest rate is not variable but fixed, although usually only for a period of time. For example, a mortgage might be taken out for twenty years, during the first five years of which the interest is fixed at 10 per cent, and after which time the interest rate is to revert to the rate current at that time. In such cases, is the duty to be charged on the ascertainable amount to be repaid?

Example 9.07.1

Joe Soap takes out a variable mortgage for 20 years in the amount of €50,000. The interest payable is unascertainable.

Duty payable on €50,000	Exempt

Example 9.07.2

Joe Soap takes out a 20-year mortgage in the amount of €50,000; the first five years are fixed at 10%. The ascertainable repayment is €50,000 capital plus 5 years at 10%.
The balance of the interest is unascertainable.

Duty payable on €50,000	Exempt

The mortgage secures the capital sum advanced only, the fixed interest rate payments are not secured by way of the mortgage, even though any interest may be recoverable under the mortgage document. Previously, such fixed rate mortgages which had the effect of the loan being repaid in instalments were liable under the bond, covenant head of charge. This has been abolished by FA 1991, s 205(6).

Example 9.07.3

Paddy takes out a €500,000 mortgage on Greenacre, repayable over 20 years. Stamp duty is chargeable on the instrument securing the mortgage. It is based on the capital sum advanced of €500,000 and not the interest payable over 20 years.

Four years later, having made no repayments he comes to an arrangement with the lending institution to place a new mortgage on the property for the original sum advanced of

---

13 *Jones v IRC* [1895] 1 QB 484.

€500,000 plus the outstanding interest in arrear of €50,000. Stamp duty shall be chargeable on €550,000.

[9.08] A security may arise without the parties involved realising that it is stampable under the mortgage head; for example, an agent acting in a financial institution on behalf of another party may have a right over the instruments concerned as security by way of contract for previous outstanding obligations by the principal to the agent. An equitable mortgage is defined as:

> ... an agreement or memorandum, under hand only, relating to the deposit of any title deeds or instruments constituting or being evidence of the title to any property whatever (other than stock or marketable security), or creating a charge on such property.[14]

In *O'Keeffe v O'Flynn, Exhams and Partners and Allied Irish Banks plc*[15] Costello J stated:

> it is well established that an agreement in writing to deposit title deeds as a security for a loan creates an equitable charge on land to which the deeds relate.

To be chargeable under general mortgage head, the document must be executed under seal, but where it relates to an equitable mortgage the agreement or memorandum recording the deposit of the title documentation by way of security is chargeable to duty.

Bond

[9.09] A bond is a personal promise to do or refrain from doing a certain act (for example, the payment of money) witnessed in an instrument under seal. The promise may be present or anticipatory.[16]

Debenture

[9.10] A debenture is an instrument which acknowledges the indebtedness of a company and which is usually charged over the assets of the company, whether by way of fixed or floating charge. However, a debenture need not be over the assets of a company but can be over the company itself. In *British India Steam Navigation Co v IRC*,[17] the court had to ascertain whether the document before them was a promissory note or debenture for stamp duty purposes. It took the view that while the document was somewhat similar to a promissory note, it also contained other matters. They held that it was chargeable under the debenture head. Grove J stated, in considering what a debenture was:

> I do not remember the term being used otherwise than in acknowledgement of indebtedness by a body corporate having power to borrow.

In the same case, Lindlay J also stated,[18] that a debenture may be 'nothing more than an acknowledgement of indebtedness'.

---

14 SDCA 1999, s 1.

15 *O'Keeffe v O'Flynn, Exhams and Partners and Allied Irish Banks plc* (1992, unreported) HC.

16 *British India Steam Navigation Co v IRC* [1881] 7 QBD 165 and 172, DC, *per* Lindley J.

17 *British India Steam Navigation Co v IRC* [1881] 7 QBD 165.

18 *British India Steam Navigation Co v IRC* [1881] 7 QBD 165 at 187.

[9.11] If a debenture comes within the definition of a marketable security, then it is not liable to duty under this head. Where the document comes within two heads of charge, then the Revenue Commissioners can choose the head of charge that yields the highest duty.[19] This rule is subject to the proviso that, where the instrument is chargeable under a particular head of charge, duty should be payable only under that head even though it may yield a lower amount of duty. Lord Blackburn stated in *North of Scotland Bank v IRC*:[20]

> ... it seems to me that where a particular document is produced and the question of which of the categories it falls into comes up for decision, then the purpose of this Act, and the persons who are administering the Act, should not be to find out that a particular section may be construed so possibly to apply to the deed in question but to find out what particular description in the ordinary use of a legal language appears to fit the deed in question best.

Covenant

[9.12] A covenant is similar to a bond and sets out obligations created between the parties; for example, it could be a covenant to pay money or a covenant in restraint of trade. The distinction between bond and covenant is that bonds are usually executed by the grantor only, whereas covenants are usually executed by both parties.

Marketable security

[9.13] Marketable security which is excluded from the mortgage head of charge is defined as 'security of such a description as to be capable of being sold in any stock market in the state'.[21] However, a mortgage of marketable securities is chargeable to stamp duty as a mortgage under this head of charge.

[9.14] Once the security is capable of being dealt with on a stock exchange in the State, it is not chargeable under this head. Debentures issued by public companies with terms applying to such debentures which render them capable of being dealt with on the stock exchange are, therefore, excluded under this head. Debentures issued by a private company are normally not capable of being listed on a stock exchange in the State. However, if the debentures from a private, unquoted company could be dealt with on the stock exchange, and the company could be converted into a public company, then these debentures may be marketable securities which could be dealt with on the stock exchange and, therefore, excluded from this head of charge. Where loan stock qualifies both as debentures and as marketable securities, it is excluded from the mortgage head of charge.

Rates and charge of stamp duty

[9.15] The charge under mortgage, bond, debenture, covenant head is divided into four separate subheadings, and stamp duty is chargeable at different rates under each heading. The four subheadings are:

---

19 *Anderson v IRC* [1939] 1 KB 341, *Speyer Bros v IRC* [1906] 1 KB 318.

20 *North of Scotland Bank v IRC* [1931] SC 149.

21 SDCA 1999, s 1.

(a) principal or primary security;
(b) collateral auxiliary additions or substituted security;
(c) equitable mortgage; and
(d) transfer, assignment or disposition.

In order to be chargeable under any of these headings, the charge must relate to property situated in the State. Where one transfer document effects a transfer of a number of mortgages, it is Revenue practice to treat this as one transfer, subject to a maximum duty of €630.

Principal or primary security

[9.16] Where the mortgage bond debenture covenant is the only or principal or primary security (other than an equitable mortgage), stamp duty rates are then as follows:

(a)	where the amount secured does not exceed €254,000	Exempt
(b)	where the amount secured exceeds €254,000 (subject to a cap of €630)	0.1%

The effective rate of stamp duty is 0.1 per cent of the amount secured, rounded up to the nearest €1.

[9.17] Where the instrument does not state the amount secured, the Revenue Commissioners will stamp the instrument on the basis of a certificate supplied by the solicitor, which accompanies the instrument, which sets out the capital sum secured (FA 1991, s 90). This would be most common where the mortgage is an all sums due mortgage which applies to any sum advanced by the bank whether now or in the future. Where the amount secured does not exceed €254,000 a certificate must be inserted in or accompany the documentation to obtain the exemption from duty.

Example 9.17.1

Mr and Mrs Smith obtain a bank loan of €33,000 secured by way of mortgage on the property enabling them to carry out renovations to their home. This is the first charge on their property.

€33,000 at 0.1%	€33
Stamp duty liability	Exempt

Example 9.17.2

Inhoc Ltd obtain an advance of €1,000,000 from a bank, which is secured by way of fixed charge over their property.

Stamp duty liability (€1,000,000 x 0.1%)	€1,000

As this amount exceeds the proviso, the duty chargeable on this mortgage is €630.

[9.18] Mortgages by their nature take different forms, in some cases for both present and future advances, while in other cases for a fixed sum. SA 1891 makes particular provisions directing the Revenue Commissioners as to the stamping of these instruments. When the instrument does not set the limit, SDCA 1999, s 58(1) directs how it is to be charged:

> ... a security for the payment or repayment of money to be lent, advanced, or paid, or which may become due upon an account current, either with or without money previously due, is to be charged, where the total amount secured or to be ultimately recoverable is in any way limited, with the same duty as the security for the amounts so limited.

[9.19] The security is stamped for the limited amount. The limit of this amount can include present advances and money to be advanced which must be expressed in the security itself.[22] In *International Power Paper Co of Newfoundland Ltd v IRC*,[23] it was held that even though the amount secured may ultimately never be advanced, once the limit is ascertainable, the full amount is chargeable to duty. The Revenue Commissioners, in consultation with the Land Registry and Registry of Deeds, issued a statement of practice as to the treatment of stamp duty on mortgages and further advances to ensure consistency in their approach.[24] Where the security instrument is for a fixed amount, it is stampable to cover that fixed amount. Duty is chargeable on the instrument where it is the only or principal or primary security involved. In *Mutual Property Insurance Co v IRC*[25] a second mortgage had been executed covenanting to pay:

(a) an amount equal to the principal security advanced by way of first mortgage;

(b) interest outstanding on these amounts; and

(c) a sum equal to the amount advanced by the second mortgage.

The court held that the second mortgage should be stamped on the aggregate amount secured by it and the first mortgage because the interest was capitalised. Where further advances were made, the Revenue Commissioners charged duty on the basis of the total amount advanced.

[9.20] The statement of practice now states that the charge to duty on these instruments is based only on the amount of the further advance without having regard to the amounts outstanding on the original advance.[26] If the further advance and earlier mortgage are consolidated into one instrument, this instrument will be chargeable to duty on the full amount secured. No allowance will be given for the duty paid on the first instrument of charge.[27] While this means that duty may be payable on the same advance twice, which is in accordance with traditional stamping practice, it does not reflect the more progressive European approach regarding capital duty.

[9.21] Where the total amount secured by any instrument is unlimited and the instrument is executed after 31 May 1973, or is deemed to be a new and separate instrument

22 *City of London Brewery Co Ltd v IRC* [1899] 1 QKB 121 CA, *Halse v Peters* [1831] 2 B & AD 807.

23 *International Power Paper Co of Newfoundland Ltd v IRC* [1933] 12 ATC 413.

24 SP-SD/3/92.

25 *Mutual Property Insurance Co v IRC* [1926] All ER 493.

26 SP-SD/3/92 para 2.2.

27 SP-SD/3/92 para 2.3.

executed after 31 May 1973, being any advance in excess of €254,000 or such greater amount as may be covered by that duty, the security shall:

(a) if unstamped, or if stamped with *ad valorem* duty to cover an amount not exceeding €254,000 , be available only for €254,000;[28] and

(b) if stamped with *ad valorem* duty to cover an amount exceeding €254,000, be available for such amount only.[29]

SDCA 1999, s 58(2) provides that if the instrument is unstamped it shall cover the amount secured up to €254,000, and where stamped will be security for any amount for which it is stamped to cover only.

Example 9.21.1

Fast Cars Ltd is a garage specialising in high-performance sports cars. It obtained an overdraft facility from the bank for €300,000 and grants a mortgage over its garage to cover all sums due by Fast Cars Ltd.

Stamp duty liability on the charge (€300,000 x 0.1%)	€300

Fast Cars Ltd increases its overdraft facility by €600,000. The security instrument has to be stamped to cover this extra overdraft facility within thirty days of the grant thereof.

Stamp duty liability on €600,000 (€600,000 x 0.1%)	€600

In Example **9.21.1**, iIf the bank failed to stamp the instrument to cover the extra overdraft facility, it could recover the sum of €254,000 advanced to Fast Cars Ltd[30] since it would be deemed to be sufficiently stamped to that extent, the instrument would not fall within the provisions of SA 1891, s 14(4) and would be admissible in evidence to enable the bank to effect the security.[31]

[9.22] The instrument for all present and future advances must be stamped to cover the full amount secured by it except where it does not exceed €254,000. There are two charging scenarios where there is a further advance:

(a) if the amount outstanding for the previous advance, together with a further advance does not exceed the amount for which the security is stamped, there is no further stamp duty liability;

(b) if the further advance and the amount outstanding on foot of the original advance exceeds the sum for which the security is stamped, duty is payable on the excess.[32] The instrument is liable to stamp duty for the amount secured by it, but where the instrument is interlinked with another instrument it may have a further liability to duty.[33]

---

28 SDCA 1999, s 58(1).

29 SDCA 1999, s 58(2).

30 SDCA 1999, s 58(2).

31 *Re Waterhouse Policy* [1937] 2 All ER 91.

32 SP-SD/3/92 para 3.1.

33 SP-SD/3/92 para 3.2.

SDCA 1999, s 58(3) provides that any amount advanced for the purchase of insurance protection, either property or life insurance, shall be reckoned as part of the amount in respect of which is chargeable with duty.

Collateral, auxiliary, additional or substituted security

[9.23] To be chargeable under this head, the instrument must be a mortgage, bond, debenture or covenant and it must be a security for the payment/repayment of money and acts as collateral, auxiliary, additional or substituted security (other than equitable mortgage) or by way of further assurance for the above-mentioned purpose and the principal or primary security must be duly stamped. Stamp duty is chargeable as follows:

(a)	where the amount secured does not exceed €254,000	Exempt
(b)	where the amount secured exceeds €254,000	€12.50

The instrument acting as a collateral security must support a primary security that is already stamped or is exempt from stamp duty. In *IRC v Ansbacher and Co*[34] there was an agreement for the sale of shares which was not executed under seal. A collateral guarantee had been entered into but it was argued that this should be stamped as the primary security, since the agreement for the sale of shares was not chargeable to duty under the mortgage head. The court held that the collateral guarantee was to be stampable under this head even though the primary instrument was not chargeable.

[9.24] The principal document must be properly stamped in accordance with the relevant stamping requirements or be exempt from duty and has to be furnished to the Revenue Commissioners with the collateral instrument so they can stamp same as a collateral security.

Example 9.24.1

Mary on purchasing the White House takes a mortgage for €480,000 to enable her to complete the transaction. The mortgage is an endowment mortgage and she assigns her endowment policy to the bank. Stamp duty is as follows:

	€
Mortgage €480,000 at 0.1%	480
Collateral security: assignment of endowment policy as a collateral security	12.50
Total liability	492.50

Example 9.24.2

Fast Cars Ltd, having redeemed its previous loan in full, decides to expand its business and borrows a further €483,000 from Graball Bank Ltd. The bank loan sanction requires a mortgage over the garage and, in addition, that the managing director puts in place a charge over his farm and residence. Stamp duty liability:

[34] *IRC v Ansbacher and Co* [1963] AC 191.

	€
Mortgage over garage premises €483,000 x 0.1%	483.00
Collateral mortgage	12.50
Total liability	495.50

Where an instrument is stampable under the section, it is stamped with an adjudication stamp.

Equitable mortgage

[9.25] An instrument that comes within the mortgage head which is an equitable mortgage, is liable to duty as follows:

(a)	where the amount secured does not exceed €254,000	Exempt
(b)	where the amount secured exceeds €254,000 (subject to a cap of €630)	0.05%

This charges an effective rate of 0.05 per cent rounded up to the nearest pound and is subject to the cap of €630.

[9.26] The equitable mortgage is defined in SDCA 1999, s 1 and relates to the lodging of title deeds of any property (other than stocks or marketable securities) as security for a loan. If an equitable interest on property is legally mortgaged, it is stampable as a primary or principal security. It is not as an equitable mortgage.

Example 9.26.1

Mary and John take a loan from the bank for €300,000. They lodge the title documentation to their private residence as security for the loan. The title documentation is lodged with the bank by way of verbal deposit. The bank manager notes the deposit. No duty is payable since no agreement or document is executed.

Example 9.26.2

Mary and John take a loan from the bank for €300,000 and agree to lodge the title documentation as security for the loan. The bank manager insists that they execute a memorandum to confirm the deposit as security for the loan.

Stamp duty liability (€300,000 x 0.05%)	€150

Example 9.26.3

Joma Ltd is expanding its business and obtains a loan from the bank for a sum of €256,000. The bank's letter of loan offer states that the security requirements are as follows:

(a) a first charge over the property owned by Joma Ltd comprising a warehouse valued at €160,000;

(b) an equitable deposit of the title documentation of John and Mary's residence. The offer is accepted by John and Mary, and they immediately lodge the title documentation to their residence with the bank;

(c) the assignment of an endowment policy with life cover over the life of John and Mary for €160,000.

The letter of offer is accepted by John and Mary.

(a) The mortgage document together with the assignment of the life policy is executed two months later. Stamp duty is as follows:

equitable mortgage chargeable within 30 days of

acceptance of letter of loan offer; €256,000 x .05% = €128

(b) the mortgage document together with the assignment of an endowment policy is executed 60 days later. Both these documents are stampable within 30 days as follows:

		€
(i)	mortgage €256,000 x 0.1%	256.00
(ii)	collateral security by way of assignment of endowment/life cover	12.50

Total stamp duty liability:		€
Equitable mortgage		128.00
First charge		254.00
	Collateral security	12.50
	Total	394.50

In practice, most lending institutions now issue letters of loan offer setting out full details in respect of a mortgage. These are accepted by the borrower. Provided the insurance cover is in place, when the solicitor furnishes an undertaking in respect of the title documentation, the majority of lending institutions are willing to advance the moneys. Such letter of loan offer could be construed as a memorandum for an equitable mortgage and might be stampable under the equitable mortgage head as the moneys are advanced on foot of the letter of loan offer duly accepted together with the undertaking from the borrower's solicitor. In practice, such letters of loan offer are not stamped.

Transfer, assignment or disposition

[9.27] With a transfer, assignment or disposition of any interest created by way of mortgage, bond, debenture or covenant (except a marketable security) or of any money or stock secured by such instrument or by any judgment, stamp duty is chargeable as follows:

(*a*)	where the amount secured does not exceed €254,000	Exempt
(*b*)	where the amount secured exceeds €254,000 (subject to a cap of €630)	0.05%

This charge is subject to the capped liability of €630. Where a mortgagee by way of instrument transfers or assigns a security, duty is chargeable on the transfer or assignment under this head. The duty is charged on the amount of the debt transferred including interest. If the transfer or assignment or disposition of the interest in the security is a voluntary transfer, the stamp duty shall be chargeable under the conveyance on sale head.[35]

[35] SDCA 1999, s 30.

[9.28] As already discussed, the Revenue Commissioners have the power to charge stamp duty under the head which yields the greatest amount of duty. If there is a voluntary disposition of the mortgagee's interest in property, the Revenue Commissioners will charge it under the conveyance on sale head. It was held that *ad valorem* duty is chargeable on the value of the mortgage passing rather than the amount secured.[36] The contract for the sale of the mortgagee's interest in the security over Irish property, is stampable under the conveyance on sale head.[37] The transfer or assignment of a mortgage not secured over Irish property falls outside the mortgage head of charge, even if it is capable of being construed as a conveyance of a debt liable to full *ad valorem* duty under s 31.

Ceiling on liability to duty

[9.29] The legislation as originally enacted did not place a ceiling on the duty payable, so that duty was payable on the total amount secured by the instrument. A ceiling on the duty payable under the charges outlined in paras **9.06, 9.07** and **9.08** was introduced with effect from 29 May 1990. It applied to mortgages or further advances executed after 29 May 1990. The maximum duty payable was £3,000.[38] If the instrument was charged with duty in excess of £3,000 prior to the passing of this section, the ceiling applied only to duty payable in respect of further advances.[39] The ceiling on the charge to duty was reduced to £500 with effect from 29 May 1991.[40] This ceiling applied to instruments stamped after the effective date (ie 29 May 1991).

[9.30] Where an instrument was stamped with duty of £500 prior to 29 May 1991, the ceiling applies to further advances made after that date subject to the proviso that the ceiling of £3,000 has not already been reached. No further duty is payable on the advances.[41] Where the instrument is stamped after the first ceiling of £3,000 was introduced (ie after 29 May 1990) but before the second ceiling of £500 was introduced (ie before 29 May 1991), any further advance is stampable subject to the proviso that the duty shall not exceed £3,000.[42]

Example 9.30.1

Jack and Jill mortgage their hill on 28 April 1990 for €2,200,000. Stamp duty on €2,200,000 at one-eight of 1% = £2,750. The rate of duty on a mortgage at that time was 25p per £200 (0.125%) or part thereof. They obtain a further advance of €700,000 on 30 April 2004.

	€
Stamp duty liability (€700,000 at 0.1%)	700
Stamp duty payable (subject to the cap of €630)	630

36 *Anderson v IRC* [1939] 1 KB 341.

37 SDCA 1999, s 31 – see **Chapter 5**.

38 FA 1990, s 110(7) and Sch 9.

39 SP-SD/3/92 para 4.2.

40 FA 1991, s 90(4) and Sch 5.

41 SP-SD/3/92 para 4.3.

42 SP-SD/3/92 para 4.4. The Statement of Practice took effect from 1 June 1992.

Example 9.30.2

Banking Ltd made an advance of £2.75m to Fast Cars Ltd and as security Fast Cars Ltd executed a first charge over the property on 1 December 1990 covering the full amount.

Stamp duty liability (£2.75m x 0.1%)	£2,750

On 1 January 1994 Banking Ltd gave a further advance to Fast Cars Ltd for £1m. Stamp duty at 0.1% equals £1,000 subject to the proviso of a full capping of £3,000.

Stamp duty now payable on 1 January 1994	£250

Example 9.30.3

John and Mary obtained a mortgage over their period residence adjoining a golf course from Green Fields Banking Ltd for €650,000.

	€
Stamp duty liability (€650,000 at 0.1%)	650
Stamp duty payable (subject to the cap of €630)	630

Due to severe weather conditions the golf course was unplayable for the winter and John and Mary now obtain a further advance of €150,000 from the Bank to tide them over.

Stamp duty (€150,000 at 0.1%)	150

This further advance is not chargeable to duty, as the capped ceiling has already been reached.

Accountable person

[9.31] Stamp duty became mandatory in respect of all instruments executed on or after 1 November 1991. In the event that duty is not paid the Revenue Commissioners are empowered to recover stamp duty from the accountable person. Under this head of charge the accountable person is the mortgagee or obligee and, where there is a transfer, assignment or disposition of the security, the transferee is liable.

Duty in certain cases

[9.32] The Stamp Act directs the Revenue Commissioners as to the application of duty in certain cases.

Transfer or retransfer of stock

[9.33] Where the instrument provides security in respect of a transfer or retransfer of any stock, duty is charged on the instrument based on the value of the amount of stock involved. If the instrument effects a transfer of such security document, or a reconveyance, release, discharge, etc of same, then duty will be charged on the instrument based on the value of the stock.[43] A reconveyance, release, discharge, surrender, warrant, vacate or renunciation of a mortgage was originally charged with duty, but such instruments are no longer stampable and the head of charge has been

[43] SDCA 1999, s 57(1).

removed from SA 1891, Sch 1. This direction as to duty in a case involving such a reconveyance, release or surrender of such a security relating to stock has no effect.

Security for the payment of any annuity or periodic payment

[9.34] A security for the payment of any rent charge, annuity, or periodic payments, by way of repayment, or in satisfaction or discharge of any loan, advance or payment intended to be so repaid, satisfied or discharged, is to be charged with the same duty as a similar security for the payment of a sum of money so lent, advanced or paid.[44]

Example 9.34.1

A agrees to make periodic payments of €2,000 per annum by way of instrument to B in discharge of a loan given by B to A of €30,000.

The instrument is stampable on €30,000.

Stamp duty = exempt.

The transfer of a security or a security for a further charge

[9.35] In the case of a transfer of security duly stamped or a grant of a further charge of money or stock, or added to the money or stock already secured, the instrument is not to be charged with any duty by reason of it providing further security for the money or stock transferred or previously secured or the interest or dividend thereof, or any further powers granted or covenants given in relation thereto. If original security already comprises a further assurance of property, this is not charged with any duty.[45]

Conveyance of the equity redemption

[9.36] Per SDCA 1999, s 57(4):

> An instrument chargeable with *ad valorem* duty as a mortgage is not to be charged with any further duty by reason of the equity of redemption in the mortgaged property being thereby conveyed or limited in any other manner than to a purchaser, or in trust for, or according to the direction of, a purchaser.

Example 9.36.1

A clause inserted into a mortgage instrument whereby the equity of redemption is held on trust by the mortgagor in favour of the lending institution is not liable to any further duty with respect to the equity of redemption.

Further instruments chargeable under the mortgage, bond debenture, covenant head

[9.37] The following instruments are also chargeable under the mortgage head:[46]

(a) a bond, accompanied with the deposit of title deeds, for making a mortgage or other security on any estate or property therein comprised;

(b) a bond, declaration, or other deed or writing for making redeemable any disposition apparently absolute, but intended only as a security;

---

44 SDCA 1999, s 57(2).

45 SDCA 1999, s 57(3).

46 SDCA 1999, Sch 1.

(c) a covenant for securing the payment or repayment of money, or the transfer or retransfer of stock; and

(d) an instrument of defeasance (a condition relating to a deed, which, when performed, renders the deed void) of any conveyance, transfer, disposition, assignment of stock, apparently absolute but intended only as a security for money or stock.

Exemptions

[9.38] It is clear from the foregoing charging provisions that any mortgage, bond, debenture, or covenant where the total amount secured by it does not exceed €254,000, is exempt. The previous threshold was €20,000.

Marketable securities

[9.39] The mortgage head of charge excludes marketable securities. A mortgage over any registered stock or marketable security is not liable to duty if the instrument is made under hand (that is not made under seal) provided that it is not a promissory note or bill of exchange.[47] A debenture may qualify as a marketable security and will be exempt from stamp duty under this head of charge.

Shares in stocks or funds of the government or the Oireachtas

[9.40] These are exempt from all stamp duties.

Ships, vessels and aircraft

[9.41] All ships, vessels, aircrafts or any interest therein are exempt from stamp duty under the general exemption provisions. The exemption for aircraft was introduced with effect from 1 October 1970.[48]

Directions to Revenue Commissioners

[9.42] Under the direction given to the Revenue Commissioners as to how to apply duty in certain cases, the following exemptions were granted:

(a) a transfer of a duly stamped security or security by way of further charge for money or stock which provides further security for the moneys already advanced or further covenants in relation thereto, or comprises a further transfer of the property;[49] and

(b) if the instrument is already charged with *ad valorem* duty, no further duty is to be applied where the equity of redemption of the property is conveyed and limited in any other manner; if it is limited in favour of a purchaser or in trust for a purchaser or according to the instructions of the purchaser, then it would be liable to *ad valorem* duty.[50]

---

47 SDCA 1999, s 107.

48 SDCA 1999, s 60.

49 SDCA 1999, s 57(3).

50 *Lord Suffield v IRC* [1908] 1 KB 865 – SDCA 1999, s 57(4).

Financial services instruments

[9.43] With the passing of FA 1991, stamp duty became a mandatory tax. Prior to this, stamp duty was a voluntary tax, the only compulsion to stamp being the inadmissibility in evidence of an unstamped document in a civil court or some other statutory requirement to have the document registered. Prior to the passing of FA 1991 the majority of instruments used in the financial services industry were left unstamped as it was felt it was commercially unnecessary. When stamp duty became mandatory, all these documents had to be legally stamped which was not commercially viable.

[9.44] Exemptions have now been introduced for the following:

(a) debt factoring agreements;

(b) swap agreements;

(c) forward agreements;

(d) financial or futures agreements;

(e) option agreements;

(f) a combination of any two or more of the instruments specified above;

(g) transfers of any of the above agreements, leases other than a lease to which any heading in the first schedule applies; and

(h) an American or Canadian depository receipt.

Provided none of these documents, other than an American or Canadian depository receipt, relate to immovable property situate in this State or stocks or marketable securities of a company having a register in this State, they are exempt from stamp duty, subject to the proviso that if an instrument is exempt from stamp duty under this head, but is chargeable under any other heading in the first schedule, it is to be chargeable with stamp duty under that heading.[51]

Loan capital and securities

[9.45] Any loan capital (which consists of debenture, stock, bond or funded debt) issued by a body corporate which has the character of borrowed money shall not be chargeable to duty in the following situations:

(a) where it is the issue, whether in bearer form or not, of any government loan or any other loan capital;[52]

(b) where it is the issue of any other loan capital; however, it shall be liable to duty where it is an instrument chargeable under the mortgage, bond, debenture, covenant head of liability, which is a charge on property situate within the State other than stock or shares in government or Oireachtas funds;[53]

(c) where it is the transfer of loan capital which does not carry the right to conversion into stocks or marketable shares nor rights similar to stocks and shares (such as the right to vote), provided it is redeemable within 30 years

---

[51] SDCA 1999, s 90(4) – see **Chapter 14**.

[52] SDCA 1999, s 85(2)(a).

[53] SDCA 1999, s 85(2)(b).

from the date of issue, has been sold for not less than 90% of its nominal value and does not carry any right to the repayment of a sum which is related to the movements of any specified indices, eg, profits earned by the company; and

(d) where it is the issue or transfer of securities issued by a TCA 1997, s 110 qualifying company operating in the course of its business.

Reliefs for security given by a subsidiary company to a holding company

[9.46] Where an instrument is chargeable under the mortgage head and the instrument is given as security by a subsidiary company to a holding company, stamp duty shall not exceed €12.50.[54] The instrument must be given by way of security to a company by a subsidiary of that company and it would be chargeable under the mortgage head. To qualify as a subsidiary of another company, the holding company must have the beneficial ownership of not less than 90 per cent of the issued share capital.[55] Finally, to be deemed duly stamped, the instrument has to be adjudicated on by the Revenue Commissioners pursuant to SDCA 1999, s 83(3). When the Revenue Commissioners adjudicate on the instrument under this section, a denoting stamp is impressed on the instrument.

A voluntary transfer of property subject to a mortgage

[9.47] The Revenue Commissioners can stamp these instruments in three different ways.

(a) The Revenue Commissioners may deduct the mortgage liability from the value of the property to arrive at the benefit passing, thereby charging the equity of redemption (the sum total of the mortgagor's right in equity over the property) with stamp duty.

Example 9.47.1

Jack transferred his property worth €98,000 to his son, Sam, subject to a mortgage of €40,000. The Revenue Commissioners can assess stamp duty on the equity of redemption (€58,000).

Stamp duty on €58,000 x 5% = Exempt

(b) The Revenue Commissioners can charge stamp duty on the amount of the mortgage as being the consideration.

Example 9.47.2

Jack transfers his commercial property worth €810,000 to his son, Sam, subject to a mortgage of €800,000. In this case the Revenue Commissioners can assess duty (using SDCA 1999, s 41) and charge the stamp duty on the amount of debt passing and the stamp duty is charged on €800,000, under the conveyance on sale head.[56]

Stamp duty on €800,000 x 9% = €7,200.

(c) The Revenue Commissioners can add any cash consideration to the amount of the mortgage.

---

54 SDCA 1999, s 83(1).

55 SDCA 1999, s 83(2).

56 SDCA 1999, s 41.

Example 9.47.3

Jack agrees to transfer his commercial property worth €98,000 to his son, Sam, subject to a mortgage of €40,000, and Sam pays his father a cash consideration of €20,000. In this case the duty is to be assessed on the consideration deemed to be passing of €60,000.

Stamp duty on €60,000 x 4% = €2,400.

The duty payable in the above examples assumes that the Revenue Commissioners do not treat each transaction as part of a larger series of transactions, ie the transfer of a commercial property valued at €98,000. The Revenue Commissioners will always choose the method which yields the greatest consideration. In all the above examples, provided the consanguinity certificate was inserted, Sam would be entitled to a half rate of stamp duty.

Bills of exchange and promissory notes

Introduction

[9.48] Bills of exchange and promissory notes provide an effective means for the transfer and payment of moneys. These documents entitle the payee to the payment of moneys in discharge of the bill of exchange or promissory note. These are commonly known as negotiable instruments, are instruments that can be passed on to third parties.

> A negotiable instrument is a chose in action, the full and legal title to which is transferable by mere delivery of the instrument with the result that complete ownership of the instrument and all the property it represents passes free from the equities to the transferee, provided the latter takes the instrument in good faith and for value.[57]

Both these instruments are defined by statute.

Statutory definitions

Bill of exchange

[9.49] A bill of exchange is an instrument signed by the drawer which is addressed to one party and demands that the person to whom it is addressed pay on demand on a fixed or determinable date a sum of money as set out on the instrument. A bill of exchange was originally defined by the Bill of Exchange Act 1882 (BEA 1882) as:

> ... an unconditional order in writing addressed by one person to another signed by the person giving it requiring the person to whom it is addressed to pay on demand or at a fixed or determinable future time, a sum certain in money to or to the order of a specified person, or to the bearer (s 3(1)).

The meaning of bill of exchange for stamp duty purposes is wider and broader than that contained in the BEA 1882. This gives rise to documents which may be stampable, but at the same time do not enjoy the benefits of the BEA 1882. The bill of exchange for the purpose of stamp duty includes:

---

57 Richardson, *Negotiable Instrument* (7th edn).

> ... a draft, order, cheque and letter of credit, and any document of writing (except a bank note) entitling or purporting to entitle any person, whether named therein or not, to payment by any other person to draw upon any other person, for any sum of money ... [58]

The expression 'bill of exchange payable on demand' is defined as including:

(a) an order for the payment of any sum of money by a bill of exchange or promissory note, or for the delivery of any bill of exchange or promissory note in satisfaction of any sum of money, or for the payment of any sum of money out of any particular fund which may or may not be available, or upon any condition or contingency which may or may not be performed or happen; and

(b) an order for the payment of any sum of money weekly, monthly or at other stated periods, and also an order for the payment by any person at any time after the date thereof of any sum of money, and sent or delivered by the person making the same to the person by whom the payment is to be made, and not to the person to whom the payment is to be made, or to any person on his behalf.[59]

[9.50] These definitions of 'bill of exchange' and 'bill of exchange payable on demand' are extremely wide and include cheques, letters of credit and promissory notes. A cheque is defined as 'a bill of exchange drawn on a bank payable on demand'.[60] The bill of exchange has to be addressed to a party requiring that party to discharge the amount due and owing on foot of the bill of exchange on demand. If the instrument is not addressed to anyone or contains the name of the person giving it, but has been signed by the acceptor, this instrument will constitute a promissory note and not a bill of exchange.[61] The sum of money must be clearly defined and the bill of exchange must be an order for the payment of same:[62]

> A letter of credit is an undertaking by a banker acting on the instruction of its customer to pay or meet the drafts drawn pursuant to it by the beneficiary of the credit in accordance with the terms laid down in the undertaking.[63]

Promissory note

[9.51] A promissory note is an unconditional promise to pay on demand a sum of money to the bearer or specified person. As with the definition of bills of exchange the definition of promissory note for stamp purposes is far broader than that contained in the BEA 1992. A promissory note is defined in the BEA 1882 as:

> ... an unconditional promise in writing made by one person to another signed by the maker undertaking to pay on demand or at a fixed or determinable future time a sum certain in money to or to the order of a specified person, or bearer.[64]

---

58 SDCA 1999, s 1(1).

59 SA 1891, s 32.

60 BEA 1882, s 73.

61 *Mason v Lack* [1929] All ER 463.

62 *Jones v Simpson* [1823] 2 BC 318.

63 *Murdoch's Dictionary of Irish Law* (4th edn, LexisNexis, 2004).

64 BEA 1882, s 83(1).

For stamp duty purposes, the meaning of promissory note:

> ... includes any document or writing (except a bank note) containing a promise to pay any sum of money.[65]

[9.52] Where a county council or municipal corporation issue bills repayable not later than twelve months from the date of issue, such bills shall be treated as promissory notes for the purposes of stamp duty and not as marketable securities, even if the bill shares secured or charged over property or some fund.[66]

[9.53] A note may be deemed to be a promissory note provided it promises the payment of any money out of any fund, whether available or not and it may be subject to a condition or contingency.[67] A bill of exchange requires the third party to discharge same on demand. If the bill of exchange is given by a party who is also liable to discharge same, then the bearer at his option can elect to have this treated as a bill of exchange or a promissory note.[68]

[9.54] The note has to be given and accepted as a promissory note to be chargeable as such.[69] In *Williamson v Ryder*[70] it was held that a promissory note which contained a condition and was payable 'on or before' the given date did not qualify as a promissory note as it did not require the maker to pay on demand or at a fixed or determinable future time. This note, however, would come within the meaning of a promissory note as set out in the Stamp Act.

[9.55] A promissory note must comprise a promise for the payment of any sum of money which must comprise the substance of the document. Lindley LJ stated:

> ... containing a promise to pay must mean that that is the substance of the document, the whole contents; it cannot mean containing a promise to pay forming one of a number of stipulations.[71]

The court held further that for the purpose of stamping, promissory notes:

> ... include documents, the contents of which consist substantially of a promise to pay a definite sum of money, and of nothing else.

If the promise to pay is not the substance of the agreement, but is merely incidental to the whole purpose of the agreement, then the document does not comprise a promissory note.[72]

[9.56] The note in writing must be more than an acknowledgment of indebtedness, and must comprise an express promise to pay. If it does not contain these elements it is merely an IOU and not a promissory note. A promise 'to pay any sum of money ... is

---

65 SDCA 1999, s 1(1).

66 SDCA 1999, s 26.

67 SDCA 1999, s 28.

68 Bill of Exchange Act 1882, s 52 – *Re British Trade Corporation Ltd* [1932] All ER 671.

69 *Yoe v Dawe* [1885] 3 WR 739.

70 *Williamson v Ryder* [1962] All ER 268 (CA).

71 *Mortgage Insurance Corporation v IRC* [1888] 21 QBD 352.

72 *Thomson v Ball* [1894] 22 R Ct of Sess 16.

deemed a promissory note for that sum of money' and the sum promised must be certain,[73] but the said sum can be paid by instalments.

[9.57] Bills of exchange and promissory notes must be distinguished from equitable assignments which comprise the assignment of a debt from one party authorising his debtor to pay a third party and are liable as assignments of debt. A bill of exchange or promissory note is an instrument creating the original liability to pay, an equitable assignment operates to transfer the original liability.

The charge to stamp duty

[9.58] Bills of exchange and promissory notes drawn or made in the State are charged to stamp duty under the head of bill of exchange and promissory notes set out in SDCA 1999, Sch 1. Cheques and drafts drawn on an account in the State are charged to stamp duty under this head of charge.[74]

The rate of duty

[9.59] Duty is charged under this head at a fixed rate of €0.15 after 1 January 2003.

Accountable persons

[9.60] Any instruments executed under this head, which are executed on or after 1 November 1991, are compulsorily chargeable to stamp duty.[75] Where the instruments are not stamped, the parties to the instrument are deemed to be the accountable persons, liable for the stamp duty.[76]

Stamping of instruments

[9.61] The form of stamp used dictates the stamping requirements.

Impressed stamp

[9.62] Instruments stamped under this head cannot be stamped after their execution with an impressed stamp.[77] The term 'execution' in this regard means signature, and the term 'impressed' means applying a stamp by means of a dye.[78] If the instrument bears an impressed stamp of the wrong denomination it may still be stamped after execution with the proper stamp on payment of the duty and a penalty of 15 cent provided the bill or note is not payable according to its tenor or, if it is, €630.[79]

Adhesive stamps

[9.63] Stamp duty on instruments under this head of charge may be denoted by adhesive stamps. The person executing the bill of exchange or promissory note must cancel the

73 *Henderson v Dawson* [1895] 22 R Ct of Sess 895.

74 SDCA 1999, Sch 1.

75 SDCA 1999, s 2.

76 SDCA 1999, s 1(1).

77 SDCA 1999, s 23.

78 SDCA 1999, s 1(1).

79 SDCA 1999, s 23.

adhesive stamp before he delivers it out of his hands, custody or power.[80] This extended the use of adhesive stamps on promissory notes executed on or after 15 February 1971.

[9.64] There is a general direction given in the Stamp Act as to the cancellation of adhesive stamps. Where the duty chargeable under this head of charge is denoted by adhesive stamp to effectively stamp the document, the person signing the instrument must cancel the stamp by:

(a) writing on or across the stamp his name or initials or the name or initials of his firm; and

(b) the true date thereof; or

(c) otherwise effectively renders the stamp incapable of being used for any other instrument, or for postal purposes; or

(d) it would be sufficient to prove that the stamp was fixed to the instrument at the proper time.[81]

The requirement that the stamp be rendered unusable for postage purposes now appears to be obsolete since the adhesive stamps used with effect from 16 February 1994 are issued only by the Revenue Commissioners.[82] Where two or more adhesive stamps have been used to denote the stamp duty, each or every stamp must be cancelled.[83] Any person who, being under a legal obligation to cancel an adhesive stamp, fails, neglects or refuses to cancel the adhesive stamp shall be liable for a fine in the amount of €630.[84]

[9.65] Every person who issues, endorses, transfers, negotiates or otherwise deals with an instrument without the correct adhesive stamp shall be liable for a fine in the amount of €630 and any person who takes, receives or deals in said instrument, shall not be entitled to recover on the instrument.[85] This could have imposed onerous conditions on anyone dealing with bills of exchange, particularly banks. Therefore, where a bill of exchange is presented for payment incorrectly stamped, an adhesive stamp may be affixed by the person honouring the instrument as if he was the original drawer of the bill of exchange which shall be deemed for stamp duty purposes to be valid and available. The adhesive stamp must be rendered incapable of reuse. The duty is recoverable from the original drawer of the bill of exchange, or deductible from the sum so payable.[86] The original drawer still remains liable for the fine of €630.[87]

[9.66] This relieving provision applies to bills of exchange only. Originally the courts took the view that, while a promissory note came within the definition of bill of exchange, it was not chargeable as a bill of exchange but chargeable as a promissory

80 SDCA 1999, s 25(1).

81 SDCA 1999, s 10(2).

82 SA 1891, s 7 substituted by SDCA 1999, s 10(1).

83 SDCA 1999, s 10(3).

84 SDCA 1999, s 10(4).

85 SDCA 1999, s 25(2).

86 SDCA 1999, s 25(3).

87 SDCA 1999, s 25(4).

note.[88] The effect of this decision was that a promissory note could not be stamped after execution. This has now been considered in Ireland in *Sparebanken Nord-Norge v Beirne & Ors*.[89] An unstamped promissory note was to be produced in evidence. The defendant argued that the promissory note was inadmissible as a document in evidence. Morris J in considering the document had to decide whether the instrument fell within the definition of promissory note, or the definition of bill of exchange pursuant to the Stamp Act. He was of the opinion that the document was a promissory note within the meaning of SDCA 1999, s 1. He also held that the document came within the definition of bill of exchange as defined by SDCA 1999, s 1. As the person to whom a bill of exchange is presented is empowered to affix an adhesive stamp which has the effect of making the bill of exchange valid and acceptable, Morris J concluded that the bill of exchange could be legally stamped after execution provided the stamping was carried out in accordance with the requirements of SDCA 1999, s 25. This applied to bills of exchange only, as opposed to promissory notes, but if the promissory note can fall within both definitions, then stamping can take place after its execution and will be effective. Certain doubts have been expressed as to the validity of the interpretation applied in this case. The Act defines a bill of exchange as:

> ... including a draft, order, cheque, letter of credit ... entitling or purporting to entitle any person whether named therein or not, to the payment by any other person, or drawn upon any person for, any sum of money... [90]

[9.67] It is clear that a bill of exchange must be addressed to a third party and is therefore exclusive of a promissory note. The Act then goes on to define a 'bill of exchange payable on demand' to include a promissory note, provided that the said promissory note does not specify the time of payment. In all other cases a promissory note cannot be a bill of exchange. Of even more importance, in enacting the relieving provision this issue was taken into account. The exception provided in, s 41(3) relates only to bills of exchange presented for payment unstamped. The section states:

> ... provided that if any bill of exchange is presented for payment unstamped, the person to whom it is presented may affix thereto an adhesive stamp...

This provision enables the party honouring the bill of exchange to affix the deficient stamp without penalty, not the holder of the bill of exchange. In the case of a promissory note, the only person who can affix the deficient stamp is the drawer since it is the drawer who honours the promissory note. It is not likely that the drawer would affix such a stamp in these circumstances since he would be rendering a document which was inadmissible against him, admissible. The section of the Act itself makes this clear:

> the person to whom it is presented may affix thereto an adhesive stamp... and cancel same, as if he had been the drawer of the bill.

The drafters of the Act therefore did not envisage that the drawer of the bill would ever affix such stamp.

---

[88] *Dettinger v Cohn* [1908] KB 582.

[89] *Sparebanken Nord-Norge v Beirne & Ors* (1992, unreported) HC.

[90] SDCA 1999, s 1.

[9.68] Any person who fraudulently removes any adhesive stamp, or attempts to use, sell or utter an adhesive stamp that has been fraudulently removed shall be guilty of an offence. On summary conviction, they shall be liable for a fine of €1,900 for offences committed before 3 March 2003 and €3,000 for any offence committed on or after 3 March 2003 and/or a term of imprisonment not exceeding 12 months. On indictment, they shall be liable for a fine of up to £10,000 and/or a term of imprisonment not exceeding 5 years.[91]

Format of stamping

[9.69] The duty chargeable on instruments can be stamped as follows:

(a) by way of impressed stamp; or

(b) by way of adhesive stamp; or

(c) under a composition agreement with the Revenue Commissioners.[92]

If the Revenue Commissioners are of the opinion that it is impractical for a person carrying on a business which involves a multiplicity of instruments which are liable to stamp duty, the Revenue Commissioners can enter into an agreement so that the person is not liable to pay stamp duty on each individual instrument, but is liable to a composite payment. The person has to furnish accounts to the Revenue Commissioners specifying the instruments involved, paying the stamp duty in bulk payment.

[9.70] The Revenue Commissioners have a total discretion as to the form, terms and conditions of such an agreement.[93] Where such an agreement has been entered into, any instrument issued which contains a statement that the stamp duty shall be paid is not chargeable to duty individually, but rather by way of composition in respect of all instruments to which the agreement relates in each relevant period of accounts. A lump sum payment is then made to the Revenue Commissioners on the delivery of the account.[94]

[9.71] To clarify the matter, the Revenue Commissioners have now issued a statement of practice entitled 'agreements as to the payment of stamp duty on instruments (composition agreements)'.[95] Composition agreements facilitate persons or institutions carrying on a business involving bills of exchange or promissory notes, for example banks. They account for stamp duty based on an accounting period which varies between two weeks and three months which is ascertained on the basis of the number of instruments involved, the amount of duty involved and the nature of the business.[96] The instruments are admissible in evidence provided they either:

---

91 SDCA 1999, s 10(4) applying TCA 1997, s 107 (3).

92 SDCA 1999, s 5.

93 SDCA 1999, s 5(2).

94 SDCA 1999, s 5(3).

95 SP-SD/3/90.

96 SP-SD/3/90 para 2.2.

(a) have a printed medallion stamp stating the stamp duty has been paid; or

(b) contain a statement that the duty has been paid or will be paid to the Revenue Commissioners.[97]

[9.72] Duty that would have arisen from the instruments during that accounting period must be paid over to the Revenue Commissioners as per the terms of the agreement and must be accompanied by accounts together with the calculation of duty.[98] The Revenue Commissioners have to be satisfied that the party benefitting from the agreement has a reliable and effective method of accounting for the duty. The Revenue Commissioners are empowered to carry out audits of accounting procedures which:

(a) ensure that the terms of the agreement are operated in full and are sufficient to enable the agreement to be carried out; and

(b) ensure that no fraud is committed.[99]

Breach of the agreement gives rise to a penalty not exceeding £100 per day and each further day for which a failure of the agreement continues, together with interest at a rate of 1 per cent per month or part thereof from the date of default.[100]

Compliance

[9.73] Compliance with these provisions is enforced in a number of ways.

Accountable persons

[9.74] As stamp duty is now mandatory, the Revenue Commissioners are empowered to recover stamp duty unpaid from accountable persons and for the purpose of this head of charge they are deemed to be the parties to the instrument.[101]

Evidentiary restrictions

[9.75] An unstamped instrument cannot be produced in evidence in civil proceedings.[102]

Recoverability

[9.76] Any person who deals with a promissory note or bill of exchange that is not properly stamped shall not be entitled to recover the money shown in the promissory note or bill of exchange or make the same available for any purpose subject to the exception for late stamping as discussed at para **9.37**.

Penalty provisions

[9.77] Where the stamp duty is denoted by way of adhesive stamp and the duty is not properly cancelled, the person who neglects or refuses to cancel the stamp shall be liable to a fine of €630.[103]

---

[97] SP-SD/3/90 para 2.3.

[98] SP-SD/3/90 para 3.

[99] SP-SD/3/90 para 4.

[100] SDCA 1999, s 5.

[101] See **Appendix 7**.

[102] SDCA 1999, s 127.

[103] SDCA 1999, s 10.

If an impressed stamp of a sufficient amount but of improper denomination is affixed on a promissory note, then stamping is subsequently liable to a penalty where:

(a) the bill or note is not payable according to its tenor – 0.15 cent;

(b) it is payable according to its tenor (ie in accordance with its terms) – €630.

General penalty

[9.78] Where a promissory note or bill of exchange is not properly stamped, any person who issues, endorses, transfers, negotiates, presents for payment or pays any bill of exchange or promissory note shall incur a fine of €630.[104]

Exemptions

[9.79] The following instruments are deemed to be exempt from stamp duty under this head of charge:

(a) a draft or order drawn by any banker in the State upon any other banker in the State, not payable to bearer or to order, and used solely for the purposes of settling or clearing any account between such bankers;

(b) a letter written by a banker in the State to another banker in the State, directing the payment of any sum of money, the same not being payable to the bearer or to the order and such letter not being sent or delivered to the person to whom payment is to be made or to any person on his behalf;

(c) a letter of credit granted in the State authorising drafts to be drawn out of the State payable in the State;

(d) a draft or order drawn by the accountant of the courts of justice;

(e) coupon or warrant for interest attached to and issued with any security or with an agreement or memorandum for the renewal or extension of time for payment of a security;

(f) bills drawn on any form supplied by the Commissioners for the purpose of remitting amounts of tax in accordance with the Income Tax (Employments) Regulations 1960 r 31(1);[105]

(g) a bill drawn on any form supplied by the Commissioners for the purposes of remitting amounts of turnover tax, wholesale tax or value added tax;

(h) a bill drawn on any form supplied by the Commissioners for the purpose of remitting amounts of tax in accordance with the Income Tax (Construction Contracts) Regulations 1971 r 10;[106]

(i) direct debits and standing orders;

(j) a bill drawn on an account outside of the State; and

(k) a bill drawn on or on behalf of the Minister by which payment in respect of prize bonds is effected.

---

[104] SDCA 1999, s 25.

[105] SI 28/1960.

[106] Inserted by FA 1971, s 44.

[9.80] The exemptions under (i) and (k) take effect from 27 March 1998 and endorsed the previous practice. The ten exemptions listed above are set out in SDCA 1999, Sch 1:

(k) non Irish bills or notes are not liable to stamp duty as this head of charge only applies to bills or promissory notes drawn in the State. If a bill or promissory note purports to be drawn outside the State even though it may have been drawn or made within the State, it shall be deemed for the purposes of this head of charge to have been drawn or made out of the State;[107]

(l) where a bill of exchange is drawn in a set and only one of the set is duly stamped the other bills shall be deemed to be exempt from duty except where they are issued or negotiated apart from the stamped bill. If it is proved that the duly stamped bill has been destroyed or lost any other bill in this set, even though unstamped, may be admitted in evidence to prove the contents of the lost or destroyed bill;[108]

(m) any instrument issued in respect of prize bonds is deemed exempt from stamp duty.[109]

Originally any bill or note issued by the Bank of England or the Bank of Ireland was exempt under this head of charge. This exemption was repealed by FA 1997, s 130 and ceased to apply to instruments with effect from 10 May 1997.

Stamp duty in respect of certain foreign bills of exchange

[9.81] A bill of exchange which is presented for acceptance or is accepted or is payable outside the State cannot be rendered invalid by virtue of the fact that it is not stamped in compliance with the head of charge. For the purposes of admitting same in evidence in a civil court of law, and in respect of the penalty provisions, the instrument shall be treated as if it may legally be stamped after the execution thereof.[110]

Bond, covenant or instrument of any kind whatsoever

[9.82] Under the mortgage bond head, any bond or covenant which was given in writing and under seal is chargeable under that head. A bond or covenant for the purpose of this head of charge (ie bill of exchange/promissory note) relates to promises not under seal. The words 'instrument of any kind whatsoever' were considered in the case of *National Telephone Co v IRC*[111] where the court held that these words were not to be read *ejusdem generis* as bond and covenant and this head of charge applied to instruments in writing which were not under seal. This head of charge which applied to annuity, etc was abolished with effect from 28 May 1992.[112]

[107] SDCA 1999, s 22.

[108] SDCA 1999, s 24.

[109] F(MP)A 1956, s 24(A).

[110] SDCA 1999, s 27.

[111] *National Telephone Co v IRC* [1900] AC 1.

[112] FA 1992, s 205(6).

Chapter 10

Specified Duties

General

[10.01] Some duties are imposed as a matter of policy by specific statutory regulations. There is little to connect them and each are dealt with individually. They appear to be more a tax levy than a charge to stamp duty. However, as the levy is charged on a document that has to be produced and on which the duty payable is stamped, these charges are technical instances of stamp duty.

Credit, charge and cash cards

[10.02] Promoters of credit and charge cards are subject to an annual duty of €40 for each credit or charge card account held.[1] In practice, the promoters of such cards are authorised to, and generally do, pass the cost to the final consumer. The duty is payable on credit or charge accounts held at the relevant dates, as set out below, even though the account may not have been held for 12 months. There are differences in the way the duty is levied depending on whether it is a charge or credit card account that is being operated.

[10.03] In general, credit cards are operated by banks or financial institutions and a credit card account is that maintained by the bank or financial institution in favour of a customer and by which that customer may use a credit card to obtain goods and services which will be billed to that account. Charge cards are identical, except the term 'credit card' is replaced with the term 'charge card'. Charge cards include supplementary cards and company charge cards but not 'in-store' cards. The term 'in-store' card is not defined in SDCA 1999 but the Revenue Commissioners in their Guidance Notes[2] state that an 'in-store' card may only be used to purchase goods and services from the person issuing the card. It is something which pertains to the internal affairs of the business which issues the cards, as opposed to the relations of that business with persons external to itself. Company charge cards are also chargeable to the duty. A company charge card is that issued to a legal person (other than an individual) which, if issued to an individual, would be a charge card as described above, or that issued to the employee, nominee or agent of such legal person. Supplementary company charge cards are also subject to the duty.

[10.04] In both cases, the duty is levied on accounts maintained for customers with an address within the State. It follows also that non-residents of Ireland are not liable to the duty; that is, persons holding such accounts with an address outside the State are exempt. Many emigrants whose address is outside Ireland, for example the United States

1 SDCA 1999, s 124(1).

2 See www.revenue.ie.

of America have either credit or charge cards. These are not the subject of the levy nor of the reporting requirements.

[10.05] Each promoter of a credit or charge card is obliged to deliver to the Revenue Commissioners a statement showing the number of relevant accounts held for the purposes of the duty. For credit card accounts, this statement is to be delivered once each year and the payment of the duty must accompany such statement. The statement is due by April 1st of each year but the promoter has a further three months from that date within which to lodge the statement.

[10.06] For charge card accounts, statements are to be delivered at the end of every quarter, and payment must accompany the statement. The charging quarters are as follows: 31 March, 30 June, 30 September and 31 December. Promoters of charge card accounts have two months from these dates within which to file the statement. For charge cards, the levy is €40 per annum. The Revenue Commissioners may consent upon request by the promoter to delivery of the statement annually, provided it includes 1 April in that year, instead of quarterly.

[10.07] In the event of a failure to deliver, the statement or the duty interest at 0.0273% per day or part thereof will run from the date that the statement should have been delivered; that is, 1 April for credit card accounts and the end of each quarter for charge card accounts, or annually with the consent of the Revenue Commissioners. If the duty is still outstanding after 1 July of the relevant year, then a further fine of €380 per day for each day the payment is not made becomes payable.

[10.08] Company charge cards are also chargeable to the duty in a similar manner. Supplementary company charge cards are also subject to duty. (A company charge card is a charge card issued to an employee on an amount held by the employer company). The promoter of the credit or charge card is entitled to pass the duty on to the account holder.[3]

[10.09] A levy of €10 per annum is imposed on cash cards that enable the holder to withdraw cash from ATMs.[4] The rate for a card with a Laser facility, but no ATM facility, is €10 per annum. A card which has both an ATM and Laser facility combined now attracts duty of €20 per annum. Cash card accounts are those maintained by banks or financial institutions through which cash transactions undertaken by a cash card will be processed. The duty only applies on those accounts where the holder has an address within the State. Accounts held by non-residents do not give rise to the charge. The bank or financial institution must deliver a statement to the Revenue Commissioners concerning the quantity of such accounts being operated, together with the relevant duty. Such statements must be furnished every year at the end of each accounting period. Failure to deliver the statement on time gives rise to a penalty of 0.0273% per day or part thereof from the due date to the date the duty is paid and, in addition, a sum of €380 per day for each day that the duty is not paid. Where a financial institution changes its accounting period so that no accounting period ends in a particular chargeable year, duty

3 SDCA 1999, s 124(7).

4 SDCA 1999, s 113.

is charged as if the accounting period had not changed. The bank or financial institution is entitled to pass the charge onto the account holder.

[10.10] A cash card which is issued on a deposit account and which has not been used during the relevant accounting period, or has been used but the average positive balance did not exceed €12.50 during the relevant period, is exempt from the reporting provisions and not liable to duty. Since 1998 the SDCA 1999, s 123(3) the levy does not apply to the issue of replacement cash cards which have been lost. Previously the Revenue had, at their discretion, waived the levy in respect of such replacement cards.

[10.11] FA 2006 amended these provisions so that the stamp duty was charged on the cards as they are used in practice. The definition of the card was extended to cover cards where both functions are used, with the onus being on the bank to identify the number of cards they have in circulation that have a single application or a dual application. The charge is €10 for each use so that €10 is charged if only one function is used and €20 if both are used (with effect from 1 January 2006).

The bank levy

[10.12] This has now expired but originally this required financial institutions to make a contribution to the Exchequer which was calculated at 50% of the deposit interest retention tax (DIRT) payable by that financial institution in 2001. This levy was capped at 0.15% of the average amount of relevant deposits of Irish residents held by any financial institutions (calculated on a group basis and excluding any government deposits and interfinancial insitution deposits). This contribution was charged like a stamp duty and payable on 20 October in each year. It is interesting to note that it was not extended in FA 2006 considering bank profits were at an all-time high.

The insurance levies

[10.13] Contracts for insurance are stampable in two distinct ways. Firstly, the policies themselves are stampable in terms of the amount insured. Secondly, the insurance companies must pay a levy on the total premiums received from business conducted within the State.

Stamp duty on assured sums

[10.14] Policies of non-life insurance and policies of life insurance are dutiable. Policies which offer life insurance for the death of any person by non- natural causes are excluded:[5]

> ... except a policy of insurance for any payment agreed to be made upon the death of any person only from accident or violence or otherwise from natural causes.[6]

The term 'insurance' covers assurance and the court held in *Prudential Assurance Co Ltd v IRC*[7] that this included endowment policies as well as term and whole of life

5 SDCA 1999, s 1.

6 *Dalby v The India & London Life Assurance Co* [1854] 15 CB 365.

7 *Prudential Assurance Co Ltd v IRC* [1904] 2 KB 658.

insurance policies, but in *General Accident Assurance v IRC*[8] a policy of insurance which provided merely for the return of premiums paid was held not to be covered by the Act.

Life insurance policies

[10.15] The assignment of life insurance policies is liable to *ad valorem* duty at the rate of 0.1% of the amount of consideration paid.

Non-life insurance policies

[10.16] All other contracts of insurance, that is policies of insurance other than life insurance, fall liable to a fixed duty of €12.50. These contracts become chargeable where the risk is located within the State. Under SDCA 1999, s 61(2) a risk is located within the State, if in the case of real property it is situated in the State, or if a vehicle of any kind is registered within the State, or where the policy is of less than four months duration for the purposes of travel insurance and where the insurance has been effected within the State. Finally, all other cases are chargeable where the policyholder has his or her habitual residence within the State. This has been extended to cover situations where the policyholder is a legal person other than an individual, if that policyholder's establishment to which the policy relates is situated in the State.[9] The concept of establishment is that defined within European Communities (Non-Life Insurance) (Amendment) (No 2) Regulations 1991 (SI/142/1991).[10] *Ad valorem* duty at 0.1% is charged on the assignment of insurance or life insurance policies on the amount of the consideration under the 'Conveyance or Transfer on sale of a policy of insurance or policy of life insurance where the risk to which the policy relates is located in the State' head of charge.[11]

[10.17] Where the policy is endorsed or varied, should the policy be restamped to take account of the increased value of the assured amount?[12] There are two possible situations. First, the variation takes place outside the terms of the policy as the policy does not itself cater for the alteration. The second situation concerns alterations and variations which are expressly provided for in the policy document. On variations outside the policy there is conflicting authority. *Prudential Assurance Co v IRC*[13] involved a life policy given on the basis that the insured was 51 years of age. In fact, it transpired that the insured was 49 years of age and entitled to a larger assured sum at the end of the policy. The original policy was altered to reflect this. The question before the court was whether or not this amounted to an increase in the duty payable. The court held it was dutiable to the extent of the increase in the sum assured. However, this case must be seen in its proper perspective. The actual case involved an action for rectification of the document to reflect the true age of the insured. In other words, it was

8 *General Accident Assurance v IRC* [1906] 8F 477.

9 SDCA 1999, s 61(2)(d).

10 FA 1992, s 208.

11 SDCA 1999, Sch 1.

12 SDCA 1999, s 62.

13 *Prudential Assurance Co v IRC* [1935] 1 KB 101.

not a variation but the amendment of a written document and liable to duty since the earlier document had not been a true representation of the contract of insurance. But dicta in that case support the proposition given in *Royal Exchange v Hope*[14] that a true variation of an existing policy does not give rise to duty. In that case an endorsement on an existing policy extending the period of cover was not a new policy and not stampable. If this proposition is true with respect to alterations outside the policy, it must be so for variations made pursuant to the contract. Even if the first proposition is incorrect, it does not automatically follow that variations made pursuant to the policy are liable to duty.

[10.18] In practice it is advisable to stamp the varied policy in respect of the increase in the amount assured. The amounts involved are relatively small compared to the consequences of a failure to stamp. Since alterations to non-life policies are specifically exempted by statute, the issue only concerns life policies which the average sum assured will be relatively small.[15] Certain documents are considered exempt from the duty, primarily, cover notes and other writings made in anticipation of a formal policy, whether life or non-life.[16] Health insurance contracts within the meaning of s 2 of the HIA 1994 are exempt from stamp duty.[17] Permanent health insurance policies and critical illness policies issued after 1 January 2001 are exempt from the €1 per policy charge.[18]

[10.19] A fine of €630 is payable by any person who receives or takes credit for any premium for a policy of insurance and who does not execute a formal policy of insurance duly stamped within one month after receiving the premium. A similar fine applies to a person who pays out on foot of a policy which has not been properly stamped.[19] An assignment of an insurance policy which has not been duly stamped renders the assignee unable to sue for recovery and prevents the insurer from validly paying out on foot of such assignment. Where a payout has occurred in error, the insurer is liable for a fine and may be sued by the original policyholder for recovery of the sums so paid. This will not apply to any insurance policy where that policy is exempt from duty.[20] No instrument shall be chargeable under this head with duty exceeding €1 only by reason that the instrument contains two or more distinct matters falling within the head of charge 'Policy of Insurance'.[21]

Non-life insurance policies – levy

[10.20] Two per cent stamp duty levy is charged on the premiums received by insurers from certain non-life insurance policies where the risk to which the policy relates is

14 *Royal Exchange v Hope* [1928] Ch 179.
15 SDCA 1999, s 109(b).
16 SDCA 1999, s 10.
17 SDCA 1999, s 110.
18 SDCA 1999, s 110A.
19 SDCA 1999, s 59.
20 SDCA 1999, s 59(2).
21 SDCA 1999, s 62).

located in the State[22] under SDCA 1999, s 125. An 'insurer' covers authorisations granted under under the First, Second and Third Non-Life Insurance Directives including the European Communities (Non-Life Insurance) Framework Regulations, 1994 or carries on the business of insurance compliance with the Assurance Companies Act, 1907. This imposes the levy on brokers to the extent that premiums are paid to them on risks located in the State.

[10.21] Under SDCA 1999, s 125(1), amounts received in respect of the following premiums are excluded from the levy:

(a) an amount received in the course of or by means of reinsurance;

(b) a premium received in respect of certain classes of business listed in the Annex to the First Council Directive 73/239/EEC of 24 July 1973;[23]

(c) a premium received in respect of a business in classes I, II, III, IV, V, VI, VII, VIII, and IX of the Annex to the First Council Directive 79/267/EEC of 5 March 1979;[24]

(d) a premium received in respect of health insurance business within the meaning of s 2 of the HIA 1994; and

(e) a premium received in respect of a contract of insurance entered into on of after 25 March 2004, the sole purpose of which is to provide for the making of payments for the reimbursement or discharge in whole or in part of fees or charges in respct of the provisions of dental services other then those involving surgical procedures carried out in a hospital by way of hospital inpatient services within the meaning of, s 2(1) of the HIA 1994.

Section 84 loans

[10.22] These loans are usually given on the basis that repayment will take the form of a reduced rate of interest in exchange for the lender participating in the profits of the borrowing company. This results in distributions being made from an Irish company to another Irish company (franked investement income) which is exempt from corporation tax. Lenders of s 84 loans must deliver to the Revenue Commissioners a financial statement, showing the relevant interest received, within 30 days of the relevant period (which is any six-month period ending on 31 January or 31 July) and payment of the relevant duty of 12 per cent on the amount of interest or distributions received by the lender on that loan over the relevant period. The duty is reduced to 8 per cent where it can be shown that the interest received by the lender is less than a 6 per cent per annum return by way of simple interest.[25]

Example 10.22.1

Company A has received a €100,000 loan from venture capitalist X who gives loan facilities based on profit performance. These loans come within s 84.

---

22 See para **[10.20]** above.

23 OJ No L228 of 16 August 1973.

24 OJ No L63, 13/3/1979.

25 SDCA 1999, s 126.

Return on the loan is to run at 2% per annum on the amount loaned, with 10% of the profits, if any. Over the relevant six-month period, Company A made a profit of €28,000.

Lender X received €2,800 from the share of the profit (10%) and €2,000 interest.

Total interest and distribution received by X = €4,800. Since this is equal to 4.8% return per annum, the financial statement to be delivered by X is liable to duty of 8%.

Duty payable	€384

Example 10.22.2

Assume the same facts as above, but that Company A had made a profit of €48,000.

	€
Lender X's share of the profit	4,800
His interest in the same	2,000
Total received by X	6,800

This is in excess of 6% simple interest on the advance.

Duty is payable at 12%.

Duty payable	816

[10.23] Failure to supply the relevant detail or the duty payable results in interest on the duty at 2.5 per cent per month, or part thereof, it is from the time the duty arose until the date paid.

The security has to fall within the relevant provisions of CTA 1976, s 84 and no allowance is given for the duty charged under these provisions against any other tax or duty payable by the lender.

Collective investments

[10.24] A conveyance or transfer of assets in a domestic fund to another such fund where the latter fund issues units to the former fund, is exempt from stamp duty.[26] The exemption applies where the transfer of assets effects a disposal not chargeable to capital gains tax by virtue of TCA 1997, s 739A. The exemption applies in respect of instruments executed on or after 23 March 2000.

Share warrants

[10.25] The definition of 'share warrant' as found in SDCA 1999, Sch 1 includes:

(a) Share Warrants issued under the provisions of the CA 1963;

(b) Stock Certificate To Bearer which is defined in SDCA 1999, s 1(1) as 'includes every stock certificate to bearer issued under any Act authorising the creation of debenture stock, county stock, corporation stock, municipal stock or funded debt, by whatever name known'; and

[26] SDCA 1999, s 88A.

(c) any instrument issued to the bearer by or on behalf of any company or body of persons formed or established in the State and having a like effect as such a share warrant or such a stock certificate expressed in the currency of the State.

The amount of duty chargeable is equal to three times the amount of the *ad valorem* duty which should be chargeable on a deed transferring stock or share(s) specified in the warrant, certificate or instrument having a like effect if the consideration were the nominal value of such share (s) or stock, ie 3 per cent.

[10.26] A penalty of €630 is imposed under SDCA 1999, s 65(2) on the issuing company or any officer of same where a share warrant or instrument having like effect is issued without being duly stamped. An officer of the company will be the managing director, secretary or other principal officer of the company. If a share warrant comes within the definition of an option agreement under SDCA 1999, s 90(1), it will be exempt from duty.

Releases and renunciations

[10.27] *Ad valorem* stamp duty is chargeable under SDCA 1999, Sch 1 on any release or renunciation where it is made for consideration or as a voluntary disposition. A disclaimer of property under a will is not chargeable to duty. Release and renunciations made otherwise than on a sale are liable to a fixed duty of €12.50 but where the following certificate is contained in the release or renunciation it will be exempt from duty:

> It is hereby certified that this instrument is a release or renunciation of property, or of a right or interest in property, which is not a release or renunciation on a sale.

Such release or renunciation does not need to be presented to the Revenue Commissioners. Care must be taken that an instrument is a release not on sale, as the Irish Courts have found a release to be chargeable to *ad valorem* duty as a conveyance on sale in *Cherry Court v Revenue Commissioners*.[27]

Surrenders

[10.28] If the effect of a surrender is to convey property, or any right or interest in the property, to another person, then the surrender is chargeable as a conveyance. Where a surrender is on sale, or operates as a voluntary disposition, it is chargeable as a conveyance on sale. A lease, or agreement for lease, made in consideration of the abandonment or surrender of an existing lease or agreement to lease relating to the same property is not chargeable to stamp duty under the provisions of SDCA 1999, s 52(1). Surrenders made otherwise than on a sale or executed on or after 24 March 1999 containing the following certificate will be exempt from stamp duty:

> It is hereby certified that the instrument is a surrender of property, or a right or interest in property, not being a surrender on sale.

---

27 *Cherry Court v Revenue Commissioners* V ITR 180.

Miscellaneous provisions

[10.29] The following documents carry a fixed charge to duty:

		€
(a)	Deed of appointment of a trustee (SDCA 1999, s 88)	12.50
(b)	Declaration of trust (save where it acts as a conveyance on sale)	12.50
(c)	Deed of covenant	12.50
(d)	Duplicate or counterpart deed (or where the original duty did not exceed €12.50 then that lesser amount)	12.50
(e)	Deed of partition/division not described in SDCA 1999	12.50
(f)	Deed of release/renunciation other than upon sale or mortgage	12.50
(g)	Deed of revocation (not being a will)	12.50
(h)	Deed of surrender (not on sale)	12.50
(i)	Transfer of marketable securities other than upon sale or mortgage	12.50
(j)	Deed of any kind not described in the First Schedule to SDCA 1999 relating to immovable property situated within the State or stocks or marketable securities of a company having its register in the State	12.50
(k)	Share warrant or stock certificate issued to bearer in the currency of this State	3 times *ad valorem* duty on nominal value
(l)	Conveyance or transfer not hereinbefore described which relates to any property situate in the State or any stocks or marketable securities situate in the State	12.50

Chapter 11

Stamp Duty on Residential and Commercial Properties

Residential property

[11.01] Residential property is defined as a building or part of a building which, at the date the conveyance or lease is executed, is used or is capable of being used as a dwelling.[1] Included within this definition are partially constructed or adapted dwellings; and dwellings which have not been adapted for non-residential use since construction.

The Revenue Commissioners' Stamp Duty Work Manual and Practices[2] states that curtilage including buildings and outhouses of up to one acre are included in the definition of residential property. This supports their view on capital gains tax. The Revenue are of the view that non-residential rates will apply to any adjoining land that exceeds this one acre. It has also been indicated by the Revenue in this manual that the local authority classing of property will have a role in deciding whether a property is residential or commercial.

[11.02] A first-time buyer is defined as a person (or where there is more than one buyer, each of such persons):

(a) who has not on any previous occasion, either individually or jointly, purchased or built on their own behalf a house (in Ireland or abroad); and

(b) where the property purchased is occupied by the purchaser, or a person on his behalf, as his or her only place of residence; and

(c) where no rent, other than rent under the rent-a-room scheme, is derived from the property for five years after the date of the current purchase.

[11.03] There are three other situations where a person may be a deemed first-time buyer. These are:

(a) separated/divorced (a spouse in a marriage which is the subject of a judicial separation, a decree of divorce or a decree of nullity): in the case of the first acquistion of a house by the spouse following the separation or divorce, provided that the spouse had in relation to the former marital home,

  (i) left that home;

  (ii) not retained an interest in that home; and

  (iii) whose separated/former spouse continues to occupy that home, which was occupied by both spouses prior to the separation or breakup of the marriage.

1 SDCA 1999, s 1.

2 At p 17.

(b) buy-out of co-owner: where two or more persons have acquired a property jointly and qualified as first-time buyers and subsequently one person buys out the other person's share in the property, they will be entitled to be treated as a first-time buyer; and

(c) trustees of certain charitable trusts: the trustees of a trust to which TCA 1997, s 189A applies whose trust funds are raised by public subscriptions for the benefit of permanently incapacitated persons, in respect of the first house(s) bought after the establishment of the trust, for occupation by the beneficiary or, if more than one, each of the beneficiaries of the trust. These may also exempt as a qualifying charity.

Example 11.03.1

Tommy is a trustee of a TCA 1997, s 189A trust of which there are four beneficiaries. Tommy executes an instrument purchasing a third property for the trust.

He is regarded as a first-time purchaser for the purpose of these provisions.

[11.04] An owner-occupier is a person who purchases a new house or apartment which is to be occupied by the purchaser, or a person on his behalf, as his only principal place of residence and no rent, other than rent under the rent-a-room scheme, is derived from the property for a period of five years from the date of the execution of the instrument.

[11.05] An investor is any person who does not qualify for first-time buyer or owner-occupier reliefs as that person (or persons in the right of the purchaser) will not occupy the property as their only or principal place of residence and rent received, if any, is not under any rent-a-room scheme. Investors are subject to the full stamp duty rates on residential property.

Rent-a-room scheme

[11.06] Although the traditional requirement for claiming relief from stamp duty either for the purchase of a new house or as a first-time purchaser was that the property be occupied exclusively by the owner and not be rented or otherwise occupied by those unconnected to the owner, there is now a provision which enables the owner-occupier of the exempt or relieved property to rent out a single room to an unconnected person without losing eligibilty for the relief or exemption. This provision is designed to ease the difficulties arising from the bouyant housing market which makes it difficult to finance a mortgage unless the assumption is made that a spare bedroom will be rented to a third party, whereby that potential rent can be taken into account in calculating the total amount which a financial institution will loan to a prospective purchaser. While the policy goal behind this is admirable, it is somewhat at odds with the caution expressed by the central bank with respect to liberal lending policies in the Irish market for house mortgages. It is part, therefore, of the failure of the government to view stamp duty as an integrated element in both the housing and credit marketplace and to interfere with stamp duty policy (albeit here beneficially) without taking all the consequences into account.

Provisions relating to residential property

[11.07] There are four main provisions in the Stamp Acts used in determining the rates and stampable consideration applicable in respect of residential property. These are as follows:

(a) section 29 dealing with purchases of residential property that are new properties in the course of construction;

(b) section 91A which states that certain smaller new residential properties may avail of a full exemption to stamp duty;

(c) section 92 which states that certain larger residential properties may avail of significant reduction in the consideration chargeable to stamp duty;

(d) section 92B, stating that first-time buyers of residential property may avail of reduced stamp duty rates on the purchase of residential property whether it is new or second-hand.

Connected contracts of sale or leases and construction

[11.08] Under SDCA 1999, ss 29 and 53, a conveyance or a lease, which is connected with a contract or arrangement for construction of a dwelling house or apartment is exposed to stamp duty on the aggregate of the consideration for the site plus the cost of the construction.

[11.09] SDCA 1999, s 29(2) specifically states 'in connection with or as part of any arrangement'. There are two factors considered by the Revenue in determining whether this test is met. Morris J in his judgment of *Carroll v Budget Travel Ltd*[3] examines the phrase 'in connection with' and concludes that the facility offered would not have been available without the contract. This principle can be equally applied to ss 29 and 53 in that the construction will be deemed to be in connection with the contract for the sale of the site where one would not have been provided without the other. Secondly, Revenue has indicated in their Statement of Practice SD/2/90 at paragraph 2.1 that the question of whether the site contract and the construction are connected is determined on the facts of each case. Under this Statement of Practice, Revenue will also have regard to the following:

(a) other information supplied to them in response to their queries;

(b) whether building has commenced prior to the execution of the instrument of sale or lease; and

(c) whether any relationship or association exists between the builder or vendor of the site.

[11.10] In determining the facts of each case under s 29(6), Revenue may require statements and/ or statutory declarations from the people concerned with the sale or lease of the land, or with the building on that land, or from the persons acting on behalf of such people. Under s 29(3), the contract for the sale and the contract or arrangement for the construction will be regarded as connected where the construction has started

3 *Carroll v Budget Travel Ltd* (7 December 1997, unreported) HC.

prior to the execution of the instrument. However, under Statement of Practice SD/2/90 paragraph 7, where a site is purchased with a partially completed dwelling house and the Revenue are satisfied that there is no connection between the sale of the site and the builder chosen to complete the construction, stamp duty will only be charged on the cost of the site and the partially completed construction.

[11.11] Section 29(4)(a) makes provision for the calculation of the amount to be charged to stamp duty where it is not possible to ascertain the aggregate consideration. Revenue may use a multiple of between 5 and 10 times the open market value of the cost of the site. If this amount is later shown to be excessive, provision is made for the refund of stamp duty. Any such application should be made within three years of the date of stamping of the instrument. It is possible to apply for a refund (within three years of the date of stamping of the instrument) where the building work on the site has not commenced on the site within two years of the stamping of the instrument. In both cases a certificate must be inserted in the instrument conveying the property stating that this provision applies. If the conveyance or lease gives effect to a site or building contract, the following certificate is inserted:

> It is hereby certified that s 29 of the SDCA 1999 applies to this instrument.

Where the conveyance or lease gives effect to a contract for a completed house, the following certificate is inserted:

> It is hereby certified that s 29 of the SDCA 1999 does not apply to this instrument.

Owner-occupier reliefs

Certain new residential property – properties under 125 sq mtrs

[11.12] An exemption from stamp duty is available under SDCA 1999, s 91A in respect of instruments conveying new apartments or dwelling houses under 125 square metres, once certain other conditions are fulfilled. The section applies to an instrument effecting the first purchase of a new dwelling house or apartment by, or on behalf of, a person who will occupy the house or apartment as his or her only or main place of residence for the specified period. The house must not have been occupied prior to the purchase and must have a floor area compliance certificate when purchased, issued by the relevant Minister (at present the Minister for the Environment, Heritage and Local Government). The certificate must certify that the house or apartment is between 38 and 125 square metres and that the house or apartment complies with certain conditions in relation to standards of construction of houses or apartments and the provision of water, sewerage and other services in the house or apartment. The purchase must be issued within a reasonable time after the property was built. In practice, it is extremely difficult to get these certificates due to a backlog in the Department. Prior to the abolition of the first-time buyers' grant the certificates were required to obtain the grant but now as they are only required for stamp duty purposes, they are certified by a Department for which they serve no purpose.

[11.13] In *Dunne v The Revenue Commissioners*[4] the court held that a house which had been lived in before it was sold and completed did not qualify for relief. McWilliam J

4 *Dunne v The Revenue Commissioners* [1992] ILRM 438.

stated that the words 'upon erection' must be understood as meaning within a reasonable time after erection. The purchase of the new house or flat must occur within a reasonable time after the property has been built.

[11.14] To qualify for the exemption, the following certificate must be inserted:

> It is hereby certified that (a) this instrument gives effect to the purchase of a dwellinghouse/apartment on the erection thereof (b) on the date of the execution of this instrument there exists a valid floor area certificate (within the meaning of, s 4(2)(b) of the Housing (Miscellaneous Provisions) Act 1979 in respect of the said dwellinghouse/apartment and (c) the purchaser or a person or persons in right of the purchaser will occupy the dwellinghouse/apartment as his/her/their only or principal place of residence for the period specified in, s 91(2) of the SDCA 1999 and that no person will derive any rent or payment in the nature of a rent (other than by virtue of a title prior to that of the purchaser) for the use of the dwellinghouse/apartment or any part of it during that period.

The instrument does not need to be presented to the Revenue Commissioners for adjudication but the requirement for the PD (particulars delivered) stamp by furnishing relevant particulars remains.[5]

[11.15] The relief granted can be clawed back if, within 5 years of the date of execution of the instrument, the property is rented (other than a rent-a-room scheme) to a third party by the taxpayer. In addition, interest on the underpayment of duty is levied on the purchaser from the date the first payment of rent is received until the fine is paid.[6] Any person who receives such rent shall notify the Revenue within six months of such receipt unless the Revenue are aware from other sources.[7] Any incorrect statement furnished to the Revenue is liable to punishment on summary conviction for a fine of up to €12,500 and/or a term of imprisonment not exceeding 12 months and on indictment, for a fine of up to €126,970 and/or a term of imprisonment not exceeding 5 years.[8]

Certain new residential property – properties over 125 sq mtrs

[11.16] Under SDCA 1999, s 92 instruments effecting the conveyance on sale of or grant of leases over new apartments or dwelling houses with a floor area greater than 125 square metres can benefit from a reduction in the amount of the consideration exposed to stamp duty once certain other conditions are met. The relief operates in the following manner:

(a) where the transaction is structured as a purchase/lease of a site with a connected construction contract for a house or apartment, then the relief reduces the amount of stampable consideration to the greater of:
    (i) the site cost, or
    (ii) 25% of the sum of the cost of the site and construction costs; and

(b) where the property being purchased is a completed new house or apartment, then the stampable consideration is reduced by 75%.

---

5 See SP-SD 1/96, **Appendix 1**.

6 SDCA 1999, s 91(2)(c)(i).

7 SDCA 1999, s 91(2)(c)(ii).

8 SDCA 1999, s 12(4) applying TCA 1997, s 1078 (3).

The stamp duty rate applicable is that applicable to the reduced value, often resulting in the reduction of the stampable consideration to below the stamp duty threshold. The Revenue Commissioners, in practice, will insist on obtaining a certificate from an architect or engineer certifying that the area of the unit is over 125 square metres.

[11.17] The relief applies to new houses or apartments purchased by, or on behalf of, a person who will occupy the house or apartment as his principal place of residence for five years or until the property is sold. The same provisions apply in respect of the property not being occupied prior to the sale and being purchased within a reasonable time after it has been built.

[11.18] The Revenue Commissioners' Stamp Duty Work Manual and Practices[9] states their view in relation to redeveloped or refurbished properties. It is stated that the Revenue do not view redeveloped or refurbished properties to be entitled to relief under SDCA 1999, s 92 and are exposed to stamp duty on the full consideration for the completed house or apartment or the site cost plus building contract price.

[11.19] The relief granted can be clawed back if within five years of the date of execution of the instrument, the property is rented (other than through a rent-a-room scheme) to a third party by the taxpayer. In addition, interest on the underpayment of duty is levied on the purchaser from the date the first payment of rent is received until the fine is paid.[10] Any person who receives such rent shall notify the Revenue within six months of such receipt unless the Revenue are aware from other sources.[11] Any incorrect statement furnished to the Revenue is liable to punishment on summary conviction for a fine of up to €12,500 and/or a term of imprisonment not exceeding 12 months and on indictment, for a fine of up to €126,970 and/or a term of imprisonment not exceeding 5 years.[12]

Old provisions

[11.20] It should be noted that the provision[13] dealt with in this section does not apply to any instruments executed on or after 6 December 2001 and has been included for reference purposes.

[11.21] Prior to the introduction of SDCA 1999, s 92, during the late 1990s, the State experienced a considerable rise in property values, making it difficult for many new purchasers to acquire their own homes. The government undertook a number of studies seeking how to maintain property values while at the same time permitting ordinary families to purchase homes at reasonable prices. The government targeted investors in property as artificially increasing property values and sought to reduce demand from investors by imposing a high level of stamp duty. This was offset by a reduction in the level of duty payable for owner-occupiers. Traditionally, exemption from duty on

---

9 At p 19.

10 SDCA 1999, s 92(a).

11 SDCA 1999, s 92(a).

12 SDCA 1999, s 12(4) applying TCA 1997, s 1078(3).

13 SDCA 1999, s 92A.

property had been confined to new house construction, the strategy being to stimulate the construction and purchase of new homes. No relief or exemption was available for secondhand, or pre-owned homes. As part of the government strategy during the house price boom, and in an effort make housing more affordable to the owner-occupier and to discourage the investor from the market, provisions were enacted for the reduction in duty payable under the conveyance or transfer head of charge in SDCA 1999, Sch 1. The net effect of these provisions was to reduce the duty payable in the event of a purchase of a new property or a pre-owned property by an owner-occupier.

[11.22] These provisons were as follows:

(a) Any instrument to which SDCA 1999, s 92 applied, that is new homes without a qualifying floor certificate, were eligible for the reduced rate of duty.[14] The section applied to instruments executed on or after 15 June 2000. However, where an instrument was executed prior to 31 January 2001 and contained a statement that it was executed solely in furtherance of a contract evidenced in writing before 15 June 2000, the relief continued to apply.

(b) Any instrument to which SDCA 1999, s 92 did not apply, that is pre-owned property, qualified for the relief for the reduced rate of duty[15] provided the instrument contained a statement on the following lines:

> It is hereby certified that this instrument gives effect to the purchase of a dwellinghouse or apartment and that the purchaser or a person or persons in right of the purchaser will occupy the dwellinghouse/apartment as his/her or their only or principal place of residence for the period specified in SDCA 1999, s 92A(2)(b) and no person will derive any rent or payment in the nature of a rent (other than by virtue of a title prior to that of the purchaser for the use of the dwellinghouse/apartment or any part of it during that period.

[11.23] Again, this section applied to instruments executed on or after 15 June 2000. However, where an instrument was executed prior to 31 January 2001 and contained a statement that it was executed solely in furtherance of a contract evidenced in writing before 15 June 2000, the relief continued to apply. The relief granted can be clawed back if, within five years, the property is rented to a third party by the taxpayer. In addition, interest on the underpayment of duty is levied at a rate of 1 per cent per month from the date the first payment of rent is received until the fine is paid.[16] Any person who receives such rent shall notify the Revenue within six months of such receipt unless the Revenue are aware from other sources.[17] The relief does not apply unless the consideration for sale or lease is wholly attributable to residential property.[18] Thus transactions for mixed property, partly residential, partly commercial, aree not eligible for the reduced duty payable.

---

14 SDCA 1999, s 92A(2)(a).

15 SDCA 1999, s 92A(2)(b).

16 SDCA 1999, s 92A(3)(a).

17 SDCA 1999, s 92A(3)(b).

18 SDCA 1999, s 92A(5).

The duty is calculated as follows:

Amount or value of consideration relating wholly to residential property	*Fraction of duty that would otherwise be payable*
Not exceeding £100,000	Nil
Exceeding £100,000 but not £150,000	Three ninths (3/9)
Exceeding £150,000 but not £200,000	Four ninths (4/9)
Exceeding £200,000 but not £250,000	Five ninths (5/9)
Exceeding £250,000 but not £300,000	Six ninths (6/9)
Exceeding £300,000 but not £500,000	Seven and a half ninths (7 ½/9)

Example 11.23.1

Fred purchased a new house for €220,000. He intended to reside in this property as his principal family residence and the instrument containes the necessary certificate to that effect. The new house did not have a floor area certificate as it was in excess of 125 square metres.

Calculation of duty	€
Consideration	220,000
Duty at 9%	19,800
Duty reduced to an amount equal to 5/9 of that which would have been payable.	
Total duty payable	11,000

Example 11.23.2

Fred purchased a pre-owned home for €140,000. He intended to reside in this property as his principal family residence and the instrument contained the necessary certificate to that effect.

Calculation of duty	€
Consideration	140,000
Duty at 9%	12,600
Duty reduced to an amount equal to 3/9 of that which would have been payable.	
Total duty payable	4,200

Relief for first-time buyers

[11.24] Under the provisions of SDCA 1999, s 92B, first-time buyers are entitled to reduced rates of stamp duty on the purchase of residential property, both new and secondhand, provided certain conditions are complied with. The effect of the relief is that instruments stampable as conveyances on sale or leases of new residential property exceeding 125 square metres and secondhand properties can avail of lower rates of stamp duty than investors and purchasers of secondhand properties. The relief applies to first-time buyers of dwelling houses and apartments purchased by, or on behalf of, a person who will occupy the house as his principal place of residence for five years or until the property is sold. No rent other than rent under the rent-a-room scheme must be derived from the property within the first five years from the date of the execution of the instrument.

[11.25] A person may qualify only once for the relief, save in the circumstances mentioned in para **[11.16]**. In addition to this, under SDCA 1999, s 92B(6), the relief does not apply where there is more than one unit of residential property being purchased or leased or where the sale or lease forms part of a larger transaction or series of transactions.

FA 2005 removed the relief under SDCA 1999, s 92B to the purchase of new houses or apartments with a floor area under 125 square metres. However, the purchase of such a dwelling house or apartment is exempted from stamp duty under SDCA 1999, s 91.

[11.26] A conveyance on sale or lease pertaining to a new house or apartment exceeding 125 square metres must contain a certificate to the effect that the purchaser or, if more than one, that each purchaser is a first-time buyer. In any other case the certificate should certify the following:

(a) each purchaser, is a first-time buyer;

(b) the instrument gives effect to the purchase of a dwelling house or apartment;

(c) the purchaser will occupy the house as his principal or main place of residence for a period of five years from the date of execution of the instrument or until the house or apartment is sold by way of bona fide sale to an unconnected party if that period is shorter than five years; if there is more than one purchaser, at least one of the purchasers should occupy the property as his principal private residence or have someone do so in their right; and

(d) no rent other than rent under the rent-a-room scheme will be derived from the property for five years from the date of the execution of the instrument.

[11.27] In addition to the requirement that the purchaser or all of the purchasers be first-time buyers, all of the purchase moneys, or party borrowing the purchase moneys must be provided by first-time buyers. In any situation where this is not the case, there will be no entitlement to the relief.

[11.28] Revenue has indicated, following the requirement of most lending institutions to have a co-mortgagor, that a first-time buyer will not be precluded from claiming the relief where:

(a) the transfer is taken in the name of the first-time buyer;

(b) it is the intention of both the first-time buyer and the co-mortgagor that the co-mortgagor is not to take a beneficial interest in the house;

(c) the other person has been joined to the mortgage solely at the request of the lending institution for the purpose of providing extra security for the moneys being advanced for the purpose; and

(d) it is not intended that the other person will be contributing to the repayment of the mortgage in the normal course.

Relief will apply where an unconditional gift of moneys is made to a first-time buyer prior to the purchase of the house. It is advisable that a declaration of the intention to make an unconditional gift of the moneys is made prior to the purchase of the house.

[11.29] Where rent is received in respect of a property to which relief under SDCA 1999, s 92B was claimed within the first five years from the date of the execution of the instrument, relief will be clawed back. The clawback is equal to the difference in the amount of duty that was paid and that which would have been owed should the relief not have applied. Under SDCA 1999, s 92B(4)(b), the first-time buyer is obliged to inform Revenue of the receipt of rent within six months after the first date of receipt. Special rules apply where first-time buyers relief and the relief under SDCA 1999, s 92 are both being clawed back. These are as follows:

(a) the amount of the penalty for loss of first-time buyers relief is the amount that would be payable if the relief under s 92 continued to apply;

(b) the penalty under s 92 will be the amount that would have been payable if first-time buyer relief had been denied (ie, as if the lower rates did not apply); and

(c) where a penalty arises under s 92B and under s 92, the total of the two penalties should not exceed the amount of the duty that would have been paid where no reliefs applied, less the amount of duty already paid.

[11.30] New measures were introduced in FA 2005 to counteract a scheme whereby the purchase or gift of property was being divided into two or more separate purchases in order to avail of lower stamp duty rates. The provisions are such that any instruments executed on or after 3 February 2005 and within a twelve-month period are to be aggregated for stamp duty purposes. Stamp duty is calculated on the aggregated value, and each transferee is made jointly and severably liable to a penalty equal to the difference between the stamp duty paid and the stamp duty due on the aggregate value plus interest from the date of execution of the first instrument.

Example 11.30.1

Fred is purchasing a new apartment that has a floor area of 150 square metres. He does not have any previous interest in property (jointly or individually). The site cost associated is €150,000 and the construction costs were €200,000. Fred will be liable to stamp duty on the greater of €150,000; or €87,500 (€350,000 x 25%). Fred is exempt from stamp duty as €150,000 is below the chargeable threshold in respect of first time buyers.

Example 11.30.2

Fred is looking at purchasing a larger house. He will be an owner-occupier. The property he is considering purchasing is a new 3 bedroomed townhouse with a floor area of 130 square metres. The house is not completed yet but will have a purchase price of €1,000,000 (€350,000 for the site and €650,000 for construction costs). Fred will be liable to stamp duty on the greater of €350,000; or €250,000 (€1,000,000 x 25%). Fred will pay stamp duty at a rate of 6% on €350,000.

Example 11.30.3

Fred is looking at purchasing a holiday home in West Cork. The house is uncompleted but the purchase price for the completed house will be €900,000 (site cost of €350,000 and construction costs of €550,000). Fred will be liable to stamp duty at investment rates as he will not occupy the house as an owner-occupier because it is a holiday home. Relief under SDCA 1999, s 92 is not available. Fred will pay stamp duty at a rate of 9% on €900,000.

Example 11.30.4

Fred is looking at entering a contract for the sale of a site and the construction of a house. Fred is looking at the house for investment purposes. The vendor of the site and the builder are connected. Construction of the house has already commenced. The purchase price of the property is €500,000 (site cost €150,000 and construction costs of €350,000). Fred will be liable to stamp duty at a rate of 7.5% on €500,000. The connected contracts rules are applied in these circumstances.

Summary

[11.31] The provisions in this area have now become relatively complex and obscure. It might be useful to summarise them in a table format:

Type of property	*Type of purchaser*	*Duty*	*Comments*
new residential property with floor area certificate	owner-occupier	exempt	s 91. Note also the rent-a-room scheme allows from 6 April 2001 an owner-occupier to rent a furnished room and still obtain the exemption.
new residential property without floor area certificate	owner-occupier	duty payable on greater of site cost or 25% of aggregate of site cost and construction costs	s 92 and rent-a-room scheme discussed above
new residential property with floor area certificate	first-time buyer	exempt	s 91. Note also the rent-a-room scheme allows from April 6, 2001 an owner-occupier to rent a furnished room and still obtain the exemption
new residential property without a floor area certificate	first-time buyer	duty payable at reduced rates on greater of site cost or 25% of aggregate of site cost and construction costs	s 92 and s 92B and rent-a-room scheme discussed above.
secondhand property	first-time buyer	reduced rates	s 92B and rent-a-room scheme discussed above

Commercial property

[11.32] There is one set of stamp duty rules in relation to commercial property unlike residential property, and they are equally applicable to owner-occupiers and investors. The basic rule in respect of fully or substantially completed commercial property is that stamp duty is charged on the purchase consideration at the rates applicable to commercial property.

Substantially completed

[11.33] Paragraph 8.2 of SD/2/90 states that the Revenue will regard properties as being 'substantially completed' where the cost of the building work completed exceeds 75% of the total cost of the building work agreed. The site architect should certify the works performed in detail and the costs of the works completed at the date of the contract for sale. Revenue Notes for Guidance at pg. 51 have indicated that stamp duty is chargeable on the value of the works completed at the date of the contract, rather than the cost to the builder of the works completed. This is unusual as stamp duty is charged on the instrument effecting the transfer of the property based on the situation at the date of the contract rather than at the date of the instrument.

Interlocked contracts

[11.34] Under SD/2/90 paragraph 8.1(b), where the contracts relating to the commercial property (ie contract of sale or lease and construction contract) are regarded as interlocked, stamp duty is charged on the aggregate of the consideration for the site and the construction at commercial property rates. 'Interlocked' is the word used in the Statement of Practice and is taken to be different to 'connected'. Revenue's view is that the contracts are interlocked where they are dependent or conditional on each other to the extent that the purchaser is not entitled to enter the contract for the sale of the site without also entering the building contract. In practice, the writer has seen the use for a contract for the sale of the land, a separate building contract and then a third agreement to connect all the contracts. This should be avoided as it interconnects the contracts with the liability to stamp duty charged on the total consideration.

Not interlocked and not substantially completed

[11.35] The Revenue Notes for Guidance[19] have indicated that where the contracts for the sale of the site and the construction are not interlocked, or where the work has not been substantially completed at the date of the sale, stamp duty should be payable on the consideration for the site plus the costs of any works done at the date of the contract. Again, the cost of the works is to be taken as the value of work done rather than the cost to the builder. The rate to be applied is the rate applicable to the chargeable consideration rather than the rate appropriate to the larger transaction.

The following conditions must be met:

Practical Application

(a) contract for the sale of the site;

(b) separate contract for the sale of the land no interconnection;

(c) architects certificate as to works done as of the date of contract;

(d) take a conveyance or transfer of the site as early as is possible; and

(e) to ensure the consideration is stated net of VAT.

---

19 At p 51.

The writer is aware of an application being made to the Revenue Commissioners on a high-profile site where the document was found to be fully liable to stamp duty on full consideration as the stamping officer passed the site every day on his way to work.

Mixed property

[11.36] Where a property being purchased consists of both residential and commercial property, the consideration should be apportioned on a just and reasonable basis as provided for under SDCA 1999, s 45(2). The residential portion and the commercial portions are treated as though they are separate transactions for the purposes of determining the applicable stamp duty rate ie the stamp duty rate is determined by the value of each portion. Independent valuations of the property should be obtained to substantiate the valuations of the commercial and residential portions.

Example 11.36.1

Fred is looking at purchasing a factory. Construction of the factory has only just begun. The site cost was €1,000,000 and the total construction costs will be €2,500,000, with €500,000 of the works being done at the date of the contract. Fred is going to employ his own builder to finish the construction of the factory. Fred will pay stamp duty at a rate of 9% on €1,500,000 (€1,000,000 + €500,000).

Example 11.36.2

Nicki and Frank decide they need a new office and agree to purchase a site and office premises in the course of construction.

The site cost was €1,000,000 with a construction cost of €4,000,000 and at the date of the contract, €1,800,000 of the work done. The architect certifies the amount of work done at the date of the contract and the contacts are not interconnected.

Stamp duty will be charged at 9% on €2,800,000 (€1,000,000 + €1,800,000).

Example 11.36.3

Nicki and Frank decide they need a new office and agree to purchase a site and office premises in the course of construction.

The site cost was €1,000,000 with a construction cost of €4,000,000 but, as the developer had a defect on title delaying the signing of the contract, €3,200,000 of the works were done at the date of the contract.

Stamp duty is charged on 9% of €5,000,000. The full consideration is liable as greater than 75% of the works are complete at the date of the contract.

Chapter 12

Stamp Duty on Marital Breakdown, Partnerships and Options

Marital breakdown

Conveyances between spouses

[12.01] Conveyances or any transfers of property between spouses are exempt from stamp duty under SDCA 1999, s 96(1). The exemption will only apply where the beneficial interest in the property or any interest thereof is passed to the spouse.[1] If any part of the beneficial interest is passed to any other person other than the spouse, then the instrument will be liable to stamp duty in full. The instrument of transfer is not required to be adjudicated upon.

[12.02] Even though spouses may be separated, they will remain legal spouses of each other until such time as they obtain a decree of judicial separation.[2] This is contrary to the treatment of spouses for capital gains tax purposes where spouses who are not living together no longer qualify for the interspouse transfer relief. This applies to any couple who are legally married even though a previous marriage may have been dissolved by an Irish or recognised foreign decree of divorce, and one of the parties to the dissolved marriage may have remarried. Any transfer of property between the spouses in a lawful marriage will be entitled to the exemption under SDCA 1999, s 96.

[12.03] Any transfer of property pursuant to SDCA 1999, s 96 does not require stamping or adjudication before being lodged with the Land Registry or Registry of Deeds, etc. Any conveyance or instrument transferring property into the joint names of spouses pursuant to the Family Home Protection Act 1976, s 14 need not be delivered to the Revenue Commissioners, nor a Particulars Delivered Form returned in respect thereof.[3] The advantage of the Family Home Protection Act exemption is that the Land Registry and Registry of Deeds fees are avoided.

Example 12.03.1

Mary and Joseph have been married for 12 years. They live in the family home which is registered in Joseph's name only. Four years ago, Joseph inherited Blackacre from his mother who had just died. Today he is in ill health and wishes to transfer the family home to Mary, and to tansfer Blackacre to Mary in trust for their two friends, Benny and Joan. Blackacre is worth €800,000 and the family home is worth €500,000.

Duty payable:

Transfer of family home	Exempt

---

1 SDCA 1999, s 96(2).

2 SDCA 1999, s 96.

3 SI 144/95, see **Appendix 3**.

Transfer of Blackacre:

Duty on €800,000 since the equitable interest is being transferred to a person other than the spouse	€72,000
Total duty payable	€72,000

Divorce

[12.04] Stamp duty is not chargeable on any instrument whereby property is transferred pursuant to an order under Part III of the Family Law (Divorce) Act 1996 or a relief order within s 23 of the Family Law Act 1995 between spouses,[4] or pursuant to an order or other determination to like effect of a court under the law of another territory made under of in consequence of a dissolution of marriage, being a dissolution that is entitled to be recognised as valid in the State.

[12.05] No duty shall be payable on any instrument arising under any order or other determination made after 10 February 2000 from a court of another jurisdiction which is recognised in this jurisdiction, which has like effect to an order granted by a court of this jurisdiction. The relief, however, does not apply where the transfer of property, in whole or in part, or the beneficial interest is made to a person other than the spouses concerned.[5]

First-time purchaser – special provisions

[12.06] A spouse who has been the subject of a decree of judicial separation, a decree of divorce, a decree of nullity or a deed of separation will be considered to be a first-time purchaser (subject to meeting all other required conditions) for the purposes of SDCA 1999, s 92B in connection with the purchase of any dwelling house or apartment after the date of granting of the relevant decree or date of execution of the deed of separation provided:[6]

(a) the acquisition of the dwelling house or apartment must be the first acquisition after the date of granting of the relevant decree of the date of the execution of the deed of separation;

(b) the spouse acquiring the dwelling house or apartment must not retain any beneficial interest in the former marital home; and

(c) the other spouse must continue to occupy the former marital home as his or her only or main residence since the date of the grant of the relevant decree of the date of the execution of the deed of separation.

Decrees of divorce, decree sof judicial separation and decrees of nullity, as defined in the Act, also apply where they are granted in a jurisdiction which is recognised in the State are effective for the purposes of SDCA 1999, s 92B(8)(a).

---

4 SDCA 1999, s 97.

5 SDCA 1999, s 97(2)(b).

6 SDCA 1999, s 92B(8)(a).

Civil decrees of nullity

[12.07] A decree of nullity means a decree granted by the High Court declaring a marriage to be null and void. A decree other than that of nullity that has same effect. After a decree of nullity has been granted, the spouses to the marriage are considered to be spouses for the purposes of stamp duty. A spouse to a marriage that has been granted a decree of nullity is entitled to qualify for relief under the provisions of SDCA 1999, s 92B(8)(a).

Partnerships

[12.08] The Partnership Act 1890, s 1(1) defines a partnership as 'the relationship which subsists between persons carrying on a business in common with a view to a profit'. Unlike a company, a partnership has no separate legal identity. The partnership is 'looked through' to the individual partners who do not enjoy limited liability. The partners of a partnership, rather than owning any partnership asset, own a share in the partnership which entitles them to a share of the partnership assets equal to their share in the partnership, and also renders them liable to the liablities of the partnership as a whole. In *Re Bainbridge ex parte Fletcher*[7] it was stated that the a share in a partnership is a chose in action giving a partner a right in the share of the partnership assets after the discharge of the liabilities of the partnership.

[12.09] Some partnership transactions give rise to a charge to stamp duty. Such transactions include:

(a) admission of a new partner;

(b) formation of a partnership;

(c) retirement of a partner; or

(d) a change in partnership shares.

A change in partnership shares, where this change is effected in writing, is chargeable to stamp duty under SDCA 1999, s 31(1)(b). The rates applicable to the change of partnership shares will be those applicable to non-residential property as under partnership law; the partnership shares are in fact choses in action.

Formation of a partnership

[12.10] A contribution to the capital of a partnership on formation is not considered to be on sale and therefore will not be liable to stamp duty. This is the case where the partners contribute cash or assets to the capital of the partnership in proportion to their entitlements in the partnership, even though this contribution may be effected by a conveyance of transfer of property. Where a partner contributes assets that exceed the level of the contribution that the partner should have made (ie equal to his partnership share), he may be entitled to compensation by way of an equality payment or a debt arising in favour of his current account. Such a payment or debt introduces the element of a sale to the contribution and as such, is chargeable to stamp duty at *ad valorem* rates as a conveyance on sale.

---

7 *Re Bainbridge ex parte Fletcher* [1878] 8 Ch D 218.

[12.11] Contributions to a limited partnership established pursuant to the Limited Partnerships Act 1907 give rise to a charge to capital duty. Contributions to an Investment Limited Partnership established pursuant to the Investment Limited Partnership Act 1994 are exempt from capital duty under SDCA 1999, s 115.

Introduction of a new partner

[12.12] Applying the above principles on the formation of a partnership, where there is no element of a sale on the introduction of a new partner and the new partner merely contributes cash or assets to the capital of an existing partnership, there will be no conveyance on sale.

[12.13] If, however, any of the following situations occur on the introduction of a new partner, there will be a charge to stamp duty as a conveyance on sale. The situations are as follows:

(a) an incoming partner's capital contribution is credited to an existing partner's capital account;

(b) an existing partner receives some or all of the cash or assets of the incoming partner; or

(c) an existing partner withdraws cash or reduces his capital in the partnership as a result of the contribution of the incoming partner;

(d) where an incoming partner contributes an assets which are subject to a mortgage or other debt; or

(e) where an incoming partner assumes a share of the partnership liabilities.

In the decision of *Christie v IRC*[8] direct payments to a partner on admission to or retirement from a partnership are chargeable as conveyances on sale. This is disctinct from a situation where a partner is merely reducing his share in the capital of the partnership.

[12.14] This case also dealt with the situation where partnership interests were transferred. In this situation, any instrument effecting a transaction where a partner receives a direct payment for his share in a partnership (by a third party or an existing partner) will be chargeable to stamp duty at *ad valorem* rates as a conveyance on sale. These principles also apply to the merger of two existing partnerships. Where there is merely a contribution of the assets of the two existing partnerships, without an assumption of the liabilites of one of the partnerships, there is no conveyance on sale. If there is an assumption of liabilites of either partnership by the other partnership there will be a conveyance on sale chargeable to stamp duty.

Incorporation of a partnership to a business

[12.15] Under *John Foster & Sons Ltd v IRC*[9] the conveyance of partnership property to a company where the partners are the shareholders of the company will be liable to stamp duty as a conveyance on sale.

---

8 *Christie v IRC* [1866] LR 2 Exch 46.

9 *John Foster & Sons Ltd v IRC* [1894] 1 QB 516.

Dissolution of a partnership

[12.16] Where the dissolution of a partnership results in the partners receiving cash directly in proportion to their shares in the partnership, there will be no charge to stamp duty. If the dissolution results in the distribution of the partnership asset *in specie* or partly *in specie*, this will be brought within the remit of the charge to stamp duty. On basic principles of the charge to stamp duty, if the dissolution of a partnership can be effected without the need for a written agreement, there will be no charge to stamp duty. SDCA 1999, s 38 applies to the dissolution of a partnership where the assets of the partnership are distributed to the partners. This section provides that the partition or division of real or heritable property for consideration exceeding €130 will be liable to stamp duty as a conveyance on sale. Lord President in his judgment in *McLeod v Inland Revenue*[10] held that a distribution of assets to the partners on the dissolution of a partnership was a partition of the partnership assets between the partners in accordance with their partnership entitlements, rather than a conveyance on sale. This judgment also recognised that the division of such assets in direct proportion to the partnership shares would be quite difficult in reality and as such any equality money paid would not trigger a stamp duty charge. Any partnership assets distributed subject to any liabilities will be chargeable under SDCA 1999, s 41 on the amount of the liabilities assumed in addition to the consideration passing.

Retirement of an existing partner

[12.17] Usually a deed of retirement will be executed in respect of an existing partner retiring. This deed will provide an undertaking that the exiting partner will discharge any existing partnership debts and will also provide an indemnity for the exiting partner on any future partnership debts or liabilities. A deed containing these provisions will be liable to stamp duty under SDCA 1999, s 41 on any liabilities assumed and consideration passing. The acquisition by way of an assignment of an exiting partner's partnership share on his retirement by the remaining partners in return for a payment will be chargeable to stamp duty as a conveyance on sale. This continues to be the case where the payment received is equal to the amount of the exiting partner's shares of the capital and undrawn profits.

[12.18] Darling J in the case of *Garnett v IRC*[11] indicated that, where the retiring partner merely withdraws the amount due to him on his capital and current accounts and does not execute an assignment of his partnership share to his co-partners but issues a receipt for the moneys received, there is no conveyance on sale.

Use of a partition

[12.19] Where partnership assets are held collectively and the partnership splits up, the properties can be divided and partitioned between the partners *in specie* without giving rise to a charge to stamp duty.

---

10 *McLeod v Inland Revenue* [1885] 22 SLR 674.

11 *Garnett v IRC* [1899] 81 LT 633.

[12.20] If a block of apartments was developed by a trading partnership and some of the units were retained by the partnership itself, they could subsequently be divided between the partners in proportion to their partnership share without giving rise to a stamp duty liability, provided always that the title to the property is freehold. Apartments can be conveyed by way of freehold with a deed of easements or service charge so that the freehold title to the apartment can be retained with a management company structure in place. The apartment building, maps and structures have to be drawn in a different manner to ensure this structure can be achieved.

Options

[12.21] In general an option is a right conferred by agreement to buy and/or a right to call for the sale of, any property at a specified price within a certain time frame. There has been an extensive body of case law in the UK that has tried to identify the exact nature of an option agreement. The question as to the nature of an option agreement relates to whether it constitutes a conditional contract or an irrevocable offer. While only the lower courts in the UK (Chancery Division) have determined the matter, the uncertainty as to the nature of an option agreement will remain until the matter comes before a higher court in Ireland or the UK. The most recent case law in the UK has decided that neither of the above classifications identifies all the elements of an option agreement and that it is a contract for sale, conditional on the exercise of the option.

[12.22] The only definition of an option in SDCA 1999, relates to, and is thus limited to financial services instruments. The definition is contained in SDCA 1999, s 90 and is as follows:

> An agreement under which the right is conferred on a party to the agreement to do, at the party's discretion either or both of the following, that is:
>
> - to buy from or sell to or buy from and sell to another party to the agreement
> - specified stocks, marketable securities, commodities or currency,
>   - an agreement conferring the right to receive certain payments and imposing the liability to make certain payments, the receipt and making of the payments being dependant on and related to certain movements in a specified stock exchange index or specified date at a price that is determined or determinable at the time of the execution of the agreement.
>   - To borrow money from or lend money to another party to the agreement for or within a specified period in consideration of the payment of interest by the party by whom the money is borrowed or to whom it is lent to the other party concerned at the rate that is determined or determinable at the time of the execution of the agreement.

This does not apply where the instrument relates to immoveable property in the State (or any right or interest in such property) or the stocks or marketable securities of a company registered in the State under SDCA 1999, s 90(1).

[12.23] Options are considered to be property in their own right under the decisions of both *Cherry Court v Revenue Commissioners*[12] and *George Wimpey & Co Ltd v IRC.*[13] An options are distinguished from a right of pre-emption or right of first refusal, which are not considered to be an interest in property as decided in *Pritchard v Briggs.*[14] There are many transactions relating to options, including the following:

(a) grant of an option;
(b) release of an option;
(c) abandonment of an option; and
(d) exercise of an option.

Grant of an option

[12.24] An instrument which grants an option is considered capable of being a conveyance on sale according to the decision of Brightman J in *Wimpey v IRC*. The definition of a conveyance on sale includes an instrument that transfers an interest in property and vests it in the buyer. An option, in effect, grants a right to a party to acquire that interest in property. Where the consideration for the grant of an option is the payment of cash, the matter is straightforward and stamp duty is assessed on the amount of cash paid. Where non-cash consideration is involved, the matter is more complicated. SDCA 1999, s 40 provides that, for the purposes of stamp duty, shares are effectively cash and SDCA 1999, s 41 makes a similar provision in relation to conveyances in consideration of a debt. In the case of *Littlewoods Mail Order Stores Ltd v IRC* the House of Lords held that to be 'on sale' as provided for under SDCA 1999, s 1, consideration must take the form of cash securities or the discharge of a debt. Where an option is granted for no consideration or insufficient consideration, it will be chargeable as a voluntary disposition under SDCA 1999, s 30. This section charges a voluntary disposition with the same duty as if the instrument was a conveyance on sale, with the substitution of the value of the property transferring with the amount or value of the consideration passing. If the option premium is below the relevant stamp duty threshold and the appropriate Finance Act certificate is included in the instrument, the option will be exempt from stamp duty.

Exercise of options

[12.25] The transfer or conveyance of property on the exercise of an option will be chargeable under the conveyance on sale head of charge, where the exercise price consists of cash consideration or some form of non-cash consideration chargeable as set out above. Where the exercise price did not represent the market value of the property at the date of the grant of the option, the transfer of the property will operate as a voluntary disposition and will be chargeable as such. A transfer of property on the exercise of an option forms part of a larger transaction or a series of transactions with the grant of the

---

[12] *Cherry Court v Revenue Commissioners* V ITR 180.

[13] *George Wimpey & Co Ltd v IRC* 2 All ER 25.

[14] *Pritchard v Briggs* [1980] All ER 299.

option. As such, in determining the rate of duty applicable to the transfer on the exercise, the option premium and the exercise price should be aggregated.

[12.26] The rates of stamp duty applicable to options are determined by SDCA 1999, Sch 1 and are as follows:

Non-residential property other than stocks or marketable securities:

Amount of value of consideration	*Rate of duty*
€	
Less than 10,000	Exempt
Between 10,001 and 20,000	1%
Between 20,001 and 30,000	2%
Between 30,001 and 40,000	3%
Between 40,001 and 70,000	4%
Between 70,001 and 80,000	5%
Between 80,001 and 100,000	6%
Between 100,001 and 120,000	7%
Between 120,001 and 150,000	8%
In excess of 150,000	9%

The rates applicable to residential property are complicated and are set out in detail in **Chapter 11**.

[12.27] For stamp duty purposes, the Revenue Commissioners are obliged to determine the value of property in accordance with the rules under CATCA 2003, s 26 (open market value). Under SDCA 1999, s 18(a) this value is to be determined without regard to, inter alia, any power the exercise of which would result in the property being revested in the transferor. This includes an option over property and any power of revocation in favour of the transferor of the property. The implications of SDCA 1999, s 18(a) are that no reduction in the market value of property transferring where there is an option over such property will be allowed where the option is in favour of the transferor of the property.

Transfer of options

[12.28] As discussed above,[15] an option is property in its own right. The transfer of an option is therefore capable of being charged to stamp duty as a conveyance on sale. Some difficulty arises in determining the rate of stamp duty applicable to the transfer of an option. If the option is property in its own right, do you look to the property over which the option is created to determine the rate, or is the rate determined by reference to the rates applied in respect of non-residential property? This has particular importance when dealing with options over shares as the rate applicable to the transfer of shares and marketable securities is 1 per cent. The question is easily answered in the case of non-residential property where the rates as set out above apply. In the case of residential property a number of different rates apply depending on the circumstances. For instance, a person cannot be an owner-occupier in respect of the transfer of an option

15 See para **[12.23]**.

as they will not be taking possession of the property. To attract the nine per cent rate of stamp duty, the consideration must be 'attributable to residential property'. As noted by Colin Fuller in his article The Stamping of Options[16], this term is broad enough to encompass an option over residential property as the value of the option derives its value from the underlying property. In the case of options over stocks and marketable securities, there are further difficulties. The one per cent rate of stamp duty only applies if the property transferring is stock or marketable securities. Clearly the transfer of an option, even though over stock or marketable securities, is not such a transfer. It is understood that in practice, the Revenue Commissioners treat transfers of options over shares as conveyances on sale of stock or marketable securities stampable at one per cent.

Release of options

[12.29] The release of an option may be exposed to stamp duty under the head of charge known as the release or renunciation of any property, or of any right or interest in any property or under the conveyance on sale head of charge. The decision in *Cherry Court v Revenue Commissioners*[17] determined that the release of an option to purchase in consideration for the allotment of shares was a release or renunciation of an interest in property. In light of this, it is clear that the release or renunciation of an option over property for consideration is chargeable to *ad valorem* stamp duty. The release head of charge refers such an instrument back to the conveyance on sale head of charge for determination of the stamp duty. If such a release is entered into otherwise than on sale and merely represents the cancellation of a purely contractual right, there will be no charge to stamp duty once the appropriate Finance Act certificate is included in the deed of release. The Revenue Commissioners operate a concession where the one per cent rate will be applied to the release of an option over stocks or marketable securities.

[12.30] The abandonment of an option is to be differentiated from the release of an option, in that abandonment occurs where an option ceases to exist because it has not been exercised before the expiry of the term of the option. Where there is consideration paid for the abandonment of an option, then this is not an abandonment of an option but rather a release. This is due to the fact that an abandonment should be a unilateral action. Barron J specifically dealt with this issue in the case of *Kearns v Dilleen*[18] and stated:

> In my view the essential element to the abandonment of anything is the giving up of the right or title to that thing… In my view there is no giving up of the right to a chattel or to the right in action or to the option whenever money is paid to the holder to induce him to do so… If you accept consideration for giving up your right under an option you are not giving up any right or title to that option but acknowledging the existence of that right and title and taking remuneration or consideration for it. A true abandonment is a unilateral action. When you give up a right for consideration your action is no longer unilateral.

Where the right is given up for consideration, it is a sale of that right as opposed to an abandonment of an interest under the option.

16 Irish Tax Review, November 2001.

17 *Cherry Court v Revenue Commissioners* V ITR 180.

18 *Kearns v Dilleen* (28 July 1997, unreported) SC.

Chapter 13

Charge and Calculation of Stamp Duty

Introduction

[13.01] The charge to stamp duty is dependent upon the instrument concerned. Where duty is chargeable, liability attaches to the accountable person as defined by SDCA 1999, s 1. The concept of accountable persons is exceptionally broad.[1]

Conveyance on sale

Commercial property

[13.02] Only sales involving cash, securities or discharge of debt are liable for duty; other conveyances are not so liable. The rates of *ad valorem* duty assessed on conveyances on sale and deemed conveyances on sale depend on the amount or value of the consideration passing under the instrument. The current rates for *ad valorem* duty are as follows:

Aggregate consideration	*Rate of duty*	*Certificate no.*
Not exceeding €10,000	*Exempt	Nos. 3A/B + 8B/C
€10,001 – €20,000	1%	Nos. 3A/B + 8B/C
€20,001 – €30,000	2%	Nos. 3A/B + 8B/C
€30,001 – €40,000	3%	Nos. 3A/B + 8B/C
€40,001 – €70,000	4%	Nos. 3A/B + 8B/C
€70,001 – €80,000	5%	Nos. 3A/B + 8B/C
€80,001 – €100,000	6%	Nos. 3A/B + 8B/C
€100,001 – €120,000	7%	Nos. 3A/B + 8B/C
€120,001 – €150,000	8%	Nos. 3A/B + 8B/C
Over €150,000	9%	Nos. 3A/B + 8B

* Where a conveyance/lease is exempt from stamp duty, the instrument need only be presented for PD (particulars delivered) stamping.

[13.03] To ensure that an instrument is deemed exempt, or to avail of the lower rate of duty, a finance certificate must be inserted in the instrument confirming that the transaction does not form part of a larger transaction, or series of transactions, in which the consideration exceeds the band of the rate sought. The certificate must confirm that the property does not comprise residential property.

[13.04] Where the full certificate is omitted, the highest rate of 9 per cent applies. The certificate should take one of the following forms:

(a) it is hereby certified that the consideration (other than rent) for the sale/ lease is wholly attributable to property which is not residential property and that the

[1] See **Appendix 7**.

transaction affected by this instrument does not form part of a larger transaction or of a series of transactions in respect of which the amount or value, or the aggregate amount or value of the consideration (other than rent) which is attributable to property which is not residential property exceeds ....(insert relevant amount).

or

(b) It is hereby certified that the consideration (other than rent) for the sale/ lease is wholly attributable to property which is not residential property.[2]

[13.05] The transaction must be a series of transactions whereby the aggregate of the amount exceeds a certain figure. For example, in *AG v Cohen*[3] a purchase of six lots at an auction was held not to be a series of transactions since each individual lot was a separate sale. The phrase 'series' must mean a connection of similar things by some likeness. The onus is on the Revenue Commissioners to prove the connection. If a connection is proven, the onus shifts to the taxpayer. An agreement whereby the legal fees of the vendor are paid by the purchaser constitutes part of the transaction and must be included.[4]

Example 13.05.1

Jack and Mary agree to purchase a warehouse for €48,000 together with the contents, valued at €3,000, which shall pass by delivery. The certificate in this case should state that the consideration does not exceed €70,000.

Duty is payable (€48,000 at 4%) €1,920

Example 13.05.2

Jack and Mary agree to purchase a strip of ground adjoining their commercial premises for €4,800. No finance certificate is inserted in the instrument.

Duty payable (€4,800 at 9%) €432

Example 13.05.3

Jack and Mary agree to purchase a new restaurant for €375,000. In this case there is a need to insert a certificate with respect to the nature of the property but not with respect to the consideration since the highest rate of duty is payable.

Duty payable (€375,000 at 9%) €33,750

Example 13.05.4

Jack agrees to sell his warehouse to Mary for €49,000, provided that Mary reimburses his legal costs of €1,200.

Duty chargeable (€50,200 at 4%) €2,008

The certificate should insert €70,000 as the figure not exceeded.

2 To be used where the consideration for the transaction exceeds €150,000 but the property is exclusively commercial, see Example **13.05.3** below.

3 *AG v Cohen* [1937] 1 KB 478.

4 For a fuller discussion, see **Chapter 4**.

Residential property

[13.06] The standard rate for residential properties varies between 3 per cent to 9 per cent for properties over €127,000. These are discussed in greater detail in this chapter. If the property is wholly residential, the following certificate has to be inserted to avail of the exemption or lower rates of duty

> it is hereby certified that the consideration (other than rent) for the sale/lease is wholly attributable to residential property and that the transaction effected by this instrument does not form part of a larger transaction or of a series of transactions in respect of which the amount or value, or the aggregate amount or value of the consideration (other than rent) which is attributable to residential property, or which would be so attributable if the contents of the residential were considered to be residential property, exceeds … (insert relevant amount).

Example 13.06.1

Bill purchases a house in the White City for €120,000. This is exempt from stamp duty.

Example 13.06.2

Bill purchases a house for €160,000, together with contents valued at €12,000. The liability to duty would be as follows:

	€
First-time purchasers	Exempt
All others @ 3%	4,440

Note: the relevant rate applicable is determined by adding the house and content consideration together but it is levied only the house consideration – see **Chapter 12**.

The above two examples require the insertion of a relevant financial certificate.

Example 13.06.3

Bill purchases a house for €950,000. No finance certificate is included. The liability to duty is as follows:

In all cases: 9%	€85,550

Commercial/residential property

[13.07] Where the property is partly residential and partly commercial, the total duty payable is calculated on the basis of the amount of the consideration apportioned to the residential and commercial elements respectively. A new certificate is required to apportion the consideration as follows:

> It is hereby certified:
>
> (a) that the consideration (other than rent) for the sale/lease is partly attributable to residential property and
>
> (b) that the transaction effected by this instrument does not form part of a larger transaction or of a series of transactions in respect of which the amount or value, or the aggregate amount or value, of the consideration (other than rent) which is attributable to residential property or which would be so attributable if the contents of the residential were considered to be residential property, exceeds … (insert relevant amount) and

(c) that the transaction effected by this instrument does not form part of a larger transaction or of a series of transactions in respect of which the amount or value, or the aggregate amount or value of the consideration (other than rent) which is attributable to property which is not residential property exceeds … (insert relevant amount).

[13.08] Where the consideration for the residential part exceeds €150,000 and/or the consideration for the non-residential part exceeds €635,000, paragraph (b) and/or (c) should be omitted from the certificate, as appropriate.

Example 13.08.1

Bill purchases a public house with residential accommodation overhead. Total consideration amounts to €650,000. The residential part is apportioned at €150,000.

Duty payable

	€
€500,000 @ 9%	45,000
€150,000 @ 3%	4,500
Total duty payable	49,500

The certificate should read as follows:

It is hereby certified (a) that the consideration (other than rent) for the sale/lease is partly attributable to residential property and (b) that the transaction effected by this instrument does not form part of a larger transaction or of a series of transactions in respect of which the amount or value, or the aggregate amount or value, of the consideration (other than rent) which is attributable to residential property or which would be so attributable if the contents of the residential were considered to be residential property, exceeds €190,000.

Example 13.08.2

Jack purchases a run-down period house, together with 110 acres of farmland, for €780,000. His main interest is in restoring the period residence. The period residence is valued at €95,000 and is in need of substantial work to restore it in full.

Stamp duty

	€
€95,000	Exempt
€685,000 @ 9%	61,650
Total duty	61,650

Example 13.08.3

Jack purchases a house with an adjoining warehouse for his business for €350,000. The house is valued at €300,000.

Stamp duty

	€
€300,000 @ 5%	15,000
€50,000 @ 4%	2,000
Total payable	17,000

The certificate should read as follows:

> It is hereby certified (a) that the consideration (other than rent) for the sale/lease is partly attributable to residential property and (b) that the transaction effected by this instrument does not form part of a larger transaction or of a series of transactions in respect of which the amount or value, or the aggregate amount or value, of the consideration (other than rent) which is attributable to residential property or which would be so attributable if the contents of the residential property were considered to be residential property, exceeds €300,000 and (c) that the transaction effected by this instrument does not form part of a larger transaction or of a series of transactions in respect of which the amount or value, or the aggregate amount or value of the consideration (other than rent) which is attributable to property which is not residential property exceeds €50,000.

Where the instrument which is chargeable with *ad valorem* duty is in any currency other than that of the State, then the duty shall be calculated on the value of that money in the currency of the State at the exchange rate prevailing at the execution of the instrument.[5]

Stocks and securities

Marketable security

[13.09] Where all or any of the consideration for conveyance on sale is discharged by way of marketable security, the *ad valorem* duty is charged on the value of the stock or security.[6] The rate of duty in the sale of stocks or marketable securities is 1 per cent of the amount or value.[7] Marketable security means any security that can be sold on any stock market in the State; stock includes any shares, loan stock or government funds, whether foreign or Irish.[8]

[13.10] *Ad valorem* duty is charged on the value of the stock or security, and the actual value of the stock involved is taken and not its nominal value.[9] The value of the marketable security is ascertained as of the date of the instrument by reference to the average price of the stocks or securities on that date.[10] The meaning of the words 'date of the instrument' was considered in *Crane Freuhauf Ltd v IRC*[11] when the court held:

> ... as the instrument was executed conditional upon the issue of the shares, the date of the instrument was deemed to be the date on which the condition was so satisfied and the shares were to be valued on that date.

Example 13.10.1

Mr Investo decides to purchase a warehouse from Mr Jones in consideration of all the shares he holds in Paddy plc, a well-known Irish public company.

---

5 SDCA 1999, s 9.
6 SDCA 1999, s 40(1).
7 SDCA 1999, Sch 1.
8 SDCA 1999, s 1.
9 *Crane Freuhauf Ltd v IRC* [1975] 1 All ER 429 at 434.
10 SDCA 1999, s 40(1).
11 *Crane Freuhauf Ltd v IRC* [1974] 1 All ER 811.

Mr Investo's holding comprises 17,250 ordinary shares of €1 each which are trading at €3.65 each at the date of the conveyance.

	€
Nominal value of shares	17,250.00
Market value of shares	62,962.50

The market value of the shares is taken into account; the nominal value is ignored.
Total consideration passing (€62,962.50 at 4%)

Stamp duty liability	2,519

The stamp duty payable on the electronic transfer of marketable securities on the Stock Exchange is charged at the same rate but in a different manner.

Non-marketable security

[13.11] Where all or any of the consideration on a conveyance on sale is discharged by way of a non-marketable security, the *ad valorem* duty charged is based on the amount due for the principal together with interest upon such security as of the date of the instrument.[12]

Example 13.11.1

A agrees to convey his warehouse to B in consideration of a loan granted by B to A of €50,000 and accrued interest of €20,000.

Stamp duty on €70,000 x 4% = €2,800.

The courts have held that the value of the shares may be arrived at by valuing the property conveyed or transferred.[13]

Example 13.11.2

Jack agrees to sell a house to Mary in consideration of shares held by Mary in Bunless Ltd, a private company. The last time any shares in this company were transferred was 50 years ago. The house is valued at €110,000.

Duty payable on €110,000	Exempt

[13.12] The Revenue Commissioners are now empowered to value the property in accordance with CATA 1976 in respect of instruments executed on or after 1 November 1991.[14] They were empowered to use the provisions of ss 15, 16 and 17, but s 17 was repealed with effect from 24 February 1993.[15] Since 23 May 1994, valuation for stamp duty purposes shall be carried out in accordance with the provisions of CATA 1976, s 15 based on market value for instruments executed after that date.[16]

12 SDCA 1999, s 40(2).

13 *Carlyon Estates v IRC* [1937] 16 ATC 337.

14 SDCA 1999, s 19.

15 FA 1993, s 134.

16 FA 1994, s 104. For a further discussion see Bohan and McCarthy, *Capital Acquisitions Tax* (2nd edn, Lexis Nexis, 2004).

[13.13] If the transaction is concerned with the exchange of shares in one company for the consideration of shares in another company, then these are charged as two separate conveyances on sale even if the whole transaction is contained within the one instrument. Where the consideration comprised stocks and securities and there is a conveyance of property (other than stock, shares or marketable securities), then the conveyance of the property shall be liable only to *ad valorem* stamp duty.

Example 13.13.1

Jack agrees to sell a house in consideration of shares held by Mary in a private company. The house is valued at €200,000.

Duty payable on transfer of house: (owner-occupier)	
	€200,000 x 4% = €8,000
Duty payable on transfer of shares:	Nil

Periodic payments

[13.14] There are special rules for calculating the duty assessable on a conveyance on sale where the consideration is payable in periodic payments.

(a) By way of periodic payments for a period not exceeding 20 years so that the aggregate amount payable can be ascertained, then the total amount payable is to be charged with *ad valorem* duty;[17]

Example 13.14.1

John agrees to sell a commercial property to Mary worth €100,000, the consideration to be discharged by instalments of €7,200 per annum for 14 years.

	€
Stamp duty on conveyance 14 x €7,200	100,800
Duty at 7%	7,056

(b) Where the period exceeds 20 years, then the duty is levied on the amount which is to be paid over 20 years in full discharge of the duty.[18]

Example 13.14.2

Gerry agrees to sell to John a commercial property for €100,000 payable by instalments over 25 years of €4,000.

	€
Duty payable 2 x €4,000	8,000
Duty is 5%	5,000

(c) Where the periodic payment is based on a life or lives in being, then the duty is chargeable on the amount that would be payable over 12 years.[19]

---

17 SDCA 1999, s 42(1).

18 SDCA 1999, s 42(2).

19 SDCA 1999, s 42(3).

Example 13.14.3

Gerry agrees to sell to John a commercial property worth €100,000 by way of instalments of €8,000 payable for John's life.

	€
Duty payable 12 x €8,000	96,000
Duty is 6%	5,760

[13.15] The payment is periodic when there is an initial payment, an end payment and at least one payment accuring between these two payments. In *Blendett v IRC*[20] a payment made at the commencement of the lease, with the balance due on the twenty-third anniversary of the lease, could not be periodic. Contrast that with *Quietlece v IRC*[21] where the balance of the purchase price was to be paid in three instalments on the twenty-third, twenty-fourth and twenty-fifth anniversary of the lease. In this case the payments were not periodic for an indefinite period since the payments occurred outside 20 years. At least one of the periodic payments must occur within the 20 year period. In *Martin v IRC*[22] an agreement for the transfer of a plot of land in consideration of £50 plus an annual payment of 1 shilling was chargeable to duty on £50 plus 20 times 1 shilling. However, the payment must be exclusively part of the terms of the bargain for sale, not incidental to the property;[23] for example, rent would be incidental to the property.

Example 13.15.1

A assigns a lease to B, the consideration for which is discharged by periodic payments.

On taking an assignment of the lease, B undertakes to take over the liability for payment of the rent of €100 per annum.

The rent is not taken into account in calculating the periodic payment.

[13.16] In *Western United Investment Co v IRC*[24] the parties entered an agreement to sell shares where the consideration was payable by 125 yearly instalments totalling £5.5 million. If there was a default on any payment, then the entire sum became due. The Revenue contended that the entire amount became chargeable to duty because of this clause but this was rejected by the court. The liability was limited to an amount equivalent to 20 years of the instalments.

[13.17] Interest on the purchase price is not chargeable.[25] The duty is based on the nominal value of the consideration.

---

20 *Blendett v IRC* [1984] STC 95.

21 *Quietlece v IRC* [1944] STC 95.

22 *Martin v IRC* [1904] 91 LT 453.

23 *Swayne v IRC* [1900] 1 QB 172.

24 *Western United Investment Co v IRC* [1958] 1 All ER 257.

25 *Hotung v Collector of Stamp Revenue* [1965] AC 766.

Example 13.17.1

John agrees to sell to Mary a commercial property worth €100,000, the consideration to be discharged by instalments of €7,200 per annum for 14 years' plus interest on each instalment to be calculated at 3% above the inter bank rate.

	€
Stamp duty on conveyance 14 x €7,200	100,800
Duty is at 7%	7,056

(Stamp duty is calculated on the nominal value of each instalment, *Hotung v The Collector of Stamp Revenue*). Where a separate instrument is executed to secure the periodic payments, then it shall only be liable to the fixed duty of €12.50.[26] Where the instrument is executed before the conveyance, the exemption does not apply.[27] New provisions concerning unascertainable consideration are now in operation, see below.[28]

Consideration in discharge of a debt

[13.18] Where the consideration is the discharge or transfer of an existing debt, it is chargeable to *ad valorem* duty to the extent of the debt, or where the debt constitutes part of the consideration, then the duty will be levied on the total consideration of which the debt forms part.[29] The debt transferred need not be the personal liability of the purchaser to become chargeable to duty.[30] It is irrelevant that the debt was considered a bad debt at the time it was discharged.[31] An obligation which forms part of the ownership obligations of property, such as rent due in the future under the terms of a lease which is being assigned, does not constitute a debt under these provisions.[32] The same is true of a transfer of shares which have only been partly paid.

[13.19] On dissolution of a partnership involving a conveyance on sale, with the purchaser assuming the liabilities of the partnership, then the liquid assets, (eg cash in hand) may be set off against the unsecured liabilities (eg trade creditors). Under a foreclosure order, a conveyance to an equitable mortgagee is liable to duty.[33] The duty on foreclosures is limited to the value of the property conveyed.[34] Foreclosure is not the normal method of enforcing a mortgage.[35]

---

26 SA 1891, s 56(4).

27 *Western United Investments v IRC*.

28 SDCA 1999, s 44 and these supersede s 42.

29 SDCA 1999, s 41.

30 *IRC v City of Glasgow Bank Liquidators* [1881] 8 R 389.

31 *IRC v North British Railway Co* [1901] 4 F 27.

32 *Swayne v IRC* [1899] 1 QB 335.

33 *Huntingdon v IRC* [1896] 1 QB 422.

34 SDCA 1999, s 149.

35 See **Chapter 4**.

Example 13.19.1

Dick agrees to sell Albert a residential property which is the subject of a €50,000 mortgage. The consideration is to consist of €35,000 cash and Albert will assume the mortgage. The property is worth €85,000.

Duty is payable on €85,000 (€35,000 cash and assumption of €50,000 debt).

Duty payable	Exempt

Example 13.19.2

Dick agrees to buy Larry's business assets for €100,000. As part of the agreement, Dick will discharge the debts of the business that were owed prior to the sale, to the value of €20,000.

Duty payable on €120,000 (€100,000 consideration plus €20,000 debts taken over).

Duty payable (at 7%)	€8,400

A clause should be inserted into the agreement appointing Dick as agent of Albert for the collection of the book debts. This would remove the charge to duty in respect of the debts.[36]

Example 13.19.3

Dick has given a mortgage to Prionsias for €100,000 secured over commercial property. Prionsias has made no payments on the mortgage and decides to transfer the property to Dick in full settlement of the debt but, due to the completion of a dump site next to the property, it is now only valued at €75,000.

Duty payable (€100,000 at 7%)	€7,000

A plea might be made to the Revenue Commissioners to restrict the duty charged to the value of the property conveyed.

Direction of duty

Multiple instruments

[13.20] Where property for which consideration is to be paid as a whole is transferred in separate parts or parcels by way of separate instruments, then each of the separate instruments shall be chargeable to duty on the distinct consideration set out in each conveyance. This will apply where there are multiple, as well as single, purchasers.[37] Cognisance must be given to the aggregation rules referred to earlier. Pursuant to SDCA 1999, s 47, the parties may select that which they consider to be the principal instrument.

[13.21] Where one property is contracted to be purchased by two or more persons and it is agreed that the property is to be divided between each purchaser, and the vendor then enters into a separate conveyance with each purcahser whereby only the part purchased by a purchaser is conveyed to a each purchaser, each conveyance is chargeable to duty on the amount of consideration referable to each individual party.[38]

---

36 See **Chapter 5** for more detail.

37 SDCA 1999, s 45(1)-(3).

38 SDCA 1999, s 45(3).

[13.22] Where more than one conveyance transfers an interest in a dwelling house as opposed to different purchasers to effect the transfer of the full interest in that dwelling house and these multiple instruments are executed within a period of twelve months, then stamp duty shall be payable on the aggregate consideration SDCA 1999, s 45A. The penalty is charged by way of clawback of stamp duty together with any interest due.

Single conveyance, multiple instruments

[13.23] Where the conveyance of a single property must be effected through multiple documents, then the leading or principle instrument shall be chargeable to *ad valorem* duty and every further instrument shall be charged with such duty as they are liable to but this duty shall not exceed the amount of the *ad valorem* duty.[39] The parties to the transaction may determine which of the several instruments shall be the principal instrument.[40]

Subpurchasers in a conveyance on sale

[13.24] Where a purchaser has contracted to resell property to a subpurchaser before the conveyance of the property from the vendor to the purchaser, as a result of which the conveyance is made direct to the subpurchaser, the duty is chargeable on the consideration moving from the subpurchaser to the purchaser, regardless of whether it is greater or smaller than the consideration paid by the purchaser to the vendor.[41] In the event of the property being resold in part or parts only to a subpurchaser or number of subpurchasers no account shall be taken of the original consideration.[42]

[13.25] This is a common commercial practice where a builder contracts to purchase land and develops it and sells the sites to the subpurchasers so that no liability to stamp duty arises to the builder. When the scheme is put in place, the parties must ensure that it is a genuine subpurchase and not a stamp duty avoidance scheme. A requirement of subsale relief is that the nature of the property does not change. Therefore the relief will only apply where the title of the property which is the subject of the sub-sale remains the same throughout the transaction, ie if the property of the first contract is freehold, then the property at the end of the chain of the subsale must also be freehold. The relief is not, however, confined to land but includes other property.

[13.26] In *Fitch Lovell Ltd v IRC*[43] the provisions were applied strictly so that they would not apply where the agreement between the purchaser and subpurchaser occurred before the agreement between the vendor and purchaser, or where the purchaser obtained a conveyance before an agreement to sell to the subpurchaser had been entered into. The property being conveyed must not be altered, it must be the same as that which was contracted for between the vendor and purchaser. In *Escoigne Properties v IRC*[44] it

---

39 SDCA 1999, s 45(4).

40 SDCA 1999, s 47.

41 SDCA 1999, s 46(1).

42 SDCA 1999, s 46(2).

43 *Fitch Lovell Ltd v IRC* [1962] 3 All ER 685.

44 *Escoigne Properties v IRC* [1958] AC 549.

was stated that the purpose of the provisions was to apply relief by charging duty on one transaction only and to avoid double duty.

[13.27] In *Maples v IRC*[45] where only part of the property is conveyed to a subpurchaser, the remainder of the property not conveyed shall be chargeable to duty in the normal manner to the extent and value of the property not so conveyed. In *Peter Bone Ltd v IRC*[46] an agreement was executed which resulted in the vendor remaining a bare trustee of property for the benefit of the purchaser and for which the vendor was the nominee of the purchaser. The court, in considering the matter, found that the agreement was a conveyance on sale.[47]

[13.28] In *McCall v Bradish Ellames*[48] the owner agreed to convey the property to the purchaser or any nominee of his, as and when desired by the purchaser. The purchaser took possession of the property but this did not cause the land to be conveyed to him. The purchaser subsequently arranged for the sale of the property to the plaintiff, the consideration to pass to the purchaser and the original owner to convey the property to the plaintiff. The plaintiff sought to put liability to duty on the earlier documents. In an action before the High Court the plaintiff obtained a declaration that the only duty payable was that which arose between the plaintiff and the purchaser. The documents between the original vendor and the purchaser were not liable to duty.

[13.29] The consideration for a conveyance under the subpurchasing section, ss 46(1)-(2) shall be ascertained without regard to any covenant, power condition or arrangement, the subject matter of the conveyance which was not contained in the original contract and without regard to consideration calculated pursuant to ss 42(2), that is periodic payments made over a period of 20 years or over a life or lives.[49] A conveyance to which SDCA 1999, s 46(4) applies shall be deemed to be a voluntary disposition.[50]

[13.30] Where a subpurchaser takes an actual conveyance of the interest of the person immediately selling to the subpurchaser and the conveyance is duly stamped, then any subsequent conveyance to that subpurchaser of the same property shall be chargeable only with such other duty as it may be liable to, but not exceeding the *ad valorem* duty. Consanguinity relief is not available where relief is obtained under the subsale provisions.[51]

Example 13.30.1

Jack contracts to sell Blackacre Farm to Jill for €200,000. Jill contracts to sell the property to Mary, the consideration for which is annual instalments of €8,000 per annum for 25 years. Jill directs Jack to convey the property directly to Mary.

---

45 *Maples v IRC* [1914] 3 KB 303.

46 *Peter Bone Ltd v IRC* [1995] STC 921.

47 For a further discussion on this see **Chapter 4**, para **4.43**.

48 *McCall v Bradish Ellames* [1950] IJR 16.

49 SDCA 1999, s 46(4)(b).

50 SDCA 1999, s 46(6).

51 SDCA 1999, s 46(5).

The consideration passing between Mary and Jill is potentially chargeable under s 56(2), that is periodic payment over a 20-year period, as discussed earlier, and as such is ignored. Duty is charged on the market value of the property, €200,000.

Duty payable (€200,000 at 9%)	€18,000

Example 13.30.2

Jack contracts to sell a residential property to Jill for €200,000. Jill contracts to sell the property to Mary, the consideration for which is 15 instalments of €20,000.
Duty is chargeable on 15 x €20,000 .[52].

Duty payable (€300,000 at 5%)	€15,000

Example 13.30.3

Jack contracts to sell to his brother his farm for €120,000. His brother, Tim, in turn agrees to sell it to Jack's son for €150,000. Tim calls on Jack to convey the property directly to Jack's son.
Neither Tim nor Jack's son is a qualified young farmer.

Duty payable (€150,000 at 9%)	€13,500

(No consanguinity relief is available under SDCA 1999, s 46(5)).

Example 13.30.4

William enters into an agreement with Hilary for the purchase of 100 acres of land for €150,000. He does not call for the conveyance to be completed. Some time later he sells 25 acres to Francois for €50,000 and a further 30 acres to Helmut for €50,000, but subjects this sale to a clause whereby William can graze cattle on this portion of the land for a period of five years. William now calls for the conveyance of the land from Hilary.
Duty payable as follows:

		€
(a)	Hilary to Francois (25 acres) (€50,000 at 4%)	2,000
(b)	Hilary to Helmut (30 acres). As the consideration consists of a right to graze cattle in favour of William, this covenant shall be ignored and duty charged on the conveyance *inter vivos*.	
	The market value of the 30 acres is €60,000 at 4%	2,400
(c)	William to Hilary (45 acres) (€67,500 at 4%)	2,700

Where a purchaser has entered into a contract on which *ad valorem* duty has been paid pursuant to SDCA 1999, s 31 and before having obtained a conveyance of the property enters into a subsale, the subsale shall be chargeable only to the extent of the excess involved.[53]

52 SDCA 1999, s 42(1).

53 SDCA 1999, s 31(2).

Covenants to improve

[13.31] With regard to any conveyance on sale for which *ad valorem* duty is chargeable, no further duty shall be charged on any covenant where the purchaser is to make substantial improvements or additions to the property in question or where the purchaser has made such improvements or additions or for any covenant given by the purchaser relating to the conveyance.[54] This shall not apply to land in respect of which there is an agreement to build dwellinghouses or apartments on it.[55]

Example 13.31.1

William conveys a derelict property adjoining his family home to Al for €2,000 provided Al covenants to repair the property. This covenant is ignored in ascertaining the consideration.

Voluntary dispositions

[13.32] Voluntary dispositions cover situations where no consideration has been paid, such as a gift, and those situations where some consideration has been paid but it is insufficient and the Revenue are of the opinion that a substantial benefit has been conferred on the transferee. A voluntary disposition is a conveyance or transfer not made in good faith or for adequate consideration.[56] Marriage shall not be regarded as valuable consideration, either in whole or in part for the disposition.

A voluntary disposition *inter vivos* is chargeable to duty as if it were a conveyance on sale and the value of the property transferred shall be the deemed consideration on which the duty is chargeable[57]

[13.33] The value placed on the property is to be determined objectively. In *Lap Shun Textiles Industrial Co Ltd v Collector of Stamp Revenue*[58] the Privy Council held that application of these provisions is not dependent upon the intention of the parties but is to be determined from an objective viewpoint. Lord Wilberforce stated that:

> the stamp duty legislation clearly proceeds by way of stamping documents according to their nature and effect and not be references to party's intentions, and any departure from this principle would require clear indication

Even if the vendor and purchaser believe that the market value was paid, if in fact the consideration was less that the true market value, the duty is payable on the true market value. All voluntary dispositions must be adjudicated and this is discussed in **Chapter 15**.

[13.34] A voluntary disposition which is subject to a power of revocation, an annuity, or other periodic payment, or an interest subject to forfeiture is to be valued without reference to such qualifications.[59] This overturns the earlier case of *Stanyforth v IRC*[60]

---

54 SDCA 1999, s 43.

55 SDCA 1999, ss 26, 53 – see *Kimbers & Co v IRC* [1936] 1 KB 132.

56 SDCA 1999, s 30(4).

57 SDCA 1999, s 30(1).

58 *Lap Shun Textiles Industrial Co Ltd v Collector of Stamp Revenue* [1976] 1 All ER 833.

59 SDCA 1999, s 18.

60 *Stanyforth v IRC* [1930] AC 339.

which held that the valuation of such a disposition was to take such power of revocation, annuity or interest subject to forfeiture into account. The net effect of the *Stanyforth v IRC* decision was to reduce the value of the property in question and therefore reduce the liability to stamp duty. In *Colreavy v Colreavy & Keenan*[61] a conveyance granted subject to the condition that the transferee should reside and care for the transferor was held to be a conveyance for valuable consideration and chargeable to duty. SDCA 1999, s 18 now states that any such right of residence, maintenance or support is not taken into account for valuation purposes, except where reserved in favour of the transferor or spouse of the transferor, and shall be limited in valuation so as not to exceed 10 per cent of the unencumbered value of the property.[62] Where the duty has been paid, it may be reclaimed where the power of revocation has been exercised within six years of the date of execution of the document.[63] The clawback is limited to the amount of excess duty that was levied.

[13.35] Finally, a voluntary disposition may involve a mortgage which attaches to the property in question. The Revenue will calculate the equity of redemption, which is the difference between the value of the property and the mortgage and will levy duty on the greater of the mortgage or the equity of redemption.

[13.36] These provisions shall not apply to the following situations:

(a) any conveyance to a body of persons incorporated by special Act where the Act prohibits the division of profit amongst its members and the property has been conveyed for the purposes of open space or for the benefit of the nation;[64]

(b) any conveyance made for nominal consideration for the purposes of securing the repayment of an advance or loan;[65]

(c) any conveyance made for effecting the appointment of a new trustee or the retirement of a trustee;[66]

(d) any conveyance under which no beneficial interest passes in the property conveyed;[67]

(e) any conveyance made to any beneficiary by a trustee;[68] and

(f) any conveyance which is a disentailing assurance not limiting any new estate other than an estate in fee simple in the person disentailing.[69]

Example 13.36.1

Tom and Jerry agree to convey Cheeseland for €30,000. The market valuation on the property is €45,000.

---

61 *Colreavy v Colreavy & Keenan* [1939] IR 71.

62 SDCA 1999, s 18(c).

63 SDCA 1999, s 18.

64 SDCA 1999, s 30(2).

65 SDCA 1999, s 5(a).

66 SDCA 1999, s 5(b).

67 SDCA 1999, s 5(c).

68 SDCA 1999, s 5(d).

69 SDCA 1999, s 5(a).

The Revenue Commissioners will deem this to confer a substantial benefit.

Stamp duty is charged on €45,000.

Example 13.36.2

Tom agrees to sell to Jerry Cheeseland subject to a right of residence and support in favour of Tom for consideration of €85,000. The market value of the property is €105,000.

The Revenue Commissioners assess the value of Tom's interest at 6% of the market value.

	€
Stamp duty chargeable on €105,000 x 6% =	98,700
Stamp duty (at 6% on €98,700)	5,922

[13.37]

Example 13.37.1

Jack gifts his property to his son. The value of the property is €190,000 subject to a mortgage of €80,000 in favour of Lendo Ltd.

The Revenue Commissioners can charge this in the following manner:

		€
(a)	under s 30(4) on the market value of the property	190,000
(b)	under s 41 on the value of the debt	80,000
(c)	on the value of the interest passing being the equity of redemption	110,000

The Revenue Commissioners may elect to levy the duty on the highest yield but in practice would elect to charge duty on the equity of redemption, ie on €110,000.

Example 13.37.2

Given the same facts as above, but that the mortgage is €110,000. The Revenue Commissioners can charge this in the following manner:

		€
(a)	under s 30(4) on the market value of the property	190,000
(b)	under s 41 on the value of the debt	110,000
(c)	on the value of the interest passing being the equity of redemption	80,000

The Revenue Commissioners may elect to levy the duty on the highest yield but in practice would usually elect to charge duty on the value of the debt passing, ie €110,000.

[13.38] There is an obligation on the parties to the instrument to disclose in an accompanying statement that an instrument operates as a voluntary disposition and supply such statement with relevant information truly and fully set out.[70] Failure to disclose such transaction means that the party shall be presumed negligent until the

[70] SDCA 1999, s 8(5).

contrary is proven.[71] A surcharge will apply to voluntary dispositions *inter vivos* where an undervaluation is submitted.[72] These provisions also apply with the necessary amendments to leases charge to duty as voluntary dispositions *inter vivos.*[73]

Unascertainable consideration

[13.39] Duty is levied on the market value of the property conveyed on any instrument where the consideration cannot be ascertained, provided that such instrument would have been liable to duty had the consideration been ascertainable. The duty is levied on the amount of consideration that could be obtained from a purchaser or tenant paying full consideration or rent for such transaction.[74] This applies only to instruments falling liable to duty under the conveyance on sale and leasehold head of charge. The operative date is for instruments executed after 30 May 1991. This provision shall not apply to any instrument coming under SDCA 1999, ss 29 and s 53(4)(a) respectively. SDCA 1999, sub-s 42(1), (2) will not apply to any instrument coming within these provisions.

[13.40] The courts have developed a principle to deal with situations where consideration is unascertainable. This has been superseded by legislative provisions as discussed above, particularly in relation to conveyances on sale under SDCA 1999, s 44(1) and leases. This principle is known as the contingency principle. The principle applies the following rules:

(a) If there is a maximum sum or cap, then stamp duty will be calculated on this maximum sum under *Underground Electric Railways and Glyn, Mills and Currie & Co v IRC*;[75]

(b) If there is a minimum sum (but no maximum), then stamp duty will be charged on this minimum sum;

(c) If there are both maximum and minimum sums, Revenue will charge the maximum;

(d) If there is an amount specified, but it is subject to variation upwards or downwards, then stamp duty is calculated on the specified amount under *Independent Television Authority v IRC*[76];

(e) If there is neither a minimum nor a maximum sum, nor a figure subject to variation then there is no amount on which *ad valorem* duty can be charged and therefore no liability to stamp duty.

[13.41] In cases where the consideration includes amounts calculated by reference to future profits, the Revenue Commissioners adopt a 'wait and see' approach, stamping the instrument as and when any additional payments are made. In cases where the parties

---

71 **Chapter 3**.

72 See para **[15.31]** ff.

73 SDCA 1999, s 54.

74 SDCA 1999, ss 44 or 55 respectively.

75 *Underground Electric Railways and Glyn, Mills and Currie & Co v IRC* (1916) 3 KB 210.

76 *Independent Television Authority v IRC* [1960] 2 All ER 481.

have provided that a future payment would not exceed a maximum figure, Revenue has applied the contingency principle charging stamp duty on the maximum figure provided.

[13.42] As discussed in **Chapter 6** the contingency rule does not apply where the consideration under the contingency is unascertainable and the duty is levied on market value only, though the issue is not conclusively resolved.

Example 13.42.1

A shopping centre is sold for €1.2 million plus a payment to the vendor equal to 15% of rents received over the next five years, subject to maximum of €200,000 and a minimum of €50,000.

Under the contingency principle, duty would be charged on €1.4 million (€1.2 million plus €200,000 even if this is never paid). Since the value of the consideration is unascertainable, the charge is calculated on the market value of the property including the right over five years rent, say €1.3 million.

Exchanges

[13.43] An exchange of property is a reciprocal transfer of ownership; that is, if A owns Blackacre and B owns Whiteacre, an agreement between A and B that the properties be swapped constitutes an exchange. Any instrument effecting an exchange of property executed after 17 June 1993 is to be charged to duty under SDCA 1999, s 37 by reference to the value of each property separately and without regard to the fact that they constitute a series of transactions. The value is to be determined as if the property were free of any encumbrance.

Example 13.43.1

Jemima agrees to exchange her residence worth €125,000 for Jim's residence worth €185,000, the balance to be paid by way of cash. Stamp duty shall be charged on each property as follows:

	€
Jemima's property to Jim €125,000 at 0%	Exempt
Jim's property to Jemima €185,000 at 3%	5,550

Partitions

[13.44] A partition is the division of land amongst owners of land in severalty; for example, A and B own Greenacre, a 100-acre plot of land and they decide to divide Greenacre into two plots of land of equal value on which A will own one division and B will own the other.

[13.45] The Revenue Commissioners have stated at pg 47 of their Guidelines:

> A partition or division of property occurs where property which was owned jointly is conveyed by the joint owners in separate parcels into their separate names

As regards a partition of real or heritable property, where consideration of greater than €130 is given, the inequality of the partition is liable to *ad valorem* duty as if a conveyance on sale had occurred.[77] The duty is levied on the consideration paid but if

[77] SDCA 1999, s 38(1).

more than one instrument is required to effect such a partition, then the duty attaches to the principal instrument only and the other instrument or instruments carry liability to a fixed duty of €12.50. It is for the parties themselves to determine which of the several instruments is the principal instrument.[78]

Example 13.45.1

A and B agree to partition their farm of 800 acres. A receives 300 acres, valued at €900,000. B receives 500 acres, valued at €1,250,000.

Liability to duty on the inequality of partition of €350,000 x 9% = €31,500.

The principal instrument is liable to duty of €31,500. The counterpart shall be held for duty of €12.50. In this case, the practice would be for B to retain the stamped instrument and A the counterpart with fixed duty of €12.50.

[13.46] The provisions apply to freehold land only and exclude duty for the partition of leasehold properties, since such leasehold properties are not real property.[79] A question arises with respect to fee farm grants. Fee farm grants can be either freehold or leasehold depending on their creation. They are freehold where they are converted from a lease for lives renewable forever under the Renewable Leasehold Conversion Act 1849. They are leasehold where they have been created by the intention of the parties, since under Deasy's Act (Landlord and Tenant (Amendment) Act 1860) no reversion is necessary to the creation of a leasehold interest. These leasehold fee farm grants are accordingly excluded from these provisions.

[13.47] Despite *Macleod v IRC*,[80] the partition of leasehold property by way of assignment becomes chargeable to duty as a conveyance on sale and the duty is levied on the consideration paid and attaches to the property of greater value. The same result applies to both freehold and leasehold properties with respect to partition, although the basis for both is different.

[13.48] If the parties are connected or associated, the adjudication stamp is required. In all other cases, there is no mandatory requirment for adjudication. As the partition would be based on valuations, it would be advisable that the instruments are adjudicated upon by the Revenue Commissioners, to ensure that the transaction is not deemed in any way to be voluntary and to satisfy the requirements of any future purchase of either property.

[13.49] For a partition it is the actual consideration paid which will form the basis of calculating the liability to duty. The consideration given may not correspond to the value received, that is it will be a voluntary partition since it will be at undervalue. In such instances, the rules discussed earlier with respect to voluntary dispositions apply. Partition can be particularly useful in the dissolution of a partnership.

---

[78] SDCA 1999, s 47.

[79] *IRC v Littlewoods Mail Order* [1962] 2 All ER 279.

[80] *Macleod v IRC* [1885] 12 R 1045.

Example 13.49.1

John and Albert decide to partition a farm they jointly own, the Fourthfield. The value of the property is €200,000. The partition is to be 3/4 to Albert and 1/4 to John.

Albert agrees to pay €50,000 to John.

Duty chargeable (€50,000 at 4%) €2,000

Example 13.49.2

Assume the same facts as above but Albert is to pay John €30,000.

The amount chargeable to duty is €50,000 being the market value of the property conveyed partition.[81]

Building contracts

[13.50] A conveyance for the sale of land and a connected contract for the construction of a dwellinghouse or apartment on the land which does not qualify for a floor area certificate[82] are chargeable to stamp duty.[83] 'Land' includes any interest in land but does not include the result of any act of building. A 'building' includes improvement or alteration to land preliminary to the erection of any building.[84] The section does not apply, nor shall it be deemed to have ever applied where the dwellinghouse or apartment was occupied by any person prior to the sale or lease of the land, other than in connection with the building contract.[85]

[13.51] 'In connection' with such a contract is not statutorily defined but in *IRC v Payne*[86] an 'arrangement' was defined as a scheme consisting of a number of steps to be taken in order to bring about a certain result. The Revenue Commissioners have stated that the question of whether the site and construction contracts are connected is a matter to be dealt with on the facts of each case and they will have regard to all the circumstances of the transaction; for example, the relationship between the builder and the vendor. If building work has commenced prior to the execution of sale of the land then it will be regarded as being chargeable under these provisions.[87] The Revenue in practice will levy duty on the value of such land and partially completed structure where it is shown to their satisfaction that there is no connection between the vendor and the builder.[88]

[13.52] In *Prudential v IRC*[89] an agreement to purchase land with partly finished buildings was executed. On the same day an agreement between the vendor and the purchaser was concluded whereby the vendor would complete the building work on the

81 SDCA 1999, s 37 as amended.

82 See **Chapter 11**.

83 SDCA 1999, s 29.

84 SDCA 1999, s 29(1)(a).

85 SDCA 1999, s 92(a)(II)(b).

86 *IRC v Payne* [1940] 23 TC 610.

87 SDCA 1999, s 29(3).

88 SP-SD/2/90 para 7.

89 *Prudential v IRC* [1904] 2 KB 658.

land in question. The question was whether the contracts were connected. The court held:

> I must therefore identify what was the subject matter of the sale. In doing so I must have regard to the commercial substance of the transaction. I must have regard to the shape, or form, which the parties have chosen for their transaction. A given commercial result can often be achieved by more than one route. If the parties have genuinely chosen one route, with legal incidents and consequences attendant on that route rather than a different route having different legal incidents or consequences for better or for worse stamp duty will be assessable accordingly. I stress the word genuinely ... I leave aside sham documents and provisions ... I am unable to characterise the transaction by which the end result was sought to be achieved as a sale of land with finished buildings thereon. That, manifestly was not the legal shape of this transaction.

[13.53] This case should, however, be contrasted with that of *Waterford Glass.*[90] Prior to FA 1998 the charge to duty under the conveyance on sale head was levied on the amount which was the greater of:

(a) the consideration for the site; or

(b) 25 per cent of the total consideration, including the building contract.

The charge to duty under the lease head was levied on the amount which was the greater of:

(a) any consideration other than rent paid in consideration of the lease of the land; or

(b) 25 per cent of the total consideration, including the building contract.

This is now covered by SDCA 1999, s 29(2), which now imposes the charge to duty.

[13.54] In the case of a conveyance on sale, the duty is levied as if the property concerned were residential property on an amount being the aggregate of any consideration paid in respect of the land and any consideration paid, or to be paid, in respect of the building contract for a dwellinghouse or apartment on that land.

[13.55] In the case of a lease under the lease head of charge, the duty is levied as if the property concerned were residential property on an amount being the aggregate of any consideration paid (other than rent) in respect of the land and any consideration paid, or to be paid, in respect of the building contract for a dwellinghouse or apartment on that land.[91] Where the aggregate value of the building contract and site value is unascertainable in the opinion of the Revenue Commissioners, then it shall be charged to duty on ten times the open market value of the property free from encumbrances, or to such lower multiple not less than five times the value of the land at the discretion of the Revenue Commissioners on the information available to them,[92] This will operate in very rare situations;[93] the general rules to unascertainable consideration do not apply.[94]

---

90 *Waterford Glass* IV ITR 187.

91 SDCA 1999, s 53(2).

92 SDCA 1999, s 29(4)(a), 53(4)(a).

93 See SP-SD/2/90.

94 SDCA 1999, s 55.

[13.56] An excess payment of duty under these provisions[95] shall be refunded provided application is made to the Revenue Commissioners within three years of stamping of the document. The refund shall include simple interest at a rate of 0.0161 per cent per day or part thereof or such other rate as the Minister may determine from time to time. Income tax shall not be deducted from this interest nor shall it be liable to income tax.[96]

[13.57] Under SDCA 1999, s 53(3) it is provided that where the construction has commenced prior to the execution of the instrument effecting the lease, the two contracts will be deemed to be connected. However, Revenue has indicated in their Notes for Guidance at pp 59 that where it can be shown that there is no connection between the lease of the land and the employment of the builder, stamp duty will be charged on the cost of the works plus the value of the works completed at the date of the lease.

[13.58] Where building has not commenced within two years of stamping of the instrument, these provisions shall be deemed not to apply to such an instrument and a refund of duty will be made upon application to the Revenue Commissioners within three years. The refund shall include simple interest at a rate of 0.0161 per cent per day or part thereof or such other rate as the Minister may determine from time to time. Income tax shall not be deducted from this interest nor shall it be liable to income tax.[97] A statutory declaration may be required by the Revenue Commissioners from any person connected with the transaction or from a solicitor to the transaction.[98] Every instrument effecting a conveyance of property shall contain a certificate certifying the liability of the instrument, if any, under the provisions of SDCA 1999, ss 29(6) and 53(6)). The Revenue Commissioners have stated the words to be used are as follows:

> It is hereby certified that, s 112 (as amended by F(No 2)A 1998) of the Finance Act 1990 applies/does not apply to this instrument.[99]

[13.59] Sections 29 and 54 do not apply where:

(a) a site is purchased, and the purchaser builds the house under his own labour;

(b) there is no connection between the sale of the site and the building of a house or apartment on the site, for example, where the purchaser contracts direct labour to build the house or apartment; or

(c) a floor area certificate is issued and the purchaser occupies the house/apartment for a period of five years.[100]

Example 13.17.1

Paddy agrees to buy a site from a farmer for €200,000. He engages a builder who is unconnected to the farmer to erect a dwellinghouse on the land for €410,000.

---

95 SDCA 1999, s 29(4)(b), 53(4)(b).

96 SDCA 1999, s 29(4)(b).

97 SDCA 1999, s 29(7), 53(7).

98 SDCA 1999, ss 29(5) and 53(5).

99 SD 5/1998 see **Appendix 7**.

100 See **Chapter 11**.

Stamp duty is chargeable on the site only, ie on €200,000.

Duty (€200,000 at 9%) €18,000

Example 13.17.2

Assume the facts as set out above except that the land is purchased from the builder.
Stamp duty is chargeable on the greater of €200,000 or 25% of €610,000.
Duty is therefore chargeable on €152,500.

Duty (€152,500 at 3%) €4,575

Commercial and industrial developments

[13.60] Statement of Practice SD/2/90 also deals with Revenue practice in relation to commercial property. While the Statement of Practice refers to interlocking site contracts and construction contracts, this is generally taken to mean that where one contract expressly refers to the other contract or where one contract could not proceed without the other going ahead. With an agreement for the sale of the site with a substantially completed building, or a contract for the sale of land and an interdependent building contract, duty is charged on the entire consideration passing for both site and building. Where the agreement is for the sale of land and a building which is not substantially completed, then the duty is charged on the market value of the site plus the value of the work completed at the date of signing the contracts, provided that the building agreement is not interdependent on the contract for sale. An architect's certificate as to the value of the work completed should be lodged with the Revenue Commissioners.[101] Substantially completed means 75 per cent or more of the total cost of the work has been completed.

[13.61] Where the building on the site is substantially completed at the date of signing of the contracts and/or the contract for the sale of the land and the building contract are interdependent, stamp duty is chargeable on the full consideration for the site and the building. Where the contract for the sale of the land and the building contract are not connected, duty is chargeable on the site only.

Example 13.61.1

Michael agrees to buy land and a substantially completed building. The sale of the land is subject to performance of the building contract with the closing of both contracts taking place simultaneously, that is interdependently.
Site purchase price is €100,000. The construction costs are €180,000.
Stamp duty on €280,000 @ 9% .

Duty payable €25,200

Example 13.61.2

Michael agrees to buy land and a partially completed retail unit from Riskit Ltd. Michael then enters into a contract with Constructit Ltd to complete the buildings.
The consideration for the site is €50,000. The value of the completed work is €20,000.

[101] SP-SD/2/90 para 8.

Duty is chargeable on €70,000.

Duty (€70,000 at 4%)	€2,800

Example 13.61.3

Michael agrees to buy a site for his commercial unit from Paddy for €82,000. He subsequently engages White House Construction Ltd to build his commercial unit for €550,000.

Stamp duty on site only €82,000 @ 6%.

Duty payable	€4,920

[13.62] In practice, the following should be borne in mind:

(a) if a purchaser intends to buy a commercial unit which is yet to be constructed, it is worth considering dividing the contracts into a building contract and a sale for site contract to mitigate the liability to duty;

(b) where the building is not substantially complete and the contracts are not interdependent, the purchaser should arrange to have an architect to inspect the site at the date of the contract;

(c) the site should be purchased at the earliest possible opportunity and this should be registered with the Revenue Commissioners with the appropriate architects certificate; and

(d) the consideration should be stated net of VAT.

Stampable contracts under s 31

[13.63] Transactions falling within this charging section are charged with the same duty as if they were conveyances on sale.

Example 13.63.1

Fred agrees to purchase a business for €120,000 which consists of a leasehold interest worth €50,000, tenants' fixtures worth €20,000, cash in bank €20,000 and goodwill valued at €30,000.

Cash to the value of €7,000 is placed in a current account and case to the value of €13,000 is placed in a deposit account of .

Fred executes a contract for the purchase of a business.

Stamp duty at contract stage (s 59)	€
Goodwill	30,000
Tenants' fixtures	20,000
Deposit account	13,000
	63,000
Stamp duty at 4%	2,520

Stamp duty at conveyance stage

Leasehold interest	50,000
Stamp duty at 4%	2,000

This is dealt with fully in **Chapter 5**.

Leases

[13.64] Stamp duty on leases for commercial premises is calculated on the premium if any and also on the annual rent. The rate of duty on the rent depends on the amount of the rent and the length of the term of the lease.

Example 13.64.1

A Ltd, a general hardware company, agrees to take a lease of a unit in a shopping centre for a term of 35 years subject to a rent of €21,000 per annum subject to five-year rent reviews. The lease is executed prior to occupation of the premises.

Stamp duty		€
Lease	€21,000 x 1%	210.00
Counterpart lease		12.50
Rent-review clause		12.50
		235.00

Example 13.64.2

As above but a premium of €50,000 is payable and the appropriate finance certificate is inserted into the lease.

Stamp duty		€
Premium in lease	€50,000 x 4%	2,000.00
Lease	€21,000 x 1%	210.00
Counterpart lease		12.50
Rent review clause		12.50
		2,235.00

It should be remembered that neither consanguinity relief nor associated companies' relief apply to the lease head of charge. In addition to this, the subsale provisions under SDCA 1999, s 46, although drafted in terms of purchase and sale, do not prohibit the relief from applying to the lease head of charge.

Mortgage bond head

[13.65] The rate chargeable on an instrument, that is a mortgage bond, debenture or a covenant, being the principal or primary security charged on property situated in the State other than shares in stocks or funds of the government or the Oireachtas, not being an equitable mortgage, is 0.1 per cent of the amount secured up to a ceiling of €635 duty.

Example 13.65.1

A places a mortgage on his property for €70,000.

	€
Stamp duty payable on mortgage	Exempt (under 254,000)

Example 13.65.2

Hidebt Ltd borrows €1.8 million to finance its ongoing business activities. It places a first charge on its factory premises in favour of Hirisk Bank Ltd.

		€
Stamp duty payable on mortgage	€1,800,000 x 0.1%	1,800

As this duty has exceeded the mortgage cap, the liability is restricted to €635.

This is dealt with fully in **Chapter 9**.

Company capital duty

[13.66] Capital duty of 0.5 per cent is payable on transactions which give rise to capital duty. The FA 2006 has abolished the charge to stamp duty on the issuing of shares on transactions executed on or after 7 December 2005.

Example 13.66.1

X Ltd issues 50,000 ordinary shares at €1 each to Fred and Mable equally.

		€
Company capital duty	€50,000 x 0.05%	25

This is dealt with fully in **Chapters 7** and **8**.

Value added tax

[13.67] In *Glenrothes Development Corporation v IRC*[102] the English court held that stamp duty was chargeable on any VAT that was payable on the consideration passing to complete the transaction. By virtue of SDCA 1999, s 56, the VAT element of the consideration is excluded from liability to duty under the conveyance on sale or lease head of charge. For the avoidance of doubt, FA 1994, s 108(2) retrospectively deemed instruments executed prior to this date validly stamped notwithstanding that they had not been stamped on the VAT element of the consideration.

Example 13.67.1

Bill purchases a dress shop for Mandy for the sum of €200,000. VAT is chargeable on the transaction.

Pre 11 April 1994	€
Stamp duty liability as follows:	
Consideration	200,000
VAT @ 12.5%	25,000
Total consideration passing	225,000
Duty at 6%	13,500

[102] *Glenrothes Development Corporation v IRC* [1993] STC 74.

Note: where the instrument has been stamped only on the €200,000 at 6%, it will be deemed to be duly and properly stamped.[103]

On or after 11 April 1994

Stamp duty liability as follows:	€
Consideration	200,000
VAT @ 13.5%	27,000
Total chargeable consideration passing	200,000
Duty at 9%	18,000

Trusts

[13.68] The mere establishment of a trust without the vesting of property on the trustees does not give rise to a charge of stamp duty. The former settlement head of charge was abolished with effect from 25 March 1999.[104] The transfer of property by a settlor to the trustees of a trust is liable to stamp duty at *ad valorem* rates as a conveyance for sale if made for valuable consideration. Usually transfers to a trust are not made for valuable consideration and are chargeable in this instance as a voluntary disposition at *ad valorem* rates under SDCA 1999, s 30. All parties are accountable persons for the purposes of this section. Some property, such as personal property such as paintings, jewellery, etc, can be effected without the necessity of a written instrument and, therefore, will not be chargeable to stamp duty. Some trusts have been created by an oral declaration that the property is to be held on trust followed some time later by a written declaration of the terms of the trust. The Revenue will seek to argue in these situations that the intention to bring into existence a written document to set out the terms of the trust always existed and as such the oral declaration and written terms constitute one transaction. This was the case in *Cohen & Moore v IRC.*[105]

[13.69] In practice, it would be quite normal for a solicitor to execute a contract in trust on behalf of a client. The solicitor would take a conveyance/transfer/assignment of the property into his own name as trustee and subsequently transfer the property onto his client. This is usually done to preserve the client's identity.

Example 13.69.1

Construct Ltd wishes to buy a large tract of land for €4.2m. They instruct their solicitor to buy the property on their behalf so that the vendor will not be aware of their identity. A declaration of trust is executed.

Stamp duty payable as follows:		€
Stamp duty on purchase of land	€4.2m @ 9%	378,000.00
Stamp duty on declaration of trust		12.50
Total duty payable		378,012.50

[103] FA 1994 s 108(2).

[104] FA 1999, s 176.

[105] *Cohen & Moore v IRC* [1933] 2 KB 126.

Care should be taken in executing the declaration of trust that it does not constitute a conveyance on sale and become liable to *ad valorem* duty, see **Chapter 4**, generally.

[13.70] The acquisition of trust property by trustees is chargeable to stamp duty as normal. Trustees are not entitled to such reliefs as owner-occupier relief or first-time buyer relief except in the latter case as provided for under SDCA 1999, s 92B(7). Appointments of trust property to a beneficiary equivalent to the benefit to which he is entitled under the trust are not chargeable to stamp duty as the beneficiary is merely taking proerty to which he is legally entitled. If property is appointed subject to a mortgage or payment of some other debt stamp duty will be chargeable on the amount of the debt assumed under the application of SDCA 1999, s 41.

[13.71] Rearrangements of interests in trust property may be liable to a charge to stamp duty at *ad valorem* rates. For example, the disposal of a beneficiary of his interest in the trust property or the release of the interest held by a life tenant to the remainderman will be liable to stamp duty at *ad valorem* rates.

[13.72] In the case of *Fuller & Anor v IRC*[106] the exercise of a power granted to the beneficiary to change the trust and direct that the trust assets be held on new trusts was held to be a voluntary disposition. The release of a remainderman's interest in certain shares to the life tenant in return for other shares was held to be chargeable to stamp duty in *Oughtred v IRC*.[107] If beneficaries vary their interests so that they become entitled to a greater interest than that which they were entitled under the original terms of the trust, the difference in the value of the original interest and the new interest will be chargeable to stamp duty at *ad valorem* rates.

[13.73] The former head of charge 'Appointment of a new trustee and Appointment in execution of a power of any property, or of any use, share or interest in any property, by an instrument not being a will" was abolished with effect from 25 March 1999.[108] As such, the deed of appointment of new trustees does not give rise to a charge to stamp duty. If the trust property is vested in the new trustees by written instrument, this will not give rise to a charge to stamp duty once the appropriate certificate confirming that it is a conveyance or transfer on any occasion not being a sale or mortgage is inserted into the instrument but is liable to the fixed charge of €12.50. Where property is vested under a bare trust, the instrument vesting legal title in the trustees will not be liable to *ad valorem* stamp duty.

Settlements

[13.74] A settlement is defined in the First Schedule of SA 1891 as any instrument, whether voluntary or upon good consideration, other than a bona fide pecuniary consideration, whereby any definite and certain principle sum of money, stock or any security (whether charged or chargeable on land or other hereditaments) is settled or agreed to be settled in any manner whatsoever.

---

[106] *Fuller & Anor v IRC* [1950] 2 All ER 976.

[107] *Oughtred v IRC* [1959] 3 All ER 623.

[108] FA 1999, s 176.

Settlements are liable to duty at a rate of 25 cent per €100 or part thereof.

Example 13.74.1

Jack agrees upon the dissolution of his marriage to settle the sum of €1 million for his ex-wife's life and thereafter to his children. This is completed by formal settlement.
Duty payable 25c per €100 or part thereof on €1 million

Duty payable	€2,500

In this case the formal settlement could have included a clause allowing for further sums to be settled at a later stage. Jack could have advanced €1,000 as the initial settlement, paying duty of €2.50. Further advancements could then have been made at a later stage without attracting duty.

[13.75] Where the settlement arises from a life insurance policy, it is liable to *ad valorem* duty provided that where no provision is contained within the policy for keeping up that policy, the duty is chargeable on the value of the policy at the date of the instrument.[109] In *Duke of Northumberland v IRC*,[110] it was held that the provision for keeping up the policy need not be in the instrument itself. The further duty is no longer applicable in any event due to the abolition of the bond, convenant head of charge.[111] Where the settlement is effect by several instruments, then only one instrument is chargeable with the duty.

Assents

[13.76] An assent is the vesting of property by the personal representative or executors, held originally by the deceased, in the beneficiaries. Once the will provides for the specific power of appropriation by the personal reprstartentatives, there will not be a charge to stamp duty on the appropriation of any assets under the terms of the will. As such, an assent will not liable to *ad valorem* duty by virtue of the Succession Act 1965, s 52(8). However, if it is executed under seal, it is liable to the fixed duty of €12.50. The assent of property to persons who are entitled to the property under the will or on an intestacy will not be liable to stamp duty. However, where the property in an estate is vested in a person or person(s) who are not entitled under the will, stamp duty will be charged at *ad valorem* rates. Where a beneficiary pays moneys to the personal representatives, stamp duty will be chargeable on the amount paid by the beneficiary to the personal representatives.

[13.77] In *GHR Co Ltd v IRC*[112] it was held that an assent based on a contract for sale entered into prior to the deceased's death was liable to *ad valorem* duty. In that case, the vendor had agreed to sell certain property to the purchaser in return for money which was to be passed to the vendor's trustees. The vendor died and his personal representatives executed an assent in favour of the purchaser. The assent was liable to *ad valorem* duty as a conveyance on sale. In practice, where there is an estate with assets

[109] SA 1891, s 104.

[110] *Duke of Northumberland v IRC* [1911] 2 KB 1011.

[111] See SDCA 1999, Sch 1.

[112] *GHR Co Ltd v IRC* [1943] KB 303.

available for distribution, the residue could be divided among the beneficiaries where one may take a property in discharge of their share and provided that asset value is equal to or less than the value of their entitlement under the terms of the estate, no stamp duty will arise.

Disclaimers on intestacy

[13.78] A disclaimer is a refusal to accept the share in an estate held by a personal representative by a beneficiary. Whilst there has been some debate on the issue, it appears that prior to the Family Law Miscellaneous Provisions Act 1997, s 6, it was not possible to disclaim on intestacy.[113] However, s 6 now clearly resolves the issue and deals with the consequences of such a disclaimer, but only with effect from 5 May 1997. The effect of a disclaimer on intestacy now is to deem that the beneficiary predeceased the intestate (and in some cases, without issue) and therefore is not entitled to benefit.

[13.79] A beneficiary is deemed to have predeceased the intestate and the Revenue in practice have allowed disclaimer on intestacy completed by the personal representatives of a surviving child to give effect to the disclaimer principles. For stamp duty purposes this could be important as a subsequent transfer by the personal representative would have been liable to *ad valorem* duties with no consanguinity relief. A disclaimer executed under seal is liable for stamp duty at a fixed rate of €12.50. If a disclaimer is made in consideration of money or money's worth, the disclaimer will to the extent that moneys are paid be liable to *ad valorem* duty. If the subsequent assent vests an estate in beneficiaries other than in the terms of the rules of intestacy, it is liable to *ad valorem* duty as a voluntary disposition to the extent of the 'arrangement'.

Deed of family arrangement

[13.80] Any variation of the terms of a will or the distribution of the assets on an intestacy by agreement between the beneficiaries will be done by deed of family arrangement. A family arrangement will not be liable to stamp duty to the extent that no consideration is paid to any beneficiary for the deed of family arrangement. In the case of *Cormack's Trustees v IRC*,[114] the renouncement of a beneficary of certain property in return for an annuity and rent-free use of a suitable premises was held not to be chargeable to stamp duty. However, where a beneficiary gives up his interest in favour of another beneficiary receiving nothing in return, the deed, to the extent of such a gift, will be liable to stamp duty as a voluntary disposition. The same applies where consideration is received for varying interests by way of a deed of family arrangement.

[13.81] An assent is needed to transfer title to an individual who is entitled by virtue of a deed of family arrangement. When such assent is presented from stamping, attention must be drawn to the existence of a deed of family arrangement. A practitioner who does not draw such attention where he is presenting an assent for stamping will be negligent and liable to pay a penalty of €1,265 plus the amount of the unpaid duty. Consanguinity

[113] *Gleeson v Feehan and Person*, (1996, unreported) SC).

[114] *Cormack's Trustees v IRC* [1924] SC 819.

relief can apply to a deed of family arrangement as it is an agreement between the beneficiaries rather than the estate.

Shares forming part of an estate

[13.82] After 25 March 1999, the transfer of shares in a company by the personal representatives to the beneficiaries under a will or intestacy effected by a stock transfer form will not be liable to stamp duty if the share transfer form contains the following certificate:

> It is hereby certified that the instrument is a conveyance on any occasion not being a sale or mortgage

Typical residential transactions

[13.83]

Example 13.83.1

Joe decides to purchase a house in the course of construction which has a floor area certificate from Construct Ltd for €170,000. He intends to reside in this property as his principal private residence. It is part of a larger development by Construct Ltd.

He finances the purchase by way of bank loan of €150,000. The stamp duty liabilities arising would be as follows:

	€
Stamp duty on deed of transfer (SDCA 1999, s 91)	Nil
Stamp duty on mortgage at 1%	Nil
Stamp duty on collateral assignment of life policy to the bank	12.50
Stamp duty on NHBGS form HB10	12.50
Stamp duty on indemnity re roads and services	12.50
Total duty payable	37.50

Example 13.83.2

John, shortly after his marriage to Mary, decides that he should transfer the property into both their names.

	€
Stamp duty on the transfer (conveyance between spouses – SDCA 1999, s 96)	Exempt

Example 13.83.3

Mabel decides to purchase Whitewater from her mother, Hilary, for €230,000. The purchase is financed by way of mortgage of €200,000, the remainder by cash.

The deed is adjudicated upon by the Revenue Commissioners who value the property at €280,000. The liability to stamp duty is as follows:

	€
Stamp duty on deed (consanguinity relief) (€280,000 x 5% x 50%)	7,000.00
Mortgage duty less than market value	Nil
Assignment of life policy	12.50
Total liability	7,012.50

If the consanguinity certificate had not been inserted into the deed, the total liability would have been €14,012.50.

Example 13.83.4

John and Mary agree to purchase a house for €282,000 financed by way of mortgage for €256,000. Stamp duty liability is as follows:

	€
Stamp duty on transfer of owner-occupier	14,100.00
Stamp duty on mortgage at 0.1%	256.00
Stamp duty on assignment of life policy	12.50
Stamp duty on counterpart mortgage	12.50
Total liability for duty	14,381.00

Valuations

[13.84] The Revenue Commissioners are empowered to ascertain the value of any property which is the subject of any instrument chargeable with stamp duty. When valuing such property the Revenue Commissioners should ascertain the value of such property in accordance with the provisions of s 26 of the Capital Acquisitions Tax Consolidation Act 2003 (CATA 2003).[115] The market value of property is the price at which the property whould fetch if sold on the open market on the date on which the property is to be valued and subject to such conditions as might be reasonably calcuated to obtain for the vendor the best price for the property CATCA 2003, s 26(2).[116]

[13.85] There are four main situations in respect of which the Revenue Commissioners will exercise their powers of valuation:

(1) where the consideration is unascertainable;[117]

(2) voluntary dispositions *inter vivos*;[118]

(3) where the consideration consists of stock or marketable securities;[119] and

(4) in the case of certain conveyances or transfers, or certain agreements, in contemplation of sale.[120]

[13.86] Under SDCA 1999, s 18 (a)–(c) regarding the valuation of property for the purposes of SDCA 1999, s 30 (voluntary dispositions *inter vivos*) or s 33 (conveyances and transfers in contemplation of sale), the value of such property is to be determined without regard to:

---

[115] SDCA 1999, s 19.

[116] For a detailed discussion please see Bohan and McCarthy *Capital Acquisitions Tax* (2nd edn, LexisNexis, 2004).

[117] SDCA 1999, s 44 and 55.

[118] SDCA 1999, s 30 and 54.

[119] SDCA 1999, s 40.

[120] SDCA 1999, s 33 and 34.

(a) any power whereby any property or any part of it or any interest in it may be revested in the disponer or any other person on the disponer's behalf;

(b) any annuity, periodic payment reserved out of the property or any part of it or any life or other interests so reserved, being an interest which is subject to forfeiture; and

(c) any right of residence, support, maintenance or other right of a similar nature. If such rights are reserved in favour of the transferor or the spouse of the transferor, regard will also be had to such rights but only to the extent that the value of such rights does not exceed 10% of the unencumbered value of the property.

Where the property is revested in the disponer by virtue of any of the powers described above within four years of the date of the original conveyance or transfer, a claim may be made for refund of the duty paid on the original conveyance or transfer.

[13.87] Shares are also subject to the open market value test above.[121] The nature of the company's business will determine which test the Revenue Commissioners apply to the valuing of the shares of a private unquoted company. The value will be ascertained by reference to a price a purchaser would pay for these shares, knowing that there may be restrictions on those shares.[122] There are three different methodologies used in valuing properties:

(a) Trading and manufacturing companies are valued based on a multiple of the maintainable after-tax profits with the multiple being selected using data from quoted companies in the same industry. The multiple used to value such quoted companies is adjusted downwards to compensate for lack of access to public markets and where the private company comparator is relatively small. The Revenue may also take account of whether the company holds or retains assets or profits not immediately required for the company's trade.

(b) Companies which own or operate business in the services industry may be valued on a mulitple of turnover, fees or commission.

(c) Investment or property holding companies are valued on the basis of their net asset value. The Revenue may require up-to-date valuations of property or investments held by such companies as the book value may not represent their true value.

[13.88] The Revenue Commissioners Work Manual and Practices[123] state that a discount will also be applied depending of the size of the shareholding. These discounts are applied as follows:

(a)	Over 75%:	0 – 5% discount;
(b)	Over 50%:	10 to 15% discount;
(c)	50%:	20 to 30% discount;

---

[121] See para **[13.55]**.

[122] *AG v Jameson* [1905] 2 IR 218.

[123] At pp 48–50.

(d)	Over 25%:	35 to 40% discount;
(e)	Up to 25%:	Valued by reference to dividends if a realistic level of dividends is paid. If no dividends are paid, discount is in the range of 50–70% using an earnings basis.

An SD4 should be submitted together with the stock transfer where the transfer relates to shares in private unquoted companies.

Chapter 14

Reliefs and Exemptions

Introduction

[14.01] Relief from duty means that the instrument is chargeable but due to statutory provision, the duty to be paid has been mitigated, in part or in full. To qualify for any relief it must be claimed, otherwise the tax is payable in the normal way. An exemption from stamp duty means that the instrument is not chargeable as it does not fall within the charging provisions of the relevant legislation or is specifically exempted. A relief is granted with respect to the rate of duty chargeable on the instrument; an exemption absolves the instrument itself. As a general rule, a relief is specific to the particular head of charge under which the instrument becomes liable. An exemption can be general or specific to the head of charge. Where the relief or exemption relates to a specific head of charge, it will be dealt with in greater detail in the relevant chapter.

Reliefs

[14.02] The reliefs available are discussed below.

Housing

[14.03] The following instruments are eligible for relief in full. Adjudication is necessary to secure the relief in each case.

Local Authority housing

[14.04] Local authority housing which is conveyed, transferred or leased by the local authority under the provisions of the Housing Acts 1966-1992 is relieved in full.[1]

Industrial and provident society housing

[14.05] Industrial and provident society housing which is conveyed, transferred or leased to a member or to a member and spouse by the society registered under the relevant Acts, is relieved in full.[2]

Shared ownership leases

[14.06] Under SDCA 1999, s 103 stamp duty is not chargeable on any instrument on a shared ownership lease (or an instrument where the lessee of a shared ownership lease exercises his or her rights under the Housing (Miscellaneous Provisions) Act 1992, s 2(1)(c)). In other words, the lessee acquires the remaining interest in the lease from the lessor provided that:

---

1 SDCA 1999, s 93.

2 SDCA 1999, s 93.

(a) such lease is not granted for a house which upon erection exceeded the maximum floor area as set out in the regulations made pursuant to Housing (Miscellaneous Provisions) Act 1979 for that time;

(b) the Revenue Commissioners are satisfied that the original instrument to the lessor has been duly stamped; and

(c) the shared ownership lease has been granted by the appropriate person.

[14.07] The 'appropriate person' is defined under the Act[3] as being any of the following:

(a) a person granted a licence under either the Central Bank Act 1971, s 9 or the Trustee Savings Banks Act 1989, s 10;

(b) the ACC Bank plc, the ICC Bank plc where there are subsisting regulations under the relevant Acts;

(c) a building society;

(d) the holder of a licence for non life insurance or life assurance pursuant to the European Community Regulations;

(e) a body approved by the Minister for the Environment under the Housing (Miscellaneous Provisions) Act 1992, s 6;

(f) a certified company (within the meaning of CA 1963, s 2 whose principal object is to provide assistance for the acquisition of housing, on a non-profit basis); or

(g) a certified society (within the meaning of Industrial and Provident Societies Acts 1893-1978 whose principal object is to provide assistance for the acquisition of housing, on a non-profit basis).

New houses and apartments

[14.08] There is provision for relief in respect of new houses and apartments. This is dealt with in detail in **Chapter 9**. Under SDCA 1999, s 92 certain larger residential properties may avail of significant reduction in the consideration chargeable to stamp duty. Where the purchaser intends to use the property as his or her only or principal residence, the consideration for the purposes of stamp duty will be the greater of 25 per cent of the total consideration payable for the completed house/apartment or consideration paid in respect of the sale of the land.[4]

This relief is subect to certain other conditions being fulfilled. Please refer to **Chapter 9**.

Rent-a-room scheme

[14.09] Although the traditional requirement for claiming relief from stamp duty either for the purchase of a new house or as a first-time purchaser was that the property be occupied exclusively by the owner and not be rented or otherwise occupied by those unconnected to the owner, there is now a provision which enables the owner-occupier of the exempt or relieved property to rent out a single room to an unconnected person

3 SDCA 1999, s 103(1).

4 SDCA 1999, s 92(1).

without losing eligibilty for the relief or exemption. This provision is designed to ease the difficulties arising from the bouyant housing market which makes it difficult to finance a mortgage unless the assumption is made that a spare bedroom will be rented to a third party, whereby that potential rent can be taken into account in calculating the total amount which a financial institution will loan to a prospective purchaser. While the policy goal behind this is admirable, it is somewhat at odds with the caution expressed by the central bank with respect to liberal lending policies in the Irish market for house mortgages. It is therefore part of the failure of the government to view stamp duty as an integrated element in both the housing and credit marketplace, and to interfere with stamp duty policy (albeit here beneficially) without taking all the consequences into account.

Charities

[14.10] Any conveyance, transfer or lease of land made by or to a body established for charitable purposes in Ireland or Northern Ireland shall be relieved from duty,[5] except where the charity executes a deed of enlargement.[6] The relief must be claimed and the instrument stamped with a denoting stamp that it is not liable to duty in accordance with SDCA 1999, s 82(2).

Example 14.10.1

The charity for relief of poverty amongst the old sea veterans purchases Blackacre by way of a 600-year lease at a premium of €100,000.

Duty payable on purchase: relieved in full, instrument must carry a denoting stamp.

The charity within six years executes a deed of enlargement pursuant to the Conveyancing Act 1881, s 65(2).

Duty payable on the enlargement	€6,000

[14.11] A charity has been defined by Lord M'Naghten in *Commissioners for Special Purposes of Income Tax v Pemsel* [1891] AC 531 as being of four kinds:

(a) trusts for the relief of poverty;

(b) trusts for the advancement of education;

(c) trusts for the advancement of religion; and

(d) trusts beneficial to the community not falling under any other heading.

All charitable trusts must be for the benefit of the public. In *Imperial Tobacco Securities Trust Co Ltd*[7] a trust for the advancement of education of children of the employees of the company, where the number of employees exceeded 110,000, was held not to be for the benefit of the public and therefore not charitable. The purposes of the trust must be charitable. Trusts relieving poverty, even 'genteel poverty' are recognised see *Re Young*[8] as are those for the advancement of education and religion.

---

5 SDCA 1999, s 82.

6 SDCA 1999, s 35(2).

7 *Imperial Tobacco Securities Trust Co Ltd* [1951] AC 297.

8 *Re Young* [1951] Ch 344.

[14.12] Trusts creating charities for a variety of miscellaneous purposes have been upheld. For example, the promotion of vegetarianism was upheld as charitable[9] as were trusts in favour of the old and infirm.[10] Political parties have been held not to be charities.[11] Purposes which aim to alter legislation are not charitable, while the abstinence movement is charitable in so far as it aims to promote abstinence from liquor.[12] An organisation that aims to bring about legislative prohibition is not charitable, but for a different view see *Farewell v Farewell.*[13]

In practice, the Revenue will seek a copy of the exemption, quoting the exemption number, issued from the Commissioner of Charitable Organisations.[14]

Consanguinity relief

[14.13] Relief is available where a conveyance effects a transfer between two people who are related by way of blood. The relief is available for both conveyance on sale and voluntary disposition. Such transactions are liable for half the duty that would have been payable under the relevant head of charge.[15] The parties must be connected in one of the following ways:

> lineal descendant, parent, grandparent, step parent, husband or wife, brother or sister of a parent or brother or sister, or lineal descendant of a parent, husband or wife or brother or sister.

[14.14] FA 2006 has extended the definition of 'child' to include foster children where that child is a transferee or lessee and has been maintained at the expense of the transferor/lessor throughout:

(a) a period of five years; or

(b) periods which together comprised at least five years, and

(c) these periods were before the person attained the age of 18 years.

[14.15] Relationship can be by way of adoption, whether in Ireland[16] or overseas,[17] or through illegitimacy[18] and now foster children in certain circumstances. Such relationships are deemed to be treated the same as if the relationship had been one of blood or by marriage. If one or more parties to the instrument does not come within the necessary relationship, then the relief is lost.

---

9 *Re Cranston, Webb v Oldfield* [1898] 1 IR 431.

10 *Re McCarthy's Will Trusts* [1958] IR 311.

11 *Goff v Gurhy* (1980, unreported) SC.

12 *Re Hood* [1931] 1 Ch 240.

13 *Farewell v Farewell* [1892] 22 OR 573.

14 Charities are controlled by the Charities Act 1961 and further reference should be made to this Act and Keane *Equity and the Law of Trusts in Ireland* (Butterworths, 1998).

15 SDCA 1999, Sch 1 para (15).

16 FA 1952, s 27.

17 FA 1972, s 45 as amended by FA 1992, s 214.

18 Status of Children Act 1987.

[14.16] A certificate of the relationship along the following lines must be inserted into the instrument. In order to avail of the relief:

> It is hereby certified by the (donee/grantee) being the person becoming entitled to the entire beneficial ownership of the property hereby (transferred/ conveyed) that he/she is related to the person immediately theretofore entitled to the entire beneficial interest in the property as a lineal (ancestor/ descendant)(set out the relationship, for example lawful daughter).

If this certificate is not inserted, the relief is lost.

Example 14.16.1

Tom conveys Blackacre to his grandchild, Emma. Blackacre is worth €300,000.
No consanguinity certificate was inserted in the instrument of transfer.

Duty payable (€300,000 at 9%)	€27,000

Example 14.16.2

Dick conveys Greenacre, valued at €400,000, to his wife, Joan and includes the necessary certificate.

Duty payable	Nil

(Conveyances between spouses are exempt entirely from duty, according to SDCA 1999, s 96 as amended by FA 1992, s 212(1) – see para **12.16**).

Example 14.16.3

Dick conveys Blueacre, valued at €1,000,000 to his wife Joan and their son, Harry and inserts the necessary certificate in the instrument.

Duty payable	4.5%	€45,000

(Conveyance is not between spouses alone and so is not exempt but it is between people of the relationship under the relief).

Example 14.16.4

Fred conveys Whiteacre to his sister, Jemima, and her husband for €1,000,000 and inserts the necessary certificate in the instrument.

Duty payable (€1,000,000 at 9%)	€90,000

Jemima's husband does not come within the ambit of the relief.

Example 14.16.5

Fred conveys Whiteacre to his sister, Jemima, for €250,000 a dwellinghouse. The property comprises valued at €100,000 and includes the necessary certificate. Subsequently Jemima conveys the property to both herself and her husband.

		€
Duty on transfer to Jemima	100,000	Nil
	150,000 @ 8%	12,000
		12,000
Duty on transfer to joint names		Nil

Total duty payable (duty is halved under SDCA 1999, Sch 1)	6,000
Duty saved	6,000

If Fred voluntarily conveyed the property to Jemina, there could be capital acquisitions tax implications that might negate the savings in duty.[19]

Transfer of a site to a child

[14.17] FA 2001 introduced SDCA 1999, s 83A which provides that the transfer or lease of a site not exceeding €254,000 from a parent to a child shall be exempt in full from stamp duty, provided the site is to be used for the construction of the child's principal private dwelling. The definition of a child will include foster children. There is a limit of one site for each child and the usual clawback provisions are expected to operate. The requirement is that the child built a dwelling house to be occupied as its sole or main residence, not that the house be the child's first residence. It should be noted that there is a corresponding relief from CGT for transferring a site to a child but no corresponding relief from CAT.

[14.18] Under SDCA 1999, s 83A(1)(a) the relief does not apply where there is a building which was used or suitable for use as a dwelling house on the site at the date of the instrument. Section 83A(1)(b) also precludes application of the relief where a dwelling house was in the course of being constructed or adapted use as a dwelling or other purpose at the date of the instrument.

[14.19] The child should be the child of the person who owns the entire beneficial interest in the site immediately before the transfer. A transfer to a child and their spouse does not qualify for the relief. As there is no provision for a clawback of this relief, the site can be transferred to the child and then subsequently, they can transfer a share of the site or property to their spouse and avail of the exemption from stamp duty on transfers between spouses. The clawback relief under CATCA 2003 may give rise to a capital acquisitions tax charge.

[14.20] Every instrument should contain a certificate certifying that the transferee of the site is the beneficial owner of the site, the value of the site, the purpose of the transfer is to allow the child construct a dwelling house which will be occupied by the child as his only or main residence and the site is the first and only transfer to that child which benefits from the relief. SDCA 1999, s 83A(4) states that the relief is subject to adjudication.

Liquidations and distribution *in specie*

[14.21] The transfer of property on liquidation by distribution *in specie* is not liable to stamp duty. It has to be proved to the satisfaction of the Revenue Commissioners that the distribution of assets is carried out in proportion to the shareholders; entitlement to participate in the distribution. The instrument effecting the transfer of the assets, where those assets are immovable property, stocks or marketable securities of a company

19 See Bohan and McCarthy *Capital Acquisitions Tax* (2nd edn, Lexis Nexis, 2004).

having a register in the state, is chargeable to a fixed duty of €12.50. However, if the instrument contains a statement certifying that the instrument is a conveyance or transfer on any occasion not being a sale of mortgage, it will be exempt.

[14.22] The Revenue Commissioners require the following to be furnished:

(a) proof that the property is being transferred in direct proportion to the transferee's entitlement to participate.;

(b) the names and addresses of the shareholders, and their shareholding as at the date of the resolution to liquidate; and

(c) a copy of the resolution resolving to wind up the company and appoint the liquidator.

These must be lodged for adjudication with form ADJN9.[20]

[14.23] There are a number of instances where distributions *in specie* on a liquidation will be chargeable to stamp duty. These are:

(a) where assets are subject to a mortgage or charge and are transferred subject to this mortgage or charge (the reasoning behind this is that a distribution *in specie* has to be of the net assets after liquidation);

(b) where the company owes a debt to the shareholders and the shareholders agree to forgive the debt in consideration for the distribution (again payment is in effect made); and

(c) where the company owes a debt to a third party and the shareholders agree to assume liability for the the debt in consideration for the distribution.

In each of the above instances, the instrument effecting the transfer will be chargeable to *ad valorem* stamp duty under SDCA 1999, s 41 on the amount of the debt assumed, owed or forgiven.

Corporate exceptions

[14.24] SDCA 1999, s 79 provides that any transfer or conveyance between associated companies is exempt from *ad valorem* duty, provided that certain conditions are met.[21] (**Chapter 8**). Any instrument effecting a reconstruction or amalgamation is exempt provided that certain conditions are met.[22] Any instrument effecting a mortgage between a company and its subsidiary which should be charged under the mortgage bond or covenant head of charge is relieved from duty but subject to a €12.50 fixed duty.[23]

Qualified young farmers

Documents executed before 25 March 2004

[14.25] Qualified young farmers who purchased or received agricultural land were relieved of the relevant charge to duty by two-thirds.[24] This section applied to

20 See **Appendix 8**.

21 See **Chapter 8**.

22 See **Chapter 8** and SDCA 1999, s 80.

23 SDCA 1999, s 83.

24 SDCA 1999, s 81(2).

instruments executed before 25 March 2004. A qualified young farmer must be under 35 years at the date of the execution of the instrument. He must have attended any full-time, third-level course for at least two years and be the holder of a Teagasc certificate of satisfactory attendance in a training course on agriculture or horticulture for a minimum of 180 hours.[25] Alternatively, the applicant had to be the holder of a qualification set out in Schedule 2 of the Act; however, certain qualifications in Schedule 2[26] also require a Teagasc certificate for satisfactory attendance at a course in farm management in excess of 80 hours. An applicant born before 1 January 1968 who held a certificate from Teagasc that his principal occupation was farming for a period of not less than three years and who has satisfactorily attended a course in agriculture or horticulture for not less than 180 hours was also eligible to claim the relief.[27]

[14.26] Agricultural land included such farm buildings, farmhouses and mansion houses (together with the land occupied therewith) as were of a character appropriate to the land.[28] The instrument effecting the transfer had to contain a certificate that the relief applied and must have been accompanied by a declaration confirming that it was the intention of the transferee to spend not less than 50 per cent of his/her working time farming and to retain ownership of the land for a period of not less than five years from the date of execution of the instrument. The PPS number must also have been furnished when the instrument was presented for stamping.[29] The interest in land transferred must not have been subject to any power of revocation exercisable by the grantor in his favour or at his discretion.[30]

[14.27] A clawback provision operates so that if the land was disposed of less than five years after purchase and was not replaced with other agricultural land within one year of the disposal, a fine equivalent to the relieved duty was levied, together with interest at 1 per cent per month or part thereof from the date of execution of the instrument. Subsequent disposal to a spouse was treated as if the transfer had occurred at the time of the original transfer.[31] Disposals between joint tenants were treated in like manner.

[14.28] If it transpired that the applicant had made a declaration which contained facts which were not true and, if known, would have resulted in the relief not being granted, then the transferee was liable for a fine equal to the difference between 125 per cent of the duty that should have been charged and the relieved duty that was charged, together with interest at 1 per cent per month or part thereof from the date of execution of the instrument.[32] An applicant cannot be fined under both sections to the extent that the fine has already been charged under another sub-heading.[33] The relief was available where

---

25 SDCA 1999, s 81(1).

26 See **Appendix 6**.

27 SDCA 1999, s 81(1)(b)(iii).

28 SDCA 1999, s 81(1).

29 SDCA 1999, s 81(3).

30 SDCA 1999, s 81(1).

31 SDCA 1999, s 81(8).

32 SDCA 1999, s 81(7)(b).

33 SDCA 1999, s 81(7)(b).

the transfer was to a joint ownership and all the joint owners were qualified young farmers or were the spouses of another qualified joint owner.[34]

[14.29] If, at the date of execution of the instrument, the applicant did not qualify as a young farmer but had completed at least one year of a prescribed course and the applicant, within a period of three years of the date of execution, completed the course, the Commissioners may refund the excess duty that would have been relieved had the applicant been a qualified young farmer at the date of execution of the instrument.[35] The five-year period of holding runs from the date of the original instrument and not the date of the refund. The refund is available on production of the original stamped deed to the Revenue Commissioners.

[14.30] To complete an application for registration in the Land Registry, the original stamped deed of transfer had to be produced to the Registrar of Titles. This may inhibit the application of this relief. To avoid this difficulty, both the original stamped deed and a counterpart duly stamped will be forwarded to the Registrar with a request to return the original.

[14.31] The provisions of this section were only available for instruments executed after 6 January 1994 and on or before 31 December 2002[36] and complementing the European Union early retirement scheme for farmers. The relief applied to both conveyance on sale and voluntary dispositions. Where consanguinity relief was also claimed, the relief under that provision was 2/3 of the duty payable after the consanguinity relief.

Example 14.31.1

Fred, who was born on 1 January 1964, has assisted his father with the work of the family farm for the last seven years. Recently Fred obtained a Diploma in Poultry Production from An Teagasc. He purchases a holding of 120 acres at an auction for €1,180,000 on 1 January 1997. Stamp duty liability on €1,180,000 at 9% would be €106,200.

To qualify for the relief under these provisions, the following steps must be taken:

1. the necessary certificate pursuant to SDCA 1999, s 81 must be included;
2. The instrument and the following requirements must be lodged to the Revenue Commissioners for adjudication:
   - (a) a declaration by Fred that for a period of five years from the date of execution of the instrument he will:
     - (i) spend 50% or more of his normal working time farming the land; and
     - (ii) retain ownership of the land.
   - (b) Fred's RSI number;
3. a certificate from An Teagasc of his qualification must be included; and.
4. proof of his age; for example, a birth certificate, should also be included.

The form attached to Statement of Practice SD2, concerning the exemption for qualified young farmers, should be completed.[37]

---

34 SDCA 1999, s 81(4).

35 SDCA 1999, s 81(5).

36 SDCA 1999, s 81(9) as substituted by FA 2001, s 126(1)(d).

37 See **Appendix 8**.

Stamp duty liability of €106,200 is reduced by 2/3 of that amount.
2/3 of €106,200= €70,800

	€
Stamp duty liability	106,200
Less reduction of 2/3	70,800
Liability to duty	35,400

Two years later Fred marries Mary and transfers the property to their joint names. Exempt from stamp duty as a conveyance between spouses.[38]

This transfer into joint names does not give rise to a clawback of the relief granted to Fred on the purchase of the holding.[39] Fred and Mary decide to sell the holding at auction on 30 January 2002.

This subsequent transfer does not give rise to a clawback of relief granted to Fred on the purchase of the holding and for the purposes of the five-year rule, the holding is deemed to have been conveyed immediately into the joint names when the relief was originally claimed (1 January 1997).

Documents executed on or after 25 March 2004 and on or before 31 December 2008

[14.32] Full relief from stamp duty is provided on the transfer of land to young trained farmers who meet certain conditions and where the instrument is executed on or after 25 March 2004 SDCA 1999, s 81A. This relief was extended further to 31 December 2008 by FA 2006. The relief applies to transfers by sale or by way of gift (ie does not extend to leases). A power to revoke the transfer, whether it be contained in the instrument conveying or transferring the land itself or otherwise, will disqualify the young trained farmer from the relief. This section also contains transitional arrangements (see sub-s (13)) which enable the educational qualifications held before 25 March 2004, for the purposes of relief under s 81, to be treated as educational qualifications for the purposes of s 81A. Instruments in respect of which relief is sought must be adjudicated. Details of the relief are contained in the Revenue Leaflet SD 2A.

[14.33] A qualified young farmer must be under 35 years at the date of the execution of the instrument. He must have achieved the required standard for entry into the third year, if a full-time course, in any discipline, of 3 or more years' duration at a third-level institute as confirmed by the institution. He must also be the holder of a certificate awarded by the Further Education and Training Awards Council (FETAC) for achieving the minimum stipulated standard in assessments completed in a Teagasc-approved training course in either or both agriculture or horticulture, the aggregate duration of which exceeded 100 hours, and in farm management, the aggregate duration of which exceeded 80 hours (s 81A(3)). Alternatively, the applicant may be the holder of a qualification set out in Schedule 2 of the Act; however, certain qualifications in Schedule 2.[40] also require a Teagasc certificate for satisfactory attendance at a course in farm management in excess of 80 hours.

---

[38] SDCA 1999, s 96.

[39] SDCA 1999, s 81(8).

[40] See **Appendix 6**.

[14.34] Where Teagasc certifies that any other qualification corresponds to a qualification which is set out in Schedule 2A and that such qualification is deemed by the National Qualifications Authority of Ireland (NQAI) to be at least at a standard equivalent to that of the Schedule 2A qualification, that qualification will be treated as a qualifying one by Revenue.

[14.35] Agricultural land includes such farm buildings, farmhouses and mansion houses (together with the land occupied therewith) as are of a character appropriate to the land.[41] The instrument effecting the transfer must contain a certificate that the relief applies and must be accompanied by a declaration confirming that it is the intention of the transferee to spend not less than 50 per cent of his/her working time farming and retain ownership of the land for a period of not less than five years from the date of execution of the instrument. The PPS number must also be furnished when the instrument is presented for stamping.[42] A clawback provision operates so that if the land is disposed of less than five years after purchase and is not replaced with other agricultural land within one year of the disposal, a fine equivalent to the relieved duty shall be levied together with interest at 1 per cent per month or part thereof from the date of execution of the instrument. Subsequent disposal to a spouse is treated as if the transfer had occurred at the time of the original transfer.[43] Disposals between joint tenants are treated in like manner. The Revenue Commissioners in practice deem the 50-hour requirement to be full-time employment so that job-sharing may render the relief unavailable.

[14.36] If it transpires that the applicant has made a declaration which contains facts which are not true and, if known, would have resulted in the relief not being granted, then the transferee shall be liable for a fine equal to the difference between 125 per cent of the duty that should have been charged and the relieved duty that was charged together with interest at 0.0273 per cent per day, or part thereof, from the date of execution of the instrument.[44] An applicant cannot be fined under both sections to the extent that the fine has already been charged under another subheading.

[14.37] The relief is available where the transfer is to joint ownership and all the joint owners are qualified young farmers or spouses of other qualified joint owners.[45]

If, at the date of execution of the instrument, the applicant does not qualify as a young farmer but has completed at least one year of a prescribed course and the applicant within a period of three years of the date of execution completes the course, the Commissioners may refund the excess duty that would have been relieved had the applicant been a qualified young farmer at the date of execution of the instrument.[46] The five-year period of holding runs from the date of the original instrument and not the date

---

41 SDCA 1999, s 81A(1).

42 SDCA 1999, s 81(7)(b).

43 SDCA 1999, s 81(8).

44 SDCA 1999, s 81A(11)(b).

45 SDCA 1999, s 81A(8).

46 SDCA 1999, s 81A(9).

of the refund. The refund is available on production of the original stamped deed to the Revenue Commissioners.

[14.38] To complete an application for registration in the Land Registry, the original stamped deed of transfer has to be produced to the Registrar of Titles. This may inhibit the application of this relief. To avoid this difficulty, both the original stamped deed and a counterpart duly stamped should be forwarded to the Registrar with a request to return the original. FA 2006 also extended the definition of agricultural property to which this relief applies to include transfers of EU Single Farm Payment Supplements.

Exemptions

Certain new residential property

[14.39] Instruments dealing with the purchase of new houses and flats of a certain floor area size are fully exempt provided that the purchaser will occupy it as his only principal residence.[47] To qualify, the instrument must effect the purchase of a new house which has not been previously occupied. Please refer to **Chapter 13** where the full details of this relief are discussed.

First-time purchasers

[14.40] In similar mode, the Government again used stamp duty as a form of assisting first-time purchasers. The reduction the level of duty payable was designed to reduce the hurdle of getting into the housing market. Accordingly, a first-time purchaser may benefit from a reduction in duty. A first-time purchaser is defined as a person who at the time of execution of the instrument had not, either solely or jointly, previously purchased or built another dwellinghouse or apartment.[48] The definition is expanded to include a dwellinghouse or apartment taken under a voluntary disposition under SDCA 1999, s 20 and 30 executed on or after 27 June 2000.[49]

There are some further specific provisions with respect to the definition of a first-time purchaser.

Dealings in shares

[14.41] The following dealings in shares are exempt under the legislation indicated:

(a) any transfer of shares in stocks or funds of the Oireachtas;[50]

(b) any transfer of shares in stocks or securities of the government or parliament of the United Kingdom of Great Britain, provided that they are registered with the Bank of Ireland in Dublin;[51]

(c) any transfer of shares in stocks or securities issued by the European Coal and Steel Community, the European Atomic Community and the European Investment Bank;

47 SDCA 1999, s 91.

48 SDCA 1999, s 92B(1).

49 SDCA 1999, s 92B(1)(b)(ii)(I) and (II).

50 SDCA 1999, s 113(a).

51 SDCA 1999, s 113(iv).

(d) any conveyance or transfer of stocks or marketable securities of a company not registered in the State iso long as it does not affect any immovable property or stocks or marketable securities situate within the State, or interest therein;[52]

(e) stamp duty shall not be chargeable on the transfer of any assets in respect of the reorganisation of an undertaking for collective investment where no chargeable gain arises under TCA 1997, s 739A – this only applies to instruments executed on or after 23 March 2000;[53]

(f) any conveyance or transfer of any stocks or other securities of the government of any territory outside the State;[54] and

(g) any transfer or conveyance of units in a collective investment undertaking provided that they do not relate to any immovable property or interest therein or stocks or marketable securities in a company other than a company which is a collective investment undertaking.[55]

Executive transactions exempted

[14.42] The following executive transactions are exempt under the legislation indicated:

(a) any transaction which gives rise to a charge to duty which would fall to be discharged from Oireachtas funds;[56]

(b) Any transfer of loan stock on any company where the payment of interest on any bond is guaranteed by the Minister or the ESB, RTE, ICC Bank plc, Bord Gáis or Irish Telecommunications Investments plc;[57]

(c) any instrument executed by or on behalf of the National Treasury Management Agency (NTMA), or the transfer of all or any right or interest so created by such instrument;[58]

(d) any bond given or assigned to a sheriff for the execution of his duties;[59]

(e) any instrument made by, to or with the Commissioners of Public Works.[60]

Disposals

[14.43] The following disposals are exempt:

(a) any disposal of foreign immovable property or an interest therein, whether by way of sale or otherwise, provided it does not relate to immovable property situate within the State or stocks or shares of a company having a register in the State;[61] and

---

52 SDCA 1999, s 88.

53 SDCA 1999, s 88A, as inserted by FA 2000, s 130.

54 SDCA 1999, s 89.

55 SDCA 1999, s 88.

56 SDCA 1999, s 111.

57 SDCA 1999, s 86 as substituted by FA 2000, s 127.

58 SDCA 1999, s 108.

59 SDCA 1999, s 113.

60 SDCA 1999, s 113.

61 SDCA 1999, s 98.

(b) any instrument disposing of any interest in a ship, vessel or aircraft no matter whether the disposal is by way of sale, transfer, mortgage or such other method.[62]

Certain conveyances

Conveyances for small consideration

[14.44] Any conveyance on sale where the aggregate consideration does not exceed €10,000 in the case of commercial property, or €127,000 in the case of residential property, is exempt from duty, provided that the instrument contains a finance certificate and a certificate as to the nature of the property.

Subsales

[14.45] Any subsale which might have given rise to double duty is now exempt from the second duty.[63]

Example 14.45.1

A purchases a €200,000 property from B and directs that the property should be conveyed to C. The document of conveyance contains two conveyances: one between A and B, the second between B and C. Both would be chargeable to duty.

	€
Duty on transfer between A and B at 4%	8,000
Duty on transfer between A and C at 4%	8,000
Total duty payable	16,000

Since it is a subsale, it is chargeable only once.	
Total duty now payable	8,000

See **Chapter 13** for more detail.

Commercial woodlands

[14.46] Where a conveyance or lease of land occurs consisting of trees that are managed on a commercial basis with a view to the realisation of profits, then the value of such trees contained in the conveyance or lease is exempt from duty, provided that the instrument contains a certificate to the effect that the trees are growing on a substantial part of the land conveyed or leased.[64] The land remains liable to duty.

Example 14.46.1

John sells Blackacre, part of which consists of a tree farm, to Jill for €1,000,000. The value of the trees growing on the land is €750,000.

---

62 SDCA 1999, s 113(b).

63 SDCA 1999, s 46.

64 SDCA 1999, s 95.

The instrument of sale contains a certificate that the trees are growing on a substantial part of the land. Amount on which duty is payable: €250,000 (€1,000,000 minus €750,000).

Duty on €250,000 at 9% = €22,500

An application should be made on form ADJN17.[65]

Petroleum and mineral licences and leases

[14.47] Any licence or lease granted under Petroleum and Other Minerals Development Act 1960, ss 8, 9, 13 or 19, or the transfer of all or any interest therein, is exempt from duty.[66]

Leases

[14.48] A lease made in consideration for the surrender or abandonment of an existing lease is exempt under SDCA 1999, s 52(1).

Mere conveyances

[14.49] A mere conveyance, other than one relating to any immovable property situate within the State, or right or interest therein, or stock or share of a company registered in the State, shall be exempt from duty.[67] A 'mere conveyance' is a transaction other than a conveyance on sale or deemed conveyance and, if not exempt, would be stamped with a fixed rate of €12.50. A mere conveyance is defined as any instrument or decree effecting the transfer or vesting of any property except by way of sale or mortgage.[68] Also included are any transfer or conveyance made for nominal consideration to secure the repayment of a loan, or where no beneficial ownership passes in the transaction, or where the transfer or conveyance is from the trustee to a beneficiary in that capacity or in the execution of a disentailing assurance.[69]

Example 14.49.1

Mary holds the legal title to Blackacre in trust for her son in fee simple. She decides to retire and appoint a new trustee as she is now too old for the position.

Duty payable (fixed duty) €12.50

Example 14.49.2

Jack gives his solicitor €800,000 to purchase a house in trust as he does not wish it to be known that he is buying the property.
The contract is executed in trust and the property is then conveyed into the solicitor's name in trust.

---

65 See **Appendix 2**.
66 SDCA 1999, s 104.
67 SDCA 1999, Sch 1.
68 SDCA 1999, s 49.
69 SDCA 1999, s 30(5). See **Chapter 8**.

	€
Stamp duty liability on €800,000	72,000
Stamp duty liability on trust deed	12.50
Total	72,012.50

Subsequently, his solicitor conveys the property into Jack's name.

	€
Liability for the mere conveyance	12.50

Conveyance where the consideration is in instalments

[14.50] No conveyance on sale coming under the charge of SDCA 1999, s 42(1), (2) or (3) which contains provision for securing payments is to be charged under these provisions, or where the provisions are contained in a separate instrument, such separate instrument is to be chargeable with a fixed duty of €12.50 only.[70] In *Western United Investments Co v IRC*[71] the court held that the exemption applies only:

> ...where you find first a conveyance on sale which is chargeable with duty, and in that document or in a separate contemporaneous or subsequent instrument a security... and it is not sufficient to find that the parties have executed a security, although they may be intending to execute a conveyance on sale thereafter.[72]

Investment and financial services transactions

Stock exchange transactions

[14.51] Any instrument transferring stocks or shares in the ordinary course of business to a designated stock exchange nominee is exempt from duty.[73]

Letters of allotment

[14.52] Any instrument which renounces or releases any letter of allotment to shares in an unquoted company shall be liable to duty as if it were an instrument renouncing or releasing any letter of allotment to share in a quoted company pursuant to Schedule 1.[74]

Scrip certificates

[14.53] A scrip certificate or scrip shall be exempt from duty.[75]

---

70 SDCA 1999, s 42(3) as amended by FA 1992, s 204(b).

71 *Western United Investments Co v IRC* [1958] 2 WLR 192.

72 See para **[13.17]** for further discussion.

73 FA 1979, s 54.

74 SDCA 1999, s 63).

75 FA 1964, s 23.

Financial services exemptions

[14.54] The following instruments are exempt from duty provided that they do not relate to any immovable property or stocks or shares situate within the State or any rights or interests therein:

(a) A debt factoring agreement undertaken in the ordinary course of business: Such an agreement is defined as the transfer, or agreement to transfer, a debt or part thereof.[76] Where the debt is secured over immovable property situate within the State, for example, a debt factoring agreement made by a builder, then the exemption is lost. Debt factoring agreements include discounting of invoices.

(b) A swap agreement, such as interest or currency swaps: A swap agreement is one where the parties agree to exchange either the payment or repayment of moneys in respect of which the parties have rights and obligations.[77]

(c) A forward agreement: A forward agreement is an agreement to buy or sell commodities, currency, money payable or receivable, stocks or marketable securities at a specified future date where the price, exchange rate, interest or share value is fixed or determinable at the time of execution of the agreement. Also covered are agreements which alter the parties' rights by reference to certain movements in a specified stock exchange index or indices.[78]

(d) A financial futures agreement: This is the forward agreement outlined above and which is currently dealt with and quoted on a recognised stock exchange or futures stock exchange.

(e) An option agreement: An option agreement is an agreement conferring a future right at one party's discretion to buy or sell, to or from another party, stocks and securities, commodities or currency, the right to receive or the liability to pay sums depending on the movements of a stock exchange index or indices, or to borrow or lend money at a rate of interest that is determined at the time of execution.[79]

Any combination of the instruments detailed above are exempt as is any transfer or agreement to transfer any such instrument or combination of such instruments. Where any of the above instruments are chargeable to duty under any other head of charge in Schedule 1, such instrument will be liable to duty under that head of charge.[80] .

American and Canadian depository receipts

[14.55] The transfer or agreement to transfer an American Depository Receipt (ADR) is exempt from duty even where it relates to immovable property or stocks or marketable securities situate within the State.

---

76 SDCA 1999, s 90(1).
77 SDCA 1999, s 90(1).
78 SDCA 1999, s 90(1).
79 SDCA 1999, s 90(1).
80 SDCA 1999, s 90(4).

Example 14.55.1

Jack holds 100,000 ADRs in Backus Inc which is traded on Wall Street. Jack agrees to transfer these ADRs for €1 million. Backus Inc owns immovable property within the State.

Duty payable	Exempt

An ADR is an instrument which acknowledges that a depository holds stock or marketable securities which are dealt with and quoted on a recognised stock exchange in the United States of America and that the holder of such instrument has rights in relation to such stock or marketable securities, including the right to receive such stocks or marketable securities from the depository. ADRs are used for US tax and ownership provisions. The exemption has now been extended to cover Canadian Depository Receipts.[81]

Issue or transfer of loan capital of a company or body corporate

[14.56] Any issue or transfer of loan capital of a company or body corporate, is exempt from stamp duty.[82] The definition of 'loan capital' includes debenture stock, bonds or funded debt or any capital raised which has the form of borrowed money.[83]

Bills

[14.57] The following bills are exempt under Schedule 1:

(a) draft or order not payable to bearer and drawn on and by a banker in the State for the purposes of settling an account between said bankers;

(b) letter between bankers directing payment of money, such letter not being sent to the person to whom payment is to be made or any other person on his behalf;

(c) letters of credit;

(d) draft or order drawn by the accountant of the courts of justice;

(e) coupon or warrant for interest attached to any security or with an agreement for the renewal or extension of payment of same;

(f) any bill supplied by the Commissioners for the purposes of remitting amounts of income tax, turnover tax, withholding tax, wholesale tax and value added tax;

(g) direct debits and standing orders;

(h) a bill drawn on an account outside the State;

(i) non-Irish bills;

(j) Bills of Exchange drawn in set, only of which one is chargeable; and

(k) instruments in respect of Prize Bonds.

---

81 SDCA 1999, s 90(1)(b).

82 SDCA 1999, s 85 – see **Chapter 9**.

83 SDCA 1999, s 85(1).

Certain instruments

Mortgages

[14.58] Instruments chargeable under the mortgage, bond, covenant debenture head where the amount secured is less than €254,000 are exempt from duty.[84]

Equity of redemption

[14.59] An instrument creating a mortgage and chargeable with *ad valorem* duty is exempt from further duty on the conveyance of the equity of redemption. If the conveyance or transfer is made to, or in trust for, or by the direction of, a purchaser, the document is liable to *ad valorem* duty.[85]

Wills

[14.60] Testamentary instruments are exempt from stamp duty.[86]

Administration

[14.61] A bond executed in order to obtain letters of administration is exempt from duty.[87]

Insurance certificates

[14.62] Any instrument which is a cover note in anticipation of a formal policy, other than a life policy, or an instrument embodying alterations to the terms and conditions of a policy of insurance, other than life insurance, is exempt.[88]

Temple Bar area

[14.63] Any land or interest in land acquired by Temple Bar Properties Limited, any subsidiary situate in the Temple Bar area as defined in the Temple Bar Area Renewal and Development Act 1991, Schedule 1 by way of instrument, shall be exempt from duty.[89]

Stock borrowing

[14.64] Any broker or dealer who is a member of the Irish Stock Exchange can claim an exemption from duty with respect to stock borrowing transactions of up to 12 months duration.[90] The transaction is exempt from duty both on the borrowing and return of such stock within the relevant 12-month period (applies to stock borrowing transactions entered into on or after 25 March 2005 – previously it was six months from the date). Stock borrowing is utilised by stock exchange dealers to facilitate the timely settlement

84 SDCA 1999, s 58.

85 SDCA 1999, s 57(4).

86 SDCA 1999, s 113(c).

87 SDCA 1999, Sch 1.

88 SDCA 1999, s 109.

89 SDCA 1999, s 100.

90 SDCA 1999, s 87.

of share or stock deals in situations where the dealer does not have sufficient shares or stocks of his own to satisfy the settlement. The stock must be quoted on a recognised stock exchange to qualify for the exemption.

[14.65] If equivalent stock is not returned to the lender within the 12-month period, the stock borrower shall pay at the expiration of 14 days therefrom, the *ad valorem* duty that would have been payable on the transaction. If the duty is not paid within the 14-day period, the borrower shall be liable for the duty plus interest at a rate of 0.0273% per day or part thereof, which shall run from the first day after the expiration of the twelve month period to the date the duty is paid, is payable. In addition, a penalty of 1% of the duty for each day the duty remains unpaid after the expiry of the 14-day period of grace is payable.[91]

[14.66] The broker or dealer shall keep full records of the stock borrowing transaction including evidence of the requirement for stock borrowing, the name and address of the lender, detailed description of the stock borrowed and returned and all relevant dates for the transactions and the form the equivalent stock took, if any, for a period of 3 years.[92]

[14.67] The records shall contain details concerning the name and address of the lender, the type, nominal value and amount of the stock borrowed, the date of transfer and return of the stock. A stock borrowing operation typically involves five transfers:

(a) transfer of stock from the lender to stock borrower;

(b) transfer on of that stock by the stock borrower to complete the sale;

(c) transfer of collateral stock from the stock borrower to the lender;

(d) return of equivalent stock to the lender; and

(e) return of the collateral stock from the lender to the stock borrower.

The purpose of SDCA 1999, s 87 is to exempt transfers (a), (b), (c) and (d) from stamp duty. The transfer at (e) is not currently within the charge to stamp duty. Equivalent stock is defined stock of an identical type, nominal value, description and amount.

Stock repo

[14.68] FA 2000 inserted specific provisions with regard to stock repo. A stock repo transaction is one in which a repo seller agrees to sell stock to a repo buyer for a cash price on the basis that the at the end of the fixed financing period the repo seller will buy back equivalent stock at a price equal to the original price plus interest. The purpose of the section is to exempt from stamp duty the stock transfer from the repo seller to the repo buyer in pursuance of a repurchase agreement and the stock return from the repo buyer to the repo seller. Stamp duty shall not be chargeable on any stock return or transfer pursuant to a stock repurchase agreement. A stock repurchase agreement arises where a person, other than an individual, enters into agreement where he or she agrees to sell stock to another on the basis that he or she will repurchase these or equivalent stocks within 12 months. If the repurchase does not take place at the expiration of the period

---

[91] SDCA 1999, s 87(3).

[92] SDCA 1999, s 87(4).

then it shall be liable for duty together with a penalty of 0.0273 per cent per day from the first day after the expiration of the 12-month period to the date the duty is paid, or payable. In addition, a penalty of 1 per cent of the duty per day for each day that the duty remains unpaid after the 14-day period of grace is payable.[93] The principal difference between stock borrowing and stock repo is that the latter is a contract of sale and repurchase, whereas the former is simply a donation coupled with an undertaking to return. The legislative impact of these provisions has been to treat both identically for stamp duty purposes.

Dublin Docklands Development Authority

[14.69] Stamp duty is exempt on any instrument whereby any land, easement, wayleave, water right or any other right is acquired by Dublin Docklands Development Authority.[94]

Miscellaneous

Intellectual property

[14.70] Stamp duty is not chargeable on the sale, transfer, or other disposition, of intellectual property as defined under SDCA 1999, s 101. This section provides an unexhaustive list of intellectual property that falls within this exemption. All goodwill associated with the intellectual property is also exempted under the section.

Assignment of housing authority mortgages

[14.71] Stamp duty is not chargeable where a housing authority transfers, sells or assigns its mortgages to a designated body.[95] The transfer of such securities by a designated body is also exempt.

Memorandum and articles of association

[14.72] With effect from 15 May 1996, there is no longer a requirement to have the memorandum and articles of association stamped as if it were a deed.[96]

Alfred Beit Foundation

[14.73] Any conveyance or transfer made by the either Alfred Lane Beit and Clementine Mabel or both of them to the Beit Foundation shall be exempt from duty.[97]

Housing Finance Agency

[14.74] Stamp duty shall not be payable with respect to any instrument connected with the securing of moneys advanced in connection with the Housing Finance Agency.[98]

---

93 SDCA 1999, s 87A.

94 SDCA 1999, s 99.

95 SDCA 1999, s 105.

96 CA 1963, s 7 and 14 as amended by FA 1996, s 112.

97 SDCA 1999, s 102.

98 SDCA 1999, s 106.

Chapter 15

Administration and Enforcement

Introduction

[15.01] Administration of stamp duty is regulated by SDCA 1999. The enforcement of the Stamp Act is the responsibility of the Revenue Commissioners. SDCA 1999, s 137 states:

> This Act shall apply to all such duties and to all fees which are for the time being directed to be collected or received by means of stamps and
>
> All duties for the time being chargeable by law as stamp duties shall be under the care and management of the Commissioners.

Since 1 November 1991 stamp duty has been a mandatory tax. To ensure that the tax is complied with, the Revenue has been given statutory powers. These powers were increased in FA 1991 to reinforce the mandatory nature of the tax. The Revenue also issue Statements of Practice which give guidance to those involved in tax affairs as to how the system operates and how they enforce the relevant provisions. These Statements of Practice have no legal affect.

Variation of rates of duty

[15.02] The SDCA 1999 prescribes the substantive extent of the application of stamp duty. The exact rates of duty payable in specific circumstances under the SDCA 1999 are set out under Schedule 1 of the Act. Any variation in the rate of duty payable normally requires an amendment to the primary legislation. However, pursuant to SDCA 1999, s 3(1), the Minister may, by order, vary the rate of duty chargeable on any particular class of instrument specified under Schedule 1, or exempt such particular class of instrument entirely. However, the Minister's power to vary such rates of duty is heavily circumscribed. First, the Minister may not make any increase in the rate of duty chargeable on any such instrument through this mechanism. Where the Minister seeks to raise the rate of duty, he or she must amend the primary legislation through the full enactment of the Oireachtas. Further, the Minister's power to act by order does not apply to any of the following:

(a) any instrument or class of instrument relating to immovable property in the State, or any right or interest therein;[1]

(b) any stock or share registered within the State;[2]

---

1 SDCA 1999, s 3(2)(a)(i).

2 SDCA 1999, s 3(2)(a)(ii).

(c) any risk situated within the State pursuant to the Insurance heading of Schedule 1;[3] and

(d) any bill of exchange or promissory note.[4]

Debt factoring agreements are not hereby excluded and the Minister may vary the rates of duty chargeable on such instruments by order.[5]

[15.03] Where the Minister makes an order varying the rate of duty chargeable pursuant to these provisions, then such order shall have statutory effect provided that the order has been laid before Dáil Éireann. However, Dáil Éireann may, within 21 days of the order being laid before it, pass a resolution annulling the relevant order.[6] The annulment of the order by the Dáil shall, however, not affect the validity of anything done under the order prior to the resolution of annulment. The Minister may, by further order, revoke or amend, any order made pursuant to these provisions. The attempt to give the Minister delegated powers to vary the rate of duty chargeable is to be welcomed; however, the provisions are severely limited and therefore of marginal use. There is considerable merit in at least allocating to the Minister the power to reduce any rate of duty chargeable under SDCA 1999 by order, without requiring a full legislative enactment.

Administration of SDCA 1999

Stamping of documents

[15.04] Every instrument to be stamped must be written in such manner as to permit the stamp to appear on the face of the instrument[7] and if more than one instrument is written on the same piece of material, every one of the instruments is to be stamped separately and distinctly with the amount of duty chargeable.[8] In order to stamp any instrument falling under a head of charge, the instrument must be presented in written form with sufficient space for the stamp to appear somewhere on the face of the instrument. Normally, the stamp appears in the margins of the instrument. If within the one instrument there is more than one transaction which falls under a head of charge, then the instrument must be separately stamped to reflect the distinct transactions and it is not sufficient to give a composite stamp.

[15.05] Stamping of documents occurs in one of two ways. The first method, which is dealt with later, is known as adjudication. The second method is normal stamping. The document is forwarded to the 'Marking Office' of the Revenue which calculates the duty payable on the face of the document. This amount is then marked on the document and when paid, a stamp to that value is impressed upon it.[9]

[15.06] In order for the Revenue to determine the correct amount of duty, it requires full disclosure of all relevant facts to be contained within the document. The relevant facts

3 SDCA 1999, s 3(2)(a)(iii).

4 SDCA 1999, s 3(2)(b).

5 SDCA 1999, s 3(3).

6 SDCA 1999, s 3(5).

7 SDCA 1999, s 6(1).

8 SDCA 1999, s 6(2).

9 SDCA 1999, s 20.

are those which would affect the liability of the instrument to duty or the amount of the duty with which any instrument is chargeable. The relevant facts may not be suitable for inclusion within the document and in that situation a statement containing such relevant facts as affect the liability to duty is to be attached to the document. These provisions are discussed more fully below.

Types of stamp

[15.07] The standard method of stamping is a form of impressed stamp which, since 1999, has taken the form of a silver hologram and a data string containing a document identification number, the date of stamping and codes representing the various transaction types and stamp types.

[15.08] The most common form of impressed stamps are subdivided into money stamps, denoting stamps and PD (particulars delivered) stamps.

(a) Money stamps (code EUR) are silver in colour and are impressed by the Revenue in the margins at the top or side of the document and indicate the exact duty paid and the date paid.

(b) Denoting stamps are used for both counterpart and collateral documents as well as documents that have been adjudicated. Where the duty chargeable on the instrument depends on the duty paid on another document, the Revenue Commissioners will, on the production of both instruments, denote on the first instrument the fact that duty was paid on the second instrument.[10] Examples of denoting stamps are as follows:

    (i) duplicate and counterpart stamps;

    (ii) collateral stamps (code COL) – a fixed head of charge under the Mortgage Bond, Debenture, Covenant Head Of Charge under Schedule 1 SDCA;

    (iii) conveyances of transfers made subsequent to a contract of agreement which was stamped pursuant to SDCA 1999, s 31;[11]

    (iv) transfers of leasehold interests made pursuant to a contract or agreement which was stamped pursuant to SDCA 1999, s 36;[12] and

    (v) leases entered into pursuant to an agreement for lease which was stamped pursuant to SDCA 1999, s 50.

    Penalty stamps are marked as P or PM where the liability to duty has been mitigated in whole or in part.

(c) PD stamps (code PD) are required for the transfer of the fee simple of any land or interest in land or for a grant of a lease for a term exceeding 14 years F(1909-10)A 1910, s 41.[13] A PD form (form ST21) must be completed providing all relevant details before the PD stamp will be impressed. Where a

---

[10] SDCA 1999, s 11.

[11] SDCA 1999, s 31(3).

[12] SDCA, s 36(2)(ii).

[13] SDCA 1999, s 12.

lease is for more than 14 years but less than 30 years, by concession, a PD stamp will be impressed without the need to fill in any PD form.

FA 1994, s 107 permitted the Revenue Commissioners to lay down regulations as to the form in which the particulars were to be delivered, the time limits within which they were to be delivered, the manner in which the land was to be described and the furnishing of tax reference numbers. These provisions aimed to give the Revenue Commissioners greater access to information concerning the property transactions of taxpayers. The principal change in the substantive application of the PD requirement was the extension to voluntary dispositions. The Revenue Commissioners issued new regulations as set out in SI/144/95 cited as Stamp Duty (Particulars to be delivered) Regulations 1995.[14]

[15.09] The Regulation refers to the following:

(a) time limits for delivery;

(b) manner in which the land is to be described; and

(c) the furnishing of tax reference numbers (in the case of an individual, a PPS number; in any other case, the reference number stated on any return form or notice issued by the Inspector of Taxes).

The Regulation applies to:

(a) the transfer on sale of the fee simple of land or any interest in land;

(b) a transfer operating as a voluntary disposition *inter vivos* of such interest in land;

(c) the grant of a lease exceeding 30 years; and

(d) the assignment of any leasehold interest in land where the unexpired residue exceeds 30 years.

The PD stamp can be impressed at either Stamp Duty Office – Dublin Castle or Cork, – Office of the Collector of Customs and Excise. It must be delivered to the Revenue Commissioners within 30 days from the date of first execution of the accompanying instrument.[15] It applies to documents executed after 31 August 1995.

A form ST21 does not need to be submitted in respect of the conveyance, transfer or leases of houses, buildings or lands by or to a housing authority (pursuant to Housing (Miscellaneous Provisions) Act 1992, s 8). It is not necessary to furnish particulars to the Revenue Commissioners in respect of any transaction creating a joint tenancy between spouses pursuant to Family Home Protection Act 1976, s 14. Failure to comply with the PD provision renders the transferor or lessor liable on summary conviction, for a fine of up to €1,900 in respect of offences committed before 3 March 2003 and €3,000 for offences committed on or after this date and/or a term of imprisonment not exceeding 12 months and on indictment, for a fine of up to €126,970 and/or a term of imprisonment not exceeding 5 years.[16]

---

14 See **Appendix 3**.

15 The form is set out in **Appendix 2**.

16 SDCA 1999, s 12(4) applying TCA 1997, s 1078 (3).

The section therefore imposes an obligation on the transferor or lessor to supply information which is exclusively within the knowledge of the transferee or lessee, namely the PPS number. This was seen to be inequitable and, in light of representation made to the Revenue Commissioners, this was amended in SDCA 1999, s 12(2) to place the obligation on the transferee or lessee. Under the present regulations, all details of the transaction and the vendor are inserted on the PD form and handed over at closing to the purchaser's solicitor who then inserts the details of the purchaser. As the declaration on the PD form is to be signed by both parties, it is recommended that these be completed by the parties to the instrument rather than by their agents.

If the PD stamp is not impressed, the instrument is not deemed to be duly stamped even if the current stamp duty has been paid and will not be admissable in evidence (except in criminal proceedings or in civil proceedings to recover stamp duty).[17]

(d) Penalty stamps (code P or PM where the penalty has been mitgated in part or in full). Where the Revenue Commissioners have elected not to subject the instrument to a penalty, or where the instrument has been held in escrow, then the instrument will be stamped accordingly.

(e) Duplicate or Counterpart Stamp (code CP or CPT): where there are several instruments evidencing the same transaction *ad valorem* stamp duty is payable on one of the instruments only. Duplicate instruments are marked with a counterpart stamp showing that they are duplicate instruments. The cost of a duplicate stamp is the lesser of the duty payable on the original instrument or €12.50.

Where it would be impractical for any person who carries on a business to stamp each instrument, the Revenue Commissioners may make a composition agreement to alleviate the need for stamping each individual document.[18]

Time for stamping

[15.10] A document becomes chargeable to duty at the time it is first executed. Once a document has been executed, it is this date of execution that governs the rates of duty payable on foot of the document and the dates for penalty payments for late or overdue liability. The instrument must be submitted to the Revenue Commissioners for stamping or adjudication within 30 days of its first execution. In practice, the Revenue Commissioners allow 44 days to elapse from the date of first execution of the instrument before penalties are levied.[19] Where the instrument has been adjudicated upon, then the duty must be paid within 14 days from the date of notice of the adjudication.

17 SDCA 1999, s 12(3).

18 **Chapter 9** and SP-SD/3/90.

19 Revenue Notes for Guidance p 22.

Refund of unused stamps

[15.11] Allowances are made for spoiled and unused stamps.[20] Where a stamp has been accidentally spoiled, or by any means rendered unfit for the purposes intended, before the instrument has been executed, or in the case of an adhesive stamp has not been affixed, a refund of the duty may be made by the Revenue Commissioners. A stamp on any bill of exchange which has not been accepted, or on any promissory note that has not been delivered, or on any bill of exchange or promissory note where the stamp has been accidentally spoiled or otherwise rendered ineffective and where an identical copy of the bill or note is produced, shall be refunded. A stamp used for the following instruments shall be refunded provided that an application is made within six years after the stamp has become spoiled or the document has been executed or dated but in the case of an executed instrument, the instrument has not or will not be given in evidence, that is, produced in a court of law:

(a) a void instrument;

(b) an instrument found unfit for the purposes intended by way of mistake or error;

(c) an instrument not made use of for any purpose whatsoever and due to the refusal of one of the parties to complete the instrument, by failing to sign, act or register the instrument, is rendered unusable;

(d) an instrument which has been accidentally spoiled and for which another instrument to the same effect has been prepared.

These provisions are limited in application and, for example, do not cover a voidable instrument (an instrument that can be set aside at the election of either one or both of the parties) nor an instrument containing a condition precedent (a clause which must be satisfied before a contract comes into existence).

[15.12] Where an instrument has been accidentally stamped with duty in excess of the correct amount, or where duty has been applied to an instrument that is not chargeable to duty, then the excess duty is refunded.[21] At common law, there is a right to repayment of any tax paid through mistake of law, together with appropriate interest: *O'Rourke v Revenue Commissioners*.[22] However, with respect to stamp duty, any claim must be made within 6 years of the date of execution. In *Byrne v Revenue Commissioners*[23] the court held that the statutory time limit for seeking a refund could not be extended by the court. Thus the legislation limits the common law right to repayment. In addition, SDCA 1999, s 153 permits the Revenue to offer other stamps to the value of the misused stamps, rather than a refund of the duty paid. Finally, any person in possession of unused and unwanted stamps may seek to have the Revenue repurchase such stamps to the same value as the purchase price. The claim must be made within 6 years of the purchase and the repurchase is at the discretion of the Revenue.[24]

---

[20] SDCA 1999, s 151.

[21] SDCA 1999, s 152.

[22] *O'Rourke v Revenue Commissioners* (December 1996, unreported) HC.

[23] *Byrne v Revenue Commissioners* [1935] IR 644.

[24] SDCA 1999, s 154.

Lost instruments

[15.13] Where an instrument has been accidentally lost, then the Revenue may issue new stamps to the value of the lost stamps in order that a new instrument be stamped to the same terms and effects as the original instrument.[25] In order to avail of this provision, the applicant must be the person by whom the lost instrument was first executed and he or she must establish that the duty was in fact paid and give an undertaking that if the lost instrument is recovered, then it shall be cancelled. The Revenue may require a statutory declaration in such instances.[26]

Power to grant licences to deal in stamps

[15.14] The Revenue may, at their discretion, grant any person a licence to deal in stamps at a specified place or places. Every person so licenced shall have a sign, displayed on some conspicuous place outside the place, with the words 'Licenced to Sell Stamp' in lettering not less than one inch in height. Failure to abide by this provision is liable to a fine of €1,265. Any person to whom a licence is granted must lodge €1,265 as a security bond.[27]

[15.15] A person who is not licensed to sell stamps, or, if licensed, is selling them at a location not specified within the licence, shall be guilty of an offence and liable, on summary conviction, for a fine of up to €1,900 and/or a term of imprisonment not exceeding 12 months and, on indictment, for a fine of up to €126,970 and/or a term of imprisonment not exceeding 5 years.[28] Any person who displays any sign indicating that they are selling stamps when they are not licensed to do so, or, if licensed, have such a sign attached at a location not specified within the licence, shall be liable for a penalty of €1,265.[29]

[15.16] Finally, any person who hawks or carries stamps on them, whether licensed or not, shall be liable, on summary conviction, for a fine of up to €1,900 and/or a term of imprisonment not exceeding 12 months and, on indictment, for a fine of up to €126,970 and/or a term of imprisonment not exceeding 5 years. In addition, such stamps shall be forfeit.[30]

Enforcement

[15.17] The following provisions empower the Revenue Commissioners to enforce the provisions of SDCA 1999 as amended.

The Revenue Commissioners' power to raise assessment of stamp duty

[15.18] The Revenue Commissioners are empowered to adjudicate the liability of stamp duty on instruments.[31] In certain circumstances instruments have to be referred to the

[25] SDCA 1999, s 155(1).

[26] SDCA 1999, s 155(2).

[27] SDCA 1999, s 146.

[28] SDCA 1999, s 147(1).

[29] SDCA 1999, s 147(2).

[30] SDCA 1999, s 149.

[31] SDCA 1999, s 20(1).

Revenue Commissioners for adjudication.[32] Prior to FA 1991, assessment was only allowed where the instruments were presented to the Revenue Commissioners. The Revenue Commissioners are now empowered on their own initiative to raise an assessment and impose a liability so that these assessments will be enforced as if the instruments had been presented to the Revenue Commissioners.[33] The Revenue Commissioners can make an assessment as to the amount of stamp duty payable to the best of their knowledge, information and belief, which they felt ought to be charged, levied and paid and the 'accountable person' shall be liable for the payment of stamp duty assessed unless the Revenue Commissioners make another assessment upon delivery of the instrument to them.[34]

[15.19] When an assessment was made by the Revenue Commissioners under the old provisions, by way of adjudication it was deemed to be final and conclusive. Under the new provisions, where it appears that the assessment is inaccurate, the Revenue Commissioners can make further assessment as they deem appropriate in the circumstances and the second assessment shall be substituted for the first assessment.[35] Where the assessment has been an underassessment the Revenue Commissioners can make additional assessment as they deem appropriate.[36]

[15.20] An instrument bearing an adjudication stamp cannot be objected to as regards the adequacy of the duty paid. Once the instrument bears the adjudication stamp, it is admissible in evidence and available for all purposes regardless of the objection raised about the adequacy of duty, unless fraud can be established. The limitation applies only if it is the party seeking to have the instrument produced in evidence who has committed the fraud. Presumably, a bona fide purchaser for value who takes without notice of any fraud can raise the instrument in evidence. The Revenue Commissioners may collect any additional duty payable, notwithstanding the fact that the instrument bears an adjudication stamp.[37]

[15.21] The adjudged duly stamped notation on an instrument has been of the utmost importance in conveyancing practice to purchasers as it ensures that the document will be admissible in evidence and the additional duty chargeable will only be collectable from the accountable person, which will protect the subsequent purchaser. Therefore no objection or requisition on title need be raised as to whether any further liability of duty arises to the vendor in respect of an instrument on title.[38] The liabilities imposed in the case of an additional substituted assessment by virtue of an undervaluation or an inaccurate statement of facts will not only include the surcharge and negligence provisions but may give rise to a late stamping penalty and interest.

---

32 *R v Registrar of Joint Stock Companies* [1882] 21 QBD 131.

33 SDCA 1999, s 20.

34 SDCA 1999, s 20(2).

35 SDCA 1999, s 20(10).

36 SDCA 1999, s 20(11).

37 SDCA 1999, s 20.

38 SDCA 1999, s 20.

[15.22] These provisions may not be used to authorise the stamping after execution of an instrument that by law cannot be stamped after execution.[39] Neither can the provisions extend to any instrument chargeable with *ad valorem* duty and made as a security for money or stock without limit.[40] Simply put this prevents individuals avoiding the mandatory nature of stamp duty by failing to stamp when the liability accrues and instead waiting until stamping becomes a practical necessity and relying on SDCA 1999, s 20 to stamp after execution.

Penalties for late payment of stamp duty

[15.23] Prior to 1 November 1991, the penalty for late payment of stamp duty was €12.50 plus an interest rate of five per cent per annum.[41] Interest was only chargeable provided the unpaid duty exceeded £10. Interest ran from the date upon which the instrument was first executed up to the time when it was stamped, subject to the provision that the amount of interest would not exceed the unpaid duty. If the instrument was executed out of the State, it could then be stamped within 30 days after it had been first received in this State. Payment of the penalty was noted on the instrument when it was stamped. The Revenue Commissioners also had power to remit any penalty they deemed fit.[42] This section also sets out the person liable for the payment of such penalty. In practice, the Revenue Commissioners were quite willing to discuss the penalty liabilities and interest charges and in cases where they felt it appropriate would mitigate the interest charged, but would impose the penalty duty of €12.50.

[15.24] New regulations were passed on 29 May 1991.[43] This should have been the effective date of these provisions; however, s 15(6) provided that this new subsection would apply with effect as and from 1 November 1991 to any instrument whenever executed. On a strict interpretation of the Act no penalty or interest charges were enforced for the period from 29 May 1991 to 1 November 1991. Tax legislation had to be strictly construed and the courts have always interpreted it and given it a strict meaning. Rowlatt J in 1921 stated:

> In a taxing Act one has to look at what is clearly said. There is no room for any intendment. There is no equity about a tax. There is no presumption as to a tax. There is nothing to be read in, nothing to be implied. One can only look fairly at the language used.[44]

[15.25] The *Inspector of Taxes v Kiernan*[45] sets out the interpretation of fiscal statutes and in particular stated:

> If a word or expression is used in a statute creating a penal or taxation liability, and there is looseness or ambiguity attaching to it, the word should be construed strictly so as to

39 SDCA 1999, s 8(b).

40 SDCA 1999, s 8(a).

41 SDCA 1999, s 14.

42 SDCA 1999, s 14(3).

43 FA 1991, s 100.

44 *Cape Brandy Syndicate v IRC* [1921] 1 KB 64.

45 *Inspector of Taxes v Kiernan* III ITR 19.

> prevent a fresh imposition of a liability from being created unfairly by the use of oblique or slack language.

[15.26] These principles were approved by the Supreme Court in the *McGrath* case[46] Finlay CJ, in delivering a judgment with which all the judges in the Supreme Court agreed, stated:

> ...the function of the courts in interpreting a statute of the Oireachtas is, however, strictly confined to ascertaining the true meaning of each statutory provision, resorting in cases of doubt or ambiguity to the consideration of the purpose and intention of the legislator to be inferred from all the provisions of the statute involved, or even of other statutes expressed to be construed with it. The courts have not got a function to add to or delete from expressed statutory provisions so as to achieve objectives which to the court appear desirable.

In that case the Revenue Commissioners had urged the court to imply into the provisions of CGTA 1975, either ss 12 or 33, a new clause to call upon the taxpayer to prove an actual loss. This was rejected by the Supreme Court.

[15.27] When interpreting the legislation strictly, it would appear that no penalty duties are payable between 29 May 1991 and 1 November 1991. However the Revenue Commissioners stated quite clearly that the penalties apply with effect from 1 November 1991 and that the old regime existed up to that date. In light of the Interpretation Act 1937, s 19(1), this was the correct view:

> ...where an act of the Oireachtas repeals the whole or a portion of a previous statute and substitute other provisions for the statute or portion of a statute so repealed, the statute or portion of a statute so repealed shall, (unless the contrary is expressly provided in the repealing Act), continue in force until the said substituted provision comes into operation.

[15.28] This had been upheld by the Supreme Court in the *ex tempore* judgment of *O'Leary v Revenue Commissioners.*[47] Obviously this has changed in light of the IA 2005. SDCA 1999, s 14 provides the following penalties:

(a) a presentation penalty of €25;[48]

(b) where the unpaid duty exceeds €30, interest on the duty at a rate of 0.0273 per cent per day or part thereof. In this regard there is no ceiling on the interest payable;

(c) (i) penalties for late stamping of 10 per cent of the unpaid duty where the stamped instrument is presented not later than six months after the date upon which it was first executed,[49] or

(ii) 20 per cent of the unpaid duty where the instrument is stamped more than six months but not later than 12 months after the date upon which it was first executed,[50] or

---

46 III ITR 683.

47 *O'Leary v Revenue Commissioners* IV ITR 357.

48 SDCA 1999, s 14(1).

49 SDCA 1999, s 14(2)(i).

50 SDCA 1999, s 14(2)(ii).

(iii) an amount equivalent to 30 per cent of the unpaid duty where such instrument is stamped more than 12 months after the date upon which the instrument was first executed.[51]

The Revenue Commissioners are also empowered to remit any penalty they think fit payable on the stamp duty[52] and such claims should be in writing and supported by documentary evidence, where relevant.[53] In practice, the Revenue Commissioners are enforcing these penalty provisions strictly. If the taxpayer is dissatisfied with a decision taken by a Revenue Officer in relation to penalties, he may have the matter re-examined by another Revenue Officer who has had no previous involvement in the case under the internal review procedure.[54] Any penalty which arises is to be chargeable and recoverable in the same manner as if it were part of the duty on the instrument to which it relates[55] and any penalty paid shall be denoted on the instrument by a particular stamp.[56]

[15.29] The statement of practice from the Revenue Commissioners sets out details of their interpretation of the penalty provisions. Where the instrument is executed prior to 1 November 1991 but is presented under the new regime, the penalty of €12.50 plus 5 per cent per annum will be payable up to 31 October 1991 and after that date interest at 1.25 per cent per month or part thereof will be charged. In calculating the time and presentation of the instrument, the 10 per cent, 20 per cent and 30 per cent surcharges shall be calculated with time running from 1 November 1991 (SP-SD/1/91 para 8.4).

Example 15.29.1

A deed of conveyance was executed in Spain on 1 December 1992 relating to a house and lands in Ireland which were sold at market value of €185,000. The deed was brought back into this jurisdiction on 5 June 1993 and presented for stamping. The liability is as follows:

	€
Stamp duty (€185,000 at 3%)	3,750
Ordinary penalty	25
Penalty interest (7 months of 8.75% of duty)	586
Surcharge 20%	1,110
Total	7,271

The payment of this penalty and duty shall be denoted on the instrument.

[15.30] FA 1992, s 201 provided an amnesty period in respect of unstamped or insufficiently stamped instruments by remitting penalties up to 30 June 1992. This section applied to instruments which were first executed before 1 November 1991 and

51 SDCA 1999, s 14(2)(iii).

52 SDCA 1999, s 14(3).

53 SP-SD/1/91 para 8.4.

54 See Statement of Practice SP – GEN/2/99 which was revised in January 2005.

55 SDCA 1999, s 14(5).

56 SDCA 1999, s 14(4).

were unstamped or insufficiently stamped on 30 January 1992. If the instrument was delivered for stamping to the Revenue Commissioners together with the unpaid duty:

(a) on or before 30 June 1992, the penalty was mitigated in full; or

(b) on or after 31 July 1992, but on or before 30 September 1992, the penalty was calculated as if the instrument was first executed on 1 June 1992.

Where the instrument is delivered together with the unpaid duty, which is insufficient or found to be insufficient by virtue of revaluation of the property, then the penalty will be mitigated in respect of the additional duty provided it was paid on or before 30 June 1992 or, in the event it was paid on or after 1 July 1992 but before 30 September 1992 the penalty was calculated with effect from 1 June 1992. A further general tax amnesty was implemented by the Waiver of Certain Tax, Interest and Penalties Act 1993 which has limited impact on stamp duty liability. These amnesties have now expired.

Surcharge provisions

[15.31] Surcharge provisions were introduced in FA 1991, s 103, to apply to transfers by way of gifts where the duty was chargeable, not on the consideration paid, but on the value of the property.[57] The purpose behind this was to counteract tax evasion and it encouraged full disclosure in respect of sales at undervalue.[58] These provisions as enacted were found to be too onerous and were reduced in FA 1994, s 103.

[15.32] On instruments executed on or after 1 November 1991, but before 23 May 1994, the surcharges were as follows:

(a) where the value of the property is 10 per cent greater than the value submitted but under 30 per cent, a surcharge of 50 per cent of the total duty payable on the instrument is charged, subject to the proviso that this does not apply where the difference between the values is less than €6,350;

(b) where the market value is greater by 30 per cent but not greater than 50 per cent of the submitted value, the surcharge is equal to the amount of duty;

(c) where the market value is greater by 50 per cent of the submitted value, then the surcharge is double the amount of the duty.

The surcharge payable shall be chargeable and recoverable as if it was part of the duty to which it relates, but the surcharge shall not be shown on the instrument to which it relates.[59]

[15.33] Under SDCA 1999, s 15, the following surcharges are to apply:

(a) where the value of the property is 15 per cent greater than the value submitted but under 30 per cent, a surcharge of 25 per cent of the total duty payable on the instrument is charged subject to the proviso that where the difference between the values is less than €6,350, no surcharge applies;[60]

---

57 SDCA 1999, s 30, s 54.

58 SP-SD/1/91, para 10.1.

59 FA 1991 ss 103(3) and (4).

60 SDCA 1999, s 15(1)(a).

(b) where the market value is greater by 30 per cent but not greater than 50 per cent of the submitted value, the surcharge is equal to 50 per cent of the amount of duty;[61]

(c) where the market value is greater by 50 per cent of the submitted value, then the surcharge is equal to the amount of the duty.[62]

The surcharge payable shall be chargeable and recoverable as if it was part of the duty to which it relates, and the surcharge shall be denoted on the instrument to which it relates.[63]

[15.34] Professional advisers should ensure that their clients are advised of their duty to submit realistic valuations. Where a formal valuation is carried out by a competent and qualified person, solicitors are entitled to assume that the value is realistic. The Revenue Commissioners have justified these provisions by stating that they are anti-evasion measures to ensure that realistic market values are placed on properties when transferring by way of gift or partial gift, and also to avoid 'under the counter' payments.[64] In practice, the surcharge will only be imposed after an appeal as to the ascertained value. These provisions are in addition to the penalty for late stamping. Where 'under the counter' payments are made the parties involved could be liable to:

(a) penalties for failure to declare the amounts involved;[65] and

(b) a surcharge under SDCA 1999, s 15.

Example 15.34.1

Pre 23 May 1994

A gives his child B a gift of a farm which they value at €100,000 with the necessary consanguinity certificate inserted. The valuation office values the farm at €160,000 and €140,000 s eventually settled on.

	€
Stamp duty (€140,000 x 8% x 50%	5,600
Surcharge penalty (undervaluation of more than 30% but less than 50%)	5,600
Total	11,200

The surcharge shall not be shown on the instrument.

Post 23 May 1994

A gives his child B, who is not a qualified young farmer, a gift of a farm which they value at €100,000 with the necessary consanguinity certificate inserted. The valuation office value the farm at €160,000 which is eventually settled at €140,000.

61 SDCA 1999, s 15(1)(b).

62 SDCA 1999, s 15(1)(c).

63 SDCA 1999, s 15(4).

64 SP-SD/1/91, paras 10.4 and 10.5.

65 SA 1891, s 15 as amended by SDCA 1999, s 14.

	€
Stamp duty as above	5,600
Surcharge penalty (undervaluation of more than 30% but less than 50%)	2,800
Total	8,400

The surcharge shall be denoted on the instrument.

Example 15.34.2

Pre 23 May 1994

House sold by A to B for €110,000 together with contents valued at €40,000.

Referred to valuation office, eventually compromised reached as follows:

	€
House value	135,000
Contents	15,000
Stamp duty on €135,000 at 6%	8,100
Penalty	4,050
Total	12,150

Additional penalties may arise under SDCA 1999, s 14 as amended.

Post 23 May 1994

House sold by A to B for €110,000 together with contents valued at €40,000.

Referred to valuation office, eventually compromised reached €135,000.

	€
House value	135,000
Contents	15,000
Stamp duty on €135,000 @ 4%	4,050
Penalty	1,350
Total	6,750

Additional penalties may arise under SA 1891, s 15 as amended, and both the penalties and surcharge shall be denoted on the instrument.

[15.35] Similar surcharge provisions apply with regard to the apportionment that arises on an instrument which is liable under the conveyance on sale or lease head of charge with respect to property that is not wholly residential. Both the vendor and purchaser must submit estimates of the apportionment between the residential and non-residential element of the consideration passing and, where such estimates are found to be at under-value, such person will be presumed to have acted negligently unless the contrary is proven.[66] Where the purchaser's estimate of the apportionment for the residential element of the consideration passing is less than the amount assessed by the Revenue

[66] SDCA 1999, s 16.

Commissioners, then, as a penalty, the duty chargeable upon the instrument shall be subject to a surcharge determined as follows:

(a) where undervaluation is between 10 per cent and 30 per cent the surcharge is 50 per cent of the loss of duty involved.

(b) where the undervaluation is greater than 30 per cent the surcharge is 100 per cent of the loss of duty involved.

No surcharge is payable where the undervaluation is less than 10 per cent.

[15.36] Where a surcharge is payable, the purchaser is entitled to recover one half from the vendor provided that where the vendor's valuation is higher than the purchaser's valuation, it shall be limited to the surcharge which would have been payable had the vendor's valuation been submitted by the purchaser.[67]

Example 15.36.1

Jack sells a public house with living accommodation overhead to Jill for €1,200,000, the residential portion of which is valued by Jill (purchaser) at €250,000. The vendor submits a valuation of €300,000. The Revenue Commissioners reach a valuation of €550,000.

Stamp duty liability on deed as presented

Public house	€950,000 @ 9%	85,500
Living accommodation	€250,000 @ 4%	10,000
Total duty		95,500

Stamp duty liability on deed

Public house	€550,000 @ 9%	49,500
Living accommodation	€650,000 @ 9%	58,500
Total duty		108,000

Surcharge

Undervaluation in excess of 30%

100% of the duty on the difference between the Revenue assessment and the purchaser's assessment; €108,000-€95,500 = €12,500

Total duty payable

Ad valorem	108,000
Surcharge	12,500
Total	120,500

Purchaser can recover 50% of what the surcharge would be if the purchaser had submitted the vendor's estimate.

---

67 SDCA 1999, s 16(4).

Stamp duty liability on deed as apportioned by vendor:

Public house	€900,000 @ 9%	81,000
Living accommodation	€300,000 @ 5%	15,000
Total duty		96,000
Surcharge in this case	€108,000-€96,000	12,000
Amount recovereable by the purchaser 50%		6,000

Where the residential property is overvalued, the section does not permit any surcharge to be applied, even where the overvaluation might have led to a potential reduction in the duty payable.

Power to inspect documents

[15.37] The Revenue Commissioners have powers to inspect documents. SDCA 1999, s 128 required every public officer having in his custody any rolls, books, records, or papers, to permit the Revenue Commissioners to inspect same and to take notes, where they were investigating any fraud or omission in relation to stamp duty. This power of inspection was extended with effect from 1 November 1991.[68] This provides that any person who is a party to any instrument or has in his custody or control any documents which on inspection would tend to secure any duty or prove or lead to the discovery of any fraud, negligence or omission in relation to any duty, shall within fourteen days of the request by way of notice in writing by the Revenue Commissioners:

(a) provide such information as the Revenue Commissioners may deem necessary; and

(b) permit any person authorised by the Revenue Commissioners to inspect such documents and take such notes, extracts, prints, print-outs and copies as he may deem appropriate.

[15.38] Failure to do so makes the person liable to a fine of €3,000, and €125 for each day of continued refusal after conviction. It is a defence for the accused to show that he is required or entitled by law to refuse the request of the Revenue Commissioners. The definition of a document has been greatly expanded and is deemed to include:

> ... any instrument, roll, book or record, any record of an entry in a document, and any information stored, maintained or preserved by means of mechanical or electronic device, whether or not stored, maintained or preserved in a legible form.[69]

This imposes greater power on the Revenue Commissioners and further liabilities on advisers. The Revenue Commissioners also have a general power of search and seizure under TCA 1997, s 905 though it is unlikely that these powers would be exercised in place of the specific stamp duty provisions.[70]

---

68 SDCA 1999, s 128(1).

69 SDCA 1999, s 128(1).

70 For a fuller discussion of these powers see Ward and Burke *Judge Irish Income Tax 2006* (Tottel Publishing, 2006).

Powers of attachment

[15.39] The Revenue Commissioners have the power of attachment for a liability to stamp duty.[71] By serving a notice of attachment on the account of the tax defaulter, the Revenue can force any debtor to discharge the liability. Where the account is in joint names a notice will be sent to each of the account holders, including the taxpayer.[72] All joint account holders will be deemed to be entitled to equal shares of the account, unless within 10 days contrary evidence is produced. The duty shall be levied on the tax defaulter's share of the account.

Miscellaneous provisions

Incorrect certificates

[15.40] The furnishing of incorrect certificates for the purpose of Schedule 1 of the SDCA 1999 shall be deemed to be an offence making the person furnishing the incorrect certificate liable, on summary conviction, for a fine of up to €1,900 in respect of offences committed before 3 March 2003, and €3,000 for offences committed on or after this date and/or a term of imprisonment not exceeding 12 months and, on indictment, for a fine of up to €126,970 and/or a term of imprisonment not exceeding 5 years.[73]

Money received for payment of stamp duty

[15.41] Any person who receives money on account to be used for the discharge of stamp duty but does not apply the money for payment of the duty, or improperly withholds same, is accountable for the said duty. The amount involved is considered a debt owing to the Minister for Finance for the benefit of the Central Fund.[74] The enforcement of this provision is the responsibility of the Revenue Commissioners who must sue to recover the amount involved, together with the costs of collection, in the High Court and the High Court can make such order as it deems just in the circumstances.[75] In *Lord Advocate v Gordon*[76] a solicitor was held liable to account for moneys deposited with him by a client for the discharge of the liability to stamp duty.

Offences for forged dies or stamps

[15.42] It is an offence for an individual to do, or cause to be done, or knowingly aid, abet or assist in any of the following:

(a) Fraudulently using a genuine stamp die to make a print or impression upon any material. It is an offence to use an official Revenue die to stamp a document without the consent of the Revenue Commissioners.[77] Since the offence is one

---

[71] TCA 1997, s 100.

[72] FA 1992, s 241.

[73] SDCA 1999, s 17 applying TCA 1997, s 1078(3).

[74] SDCA 1999, s 138(1).

[75] SDCA 1999, s 138(2) and (3).

[76] *Lord Advocate v Gordon* [1901] SLT 439.

[77] SDCA 1999, s 139(a).

of fraud, intent must be shown and negligence or recklessness is insufficient.[78] It shall also be an offence to knowingly sell or expose for sale such fraudulently impressed stamp from a genuine die.[79]

Example 15.42.1

A finds himself in the Stamp Office with a number of documents to be stamped. Whilst the Revenue Officer is not looking, A impresses one of the documents with an official die. A has committed a felony.

Example 15.42.2

Assume the facts as above but that A impresses a blank sheet of paper with a stamp to the value of €2,000. A now seeks to sell the paper for €500. A has committed a felony.

(b) Fraudulently mutilate, tear or otherwise interfere with any stamp for the purposes and intent of putting the stamp, or part thereof, to some use.[80]

Example 15.42.3

A has executed a document for which the liability to duty is €4,000. A discovers an old document which has been stamped with duty to the value of €3,000. A tears off the stamp from the old document and sticks it on the new document. He then adds the additional duty required. A has committed a felony.

(c) Fraudulently erase or remove from any stamped document any material thereon with the intention to use the stamp which has been placed upon the material.[81] It is an offence to erase the names of the parties on a prior executed document and insert different names thereon, or to do likewise with the identity of the property in question.

Example 15.42.4

A executes a document which sells Blackacre to B. Stamp duty of €4,500 is impressed on the document. B now sells Blackacre to C for which the relevant duty is €4,500.

C now erases both A's and B's name from the original document and replaces them with B and C (B now being the vendor would be inserted where A was, C now the purchaser is inserted where B was).

C is liable to be prosecuted for the commission of a felony.

(d) To be knowingly and without lawful excuse in possession of any fraudulent stamp die as set out in the preceding sections.[82]

Example 15.42.5

A finds himself in the Stamp Office with a number of documents to be stamped. Whilst the Revenue official has his back turned, A picks up a piece of paper upon which a stamp has been impressed and retains it. Before A leaves the Office, a

---

78 SDCA 1999, s 139(a).

79 SDCA 1999, s 139(f)).

80 SDCA 1999, s 139(b), (c) and (d).

81 SDCA 1999, s 139(e).

82 SDCA 1999, s 139(g).

Revenue official stops him and confiscates the paper. A is guilty of a felony for possession.

[15.43] The relevant charging provision is TCA 1997, s 1078(2) and a person found liable for such an offence shall be liable, on summary conviction, for a fine of up to €1,900 in respect of offences committed before 3 March 2003, and €3,000 for offences committed after this date and/or a term of imprisonment not exceeding 12 months and, on indictment, for a fine of up to €126,970 and/or a term of imprisonment not exceeding 5 years.

[15.44] In order to detect the presence of such fraudulent dies, the District Judge may, on sworn information that there is just cause to suspect a person, issue a warrant enabling every property owned, or in the control of the said person, to be searched and any evidence to be seized. Afterwards, such stamps or dies must be handed over to the Revenue Commissioners.[83] Any District Judge who has reasonable suspicion that stamps have been stolen or fraudulently obtained and are now concealed within the jurisdiction of the District, may sign such order as to enable the stamps to be seized and such warrant as to bring the person in whose possession the stamps or dies were found before the courts.[84] If no satisfactory explanation for the possession of these stamps is forthcoming then they shall be regarded as forfeit and delivered to the Revenue Commissioners,[85] unless within six months any person proves to the satisfaction of the Revenue Commissioners that they purchased the stamps legitimately and that the stamps were then stolen, or fraudulently obtained from him or her in some manner, and they shall be entitled to have the stamps returned.[86]

[15.45] If a person who is licensed to hold such stamps is found in possession of forged stamps, then the presumption of guilt shall apply unless and until a satisfactory explanation proving that person's innocence is forthcoming.[87] In such cases the Revenue Commissioners may themselves authorise their own warrant for the forcible entry, search and seizure of the stamps from such person's property between the hours of 9am and 7pm.[88] All members of the gardaí are required to give assistance in the execution of such warrant when requested to so do[89] and it shall be an offence to in any way prevent the execution of such warrant, by either simple refusal or forcible prevention, subject to a fine of €1,265.[90] A member of the Garda Síochãin who refuses to assist the execution of such a warrant may be similarly liable.

[15.46] Where stamps are seized under a warrant, then an acknowledgment of the stamps, consisting of the number, particulars and amount, shall, if requested, be

83 SDCA 1999, s 140.
84 SDCA 1999, s 141(1).
85 SDCA 1999, s 141(2).
86 SDCA 1999, s 141(3).
87 SDCA 1999, s 142(1).
88 SDCA 1999, s 142(2).
89 SDCA 1999, s 142(3).
90 SDCA 1999, s 142(4).

delivered to the person from whom such stamps have been seized.[91] It shall be an offence to deface an adhesive stamp without lawful cause and a person who so defaces such stamp shall be subject to a fine of €630.[92]

[15.47] Finally, any person who in any form contrives to use a die so as to defraud the State from any duty which is not specially prohibited by law, shall be guilty of an offence and a person found liable for such an offence shall be liable, on summary conviction, for a fine of up to up to €1,900 in respect of offences committed before 3 March 2003, and €3,000 for offences committed after this date and/or a term of imprisonment not exceeding 12 months and, on indictment, for a fine of up to €126,970 and/or a term of imprisonment not exceeding 5 years.[93] This appears to be a catch-all offence under these provisions.

Forgeries Act 1913

[15.48] It is a felony to forge any die provided, made by or used by the Revenue Commissioners with the intent to defraud or deceive and it is punishable by penal servitude for a term not exceeding fourteen years.[94] It shall be a felony for someone to knowingly have in his possession forged dies without lawful authority (the burden of proof shall rest with the accused).[95]

Definitions

[15.49] The term 'die' includes any plate, type, tool, implement, apparatus, appliance, device, process or any other means whatsoever, used under the direction of the Commissioners for expressing or denoting any duty, rate of duty, or the fact that any duty or rate of duty or penalty has been paid, or that the instrument is duly stamped, or is not chargeable with any duty or for denoting any fee, and also any part of any such plate, type, tool, implement, apparatus, appliance, device, process and any such other means whatsoever.[96] The term 'stamp' means:

(a) any stamp, image, type, mark, seal, impression, imprint, perforation whatsoever impressed by means of a die; or

(b) any receipt in whatever form issued by or under the direction of the Commissioners; or

(c) any adhesive stamp issued by or under the direction of the Commissioners, for denoting any duty or fee.[97]

---

91 SDCA 1999, s 143.

92 SDCA 1999, s 144(4).

93 TCA 1997, s 1078(2).

94 Forgeries Act 1913, s 5.

95 Forgeries Act 1913, s 8(2).

96 SDCA 1999, s 1.

97 SDCA 1999, s 1.

Duties of relevant persons in relation to certain revenue offences

[15.50] The following provision assists the Revenue Commissioners in the enforcement of the provisions of SA 1891, as amended. Under TCA 1997, any relevant person, during an examination of the accounts of a company or whilst assisting or advising the company in the preparation of its accounts, becomes aware that the company has committed, or is in the course of committing, relevant material offences, shall communicate particulars of the offence to the company in writing and require that the company rectify the situation (or report the offence to the appropriate officer) within 6 months from date of notification. The relevant person must satisfy himself that remedial action has taken place or he must cease to act or advise the company for a period of three years after serving the notification of the offences on the company or from the time the relevant person has satisfied himself that such remedial action has taken place, whichever is the earlier.[98] Where the relevant person is an auditor and ceases to act in accordance with these provisions, he should inform the company in writing that he is resigning and serve a copy of this notice in writing to an appropriate officer within 14 days of notifying the company.[99] This provision does not apply to relevant persons who are not auditors.

[15.51] A relevant person found guilty of an offence under this section shall be liable to a fine of €1,265 on summary conviction (minimum of €300) and of €6,345 on indictment or term not exceeding two years imprisonment or both.[100] There is a time limit of six years within which prosecutions should be brought.[101] It shall be a good defence to show that the relevant person was, in the ordinary scope of his business, unaware of the offence being committed by the company.[102] It is a good defence for legal advisers to not report such offences where they are assisting or advising a company in preparing or conducting legal proceedings, extant or pending, at a time which is 6 months after the communication.[103] The effective date of this provision with respect to stamp duty is on instruments executed on or after 30 June 1995.[104] A 'relevant person' is an auditor appointed pursuant to CA 1963, s 160, an external adviser engaged in assisting or advising a company, for reward. Effectively, employees of the company are not relevant persons.[105] The appropriate officer is appointed by the Revenue Commissioners and notified in Iris Oifiguil.[106]

---

[98] TCA 1997, s 1079(3).

[99] TCA 1997, s 1079.

[100] TCA 1997, s 1079(7).

[101] TCA 1997, s 1079(9).

[102] TCA 1997, s 1079(10).

[103] TCA 1997, s 1079(4).

[104] FA 1995, s 172(11)(e).

[105] TCA 1997, s 1079(2).

[106] TCA 1997, s 1079(12).

FOIA and FOI(A)A 2003

[15.52] Under these Acts, members of the public have, with exceptions, the right to access to information held by public bodies, including the right to amend official information which is inaccurate, incomplete or misleading, where appropriate. Finally, but of utmost importance in terms of stamp duty, a member of the public has the legal right to obtain reasons for decisions affecting himself. In light of the recent changes in stamp duty and the complexity introduced by the FA 2006, the right of the taxpayer to obtain information as to the Revenue's basis for assessment to duty could be of considerable benefit. In the event that this information is not forthcoming or the information is not what the taxpayer feels he is entitled to, the taxpayer must first carry out an internal review and, after this process has been exhausted, an application can be made to the Office of the Information Commissioner.

[15.53] For further information concerning the Freedom of Information Act and the Revenue Commissioners, see Guide to Stucture, Functions and Records of the Office of the Revenue Commissioners, s 15 FOI Act Reference Book (Ver 1-April 98).

CREST

[15.54] The imposition of duty on the electronic transfer of shares by way of the CREST system of trading has necessitated some modifications to the collection of stamp duty in light of the absence of an instrument upon which to impress the duty. The transfer of title through CREST, or any other relevant system, shall be deemed to be an executed conveyance and the date of execution will be deemed to be the date that the operator instruction is generated.[107] The terms 'operator instruction' and 'generate' shall have the same meaning as under the Companies Act 1990 (Uncertificated Securities) Regulations 1996.[108]

[15.55] Such transactions are liable to *ad valorem* duty to the amount of 1 per cent of the consideration of the transaction under the 'Conveyance or transfer or sale of any stock or marketable securities' in Schedule .1[109] The transferee is the accountable person for the duty and it becomes due and payable on the date on which the operator instruction is generated. The operator instruction is deemed to be duly stamped only when the duty has been paid to the Commissioners, the collection of which may be determined by agreement between the Commissioners and the operator of the system.[110] Failure to make payment of the duty within 30 days of the operator instruction renders the transaction liable to similar penalties as arise for failure to stamp an instrument. The Revenue is entitled to make assessments on the transferee where it appears to them that either insufficient duty or no duty has been paid. These transactions are liable for fines, interest and penalties as if there had been an instrument upon which duty could have been impressed.

---

[107] SDCA 1999, s 69(1).

[108] SDCA 1999, s 68(2).

[109] SDCA 1999, s 70.

[110] SDCA 1999, s 72.

[15.56] Certain transactions are exempt from liability to duty,[111] however, the CREST system member must retain appropriate records in sufficient detail to enable the Revenue to determine that the transfer was not liable to duty, for a period of three years.[112] Failure to keep such records renders the system operator liable to a fine of €1,265.[113] An instrument liable to duty under SDCA 1999, s 69 shall not be liable under the 'Conveyance or transfer of any kind not already described' head.[114] In addition, an instrument which retransfers, in completion of a separate contract of sale to the purchasers shall not be liable to duty under SDCA 1999, s 69, provided that both contracts are due for completion on the same day and are in fact completed within 25 days after the making or the earliest contract.[115] Finally, such transfers under SDCA 1999, s 69, are not be liable to any other duty, including fixed duties.[116] These exemptions are designed to encourage the use of electronic transfer of shares and marketable securities by:

(a) abolishing fixed duties with respect to such transactions; and

(b) maintaining the sub-sale provisions where a transfer of shares prior to their acquisition will benefit from an exemption to duty.

An instrument under SDCA 1999, s 69 shall not be liable to duty where the securities are transferred to a market maker acting in the ordinary course of business.[117] This exempts from liability the deposit of legal title into the electronic CREST system, which should encourage people to convert paper shares to electronic holdings. A claim may be made for the repayment of an overpayment of duty within six years.[118] The claim must set out the grounds on which the repayment is being claimed, the computation of the repayment being claimed, and any supporting documentation required by the Revenue.[119] In certain situations, the claim may have to be made on a particular form and by the twnety-first day of the month following the month in which the overpayment has been made.[120] Where the claimant is not resident in the State, the Revenue may require that he appoint a tax representative who has a business establishment within the State and is approved by the Revenue, who shall be personally liable to the Revenue in the event of an incorrect claim.[121]

[15.57] Stamp duty is not chargeable on any instrument which transfers securities to a member firm acting on its own behalf in the ordinary course of business.[122] The aim is to

---

111 SDCA 1999, s 73.

112 SDCA 1999, s 76(1).

113 SDCA 1999, 76(2).

114 SDCA 1999, s 73(1)(a).

115 SDCA 1999, s 73(1)(b).

116 SDCA 1999, s 73(2).

117 SDCA 1999, s 74.

118 SDCA 1999, s 77.

119 SDCA 1999, s 77(2).

120 SDCA 1999, s 77(2)(e) referring to overpayments pursuant to SDCA 1999, s 73(1)(b)).

121 SDCA 1999, s 77(3) and (4).

122 SDCA 1999, s 75(1).

exclude liability to duty for shares purchased by market makers with the intention of selling them on within a short period of time. In essence, it covers the temporary purchase of shares in the ordinary course of business. However, if these securities are not transferred to a bona fide purchaser within 30 days, then the instrument shall be liable to the full *ad valorem* duty within 14 days.[123] A member firm that fails to pay any sum due to the Revenue shall be liable to pay interest at a rate of 1 per cent per month or part thereof plus a penalty in the amount of 1 per cent of the duty per day together with the duty payable.[124] Where a member firm is claiming relief under SDCA 1999, s 75, then they shall provide the Revenue with a statement containing the following details and certificates:

(a) details of the transactions, including details of the shares, nominal value etc;

(b) details of what part, if any, of the shares have been transferred within 30 days, including the date of transfer;

(c) the amount of duty for which the transaction was liable and the amount of the actual duty paid; and

(d) a certificate that the firm was acting in the ordinary course of business and that the shares were transferred to a bona fide purchaser within 30 days.[125]

A member firm who fails to deliver such a statement is liable for a fine of €1,265.[126]

[15.58] We have already seen that a system operator is required to keep records of s 69 transactions for a period of 3 years. Failure to keep such records renders the system operator liable to a fine of €1,265.[127] In addition, where a system operator negligently or fraudulently enters an incorrect instruction which gives rise to an exemption to duty or an underpayment of duty, then they shall be liable to a fine of €1,265, together with the difference between the duty which was paid and the duty which should have been paid on the transaction. Where the incorrect instruction arises from fraud, then twice the difference in the duty is payable.[128] A system member is deemed to have acted negligently where the incorrect instruction should have come to their attention if they were acting with reasonable care.[129] The Revenue Commissioners are entitled to make such regulations to enable them to administer these provisions.[130]

Share warrants and stock certificates to bearer

[15.59] An instrument which can be used for the purpose of assigning or transferring any right or interest in a share or stock which is regarded by the sale market as being effective simply by way of delivery, shall be deemed to be a share warrant or stock

123 SDCA 1999, s 75(2).
124 SDCA 1999, s 75(3).
125 SDCA 1999, s 75(4).
126 SDCA 1999, s 75(5).
127 SDCA 1999, s 76.
128 SDCA 1999, s 76(3).
129 SDCA 1999, s 76(4).
130 SDCA 1999, s 78.

certificate to bearer. If a share warrant or like instrument is issued without being stamped, then any director or officer of the company shall be liable to a fine of €635.[131]

[15.60] Where the holder of a stock certificate to bearer, or instrument having like effect, had been entered on a register as the owner of the share of stock described in the certificate, the certificate shall be forthwith cancelled and be incapable of being re-issued to any person.[132] Any person who issues such a certificate shall incur a fine of €635.[133]

Time limits for reopening stamp duty decisions

[15.61] With effect from 1 January 2005, the Revenue Commissioners can only make enquiries or raise assessments in relation to under assessments of stamp duty for a period of four years from the date the instrument was stamped or, in the case of CREST, the date the operator instruction was made.[134]

[15.62] This time limit does not apply where the Revenue Commissioners have reasonable grounds for believing that any form of fraud or neglect has been committed by or on behalf of any person in connection with or in relation to any instrument.[135] The term 'neglect' is defined as negligence or failure to deliver a chargeable instrument or statement of liability to the Revenue Commissioners or failure to enter a correct instruction into the CREST system.[136] This provision may have the effect of limiting the ability of the Revenue Commissioners to recover stamp duty, but the parties shall require the document to be stamped to enable them enforce the document in a court of law.

Time Limits for claiming repayment of stamp duty

[15.63] With effect from 31 October 2003, a time limit of four years applies to the making of a valid claim (within the meaning of SDCA 1999, s 159A(1)) for the repayment of stamp duty. The four-year period runs from the date the instrument was stamped or, in the case of CREST, the date the operator instruction was made.

Interest on repayments of stamp duty

[15.64] SDCA 1999, s 159B provides that interest on a 'repayment' (which includes the duty and any interest, penalty or surcharge thereon) will be made where the repayment has not been made within 183 days after a valid claim. Interest is paid at a rate of 0.011 per cent per day or part thereof for the period commencing from the relevant date and ending on the date of payment.

---

131 SDCA 1999, s 65.
132 SDCA 1999, s 66.
133 SDCA 1999, s 66(2).
134 SDCA 1999, s 159C.
135 SDCA 1999, s 159C(4).
136 SDCA 1999, s 159C(1)).

Chapter 16

Adjudication and Appeals

Adjudication – introduction

[16.01] Adjudication of an instrument for stamp duty purposes involves the Revenue Commissioners determining the correct amount of duty that is owing on the instrument, if any. The effect is to finalise the amount of duty on any instrument and an instrument which has been adjudicated upon is admissible in evidence and available for all purposes notwithstanding any objection relating to duty.[1] In *BTR plc v IRC*[2] Harman J stated:

> Under the Stamp Act there is no hearing, no evidence is adduced or oral argument presented before the Commissioners of Inland Revenue, who are themselves the assessing authority, and the case contains no express findings of fact, nor any reasoning leading to a conclusion; indeed there is no true judicial process at all. Both the appellant taxpayer and the Crown agree in argument before me that the procedure are thoroughly unsatisfactory.

There are three instances where adjudication is available to the taxpayer. First, where the amount of duty assessed by the marking office is unacceptable to the party to the instrument. Second, the parties to the instrument may wish to prevent any questions arising in the future as to the correct amount of duty paid, particularly where the transaction is complex. Third, certain transactions are required by virtue of the law to be adjudicated upon. The Revenue Commissioners may themselves raise an assessment by way of adjudication.

Dissatisfaction with the marking office assessment

[16.02] Where an instrument has been presented to the stamp office for stamping and the relevant officer marks on it an amount of duty for payment which the taxpayer feels is incorrect, the instrument may voluntarily be submitted for adjudication. Where the taxpayer is dissatisfied with the assessment, in accordance with the Charter of Rights issued by the Revenue Commissioners, said taxpayer may ask to have the matter reviewed internally by a higher officer who has had no previous involvement in the case. A taxpayer who is still dissatisfied retains all rights to refer the matter to the Appeals Commissioners. This procedure provides a time and cost efficient means of having the matter disposed of. In any event, a taxpayer has a legal right to seek to have the matter referred to the Appeals Commissioners and is not obligated to pursue the internal review before so doing.[3]

---

1 SDCA 1999, s 20.

2 *BTR plc v IRC* [1986] STC 433.

3 For further details see Appendix 1 (SD3 Statement of Practice on Review and Appeal Procedures May 1996).

Voluntary submission

[16.03] Where the taxpayer desires to conclusively determine the issue of liability to duty, he may opt to submit the instrument for adjudication and gain statutory protection with respect to the validity of the instrument in evidence. Furthermore, the taxpayer is no longer liable for fines or penalties if it transpires that the assessment is incorrect.

Obligatory adjudication

Assessment of any executed instrument

[16.04] With effect from 1 November 1994 the Revenue Commissioners may assess any executed instrument to duty.[4] Where the instrument is not presented to the Revenue Commissioners they may raise such assessment as they believe ought to be charged given all the facts within their knowledge, information and belief. The accountable person shall be liable for the duty so assessed. If the instrument is subsequently delivered to the Revenue Commissioners, they may make such other assessment as they see fit.[5]

Voluntary dispositions

[16.05] Instruments effecting a voluntary disposition or operating as a voluntary disposition for less than market value must be adjudicated upon.[6] This is also the case where the instrument is a voluntary disposition with a right of revocation.[7]

Certain conveyances

[16.06] Adjudication is obligatory for the following conveyances:

(a) conveyances between blood relations where the consanguinity relief is claimed;

(b) conveyances in contemplation of a sale;[8]

(c) conveyances or leases of new houses or flats which qualify for relief;[9]

(d) conveyances to subpurchasers;[10]

(e) leases which are deemed to operate as voluntary dispositions inter vivos;[11]

(f) conveyances in consideration of marriage;[12]

---

4 SDCA 1999, s 20(1).

5 SDCA 1999, s 20(2).

6 SDCA 1999, s 30(1).

7 SDCA 1999, s 33.

8 SDCA 1999, s 33(3).

9 SDCA 1999, s 91.

10 SDCA 1999, s 46(6).

11 SDCA 1999, s 54(2).

12 SDCA 1999, s 30. Note: Marriage is not sufficient consideration in the legal sense to render an agreement enforceable. This provision concerns conveyances which take place arising from a marriage and that consideration is not valuable consideration, and the transaction is treated as a voluntary disposition *inter vivos*.

(g) conveyances involving reconstruction or amalgamations of companies and which qualify for the exemption,[13] and conveyances between associated companies where the 0 per cent rate is claimed;[14]

(h) conveyances or transfers to young trained farmers of agricultural land;[15]

(i) conveyances or transfers of property availing of farm consolidation relief;[16] and

(j) the transfer of a site to a child.[17]

Certain corporate transactions

[16.07] Adjudication is obligatory for the following corporate transactions:

(a) the statement in connection with the issue of shares on the reconstruction or amalgamation which qualify for relief and which is filed with the Registrar of Companies;[18] and

(b) SDCA 1999, s 120 transactions which are exempt from capital duty.

Miscellaneous

[16.08] Obligatory adjudication also applies to the following:

(a) a mortgage, bond or covenant which is given to a company by its subsidiary, provided it owns not less than 90 per cent of the issued share capital of the company;[19] and

(b) an instrument which must be registered and is required to be adjudicated upon must be so adjudicated.[20]

Adjudication of an instrument does not authorise the stamping of a document after execution which cannot legally be so stamped. A statutory declaration for adjudication purposes cannot be used by any person in any proceedings whatsoever except where it relates to the amount of duty.

[16.09] Since stamp duty is now a mandatory tax, the process of adjudication might appear to offer a solution to the taxpayer in determining the best way to arrange a transaction so as to reduce the liability to duty or to decide not to proceed with the transaction. However, once presented for adjudication, the instrument has already come into existence and is liable to duty. The duty cannot be avoided. A taxpayer will only present an instrument for adjudication provided that he wishes the transaction to proceed irrespective of the liability to duty. The need for some predetermination of the liability without creating a binding obligation on the taxpayer is worthy of consideration by the Revenue Commissioners.

---

13 SDCA 1999, s 80.

14 SDCA 1999, s 79.

15 SDCA 1999, s 81.

16 SDCA 199, s 81B.

17 SDCA 1999, s 83A.

18 SDCA 1999, s 19.

19 SDCA 1999, s 83.

20 *R v Registrar of Joint Stock Companies* [1882] 21 QBD 131.

[16.10] One possibility is to present the instrument executed by one of the parties only to the transaction, for adjudication. Once adjudicated upon, the duty becomes immediately payable but if the instrument is subsequently not completed there is provision for the return of the unused stamp duty. Alternatively, the contract can be made conditional on the adjudication not exceeding a certain figure and, if it does exceed this figure, the instrument is no longer effective.[21]

Procedure for adjudication

[16.11] The taxpayer must prepare either a copy of the instrument or an abstract memorial of it. In practice, a copy is invariably used. Any additional information not available from the instrument, or a report as to the valuation of the transaction being effected by the instrument, should be prepared at the same time. The Revenue Commissioners may call for further supporting documentation as they require or as set out in the warrant of adjudication.[22] These documents together with the warrant for adjudication are submitted to the Revenue Commissioners.[23] In the case of a transfer of shares in private companies where the parties are related, the following must be submitted for adjudication:

(a) original stock transfer form, together with copy;

(b) adjudication warrant;

(c) completed form SD4;[24]

(d) copies of companies' latest audited accounts; and

(e) any relevant agreement.

[16.12] The Revenue Commissioners decide whether the instrument is liable to any duty. If it is not liable, they will place an adjudication stamp on the instrument which will confirm this.[25] The stamp normally reads: 'adjudged not chargeable with any duty' or 'AEUR-Exempt'. If the Revenue Commissioners decide that duty is payable, then they will notify the taxpayer as to the amount of the duty and the taxpayer has 14 days within which to pay the duty. When the duty is paid, the instrument will be stamped in the following terms: 'adjudged duly stamped' or 'AEUR' as well as the duty paid. If for any reason and at any time it appears that an instrument has been incorrectly stamped, the Revenue Commissioners may substitute such proper assessment as they see fit.[26]

Appeals

[16.13] If the taxpayer is dissatisfied with the adjudication then there is a right of appeal. The system was altered in 1994. Prior to this the appeal was to the High Court by way of case stated.[27] In the case of the valuation of stocks or shares in a private company

---

21 See **Chapter 13**.

22 SDCA 1999, s 20(3).

23 **Appendix 8**.

24 See **Appendix 2**.

25 SDCA 1999, s 20(4).

26 SDCA 1999, s 20(10), (11).

27 SDCA 1999, s 2).

however an appeal could be made to the Appeal Commissioners or in the case of land, an appeal lay to the Land Value Reference Committee.

[16.14] The duty adjudicated had to be paid within 14 days and it was not stayed by the lodging of an appeal. The appeal had to be made within 21 days of the assessment of the Revenue Commissioners. Once application was made, the Revenue Commissioners would state the case and deliver it to the taxpayer and the case would be set down for hearing after seven days of the case being so stated. Whilst the procedure was by way of case stated, oral evidence could be admitted, but only in rare circumstances.[28] It was open to the High Court to make such order as it saw fit. If the High Court was of the opinion that the assessment was excessive, then it would order the repayment of any such excess duty and fine or penalty, if any, to the taxpayer. No interest was allowable on the overpayment of duty. The High Court could confirm the decision of the Revenue Commissioners and the appeal was dismissed. In both cases, the court could make the appropriate order as to costs. The decision of the court is an order, not a judgment, and no right of appeal lies to the Supreme Court.[29]

[16.15] Since 1994, new provisions apply. Where an appeal is as to the amount of the duty payable, then a right of appeal by the accountable person lies to the Appeal Commissioners, provided that the duty has been paid in accordance with the assessment.[30] The appeal provisions of TCA 1997, Pt 40 Ch 1 shall apply to appeals from stamp duty, subject to certain modifications. Notice of intention to appeal must be made in writing to the Revenue Commissioners within 30 days of the assessment being raised.[31] Since the passing of FA 1995, notification of an appeal shall be made to an inspector, or other officer, of the Revenue Commissioners.[32] In the case of stamp duty, the relevant officer of the Revenue Commissioners is the Marking Officer. If the inspector or other officer of the Revenue Commissioners feels that the person making the appeal is not entitled to do so, then the inspector or other such officer shall serve notice on that person that the application for appeal is refused and give reasons for such refusal.[33] A person who has been refused the right to make an appeal, may appeal this finding to the Appeal Commissioners by written notification to the Appeal Commissioners within 15 days of being so refused.[34] On notification, the Appeal Commissioners shall request the inspector or other officer of the Revenue Commissioners to produce a copy of the notification sent to the person refusing the right to appeal and the reasons thereto. On receipt of this, the Appeal Commissioners shall, as soon as possible, either refuse the application for appeal setting out the grounds for refusal, allow the application for appeal notifying the parties concerned or arrange a hearing to determine the issue.[35] Where an inspector or other officer of the Revenue

[28] *Speyer Bros v IRC* [1906] 1 KB 318.

[29] *Onslow v Commissioners for Inland Revenue* [1890] 25 QBD 465.

[30] SDCA 1999, s 21(2).

[31] SDCA 1999, s 21(3).

[32] TCA 1997, s 933.

[33] TCA 1997, s 933.

[34] TCA 1997, s 933.

Commissioners proposes to withdraw a listing of an appeal from the Appeal Commissioners, where he believes that the appeal can be settled by agreement without resort to an appeal, he must notify the taxpayer in writing and secure the taxpayer's agreement before the appeal may be withdrawn from the listing.[36]

[16.16] The Appeal Commissioners are entitled to summon any person to give evidence on oath and to hear pleadings by any barrister, solicitor, accountant or member of the Institute of Taxation in Ireland or the taxpayer, as they deem fit. Where a person who has been duly summoned by the Appeals Commissioners neglects or refuses to appear, or to take any oath, or answer any lawful question surrounding the appeal, they shall be liable to a fine of €950.[37] An agent shall only be liable to a fine for neglecting or failing to appear.

[16.17] The Appeal Commissioners also have the power to request evidence by issuing a precept requiring the appellant to produce a schedule of information concerning the appellant's trade, profession, employment or property and the amount of his profits, or gains.[38] The grounds for dismissing an appeal have been extended to include those situations where the appellant has not co-operated with the Appeal Commissioners in the production of evidence or the answering of questions sought by the Appeal Commissioners.[39] It is for the appellant to prove his or her case on the balance of probabilities (that is, whether the appellant's version is more likely to be true than not; mathematically speaking, whether the appellant can prove his or her case 51 per cent). Having heard the case, the Appeal Commissioners must transmit the result of their decision within 10 days to the Marking Officer.[40] Once the Appeal Commissioners render their decision, a taxpayer may appeal to the Circuit Court for a full re-hearing of the case, within 10 days of the decision (or 12 days where the Commissioners send the determination of the appeal by post).[41] Where no appeal is lodged, or where there is no attendance at an appeal, the determination shall become final and conclusive. The Revenue Commissioners have no such right of appeal. On appeal to the Circuit Court, any barrister, solicitor, accountant, Member of the Institute of Taxation, or such other person as the court may deem fit, can be heard.

[16.18] Either the taxpayer or the Revenue Commissioners may within 21 days of the decision send a notice to the Clerk of the Commissioners that a point of law is in question and require that the Appeal Commissioners make a case stated to the High Court. However, immediately following the determination of the Commissioners (or within 12 days of receiving a decision sent by post), the dissatisfied party must express

35 TCA 1997, s 933.

36 TCA 1997, s 933.

37 TCA 1997, s 939.

38 TCA 1997, s 935.

39 TCA 1997, s 933.

40 TCA 1997, s 934(7).

41 TCA 1997, s 933.

this dissatisfaction to the Commissioners,[42] although in certain circumstances failure to do so may not be fatal.[43] No appeal can be made on a question of fact to the High Court.

[16.19] The costs of the appeal are carried by each side, except where the case is sent to the High Court by way of case stated. In these situations, the ordinary rules of cost apply, with costs being awarded against the party who loses. Whilst the Circuit Court appears to have the jurisdiction to award costs, the practice has been not to make any award as to costs[44] In *Arida v Inspector of Taxes*[45] the validity of an award of costs by the Dublin Circuit Court to the taxpayer, on the basis that the appeal arose from the unreasonable action of the Revenue Commissioners, is currently under consideration by the Supreme Court. Where an appellant believes that the listing of his appeal is being delayed by the inspector or other officer of the Revenue Commissioners, a written application may be made directly to the Appeal Commissioners requesting an early listing. In order for the Appeal Commissioners to grant this early listing, they must be satisfied on the basis of the information submitted to the inspector or other officer of the Revenue Commissioners, that the appeal is likely to be determined on the first occasion it comes for hearing by the Appeal Commissioners. These provisions apply only to instruments executed after the passing of the Act, 23 May 1994.[46]

Time limits

[16.20] Since 1 January 2005 the Revenue Commissioners can only make enquiries or raise assessments in relation to assessments of stamp duty for a period of four years from the date the instrument was stamped or the date on which the relevant statement was delivered to the Revenue Commissioners. In the case of CREST, this date is the date the operator instruction was made.[47] This four-year period does not apply where the Revenue Commissioners have reasonable grounds for believing that any form of neglect or fraud has been committed by or on the behalf of any person in connection with or in relation to the instrument.[48] SDCA 1999, s 159C(1) defines neglect as negligence or failure to deliver a chargeable instrument or statement of liability to the Revenue Commissioners or failure to enter a correct instruction into the CREST system. The time limit of 4 years applies for the making of a valid claim for the repayment of stamp duty within the meaning of SDCA 1999, s 159B.[49] The four-year limit runs from the date on which the relevant statement was delivered to the Revenue Commissioners or the date the instruction was made in respect of the CREST system.

---

42 *The State Multiprint Label Systems v Mr Justice Neylon* III ITR 159.

43 *Michael Buiread v Martin E Carr* IV ITR 505.

44 For a fuller discussion, see *Judge, Irish Income Tax 2005*, para 2.2 et seq.

45 *Arida v Inspector of Taxes* IV ITR 401.

46 See SD 3 – May 1996, Review of Appeal Procedures.

47 SDCA 1999, s 159C.

48 SDCA 1999, s 159C(4).

49 SDCA 1999, s 159A(1).

Valuations

[16.21] The Revenue Commissioners were empowered to determine the valuation of property under SDCA 1999, s 19, which provides that in valuing such property the Revenue Commissioners ascertain the value in accordance with s 26 of the CATCA 2003 which is the open market value basis of valuation. The Revenue Commissioners are empowered to inspect the property at reasonable times but the costs of the determination will be defrayed by the Commissioners. In *Findlays Trustees v IRC*[50] Fleming LJ stated:

> It must be assumed that the transaction takes place between a willing seller and a willing purchaser and that the purchaser is a person of reasonable prudence who has informed himself in regard to all the relevant facts ...

[16.22] In *Gray v IRC*[51] Hoffman LJ in considering 'sale in the open market' said:

> The property must be assumed to have been capable of sale in the open market even if in fact it was inherently unassignable or held subject to restrictions on sale. The question is what a purchaser in the open market would have paid to enjoy whatever right attached to the property at the relevant date.
>
> Furthermore the hypothesis must be applied to the property as it actually existed and not to some other property, even if in real life a vendor would have been likely to make some changes or improvements before putting it on the market. To this extent, but only to this extent, the express term of statute must introduce an element of artificiality into the hypothesis.
>
> In all other respects the theme which runs through the authorities is that one assumes that the hypothetical vendor and purchaser did whatever reasonable people buying or selling such property would be likely to have done in real life ...
>
> It is often said that the hypothetical vendor and the purchaser must be assumed to have been 'willing' but I doubt if this adds anything to the assumption that they must have behaved as one would reasonably expect of prudent parties who have in fact agreed a sale on the relevant date. It does not mean that having calculated the price which the property might reasonably have been expected to fetch in the way I have described, one then asks whether the hypothetical parties would have been pleased or disappointed with the result; for example by reference to what the property might have been worth at a different time ...

[16.23] Valuations of property pursuant to SDCA 1999, s 30 (voluntary dispositions) and s 34 (contracts in contemplation of a sale) are to be made without regard to any power, annuity or periodic payment reserved to which the property is subject. In addition, no regard shall be had to any right of residence, support, maintenance, or other right of a similar nature to which the property is subject, save where such right is for the benefit of the transferor, or spouse of the transferor, subject to a maximum of 10 per cent of the value of the unencumbered property.[52] Also worth noting is that the Revenue Commissioners at p 41 of the Revenue Notes for Guidance, where a voluntary disposition *inter vivos* is subject to a mortgage, allow a deduction of the mortgage

---

50 *Findlays Trustees v IRC* [1938] 22 ATC 437.

51 *Gray v IRC* [1994] STC 360.

52 SDCA 1999, s 18.

liability in arriving at the value of the benefit. Where an instrument operates or is deemed to operate as a voluntary conveyance, such fact must be disclosed to the Revenue Commissioners as part of the duty under SDCA 1999, s 8(2) to disclose all facts and circumstances affecting the liability of an instrument to duty and amount thereof. This statement must also contain a statement of the value of the property with regard to the provisions under SDCA 1999, s 54.

[16.24] The Revenue Commissioners employ a number of practices when valuing shares in a private company. These will depend on the nature of the company's activities.

(a) Trading and manufacturing companies are normally valued based on a multiple of the maintainable profits after tax, with the multiple being selected using data from quoted companies in the same industry. This multiple will be adjusted downwards to take into account certain elements such as lack of access to public markets or the size of the private company. Assets which are not required for the company's trade may also be factored into the valuation of the company.

(b) Investment or property-holding companies are normally valued on the basis of their net asset value. The Revenue Commissioners may require recent valuations of the property of investments held by the company.

(c) Companies which own or operate business in the services sector (eg insurance brokers, consulting engineers, etc) may be valued on a multiple of their turnover, fees or commission.

(d) The Revenue Commissioners also operate a discount in the valuation, depending on the size of the shareholding transferring.

   (i) Over 75% = 0 – 5% discount
   (ii) Over 50% = 10 – 15% discount
   (iii) 50% = 20 – 30% discount
   (iv) Over 25% = 35 – 40% discount
   (v) Up to 25% = valued by reference to dividends where they are paid. If no dividends are paid, a discount in the range of 50–70% is applied. [53]

[16.25] SDCA 1999, s 21(5)(b) prohibits any appeal on the value of land under SDCA 1999, s 21(2) described above. According to SDCA 1999, s 21(5)(a), an appeal on the valuation of land, a referral to the Land Value Reference Committee determines an appeal by a dissatisfied taxpayer provided such an appeal is lodged within 30 days of the determination.[54] The referee is appointed from the panel and such referee shall determine the true valuation of the property in consultation with the Revenue and the taxpayer or their agents and may make an order for such costs as he sees fit. An appeal from the referee lies to the High Court. Where the property does not exceed €635, the appeal lies to the Circuit Court where the appellant resides or the property is located and is taken to the High Court. There is a further right of appeal to the Supreme Court.

---

[53] For further details, see Bohan and McCarthy, *Capital Acquisitions Tax* (2nd edn, LexisNexis, 2004).

[54] F(1909-10)A, s 33 as amended by Property Values (Arbitrations and Appeals) Act 1960.

APPENDICES

Appendix 1

Statements of Practice

STATEMENTS OF PRACTICE (SP-SD/1/90)

Levy on Investments in Collective Investment Undertakings

1. Introduction

Section 109 of the Finance Act, 1990 imposes a levy of 3% on all investments in units of collective investment undertakings or other similar investment vehicles. This Statement of Practice is intended to provide guidance in relation to the implementation of the section.

2. Accountability

General

2.1 An accountable person is a person from whom the levy may be recovered. All persons who are involved as active participants in the sale or purchase of units are accountable persons. They include the trustees who are the persons legally responsible for the fund; the management company, as it is this entity which manages the fund and in many ways facilitates a market in units; a broker or intermediary who is usually the person an investor actually deals with; and the unit holder i.e. the investor. Any other person, including a corporate person, who actually sells units or provides facilities for a market in units is accountable. In general the provision of facilities will involve an element of handling funds invested. Where a person's role in the marketing of funds is purely advisory he will not be accountable.

2.2 With regard to all unit holders, other than trustees or a management company, persons are only accountable in respect of those units in whose sale they were actively involved eg a broker who has sold units in an undertaking will not be an accountable person in respect of units sold in an unrelated transaction in the same undertaking by another broker-

'Block' Remitters

2.3 It is desirable for all concerned that the level of administration involved in compliance be minimised. Accordingly the section provides that one person may act as a remitter of the levy on behalf of several accountable persons. Such "block" remittance agreements will discharge the accountability of the participating accountable persons other than that of the remitter in the group. Before any such discharge of accountability can take place however a person who is to be a remitter on behalf of several accountable persons should get agreement from the Revenue Commissioners, and persons on whose behalf the levy is to be remitted must satisfy themselves as to the intentions and integrity of the remitter. In general the agreement of the Revenue Commissioners will be forthcoming so long as the remitter, if a company, has a registered office in the State and in the case of a non-corporate person he or she is resident in the State. The Revenue Commissioners may require a person who is to be a remitter to enter into a security bond – this however will not be the norm.

Accountability of Brokers etc

2.4 The most likely context in which "block' remittance will take place is where a management company will remit the levy on behalf of all those brokers, etc. selling units in an undertaking which it manages. In such a case a written undertaking to the brokers from the management company that the management company will pay the levy on the broker's behalf when relied on by a broker in good faith, will discharge him or her from accountability for paying the levy. The broker's accountability will also be discharged if he or she acts in good faith upon any form of written undertaking from a remitter – such as a contract note. The undertaking need not however be a formal agreement between parties.

Accountability of Unit Holders/Investors

2.5 Unit holders should take the following steps which, in general, will discharge their accountability for the levy:

(*a*) Satisfy themselves that the person from whom they are purchasing units is registered for that purpose. They can do this by asking to see that person's registration certificate. If they are in any doubt they should check with the Office of the Revenue Commissioners. A register will be maintained by the Commissioners for public inspection.

(*b*) They should receive a written undertaking from the person selling the units that that person will remit the levy to the Revenue Commissioners on their behalf or that it is being remitted by the management company or other remitter. The written undertaking may form part of a receipt for money or be in any other form. In the case of a group remitter the unit holder would be well advised to inspect the undertaking from the management company, or other remitter, to the persons from whom they are purchasing the units.

2.6 In all cases an accountable person is required only to take reasonable steps to ensure compliance with this provision and to act in good faith.

3. Undertaking

3.1 The undertaking is the entity investment in which triggers the charge to the levy. The best known model for this entity is the unit trust. Accordingly investment in investment vehicles which exhibit essential features of a unit trust, although structured somewhat differently or calling themselves something different will be liable to the levy. The principal features of a unit trust type undertaking include (i) the collective investment of funds raised from a wide range of investors; (ii) that investment is distributed over a large portfolio of investments so as to spread risk; (iii) the investment portfolio is divided into units or shares and the value of each unit or share is determined by the performance of the underlying investments; (iv) all profits from the management of the portfolio, with the exception of expenses, are for the benefit of the unit holders or shareholders, either as income, enhanced unit or share value or the issue of additional units or shares.

3.2 While the unit trust therefore forms the basic model for the undertaking in the context of the levy the legislation acknowledges that there are variations on that model. An exhaustive list of relevant undertakings, even if possible, would not be desirable because of the many possibilities that can arise in the investment market. In cases of doubt the Revenue Commissioners will decide the matter, subject to usual appeal procedures. In doing so the Revenue Commissioners will look to the objects, structure and activities of the undertaking. Given their many similarities with a unit trust, investment companies or investment trusts are undertakings for the purpose of this levy. The levy, however, does not apply to investment in holding companies whose value is based upon controlling interests in subsidiaries.

4. Registration

4.1 Everyone who is an accountable person as set out in paragraph 2 above must register with the Revenue Commissioners. The sole exception to this requirement is a person who is accountable only because he or she holds units as an investor. This registration might be termed the principal registration and it is intended to signal to the Revenue Commissioners that person's involvement in the marketing of units generally rather than an involvement in respect of a particular undertaking.

4.2 Different registration requirements will apply for remitters and for persons who are obliged to register simply because they are involved only in the marketing of units and are not remitters.

4.3 Where an accountable person acts as a remitter of the levy to the Revenue Commissioners in respect of units of particular undertakings that person must register separately in respect of each such undertaking. The aim of this requirement is to enable accountability to be more accurately ascertained in the event of disagreement over or uncertainty about the payment of the levy on any block of units.

4.4 Where an accountable person, who has fulfilled the so-called principal registration requirements, is part of group remittance arrangements in respect of one or more particular undertakings and he or she is not the remitter for that group or groups, it is not necessary for that person to register separately in respect of each undertaking.

4.5 Where an accountable person is a branch or sub-office of a company it will be sufficient, where the company head office is the remitter of the levy on behalf of all such branches, that the head office only register. An obvious example would be banks with branch networks. Banks providing exchange control facilities are not obliged to register specifically for this purpose.

4.6 A person who 'is an accountable person on the passing of the Act has 60 days to register. Thereafter registration must be completed 14 days prior to the commencement of the sale of units. This lime limit applies to what might be called the principal registration. It does not apply where an already registered person wishes to register in respect of a particular undertaking. In this case, and where the accountable person is also the remitter of levy payments, he or she must register within 14 days of the sale of units in that undertaking.

4.7 Registration will be effected by completing the Form of Registration which is available on request from the Office of the Revenue Commissioners. A sample copy is attached to this Statement of Practice.

5. Non Residents

5.1 The levy imposed by Section 109 applies only to investments by Irish residents. To ensure uniformity among operators in the investment fund industry in regard to the criteria they adopt when establishing the residency status of an investor, a person claiming foreign residence will be obliged to make a formal declaration to this effect. A sample copy of such a declaration is attached.

Penalties

1. There are several provisions for penalties in the section. Penalties apply (1) where an incomplete or inaccurate statement is furnished and/or an inadequate payment of duty is made; (2) where an accountable person fails to deliver a statement and/or to pay, the duty and/or interest following notice in writing from the Revenue Commissioners to do so; (3) where an accountable person fails to register; and (4) where an investor purchases units in an undertaking from an unregistered person unless the investor delivers a statement and pays the duty within thirty days. Penalties of up to £20,000 or 25% of the sum invested can be imposed.
2. Interest is chargeable on late payments of the levy at a rate of 1.25% per month or part of a month.

Other Issues

1. A transfer of units by gift or inheritance will not give rise to the levy charge-,
2. A transfer of units between unit holders will be liable to the levy under subsection (16) of the section;
3. A transfer of investment within an umbrella fund structure is exempt from the levy but otherwise switching from one fund to another is liable;

4. The transfer of units by the use of bearer instruments, although infrequent, is specifically covered by the provisions of subsection (16).
5. Switching from one class of shareholding to another class within the same undertaking does not give rise to a levy charge.

Further Information

Any further information or copies of forms may be had by writing to. The Office of the Revenue Commissioners, Capital Taxes Branch (Stamp Duty), Room 208, Stamping Building, Dublin Castle, Dublin 2 or by telephoning 01 6792777, Extns: 2193, 2273, 2274. Fax No: 01-6793261.

Notes on Completion

The general scheme of Section 109 of the Finance Act, 1990 is to impose a levy of 3% on the gross investment by a person in a collective investment undertaking or any other similar investment vehicle. All accountable persons other than a person who is an accountable person solely because he owns units in an undertaking must register with the Revenue Commissioners. Significant penalties apply in the event of failure to register.

Note: A person who intends to become an accountable person must register a such not later than fourteen days prior to providing facilities in relation to the marketing of units.

This application for registration should be typewritten or completed in block capitals.

1. The full name of the applicant for registration must be shown. If the applicant is a registered body corporate the registration number should be shown in brackets after the name eg ABC Financial Services Ltd. (Cert No: 123456).
   If the applicant trades under a business name this must also be shown, for example, John Smith and Patrick Murphy t/a XYZ Investment Brokers.
2. The full postal address of the applicant's principal place of business must be shown. As all official communications from the Office of the Revenue Commissioners will be forwarded to this address any change must be notified to the Commissioners immediately.
3. As all persons involved in a market in collective investment undertakings are accountable persons all applicable for registration must state in what capacity they are applying for registration. The terms trustee and management company are self-explanatory in this context. Agent includes any person who acts in a transaction involving the sale or purchase of units on behalf of another. Intermediary includes a person who is an intermediary as defined in FA 1989 s 19. Broker includes stockbroker and investment broker.
4. All accountable persons must register at least once. In addition where an accountable person is not part of an arrangement under subsection (2) of section 109 (whereby one person undertakes to remit the levy on behalf of others who are accountable persons in respect of an undertaking) the accountable person must register separately in respect of *each* such undertaking.

When completed the application should be signed by the applicant for registration and the signatory's name and status (eg Partner/Secretary/Director) should be stated.

STATEMENT OF PRACTICE (SP-SD/2/90)

Stamp Duty on Purchases of New Residential Properties

1. Introduction and Scope

1.1 FA 1990 s 112 introduces changes to the way in which stamp duty is to be charged on transfers of new houses or apartments. The background to the section is provided for by the statement made by the Minister for Finance in his budget on 31 January 1990 when he announced his intention to introduce legislation to counter the loss of revenue which results from "a practice... whereby the intending purchaser of a new house can reduce his exposure to stamp duty by entering into separate agreements for the purchase of a site and the construction of a house on it".

1.2 As a result of the new section, stamp duty will be charged on the combined cost of the site and the building, irrespective of whether separate contracts are entered into or not, where the sale of the site and the construction of a house or apartment on that site are connected.

1.3 The section does not alter the position of the following:

(*a*) Transfers of houses and apartments of under 1,346 square feet (125 square metres) in floor area, in respect of which a floor-area certificate has been issued and which are exempt under FA 1969 s 49.

(*b*) Purchases of sites where it can be shown that no connection or arrangement exists between the sale of the site and the building of a house or apartment on that site, eg where a person buys a site and employs a builder unconnected with the sale of the site.

(*c*) Transfers of sites on which the transferee will build a house by his own labour.

2. Meaning of Connection or Arrangement

2.1 The question of the existence of a connection or arrangement, insofar as the transfer of the site and the building of a house or apartment on that site are concerned, will be determined by the facts of each case. In particular, the Revenue Commissioners will have regard to the following:

(*a*) whether building has commenced prior to the execution of any instrument of sale or lease;

(*b*) whether any relationship or association exists between the builder and the vendor of the site.

2.2 In determining the facts of a case, the Revenue Commissioners may require statements and/or statutory declarations from people concerned with the sale or lease of the land, or with building on that land, or from the persons acting on behalf of such people. The Commissioners will also have regard to other information supplied to them in response to queries.

3. Fall-Back Arrangements (s 3(a))

3.1 The section provides for stamp duty to be assessed on an amount equal to not more than 10 times and not less than 5 times (as the Revenue Commissioners consider appropriate) the value of the site if the total consideration on which the stamp duty assessment is to be based cannot, in the opinion of the Revenue Commissioners, be ascertained when the instrument is presented for stamping. This would arise where information regarding the cost of the building is not available. This type of situation is likely to be extremely unusual and the likelihood is that this option will be exercised only in very exceptional circumstances.

4. Refunds of Excess Duty

4.1 Where the stamp duty has been charged on the basis outlined at para **3.1** above, and is later shown to have been excessive, a refund of duty will be made. For a refund application to succeed, it will be necessary to prove to the satisfaction of the Revenue Commissioners that the duty paid exceeded the amount which would have been initially payable had the combined value of the site and the building been known and available at the date of the stamping of the instrument. The application for refund must be made within 3 years of the stamping of the instrument.

4.2 A refund of stamp duty will also be made in cases where, 2 years after the stamping of the relevant instrument, building has not commenced on the site. The refund would relate to the duty attributed to the cost of building the house or apartment. In this case also, the application for refund must be made within 3 years of the instrument being stamped.

5. Form of Certificate (s (5))

5.1 The section applies to instruments executed on or after 1 September 1990. Under the provisions of s (5), it will be necessary from that date for every instrument which transfers or leases land to contain a statement "in such form as the Revenue Commissioners may specify", certifying whether or not it comes within the ambit of this section. The form of words is to be as follows:

(*a*) *in cases where the instrument comes within the provisions of the section:*

"it is hereby certified, for the purposes of the stamping of this instrument, that this is an instrument to which the provisions of FA 1990 s 112 apply"

(*b*) *in cases where the instrument does not come within the provisions of the section:*

"it is hereby certified, for the purposes of the stamping of this instrument, that this is an instrument to which the provisions of FA 1990 s 112 do not apply for the reason that... (adding the reason ie specifying the type of property being transferred or leased, for example, agricultural land, existing houses etc.

5.2 Incorrect certificates included in an instrument will be deemed to be incorrect statements for the purposes of FA 1983 s 94.

5.3 In order to ensure that documents are dealt with speedily, the certificate specified above should be included in transfers and leases of land from 1 September 1990. However, in order to allow an adjustment period for taxpayers and practitioners this requirement will not be rigorously applied during the first two months of the implementation of the legislation ie until after 1 November 1990. With effect from 1 November 1990, any instrument effecting a transfer or lease of land which does not contain an appropriate certificate, will not be accepted for stamping.

6. Date of Application

6.1 As already stated, the section applies to instruments executed on or after 1 September 1990. The signing of a contract prior to that date will not, therefore, avoid the effects of the new legislation unless the conveyance is also completed (and not merely signed) before that date.

6.2 Where any sale to which the provisions of s 112 would apply has been completed prior to 1 September 1990, except only that the instrument of sale has not been stamped prior to that date, the Revenue Commissioners will accept that the provisions of s 112 will not apply to any such instrument.

7. Sites Containing Partially Completed Dwellings

7.1 Where a person enters into a contract for the purchase of a site on which construction work has already commenced, and where it is shown to the satisfaction of the Revenue Commissioners that there is no connection between the sale of the site and the employment of the builder chosen to complete the construction work, then stamp duty will be based on the amount paid for the site and the partially completed structure.

8. Commercial and Industrial Developments

8.1 For properties other than houses and apartments (eg commercial and industrial units):

(*a*) where the building on the site is not substantially completed at the date of signing of contracts and where the contract for the sale of the site and the building agreement are not interlocked, stamp duty will be assessed on the market value of the site together with the cost of the works done at the date of signing of the contracts. (A certificate from the site architect should be produced, detailing the works performed and the cost of such works at the date of the sale. This certificate, if incorrect, would be an incorrect statement for the purposes of FA 1983 s 94, attracting the sanctions provided for in that Act).

(*b*) where the building on the site is substantially completed at the date of signing of contracts;

and/or

the contract for the sale of the site and the building agreement is interlocked, stamp duty will be assessed on the entire consideration passing for the site and the building.

8.2 As a general guideline, properties will be regarded by the Revenue Commissioners as "substantially completed" where the cost of the building work completed exceeds 75% of the total cost of the building work agreed.

9. Miscellaneous

9.1 The provisions of FA 1990 s 112 replace all previous practices in relation to the stamping of new "non grant-type" houses and apartments, including those practices summarised in the Law Society's *Gazette* in November 1976.

9.2 This Statement of Practice is issued for general guidance only and is not a comprehensive legal interpretation of the section.

Statement of Practice (SP-SD/3/90)

Agreements as to Payments of Stamp Duty on Instruments (Composition Agreements)

1. Introduction

1.1 FA 1990 s 113 enables the Revenue Commissioners to enter into an agreement for composition of stamp duty with any person carrying on a business which involves instruments liable to stamp duty. The section extends the range of persons with whom the Commissioners can enter into such "composition agreements" and supersedes four earlier sections relating specifically to agreements with insurance companies (FA 1950 s 19), banks (FA 1958 s 57), bodies corporate (FA 1964 s 24) and the Stock Exchange (FA 1979 s 55).

2. Description

2.1 The essential feature of a composition agreement is that instruments which are liable to stamp duty and which are covered by an agreement need no longer be individually stamped. The agreement provides that duty which would otherwise have been paid on each individual instrument will be paid by way of composition ie a bulk payment will be made at the end of an accounting period equal to the total stamp duty which would have been paid, but for the operation of the agreement, on all instruments executed in that period. Agreements are entered into at the discretion of the Office of the Revenue Commissioners. They are of most benefit in circumstances where an institution issues a large number of standard instruments which are liable to stamp duty.

2.2 The term accounting period as referred to at **2.1** above is the period during which stamp duty is held by the other party to the agreement in respect of instruments executed during that time. The period at present varies between two weeks and three months. The length of the period depends upon the number of instruments likely to be executed, the amount of duty arising on such instruments and any special features of the business which gives rise to the instruments.

2.3 Instruments issued under an agreement must contain a statement that the appropriate duty has been or will be paid to the Revenue Commissioners in accordance with the provisions of the section. Alternatively the instruments must carry a printed medallion stamp (as do cheques at present) which states that stamp duty has been paid. The certificate or medallion stamp is sufficient to satisfy the provisions of the Stamp Act 1891 s 14 (Production of Instruments in Evidence).

3. Payment of Duty

3.1 The amount of duty to be paid to the Office of the Revenue Commissioners in respect of an accounting period will be equal to that aggregate of the amounts of duty which, but for the operation of the agreement, would have been chargeable on all of the instruments issued during that period. Payment of the duty must be made within a short interval of the end of the accounting period as provided for in the agreement. The length of the interval will depend on any special features relevant to the business creating the instruments and may therefore vary from one type of business to another. It is a matter to be agreed upon with the other party before an agreement is concluded.

3.2 Payment of duty under composition agreements must also be accompanied by accounts and any other relevant documentation showing how the payment was calculated. The actual information which the Office of the Revenue Commissioners will require is also a matter to be agreed prior to the conclusion of an agreement.

3.3 Failure to deliver a payment and/or accounts may result in a penalty of up to £100 per day for each day on which such failure continues. Provision is also made for interest charges on late payments at the rate of 1.25% per month or part of a month from the date when the default beings.

4. Supervision

4.1 The Office of the Revenue Commissioners will enter into a composition agreement only when satisfied that the other party to an agreement can establish a reliable and effective method for accounting for the duty payable.

4.2 After entering into an agreement the Revenue Commissioners will, from time to time as part of their care and management obligations, conduct regular audits of the accounting procedures used by parties to composition agreements to ensure compliance with the terms of the agreement. These audits have two aims. Firstly they ensure that agreed procedures are operating and are adequate to fulfil the obligations imposed by the agreement. Secondly audits are aimed at detecting any fraud.

5. Further Information

5.1 Any further information regarding composition agreements may be obtained by writing to: The Office of the Revenue Commissioners, Capital Taxes Branch (Stamp Duty), 2nd Floor, Stamping Building, Dublin Castle, Dublin 2 or by telephoning 01-6792777 Extns: 2251, 2252, 2254. Fax No: 01-6793261.

STATEMENT OF PRACTICE (SP-SD/4/90)

Stamp duty – Revised Stamping Procedures

The Revenue Commissioners have decided to introduce changes to the procedure for stamping counterpart and collateral instruments. These changes are to be introduced in the interests of improving the service provided to taxpayers and their agents.

Counterpart Instruments

At present counterpart instruments are impressed with a £10 "money" stamp and a blue stamp indicating that the instrument is a duplicate or counterpart and that the original instrument is fully and properly stamped. With effect from 1 January 1991 this blue stamp will be impressed in green and it will attract the £10 charge for duplicate or counterpart instruments. The £10 "money" stamp will no longer be impressed. Thus the number of stamps will be reduced from two to one.

Collateral Instruments

At present collateral instruments are impressed with a green £10 "money" stamp and with blue stamps duplicating those impressed on the original or principal instrument. With effect from 1 January 1991 a single stamp only will be impressed in green stating that the instrument is a collateral instrument and that the principal instrument is fully and properly stamped. This stamp will attract the £10 charge for collateral instruments. The £10 "money" stamp will not be impressed. As a result of this change to stamping procedures the number of stamps will be reduced from an average of six per instrument to one.

Following the introduction of these revised stamping procedures the Stamp Duty Offices in Dublin and Cork will be able to provide a stamping service on demand for original, counterpart and collateral instruments for those who attend at the public offices. At present it is necessary to hold instruments for a time where counterpart and collateral stamping is required. In the case of instruments submitted for stamping by post is it anticipated that these changes will eliminate any significant delay in returning instruments, properly stamped, to taxpayers or their agents. These changes to stamping procedures are also an integral part of plans to upgrade the stamping facilities in our Cork Office so that a full service can be provided there early in 1991.

Statement of Practice (SP-SD/1/91)

Collection and Enforcement of Stamp Duty
Finance Act 1991

1. Introduction

1.1 This Statement of Practice relates to provisions for the collection and enforcement of Stamp Duties as amended in the Finance Act, 1991 – ss 94 to 100 and s 130. These sections bring stamp duty into line with the collection and enforcement provisions of other taxes. For the majority of those who pay stamp duty, its changed status will make little practical difference. However, those liable to duty will suffer higher penalties for late payment of duty and there are considerably strengthened provisions to combat evasion. The provisions of the Act are not retrospective. In order to provide time for taxpayers and tax practitioners to become aware of the provisions, the Act provides that they will apply only to instruments executed on or after 1 November 1991. This statement sets out the background to the changes and outlines the provisions. It also, where necessary, explains the rationale behind the provisions and indicates how they will be implemented by the Revenue Commissioners.

2. Background

2.1 As structured at present the Stamp Act 1891 imposes no direct obligation on taxpayers to pay duty on chargeable instruments, and in general it does not specify who should pay the duty. In these respects stamp duty is unique among taxes and is, for this reason, sometimes referred to as a voluntary tax. In practice, of course, many, if not most, instruments have been and continue to be stamped because of the indirect obligations to pay duty created by the 1891 Act. That Act provides that unstamped or insufficiently stamped instruments cannot be used in evidence in civil proceedings. It also imposes obligations on people charged with the responsibility for registering title to property to ensure that instruments are properly stamped and it imposes interest charges for late payment of duty. While these provisions have been reasonably successful in ensuring the payment of duty on many instruments the collection and enforcement powers in the 1891 Act are not sufficient to deal effectively with evasion and avoidance of duty. The 1991 Act also makes changes to interest and other penalty provisions which are largely designed to compensate for the erosion of monetary values since 1891 – the date when many of these penalties were last fixed.

3. Principal Provisions – Summary

3.1 The main features of the revised stamp duty regimes for instruments executed on or after 1 November 1991 are:

(a) the payment of stamp duty will be mandatory ie once an instrument which is liable to duty is executed duty must be paid and an unpaid duty liability will be a debt due to the State which can be enforced in the same manner as other taxes (s 94),

(b) payment of duty must be made not later than 30 days after execution of an instrument, unless the instrument is lodged for adjudication within that period.

In the latter case payment must be made within fourteen days of the issuing of an assessment (s 94),

(c) accountable person are specified. These are liable to pay the duty and penalties (s 96),

(d) there will be significant new penalties for fraud, and for negligence in the preparation of instruments and their presentation for stamping (s 97),

(e) transfers of property for less than full consideration must be brought specifically to the attention of the Commissioners and a statement of market value for the property must be provided (s 97(5)),

(f) the Revenue Commissioners may raise assessments of duty, correcting assessments and additional assessments even where an instrument is not presented to them (s 98),

(g) penalties for late payment of duty are substantially revised and increased in some cases. These penalties will apply to all instruments whenever executed, if presented late for stamping on or after 1 November 1991 (s 100),

(h) the impression of an adjudication stamp on an instrument will not prevent the Commissioners from recovering additional duty where due (s 94 in conjunction with s 12 of the 1891 Act),

(i) a wide range of people will be obliged to provide information relevant to a stamp duty liability (s 101),

(j) understatement of market value in the case of gifts or deemed gifts and understatement of consideration paid will expose parties to the deed to surcharges of up to 200% of the duty payable, as well as to prosecution for negligence or fraud (s 103),

(k) no change is made to the collection and enforcement procedures which already apply to instruments executed before 1 November 1991.

4. Mandatory Stamp Duty

4.1 Section 1 of the Stamp Act 1891 does not contain any obligation to pay the stamp duty charges set out in the schedule to the Act – neither as stated above does any other provision in the 1891 Act. Section 94 of the Finance Act, 1991 amends s 1 by putting stamp duty, as regards collection and enforcement, on a similar basis to the other taxes. The section provides that an instrument which is specified in the First Schedule to the Stamp Act, 1891 and which is executed in the State or which, wherever executed, refers to property situated or things done or to be done in the State shall be chargeable with stamp duty. It thus directly imposes a charge to stamp duty on such instruments. This provision does not impose any new charges; neither does it make any changes to the range of instruments chargeable to duty heretofore.

4.2 The provision in the Stamp Act, 1891 that an instrument which relates to anything done or to be done in the State is chargeable with stamp duty is capable of a very broad interpretation. In practice, the view of the Revenue Commissioners in relation to this criterion is that the instrument and/or the underlying transaction should relate to, or involve, a substantive action or obligation to be carried out or undertaken in the State. An illustration of this view would be where an instrument is executed abroad relating to foreign property where the only connection with Ireland is that one of the parties is an

Irish resident. The Commissioners' view is that in such a case the instrument would not be liable to duty.

4.3 The Finance Act, 1991 provides that duty must be paid within certain time limits. In general taxpayers have 30 days within which to discharge a liability to duty. In some cases, a taxpayer may submit an instrument to the Revenue Commissioners who will effectively raise an assessment of duty payable. In such a case the taxpayer will have fourteen days from the date of the assessment to pay the duty.

4.4 In the event of non-payment of duty on a chargeable instrument the Revenue Commissioners can proceed for payment in the same manner as for other taxes. Apart from seeking payment through the Courts the Commissioners may use powers of attachment (s 130) or instruct a Sheriff to collect unpaid duty (s 108). The powers of enforcement and collection apply to penalties in the same way as they do to the duty itself.

4.5 Until the passing of the Finance Act, 1991 an unstamped instrument was admissible in evidence only in criminal proceedings. The Act (s 99) now provides that an unstamped instrument may also be admitted in evidence in proceedings by the Commissioners to recover stamp duty.

5. Accountable Persons

5.1 The 1891 Act did not, in general, specify who should pay stamp duty in the event of the execution of a chargeable instrument. This was consistent with the absence of a direct statutory obligation to pay duty. In practice, however, where duty was significant there has been a convention about payment – eg purchasers pay in the case of sales. As stamp duty is now to be a directly enforceable tax, it is necessary that the Revenue Commissioners be in a position to identify individuals as being responsible for the payment of the duty. It is also desirable from the viewpoint of the parties that the person(s) liable to the tax is clearly identifiable so that the other can be satisfied that they have no obligation to discharge in this respect.

5.2 Section 96 of the Finance Act sets out who are to be the accountable persons. In doing so it, in general, follows existing conventions as to payment in the case of *ad valorem* duties. In the case of conveyances on sale the purchaser or transferee will be accountable for paying duty. In the case of mortgages, bonds, debentures, covenants and related instruments the mortgagee, covenantee or obligee will be accountable. The settlor will be liable in the case of settlements. Although the duty on duplicate or counterpart instrument is usually a fixed charge of £10 it is provided that the accountable person for this duty shall be the person who is accountable for the duty on the principal or original instrument.

5.3 The payment of duty in the case of gifts is an exception to the general scheme of accountability relating to *ad valorem* duty. In the case of gifts or deemed gifts the parties to the deed are accountable for the payment of duty. Paragraph **10.1** deals in more detail with the concept of a deemed gift. Its practical impact in the context of accountability will most often arise in cases of evasion of stamp duty by the understatement of consideration paid for property in the deed of transfer and where fraud cannot be established. In such a case both the vendor and the purchaser of the property will be liable to pay any unpaid duty and penalties.

5.4 All parties to instruments attracting fixed duties are accountable persons for the purposes of stamp duty. Instruments (and the duty payable) in this category include, cheques (7p), deeds of exchange (£5), general deeds (£5)

6. Preparation and Presentation of Instruments

6.1 Section 97 of the Act re-enacts s 5 of the 1891 Act in an expanded form. This latter section was the main provision which up to now obliged taxpayers to come forward with all relevant information when presenting the instrument for stamping. Section 5 as originally enacted also provides for penalties in the event of fraud. It is not always practical, however, to set out all the facts affecting a stamp duty liability in the instrument itself, as the existing s 5 of the 1891 Act provides. Accordingly the Finance Act now provides that further information can be set out in an accompanying statement. Essentially the Act seeks to maintain and re-enforce the practice whereby taxpayers or their agents provide relevant information from the outset without prompting from the Revenue Commissioners. This is in the interest of the taxpayers and their agents. Cases can be dealt with more speedily, and it makes for a more efficient administration of the tax. This approach is also consistent with the concept of self-assessment which now applies across the major tax heads.

6.2 Where s 5(2) of the 1891 Act (as amended by s 97) uses the word "practicable" in relation to the setting out of information in a deed the intention is that those who prepare deeds should draft them on the basis of normal drafting conventions and practice. Any information which is not covered by those conventions or practice but which is relevant to the stamp duty charge should be set out in the accompanying statement.

6.3 The 1891 Act provided for penalties for fraud in relation to the provision of information and preparation of instruments. Section 97 of the 1991 Finance Act, in addition, now provides for penalties in the case of negligence on the part of parties to deeds or people who draw up deeds or provide statements. The concept of negligence is potentially very wide-ranging and ultimately in any given case the courts will decide the matter on the facts. In deciding whether actions constitute negligence the Revenue Commissioners will have to consider how a court might view those actions. To assist in determining the kind of conduct which will be considered negligent the Act sets down two specific instances.

6.4 First, where an error in a deed which affects the liability of the deed to duty comes to the attention of any of the parties they are obliged to inform the Revenue Commissioners without delay. Failure to do so will constitute negligence. The fact that the error was not actually noticed will not be a defence if it would have been noticed had a person taken reasonable care.

6.5 The second instance arises in the context of gifts or deemed gifts. Where a transfer of property is made by way of a full or partial gift, stamp duty has been payable since the Finance Act, 1910 on the value of the property and not on the consideration, if any, paid. However, it is not always apparent to the Revenue Commissioners from the instrument presented for stamping that a transfer is a gift eg where some consideration is paid for property. Subsection (5) of s 97 now obliges all parties to a deed to ensure that the Commissioners are aware that the transfer is to be assessed to duty as a gift and the market value of the property must be stated. Failure to do either will be negligence on their part, unless the contrary is proven.

6.6 This provision will also have a role in dealing with evasion of duty by so-called "under-the-counter" payments. The rationale behind this approach is dealt with further in this statement at para **10.5**. Where a transfer of property involving such evasion cannot be prosecuted under fraud provisions, for lack of evidence, it will be open to the Revenue Commissioners to deem the transfer to be a gift since it has been made for a stated purchase price substantially less than market value. Accordingly, all parties to such attempts at evasion will in future be leaving themselves open to prosecution for negligence.

6.7 Subsection 6 of s 96 of the Act contains provisions intended to assist people in genuine doubt about any matter relevant to a duty liability. In such a case, if a person brings the matter to the attention of the Revenue Commissioners when submitting any instrument for stamping or assessment he/she will be deemed to have made a full and true disclosure with regard to the matter in doubt.

7. Assessment of Duty

7.1 Because stamp duty is not a mandatory tax the 1891 Act provides for assessment only where an instrument is presented to the Commissioners by a person who requires them to make an assessment. Section 94 of the Finance Act now gives the Commissioners power to raise assessments for stamp duty. This brings stamp duty into line with the other main taxes.

7.2 The failure by a person to deliver a chargeable instrument for stamping or assessment will not for the future inhibit the Commissioners in raising duty assessments. These can be raised on the basis of the best information available to the Commissioners. These assessments will be enforceable against the accountable person in the same way as if an instrument had been delivered.

7.3 Section 98 of the 1991 Finance Act amends s 12 of the 1891 Act by expanding the circumstances where assessments of duty can be made. The interaction between s 12(5) and the power of the Revenue Commissioners to raise additional or correcting assessment is worthy of note. At present where an instrument bears an adjudication stamp s (5) provides that no objection may be raised as to the adequacy of the duty paid. That position remains unaltered by the provisions of the Finance Act. In other words, once an instrument bears an adjudication stamp it is, as has always been the case, admissible in evidence and available for all purposes regardless of objections raised about the adequacy of the duty unless fraud can be established. However, if an instrument executed after 1 November 1991 is insufficiently stamped the accountable person may be proceeded against for the balance of duty notwithstanding the fact that the instrument bears an adjudication stamp. Those proceedings will not, however, in any way diminish the legal effect of the instrument itself.

8. Late Payment of Duty – Penalty Provisions

8.1 The penalty provisions relating to the late payment of stamp duty have remained largely unchanged since 1891. The Act now revises these penalties and brings them into line with current monetary values.

8.2 The existing statutory penalty for late payment of stamp duty is £10 plus 5% per annum. This is to be replaced by a penalty of £20 plus 1.25% per month or part of a month. This penalty is intended to compensate the exchequer for the loss of revenue from tax which has not been paid on time.

8.3 At present the 1891 Act provides for a further penalty, of the amount of the duty, where certain instruments, chargeable with *ad valorem* duty, are delivered late for stamping. This further penalty has fallen largely into disuse. However, this type of penalty has a role in creating a compliance environment where instruments are presented for assessment and stamping without delay. Accordingly s 100(2) of the Act provides that the accountable person shall be liable to further penalties as follows:

(1) 10% of the duty where there is a delay in presenting instruments of more than 1 month but not more than 6 months.

(2) 20% of the duty where there is a delay of more than 6 months but not more than 12 months.

(3) 30% of the duty where there is a delay of over 12 months.

8.4 It will be the general practice of the Revenue Commissioners to impose these penalties where instruments are presented late for stamping. The penalties will not be reserved for cases of serious delay only. Inevitably there will be taxpayers who although acting in good faith find that a penalty applies to them. The Revenue Commissioners have a discretion in such cases, depending on the particular circumstances, to mitigate the penalty. Claims for mitigation of penalties should be in writing and supported by documentary evidence where relevant.

8.5 The new penalties apply with effect from 1 November 1991. After that date the following will be the penalty regime for instruments executed prior to 1 November 1991:

(*a*) Where an instrument is executed prior to 1 November 1991 but presented for stamping after this date it will be charged under the existing penalty regime – £10 plus interest at 5% per annum up to 31 October 1991. Thereafter interest will be charged at 1.25% per month or part of a month under the revised penalty regime.

(*b*) Where the instrument referred to at (*a*) is presented for stamping later than 30 days after 1 November but not later than 6 months after that date the additional penalty of 10% of the duty will apply.

(*c*) The further penalties of (*a*) 20% and (*b*) 30% of duty will apply to pre-November 1991 instruments which are presented for stamping (*a*) between 6 months and 12 months and (*b*) later than 12 months from 1 November 1991, respectively.

8.6 Section 100, in particular s (6), effectively abolishes the provision in s 15 of the 1891 Act whereby instruments executed abroad become liable to penalties for late stamping only if unstamped for longer than 30 days after being brought into the country. Such instruments executed after 1 November 1991 will be in the same position as instruments executed in the State ie duty must be paid within 30 days of execution or penalties for late payment will apply.

8.7 Where an instrument has been executed abroad prior to 1 November 1991 interest and penalties for late payment of duty will be chargeable only if the instrument is not stamped within 30 days of being brought into the country. Interest and penalties will apply to such instruments with effect only from the date of their introduction into the country, not the date of execution. This preserves the penalty and interest regime which existed for such instruments prior to the Finance Act. The interest and penalties imposed after 1 November 1991 will be those provided in the Finance Act, 1991.

9. Information and Investigation

9.1 Section 101 of the Act greatly extends the scope of the existing s 16 of the Stamp Act, 1891. As provided in the 1891 Act only public officers were obliged to provide access to information for the purposes of investigating the existence and extent of a charge to duty or the existence of fraud, negligence or omission in relation to duty. Any person who is a party to an instrument or who has a document in his control or custody which is relevant to an investigation may now be required to provide this information.

9.2 The Act now makes provision for the verification of information provided and, for the taking of notes, or copies for reference or future evidence. Failure to co-operate with the provisions of s 101 will attract a fine of up to £100 per day during which the failure to co-operate continues. Under no circumstances will the Revenue Commissioners require a person to give information where he/she has a legal right to refuse. Subsection (2) of the section allows a person to refuse inspection where he has a legal right to do so, such as where privilege can be established.

9.3 The provisions of this section apply only to instruments executed on or after 1 November 1991. However, the Revenue Commissioners may use the provisions where it has been claimed that an instrument was executed before 1 November 1991 but they have grounds for suspecting that this may not be the case. This will be used to counter any attempt to back date instruments so as to escape the more effective duty enforcement provisions. In these circumstances the power will cease to be applicable if it is proven that the instrument was in fact executed after 1 November 1991.

10. Statements of Market Value and Surcharges

10.1 In general stamp duty is charged on the consideration paid for property. In the case of transfers which are gifts however, stamp duty is charged not upon any consideration paid but upon the value of the property – s 74 Finance (1909-10) Act, 1910. The section also provides for circumstances where, because the consideration paid for property is so low as to confer a substantial benefit on a purchaser, stamp duty may be charged on the basis of the value of the property. This legislation is now further strengthened in the Finance Act (s 103) so as to counter evasion and to encourage early disclosure of sales for substantially less than full consideration. Section 97(5) as referred to in para 6.5 obliges parties to an instrument to inform the Revenue Commissioners where an interest in property is transferred for less than full consideration. Section 97(5) also obliges the parties to state a market value for the property concerned. Failure to do either will lead to a prosecution for negligence.

10.2 Once a market value is stated for property the Revenue Commissioners may accept or reject it. If a higher "ascertained" value (see para **10.3**) is established surcharges for undervaluation will be imposed. The surcharges are as follows:

(*a*) 50% of the duty chargeable where the understatement of value is between 10% and 30% with a proviso that an understatement by less than £5,000 will attract no surcharge;

(*b*) 100% of the duty chargeable where the understatement of value is between 30% and 50%;

(*c*) 200% of the duty chargeable where the understatement of value is greater than 50%.

10.3 The amount of surcharge imposed depends upon the degree of deviation from what the legislation refers to as the "ascertained value". In practice the ascertained value will be the value established after any appeals against valuation have been determined. There are effectively four stages in the valuation process to which a taxpayer may have recourse before a surcharge is imposed. Firstly the taxpayer or his/her agent will make a valuation. The Revenue Commissioners will also make a valuation – often with the assistance of the Valuation Office. Where agreement cannot be reached the taxpayer may appeal to the Land Values Reference Committee and from there to the Circuit Court.

10.4 The provisions relating to surcharges are anti-evasion measures and they are aimed at two instances of evasion in particular. The first involves transfers or assignments which are outright or partial gifts. Taxpayers are encouraged, by the serious penalties for default, to state realistic market values when paying duty.

10.5 The second form of evasion which is targeted by this section are so-called "under-the-counter" payments. These transactions constitute fraud and they will be dealt with as such where fraud can be proven. The investigation provisions in s 101 of the Act will greatly enhance Revenue's powers in this area. In addition where there is suspicion of fraud because property has changed hands for a stated value which is clearly less than the market value the provisions regarding the purchase of property for less than full value will provide an alternative course of action against evaders. Parties to the transaction will be liable to penalties under s 97 of the Act for failure to declare that a deemed gift was involved. Secondly, they will be liable to surcharge under the provisions of s 101.

Statement of Practice (SP-SD/1/92)

Amnesty for Stamp Duties

1. Introduction

1.1 In his budget speech on 29 January, the Minister for Finance announced an amnesty to encourage the payment of stamp duties outstanding on documents executed prior to 1 November 1991. The amnesty as proposed will apply to interest and other penalties for the late payment of duty. It is effective from 30 January 1992. Because of the revised stamp duty regime brought about by FA 1991 interest and penalties on duty outstanding on documents executed prior to 1 November 1991 can in many cases be very substantial. The amnesty will give taxpayers a once-off opportunity to settle any long outstanding stamp duty liabilities without payment of interest or penalties.

2. Details of Amnesty

(i) the amnesty will apply to instruments executed prior to 1 November 1991 only;
(ii) during the period of the amnesty interest or any other penalty for late payment of duty will be mitigated;
(iii) full mitigation will apply to duty paid from 30 January 1992 to 30 June 1992. Instruments executed prior to 1 November 1991 and on which duty is paid during that period will not be charged any interest or other penalty for late payment;
(iv) interest and other penalties will again commence from 1 July 1992;
(v) where duty is paid on any instrument executed prior to 1 November 1991, between 1 July 1992 and 30 September 1992, interest and other penalties will be charged only from 1 July 1992;
(vi) the amnesty will end on 30 September 1992;
(vii) where duty is paid on any instrument executed prior to 1 November 1991, on or after 1 October 1992, interest and other penalties for late payment will be charged from the date of execution of that instrument;
(viii) the amnesty will not apply to companies capital duty, to duty payable on credit and charge cards or to duty payable by way of levies;
(ix) the amnesty will apply to any duty payable as a result of the withdrawal of reliefs under FA 1965 s 31 (reconstructions and amalgamations) and FA 1952 s 19 (transactions between associated companies).

3. Revised Stamp Duty Regime

3.1 FA 1991 substantially altered the collection and enforcement of stamp duty. The following changes to the stamp duty regime were made:

(*a*) payment of stamp duty was made mandatory within 30 days of the execution of an instrument;
(*b*) interest and penalties for late payment were substantially increased;
(*c*) greater responsibility was imposed on taxpayers and their agents to ensure that all relevant information is provided to the Revenue Commissioners when instruments are presented for stamping;

(*d*) the Commissioners were given greatly improved powers of investigation and assessment;

(*e*) surcharges were introduced for the understatement of consideration or market value.

3.2 The revised stamp duty regime applies only to instruments executed on or after 1 November 1991. Instruments executed prior to that date are not affected. However, the revised penalties for late payment of stamp duty apply to these instruments with effect from 1 November 1991. Accordingly, where the stamp duty on an instrument, executed prior to 1 November 1991, is paid after that date a range of interest charges and penalties will apply. With regard to interest, this will be charged on outstanding duty at 5% per annum up to 31 October 1991 and at 1.25% per month or part of a month thereafter. The penalties of 10%, 20% and 30% of the duty provided by FA 1991 will apply to the outstanding duty as if the instrument had been executed on 1 November 1991. In practice this means that all such instruments are now liable to a penalty charge of 10% of duty in addition to interest. With effect from 1 May 1992 any such instrument would attract a penalty of 20% of duty plus interest and on 1 November 1992 it would attract a penalty of 30% of duty plus interest.

Increase in Certain Stamp Duty Charges

In his budget speech the Minister for Finance announced that certain legal documents which at present attract a stamp duty charge of £5 would, for the future, attract a £10 charge. The increase in duty will apply only to those documents which are executed on or after 1 February 1992. Documents executed before 1 February, but which are stamped on or after that date will remain chargeable at £5. The documents fall under a number of residual charging provisions in stamp duty law. The following is a full list:

Stamp Act 1891

First Schedule Headings

Appointment of a new trustee;

Bond not charged under the bond, covenant heading;

Conveyance not chargeable with *ad valorem* duty;

Covenant;

Declaration of any use or trust;

Deed – any document under seal not charged under any other heading, eg a grant of a right of way, appointment of a receiver of property;

Instruments effecting a exchange;

Marketable security – a deed which is not a transfer on sale;

Instrument effecting a partition or division of property;

Release of renunciation of property or a right to property;

Revocation (eg a trust);

Surrender of any property or a right to property.

Stamp Act 1891

s 56	an instrument securing payments where property is purchased by periodical payments;
s 59	contract for the sale of certain property – no lands;
s 62	appointment of new trustee;
s 106	where several instruments are executed for the purposes of settling property only one is to be charged with *ad valorem* duty where the duty exceeds £5;

FA 1902

s 9	an instrument effecting the retirement of a trustee;

FA 1920

s 42	a transfer of stock to a dealer to facilitate a market in stocks. This charge arises very infrequently;

FA 1961

s 30	the duty on mortgage from a company to a subsidiary is not to exceed £5.

STATEMENT OF PRACTICE (SP-SD/2/92)

Use of Registered Post in Stamp Duty

The Delivery by Mail of Stamped Instruments – Permanent Suspension of Registered Post

1. Background

Until 1989 it had been the practice of the Revenue Commissioners to use registered post when returning stamped instruments to taxpayers and their agents. This use of registered post had to be suspended late in 1988 because of an industrial dispute in An Post and documents were despatched by ordinary post. The experience with the security of the ordinary post was sufficiently satisfactory during the period of the dispute to justify a subsequent pilot study involving the general suspension of the use of registered post for a trial period.

2. Results of the Pilot Study

The operation of the pilot study has been reviewed and the results are very positive:

- there has been no increase in the number of instruments mislaid in the post – the incidence of loss continues to be very low;
- there appears to be an overwhelming acceptance by taxpayers and their agents that the use of non-registered post is adequately reliable;
- no cases have been brought to the attention of the Revenue Commissioners where taxpayers suffered significant financial loss due to the loss of instruments;
- administrative savings and savings on postal costs have been significant;

3. Implications

These results indicate that:

- the ordinary postal service is highly reliable and as a result the probability of the loss of instruments is very low;
- in the unlikely event of the loss of instruments the damage caused to a taxpayer is unlikely to be significant and is in general easily remedied;
- given the low probability of loss and the fact that where loss of an instrument does occur the cost to the taxpayer is, in general small, the very significant costs associated with returning all instruments by registered post cannot be justified given the duty of the Revenue Commissioners to conduct their care and management functions in a cost effective manner;
- the administration associated with the use of registered post makes a large and, in the view of the Revenue Commissioners, unnecessary demand on staff resources which detracts from the postal stamping service and from administration of taxes generally.

Accordingly, the Revenue Commissioners have decided permanently to suspend the use of registered post for the return of stamped instruments. All instruments submitted through the postal stamping service will be returned to taxpayers or their agents by ordinary post.

4. Alternative Arrangements

While the Revenue Commissioners are satisfied that in all the circumstances the use of the ordinary postal service is an adequate method of returning instruments to taxpayers or their agents some people may wish to take special precautions. In such cases the Revenue Commissioners will provide facilities so that instruments can be collected from the Stamp Duty offices in Dublin or Cork. Where taxpayers or their agents wish to avail of this service they should indicate as such when submitting the instruments for stamping so that they can be contacted by the Stamp Duty Office when the instruments are ready for collection.

STATEMENT OF PRACTICE (SP-SD/3/92)

Stamp Duty on Mortgages and Further Advances

1. Introduction

1.1 This Statement of Practice has been produced in consultation with the Land Registry and the Registry of Deeds. The purpose of the Statement is to ensure a consistent approach in the treatment of mortgages and further advances by the Revenue Commissioners, in charging stamp duty and by the Registries, in registering charges.

2. Fixed Sum Mortgages and Deeds of Further Charge

2.1 Where an instrument acts as a security for a fixed amount the instrument must be stamped with duty to cover the amount stated in the instrument unless duty is not chargeable because the amount does not exceed £20,000.

2.2 It is now common practice, in the case of fixed sum mortgages, to make further advances from time to time to the mortgagor. Various instruments are employed to effect these advances. Deeds of further charge are the most common type of instrument used. Heretofore it has been die practice of the Revenue Commissioners to charge duty on such instruments by reference to the amount outstanding on the first mortgage. These further advances are registered by the Registries, however, as separate independent charges. In order to bring consistency to the practice of the Revenue Commissioners and the Registries stamp duty will henceforth be charged on these instruments without any reference to amounts outstanding on previous advances. Where the further advance does not exceed £20,000 no stamp duty shall be chargeable. This approach will apply to all instruments presented for stamping from the date of this Statement. It will be adopted whether or not the deed of further charge makes reference to any sum previously advanced or outstanding.

2.3 Where mortgages are consolidated, stamp duty is payable on the entire sum secured by the instrument without any allowance for duty already paid. This applies only where an earlier mortgage in respect of which sums remain unpaid is discharged and the outstanding sums are consolidated in a new instrument with a further advance. Although this may appear to impose a double charge to duty on part of the amount secured this outcome is consistent with the position of stamp duty as a tax on instruments not property or transactions. It is also consistent with the treatment of different instruments as separately stampable.

3. Unlimited Mortgages and Further Advances

3.1 In the case of mortgages which are stated to be for all "present and future advances" or a similar form of wording they must be stamped to cover the highest sum at any time secured unless that amount does not exceed £20,000. Where such an instrument has been stamped to cover a particular amount and a further advance is made there are two possible charge scenarios.

(*a*) If the total amount of a further advance and the amount outstanding from previous advances does not exceed the amount for which the mortgage is already stamped to cover, no additional duty is payable.

(*b*) If the total amount of a further advance and the outstanding borrowings exceed the amount for which the mortgage is stamped to cover duty is payable – but only on the excess. Duty is paid on the excess according to the rates applying on the date of the further advance.

3.2 In all cases an instrument is liable to duty only in respect of the amount for which it is security. The duty is not effected by amounts which may be advanced under other loan instruments or equitable mortgages. These instruments will be charged separately to duty, unless of course the instruments themselves contain term interlinking them which may have stamp duty implications.

4. Capped Mortgages

4.1 The Finance Act 1990, introduced a cap on the duty payable under the Mortgage heading in the schedule of stamp duty charges. The cap applies only to mortgages or further advances made on or after 30 May, 1990. Any mortgage executed after that date which has a duty charge capped at £3,000 is capped for all future advances i.e. no further duty is payable.

4.2 Where an instrument has already been stamped with stamp duty of £3,000 or more prior to 30 May, 1990, capping will apply only to the duty payable (if any – see **3.1**(*a*)) in respect of further advances made after 30 May, 1990 – the date of introduction of this maximum charge.

4.3 The Finance Act, 1991, reduced the maximum charge from £3,000 to £500 – effective from 29 May 1991. In the case of instruments which were already stamped with duty of £500 or more prior to 29 May 1991, capping will apply only to advances made after 29 May, 1991. This, of course, is subject to paras 4.1 and 4.2 ie if an instrument has already been capped at £3,000 no duty is payable on that instrument in respect of any future advances.

4.4 Where an instrument has been stamped between the 30 May, 1990 and 28 May, 1991 inclusive with an amount in excess of £2,500 and a further advance is made the instrument will be stamped with additional duty subject to the proviso that the total duty paid since 30 May, 1990 shall not exceed £3,000.

Statement of Practice (SP-SD 1/94)

Stamp Duty on Instruments used in the Insurance Industry

1. Introduction

1.1 The insurance industry uses a wide range of instruments. Many of these are customised for a particular company or product. For this reason it would be impractical and not very useful to provide a list of documents by name and state the stamp duty payable. Instead, this Statement of Practice sets out the basic principles according to which the stamp duty on insurance related instruments can be ascertained. The statement also deals with the stamp duty treatment of group policies.

2. Main Heads of Charge

2.1 The First Schedule to the Stamp Act, 1891, contains three heads of charge relating to insurance policies. In the case of life – insurance, duty is charged *ad valorem*, i.e. according to the value of the sum assured. Where that sum exceeds £50 but does not exceed £1,000, duty is charged at the rate of 10p per £100 or part of £100. Where the sum assured in respect of a life policy exceeds £1,000, duty is charged at a rate of £1 per £1,000 or part of £1,000 of that sum. Apart from these *ad valorem* duties there are two fixed-charge duties. If a policy of life insurance is made for a period that does not exceed two years, a fixed duty of 10p is payable. In the case of all other policies, a fixed duty of £1 is payable. Included in this latter category of charge are car and household insurance.

2.2 In addition to policies, insurance companies use a great many more chargeable instruments in the normal course of their business. These, overwhelmingly, are instruments attracting fixed £10 duties, most usually under the "Appointment of a new trustee", "Declaration of trust", and general "Deed" heads of charge. Paragraph 8 provides details on these instruments.

2.3 It should be noted that the duties imposed under the heads of charge relating to insurance policies in the First Schedule to the Stamp Act, 1891, are chargeable only where the risk to which a policy relates is located in the State. Section 208 of the Finance Act, 1992, sets out the criteria which locate a risk in the State.

3. Policy of Life Insurance

3.1 As for the most part it will be life policies which give rise to the greatest amount of duty, it is important that there should be certainty about what constitutes a policy of life insurance.

Section 98(1) of the Stamp Act, 1891, provides a definition:

> "For the purposes of this Act the expression "policy of life insurance" means a policy of insurance upon any life or lives or upon any event or contingency relating to or depending upon any life or lives except a policy of insurance for any payment agreed to be made upon the death of any person only from accident or violence or otherwise than from a natural cause".

This definition comprehends term, whole of life and endowment policies.

3.2 Section 91 of the Act in turn defines "policy of insurance", as used in the above definition. It includes "every writing whereby any contract of insurance is made or agreed to be made, or is evidenced". It also provides that the expression "insurance" includes assurance.

3.3 A policy which contains a provision for the payment of money upon the death of any person is liable to duty as a policy of life insurance. So too is a policy which provides for the payment of money upon the attainment by any person of a specified age. Clearly, a policy which provides for the payment of money upon the death of, or the attainment of a specified age by, any person is a policy of life insurance. The duty on such a policy is calculated by reference to the higher of the two sums assured. Where a policy provides for the payment of a sum on the attainment by the insured of a specific age and an additional sum on his/her subsequent death, duty is charged on the total of the two sums. It should be noted that where a policy provides for nothing more than the return of premiums paid on the death of the insured it is not liable to duty as a policy of life insurance.

3.4 If the sum assured by a life policy is increased, any written endorsement of the increase is itself chargeable to duty as a life policy. A written endorsement includes a memorandum on the original policy or a letter to the policyholder recording the increase in cover. Assuming duty has been paid on the original policy, duty in this instance is payable in respect of the increase in cover provided. Increases in sums assured due to indexation, profits or bonuses require special consideration. The underlying principle is that if an additional sum assured can be ascertained on the date of execution of the policy, that sum is chargeable to duty. In the case of *term* policies (policies for periods other than whole of life), any guaranteed profits, bonuses or level of indexation must be taken into account when ascertaining the sum assured for stamp duty purposes. Increases to the sum assured which are dependent on an uncertain level of indexation, such as a consumer price index, are indeterminable on the date of execution of the policy and thus not chargeable to duty. Where a policy provides for an increase to the sum assured calculated by reference to the higher of a guaranteed level of indexation or a consumer price index, stamp duty is payable on the additional sum assured provided by the guaranteed level of indexation. In the case of *whole of life* policies, unless an additional amount payable on death is specified or can be ascertained, no account need be taken of increases to the sum assured calculated by reference to indexation, bonuses or profits for the purposes of calculating stamp duty

3.5 Some life policies provide cover for a limited period only, with an option to renew. Clearly these policies are liable to duty when executed. A liability also arises if, on conversion, a new policy is issued. Duty is then payable in respect of the sum assured. Allowance will not be made for duty paid on the earlier policy, as it is a separate instrument. If, however, a new policy is not issued, duty is payable only if the sum assured by the existing policy is increased and then only in respect of the increase.

3.6 It should be noted that the definition of life insurance policy provides an exception for a payment to be made on the death of a person only from accident, violence or otherwise than from a natural cause. The word "only" is important since its effect is that a policy of insurance which provides cover for death from natural causes or from accident is liable to duty as a life policy. However, if the policy provides for separate sums depending on the circumstances of death, duty is payable only in respect of the sum assured on death from natural causes.

4. General Stamp Duty Principles

4.1 Central to the imposition of a stamp duty charge is the requirement that there must be an instrument or document. Furthermore, the instrument must be one which falls into one of the heads of charge in the First Schedule to the Stamp Act, 1891. In deciding whether or not this is the case, one must consider the effect of the instrument. It is this, rather than how the instrument is described, which determines whether duty is payable and, if so, how much. It is essential that attention is focused on what the instrument achieves, rather than how it is commonly classified, when assessing its liability to duty.

4.2 Another principle of particular relevance in an insurance context is that for duty to be charged *ad valorem*, it must be possible to determine a sum on which to base the stamp duty charge when the instrument is executed. If no sum can be ascertained, no duty is payable, except in some cases a fixed charge. A savings contract where the death benefit is calculated on death as the unit value of the policy, and no minimum sum is guaranteed, will come within this category. It will be liable to a £1 charge only, even if it falls within the definition of "life insurance policy" as no sum assured can be ascertained on the date of execution. The same is true for policies where the benefit payable on death is specified as the encashment value of the policy on the date of death, and no minimum sum is guaranteed.

4.3 Circumstances do exist where although a definite sum cannot be ascertained on the date of execution, either a minimum or a maximum sum can. An example of a situation where a minimum sum is ascertainable is a savings contract where the death benefit is calculated on death as a multiple of the amount paid in premiums. In this case, on the date of execution, a minimum sum assured is clearly ascertainable as the relevant multiple of the first premium. Duty is payable in respect of this sum.

4.4 If, on the other hand, a maximum sum assured is ascertainable, duty is payable on this sum. In the case of some joint life policies, the sum payable may vary, depending on which of the two people dies first. In that case both a minimum and a maximum sum assured is ascertainable. Duty is always paid on the greater sum.

4.5 Stamp duty law provides that where an instrument contains or relates to several distinct matters, it is to be charged to duty as if each of these matters constituted a separate instrument. This situation is most likely to arise in an insurance context where there is a life policy providing dual cover or spouse cover. In these cases, duty is payable on the combined sum assured as if there were separate policies for each of the lives insured.

4.6 Finally, as is the case in other areas of stamp duty, a contingency principle operates in relation to policies of insurance. Where a policy provides for additional cover contingent on the occurrence of certain circumstances, the stamp duty liability must be calculated with reference to the maximum amount payable under the terms of the policy.

5. Group Policies

5.1 In the case of group life policies, when the policy is first executed duty is payable on the total sum assured in respect of all members of the group. Thereafter, no additional duty is payable unless there is an increase in the life assurance benefits provided by the policy. To ascertain if this has happened and to provide for fluctuations in the number of members in the group certain arrangements must be made. The duty payable will need to be reviewed at intervals during the life of the policy. Such reviews should take place when an insurer is making returns to the Revenue Commissioners arising under its composition agreement. In the course of these reviews duty should be charged on the total of the sum assured to people who are current members of the group *plus* any benefits paid in respect of former members. Allowance is given for duty already paid.

5.2 Prior to 28 May, 1992, retirement benefits were chargeable to duty under the Bond, Covenant head of charge in the First Schedule to the Stamp Act, 1891. Since the abolition of the Bond, Covenant head of charge, with effect from 28 May, 1992, such benefits are no longer chargeable to duty. Consequently, duty on group life and pension policies is now calculated by reference only to the total sum assured on lives plus any benefits paid in respect of former members. Such benefits do not include dependents pensions. Pension policies for individuals and pure group pension policies are also no longer chargeable to duty.

5.3 To accommodate the fluctuating nature of the group, a member is allowed to withdraw and another member to take his/her place, without any additional duty being paid, provided the withdrawing member derives no benefit.

6. Cancellation of Policies

6.1 Once a policy is executed and is effective for the purpose intended and is acted upon, there can be no refund of the stamp duty paid due to its cancellation. An exception arises where a policy is cancelled during the prescribed "cooling-off" period. In such a case, allowance for a cancelled policy can be made in the return due under the terms of the composition agreement. Outside the cooling-off period, where a policy is cancelled and rendered inoperative before becoming effective or is found to have been absolutely void since inception, duty, if paid, may be refunded. This will normally be done by offsetting any refunds claimed against any stamp duty liabilities arising when the insurer submits accounts to the Commissioners. Any such offsets should be brought specifically to the notice of the Commissioners and an explanation of the circumstances provided. A claim for a refund must be made within six years of the date of execution of the policy.

7. Miscellaneous Policies

- Critical Illness: Duty is £1 unless the policy also provides life cover. Where life cover is provided duty is charged at the rate of £1 per £1,000 or part of £1,000 of the ascertainable sum assured *plus* £1.
- Permanent Health Insurance: Duty is £1 per policy.

- Group Permanent Health Insurance: Duty is £1 per policy.
- Single Premium Life Policies: Duty is payable at the rate of £1 per £1,000 or part of £1,000 of the sum assured.

8. Non-Policy Instruments

8.1 The following are some of the more commonly occurring general instruments used by the insurance industry. The liability of these instruments depends on whether they fall, by virtue of the transaction effected by them, into one of the stamp duty heads of charge.

Declaration of Trust: Liable to £10 duty under the "Declaration" head of charge.

Declaration of Trust Pension Arrangement: Liable to £10 duty as a declaration of trust.

Assignment to Trust:

(a) Where no beneficial interest in the policy passes from the policyholder to another party no duty is payable.

(b) Where a beneficial interest in the policy passes from the policyholder to another party duty is payable at the rate of £1 per £1,000 or part of £1,000 of the surrender value of the policy on the date of assignment. The calculation of the surrender value is made without reference to any rights retained by the original policyholder. As virtually all assignments to trust involving changes in beneficial interest constitute voluntary dispositions such instruments must be submitted to the Commissioners for adjudication.

Letter of Exchange: Duty is not payable except in those cases where the document also acts as an appointment of trustees. In that case, it is liable to £10 duty.

Trust Deed – Principal Employer: Liable to duty of £10 as a declaration of trust.

Interim Trust Deed: Liable to duty of £10 as a declaration of trust.

Standard Deed and Rules for Defined Benefit Schemes: No duty.

Deed of Appointment and Removal: Liable to duty of £10 as an appointment of trustees.

Deed of Substitution of Principal Employer: Liable to duty of £10 where it acts as an appointment of trustees. **Deeds of Amendment and Adherence:** No duty.

8.2 In the case of some of these instruments they may effect two separate transactions, e.g. a declaration of trust and an appointment of trustees. The Commissioners, in these cases, will impose a £10 charge in respect of each transaction.

8.3 An important caveat should be noted in respect of the outline of charges on these instruments. If they go beyond a declaration of trust or appointment of trustees, they may fall within other heads of charge, albeit that they bear the titles referred to above.

9. Payment

9.1 The payment of stamp duty is mandatory within 30 days of the execution of the instrument. In general, an instrument which is – liable to stamp duty must be physically stamped by the Revenue Commissioners. An instrument liable to stamp duty which has not been stamped cannot be used in legal proceedings or for any purpose.

9.2 For the most part, it is impractical for insurance companies to have documents stamped individually. In recognition of this, the Revenue Commissioners have entered into agreements with most of the companies for the payment of duty by composition. Under a composition agreement, the instrument which is liable to duty is absolved from the requirement that it be stamped. Instead, the other party to the agreement must pay at regular intervals to the Commissioners the duty which would have been paid on all the instruments executed in a period. This obviates the need for stamping documents and simplifies administration for taxpayers and the Commissioners. For further information on composition agreements see Statement of Practice SP-SD/3/90: Agreements as to Payments of Stamp Duty on Instruments (Composition Agreements).

STATEMENT OF PRACTICE (SP-SD 1/96)

Exempt New Houses

Procedures under Section 113, Finance Act, 1996

Introduction

1.1 The Finance Act, 1996, simplifies procedures for claiming stamp duty exemption in respect of new houses or apartments i.e., houses or apartments which are entirely exempt under the provisions of Section 49, Finance Act, 1969. It is no longer necessary to present such instruments to the Revenue Commissioners in order to qualify for the exemption. This Statement of Practice sets out the new procedures which apply to instruments executed on or after 15 May, 1996.

1.2 The requirement that such deeds be Impressed with the "particulars Delivered" (PD) stamp still remains.

2. Background

2.1 Section 49, Finance Act, 1969, refers to new houses and apartments which come within certain floor area limits laid down by the Department of the Environment.

2.2 Under Section 49, an instrument giving effect to the purchase of a house or apartment upon the erection thereof, is exempt from stamp duty provided that it is shown to the satisfaction of the Revenue Commissioners that a floor area certificate has been issued by the Department of the Environment in respect of same. The floor area certificate certifies that, on the basis of the information available to the Minister for the Environments the floor area of the house or apartment is within the limits as laid down under Regulations made by the Minister. As the exemption could not be granted unless the Revenue Commissioners were satisfied' in practice all such instruments were adjudged.

2.3 Instruments executed prior to 15 May, 1996 had to be stamped "adjudged not chargeable with any stamp duty" before registration could take place in the Land Registry or the Registry of Deeds.

3. Section 113, Finance Act, 1996

3.1 This section applies to instruments executed on or after 15 May, 1996. It provides that the exemption from stamp duty shall apply where the instrument contains a statement, in such form as the Revenue Commissioners may specify, certifying that:

- the instrument gives effect to the purchase of a house or apartment upon the erection thereof, *and*
- on the date of execution of the instrument there exists a valid floor area certificate in respect of the said house or apartment.

The form of words is to be as follows:

"It is hereby certified that -

- this instrument gives effect to the purchase of a house/apartment [delete as appropriate] upon the erection thereof; *and*
- on the date of execution of this instrument, there exists a valid floor area certificate (within the meaning of Section 4(2)(b) Housing Miscellaneous Provisions Act, 1979) in respect of the said house/apartment [delete as appropriate]."

3.2 There is no need to present the instruments to the Revenue Commissioners in order to obtain the exemption. The requirement to have the deed stamped "adjudged not chargeable with any stamp duty" has been removed.

3.3 Where an instrument contains a certificate as at 3.1, the Land Registry and the Registry of Deeds will accept such instruments without the adjudged stamp for the purposes of registering title. There is still, however, a requirement to have the PD stamp impressed.

3.4 The furnishing of an incorrect statement under Section 1 13, Finance Act, 1996 shall be deemed to be the delivery of an incorrect statement for the purposes of Section 94, Finance Act, 1983.

4. Particulars Delivered

4.1 There is no change in the requirement to furnish particulars and to have the "Particulars Delivered" stamp impressed on instruments giving effect to the purchase of exempt new houses/apartments.

4.2 Where conveyances, transfers or leases of houses, buildings or land are made by or to a housing authority to which section 8 of the Housing (Miscellaneous Provisions) Act, 1992 (No. 18 of 1992) apply, there is no requirement to furnish particulars or to have a "Particulars Delivered" stamp impressed.

5. Miscellaneous

5.1 This Statement of Practice has been produced in consultation with the Land Registry and the Registry of Deeds.

5.2 In order to ensure that exemption is only granted in appropriate cases, selected cases will be subject to audit.

5.3 This Statement of Practice is issued for general guidance only and is not a comprehensive legal interpretation of the legislation.

Appendix 2

Stamp Duties Regulations

FINANCE ACT 1920 LAND REGULATIONS

Made by the Revenue Commissioners under section 4 of the Finance (1909-10) Act, 1910, as amended by the Finance Act, 1920

Presentation of instruments

Production of instruments in evidence

(1) Having regard to the provisions of Part I of the Finance (1909-10) Act, 1910, as amended by the Finance Act, 1920, it is necessary that, on the occasion of any transfer on sale of the fee simple of any land or of any interest in land, or on the grant of any lease of any land, for a term exceeding fourteen years, the transferor or lessor shall present to the Revenue Commissioners the instrument by means of which the transfer or the lease is agreed or agreed to be effected, or reasonable particulars thereof. The land in question is only such as is situate within the State.

(2) Under the arrangements made by the Commissioners the instrument or the required particulars thereof, may be presented at ... the following Stamp Offices at which the stamp mentioned in section 4, sub-section 3, of the Finance (1909-10) Act, 1910, as amended by the Finance Act, 1920, will be impressed:

Dublin Castle, Dublin

Cork, The Office of the Collector of Customs and Excise.

The forms referred to in these Regulations may be obtained at ... the above-mentioned offices, ... and at or through any Money Order Office authorised to transact Inland Revenue business.

(3) If the instrument itself be presented the presentation should take place, if possible, after execution by the transferor or lessor. The instrument must be accompanied either by a copy, or by an abstract such (but containing the further particulars required) as is presented with an instrument lodged for adjudication under section 12 of the Stamp Act, 1891. The abstract should set out fully, for purposes of identification, the description of the property sold or leased, and if the instrument contains or refers to a plan, a copy of

such plan should be furnished. A full statement should be made, in so far as they affect the consideration, of any easements or reservations affecting the land, of any covenant restricting its use, and of any agreement or obligation to repair, or to pay outgoings. Any covenant or undertaking or liability to discharge any incumbrance, and any covenant or undertaking to erect buildings or to expend any sums upon the property, should be set out in sufficient abstract. The official form of application for a "Particulars Delivered" stamp, duly filled up and signed, should also be lodged. The official form of abstract can be used if desired.

(4) The instrument, the abstract and the form of application, when presented, will be retained by the proper officer of the Commissioners for examination, a ticket being given by way of receipt, to the person presenting them.

(5) Assuming that the various documents or papers so presented are found on examination to contain the particulars necessary, the instrument will be impressed with the "Particulars Delivered" stamp, and will be returned on presentation of the ticket after the expiration of the time mentioned therein.

(6) Where an instrument is so stamped it will be deemed to be duly stamped so far as respects, the provisions of Part I of the Finance (1909-10) Act, 1910, as amended by the Finance Act, 1920. Unless so stamped the instrument cannot, except in criminal proceedings, be given in evidence, or be made available for any purpose whatever.

(7) The Act, (section 4, sub-section 7) provides that where any agreement for a transfer, or agreement for a lease, is stamped with the special stamp provided, it will not be necessary to stamp in a similar manner any conveyance, assignment, or lease made subsequently to and in conformity with the agreement. But, if desired, a corresponding stamp will be impressed on the conveyance, assignment, or lease on presentation of both instruments .... Similarly a duplicate of any instrument which has been stamped in accordance with the above section will be impressed with a corresponding stamp on both documents being produced at the Office for the purpose.

If, however, an agreement for a transfer is intended to be followed shortly by an actual conveyance, the Commissioners will not require the agreement, or particulars thereof, to be presented under these Regulations, but will accept the presentation in due course of the actual conveyance, or particulars thereof, as a compliance with the provisions of the Act. But an agreement for a lease, or particulars thereof, should be presented without waiting for the actual lease.

(8) The fact that an instrument has been presented under these Regulations, and stamped with the "Particulars Delivered" stamp, will not in any way affect the liability of the instrument to the ordinary Stamp Duty imposed by the Stamp Act, 1891, or any amending Act. It will be necessary therefore that the instrument, if not drawn on material duly stamped, be presented within thirty days of execution, to be impressed with the proper ordinary Stamp Duty (Stamp Act, 1891, section 15). Should, however, the transferor or lessor desire to have this duty impressed at the same time as the "Particulars Delivered" stamp, so as to avoid the necessity for a second presentation of the instrument, he should pay the amount of the duty when presenting the instrument, abstract &c. ...

(9) In the case of instruments lodged at the Head Office in Dublin Castle, Dublin, for adjudication under section 12 of the Stamp Act, 1891, the application for the "Particulars Delivered" stamp may be made at the same time, the application form being accompanied by a separate copy or abstract of the instrument, any abstract to contain a full statement as regards easements, covenants, &c. The "Particulars Delivered" stamp will then be impressed when the instrument is stamped with the adjudication stamp.

Presentation of Particulars

(10) If the instrument itself be not presented by the transferor or lessor, reasonable particulars thereof, in the form of the various documents mentioned in paragraph 3, must be furnished by him. Such particulars can be lodged at ... the offices mentioned in paragraph 2, and a receipt will be given therefor. The transferor or lessor should at the same time lodge the form of application duly filled up.

(11) The presentation of such particulars, in lieu of the instrument itself, will free the transferor or lessor from liability to the fine imposed by section 4, sub-section 2, of the Finance (1909-10) Act, 1910, as amended. But the instrument will not be "duly stamped" until it bears, in addition to the ordinary Stamp Duty to which it is liable, the special stamp mentioned in paragraph 5. Provided, however, the necessary particulars, as above, have been furnished by the transferor or lessor, the appropriate stamp will be impressed at any future date, if the instrument and the receipt for the particulars are lodged for the requisite length of time at the Head Office, Dublin Castle.

Presentation at Other Offices

(12) Where it is not possible or convenient to present the instrument or the required particulars at one of the offices mentioned in paragraph 2, it will be open to the transferor or lessor to lodge the various documents (including the form of application) at ... any Money Order Office authorised to transact Inland Revenue business, with a request that they may be forwarded to the Head Office, in the same way as documents requiring to be stamped with the ordinary Stamp Duties may now be lodged. In such cases the examination of the documents will be made at the Head Office only, and in due course the conveyance or lease or agreement, stamped as required by Part I of the Finance (1909-10) Act, 1910, as amended by the Finance Act, 1920, will be returned to the ... Post Office for delivery to the transferor or lessor on personal application for it.

Correspondence

(13) Should occasion arise for correspondence in connection with the presentation of an instrument or the delivery of particulars, the letter should be addressed to the Secretary, Revenue Commissioners, Dublin Castle, the envelope being marked in the left-hand corner "Particulars Delivered".

(14) ....

IRELAND

[(15) Paragraphs (1) to (12) of these Regulations shall not apply to conveyances or leases of houses by a housing authority, within the meaning of the Housing Act, 1966

(No 21 of 1966), under section 90 of that Act, and it shall not be necessary to present such conveyances or leases to the Commissioners or to furnish them with reasonable particulars thereof.][1]

With this exception paragraphs 1 to 12 of the above Regulations shall apply in Ireland to all conveyances on sale and leases exceeding 14 years.

Amendments

1 Substituted by SI 181/1977 with effect from 4 July 1977.

AMENDMENT

Particulars delivered

Order made by Commissioners on 13th May, 1921

The Board have decided to dispense with the presentation of particulars (Forms A and B) of all Leases for a term not exceeding 30 years, and Assignments of Leases, when the unexpired term does not exceed 30 years. On and after 18th May, 1921, the Particulars Delivered stamp required under the provisions of section 4(2) of the Finance (1909-10) Act, 1910, may be impressed, without question, on all such instruments.

In future it will not be necessary to furnish a plan of the property, except in the case of vacant building plots, or where the particulars given in paragraph 5 of the Particulars Delivered Form B, or in the copy or abstract, are insufficient for identification purposes and cannot be supplemented in any other way.

Order made by the Revenue Commissioners on 11 August 1970

The Revenue Commissioners have decided to dispense with the presentation of particulars (Forms A and B) in all cases of sales or leases of houses by a housing authority under the provisions of Section 90, Housing Act, 1966, and it shall no longer be necessary to present the transfer orders effecting such sales or leases to the Commissioners or to furnish them with "reasonable particulars" thereof.

PROPERTY VALUES (ARBITRATIONS AND APPEALS) RULES 1961

(SI No 91 of 1961)

We, the Reference Committee, in exercise of the powers conferred on us by section 33 of the Finance (1909-10) Act, 1910, the Acquisition of Land (Assessment of Compensation) Act, 1919, and sections 3 and 4 of the Property Values (Arbitrations and Appeals) Act, 1960 (No 45 of 1960), hereby make the following Rules, with the approval of the Minister for Finance in so far as they are made under the said section 33:

1. These Rules may be cited as the Property Values (Arbitrations and Appeals) Rules, 1961.

2. The Interpretation Act, 1937 (No 38 of 1937), applies to these Rules.

3. (1) In these Rules -

"the Act of 1910" means the Finance (1909-10) Act, 1910;

"the Act of 1919" means the Acquisition of Land (Assessment of Compensation) Act, 1919;

"question" means a question referred to in section 1 of the Act of 1919;

"the Reference Committee" means the Reference Committee established by section 1 of the Act of 1919, as amended by the Acquisition of Land (Reference Committee) Act, 1925 (No 22 of 1925);

"the Rules of 1911" means the Land Values (Referee) (Ireland) Rules, 1911;

"the Rules of 1920" means the Acquisition of Land (Assessment of Compensation) Rules, 1920.

(2) These Rules shall, in so far as they amend the Rules of 1911, be construed as one with the Rules of 1911 and shall, in so far as they amend the Rules of 1920, be construed as one with the Rules of 1920.

4. (1) An appeal under section 33 of the Act of 1910 to a property arbitrator may be made by sending to the Reference Committee and to the Revenue Commissioners within the period provided for by the Rules of 1911 or in a form to the like effect specifying the matter to which the appeal relates and giving particulars of the grounds of the appeal.

(2) The Revenue Commissioners shall cause printed copies of the forms of notices of appeal set out in Schedule to the Rules of 1911 to be furnished free of charge on application by any person to the Revenue Commissioners or to any person authorised by the Revenue Commissioners to furnish the forms.

5. Whenever the Reference Committee receives, pursuant to Rule 4 of these Rules, a notice of appeal in writing, it shall, as soon as may be, nominate a property arbitrator for the purpose of the reference and determination of the appeal to which the notice relates, and shall, as soon as it has nominated the property arbitrator, inform the Revenue Commissioners and the appellant of his name and address.

6. In the Rules of 1911—

(*a*) references to the Reference Committee for Ireland constituted under section 33 of the Act of 1910, shall be construed as references to the Reference Committee,

(*b*) references to a referee and the reference in Rule 8 to the referee selected shall be construed as references to a property arbitrator nominated under these Rules, and

(*c*) Rules 3, 7, 11 and 14 shall be revoked.

7. (1) Where a question has arisen, any party to or affected by, the acquisition in relation to which the question has arisen—

(*a*) may, at any time after expiration of fourteen days from the date on which notice to treat was served in relation to the acquisition, send to the Reference Committee an application in writing for the nomination of a property arbitrator for the purposes of the reference and determination of the question, and

(*b*) shall, if he sends the application specified in paragraph (*a*) of this Rule, as soon as may be after such sending, send a copy thereof to every other party to, or affected by, the acquisition aforesaid.

(2) An application under this Rule shall be in writing and shall specify the parties to, or affected by the acquisition, the land to be acquired, the nature of the question to which the application relates, the statutory provisions under which the question arises and, if compensation is claimed, the interest in respect of which it is claimed.

8. Whenever the Reference Committee receives, pursuant to Rule 7 of these Rules, a valid application in writing for the appointment of a property arbitrator, it shall, as soon as may be, nominate a property arbitrator for the purpose of the reference and determination of the question to which the notice relates, and shall, as soon as it has nominated the property arbitrator, inform the parties to, or affected by, the acquisition in relation to which the question has arisen of his name and address.

9. In the Rules of 1920—

(*a*) the definition of "arbitrator" in Rule 2 shall be deleted,

(*b*) "nomination" shall be substituted for "appointment" in each place where it occurs and "nominated" shall be substituted for "appointed" in each place where it occurs,

(*c*) references to an official arbitrator shall be construed as references to a property arbitrator nominated under these Rules, and

(*d*) Rules 3, 4, 6 and 9 and the Schedule shall be revoked.

10. The Reference Committee may, in the case of the death or incapacity of a property arbitrator nominated for the purposes of the reference and determination of an appeal under section 33 of the Act of 1910 or a question, or if it is shown to the Reference Committee that it is expedient so to do, in any other case, at any time before the determination of the appeal or question, as the case may be, revoke the nomination of the property arbitrator and nominate another property arbitrator for the purposes of the reference and determination of the appeal or question, as the case may be, and the

Reference Committee shall as soon as it has nominated the other property arbitrator, inform—

(*a*) in the case of an appeal, the Revenue Commissioners and the appellant, and
(*b*) in the case of a question, every party to, or affected by, the acquisition to which the question relates,

of the name and address of the other property arbitrator.

11. Any notice or other document required or authorised by the Rules of 1911, the Rules of 1920 or these Rules to be sent to the Reference Committee or any other person shall be deemed to be duly sent by post—

(*a*) in the case of the Reference Committee, to the Secretary of the Reference Committee, Four Courts, Dublin, and
(*b*) in the case of any other person, to his usual address.

12. These Rules shall not have effect in respect of—

(*a*) any appeal under section 33 of the Act of 1910 in relation to which a referee has been selected under the Rules of 1911 before the 21st day of December, 1960 or
(*b*) any question in relation to which an official arbitrator has been selected under the Rules of 1920 before the 21st day of December, 1960.

EUROPEAN COMMUNITIES (NON-LIFE INSURANCE) (AMENDMENT) (NO 2) REGULATIONS 1991

(SI No 142 of 1991)

1. (1) These Regulations may be cited as the European Communities (Non-Life Insurance) (Amendment) (No 2) Regulations, 1991, and shall come into operation on the 17th June, 1991.

(2) These Regulations shall be construed as one with the Principal Regulations, as amended.

...

4. (1) Article 291) of the Principal Regulations is hereby amended by the addition of the following definitions—

"the first Directive" means EEC Council Directive 72/239/EEC [OJ No L 228, 16.8.1973, p 3];

"the second Directive" means EEC Council Directive 88/357/EEC [OJ No L 172, 4.7.1988, p 1];

"undertaking", except where the context otherwise requires, means—

(i) 'for the purposes of carrying on non-life insurance in the State from an establishment in the State:
the holder of an authorisation under Article 6 or Article 23 of the first Directive;

(ii) for the purposes of carrying on non-life insurance by way of services into the State from an establishment in another Member State:
the holder of an authorisation under Article 6 of the first Directive;

"establishment" means the head office, agency or branch of an undertaking subject to Article 3 of the second Directive;

"Member State where the risk is situated" means:

(i) the Member State in which the property is situated, where the insurance relates either to buildings or to buildings and their contents, in so far as the contents are covered by the same insurance policy,

(ii) the Member State of registration, where the insurance relates to vehicles of any type,

(iii) the Member State where the policyholder took out the policy in the case of policies of a duration of four months or less covering travel or holiday risks, whatever the class concerned,

(iv) the Member State where the policyholder has his habitual residence or, if the policyholder is a legal person, the Member State where the latter's establishment, to which the contract relates, is situated, in all cases not explicitly covered by the foregoing subparagraphs;

"Member State of establishment" means the Member State in which the establishment covering the risk is situated;

"Member State of provision of services" means the Member State in which the risk is situated when it is covered by an establishment situated in another Member State;

"large risks" has the meaning assigned to it by Article 3A of the Principal Regulations, inserted by Article 5 of these Regulations.

(2) Article 2 of the Principal Regulations is hereby amended by the substitution, for subarticle (2) , of the following:

> "(2) In these Regulations any word or phrase to which a meaning is assigned by the first Directive or by the second Directive has that meaning."

...

STAMP DUTY (PARTICULARS TO BE DELIVERED) REGULATIONS 1995

(SI No 144 of 1995)

The Revenue Commissioners, in exercise of the powers conferred on them by section 107 (as amended by section 149 of the Finance Act 1995 (No 8 of 1995)) of the Finance Act 1994 (No 13 of 1994), hereby make the following regulations.

1. These Regulations may be cited as the Stamp Duty (Particulars to be Delivered) Regulations 1995.

2. These Regulations shall have effect in relation to any instrument executed on or after 1 September 1995.

3. In these Regulations "particulars to be delivered" means the particulars to be delivered for the purposes of section 107 of the Finance Act 1994 (No 13 of 1994).

4. Subject to Regulation 5, these Regulations shall apply to:

(*a*) any conveyance or other transfer on sale of the fee simple of any land or interest in land;

(*b*) any conveyance or other transfer operating as a voluntary disposition *inter vivos* for the fee simple of any land or interest in land;

(*c*) the grant of any lease of any land for a term where the unexpired term of that lease exceeds 30 years;

(*d*) the assignment of any lease of any land where the unexpired term of that lease exceeds 30 years.

5. These Regulations shall not apply to—

(*a*) any transaction creating a joint tenancy between spouses to which section 14 of the Family Home Protection Act 1976 (No 27 of 1976) relates and it shall not be necessary to present the instrument concerned to the Revenue Commissioners or to furnish them with particulars thereof, or

(*b*) conveyances, transfers or lease of houses, buildings or land by or to a housing authority to which section 8 of the Housing (Miscellaneous Provisions) Act 1992 (No 18 of 1992) relates and it shall not be necessary to present such conveyance, transfer or lease to the Revenue Commissioners or to furnish them with particulars thereof.

6(1). The particulars to be delivered shall contain the information required in the form (in this Regulation referred to as "the first mentioned form") which is set out in the Schedule to these Regulations and shall:

(*a*) be in the first mentioned form, or

(*b*) where the printed document containing those particulars has been produced with computer assistance in a form other than the first mentioned form, be in such order and layout as approximates to the first mentioned form as the Revenue Commissioners may agree to, and any such form, duly completed and signed together with a copy thereof, shall be presented and lodged along with the instrument concerned at one of the offices of the Revenue Commissioners specified in Regulation 7 of these Regulations before the expiration of 30 days after that instrument is first executed.

6(2). In the first mentioned form the reference to "Tax No" means:

(i) in the case of an individual who has a number known as the Revenue and Social Insurance (RSI) number, such number;

(ii) in the case of any other person, the reference number stated on any return form or notice of assessment issued to that person by an inspector of taxes.

6(3). For convenience of reference there are set out in the Schedule to these Regulations, after the first mentioned form, notes for the completion of that form.

7. The particulars to be delivered shall be presented at either of the following offices of the Revenue Commissioners at which the stamp known as "Particulars Delivered" is impressed.

(*a*) The Stamp Duty Office, Capital Taxes Division, Stamping Building, Dublin Castle, Dublin 2;

(*b*) The Stamp Duty Office, Customs and Excise, Government Buildings, Sullivans Quay, Cork.

8. If a form duly presented and lodged for the purposes of these Regulations is found on examination to contain the particulars necessary, the instrument to which that form relates shall be impressed with the stamp known as "Particulars Delivered" and that instrument shall be returned to the person who presented it.

Appendix 3

Council Directives

COUNCIL DIRECTIVE

of 17 July 1969

69/335/EEC

(OJ 1969 L249/25)

Concerning indirect taxes on the raising of capital amended by Council Directive of 9 April 1973 (73/79) and modified by Adaptation Council Decision of 1 January 1973 (OJ 1973, L2, 1.1.1973 p 1)

THE COUNCIL OF THE EUROPEAN COMMUNITIES

Having regard to the Treaty establishing the European Economic Community, in particular Articles 99 and 100 thereof;

Having regard to the proposal from the Commission;

Having regard to the Opinion of the European Parliament [OJ No 119 3 July, 1965, p 2057/65];

Having regard to the Opinion of the Economic and Social Committee [OJ No 134, 23 July 1965, p 2227/65];

Whereas the objective of the Treaty is to create an economic union whose characteristics are similar to those of a domestic market and whereas one of the essential conditions for achieving this is the promotion of the free movement of capital;

Whereas the indirect taxes on the raising of capital, in force in the Member States at the present time, namely the duty chargeable on contributions of capital to companies and firms and the stamp duty on securities, give rise to discrimination, double taxation and disparities which interfere with the free movement of capital and which, consequently, must be eliminated by harmonisation;

Whereas the harmonisation of such taxes on the raising of capital must be arranged in such a way as to minimise the budgetary repercussions for Member States;

Whereas the charging of stamp duty by a Member State on securities from other Member States introduced into or issued within its territory is contrary to the concept of a common market whose characteristics are those of a domestic market; whereas, in addition, it has become evident that the retention of stamp duty on the issue of securities in respect of internal loans and on the introduction or issue on the market of a Member State of foreign securities is both undesirable from the economic point of view and inconsistent with current developments in the tax laws of the Member States in this field;

Whereas, in these circumstances, it is advisable to abolish the stamp duty on securities, regardless of the origin of such securities, and regardless of whether they represent a company's own capital or its loan capital;

Whereas it is inherent in the concept of a common market whose characteristics are those of a domestic market that duty on the raising of capital within the common market by a company or firm should be charged only once and that the level of this duty should be the same in all Member States so as not to interfere with the movement of capital;

Whereas, therefore, this duty should be harmonised, with regard both to its structures and to its rates;

Whereas the retention of other indirect taxes with the same characteristics as the capital duty or the stamp duty on securities might frustrate the purpose of the measures provided for in this Directive and those taxes should therefore be abolished;

HAS ADOPTED THIS DIRECTIVE:

Article 1

Member States shall charge on contributions of capital to capital companies a duty harmonised in accordance with the provisions of Articles 2 to 9 and hereinafter called **"capital duty"**.

Case law

Capital duty could be levied on a waiver by a parent company in whole or in part of a claim against its subsidiary on the grounds that it both lead to an increase in the assets of the company and the value of the shares of the company. *Delkakabel BV v Staatssecretaris Financien* [1993] 1 CMLR 116.

A Member State was not entitled to charge capital duty solely on the basis of an increase in the nominal capital which did not contribute to the economic strengthening of the company. Ministeriet for Skatter OG Afgifter Mod Investeringsforeningen Dansk Sparinvest, Judgment of the Court 2 February 1988.

Article 2

1. Transactions subject to capital duty shall only be taxable in the Member State in whose territory the effective centre of management of a capital company is situated at the time when such transactions take place.

2. When the effective centre of management of a capital company is situated in a third country and its registered office is situated in a Member State, transactions subject to capital duty shall be taxable in the Member State where the registered office is situate.

3. When the registered office and the effective centre of management of a capital company are situated in a third country, the supplying of fixed or working capital to a branch situated in a Member State may be taxed in the member State in whose territory the branch is situated.

Article 3

[**1.** For the purposes of this Directive, the expression **"capital company"** means:

(*a*) companies under Belgian, Danish, German, French, [Hellenic,] Irish, Italian, Luxembourg, Netherlands [Portuguese,] [Spanish,] and United Kingdom law, known respectively as:

-- société anonyme/naamloze vennootschap, aktieselskab, aktiengesellschaft, société anonyme, companies incorporated with limited liability, società per azione, société anonyme, naamloze vennoorschap, companies incorporated with limited liability, [*Ανωυυμος* ' *Εταιρεια* ';] [sociedad anonima; sociedade anonima;]

-- société commandite par actions/commanditaire vennootschap op sandelen, kommandit-aktieselskab, Kommanditgesellschaft auf Aktien, société en commandite par actions, società in accommandita per azione, société en commandite par actions, commanditaire veennootschap op sandelen; [*Κατα μετοχας ετερορυθμος εταιρεια*]; [sociedad commandetaria por acciones; sociedada em comandita por accoes;]

-- société de personnes à responsabilité limitée/personenvennootschap met beperkte ansprakelijkheid, Gesellschaft mit beschrankter Haftung, société a responsabilité limitée, società a responsabilità limitata, société à responsabilité limitée.] [*Εταιρεια* περιωρισμενης ευθυωης] [sociedad de responsabilidad limitada sociedade por quotas].]

(*b*) any company, firm, association or legal person the shares in whose capital or assets can be dealt in on a stock exchange;

(*c*) any company, firm, association or legal person operating for profit, whose members have the right to dispose of their shares to third parties without prior authorisation and are only responsible for the debts for the debts of the company, firm, association or legal person to the extent of their shares.

2. For the purposes of the application of this Directive, any other company, firm, association or legal person operating for profits shall be deemed to be a capital company. However a Member State shall have the right not to consider it as such for the purpose of charging capital duty.

Case law

In *Amro Aaneden Fonds v Inspecteur der Registratie EN Successie*, the court ruled that the object of article 3(2) was to prevent the choice of a particular legal form leading to a different fiscal treatment of activities which in substance and economically were the same. Accordingly, it ruled that a grouping of persons which did not have legal personality and whose members provided capital for a separate fund with a view to making profits was to be deemed to be a capital company. However the court ruled that this article gave a discretion to Member States to determine whether or not such a grouping was to be regarded as a "capital company" for the purposes of charging capital duty.

Article 4

1. The following transactions shall be subject to capital duty:

(*a*) the formation of a capital company;

(*b*) the conversion into a capital company of a company, firm, association or legal person which is not a capital company;

(*c*) an increase in the capital of a capital company by contribution of assets of any kind;

(*d*) an increase in the assets of a capital company by contribution of assets of any kind, in consideration, not of shares in the capital or assets of the company, but of rights of the same kind as those of members, such as voting rights, a share in the profits or a share in the surplus upon liquidation;

(*e*) the transfer from a third company to a Member State of the effective centre of management of a company, firm, association or legal person, whose registered office is in a third country and which is considered in that Member State, for the purposes of charging capital duty, as a capital company;

(*f*) the transfer from a third country to a Member State of the registered office of a company, firm, association or legal person, whose effective centre of management is in a third country and which is considered in that Member State, for the purposes of charging capital duty, as a capital company;

(*g*) the transfer from a Member State to another Member State of the effective centre of management of a company, firm, association or legal person which is considered in the latter Member State, for the purposes of charging capital duty, as a capital company, but is not so considered in the other Member State;

(*h*) the transfer from a Member State to another Member State of the registered office of a company, firm, association or legal person, whose effective centre of management is in a third country and which is considered in the latter Member State, for the purposes of charging capital duty, as a capital company, but is not so considered in the other Member State.

[**2.** The following transactions may, to the extent that they were taxed at the rate of 1% as at 1 July 1984, continue to be subject to capital duty:][1]

(*a*) an increase in the capital of a capital company by capitalisation of profits or of permanent or temporary reserves;

(*b*) an increase in the assets of a capital company through the provision of services by a member which do not entail an increase in the company's capital, but which do result in variation in the rights in the company or which may increase the value of the company's shares;

(*c*) a loan taken up by a capital company, if the creditor is entailed to a share in the profits of the company;

(*d*) a loan taken up by a capital company with a member or a member's spouse or child, or a loan taken up with a third party, if it is guaranteed by a member, on condition that such loans have the same function as an increase in the company's capital.

[However, the Hellenic Republic shall determine which of the transactions listed above it will be subject to capital duty.][2]

3. Formation, within the meaning of paragraph 1(*a*), shall not include any alteration of the constituent instrument or regulations of a capital company and in particular:

(*a*) the conversion of a capital company into a different type of capital company;

(*b*) the transfer from a Member State to another Member State of the effective centre of management or of the registered office of a company, firm, association or legal person which is considered in both Member States, for the purposes of charging capital duty, as a capital company;

(*c*) a change in the objects of a capital company;

(*d*) the extension of the period of existence of a capital company.

Amendments

1 Substituted by Council Directive 85/303/EEC of 10 June 1985, art 1 with effect from 1 January 1986.

2 Inserted by Council Directive 85/303/EEC of 10 June 1985, art 1 with effect from 1 January 1986.

Case law

The granting of an interest-free loan which allowed a company to have capital available without having to bear its cost and which resulted in a saving in interest was an increase in the assets of a company within the meaning of article 4(2)(b) of this Directive as it allowed a company to avoid expenditure which it would otherwise have to bear. *Trave Schiffahrts-GmbH and Co KG v Finanzamt Kiel-Nord* [1992] 3 CMLR 777.

The absorption of a company's losses by a shareholder, pursuant to a profit and loss transfer agreement, concluded before those losses determined, did not increase the assets of that company for the purposes of article 4(2)(b) and was not, therefore, a chargeable transaction. *Waldrich Siegen Werkzeugnaschinen GmbH v Finanzamt Hagen* ECJ 38/88. See also *Commerz-Credit AG v Finamzamt Saarbruecken* ECJ 50/91.

Article 5

1. The duty shall be charged:

(*a*) in the case of formation of a capital company or of an increase in its capital or assets, as referred to in Article 4(1)(*a*), (*c*) and (*d*): on the actual value of assets of any kind contributed or to be contributed by the members, after the deduction of liabilities assumed and of expenses borne by the company as a result of each contribution. Member States may postpone the charging of capital duty until the contributions have been effected;

(*b*) in the case of conversion into a capital company or of the transfer of the effective centre of management or of the registered office of a capital company, as referred to in Article 4(1)(*b*), (*e*), (*f*), (*g*) and (*h*): on the actual value of the assets of any kind belonging to the company at the time of the conversion or transfer, after the deduction of liabilities and expenses for which the company is responsible at that time;

(*c*) in the case of an increase in the capital by capitalisation of profits reserves, or provisions, as referred to in Article 4(2)(*a*): on the nominal amount of such increase;

(*d*) in the case of an increase in the assets, as referred to in Article 4(2)(*b*): on the actual value of the services provided, after deduction of the liabilities assumed and the expenses borne by the company as a result of the provision of such services;

(*e*) in the case of loans referred to in Article (2)(*c*) and (*d*): on the nominal amount of the loan taken up.

[**2.** In the cases referred to in paragraph 1(*a*) and (*b*), Member States may base the amount on which to charge capital duty on the actual value of the shares in the company allotted or belonging to each member. This does not apply, to those cases in which contributions are made only in cash. The amount on which duty is charged shall in no circumstances be less than the nominal amount of the shares in the company allotted or belonging to each member.][1]

3. The amount on which the duty is charged in the case of an increase in capital shall not include:

the amount of the assets belonging to the capital company which are allocated to the increase in capital and which have already been subjected to capital duty;
the amount of the loans taken up by the capital company which are converted into shares in the company and which have already been subjected to capital duty.

Amendments

1 Para (2) substituted by Council Directive 74/553/EEC of 7 November 1974, art 1.

Article 6

1. Each Member State may exclude from the basis of assessment, as determined in accordance with Article 5, the amount of the capital contributed by a member with unlimited liability for the obligations of a capital company as well as one share of such a member in the company's assets.

2. Where a member State exercises the power provided for in paragraph 1 the following shall be subject to capital duty:

the transfer of the effective centre of management of a capital company to another Member State which does not exercise that power;
the transfer of the registered office of a capital company whose effective centre of management is in a third country to another Member State which does not

exercise that power;

any transaction as a result of which the liability of a member is limited to his share in the company's capital, in particular when the limitation of liability results from the conversion of a capital company into a different type of capital company.

Capital duty shall be charged in all such cases on the value of the share the company's assets belonging to members with unlimited liability for the company's obligations.

[Article 7

1. Member States shall exempt from capital duty transactions, other than those referred to in Article 9, which were, as at 1 July 1984, exempted or taxed at a rate of 0,50% or less.

The exemption shall be subject to the conditions which were applicable, on that date, for the grant of the exemption or, as the case may be, for imposition at a rate of 0,50% or less.

The Hellenic Republic shall determine which transactions it shall exempt from capital duty.

2. Member States may either exempt from capital duty all transactions other than those referred to in paragraph 1 or charge duty on them at a single rate not exceeding 1%.

3. In the case of an increase in a company's capital in accordance with Article 4(1)(*c*), following a reduction in the company's capital as a result of losses sustained, that part of the increase which corresponds to the reduction in capital may be exempted, provided this increase occurs within four years of the reduction in capital.][1]

Amendments

1 Art (7) substituted by Council Directive 85/303/EEC of 10 June 1985 with effect from 1 January 1985.

Article 8

[Subject to Article 7(1), Member States may exempt from capital duty the transactions referred to in Article 4(1) and (2) concerning:][1]

capital companies which supply public services, such as public transport undertakings, port authorities or undertakings supplying water, gas or electricity, in cases where the State or regional or local authorities own at least half of the company's capital;

capital companies which, in accordance with their regulations and in fact, pursue exclusively and directly cultural, charitable, relief or educational objectives.

Amendments

1 Substituted by Council Directive 85/303/EEC of 10 June 1985 with effect from 1 January 1986.

Article 9

Certain types of transactions or of capital companies may be the subject of exemptions, reductions or increases in rates in order to achieve fairness in taxation, or for social considerations, or to enable a Member State to deal with special situations. The Member State which proposed to take such a measure shall refer the matter to the Commission in good time, having regard to the application of Article 102 of the Treaty.

Article 10

Apart from capital duty, Member States shall not charge, with regard to companies, firms, associations or legal persons operating for profits, any taxes whatsoever:

(*a*) in respect of the transactions referred to in Article 4;

(*b*) in respect of contributions, loans or the provision of services, occurring as part of the transactions referred to in Article 4;

(*c*) in respect of registration or any other formality required before the commencement of business to which a company, firm, association or legal person operating for profit may be subject by reason of its legal form.

Article 11

Member States shall not subject to any form of taxation whatsoever:

(*a*) the creation, issue, admission to quotation on a stock exchange, making available on the market or dealing in stocks, shares or other securities of the same type, or of the certificates representing such securities, by whomsoever issued;

(*b*) loans, including government bonds, raised by the issue of debentures or other negotiable securities, by whomsoever issued, or any formalities relating thereto, or the creation, issue, admission to quotation on a stock exchange, making available on the market or dealing in such debentures or other negotiable securities.

Case law

Articles 10 and 11 of the Directive mean that it is not possible for Member States to subject "capital companies" to taxes or duties other than capital duty and the duties mentioned in Article 12. *Spa Maxi DI Ufficio del Registro de Bolzana* ECJ 15/88.

Article 12

1. Notwithstanding Articles 10 and 11, Member States may charge:

(*a*) duties on the transfer of securities, whether charged at a flat rate or not;

(*b*) transfer duties, including land registration taxes, on the transfer, to a company, firm, association or legal person operating for profit, of businesses or immovable property situated within their territory;

(*c*) transfer duties on assets of any kind transferred to a company, firm, association or legal person operating for profit, in so far as such property is transferred for a consideration other than shares in the company;

(*d*) duties on the creation, registration or discharge of mortgages or other charges on land or other property;

(*e*) duties paid by way of fees or dues;

(*f*) value added tax.

2. The duties and taxes referred to in paragraph 1(*b*), (*c*), (*d*) and (*e*) shall be the same, whether the effective centre of management or the registered office of the company, firm, association or legal person operating for profit is situated within the territory of the Member State charging the duties or taxes or not; nor may these duties and taxes exceed those which are applicable to like transactions in the Member State charging them.

Article 13

Member States shall bring into force by 1 January 1972 such provisions by way of law, regulation or administrative action as may be necessary to comply with the provisions of this Directive and shall forthwith inform the Commission thereof.

Article 14

Member States shall ensure that the texts of the main provisions of internal law which subsequently adopt in the field covered by this Directive are forwarded to the Commission.

Article 15

This Directive is addressed to the Member States.

Appendix 4

Stamp Duty (Exemptions Miscellaneous Acts)

Broadcasting Authority Act 1960, s 32
Building Societies Act 1989, s 118
Canals Act 1986, s 2
Central Bank Act 1971, ss 42 and 48
Charitable Loan Societies (Ireland) Act 1843, s 26
Common Law Procedure Amendment Act (Ireland) 1856 s 36
Companies Act 1990, s 208
Companies Act 1963, ss 64, 65 and 95
Congested Districts Board (Ireland) Act 1899, s 3
Diplomatic Relations and Immunities Act 1967 Articles 23, 28, 34 and 49
Diseases of Animals Act 1966, s 6
Electricity (Supply) Act, 1927, s 95
Erne Drainage and Development Act 1950, s 12
Export Promotion Act 1959, s 6
Family Home Protection Act 1976, s 12
Fire Services Act 1981, s 17
Fisheries Act 1980, s 62
Forestry Act 1946, ss 19, 20, 21 and 26
Foyle Fisheries Act 1952, s 9
Friendly Societies Act 1896, s 33
Glebe Loans (Ireland) Act 1879, s 8
Grass Meal (Production) Act 1953, s 4(2)
Great Northern Railway Act 1958, s 4
Harbours Act 1996, s 98
Higher Education Authority Act 1971, s 18
Hospitals Federation and Amalgamation Act 1961, s 19
Housing (Miscellaneous Provisions) Act 1992, s 8
Housing Finance Agency Act 1981, s 16
Industrial Development Act 1986, s 17
Industrial Development Act 1995, s 9
Irish Film Board Act 1980, s 33
Irish Land Act 1903, s 50
Irish Land Act 1909, s 10
Irish News Agency Act 1949, s 4(3)
Land Act 1931, s 2
Land Act 1950, ss 27, 28 and 30
Land Act 1965, s 5

Landed Property Improvement (Ireland) Act 1847, s 59
Marine Institute Act 1991, s 20
Merchant Shipping Act 1894, ss 108, 196, 309, 320, 342, 395, 563 and 721
National College of Art and Design Act 1971, s 29
National Film Studios of Ireland Limited Act 1980, s 17
National Stud Act 1945, s 5(3) and (4)
Postal and Telecommunications Services Act 1983, ss 43, 68 and 106
Railways Act 1924, s 9
Sea Fisheries Act 1952, s 30
Social Welfare (Consolidation) Act 1981, s 302
State Property Act 1954, s 6
Statute of Limitations 1957, s 60
Succession Act 1965, s 52
The Institute of Civil Engineers of Ireland (Charter Amendment) Act 1969, s 11
Transport Act 1944, s 58(3) and (4)
Transport Act 1950, ss 26, 27, 38, 39, 40, 42 and 67
Trustee Savings Banks Act 1989, s 64
Údarás na Gaeltachta Act 1979, s 25
Wildlife Act 1976, s 14 and 55

Appendix 5

Certificate of Escrow

To:

Revenue Commissioners,

Stamps Branch,

Dublin Castle,

Dublin 2.

Dear Sirs,

We hereby certify that the effective date of delivery of this instrument was the day of , 20 by reason of the fact that the delivery was subject to the title being rectified.

Yours faithfully,

Solicitor

(The necessary details for placing the deed in escrow should be inserted in the certificate of escrow).

Appendix 6

SDCA 1999, Schedules

SCHEDULE 1

Stamp Duties on Instruments

[*Section 2*]

Heading	*Duty*
AGREEMENT or CONTRACT, accompanied with a deposit.	
See MORTGAGE, etc.	
AGREEMENT for a Lease, or for any letting.	
See LEASE.	
AGREEMENT for sale of property.	
See CONVEYANCE or TRANSFER on sale.	
ANNUITY.	
Conveyance in consideration of.	
See CONVEYANCE or TRANSFER on sale.	
Purchase of.	
See CONVEYANCE or TRANSFER on sale.	
Creation of, by way of security.	
See MORTGAGE, etc.	
ASSIGNMENT.	
By way of security, or of any security.	
See MORTGAGE, etc.	
On a sale or otherwise.	
See CONVEYANCE or TRANSFER.	
ASSURANCE.	
See POLICY.	
BILL OF EXCHANGE or PROMISSORY NOTE.	
Where drawn on an account in the State	7p
In any other case:	
where drawn or made in the State	7p.

Exemptions

(1) Draft or order drawn by any banker in the State on any other banker in the State, not payable to bearer or to order, and used solely for the purpose of settling or clearing any account between such bankers.

(2) Letter written by a banker in the State to any other banker in the State, directing the payment of any sum of money, the same not being payable to bearer or to order, and such letter not being sent or delivered to the person to whom payment is to be made or to any person on such person's behalf.

(3) Letter of credit granted in the State, authorising drafts to be drawn out of the State payable in the State.

(4) Draft or order drawn by the Accountant of the Courts of Justice.

(5) Coupon or warrant for interest attached to and issued with any security, or with an agreement or memorandum for the renewal or extension of time for payment of a security.

(6) Coupon for interest on a marketable security being one of a set of coupons whether issued with the security or subsequently issued in a sheet.

(7) Bill drawn on any form supplied by the Commissioners for the purpose of remitting amounts of tax in accordance with Regulation 31(1) of the Income Tax (Employments) Regulations, 1960 (SI No 28 of 1960).

(8) Bill drawn on any form supplied by the Commissioners for the purpose of remitting amounts of turnover tax, wholesale tax, or value-added tax.

(9) Bill drawn on any form supplied by the Commissioners for the purpose of remitting amounts of tax in accordance with Regulation 10 of the Income Tax (Construction Contracts) Regulations, 1971 (SI No 1 of 1971).

(10) Direct debits and standing orders.

(11) Bill drawn on an account outside the State.

(12) Bill drawn on or on behalf of the Minister by which payment in respect of prize bonds is effected.

BILL OF SALE.

Absolute.

See CONVEYANCE or TRANSFER on sale.

By way of security.

See MORTGAGE, etc.

BOND in relation to any annuity on the original creation and sale of that annuity.

See CONVEYANCE or TRANSFER on sale.

BOND, accompanied with a deposit of title deeds, for making a mortgage or other security on any estate or property comprised in the mortgage or other security.

See MORTGAGE, etc.

BOND, DECLARATION, or other DEED or WRITING for making redeemable any disposition apparently absolute, but intended only as a security.

See MORTGAGE, etc.

CHEQUE.

See BILL OF EXCHANGE.

CONTRACT.

See AGREEMENT.

CONVEYANCE or TRANSFER on sale of any stocks or marketable securities

1 per cent of the consideration but where the calculation results in an amount which is not a multiple of £1 the amount so calculated shall be rounded up to the nearest £.

Exemption

Foreign loan security issued by or on behalf of a company or body of persons corporate or unincorporate formed or established in the State. For the purposes of this exemption a "foreign loan security" means a security issued outside the State in respect of a loan which is expressed in a currency other than the currency of the State and is neither offered for subscription in the State nor offered for subscription with a view to an offer for sale in the State of securities in respect of the loan.

CONVEYANCE or TRANSFER on sale of a policy of insurance or a policy of life insurance where the risk to which the policy relates is located in the State

0. 1 per cent of the consideration but where the calculation results in an amount which is not a multiple of £1 the amount so calculated shall be rounded up to the nearest £.

CONVEYANCE or TRANSFER on sale of any property other than stocks or marketable securities or a policy of insurance or a policy of life insurance.

[(1) Where the amount or value of the consideration for the sale which is attributable to residential property, or would be so attributable if the contents of residential property were considered to be residential property, does not exceed £100,000 and the instrument contains a statement certifying that the consideration for the sale is, as the case may be—

(*a*) wholly attributable to residential property, or

(*b*) partly attributable to residential property,

and that the transaction effected by that instrument does not form part of a larger transaction or of a series of transactions in respect of which the amount or value, or the aggregate amount or value, of the consideration which is attributable to residential property, or which would be so attributable if the contents of residential property were considered to be residential property, exceeds £100,000

9 per cent of the consideration which is attributable to residential property but where the calculation results in an amount which is not a multiple of £1 the amount so calculated shall be rounded up to the nearest £.

(2) Where paragraph (1) does not apply and the amount or value of the consideration for the sale which is attributable to residential property, or would be so attributable if the contents of residential property were considered to be residential property, does not exceed £150,000 and the instrument contains a statement certifying that the consideration for the sale is, as the case may be—

(*a*) wholly attributable to residential property, or

(*b*) partly attributable to residential property,

and that the transaction effected by that instrument does not form part of a larger transaction or of a series of transactions in respect of which the amount or value, or the aggregate amount or value, of the consideration which is attributable to residential property, or which would be so attributable if the contents of residential property were considered to be residential property, exceeds £150,000

9 per cent of the consideration which is attributable to residential property but where the calculation results in an amount which is not a multiple of £1 the amount so calculated shall be rounded up to the nearest £.

(3) Where paragraphs (1) and (2) do not apply and the amount or value of the consideration for the sale which is attributable to residential property, or would be so attributable if the contents of residential property were considered to be residential property, does not exceed £200,000 and the instrument contains a statement certifying that the consideration for the sale is, as the case may be—

(*a*) wholly attributable to residential property, or

(*b*) partly attributable to residential property,

and that the transaction effected by that instrument does not form part of a larger transaction or of a series of transactions in respect of which the amount or value, or the aggregate amount or value, of the consideration which is attributable to residential property, or which would be so attributable if the contents of residential property were considered to be residential property, exceeds £200,000

9 per cent of the consideration which is attributable to residential property but where the calculation results in an amount which is not a multiple of £1 the amount so calculated shall be rounded up to the nearest £.

(4) Where paragraphs (1) to (3) do not apply and the amount or value of the consideration for the sale which is attributable to residential property, or would be so attributable if the contents of residential property were considered to be residential property, does not exceed £250,000 and the instrument contains a statement certifying that the consideration for the sale is, as the case may be—

(*a*) wholly attributable to residential property, or

(*b*) partly attributable to residential property,

and that the transaction effected by that instrument does riot form part of a larger transaction or of a series of transactions in respect of which the amount or value, or the aggregate amount or value, of the consideration which is attributable to residential property, or which would be so attributable if the contents of residential property were considered to be residential property, exceeds £250,000

9 per cent of the consideration which is attributable to residential property but where the calculation results in an amount which is not a multiple of £1 the amount so calculated shall be rounded up to the nearest £.

(5) Where paragraphs (1) to (4) do not apply and the amount or value of the consideration for the sale which is attributable to residential property, or would be so attributable if the contents of residential property were considered to be residential property, does not exceed £300,000 and the instrument contains a statement certifying that the consideration for the sale is, as the case may be—

(*a*) wholly attributable to residential property, or

(*b*) partly attributable to residential property,

and that the transaction effected by that instrument does not form part of a larger transaction or of a series of transactions in respect of which the amount or value, or the aggregate amount or value, of the consideration which is attributable to residential property, or which residential property, or which would be so attributable if the contents of residential property were considered to be residential property, exceeds £300,000

9 per cent of the consideration which is attributable to residential property but where the calculation results in an amount which is not a multiple of £1 the amount so calculated shall be rounded up to the nearest £.

(6) Where paragraphs (1) to (5) do not apply and the amount or value of the consideration for the sale which is attributable to residential property, or would be so attributable if the contents of residential property were considered to be residential property, does not exceed £500,000 and the instrument contains a statement certifying that the consideration for the sale is, as the case may be—

(*a*) wholly attributable to residential property, or

(*b*) partly attributable to residential property,

and that the transaction effected by that instrument does not form part of a larger transaction or of a series of transactions in respect of which the amount or value, or the aggregate amount or value, of the consideration which is attributable to residential property, or which would be so attributable if the contents of residential property were considered to be residential property, exceeds £500,000

9 per cent of the consideration which is attributable to residential property but where the calculation results in an amount which is not a multiple of £1 the amount so calculated shall be rounded up to the nearest £.

(6A) Where paragraphs (1) to (6) do not apply and the amount or value of the consideration for the sale is wholly or partly attributable to residential property

9 per cent of the consideration which is attributable to residential property but where the calculation results in an amount which is not a multiple of £1 the amount so calculated shall be rounded up to the nearest £.][1]

(7) Where the amount or value of the consideration for the sale which is attributable to property which is not residential property does not exceed £5,000 and the instrument contains a statement certifying that the consideration for the sale is, as the case may be—

(*a*) wholly attributable to property which is not residential property, or

(*b*) partly attributable to residential property,

and that the transaction effected by that instrument does not form part of a larger transaction or of a series of transactions in respect of which the amount or value, or the aggregate amount or value, of the consideration which is attributable to property which is not residential property exceeds £5,000:

for the consideration which is attributable to property which is not residential property — Exempt.

(8) Where paragraph (7) does not apply and the amount or value of the consideration for the sale which is attributable to property which is not residential property does not exceed £10,000 and the instrument contains a statement certifying that the consideration for the sale is, as the case may be—

(*a*) wholly attributable to property which is not residential property, or

(*b*) partly attributable to residential property,

and that the transaction effected by that instrument does not form part of a larger transaction or of a series of transactions in respect of which the amount or value, or the aggregate amount or value, of the consideration which is attributable to property which is not residential property exceeds £10,000

1 per cent of the consideration which is attributable to property which is not residential property but where the calculation results in an amount which is not a multiple of £1 the amount so calculated shall be rounded up to the nearest £.

(9) Where paragraphs (7) and (8) do not apply and the amount or value of the consideration for the sale which is attributable to property which is not residential property does not exceed £15,000 and the instrument contains a statement certifying that the consideration for the sale is, as the case may be—

(a) wholly attributable to property which is not residential property, or

(b) partly attributable to residential property,

and that the transaction effected by that instrument does not form part of a larger transaction or of a series of transactions in respect of which the amount or value, or the aggregate amount or value, of the consideration which is attributable to property which is not residential property exceeds £15,000

2 per cent of the consideration which is attributable to property which is not residential property but where the calculation results in an amount which is not a multiple of £1 the amount so calculated shall be rounded up to the nearest £.

(10) Where paragraphs (7) to (9) do not apply and the amount or value of the consideration for the sale which is attributable to property which is not residential property does not exceed £25,000 and the instrument contains a statement certifying that the consideration for the sale is, as the case may be—

(a) wholly attributable to property which is not residential property, or

(b) partly attributable to residential property,

and that the transaction effected by that instrument does not form part of a larger transaction or of a series of transactions in respect of which the amount or value, or the aggregate amount or value, of the consideration which is attributable to property which is not residential property exceeds £25,000

3 per cent of the consideration which is attributable to property which is not residential property but where the calculation results in an amount which is not a multiple of £1 the amount so calculated shall be rounded up to the nearest £.

(11) Where paragraphs (7) to (10) do not apply and the amount or value of the consideration for the sale which is attributable to property which is not residential property does not exceed £50,000 and the instrument contains a statement certifying that the consideration for the sale is, as the case may be—

(*a*) wholly attributable to property which is not residential property, or

(*b*) partly attributable to residential property,

and that the transaction effected by that instrument does not form part of a larger transaction or of a series of transactions in respect of which the amount or value, or the aggregate amount or value, of the consideration which is attributable to property which is not residential property exceeds £50,000

4 per cent of the consideration which is attributable to property which is not residential property but where the calculation results in an amount which is not a multiple of £1 the amount so calculated shall be rounded up to the nearest £.

(12) Where paragraphs (7) to (11) do not apply and the amount or value of the consideration for the sale which is attributable to property which is not residential property does not exceed £60,000 and the instrument contains a statement certifying that the consideration for the sale is, as the case may be— (*a*) wholly attributable to property which is not residential property, or (*b*) partly attributable to residential property, and that the transaction effected by that instrument does not form part of a larger transaction or of a series of transactions in respect of which the amount or value, or the aggregate amount or value, of the consideration which is attributable to property which is not residential property exceeds £60,000	5 per cent of the consideration which is attributable to property which is not residential property but where the calculation results in an amount which is not a multiple of £1 the amount so calculated shall be rounded up to the nearest £.
(13) Where paragraphs (7) to (12) do not apply and the instrument contains a statement certifying that the consideration for the sale is, as the case may be— (*a*) wholly attributable to property which is not residential property, or (*b*) partly attributable to residential property	6 per cent of the consideration which is attributable to property which is not residential property but where the calculation results in an amount which is not a multiple of £1 the amount so calculated shall be rounded up to the nearest £.
(14) Where paragraphs (7) to (13) do not apply and the amount or value of the consideration for the sale is wholly or partly attributable to property which is not residential property	

9 per cent of the consideration which is attributable to property which is not residential property but where the calculation results in an amount which is not a multiple of £1 the amount so calculated shall be rounded up to the nearest £.

[(15) Where in the case of a conveyance or transfer on sale or in the case of a conveyance or transfer operating as a voluntary disposition inter vivos the instrument contains a certificate by the party to whom the property is being conveyed or transferred to the effect that the person becoming entitled to the entire beneficial interest in the property (or, where more than one person becomes entitled to a beneficial interest in the property, each of them) is related to the person or each of the persons immediately theretofore entitled to the entire beneficial interest in the property in one or other of the following ways, that is, as a lineal descendant, parent, grandparent, step-parent, husband or wife, brother or sister of a parent or brother or sister, or lineal descendant of a parent, husband or wife or brother or sister

a duty of an amount equal to one-half of the *ad valorem* stamp duty which, but for the provisions of this paragraph, would be chargeable under this heading but where the calculation results in an amount which is not a multiple of £1 the amount so calculated shall be rounded up to the nearest £.][2]

CONVEYANCE or TRANSFER by way of security of any property, or of any security.

See MORTGAGE, etc.

CONVEYANCE or TRANSFER of any kind not already described in this Schedule.

where such instrument relates to—

(*a*) immovable property situated in the State, or any right over or interest in such property, or

(*b*) the stocks or marketable securities of a company having a register in the State. £10

Exemption.

Instrument which contains a statement certifying that the instrument is a conveyance or transfer on any occasion, not being a sale or mortgage.

COUNTERPART.

See DUPLICATE.

COVENANT for securing the payment or repayment of money, or the transfer or retransfer of stock.

See MORTGAGE, etc.

COVENANT in relation to any annuity on the original creation and sale of that annuity.

See CONVEYANCE or TRANSFER on sale.

DEFEAZANCE. Instrument of defeazance of any conveyance, transfer or disposition, apparently absolute, but intended only as a security for money or stock.

See MORTGAGE, etc.

DEPOSIT of title deeds.

See MORTGAGE, etc.

DRAFT for money.

See BILL OF EXCHANGE.

DUPLICATE or COUNTERPART of any instrument chargeable with any duty.

Where such duty does not amount to £10	The same duty as the original instrument.
In any other case	£10.

EQUITABLE MORTGAGE.

See MORTGAGE, etc.

EXCHANGE - instruments effecting.

In the case specified in section 37, see that section.	
In any other case	£10.

Exemption

Instrument which contains a statement certifying that the instrument is an instrument effecting an exchange which is not an exchange which is specified in section 37.

FURTHER CHARGE or FURTHER SECURITY.

See MORTGAGE, etc.

INSURANCE.

See POLICY.

LEASE.

(1) For any indefinite term or any term not exceeding 35 years of any dwellinghouse, part of a dwellinghouse, or apartment at a rent not exceeding [£15,000][3] per annum

Exempt.

(2) For any definite term less than a year of any lands, tenements or heritable subjects

The same duty as a lease for a year at the rent reserved for the definite term.

(3) For any other definite term or for any indefinite term of any lands, tenements, or heritable subjects—

[(*a*) where the consideration, or any part of the consideration (other than rent), moving either to the lessor or to any other person, consists of any money, stock or security, and—

(i) the amount or value of such consideration which is attributable to residential property, or would be so attributable if the contents of residential property were considered to be residential property, does not exceed £100,000 and the lease contains a statement certifying that the consideration (other than rent) for the lease is, as the case may be—

(I) wholly attributable to residential property, or

(II) partly attributable to residential property,

and that the transaction effected by that instrument does not form part of a larger transaction or of a series of transactions in respect of which the amount or value, or the aggregate amount or value, of the consideration (other than rent) which is attributable to residential property, or which would be so attributable if the contents of residential property were considered to be residential property, exceeds £100,000

9 per cent of the consideration which is attributable to residential property but where the calculation results in an amount which is not a multiple of £1 the amount so calculated shall be rounded up to the nearest £.

(ii) the amount or value of such consideration which is attributable to residential property, or would be so attributable if the contents of residential property were considered to be residential property, does not exceed £150,000 and the lease contains a statement certifying that the consideration (other than rent) for the lease is, as the case may be—

(I) wholly attributable to residential property, or

(II) partly attributable to residential property,

and that the transaction effected by that instrument does not form part of a larger transaction or of a series of transactions in respect of which the amount or value, or the aggregate amount or value, of the consideration (other than rent) which is attributable to residential property, or which would be so attributable if the contents of residential property were considered to be residential property, exceeds £150,000 and clause (i) does not apply

9 per cent of the consideration which is attributable to residential property but where the calculation results in an amount which is not a multiple of £1 the amount so calculated shall be rounded up to the nearest £.

(iii) the amount or value of such consideration which is attributable to residential property. or would be so attributable if the contents of residential property were considered to be residential property, does riot exceed £200,000 and the lease contains a statement certifying that the consideration (other than rent) for the lease is, as the case may be—

(I) wholly attributable to residential property, or

(II) partly attributable to residential property,

and that the transaction effected by that instrument does not form part of a larger transaction or of a series of transactions in respect of which the amount or value, or the aggregate amount or value, of the consideration (other than rent) which is attributable to residential property, or which would be so attributable if the contents of residential property were considered to be residential property, exceeds £200,000 and clauses (i) and (ii) do not apply

9 per cent of the consideration which is attributable to residential property but where the calculation results in an amount which is not a multiple of £1 the amount so calculated shall be rounded up to the nearest £.

(iv) the amount or value of such consideration which is attributable to residential property, or would be so attributable if the contents of residential property were considered to be residential property, does not exceed £250,000 and the lease contains a statement certifying that the consideration (other than rent) for the lease is, as the case may be—

(I) wholly attributable to residential property, or

(II) partly attributable to residential property,

and that the transaction effected by that instrument does not form part of a larger transaction or of a series of transactions in respect of which the amount or value, or the aggregate amount or value, of the consideration (other than rent) which is attributable to residential property, or which would be so attributable if the contents of residential property were considered to be residential property, exceeds £250,000 and clauses (i) to (iii) do not apply

9 per cent of the consideration which is attributable to residential property but where the calculation results in an amount which is not a multiple of £1 the amount so calculated shall be rounded up to the nearest £.

(v) the amount or value of such consideration which is attributable to residential property, or would be so attributable if the contents of residential property were considered to be residential property, does not exceed £300,000 and the lease contains a statement certifying that the consideration (other than rent) for the lease is, as the case may be—

(I) wholly attributable to residential property, or

(II) partly attributable to residential property,

and that the transaction effected by that instrument does not form part of a larger transaction or of a series of transactions in respect of which the amount or value, or the aggregate amount or value, of the consideration (other than rent) which is attributable to residential property, or which would be so attributable if the contents of residential property were considered to be residential property, exceeds £300,000 and clauses (i) to (iv) do not apply

9 per cent of the consideration which is attributable to residential property but where the calculation results in an amount which is not a multiple of £1 the amount so calculated shall be rounded up to the nearest £.

(vi) the amount or value of such consideration which is attributable to residential property, or would be so attributable if the contents of residential property were considered to be residential property, does not exceed £500,000 and the lease contains a statement certifying that the consideration (other than rent) for the lease is, as the case may be—

(I) wholly attributable to residential property, or

(II) partly attributable to residential property,

and that the transaction effected by that instrument does not form part of a larger transaction or of a series of transactions in respect of which the amount or value, or the aggregate amount or value, of the consideration (other than rent) which is attributable to residential property, or which would be so attributable if the contents of residential property were considered to be residential property, exceeds £500,000 and clauses (i) to (v) do not apply

9 per cent of the consideration which is attributable to residential property but where the calculation results in an amount which is not a multiple of £1 the amount so calculated shall be rounded up to the nearest £.

(vii) the amount or value of such consideration is wholly or partly attributable to residential property and clauses (i) to (vi) do not apply

9 per cent of the consideration which is attributable to residential property but where the calculation results in an amount which is not a multiple of £1 the amount so calculated shall be rounded up to the nearest £.][4]

(b) where the consideration, or any part of the consideration (other than rent), moving either to the lessor or to any other person, consists of any money, stock or security, and—

(i) the amount or value of such consideration which is attributable to property which is not residential property does not exceed £5,000 and the lease contains a statement certifying that the consideration for the lease is, as the case may be—

(I) wholly attributable to property which is not residential property, or

(II) partly attributable to residential property,

and that the transaction effected by that instrument does not form part of a larger transaction or of a series of transactions, in respect of which the amount or value, or the aggregate amount or value, of the consideration (other than rent) which is attributable to property which is not residential property exceeds £5,000:

for the consideration which is attributable to property which is not residential property — Exempt.

(ii) the amount or value of such consideration which is attributable to property which is not residential property does not exceed £10,000 and the lease contains a statement certifying that the consideration for the lease is, as the case may be—

(I) wholly attributable to property which is not residential property, or

(II) partly attributable to residential property,

and that the transaction effected by that instrument does not form part of a larger transaction or of a series of transactions in respect of which the amount or value, or the aggregate amount or value, of the consideration (other than rent) which is attributable to property which is not residential property exceeds £10,000 and clause (i) does not apply

1 per cent of the consideration which is attributable to property which is not residential property but where the calculation results in an amount which is not a multiple of £1 the amount so calculated shall be rounded up to the nearest £.

(iii) the amount or value of such consideration which is attributable to property which is not residential property does not exceed £15,000 and the lease contains a statement certifying that the consideration for the lease is, as the case may be—

(I) wholly attributable to property which is not residential property, or

(II) partly attributable to residential property,

and that the transaction effected by that instrument does not form part of a larger transaction or of a series of transactions in respect of which the amount or value, or the aggregate amount or value, of the consideration (other than rent) which is attributable to property which is not residential property exceeds £ 15,000 and clauses (i) and (ii) do not apply

2 per cent of the consideration which is attributable to property which is not residential property but where the calculation results in an amount which is not a multiple of £1 the amount so calculated shall be rounded up to the nearest £.

(iv) the amount or value of such consideration which is attributable to property which is not residential property does not exceed £25,000 and the lease contains a statement certifying that the consideration for the lease is, as the case may be—

(I) wholly attributable to property which is not residential property, or

(II) partly attributable to residential property,

and that the transaction effected by that instrument does not form part of a larger transaction or of a series of transactions in respect of which the amount or value, or the aggregate amount or value, of the consideration (other than rent) which is attributable to property which is not residential property exceeds £25,000 and clauses (i) to (iii) do not apply

3 per cent of the consideration which is attributable to property which is not residential property but where the calculation results in an amount which is not a multiple of £1 the amount so calculated shall be rounded up to the nearest £.

(v) the amount or value of such consideration which is attributable to property which is not residential property does not exceed £50,000 and the lease contains a statement certifying that the consideration for the lease is, as the case may be—

(I) wholly attributable to property which is not residential property, or

(II) partly attributable to residential property,

and that the transaction effected by that instrument does not form part of a larger transaction or of a series of transactions in respect of which the amount or value, or the aggregate amount or value, of the consideration (other than rent) which is attributable to property which is not residential property exceeds £50,000 and clauses (i) to (iv) do not apply

4 per cent of the consideration which is attributable to property which is not residential property but where the calculation results in an amount which is not a multiple of £1 the amount so calculated shall be rounded up to the nearest £.

(vi) the amount or value of such consideration which is attributable to property which is not residential property does not exceed £60,000 and the lease contains a statement certifying that the consideration for the lease is, as the case may be—

(I) wholly attributable to proper which is not residential property, or

(II) partly attributable to residential property,

and that the transaction effected by that instrument does not form part of a larger transaction or of a series of transactions in respect of which the amount or value, or the aggregate amount or value, of the consideration (other than rent) which is attributable to property which is not residential property exceeds £60,000 and clauses (i) to (v) do not apply

5 per cent of the consideration which is attributable to property which is not residential property but where the calculation results in an amount which is not a multiple of £1 the amount so calculated shall be rounded up to the nearest £.

(vii) the instrument contains a statement certifying that the consideration for the lease is, as the case may be—

(I) wholly attributable to property which is not residential property, or

(II) partly attributable to residential property,

and clauses (i) to (vi) do not apply

6 per cent of the consideration which is attributable to property which is not residential property but where the calculation results in an amount which is not a multiple of £1 the amount so calculated shall be rounded up to the nearest £.

(viii) the amount or value of such consideration is wholly or partly attributable to property which is not residential property and clauses (i) to (vii) do not apply

	9 per cent of the consideration which is attributable to property which is not residential property but where the calculation results in an amount which is not a multiple of £1 the amount so calculated shall be rounded up to the nearest £.
(*c*) where the consideration or any part of the consideration is any rent, in respect of such consideration, whether reserved as a yearly rent or otherwise:	
(i) if the term does not exceed 35 years or is indefinite	1 per cent of the average annual rent but where the calculation results in an amount which is not a multiple of £1 the amount so calculated shall be rounded up to the nearest £.
(ii) if the term exceeds 35 years but does not exceed 100 years	6 per cent of the average annual rent but where the calculation results in an amount which is not a multiple of £1 the amount so calculated shall be rounded up to the nearest £.
(iii) if the term exceeds 100 years	12 per cent of the average annual rent but where the calculation results in an amount which is not a multiple of £1 the amount so calculated shall be rounded up to the nearest £.
(4) Lease made subsequently to, and in conformity with, an agreement duly stamped under the provisions of section 50	£10
(5) Of any other kind not already described under this heading which relates to immovable property situated in the State or to any right over or interest in such property	£10

LETTER OF CREDIT.

See BILL OF EXCHANGE.

MORTGAGE, BOND, DEBENTURE, COVENANT (except a marketable security) which is a security for the payment or repayment of money which is a charge or incumbrance on property situated in the State other than shares in stocks or funds of the Government or the Oireachtas.	
(1) Being the only or principal or primary security (other than an equitable mortgage):	
where the amount secured does not exceed £20,000	Exempt.
where the amount secured exceeds £20,000	0. 1 percent of the amount secured and where the calculation results in an amount which is not a multiple of £1 the amount so calculated shall be rounded up to the nearest £ but in no case shall the duty so charged exceed £500.
(2) Being a collateral, or auxiliary, or additional, or substituted security (other than an equitable mortgage), or by way of further assurance for the above-mentioned purpose where the principal or primary security is not chargeable to duty or is duly stamped:	
where the amount secured does not exceed £20,000	Exempt.
where the amount secured exceeds £20,000	£10.
(3) Being an equitable mortgage:	
where the amount secured does not exceed £20,000	Exempt
where the amount secured exceeds £20,000	0.05 per cent of the amount secured and where the calculation results in an amount which is not a multiple of £ 1 the amount so calculated shall be rounded up to the nearest £ but in no case shall the duty so charged exceed £500.
(4) Transfer, assignment or disposition of any such mortgage, bond, debenture, or covenant (except a marketable security) or of any money or stock secured by any such instrument or by any judgement:	

where the amount secured does not exceed £20,000	Exempt.
where the amount secured exceeds £20,000	0.05 per cent of the amount transferred, assigned, or disposed, exclusive of interest which is not in arrear and where the calculation results in an amount which is not a multiple of £1 the amount so calculated shall be rounded up to the nearest £ but in no case shall the duty so charged exceed £500.
where any further money is added to the money already secured	The same duty as a principal security for such further money.
MORTGAGE OF STOCK or MARKETABLE SECURITY.	
By deed. See MORTGAGE, etc.	
ORDER for the payment of money.	
See BILL OF EXCHANGE.	
PARTITION or DIVISION - instruments effecting.	
In the case specified in section 38, see that section.	
POLICY OF LIFE INSURANCE made for a period exceeding 2 years where the risk to which the policy relates is located in the State.	
Where the sum insured exceeds £50	0. 1 per cent of the amount insured but where the calculation results in an amount which is not a multiple of £1 the amount so calculated shall be rounded up to the nearest £.
POLICY OF INSURANCE other than Life Insurance where the risk to which the policy relates is located in the State.	
Where there is one premium only and the amount of that premium equals or exceeds £15 or, where there is more than one premium and the total amount payable in respect of that premium in any period of 12 months equals or exceeds £15	£1.

PROMISSORY NOTE.

See BILL OF EXCHANGE.

RELEASE or RENUNCIATION of any property, or of any right or interest in any property.

On a sale.

See CONVEYANCE or TRANSFER on sale.

In any other case — £10.

Exemption

Instrument which contains a statement certifying that the instrument is a release or renunciation of property, or of a right or interest in property, which is not a release or renunciation on a sale.

SHARE WARRANT issued under the provisions of the Companies Act, 1963, and **STOCK CERTIFICATE to bearer,** and any instrument to bearer issued by or on behalf of any company or body of persons formed or established in the State and having a like effect as such a share warrant or such a stock certificate to bearer, expressed in the currency of the State — A duty of an amount equal to 3 times the amount of the *ad valorem* stamp duty which would be chargeable on a deed transferring the share or shares or stock specified in the warrant or certificate or instrument having a like effect as such a warrant or certificate if the consideration for the transfer were the nominal value of such share or shares or stock.

SURRENDER of any property, or of any right or interest in any property.

On a sale.

See CONVEYANCE or TRANSFER.

In any other case — £10.

Exemption

Instrument which contains a statement certifying that the instrument is a surrender of property, or of a right or interest in property, not being a surrender on a sale.

TRANSFER.

See CONVEYANCE or TRANSFER.

Amendments

1 Heading "CONVEYANCE or TRANSFER on sale of any property other than stocks or marketable securities or a policy of insurance or a policy of life insurance" paras (1) to (6) substituted by F(No2)A 2000 s 3(*a*) and Sch Pt 1 with effect for instruments executed on or after 15 June 2000. However, where an instrument executed on or before 31 January 2001 would increase the duty chargeable on the instrument and the instrument contains a statement certifying that the instrument was executed solely in pursuance of a contract which was evidenced in writing before 15 June 2000, the substitution does not apply; previously:

(1) Where the amount or value of the consideration for the sale which is attributable to residential property, or would be so attributable if the contents of residential property were considered to be residential property, does not exceed £60,000 and the instrument contains a statement certifying that the consideration for the sale is, as the case may be—

(*a*) wholly attributable to residential property, or

(*b*) partly attributable to residential property,

and that the transaction effected by that instrument does not form part of a larger transaction or of a series of transactions in respect of which the amount or value, or the aggregate amount or value, of the consideration which is attributable to residential property, or which would be so attributable if the contents of residential property were considered to be residential property, exceeds £60,000:

for the consideration which is attributable to residential property — Exempt.

(2) Where paragraph (1) does not apply and the amount or value of the consideration for the sale which is attributable to residential property, or would be so attributable if the contents of residential property were considered to be residential property, does not exceed £100,000 and the instrument contains a statement certifying that the consideration for the sale is, as the case may be—

(*a*) wholly attributable to residential property, or

(*b*) partly attributable to residential property,

and that the transaction effected by that instrument does not form part of a larger transaction or of a series of transactions in respect of which the amount or value, or the aggregate amount or value, of the consideration which is attributable to residential property, or which would be so attributable if the contents of residential property were considered to be residential property, exceeds £100,000

3 per cent of the consideration which is attributable to residential property but where the calculation results in an amount which is not a multiple of £1 the amount so calculated shall be rounded up to the nearest £.

(3) Where paragraphs (1) and (2) do not apply and the amount or value of the consideration for the sale which is attributable to residential property, or would be so attributable if the contents of residential property were considered to be residential property, does not exceed £170,000 and the instrument contains a statement certifying that the consideration for the sale is, as the case may be—

(*a*) wholly attributable to residential property, or

(*b*) partly attributable to residential property,

and that the transaction effected by that instrument does not form part of a larger transaction or of a series of transactions in respect of which the amount or value, or the aggregate amount or value, of the consideration which is attributable to residential property, or which would be so attributable if the contents of residential property were considered to be residential property, exceeds £170,000

4 per cent of the consideration which is attributable to residential property but where the calculation results in an amount which is not a multiple of £1 the amount so calculated shall be rounded up to the nearest £.

(4) Where paragraphs (1) to (3) do not apply and the amount or value of the consideration for the sale which is attributable to residential property, or would be so attributable if the contents of residential property were considered to be residential property, does not exceed £250,000 and the instrument contains a statement certifying that the consideration for the sale is, as the case may be—

(*a*) wholly attributable to residential property, or

(*b*) partly attributable to residential property,

and that the transaction effected by that instrument does not form part of a larger transaction or of a series of transactions in respect of which the amount or value, or the aggregate amount or value, of the consideration which is attributable to residential property, or which would be so attributable if the contents of residential property were considered to be residential property, exceeds £250,000

5 per cent of the consideration which is attributable to residential property but where the calculation results in an amount which is not a multiple of £1 the amount so calculated shall be rounded up to the nearest £.

(5) Where paragraphs (1) to (4) do not apply and the amount or value of the consideration for the sale which is attributable to residential property, or would be so attributable if the contents of residential property were considered to be residential property, does not exceed £500,000 and the instrument contains a statement certifying that the consideration for the sale is, as the case may be—

(*a*) wholly attributable to residential property, or

(*b*) partly attributable to residential property,

and that the transaction effected by that instrument does not form part of a larger transaction or of a series of transactions in respect of which the amount or value, or the aggregate amount or value, of the consideration which is attributable to residential property, or which would be so attributable if the contents of residential property were considered to be residential property, exceeds £500,000

7 per cent of the consideration which is attributable to residential property but where the calculation results in an amount which is not a multiple of £1 the amount so calculated shall be rounded up to the nearest £.

(6) Where paragraphs (1) to (5) do not apply and the amount or value of the consideration for the sale is wholly or partly attributable to residential property

9 per cent of the consideration which is attributable to residential property but where the calculation results in an amount which is not a multiple of £1 the amount so calculated shall be rounded up to the nearest £.

2 Para (15) substituted by FA 2000, s 133(1)(*a*) in relation to instruments executed on or after 10 February 2000.

3 Substituted by FA 2000, s 133(1)(*b*) in relation to instruments executed on or after 1 December 1999; previously "£6,000".

4 Heading of "Lease" para (3)(*a*) substituted by F(No2)A 2000, s 3(*b*) and Sch Pt 2 with effect for instruments executed on or after 15 June 2000. However, where an instrument executed on or before 31 January 2001 would increase the duty chargeable on the instrument and the instrument contains a statement certifying that the instrument was executed solely in pursuance of a contract which was evidenced in writing before 15 June 2000, the substitution does not apply; previously:

(*a*) where the consideration, or any part of the consideration (other than rent), moving either to the lessor or to any other person, consists of any money, stock or security, and—

(i) the amount or value of such consideration which is attributable to residential property, or would be so attributable if the contents of residential property were considered to be residential property, does not exceed £60,000 and the lease contains a statement certifying that the consideration (other than rent) for the lease is, as the case may be—

(I) wholly attributable to residential property, or

(II) partly attributable to residential property,

and that the transaction effected by that instrument does not form part of a larger transaction or of a series of transactions, in respect of which the amount or value, or the aggregate amount or value, of the consideration (other than rent) which is attributable to residential property, or which would be so attributable if the contents of residential property were considered to be residential property, exceeds £60,000:

for the consideration which is attributable to residential property

(ii) the amount or value of such consideration which is attributable to residential property, or would be so attributable if the contents of residential property were considered to be residential property, does not exceed £100,000 and the lease contains a statement certifying that the consideration (other than rent) for the lease is, as the case may be—

(I) wholly attributable to residential property, or

(II) partly attributable to residential property,

and that the transaction effected by that instrument does not form part of a larger transaction or of a series of transactions in respect of which the amount or value, or the aggregate amount or value, of the consideration (other than rent) which is attributable to residential property, or which would be so attributable if the contents of residential property were considered to be residential property, exceeds £100,000 and clause (i) does not apply

3 per cent of the consideration which is attributable to residential property but where the calculation results in an amount which is not a multiple of £ 1 the amount so calculated shall be rounded up to the nearest £.

(iii) the amount or value of such consideration which is attributable to residential property, or would be so attributable if the contents of residential property were considered to be residential property, does not exceed £170,000 and the lease contains a statement certifying that the consideration (other than rent) for the lease is, as the case may be—

(I) wholly attributable to residential property, or

(II) partly attributable to residential property,

and that the transaction effected by that instrument does not form part of a larger transaction or of a series of transactions in respect of which the amount or value, or the aggregate amount or value, of the consideration (other than rent) which is attributable to residential property, or which would be so attributable if the contents of residential property were considered to be residential property, exceeds £170,000 and clauses (i) and (ii) do not apply

4 per cent of the consideration which is attributable to residential property but where the calculation results in an amount which is not a multiple of £1 the amount so calculated shall be rounded up to the nearest £.

(iv) the amount or value of such consideration which is attributable to residential property, or would be so attributable if the contents of residential property were considered to be residential property, does not exceed £250,000 and the lease contains a statement certifying that the consideration (other than rent) for the lease is, as the case may be—

(I) wholly attributable to residential property, or

(II) partly attributable to residential property,

and that the transaction effected by that instrument does not form part of a larger transaction or of a series of transactions in respect of which the amount or value, or the aggregate amount or value, of the consideration (other than rent) which is attributable to residential property, or which would be so attributable if the contents of residential property were considered to be residential property, exceeds £250,000 and clauses (i) to (iii) do not apply

5 per cent of the consideration which is attributable to residential property but where the calculation results in an amount which is not a multiple of £1 the amount so calculated shall be rounded up to the nearest £.

(v) the amount or value of such consideration which is attributable to residential property, or would be so attributable if the contents of residential property were considered to be residential property, does not exceed £500,000 and the lease contains a statement certifying that the consideration (other than rent) for the lease is, as the case may be—

(I) wholly attributable to residential property, or

(II) partly attributable to residential property,

and that the transaction effected by that instrument does not form part of a larger transaction or of a series of transactions in respect of which the amount or value, or the aggregate amount or value, of the consideration (other than rent) which is attributable to residential property, or which would be so attributable if the contents of residential property were considered to be residential property, exceeds £500,000 and clauses (i) to (iv) do not apply

7 per cent of the consideration which is attributable to residential property but where the calculation results in an amount which is not a multiple of £1 the amount so calculated shall be rounded up to the nearest £.

(vi) the amount or value of such consideration is wholly or partly attributable to residential property and clauses (i) to (v) do not apply

9 per cent of the consideration which is attributable to residential property but where the calculation results in an amount which is not a multiple of £1 the amount so calculated shall be rounded up to the nearest £.

Notes

Heading "CONVEYANCE or TRANSFER on sale of any property other than stocks or marketable securities or a policy of insurance or a policy of life insurance" para (8) is deemed to have had effect for the period subsequent to the substitution made by FA 1997, s 117(*a*) and prior to F(No 2)A 1998, s 7(*a*) except in relation to an appeal made under SA 1891 s 13 before 2 March 1999:

"(8) Of any other kind whatsoever not hereinbefore described by reference to a consideration for which a rate of duty has already been specified at paragraphs (1) to (7):
for every £100, or fractional part—
of £100, of the consideration .... £9.00".

Heading "LEASE" para (3)(a)(viii) is deemed to have had effect for the period subsequent to the substitution made by FA 1997 s 117(a) and prior to F(No 2) A 1998, s 7(a) except in relation to an appeal made under SA 1891 s 13 before 2 March 1999:

"(viii)the case is of any other kind whatsoever not hereinbefore described by reference to a consideration for which a rate of duty has already been specified at clauses (i) to (vii):
for every £100, or fractional part of £100, of the consideration............................£9.00"

Former enactment

SA 1891, Sch 1; FA 1899, s 5(1)

SCHEDULE 2

Qualifications for applying for relief from Stamp Duty in respect of Transfers to Young Trained Farmers

1. Qualifications awarded by Teagasc:

(*a*) Certificate in Farming;

(*b*) Diploma in Commercial Horticulture;

(*c*) Diploma in Amenity Horticulture;

(*d*) Diploma in Pig Production;

(*e*) Diploma in Poultry Production.

2. Qualifications awarded by the Farm Apprenticeship Board:

(*a*) Certificate in Farm Management;

(*b*) Certificate in Farm Husbandry;

(*c*) Trainee Farmer Certificate.

3. Qualifications awarded by a third-level institution:

(*a*) Degree in Agricultural Science awarded by the National University of Ireland through University College Dublin, National University of Ireland, Dublin;

(*b*) Degree in Horticultural Science awarded by the National University of Ireland through University College Dublin, National University of Ireland, Dublin;

(*c*) Degree in Veterinary Science awarded by the National University of Ireland through University College Dublin, National University of Ireland, Dublin:

(*d*) Degree in Rural Science awarded by the National University of Ireland through University College Cork-National University of Ireland, Cork or by the University of Limerick;

(*e*) Diploma in Rural Science awarded by the National University of Ireland through University College Cork-National University of Ireland, Cork;

(*f*) Degree in Dairy Science awarded by the National University of Ireland through University College Cork - National University of Ireland, Cork;

(*g*) Diploma in Dairy Science awarded by the National University of Ireland through University College-Cork National University of Ireland, Cork.

4. Certificates awarded by the National Council for Educational Awards:

(*a*) National Certificate in Agricultural Science studied through Kildalton Agricultural College and Waterford Institute of Technology;

(*b*) National Certificate in Business Studies (Agri-business) studied through the Franciscan Brothers Agricultural College, Mountbellew, and Galway-Mayo Institute of Technology.

Former enactment
FA 1994 s 112, Sch 6.

SCHEDULE 3

Enactments Repealed or Revoked

[*Section 160*]

PART 1

Acts Repealed

Session and Chapter or Year and Number	Short Title	Extent of Repeal
(1)	(2)	(3)
54 & 55 Vict., c.38.	Stamp Duties Management Act, 1891.	The whole Act, in so far as it is unrepealed.
54 & 55 Vict., c.39.	Stamp Act, 1891.	The whole Act, in so far as it is unrepealed.
57 & 58 Vict., c.30.	Finance Act, 1894.	Section 39.
58 Vict., c. 16.	Finance Act, 1895.	Section 16 and the Schedule.
60 & 61 Vict., c.24.	Finance Act, 1897.	Section 8.
61 & 62 Vict., c.10.	Finance Act, 1898.	Sections 5 and 6.
61 & 62 Vict., c.46.	Revenue Act, 1898.	Sections 7, 10 and 13.
62 & 63 Vict., c.9.	Finance Act, 1899.	Sections 5, 6 and 14.
63 Vict., c. 7.	Finance Act, 1900.	Section 10.
3 Edw. 7, c.46.	Revenue Act, 1903.	Section 9.
9 Edw. 7, c.43.	Revenue Act, 1909.	Sections 7 and 8.
10 Edw. 7, c.8.	Finance (1909-10) Act, 1910.	Sections 4 and 74.
10 & 11 Geo. 5, c. 18.	Finance Act, 1920.	Sections 37 and 43.
12 & 13 Geo. 5, c. 17.	Finance Act, 1922.	Sections 46 and 47.

No 27 of 1924.	Finance Act, 1924.	Section 38, in so far as it relates to stamp duties.
No 35 of 1926.	Finance Act, 1926.	Section 39, in so far as it relates to stamp duties.
No 5 of 1929.	Finance (Customs and Stamp Duties) Act, 1929.	Section 5.
No 32 of 1929.	Finance Act, 1929.	Section 36.
No 31 of 1931.	Finance Act, 1931.	Section 32.
No 20 of 1932.	Finance Act, 1932.	Section 50.
No 15 of 1933.	Finance Act, 1933.	Sections 40, 41 and 43.
No 31 of 1934.	Finance Act, 1934.	Section 34.
No 7 of 1935.	Finance (Miscellaneous Provisions) Act, 1935.	Section 6 and Part II of the Schedule.
No 31 of 1936.	Finance Act, 1936.	Section 25.
No 14 of 1942.	Finance Act, 1942.	Section 21.
No 16 of 1943.	Finance Act, 1943.	Sections 14 to 16.
No 13 of 1949.	Finance Act, 1949.	Section 24.
No 14 of 1952.	Finance Act, 1952.	Section 19.
No 22 of 1954.	Finance Act, 1954.	Section 23.
No 36 of 1954.	Solicitors Act, 1954.	Section 72.
No 13 of 1955.	Finance Act, 1955.	Section 16.
No 25 of 1958.	Finance Act, 1958.	Sections 59 and 60.
No 18 of 1959.	Finance Act, 1959.	Sections 75(4) and 76.
No 19 of 1960.	Finance Act, 1960.	Section 36.
No 23 of 1961.	Finance Act, 1961.	Sections 29 and 30.
No 15 of 1962.	Finance Act, 1962.	Sections 17 and 18.
No 23 of 1963.	Finance Act, 1963.	Sections 40, 41 and 43.
No 22 of 1965.	Finance Act, 1965.	Section 31.
No 17 of 1967.	Finance Act, 1967.	Section 20.
No 21 of 1969.	Finance Act, 1969.	Sections 49 and 50.
No 14 of 1970.	Finance Act, 1970.	Sections 40 to 47 and the First Schedule.
No 23 of 1971.	Finance Act, 1971.	Sections 43 and 44.
No 19 of 1972.	Finance Act, 1972.	Section 35.

No 22 of 1972.	Value-Added Tax Act, 1972.	Section 38(4).
No 19 of 1973.	Finance Act, 1973.	Sections 62 to 75 and section 92(6).
No 27 of 1974.	Finance Act, 1974.	Sections 81 to 83.
No 6 of 1975.	Finance Act, 1975.	Sections 48 and 49 and the Fourth Schedule.
No 16 of 1976.	Finance Act, 1976.	Sections 47 and 48.
No 18 of 1977.	Finance Act, 1977.	Sections 47 and 48.
No 21 of 1978.	Finance Act, 1978.	Sections 31 to 35.
No 11 of 1979.	Finance Act, 1979.	Sections 50 to 53 and section 56.
No 14 of 1980.	Finance Act, 1980.	Sections 85 to 87.
No 16 of 1981.	Finance Act, 1981.	Sections 47 to 50.
No 28 of 1981.	Finance (No 2) Act, 1981.	Sections 16 and 17.
No 14 of 1982.	Finance Act, 1982.	Sections 91 to 96 and the Fourth Schedule.
No 15 of 1983.	Finance Act, 1983.	Sections 90 to 93.
No 24 of 1983.	Postal and Telecommunications Services Act, 1983.	Section 5(4)(*c*).
No 9 of 1984.	Finance Act, 1984.	Sections 97 to 103.
No 10 of 1985.	Finance Act, 1985.	Sections 55 to 57.
No 13 of 1986.	Finance Act, 1986.	Sections 92 to 99 and section 101.
No 10 of 1987.	Finance Act, 1987.	Sections 48 and 49.
No 12 of 1988.	Finance Act, 1988.	Sections 64 and 65.
No 10 of 1989.	Finance Act, 1989.	Sections 64, 66, 67, 68, 71 and 72.
No 10 of 1990.	Finance Act, 1990.	Sections 108 to 116, sections 118 and 120 and the Ninth Schedule.
No 13 of 1991.	Finance Act, 1991.	Sections 88 to 106, sections 108 to 111 and the Fifth Schedule.

No 9 of 1992.	Finance Act, 1992.	Sections 199 to 211, section 213, sections 215 to 217 and the Seventh Schedule.
No 28 of 1992.	Finance (No 2) Act, 1992.	Section 28.
No 13 of 1993.	Finance Act, 1993.	Sections 100 to 106.
No 13 of 1994.	Finance Act, 1994.	Sections 102 to 109, sections 111, 112 and 161(4) and the Sixth Schedule.
No 8 of 1995.	Finance Act, 1995.	Sections 142 to 150.
No 9 of 1996.	Finance Act, 1996.	Sections 101 to 111, sections 113 to 119 and the Fourth Schedule.
No 25 of 1996.	Disclosure of Certain Information for Taxation and Other Purposes Act, 1996.	Section 7.
No 31 of 1996.	Criminal Assets Bureau Act, 1996.	Section 24(3).
No 22 of 1997.	Finance Act, 1997.	Sections 115 to 130 and the Eighth Schedule.
No 3 of 1998.	Finance Act, 1998.	Sections 118 to 125 and Schedule 8.
No 15 of 1998.	Finance (No 2) Act, 1998.	Sections 5 to 14 and the Schedule.
No 2 of 1999.	Finance Act, 1999.	Sections 140 to 197 and Schedules 5 and 6.

PART 2

Statutory Instrument Revoked

Year and Number	Citation	Extent of Revocation
No 4 of 1923.	Inland Revenue (Adaptation of Taxing Acts) Order, 1923.	Paragraphs 16 and 17.

SCHEDULE 4

Consequential Amendments

[*Section 162*]

In the enactments specified in column (1) of the following Table for the words set out or referred to in column (2), there shall be substituted the words set out in the corresponding entry in column (3).

Enactment amended (1)	Words to be replaced (2)	Words to be substituted (3)
Forgery Act, 1913: section 8(2)(*b*)	Stamp Duties Management Act, 1891 (as amended by the Finance Act, 1989)	Part 11 of the Stamp Duties Consolidation Act, 1999
section 18(1A)	Stamp Duties Management Act, 1891 (as amended by the Finance Act, 1989)	Part 11 of the Stamp Duties Consolidation Act, 1999
Electricity (Supply) Act, 1927, section 95	section fifty-nine of the Stamp Act, 1891	section 31 of the Stamp Duties Consolidation Act, 1999
Statute of Limitations, 1957, section 60	Stamp Act, 1891	Stamp Duties Consolidation Act, 1999
Companies Act, 1963: section 58(2)	Stamp Act, 1891	Stamp Duties Consolidation Act, 1999
section 58(2)	section 12	section 20
Stock Transfer Act, 1963: section 4(3)	section 74 of the Finance (1909-10) Act, 1910	section 30 of the Stamp Duties Consolidation Act, 1999
section 4(4)	subsection (4) or (5) of section 58 of the Stamp Act, 1891	subsection (1) or (2) of section 46 of the Stamp Duties Consolidation Act, 1999
Finance Act, 1980, section 78(6)	Stamp Duties Management Act, 1891	Part 11 of the Stamp Duties Consolidation Act, 1999

Housing Finance Agency Act, 1981, section 16	section 44 of the Finance Act, 1970 said section 44	section 86 of the Stamp Duties Consolidation Act, 1999 that section 86
Postal and Telecommunications Services Act, 1983: section 5 (4) (*b*) section 69(2) section 69(3) section 69(5) section 69(8)	 Stamp Act, 1891 sections 4, 6, 13 and 16 to 20 of the Stamp Duties Management Act, 1891 section 16 or 17 of the Stamp Duties Management Act, 1891 section 9 of the Stamp Act, 1891 section 18(2) of the Stamp Duties Management Act, 1891	 Stamp Duties Consolidation Act, 1999 sections 139 to 144 and 147 and 149 of the Stamp Duties Consolidation Act, 1999 section 140 or 141 of the Stamp Duties Consolidation Act, 1999 section 10(5) of the Stamp Duties Consolidation Act, 1999 section 142(2) of the Stamp Duties Consolidation Act, 1999
Finance Act, 1989: section 48(1) section 48(3)	 Stamp Duties Management Act, 1891 Stamp Duties Management Act, 1891	 Part 11 of the Stamp Duties Consolidation Act, 1999 Part 11 of the Stamp Duties Consolidation Act, 1999
Building Societies Act, 1989, section 118(2)	sections 67 to 75 of the Finance Act, 1973	Part 8 of the Stamp Duties Consolidation Act, 1999
Trustee Savings Banks Act, 1989, section 64	sections 67 to 75 of the Finance Act, 1973	Part 8 of the Stamp Duties Consolidation Act, 1999
Companies Act, 1990, section 208, para (*c*)	section 68 of the Finance Act, 1973 section 69 of the Finance Act, 1973	section 116 of the Stamp Duties Consolidation Act, 1999 section 117 of the Stamp Duties Consolidation Act, 1999

Solicitors (Amendment) Act, 1994, section 72(1)	section 24 of the Stamp Duties Management Act, 1891	section 157 of the Stamp Duties Consolidation Act, 1999
Stamp Duty (Particulars to be Delivered) Regulations, 1995 (SI No 144 of 1995)	section 107 of the Finance Act, 1994 (No 13 of 1994)	section 12 of the Stamp Duties Consolidation Act, 1999
Taxes Consolidation Act, 1997:		
section 487(1)(*a*) in paragraph (iii)(II) of the definition of "accounting profit"	section 94 of the Finance Act, 1986	section 126 of the Stamp Duties Consolidation Act, 1999
section 905(2)(*c*)(iii)	section 16 of the Stamp Act, 1891	section 128 of the Stamp Duties Consolidation Act, 1999
section 1002(1)(*a*), in the definition of "the Acts"	Stamp Act, 1891	Stamp Duties Consolidation Act, 1999
section 1089(1)	section 15 of the Stamp Act, 1891, and subsections (2) and (3) of section 69 of the Finance Act, 1973	section 14 and subsections (3) and (4) of section 117 of the Stamp Duties Consolidation Act, 1999

Appendix 7

Wording of Certificates in Conveyances/Leases

Cert. No.	**Wording of Certificates** (delete as appropriate) Note: Knowingly furnishing an incorrect certificate is a Revenue Offence
1	"It is hereby certified that— (a) this instrument gives effect to the purchase of a dwellinghouse/ apartment on the erection of that dwellinghouse/apartment, (b) on the date of execution of this instrument, there exists a valid floor area certificate (within the meaning of section 4(2)(b) of the Housing (Miscellaneous Provisions) Act, 1979) in respect of the said dwellinghouse/ apartment, and (c) the purchaser/one or more of the purchasers/a person or persons in right of the purchaser/a person or persons in right of one or more of the purchasers will occupy the dwellinghouse/apartment as his/her/their only or principal place of residence for the period specified in section 91(2)(b)(ii) (new dwellinghouse/ apartment with floor area certificate) of the Stamp Duties Consolidation Act, 1999, and that no person (other than a person who, while in such occupation, derives rent or payment in the nature of rent in consideration for the provision, on or after 6 April 2001, of furnished residential accommodation in part of the dwellinghouse/apartment concerned or other than by virtue of a title prior to that of the purchaser) will derive any rent or payment in the nature of rent for the use of the dwellinghouse/ apartment or any part of it during that period."
2A	"It is hereby certified that section 29 (conveyance on sale combined with building agreement for dwellinghouse/apartment) of the Stamp Duties Consolidation Act, 1999, applies to this instrument."
2B	"It is hereby certified that section 53 (lease combined with building agreement for dwellinghouse/apartment) of the Stamp Duties Consolidation Act, 1999, applies to this instrument."
3A	"It is hereby certified that section 29 (conveyance on sale combined with building agreement for dwellinghouse/apartment) of the Stamp Duties Consolidation Act, 1999, does not apply to this instrument."
3B	"It is hereby certified that section 53 (lease combined with building agreement for dwellinghouse/apartment) of the Stamp Duties Consolidation Act, 1999, does not apply to this instrument."

4A	"It is hereby certified that this instrument gives effect to the purchase of a dwellinghouse/apartment on the erection of that dwellinghouse/apartment and that sections 29 (conveyance on sale combined with building agreement for dwellinghouse/apartment) and 91 (new dwellinghouse/apartment with floor area certificate) of the Stamp Duties Consolidation Act, 1999, do not apply."
4B	"It is hereby certified that this instrument gives effect to the purchase of a dwellinghouse/apartment on the erection of that dwellinghouse/apartment and that sections 53 (lease combined with building agreement for dwellinghouse/ apartment) and 91 (new dwellinghouse/apartment with floor area certificate) of the Stamp Duties Consolidation Act, 1999, do not apply."
5	"It is hereby certified that this instrument gives effect to the purchase of a dwellinghouse/apartment"
6	"It is hereby certified that the purchaser/each of the purchasers is a first-time purchaser as defined in section 92B(1) (residential property first-time purchaser relief) of the Stamp Duties Consolidation Act, 1999."
7A	"It is hereby certified that the purchaser/one or more of the purchasers/a person or persons in right of the purchaser/a person or persons in right of one or more of the purchasers will occupy the dwellinghouse/ apartment as his/ her/their only or principal place of residence for the period specified in section 92(1)(b)(ii) (new dwellinghouse/apartment with no floor area certificate) of the Stamp Duties Consolidation Act, 1999, and that no person (other than a person who, while in such occupation, derives rent or payment in the nature of rent in consideration for the provision, on or after 6 April 2001, of furnished residential accommodation in part of the dwellinghouse/apartment concerned or other than by virtue of a title prior to that of the purchaser) will derive any rent or payment in the nature of rent for the use of the dwellinghouse/ apartment or any part of it during that period."
7B	"It is hereby certified that the purchaser/one or more of the purchasers/a person or persons in right of the purchaser/a person or persons in right of one or more of the purchasers will occupy the dwellinghouse/ apartment as his/ her/their only or principal place of residence for the period specified in section 92B(3)(b)(ii) (residential property first-time purchaser relief) of the Stamp Duties Consolidation Act, 1999, and that no person (other than a person who, while in such occupation, derives rent or payment in the nature of rent in consideration for the provision, on or after 6 April 2001, of furnished residential accommodation in part of the dwellinghouse/apartment concerned or other than by virtue of a title prior to that of the purchaser) will derive any rent or payment in the nature of rent for the use of the dwellinghouse/ apartment or any part of it during that period."
8A	"It is hereby certified that the consideration (other than rent) for the sale/lease is wholly attributable to residential property and that the transaction effected by this instrument does not form part of a larger transaction or of a series of transactions in respect of which the amount or value, or the aggregate amount or value, of the consideration (other than rent) which is attributable to residential property, or which would be so attributable if the contents of residential property were considered to be residential property, exceeds €127,000 / €190,500 / €254,000 / €317,500 / €381,000 / €635,000."

8B	"It is hereby certified (a) that the consideration (other than rent) for the sale/ lease is partly attributable to residential property, and (b) that the transaction effected by this instrument does not form part of a larger transaction or of a series of transactions in respect of which the amount or value, or the aggregate amount or value, of the consideration (other than rent) which is attributable to residential property, or which would be so attributable if the contents of residential property were considered to be residential property exceeds €127,000 / €190,500 / €254,000 / €317,500 / €381,000 / €635,000, and (c) that the transaction effected by this instrument does not form part of a larger transaction or of a series of transactions in respect of which the amount or value, or the aggregate amount or value, of the consideration (other than rent) which is attributable to property which is not residential property exceeds €10,000/ €20,000/ €30,000/ €40,000/ €70.000/ €80,000/ €100,000/ €120,000/ €150,000."
8C	"It is hereby certified that the consideration (other than rent) for the sale/lease is wholly attributable to property which is not residential property and that the transaction effected by this instrument does not form part of a larger transaction or of a series of transactions in respect of which the amount or value, or the aggregate amount or value, of the consideration (other than rent) which is attributable to property which is not residential property exceeds €10,000 / €20,000 / €30,000/ €40,000 / €70,000 / €80,000/ €100,000/ €120,000/ €150,000."
9	"It is hereby certified that (a) the instrument gives effect to the transfer/ conveyance/lease of a site as defined in section 83A (transfer of site to child) of the Stamp Duties Consolidation Act, 1999, (b) the person becoming entitled to the entire beneficial interest in the site is a child of the person (or of each of the persons) immediately heretofore entitled to the entire beneficial interest in the site,(c) at the date of this instrument, the value of the site does not exceed €254,000 and that the transaction hereby effected does not form part of a larger transaction or of a series of transactions whereby property with a value in excess of €254,000 is conveyed/transferred/leased to that child,(d) the purpose of the conveyance/transfer/lease is to enable that child to construct a dwellinghouse thereon which will be occupied by that child as his/ her only or main residence, and (e) the transaction hereby effected is the first and only conveyance/transfer/lease of a site for the benefit of that child which contains this certificate."
10	"It is hereby certified by the party (or parties) becoming entitled to the entire beneficial interest in the property that the person (or each of the persons) becoming entitled to the entire beneficial interest in the property is related to the person (or each of the persons) immediately theretofore entitled to the entire beneficial interest in the property as a (state relationship(s))."
11	"It is hereby certified that section 81 (young trained farmers) of the Stamp Duties Consolidation Act, 1999, applies to this instrument."
12	"It is hereby certified for the purposes of section 95 (commercial woodlands) of the Stamp Duties Consolidation Act, 1999, that trees (within the meaning of that section) are growing on a substantial part of the land the subject of this instrument."

13A	"It is hereby certified that this instrument is a conveyance or transfer on any occasion, not being a sale or mortgage."
13B	"It is hereby certified that this instrument is an instrument effecting an exchange which is not an exchange which is specified in section 37 (exchanges) of the Stamp Duties Consolidation Act, 1999."
13C	"It is hereby certified that this instrument is a release or renunciation of property, or of a right or interest in property, which is not a release or renunciation on a sale."
13D	"It is hereby certified that this instrument is a surrender of property, or of a right or interest in property, which is not a surrender on a sale."

Appendix 8

Revenue Forms/Company Office Forms

Form A1: CRO Formation of a Company

COMPANIES REGISTRATION OFFICE
AN OIFIG UM CHLÁRÚ CUIDEACHTAÍ

Application to incorporate a company

Section 3 and 3A (inserted by section 101 Company Law Enforcement Act 2001) Companies (Amendment) Act 1982
Section 5 Companies (Amendment) Act 1983
European Communities (Single-Member Private Limited Companies) Regulations 1994
Sections 42 and 43, section 44 (other than subsection (2)) and section 45 (other than subsections (3)(b) and (5)) Companies (Amendment)(No. 2) Act 1999
Section 117 Stamp Duties Consolidation Act 1999
Companies Act 1990 (Form and Content of Documents Delivered to Registrar) Regulations 2002

CRO receipt date stamp

Companies Acts 1963 to 2003

A1

Tick box if bond is attached ☐
note seven

Company number *for official use*

Please complete using black typescript or BOLD CAPITALS, referring to explanatory notes

Company name
in full/note one

Limited

Registered office
note two

Memorandum
delivered by an agent

Where a person as agent for the subscribers to the memorandum delivers the memorandum to the Registrar of Companies, place a tick in the box below and give the agent's details.

Tick box ☐

Name

Address

Secretary details

Please give details below of the person who has consented in writing to become secretary.

Surname

Forename
note three

Former surname

Former forename
note four

Residential address
note three

Consent

I hereby consent to act as secretary of the aforementioned company and I acknowledge that as secretary I have legal duties and obligations imposed by the Companies Acts.

Signature

Date

Presenter details
note five

Name

Address

DX number

DX exchange

Telephone number

Fax number

E-mail

Reference number

Form effective date: 15 February 2005

Director details
including shadow/ alternate directors

Please give details below of the persons who have consented in writing to become directors.
note six

Surname

Forename
note three

Former surname

Former forename
note four

Date of birth — Day / Month / Year

Irish resident
note seven

Residential address
note three

Business occupation

Nationality

Alternate director
note eight

Full director appointing alternate director
note eight

Other directorships — Company *note nine* / Place of incorporation *note ten* / Company number

Consent

I hereby consent to act as director of the aforementioned company and I acknowledge that as director I have legal duties and obligations imposed by the Companies Acts, other enactments and at common law.

Signature

Date

Surname

Forename
note three

Former surname

Former forename
note four

Date of birth — Day / Month / Year

Irish resident
note seven

Residential address
note three

Business occupation

Nationality

Alternate director
note eight

Full director appointing alternate director
note eight

Other directorships — Company *note nine* / Place of incorporation *note ten* / Company number

Consent

I hereby consent to act as director of the aforementioned company and I acknowledge that as director I have legal duties and obligations imposed by the Companies Acts, other enactments and at common law.

Signature

Date

Director details *contd*

Surname

Forename *note three*

Former surname

Former forename *note four*

Date of birth — Day / Month / Year

Irish resident *note seven*

Residential address *note three*

Business occupation

Nationality

Alternate director *note eight*

Full director appointing alternate director *note eight*

Other directorships

Company *note nine* | Place of incorporation *note ten* | Company number

Consent

I hereby consent to act as director of the aforementioned company and I acknowledge that as director I have legal duties and obligations imposed by the Companies Acts, other enactments and at common law.

Signature

Date

Subscribers to memorandum

note eleven

Signature(s)	Subscriber	Agent	Date

Tick one box only

Company capital and stamp duty statement

note twelve

Total value authorised shares €/__

Total number authorised shares

made up as follows:

Class of authorised shares | Number in each class | Value per share €/__

Total value issued shares €/__

Total number issued shares

made up as follows:

Class of shares issued | Number in each class | Consideration for each share *note thirteen*

Declaration of compliance and section 42(2) declaration

note fourteen

I
name in bold capitals

of
residential address

do solemnly and sincerely declare that I am a *note fifteen*

Director ☐ Secretary ☐ Solicitor engaged in the formation of the company ☐

and that all the requirements of the Companies Acts 1963 to 2003 in respect of the registration of the said company, and of matters precedent and incidental thereto have been complied with and that Form A1 has been completed in accordance with the Notes on Completion of Form A1.

I further declare that the purpose, or one of the purposes, for which the company is being formed is the carrying on by it of an activity in the State and that it appears to me that either

(a) the activity can be classified in accordance with the relevant classification system as follows:

NACE Code ☐☐ – ☐☐
note sixteen

and that the general nature of the activity is *note sixteen*

or (b) **that** the activity cannot be so classified but is precisely described as follows: *note seventeen*

I further declare that the place or places in the State where it is proposed to carry on the activity is/are *note eighteen*

and that the place where the central administration of the company will normally be carried on will be *note eighteen*

I further declare that this form, including the company capital and stamp duty statement which is required by section 117 Stamp Duties Consolidation Act 1999, has been fully and accurately completed.

And I make this solemn declaration conscientiously believing the same to be true and by virtue of the Statutory Declarations Act 1938.

Signature of declarant *name as at top of page*

In the presence of *signature of witness*

Commissioner for oaths ☐ Practising solicitor ☐

Notary public ☐ Peace commissioner ☐

Name of witness *in bold capitals or typescript*

Declared before me by *declarant's name in bold capitals or typescript*

☐ who is personally known to me **or** ☐ who is identified to me by *note fifteen*

who is personally known to me at *note eighteen*

This ____________ day of ________________ 20 _____

NOTES ON COMPLETION OF FORM A1

These notes should be read in conjunction with the relevant legislation.

General This form must be completed correctly, in full and in accordance with the following notes. Every section of the form must be completed. Where "not applicable", "nil" or "none" is appropriate, please state. Where €/_ appears, please insert/delete as appropriate. Where /_ applies, give the relevant currency, if not euro. Where the space provided on Form A1 is considered inadequate, the information should be presented on a continuation sheet in the same format as the relevant section in the form. The use of a continuation sheet must be so indicated in the relevant section.

note one The proposed company name must be given in full and must correspond **exactly** with the company name given on the accompanying memorandum and articles of association.

note two A **full** postal address in the State at which post is capable of being readily delivered by the postal service must be given. A P.O. Box will not suffice.

note three Insert full name (initials will not suffice) and the usual residential address. Where the secretary is a firm, the name of the firm and registered address ought to be stated. Where a person is signing on behalf of a company which is the secretary, he/she should state that he/she is signing for and on behalf of the company which is acting as secretary. His/her name should be printed in bold capitals or typescript below the signature.

note four Any former forename and surname must also be stated. However, it does not include the following: (a) in the case of a person usually known by a title different from his/her surname, the name by which he/she is known previous to the adoption of a succession to the title; (b) in the case of any person, a former forename or surname where the forename or surname was changed or disused before the person bearing the name attained the age of 18 years or has been changed or disused for a period of not less than 20 years; (c) in the case of a married woman, the name or surname by which she was known previous to her marriage.

note five This section must be completed by the person who is presenting the application form to the Registrar. This may be either the applicant or a person on his/her behalf. The certificate of incorporation will be issued by hand or by registered post to the presenter.

note six All company types must have a minimum of two directors.
Where a person who has consented to be a director of this company is currently disqualified under the law of another state from being appointed or acting as a director or secretary of a body corporate or undertaking, he/she must complete Form B74 which must be submitted to CRO **with** Form A1. Otherwise he/she will be deemed to be disqualified from acting as a director of an Irish-registered company for the balance remaining of his/her foreign disqualification.
'Shadow director' means a person in accordance with whose directions or instructions the directors of a company are accustomed to act.

note seven Every company must have at least one Irish-resident full director or a bond pursuant to s43(3) Companies (Amendment)(No.2) Act 1999. Note that an Irish-resident alternate director is not sufficent for the purposes of s43 of that Act. Place a tick in the "Irish resident" box if the director is resident in the State in accordance with s43 of the 1999 Act as defined by s44(8) and (9) of that Act. If no full director is so resident, a valid bond must be furnished **with** the application. (Note that "Irish resident" means resident in the Republic of Ireland.) For further information on the bond, see CRO Information Leaflet No. 17.

note eight Tick the box if the director appointed is an alternate/substitute director. Where the box is ticked, the name of the full director appointing the alternate/substitute director must also be inserted in the space provided.
If the company's articles so permit and subject to compliance with those articles, a director may appoint a person to be an alternate/substitute director on his/her behalf. The appointment of any person to act as director is notifiable by a company to the CRO, regardless of how that appointment is described. The company is statutorily obliged to notify the CRO of the addition to and removal of each person from its register of directors. In the event that a full director who has appointed an alternate director ceases to act as a director, the company is required to notify the CRO of the termination of appointment of the full director **and** his/her alternate. Note: CRO accepts no responsibility for maintaining the link between a full director and his/her alternate.

note nine State the company name and number of other bodies corporate, whether incorporated in the State or elsewhere, of which the person is or has been director. Exceptions to this rule are made for bodies (a) of which the person has not been a director at any time during the past 10 years; (b) which the company is (or was at the relevant time) a wholly owned subsidiary; (c) which are (or were at the relevant time) wholly owned subsidiaries of the company.
Pursuant to s45(1) Companies (Amendment)(No.2) Act 1999, a person shall not at a particular time be a director of more than 25 companies. However, under s45(3) of the Act, certain directorships are not reckoned for the purposes of s45(1). For further information, see CRO Information Leaflet No.1.

note ten Place of incorporation if outside the State.

note eleven The subscribers in this section **must** correspond with the subscribers to the accompanying memorandum and articles of association except where an agent signs this section on behalf of the subscriber(s). Where the space is inadequate, the signatures must be presented on a continuation sheet in the **same format** as this section.

note twelve Where applicable, the details must correspond **exactly** with the share details given in the accompanying memorandum and articles of association. Capital duty is also payable at the time of registration where the company is limited by shares and is charged at the rate of 0.5% on issued share capital subject to a minimum of €1.

note thirteen Indicate cash or stock.

note fourteen The statutory declaration is a declaration of compliance with all the legal requirements relating to the incorporation of a company. **It must be signed by either a solicitor who is forming the company or the director or secretary in the presence of either a commissioner of oaths, notary public, solicitor or peace commissioner.** As the declaration confirms that all other registration requirements have been completed, it must be signed after the form has been completed in full, and so the date of declaration must not predate the dates of other signatures which appear on the form and accompanying memorandum and articles of association.

note fifteen Tick the relevant box.

note sixteen	The NACE code is the common basis for statistical classifications of economic activities within the E.U. The code is available on www.cro.ie. The four digit NACE code and general nature of the activity **must** correspond with the proposed company's principal objective in the accompanying memorandum of association. Where there are two or more activities, give details of the principal activity in the State.
note seventeen	As all activities can be classified under the NACE code, it should rarely be necessary to complete (b).
note eighteen	Full postal address must be given. A P.O. Box will not suffice.

Checklist

Page 1	Does the company name correspond exactly with that given on the accompanying memorandum and articles of association?	☐
	If the memorandum is delivered by an agent, are the relevant details entered correctly?	☐
	Is a full postal address in the State for the registered office given?	☐
	Are the secretary's details given in full (in bold capitals/typescript)?	☐
	Are the presenter's details given and is the postal address legible and correct?	☐
	If a bond is attached, is the relevant box ticked?	☐
Page 2	Is there a minimum of two full directors and are their details, including their usual residential addresses, given in full (in bold capitals/typescript)?	☐
	Where none of the full directors is Irish-resident, is a bond attached and does it meet the effective date requirements? See CRO Information Leaflet 17.	☐
	Where appropriate, is Form B74 (Statement of Director's Disqualifications) attached?	☐
Page 3	Does the number of subscribers correspond with that on the accompanying memorandum and articles of association?	☐
	Where applicable, is the capital duty statement completed in full and do the details correspond with the share capital details in the accompanying memorandum and articles of association?	☐
Page 4	Is the correct NACE code applied and does it correspond with the description of the general nature of the activity and the main object in the accompanying memorandum of association?	☐
	Are full postal addresses for the place(s) of activity and central administration given?	☐
	Is the statutory declaration completed in full and does the declaration date not precede all other dates given on Form A1 and the accompanying memorandum and articles of association?	☐
General	Are all signatures and dates given where requested?	☐
	Are the accompanying memorandum and articles of association completed in full and are full details of occupations and addresses given for the subscribers and witness?	☐
	Where the company is limited by shares, is the capital duty, at a rate of 0.5% on the issued share capital, at a minimum of €1, paid with the prescribed fee accompanying the form?	☐

Further information

Changes After registration, you must notify the CRO of any changes to the registered company details. The following forms are the principal ones completed and submitted to the CRO (for the full list go to www.cro.ie):

B2	Notice of change in the situation of the registered office
B3	Notice of the places where the register of members, register of debenture holders, register of directors' and secretary's interests in shares and debentures, and directors' service contracts/memoranda are kept
B4/G1	Notice of increase in authorised capital
B5	Return of allotments (increase in issued share capital)
B10	Notice of change of directors or secretaries or in their particulars
B67	Section 44 certificate
B69	Statutory declaration that person has ceased to act as secretary/director
B70	Notification of death of director/secretary
G1Q/G1	Change of company name
D1/D4/D6/D12/M1/M2	Re-registration of company status

CRO address When you have completed and signed the form, please send with the prescribed fee to the Registrar of Companies at:
Parnell House, 14 Parnell Square, Dublin 1
DX 145001 Parnell House

Payment If paying by cheque, postal order or bank draft, please make the fee payable to the Companies Registration Office. Cheques or bankdrafts must be drawn on a bank in the Republic of Ireland.

Please *carefully* study the explanatory notes overleaf. A Form A1 that is not completed correctly or is not accompanied by the correct documents or fee is liable to be rejected and returned to the presenter by the CRO.

FURTHER INFORMATION ON COMPLETION OF FORM A1, INCLUDING THE PRESCRIBED FEE, IS AVAILABLE FROM INFORMATION LEAFLET NO. 1, "COMPANY INCORPORATION", FROM www.cro.ie OR BY E-MAIL info@cro.ie

Form B1: CRO Annual Return

IMPORTANT CHANGE TO FORM B1
A new section has been inserted into this form.
This page is for your information only.

Do not complete

Tick box if bond is attached ☐
note sixteen

Company number ☐☐☐☐☐☐

B1

Please complete using black typescript or BOLD CAPITALS, referring to explanatory notes

Company name *in full* ______________________ Limited

Return made up to *note one* Day ☐☐ Month ☐☐ Year ☐☐☐☐

If the return is made up to a date earlier than the existing ARD, do you wish to retain the anniversary of the existing ARD for next year? *note two* Yes ☐ No ☐

Companies that wish to file their annual return prior to their ARD

It is now possible for a company to make a return up to an earlier date than its ARD without changing its ARD for future years.

Under the previous rules, a company with, for example an ARD of 31 December 2004, would have had to wait until December 2004 to file its annual return if it wanted to retain 31 December as its ARD in future years.

Under the new rules, a company ready to file early can make the return up to a date earlier than its ARD. However, the company must then decide to either:

(a) retain the same ARD for next year, or
(b) move the ARD to the anniversary of that earlier date for next year.

If the company decides (a), the "Yes" box must be ticked. If it decides (b), the "No" box must be ticked.

* * * * * * * * * * * * * *

A company is statutorily obliged to file an annual return with CRO once at least in every calendar year. Accordingly, where an annual return is made up to a date in the calendar year prior to the company's next ARD, the effect of ticking the "Yes" box is to retain the company's next ARD as it is. For instance, a company with its next ARD falling on 31 March 2005, which files a further annual return in 2004 made up to 31 October 2004 and ticks the "Yes" box, will have a 2005 ARD of 31 March 2005. If it ticks the "No" box, its 2005 ARD will be 31 October 2005.

If your company's return is being made up to a date earlier than its existing ARD and neither box is ticked, the form will be returned to the presenter for correction.

If the return is being filed with a Form B73, and the return is made up to a date earlier than the company's next ARD, the "Yes" box should NOT be ticked as the ARD cannot be extended and retained at the same time.

The question applies only to those companies that are filing a return made up to a date earlier than their ARD. If your company files a return made up to its ARD and ticks either of the boxes, this information will be ignored by the CRO as it is legally meaningless. As a matter of law, where a company makes a return up to its ARD, its ARD in the following year is the anniversary of its ARD.

* * * * * * * * * * * * * *

The first return of a new company must be made up to its ARD which is six months after its date of incorporation. Accordingly, this section of the form does not apply to a new company filing its first return post-incorporation.

Companies Registration Office

Annual return
Sections 125, 127, 128 Companies Act 1963
Section 7 Companies (Amendment) Act 1986
Section 26 Electoral Act 1997
Sections 43, 44 Companies (Amendment)(No. 2) Act 1999
Section 249A Companies Act 1990 (inserted by section 107 Company Law Enforcement Act 2001)
Companies Act 1990 (Form and Content of Documents Delivered to Registrar) Regulations 2002

CRO receipt date stamp

Companies Acts 1963 to 2003

B1

Tick box if bond is attached ☐
note sixteen

Company number ☐☐☐☐☐☐

Please complete using black typescript or BOLD CAPITALS, referring to explanatory notes

Company name *in full* ______________________ Limited

Return made up to *note one* — Day ☐☐ Month ☐☐ Year ☐☐☐☐

If the return is made up to a date earlier than the existing ARD, do you wish to retain the anniversary of the existing ARD for next year? *note two* — Yes ☐ No ☐

Financial year *note three* — **From** Day ☐☐ Month ☐☐ Year ☐☐☐☐ **To** Day ☐☐ Month ☐☐ Year ☐☐☐☐

The company is claiming the exemption from audit in respect of the financial year covered by the accounts attached to this return. ☐

Registered office *note four*

Other addresses *note five* — Address | Register(s)/documents held at this address

Secretary
Surname | Former surname
Forename | Former forename
note six | *note seven*

Residential address *note six*

Donations for political purposes *note eight* — Name of person or political party to whom donation was made | Value of donation €/__

Presenter details — Person to whom queries can be addressed
Name
Address
DX number | DX exchange
Telephone number | Fax number
E-mail | Reference number

Authorised share capital *note nine*

Total

€/__

made up as follows:

Class	Number of shares	Nominal value per share €/__

Issued share capital *(insert nominal values)*

Total

€/__

made up as follows:

Paid up on shares issued for cash	€/__	
Considered paid on other shares	€/__	
Total calls unpaid	€/__	(E)
Total not yet called	€/__	(F)

The sum of these figures must equal the total issued share capital.

Total standing to credit of Capital Conversion Reserve Fund *note ten* €/__

Shares issued

Consideration – all cash

Class	Number of shares	Total nominal value €/__	Total premium paid €/__	Total amount paid €/__
Totals	(A)			(C)

Consideration – not all cash

Class	Number of shares	Total nominal value €/__	Total premium considered paid €/__	Total amount considered paid €/__
Totals	(B)			(D)

Totals

Total number of shares issued **(A)** + **(B)**

This total must agree with the total number of shares held by existing members as stated in the **List of past and present members** section of the return.

Total paid and unpaid and considered paid **(C)** + **(D)** + **(E)** + **(F)** €/__

Other share/ debenture details *note eleven*

List of past and present members

Persons holding shares on the date to which the annual return has been made up for 20_________ (insert year) and of persons who have held shares therein at any time since the date of the last return, or in the case of the first return, the date of incorporation of the company. *note twelve*

☐ Tick box if the list of past and present members is submitted on CD.

notes six and thirteen		Share class	Numbers held *note fourteen*	Number transferred & date *note fifteen*	Particulars of transferee *note fifteen*
Name					
Address					
Folio no.					
Name					
Address					
Folio no.					
Name					
Address					
Folio no.					
Name					
Address					
Folio no.					
Name					
Address					
Folio no.					
Name					
Address					
Folio no.					
Name					
Address					
Folio no.					

Total number held ☐

The total number of shares held must agree with the total number of issued shares given in the **Shares issued** section (total of **(A)** plus **(B)**).

Directors
including shadow/alternate directors, if any

Surname
Forename
note six

Former surname
Former forename
note seven

Date of birth — Day / Month / Year

Irish resident *note sixteen* ☐ Alternate director *note seventeen* ☐

Residential address
note six

Business occupation

Nationality

Other directorships

Company *note eighteen* | Place of incorporation *note nineteen* | Company number

---

Surname
Forename
note six

Former surname
Former forename
note seven

Date of birth — Day / Month / Year

Irish resident *note sixteen* ☐ Alternate director *note seventeen* ☐

Residential address
note six

Business occupation

Nationality

Other directorships

Company *note eighteen* | Place of incorporation *note nineteen* | Company number

---

Surname
Forename
note six

Former surname
Former forename
note seven

Date of birth — Day / Month / Year

Irish resident *note sixteen* ☐ Alternate director *note seventeen* ☐

Residential address
note six

Business occupation

Nationality

Other directorships

Company *note eighteen* | Place of incorporation *note nineteen* | Company number

---

Certification

We hereby certify that (i) this form has been completed in accordance with the Notes on Completion of Form B1, (ii) contains the particulars in respect of the company as at the date to which the return is made up and that (iii) *note twenty*

The company is not a private company. ☐

The company is a private company and has not since the date of the last annual return (or the date of incorporation if this is the first return) issued any invitation to the public to subscribe for any shares or debentures in the company. ☐

The company is a private company with more than 50 members, the excess of the number of members over 50 consisting wholly of persons who, under section 33(1)(b) Companies Act 1963, are not included in reckoning the number of 50. ☐

Signed

Director

Secretary

Name *in bold capitals or typescript*

NOTES ON COMPLETION OF FORM B1

These notes should be read in conjunction with the relevant legislation.

General This form must be completed correctly, in full and in accordance with the following notes. Every section of the form must be completed. Where "not applicable", "nil" or "none" is appropriate, please state. Where **€/_** appear, please insert/delete as appropriate. Where ***/_*** applies, give the relevant currency, if not euro. Where the space provided on Form B1 is considered inadequate, the information should be presented on a continuation sheet in the same format as the relevant section in the form. The use of a continuation sheet must be so indicated in the relevant section.

note one A company is required to file with this return any returns that may be outstanding in respect of previous years. There must be no gap between the effective date of the previous year's return (if applicable) and the period covered by this return. Pursuant to s127 Companies Act 1963, a company's return must be made up to a date not later than its Annual Return Date (ARD). However, a new company filing its first return post-incorporation must make that return up to its ARD. The return must be filed with the Registrar within 28 days of the company's ARD, or, where the return has been made up to a date earlier than the company's ARD, within 28 days of that earlier date. S127 sets out the manner in which a company's ARD is determined and in which it may be altered. There are severe penalties for late filing of the return. *Returns made up to a date prior to 1 March 2002*: If this form is being used to file such a return, the return ought to be made up to the date which was 14 days after the company's AGM for the year in question and was required to have been delivered to the CRO within 60 days of the AGM. All other notes are also applicable to such returns. The late filing penalty will be charged in respect of any such return.

note two This section must be completed if this return is being made up to a date earlier than the company's existing ARD. Where the company elects to retain the anniversary of its existing ARD for next year, the "Yes" box must be ticked. Where it elects that its ARD in the following year will be the anniversary of the date to which this return is made up, the "No" box must be ticked. If neither box is ticked, the form will be returned for correction. This section does not apply to a new company filing its first return post-incorporation.

note three (i) If the return is filed with Form B73, or it is the first return of a company incorporated since 1 March 2002, no accounts need be attached and financial year details are not required. Otherwise, give the date of the commencement and completion of the financial year covered by the accounts presented or to be presented to the AGM of the company for that year. Pursuant to s7(1A) Companies (Amendment) Act 1986 (inserted by s64 Company Law Enforcement Act 2001), the accounts must be made up to a date **not earlier by more than nine months** than the date to which the return is made up. In the case of the first return since the company's incorporation, the period since incorporation is required to be covered by the accounts. In any other case, the accounts are required to cover the period since the last set of accounts filed with the CRO.

(ii) Certain unlimited companies **are** required to prepare accounts and annex them to Form B1: Unlimited companies and partnerships where **all** the members, who **do not** have a limit on their liabilities, are companies limited by shares or guarantee, or their equivalent if not covered by the laws of the State, or a combination of these undertakings; unlimited companies and partnerships where **all** the members, who **do not** have a limit on their liabilities, are themselves unlimited companies or partnerships of the type aforementioned that are governed by the laws of the State or equivalent bodies governed by the laws of an EU Member State or combinations of these undertakings. Unlimited companies which do not come under either of these categories do not have to file accounts nor give details of their financial year.

(iii) To avail of an audit exemption, certain conditions must be satisfied. For further information see CRO Information Leaflet No. 10.

(iv) Private unlimited companies, private not-for-profit companies and certain companies with charitable objects, while exempt from annexing accounts to Form B1, are required by s128(6B) Companies Act 1963 to annex a special auditor's report to Form B1.

note four Give the address at the date of this return. Any change of registered office must be notified to the CRO. Form B2 ought to be used for this purpose.

note five If not kept at the registered office, state the address(es) where the register of members, register of debenture holders, and register of directors' and secretary's interests in shares and debentures of the company are kept, and where copies of directors' service contracts/memoranda of same (if applicable) are retained. Where the records are retained at an accessible website, the CRO should be notified of the relevant website address.

note six Insert the full name (initials will not suffice) and usual residential address. Where the secretary is a body corporate, its company name and registered office must be stated. Where the secretary is a firm, and all the partners are joint secretaries of the company, the name and principal office of the firm will be accepted.

note seven Any former forename and surname must also be stated. This does not include (a) in the case of a person usually known by a title different from his surname, the name by which he was known previous to the adoption of or succession to the title; or (b) in the case of any person, a former forename or surname where that name or surname was changed or disused before the person bearing the name attained age 18 years or has been changed or disused for a period of not less than 20 years; or (c) in the case of a married woman, the name or surname by which she was known prior to the marriage.

note eight S26 Electoral Act 1997 requires details of contributions for political purposes, in excess of € 5,079 **in the aggregate**, to any political party, member of the Dáil or Seanad, MEP or candidate in any Dáil, Seanad or European election, made by the company in the year to which the annual return relates (i.e. the period since the effective date of the previous year's annual return, up to and including the effective date of the current return), to be declared in the annual return and directors' report of the company in respect of that year. The particulars must be sufficient to identify the value of each such donation and the person to whom the donation was made. A wide definition of donation is set out in s22/s46 of the 1997 Act and includes services supplied without charge, a donation of property or goods, or the free use of same.

note nine Where a company has converted any of its shares into stock, then, where appropriate, the references to shares shall be taken as references to stock and references to number of shares shall be taken as references to amount of stock. The second page does **not** apply to a guarantee company without a share capital.

note ten Insert, where applicable. (If share capital has been renominalised pursuant to s26 Economic and Monetary Union Act 1998 and there has been a decrease in the whole or part of the authorised and issued share capital or in a class of shares as a result of the renominalisation (26(4)(a).)

note eleven Details of shares forfeited, shares/debentures issued at a discount, or on which a commission was paid including share class, number of shares and amounts in each case.

note twelve A full list is required with all returns. However, this requirement does not apply to a guarantee company without a share capital. Where joint shareholders exist, name either all joint shareholders or the first shareholder and "Another".

note thirteen Where there are more than seven shareholders, the list should be given on a continuation sheet in alphabetical order.

note fourteen Give the total number of shares held by each member.

note fifteen Applicable to private companies only. Furnish particulars of shares transferred, the date of registration of each transfer and the number of shares transferred on each date since the date of the last return, or in the case of the first return, of the incorporation of the company, by persons who are still members and persons who have ceased to be members.

note sixteen Every company must have at least one full-time Irish resident director **or** a bond or certificate in place pursuant to s43(3) and s44 Companies (Amendment)(No.2) Act 1999. Note that an Irish resident alternate director is not sufficient for the purposes of s43. Place a tick in the "Irish resident" box if the director is resident in the State in accordance with s43 of the 1999 Act as defined by s44(8) and (9) of that Act. If no full-time director is so resident and no certificate has been granted, a valid bond must be furnished with the return, unless same has already been delivered to the CRO on behalf of the company. (Please note that "Irish resident" means resident in the Republic of Ireland.) For further information see CRO Information Leaflet No. 17.

note seventeen Please tick the box if the director is an alternate (substitute) director. If the company's articles so permit and subject to compliance with those articles, a director may appoint a person to be an alternate director on his/her behalf. The appointment of any person to act as director is notifiable by a company to the CRO, regardless of how the appointment is described. The company is statutorily obliged to notify the CRO of the addition to and removal of each person from its register. In the event that a full-time director who has appointed an alternate director ceases to act as director, the company is required to notify the CRO of the termination of appointment of the full-time director **and** of his/her alternate. Note: The CRO accepts no responsibility for maintaining the link between a full-time director and his/her alternate.

note eighteen Company name and number of other bodies corporate, whether incorporated in the State or elsewhere, except for bodies (a) of which the person has not been a director at any time during the past ten years; (b) of which the company is (or was at the relevant time) a wholly owned subsidiary; or (c) which are (or were at the relevant time) wholly owned subsidiaries of the company.
Pursuant to s45(1) Companies (Amendment)(No.2) Act 1999, a person shall not at a particular time be a director of more than 25 companies. However, under s45(3), certain directorships are not reckoned for the purposes of s45(1).

note nineteen Place of incorporation if outside the State.

note twenty Tick the relevant box(es).

Checklist of documents annexed

- Balance Sheet S128 Companies Act 1963 (CA 63); S7 & S18 Companies (Amendment) Act 1986 (CAA 86) ☐
- Profit and Loss Account S7 and S18 CAA 86 ☐
- Notes to the Accounts Schedule of CAA 86 (refer specifically to s12 for notes required in the case of small/medium sized businesses) ☐
- Directors' Report S128 CA 63; S7 & S18 CAA 86 ☐
- Auditor's Report S128 CA 63; S7 & S18 CAA 86 ☐
- Special auditor's report duly certified by a director and secretary to be a true copy of the report S128(6B) CA 63 ☐
- Overall Certification The Acts require that the balance sheet, profit and loss account, directors' report and auditor's report be certified by both director and secretary to be a true copy as laid or to be laid before the A.G.M. or sent to the sole member in accordance with the single member private limited company regulations. In the case of full accounts, an overall certification will be sufficient ☐
- Guarantee by parent undertaking of the liabilities of subsidiary undertaking S17 CAA 86 as amended ☐
- Declaration of consent by shareholders of subsidiary to exemption S17 CAA 86 as amended ☐
- Notification to shareholders of Guarantee S17 CAA 86 as amended ☐
- Note stating company has availed of exemptions in s17 CAA 86, as amended ☐
- Accounting documents
  - Reg 39 E.C. (Companies: Group Accounts) Regulations 1992 ☐
  - Reg 7 E.C. (Credit Institutions: Accounts) Regulations 1992 ☐
  - Reg 7 E.C. (Accounts) Regulations 1993 ☐
  - Regs 5, 17 E.C. (Insurance Undertakings: Accounts) Regulations 1996 ☐
- Section 43 bond See note sixteen above. ☐
- Form B73 Nomination of a new ARD ☐

Further information

Professional advice If you have a problem completing this annual return, and in particular are unclear of the requirements pertaining to a company's ARD, you should consult your professional adviser.

Change in details Where applicable, the particulars given on Form B1 must accord with the particulars contained in the documentation already delivered to the CRO. The most common forms used to notify the CRO of any changes to the company details are:

- B2 Notice of change in the situation of the registered office
- B3 Notice of places where register of members, register of debenture holders, register of directors' and secretary's interests in shares and debentures, and directors' service contracts/memoranda are kept
- B4/G1 Notice of increase in authorised capital
- B5 Return of allotments (increase in issued share capital)
- B10 Notice of change of directors or secretaries or in their particulars

CRO address When you have completed and signed the form, please send with the prescribed fee to the Registrar of Companies at:
Parnell House, 14 Parnell Square, Dublin 1
DX 145001 Parnell House

Please *carefully* study the explanatory notes overleaf. A Form B1 that is not completed correctly or is not accompanied by the correct documents or fee is liable to be rejected and returned to the presenter by the CRO pursuant to section 249A Companies Act 1990 (inserted by section 107 Company Law Enforcement Act 2001). Unless the document, duly corrected, is relodged in the CRO within 14 days, it will be deemed to have never been delivered to the CRO.

FURTHER INFORMATION ON COMPLETION OF FORM B1, INCLUDING THE PRESCRIBED FEE, IS AVAILABLE FROM www.cro.ie OR BY E-MAIL info@cro.ie

Form B2: CRO Notice of Change in Registered Office

CRO COMPANIES REGISTRATION OFFICE
AN OIFIG UM CHLÁRÚ CUIDEACHTAÍ

Notice of change in registered office address
Section 113(3) Companies Act 1963 (inserted by section 4 Companies (Amendment) Act 1982)
Section 249A Companies Act 1990 (inserted by section 107 Company Law Enforcement Act 2001)
Companies Act 1990 (Form and Content of Documents Delivered to Registrar) Regulations 2002

CRO receipt date stamp
Companies Acts 1963 to 2003

Company number

B2

Please complete using black typescript or BOLD CAPITALS, referring to explanatory notes

Company name *in full* ______ Limited

Change

Registered office address *note one*

Date of change Day Month Year

Certification

I hereby certify that the particulars contained in this form are correct and have been given in accordance with the Notes on Completion of Form B2.

Signature

Name *in bold capitals or typescript*

Director Secretary *note two*

Date

Presenter details

Name		
Address		
DX number		DX exchange
Telephone number		Fax number
E-mail		Reference number

Form effective date: 15 February 2005

NOTES ON COMPLETION OF FORM B2
These notes should be read in conjunction with the relevant legislation.

General This form must be completed correctly, in full and in accordance with the following notes. Every section of the form must be completed.
Where "not applicable", "nil" or "none" is appropriate, please state.

note one A **full** postal address in the State at which post is capable of being readily delivered by the postal service must be given. A P.O. Box will not suffice.

note two Tick the relevant box(es). This form **must** be certified by a current officer of the company.

Further information

CRO address When you have completed and signed the form, please send with the accompanying fee to the Registrar of Companies at:

Parnell House, 14 Parnell Square, Dublin 1

DX 145001 Parnell House

Payment If paying by cheque, postal order or bank draft, please make the fee payable to the Companies Registration Office. Cheques or bankdrafts must be drawn on a bank in the Republic of Ireland.

Please *carefully* study the explanatory notes above. A Form B2 that is not completed correctly or is not accompanied by the correct fee is liable to be rejected and returned to the presenter by the CRO pursuant to section 249A Companies Act 1990 (inserted by section 107 Company Law Enforcement Act 2001). Unless the document, duly corrected, is relodged in the CRO within 14 days, it will be deemed to have never been delivered to the CRO.

FURTHER INFORMATION ON COMPLETION OF FORM B2, INCLUDING THE PRESCRIBED FEE, IS AVAILABLE FROM www.cro.ie OR BY E-MAIL info@cro.ie

Form B5: CRO Return of Allotments

This form should be lodged with the Revenue Commissioners, Companies Capital Duty Section, Capital Taxes Division, Stamping Building, Dublin Castle, Dublin 2, who will forward it to the Companies Registration Office.

Companies Registration Office
Companies Capital Duty

Return of allotments Companies Acts, 1963 to 2001

B5
Euro

Section 58, Companies Act, 1963
Sections 114 to 122, Stamp Duties Consolidation Act, 1999

The return must be delivered within one month after the allotment

Company number

Company name *in full*

______________________________ Limited

Effective centre of management if outside the State

Registered office

Note One
The period between the first and last dates should not exceed one month.

Note Two
When the return includes several allotments made on different dates, the dates of only the first and last of such allotments should be entered and the registration of the return should be effected within one month of the first date.

Date of allotment(s) made on ______________
notes one and two
or made from ______________ to ______________

A

Allottees — **These details are not required in a case where shares are allotted to the members on a capitalisation or provisionally allotted on a rights issue.**

Full name and address	Share class	Number of shares allotted

Presenter's Name Address

Telephone Number Reference

Page 2

B

Consideration for allotment(s) consists of (✓ as appropriate)

Cash ☐ Complete Section C

Non-Cash ☐ Complete Section D

Both Cash and Non-Cash Complete Sections C & D ☐

Shares allotted in consideration of capitalisation of profits or reserves only (Section 116 (i) Stamp Duties Consolidation Act, 1999) ☐

Exemption claimed under Section 119, Stamp Duties Consolidation Act, 1999 ☐

Relief claimed in respect of the redemption of shares ☐

C

Allotment(s) for cash consideration

Number of shares	Share class	Nominal value per share	Amount paid or due and payable on each share	Amount paid or due including premium

Denomination ______________

Conversion rate, if any ______________

Total value of consideration €

Enter this amount in page 3 section E1

D

Allotment(s) for non-cash consideration *note three*

Note Three
Form 52 (in duplicate) or contract in writing (in duplicate) must be filed with Stamps Adjudication Branch, Revenue Commissioners, at the same time as form B5 is filed with Capital Duty Branch, Revenue Commissioners. On its return to the presenter, it must then be submitted with filing fee to the **Registrar of Companies** pursuant to s.58 Companies Act, 1963.

Number of shares	Share class	Nominal value per share	Amount to be treated as paid on each share

Full details of consideration

____

____

____

Denomination ______________

Conversion rate, if any ______________

Total value of consideration *note four* €

Enter this amount in page 3 section E2

Note Four
The total value of the consideration must be stated for allotments for non-cash consideration.

I hereby certify that the particulars contained in this form are correct ☐ Director ☐ Company secretary

Signature ______________ Date ______________

Name *Block letters please* ______________

Page 3

Companies Capital Duty

Calculation of Duty

Company Number

Statement required under
Section 117 Stamp Duties Consolidation Act 1999

Date of allotment(s) made on ____________________

notes one and two

or made from ____________ to ____________

E

Value of assets contributed or to be contributed.

1. Total from Section C €
2. Total from Section D €
3. Total 1 + 2 above €
4. Expenses *note five* €
5. Total 3 - 4 €

F

Nominal value of shares allotted

1. Amount/Denomination
2. Conversion Rate
3. Amount in € €

Note Five
Ascertained in accordance with the provisions of Section 118 Stamp Duties Consolidation Act 1999. Full details, including copies of invoices / receipts, must be submitted with this form.

Greater amount of boxes E5 or F3

€

Rate of Duty
0.5% from 02/12/2004
1.00% prior to 02/12/2004
Amount calculated to be rounded down to nearest €, subject to a minimum of €1.00

€ [TOTAL DUTY]

+

Interest for ________ days
note six

€ [INTEREST]

€ [TOTAL CCD]

Note Six
Interest at the rate of 0.0273% per day or part of a day is charged on duty not paid within one month of the date of the allotment.

+

€12 Companies Office Registration Fee

TOTAL DUE (CCD + Reg. Fee) €

Companies Capital Duty must be paid before lodgement of this return with the Companies Registration Office.

Form B10: CRO Notice of Change in Directors

Notice of change in directors or secretaries or in their particulars

S195 Companies Act 1963 (inserted by s51 Companies Act 1990, and amended by s47 Companies (Amendment)(No. 2) Act 1999 and by s91 Company Law Enforcement Act 2001)
S249A Companies Act 1990 (inserted by s107 Company Law Enforcement Act 2001)
S43, s44 (other than subsection (2)) and s45 (other than subsections (3)(b) and (5)) Companies (Amendment)(No. 2) Act 1999
Companies Act 1990 (Form and Content of Documents Delivered to Registrar) Regulations 2002

CRO COMPANIES REGISTRATION OFFICE
AN OIFIG UM CHLÁRÚ CUIDEACHTAÍ

CRO receipt date stamp

Companies Acts 1963 to 2003

B10

Tick box if bond is attached ☐ *note six*

Company number ☐☐☐☐☐☐

Please complete using black typescript or BOLD CAPITALS, referring to explanatory notes

Company name *in full* ________________ Limited

Change(s) *note one* ________________

Date change(s) take(s) effect — Day ☐☐ Month ☐☐ Year ☐☐☐☐

New secretary/director ***including shadow/ alternate director***

Please give details below of the person who has consented in writing to become secretary and/or director. ***(continued overleaf)*** *note two*

Surname		Former surname	
Forename *note three*		Former forename *note four*	
Date of birth *note five*	Day ☐☐ Month ☐☐ Year ☐☐☐☐	Irish resident *note six* ☐	Alternate director *note seven* ☐
Residential address *note three*			
Business occupation *note five*		Nationality *note five*	

Other directorships

Company *note eight*	Place of incorporation *note nine*	Company number

Consent *note ten*

I hereby consent to act as:

☐ director of the aforementioned company and I acknowledge that as director I have legal duties and obligations imposed by the Companies Acts, other enactments and at common law.

☐ secretary of the aforementioned company and I acknowledge that as secretary I have legal duties and obligations imposed by the Companies Acts.

Signature ________________ Date ________________

Continue overleaf for certification

Presenter details

Name			
Address			
DX number		DX exchange	
Telephone number		Fax number	
E-mail		Reference number	

Form effective date: 15 February 2005

New secretary/director
including shadow/alternate director

Surname | Former surname
Forename *note three* | Former forename *note four*

Date of birth *note five* — Day / Month / Year | Irish resident *note six* ☐ | Alternate director *note seven* ☐

Residential address *note three*

Business occupation *note five* | Nationality *note five*

Other directorships — Company *note eight* | Place of incorporation *note nine* | Company number

Consent *note ten*
I hereby consent to act as:

☐ director of the aforementioned company and I acknowledge that as director I have legal duties and obligations imposed by the Companies Acts, other enactments and at common law.

☐ secretary of the aforementioned company and I acknowledge that as secretary I have legal duties and obligations imposed by the Companies Acts.

Signature | Date

Surname | Former surname
Forename *note three* | Former forename *note four*

Date of birth *note five* — Day / Month / Year | Irish resident *note six* ☐ | Alternate director *note seven* ☐

Residential address *note three*

Business occupation *note five* | Nationality *note five*

Other directorships — Company *note eight* | Place of incorporation *note nine* | Company number

Consent *note ten*
I hereby consent to act as:

☐ director of the aforementioned company and I acknowledge that as director I have legal duties and obligations imposed by the Companies Acts, other enactments and at common law.

☐ secretary of the aforementioned company and I acknowledge that as secretary I have legal duties and obligations imposed by the Companies Acts.

Signature | Date

Certification

I hereby certify that the particulars contained in this form are correct and have been given in accordance with the Notes on Completion of Form B10.

Signature | Name *in bold capitals or typescript*

☐ Director ☐ Secretary *note eleven* | Date

NOTES ON COMPLETION OF FORM B10

These notes should be read in conjunction with the relevant legislation.

General This form must be completed correctly, in full and in accordance with the following notes. Every section of the form must be completed. Where "not applicable", "nil" or "none" is appropriate, please state. Where the space provided on Form B10 is considered inadequate, the information should be presented on a continuation sheet in the same format as the relevant section in the form. The use of a continuation sheet must be so indicated in the relevant section. Where another Form B10 is used as a continuation sheet, it ought not to be completed in full and certified as to do so will result in it being treated as a separate form and incurring a separate filing fee. It should be headed "Continuation Sheet".

note one Give details of change(s) eg appointment/resignation of a company officer, and specify date when same took effect. Only changes which occur on the same date may be registered by this notification. Otherwise, separate notifications should be made. Where the space provided here is considered inadequate a contination sheet(s) should be attached. If a new director/secretary has been appointed, also complete the **New secretary/director** section.

note two Where a director being appointed is disqualified under the law of another state (whether pursuant to an order of a judge, or a tribunal or otherwise) from being appointed or acting as a director or secretary of a body corporate or an undertaking, Form B10 **must** be accompanied by Form B74 (Statement of Director's Disqualifications). Failure to file Form B74 where one is required results in the automatic disqualification of the person concerned from acting as a company officer in Ireland for the balance remaining of his/her foreign disqualification.

note three Insert the full name (initials will not suffice) and usual residential address. Where the secretary is a firm, the corporate name and registered address of the firm must be stated.

note four Any former forename and surname must also be stated. However, it does not include the following: (a) In the case of a person usually known by a title different from his/her surname, the name by which he/she is known previous to the adoption of a succession to the title; (b) in the case of any person, a former forename or surname where the forename or surname was changed or disused before the person bearing the name attained the age of 18 years or has been changed or disused for a period of not less than 20 years; (c) in the case of a married woman, the name or surname by which she was known previous to her marriage.

note five Applicable to directors only.

note six Applicable to directors only. Every company must have at least one Irish resident full director **or** a bond or certificate in place pursuant to s43(3) and s44 Companies (Amendment)(No.2) Act 1999. Note that an Irish resident alternate director is not sufficent for the purposes of s43 of that Act. Place a tick in the "Irish resident" box if the director is resident in the State in accordance with s43 of the 1999 Act as defined by s44(8) and (9). If no full director is so resident and no certificate has been granted, a valid bond must be furnished with Form B10, unless same has already been delivered to the CRO on behalf of the company. (Please note that "Irish resident" means resident in the Republic of Ireland.) For further information see CRO Information Leaflet No. 17.

note seven Applicable to directors only. If the company's articles so permit, and subject to compliance with those articles, a full director may appoint a person to be an alternate or substitute director on his/her behalf. The appointment of any person to act as director is notifiable by a company to the CRO, regardless of how the appointment is described. The company is statutorily obliged to notify the CRO of the addition to and removal of each person from its register. In the event that a full director who has appointed an alternate director ceases to act as director, the company is required to notify the CRO of the termination of appointment of the full director **and** of his/her alternate. Note: CRO accepts no responsibility for maintaining the link between a full director and his/her alternate.

note eight Applicable to directors only. State the company name and number of other bodies corporate, whether incorporated in the State or elsewhere, of which the person is or has been director. Exceptions to this rule are made for bodies (a) of which the person has not been a director at any time during the past 10 years; (b) which the company is (or was at the relevant time) a wholly owned subsidiary; (c) which are (or were at the relevant time) wholly owned subsidiaries of the company.
Pursuant to s45(1) Companies (Amendment)(No.2) Act 1999, a person shall not at a particular time be a director of more than 25 Irish-registered companies. However, under s45(3) of the Act, certain directorships are not reckoned for the purposes of s45(1). For further information, see CRO Information Leaflet No.1.

note nine Place of incorporation if outside the State.

note ten Tick the relevant box(es).

note eleven Tick the relevant box(es). This form **must** be certified by a current officer of the company. Where another Form B10 is used as a continuation sheet, it ought not to be completed in full and certified as to do so will result in it being treated as a separate form and incurring a separate filing fee. It should be headed "Continuation Sheet".

Further information

CRO address When you have completed and signed the form, please send with the accompanying fee to the Registrar of Companies at:

Parnell House, 14 Parnell Square, Dublin 1
DX 145001 Parnell House

Payment If paying by cheque, postal order or bank draft, please make the fee payable to the Companies Registration Office. Cheques or bankdrafts must be drawn on a bank in the Republic of Ireland.

Please *carefully* study the explanatory notes above. A Form B10 that is not completed correctly or is not accompanied by the correct documents or fee is liable to be rejected and returned to the presenter by the CRO pursuant to section 249A Companies Act 1990 (inserted by section 107 Company Law Enforcement Act 2001). Unless the document, duly corrected, is relodged in the CRO within 14 days, it will be deemed to have never been delivered to the CRO.

FURTHER INFORMATION ON COMPLETION OF FORM B10, INCLUDING THE PRESCRIBED FEE, IS AVAILABLE FROM www.cro.ie OR BY E-MAIL info@cro.ie

Form ADJN6: Statutory Declaration

Stamps Office,
Revenue Commissioners,
Dublin Castle.

Telephone: 01-6475000
Fax: 01-6793261

Public Office Hours
10.00a.m. to 4.30p.m.

DRAFT STATUTORY DECLARATION

(Claim for relief under Section 79 of the Stamp Duties Consolidation Act, 1999, for transfers between associated companies)

IN THE MATTER OF

Section 79 of the Stamp Duties Consolidation Act, 1999

and

IN THE MATTER OF

[Name of Transferor] and [Name of Transferee]

STATUTORY DECLARATION

I, [name, address and description], aged 18 years and upwards DO SOLEMNLY AND SINCERELY DECLARE as follows:

1. I am [the solicitor for/a director of/the secretary of] [name of Transferor/ee] and as such I am acquainted with the transaction to which this declaration refers.

Form ADJN 6

Notes. re. paragraphs 2 & 3

If a body corporate is not a limited company, adapt the wording accordingly.

The italicised words may be deleted where the shareholding of the particular body corporate is not relevant for the purpose of determining the qualifying association between the transferor and transferee.

Particulars of relevant shareholders **must be verified** by a certificate from the secretary of the body corporate and must be appended to this Declaration.

2. [Name of Transferor] (hereinafter called "the Transferor") was incorporated under Registered No. [reg. no.] on [date] under [relevant legislation] as a [public/private] company limited by shares *and has an authorised share capital of [€ amount] divided into [no. and type] shares of [nominal value] each, of which [no. and type] shares have been issued, particulars of the holders of which are set out in the SCHEDULE hereto.*

3. [Name of Transferee] (hereinafter called "the Transferee") was incorporated under Registered No. [reg. no.] on [date] under [relevant legislation] as a [public/private] company limited by shares *and has an authorised share capital of [€ amount] divided into [no. and type] shares of [nominal value] each, of which [no. and type] shares have been issued, particulars of the holders of which are set out in the SCHEDULE hereto.*

Delete paragraph 4 if not applicable and renumber following paragraphs.

4. Particulars of the holders of shares in other bodies corporate which are relevant for the purpose of determining the qualifying association between the Transferor and Transferee for the relief claimed herein are also set out in the SCHEDULE hereto.

5. The instrument of [conveyance/transfer/assignment] dated [date], which has been submitted herein for adjudication, has been entered into by the parties thereto for the purpose of [state purpose].

Delete the italicised alternative that is not applicable.

6. At the date of execution of the said instrument, the Transferor and the Transferee were associated with each other, that is to say *the [Transferor/ee] was the beneficial owner of not less than ninety per cent. of the issued share capital of the [Transferor/ee] OR [name of body corporate] was the beneficial owner of not less than ninety per cent. of the issued share capital of each of the Transferor and the Transferee* either directly or as otherwise provided for by Section 79(3) AND FURTHERMORE at that date

Delete the italicised alternative that is not applicable.

(a) *the [Transferor/ee] was beneficially entitled to not less than ninety per cent. of any profits available for distribution to the shareholders of the [Transferor/ee] OR [name of body corporate] was beneficially entitled to not less than ninety per cent. of any profits available for distribution to the shareholders of each of the Transferor and the Transferee* and

Delete the italicised alternative that is not applicable.

(b) *the [Transferor/ee] would be beneficially entitled to not less than ninety per cent. of any assets of the [Transferor/ee] available for distribution to its shareholders on a winding up OR [name of body corporate] would be beneficially entitled to not less than ninety per cent. of any assets of each of the Transferor and the Transferee available for distribution to the shareholders of each on a winding up*

either directly or as otherwise provided for by Section 79(4).

7. The effect of the said instrument is to [convey/transfer/assign] a beneficial interest in the property from the Transferor to the Transferee.

8. The amount of the consideration for the [conveyance/transfer/assignment] was [€ amount], being found and satisfied by way of [state how, e.g. cash, loan, shares, etc.].

9. The said instrument was not executed in pursuance of or in connection with an arrangement whereunder

   (i) the consideration, or any part of the consideration, for the [conveyance/transfer/assignment] was to be provided or received, directly or indirectly, by a person other than a body corporate which at the time of the execution of the instrument was associated within the meaning of Section 79(3) with either the Transferor or the Transferee, or

   (ii) the beneficial interest being [conveyed/transferred/assigned] was previously conveyed or transferred, directly or indirectly, by such a person, or

   (iii) the Transferor and the Transferee were to cease to be associated within the meaning of Section 79(3) and Section 79(4).

10. It is intended that the association between the Transferor and the Transferee within the meaning of Section 79(3) shall be maintained for a period of at least 2 years from the date of the said instrument.

11. I make this Declaration from facts within my own knowledge conscientiously believing the same to be true and by virtue of the Statutory Declarations Act, 1938.

Sworn, etc

Please turn over ➡

SCHEDULE

[NAME OF BODY CORPORATE]

BENEFICIAL HOLDERS OF SHARES

Name of Holder	No. of Shares	Denomination
1.		
2.		
3.		
4.		
5.		

(etc.)

Company Director/Secretary

Note:

Particulars in the above format must be furnished in this schedule in respect of all bodies corporate, the shareholders of which are relevant for the purpose of determining the qualifying association between the transferor and the transferee. In the case of a complex group structure a schematic diagram setting out the overall relationship within the group should also be furnished.

Revenue

Form ADJN7: Reconstructions and Amalgamations

Form ADJN7: Reconstructions and Amalgamations

Revenue

Office of the Revenue Commissioners
Capital Taxes Division
Stamping Building
Dublin Castle
Dublin 2
Ireland

Oifig na gCoimisinéirí Ioncaim
Rannán Cánacha Caipitiúla
Áras Stampála
Caisleán Bhaile Átha Cliath
Baile Átha Cliath 2
Éire

December 3, 1998

Adjn. Ref: /

your ref:

PARTIES:

With reference to your application for relief under Section 31 of the Finance Act, 1965, please comply with the requirements marked "X" below.

[ ] 1. Furnish a statutory declaration by a solicitor setting out in detail, point by point, how the scheme satisfies all the conditions of Section 31.

[ ] 2. Furnish copies of the share certificates issued by the transferee company.

[ ] 3. Furnish a copy of the resolution whereby the nominal capital of the transferee company was increased for the purpose of acquiring the undertaking/shares in the existing company.

[ ] 4. Furnish a copy of the memorandum of association of the transferee company wherein one of its objects is stated to be the acquisition of the undertaking/shares in the existing company.

[ ] 5. Furnish a copy of the resolution, Act or other authority for the issue by the transferee company of its unissued share capital for the purpose of acquiring the undertaking/shares in the existing company.

[ ] 6. Furnish copies of any memoranda of agreement entered into in relation to the scheme.

[ ] 7. Amend/complete the share transfer forms to show the number of shares alloted in the transferee company as part/all of the consideration for the transfers.

[ ] 8. Date the share transfer forms.

[ ] 9. Furnish copies of the audited accounts of the existing company for the three years prior to the acquisition of its undertaking by the transferee company.

[ ]

Form ADJN 14: Section 59 Contracts

Stamps Ref: ____________________

(Quote in all communications)

Stamps Office,
Revenue Commissioners,
Dublin Castle,
Dublin 2.

Phone: 01-6475000
Fax: 01-6793261

APPORTIONMENT OF CONSIDERATION IN RESPECT OF AGREEMENTS CHARGEABLE UNDER SECTION 31 OF THE STAMP DUTIES CONSOLIDATION ACT, 1999

Your Ref: ______________________ Date: ____________________

Parties: ____

The agreement submitted appears to be liable to ad valorem duty under Section 31(1) of the Stamp Duties Consolidation Act, 1999. Please apportion the total consideration (i.e. cash, shares, debentures and liabilities assumed by the purchaser) under the appropriate heads listed below. If no apportionment can be made, duty is chargeable on the agreement based on the total consideration passing.

ASSETS		**CONSIDERATION**	
Goodwill	€ ________	Cash	€ ________
Tenants and Trade fixtures and fittings	€ ________		
Book and other debts (including money on deposit at bank or elsewhere)	€ ________	Shares	€ ________
Benefit of Contracts	€ ________		
Patents, Designs, Trade Marks, Licences and Copyrights	€ ________	Debentures	€ ________
Equitable estates or interests in land or whatever tenure, whether in the State or abroad	€ ________	Vendor's liabilities (e.g. mortgages, etc) assumed by the purchaser	€ ________
Subtotal (consideration on which ad valorem duty is chargeable on the agreement)	€ ________		
Legal interest in freeholds, leaseholds and copyholds	€ ________		
Loose plant, loose machinery, stock-in-trade and furniture	€ ________		
Foreign property (other than above)	€ ________		
Ships	€ ________		
Cash in hand or on current account at bankers, bills of exchange, etc.	€ ________		
Total Value	€ ________	**Total Consideration**	€ ________

I hereby certify that the particulars shown in this form are in every respect fully and truly stated according to the best of my judgement and belief, and that no part of the value apportioned to loose plant and machinery represents plant or machinery which was not in a state of actual severance at the date of the sale.

Signed: ______________________________

Date: ______________________________

Revenue

FORM ADJN 14

Form ADJN20: Woodlands Exemption

STAMP DUTY
WOODLANDS EXEMPTION

With reference to your application for relief under Section 95 of the Stamp Duties Consolidation Act, 1999, please provide the following information:

Stamps Ref. ______ Your Ref. ______
(quote in all communications)

Parties ______

1. Details of lands

Townland ______ County ______

O.S. Sheet No. ______ Folio No. ______

Age of plantation ______ Did plantation receive Forest Grant Aid?(✓) Yes ☐ No ☐

Ref No. ______

Furnish a 6" O.S. map clearly outlining the property

For Official Use Only
(Inspector's Report)

Agreed ☐ Not Agreed ☐

Comments

2. Basis of qualification for exemption

(a) area (hectares) of lands sold/ leased: ______

(b) area (hectares) of commerical woodlands (within the meaning of Section 120) comprised in (a): ______

(c) area (b) expressed as % of area (a): ______

For Official Use Only
(Inspector's Report)

Agreed ☐ Not Agreed ☐

Comments

3. Apportionment for exemption:

(a) value of lands (incl. trees) sold/ leased: € ______

(b) value of trees growing on lands: € ______

______
Inspector's signature

Signature of applicant: ______

Date ______

Form ADJN 120

This form on completion should be sent to:
Stamps Office, Revenue Commissioners, Dublin Castle.
Phone: 01 - 6475000 Fax: 01 - 6793261

Revenue

Form SD2: Application for Relief on the Transfer of Land to Young Trained Farmers

Application for Relief on the Transfer of Land to Young Trained Farmers under Section 81A of the Stamp Duties Consolidation Act, 1999

Please complete sections 1, 2 and 3 in type or in block capitals

1. Date of execution of Deed of Transfer   /   /

2. Person claiming the relief

Name

Address

Date of Birth   /   /

PPS No.

3. Qualification held

State category
(see qualifications listed on pages 8-10)

DECLARATION

I declare that all of the particulars given by me in relation to this claim are correct. I further declare that it is my intention to -

(i) spend not less than 50% of my normal working time farming the land;
and
(ii) retain ownership of the land *for a period of 5 years from the date at 1 above.*

Signed:

Date: /   /

Claimants may be asked to produce evidence in support of the information given on this form.

Penalties will be imposed, under Section 81A of the Stamp Duties Consolidation Act 1999, for providing false information.

SD2A

Form SD4: Private Company Share Valuation Form

STAMP DUTY
TRANSFER OF UNQUOTED SHARES

Stamp Duty Ref. No.

Agent's Ref. No.

PART 1 WHEN TO USE THIS FORM

Completion of this form will assist the speedy processing of **transfers on sale** of unquoted shares. Although completion of Parts 2 - 4 is not obligatory the details requested in Parts 5 - 7 may, in certain circumstances, have to be furnished to facilitate a valuation of the shares.

Where the **fixed rate of duty** applies, complete the certificate on the reverse side of the stock transfer form.
Where a **relief or exemption** from stamp duty is being claimed, an appropriate application for the relief or exemption should be made.

Where a transfer operates as a **voluntary disposition,** or is deemed to operate as a voluntary disposition, Parts 5 - 7 of this form ***must*** be completed (see Part 3 below). The transfer ***must*** be lodged for adjudication, accompanied by a warrant for adjudication and this form, both appropriately completed.

PART 2 GENERAL INFORMATION

Name of company

Nature of business

Date of transfer | Shares transferred (No. & Type)

Transferor

Transferee

PART 3 TRANSACTION DETAILS

1. Amount of consideration shown on the share transfer form. €
2. Does the consideration comprise solely of a once-off monetary payment which is shown on the share transfer form? (✓) Yes ☐ No ☐

   If "No" please furnish a copy of the Share Purchase Agreement and

   (a) if the entire consideration is ascertainable supply full details and state the total amount of the consideration (on a separate sheet)

   or

   (b) if the entire consideration is unascertainable Parts 5 - 7 of this form ***must*** be completed and the transfer lodged for adjudication together with a completed adjudication warrant.
3. Does the consideration represent the full market value of the shares transferred? (✓) Yes ☐ No ☐

   If "No" the transfer may be deemed to operate as a voluntary disposition (see Part 1 above).
4. Are the parties related/associated in any manner?(✓) Yes ☐ No ☐

   If "Yes" tick the relevant box below (✓)

   ☐ * Related by blood/marriage.

   ☐ * Intragroup transfer (other than where relief is claimed under S79 or S80 Stamp Duties Consolidation Act, 1999).

   ☐ Co-shareholders in the company.

Transactions are subject to audit. Penalties may be incurred where incorrect information is given.

* If you have ticked this box you ***must*** complete Parts 5 - 7 and lodge the transfer for examination. Following examination the Commissioners may be able to process the transfer without formal adjudication.

Revenue

PART 4 CERTIFICATE

I certify to the best of my knowledge, information and belief, all due enquiries having been made, that the details given above are true and complete and that all the relevant facts and circumstances required under Section 8 of the Stamp Duties Consolidation Act, 1999, have been fully and truly set forth.

Signed | Date

Form S.D.4

STAMP DUTY
TRANSFER OF UNQUOTED SHARES

Stamp Duty Ref. No.

Agent's Ref. No.

PART 5 GENERAL INFORMATION

Name of company

Business location

Date of incorporation | Nature of Business

Issued share capital | Ords: | Prefs: | Others:

Shares to be valued | Ords: | Prefs: | Others:

Date of transfer | Consideration paid per share | Value submitted per share

PART 6 VALUATION DETAILS

Indicate the basis of valuation for the shares being transferred: (✓) Earnings ☐; Assets ☐; Dividend yield ☐; Hybrid ☐; Other ☐

Provide a full set of the company's latest audited accounts for the period immediately preceding the date of transfer and set out the information requested below regarding the earnings or assets values, depending on the method of valuation used.

VALUATION BASED ON EARNINGS (i.e. PROFITS)

Information from relevant audited accounts:

Turnover € | Pre-tax profits € | After tax profits €

The multiple of earnings used in your calculation | The earnings valuation of the company €

The earnings value per share € | Discount % *(if applicable)* | Value per share €

VALUATION BASED ON ASSETS

The market value of all property and investments held by the company and its subsidiaries or associate companies must be substituted for their book values when calculating the adjusted assets value of the company.

Book assets value €

State the increase which arises on substituting market value for net book value of any property held €

State the increase which arises on substituting market value for net book value of investments held €

Adjusted assets value €

After tax profits earned since date of last accounts €

Revised net assets value of the company €

Net assets value per share € | Discount % *(if applicable)* | Value per share €

VALUATION BASED ON DIVIDEND YIELD

If this method is used state on a separate sheet the basis on which it is calculated.

If the valuation is based on a methodology other than that outlined above or on a combination (hybrid method) of earnings/assets/dividend yield, outline on a separate sheet how the valuation was arrived at.

You should note that

- the information supplied may be sufficient to allow valuation to proceed without further query.
- in the event that the value offered is found to be understated, appropriate surcharges as provided for under Section 15 of the Stamp Duties Consolidation Act, 1999, may be imposed.
- the acceptance of a value for Stamp Duty purposes is entirely without prejudice to any valuation of shares in the same company for any other Revenue purposes.

Transactions are subject to audit. Penalties may be incurred where incorrect information is given.

PART 7 CERTIFICATE

I certify to the best of my knowledge, information and belief, all due enquiries having been made, that the details given above are true and complete and that all the relevant facts and circumstances required under Section 8 of the Stamp Duties Consolidation Act, 1999, have been fully and truly set forth.

Signed | Date

Form SD10: Certificates Required in Deed

SD 10 (A)

STAMP DUTY

(Stamp Duties Consolidation Act 1999,
as amended up to
and including the Finance Act 2005.)

Revenue Certificates Required In Deeds

Note: This document is also available in electronic form on our Revenue website at - *www.revenue.ie*

Further information may be obtained at - **Lo-Call: 1890 48 25 82 (Dublin)**
Tel: (021) 43 25 000 (Cork)
Tel: (091) 53 63 00 (Galway)

Revenue

April 2005

This leaflet sets out in Table 4 the wording of all the certificates referred to in the Stamp Duties Consolidation Act 1999 (as amended by subsequent Finance Acts up to and including the Finance Act 2005) which are required to be inserted in instruments for Revenue purposes.

The leaflet is for general guidance only and should not be regarded as a legal interpretation.

Residential Property

What is residential property?

Residential property is defined in Section 1 of the Stamp Duties Consolidation Act 1999 and in broad terms it includes (i) a building which was used or was suitable for use as a dwelling at the date of the conveyance or transfer and (ii) the curtilage of the residential property up to an acre.

The rates of stamp duty and the certification required is dependent on the status of the purchaser(s) and on whether the property is new or second-hand. The rates of stamp duty for residential property transactions are contained in Table 1 and the certification required is set out in Table 3.

The following is a short explanation of some of the terms used.

Who is a First Time Buyer?

A First Time Buyer is a person, (or, where there is more than one buyer, each of such persons):

- who has not on any previous occasion, either individually or jointly, purchased or built on his/her own behalf a house (in Ireland or abroad) and
- where the property purchased is occupied by the purchaser, or a person on his behalf, as his/her only or principal place of residence and
- where no rent, other than rent under the rent-a-room-scheme, is derived from the property for five years after the date of the current purchase.

Is there provision for any special situations in relation to the scope of the definition of a First Time Buyer?

Yes. There are two particular situations where a person is deemed to be a First Time Buyer.

(a) The ***trustees*** of a trust (to which section 189A of the Taxes Consolidation Act 1997 applies), whose trust funds are raised by ***public*** subscriptions for the benefit of permanently incapacitated persons, in respect of the first house(s) bought after the establishment of the trust, for occupation by the beneficiary or if more than one, each of the beneficiaries.

b) A ***spouse*** to a marriage the subject of a decree of ***judicial separation***, a ***deed of separation***, a decree of ***divorce*** or a decree of ***nullity*** in the case of the first acquisition of a house by the spouse following the separation or divorce provided that the spouse had, in relation to the former marital home,

- left that home;
- not retained an interest in that home;
- whose separated/former spouse continues to occupy that home, which home was occupied by both spouses prior to the separation or dissolution of the marriage.

Who is an Owner Occupier?

An Owner Occupier is a person who purchases a ***new*** house/apartment which is to be occupied by the purchaser, or a person on his behalf, as his only or principal place of residence and no rent, other than rent under the rent-a-room scheme, is derived from the property for a period of five years from the date of the purchase.

Who is an Investor?

An Investor is any person who does not qualify for First Time Buyer or Owner Occupier reliefs as that person (or persons in right of the purchaser) will not occupy the property as their only or principal place of residence and rent received, if any, is not under the Rent-a Room scheme. Investors acquiring new and second hand residential property are subject to the full rate of stamp duty as shown in Table 1 and 3.

What is the rent-a-room scheme?

Under this scheme there is no clawback of the First Time Buyer or Owner Occupier reliefs where rent is received by the person in occupation of the house, on or after 6 April 2001, for the letting of furnished accommodation in ***part*** of the house.

When does a clawback arise?

A clawback arises if rent is obtained from the letting of the house, other than under the rent-a-room scheme. The clawback amounts to the difference between the higher stamp duty rates and the duty paid and it becomes payable on the date that rent is first received from the property.

Non-residential Property

Non- residential property includes all types of property other than residential property, stocks or marketable securities and policies of insurance or life insurance.

The rates of stamp duty and the certification required for non-residential property transactions are set out in Table 2.

Mixed Property

In a mixed property situation the residential portion of the property is not aggregated with the non-residential portion for the purposes of determining the appropriate rate of stamp duty. The consideration should be apportioned between the residential and non-residential elements and each type of property should be separately certified to the applicable threshold (see certificate No. 8B in Table 4).

A copy of the Apportionment Form is available at Appendix 2 of the Guidance Notes issued in relation to the Stamp Duties Consolidation Act 1999. These Guidance Notes are available on the Revenue web site.

Gifts

A transfer by way of gift is chargeable in the same manner as a transfer on sale with the substitution of the market value of the property for the consideration. In the case of a gift the appropriate transaction certificate (see Nos. 8A-C in Table 4) should be adapted as follows:

- in certificate No. 8A-C substitute "value of the property conveyed or transferred/leased" for "consideration (other than rent) for the sale/lease" in line 1 of each certificate, and

- in certificate No. 8A-C substitute "property conveyed or transferred/leased" for "consideration (other than rent)" in line 3/4 of each certificate and also in line 7/8 of certificate No. 8B.

Reliefs/Exemptions

Consanguinity Relief

This relief is provided for in paragraph (15) of the heading "CONVEYANCE or TRANSFER on sale of any property other than stocks or marketable securities or a policy of insurance or a policy of life insurance" in Schedule 1 of the Stamp Duties Consolidation Act 1999. Where the relief applies the stamp duty is reduced to an amount equal to one-half of the ad valorem duty which would otherwise be payable. This relief does not apply to leases or to the transfer of stocks or marketable securities.

The wording of the certificate to be included in the instrument is set out at No. 10 in Table 4 and adjudication is required in conjunction with the relief.

Young Trained Farmer Exemption

Section 81A of the Stamp Duties Consolidation Act 1999 provides for an exemption from stamp duty on certain conveyances/transfers of property to young trained farmers. The parties do not have to be related and the relief applies to both sales and gifts but does not apply to leases. Full details of the relief are contained in Leaflet SD2A.

Where relief is claimed the instrument should contain certificate No. 11 in Table 4. Adjudication is also required.

Woodlands Relief

This relief is contained in Section 95 of the Stamp Duties Consolidation Act 1999 which excludes from the charge to stamp duty that portion of the consideration attributable to trees growing on lands for commercial purposes. The relief only applies to sales and the consideration must be apportioned between the lands and the trees and the rate of duty chargeable on the lands is determined by the amount of the total consideration for the sale.

Where this relief is claimed the instrument should contain certificate No. 12 in Table 4. While the section does not provide for adjudication it is in practice required.

New houses/apartments with floor area compliance certificate

Section 91A of the Stamp Duties Consolidation Act 1999 provides for an exemption from stamp duty for an owner occupier of a new house/apartment to which a floor area compliance certificate applies.

A floor area compliance certificate is issued by the Minister for the Environment, Heritage and Local Government where the floor area of the new house/apartment is not less than 38 sq. m. and not greater than 125 sq. m. and the house/apartment complies with certain conditions set down in regulations (**Housing (Floor Area Compliance Certificate Inspection) Regulations, 2004 (SI 128/04)**) made by that Minister.

For instruments executed on or after 1 April 2004, a valid floor area certificate, within the meaning of section 91 of the Stamp Duties Consolidation Act 1999, issued in respect of a house/apartment will be treated as a valid floor area compliance certificate for the purposes of section 91A.

Where this exemption is claimed the instrument should contain certificate No. 1 in Table 4.

First time buyer relief, under section 92B of the Stamp Duties Consolidation Act 1999, is not available for instruments executed on or after 1 March 2005 which give effect to the purchase of a new house/apartment with a floor area of not less than 38 sq. m. and not greater than 125 sq. m. where a Floor Area Compliance Certificate has not been obtained.

New large houses/apartments without a floor area compliance certificate

Section 92 of the Stamp Duties Consolidation Act 1999 provides for a relief from stamp duty for an owner occupier of a new houses/apartment. The stamp duty is charged on the site value or one quarter of the total value of the property whichever is the greater.

For instruments executed on or after 1 July 2004 (other than instruments executed in pursuance of binding contracts entered into before 1 April 2004) the relief will only apply where the floor area of the house is greater than 125 sq. m. and is so certified by a qualified architect, engineer or surveyor, as set down in regulations (**Housing (Floor Area Compliance Certificate Inspection) Regulations, 2004 (SI 128/04)**) made by the Minister for the Environment, Heritage and Local Government. These instruments should contain the appropriate certificates referred to in Table 3 the wording of which is shown in Table 4. Instruments, other than these, should be certified in accordance with the position as set out in the ***May 2003 edition of Leaflet SD 10.***

Transfer of site from parent to child

This exemption was introduced under the Finance Act 2001 by the insertion of Section 83A in the Stamp Duties Consolidation Act 1999. It applies to instruments executed on or after 6 December 2000 and adjudication is required. The requirements for the exemption are included in the wording of the certificate to be endorsed in the instrument as set out at certificate No.9 in Table 4. In addition certificate No. 3A or No. 3B in Table 4 as appropriate should be endorsed in the instrument.

Farm Consolidation Relief

This relief was introduced under the Finance Act 2005 by the insertion of Section 81B into the Stamp Duties Consolidation Act 1999. Section 81B provides for a stamp duty relief which applies in respect of an exchange of land between two farmers for the purposes of consolidating each farmer's holding.

The relief provides that where there is a valid consolidation certificate in existence at the time of an exchange of lands, no stamp duty will be charged on an exchange of such lands where the lands are of equal value. In a case where the lands exchanged are not of equal value, stamp duty will only be charged on the amount of the difference in the value of the lands concerned. This stamp duty is payable by the person or persons to whom the land which is of greater value is transferred. Where consideration is paid in respect of the difference (or part of the difference) in those values, it must be payable in cash.

The relief applies to instruments executed on or after 1 July 2005 and on or before 30 June 2007 and where the relief is claimed the instrument should contain certificate No. 11B in Table 4. Adjudication is required where the relief is being claimed.

Further details regarding the relief are available at ***www.revenue.ie*** and a leaflet, which will contain an application form for claiming the relief, will be published shortly.

Fixed Duty of €12.50

Instruments which contain the following certificate(s) are exempt from the €12.50 stamp duty imposed under the heads of charge referred to below and need not be presented for stamping.

"CONVEYANCE or TRANSFER of any kind not already described in Schedule 1"

Certificate No.13A in Table 4

"EXCHANGE" (other than an exchange relating to immovable property which is chargeable to ad valorem duty under Section 37 of the Stamp Duties Consolidation Act 1999)

Certificate No.13B in Table 4

"RELEASE or RENUNCIATION of any property, or of any right or interest in any property"

Certificate No.13C in Table 4

"SURRENDER of any property, or of any right or interest in any property"

Certificate No.13D in Table 4

Further Information

Further information may be obtained from the addresses and telephone numbers listed below. We look forward to helping you.

Dublin Stamping District,
Dublin Region,
Stamping Building,
Dublin Castle,
Dublin 2.
Lo-call: 1890 48 25 82

Cork Stamp Duty Office,
South West Region,
Government Buildings,
Sullivan's Quay,
Cork.
Tel: (021) 43 25 000

Galway Stamp Duty Office,
Border Midlands West Region,
Custom House,
Flood Street,
Galway.
Tel: (091) 53 63 00

Table 1

Rates of stamp duty for Conveyances on Sale or Lease Premiums of Residential Property

Aggregate Consideration	***First Time Buyer Rate*** Pre 2 December 2004	***First Time Buyer Rate*** On/After 2 December 2004	***Full Rate***
Less than €127,000	Exempt	Exempt	Exempt
€127,001 - €190,500	Exempt	Exempt	3%
€190,501 - €254,000	3%	Exempt	4%
€254,001 - €317,500	3.75%	Exempt	5%
€317,501 - €381,000	4.5%	3%	6%
€381,001 - €635,000	7.5%	6%	7.5%
Over €635,000	9%	9%	9%

N.B. Where applicable VAT should be excluded from the chargeable consideration.

Table 2

Rates of stamp duty for Conveyances on Sale or Lease Premiums of Non -Residential Property

Aggregate Consideration	**Rate of Duty**	**Certificate No.**
Not exceeding €10,000	*Exempt	Nos. 3A/B + 8B/C
€10,001 - €20,000	1%	Nos. 3A/B + 8B/C
€20,001 - €30,000	2%	Nos. 3A/B + 8B/C
€30,001 - €40,000	3%	Nos. 3A/B + 8B/C
€40,001 - €70,000	4%	Nos. 3A/B + 8B/C
€70,001 - €80,000	5%	Nos. 3A/B + 8B/C
€80,001 - €100,000	6%	Nos. 3A/B + 8B/C
€100,001 - €120,000	7%	Nos. 3A/B + 8B/C
€120,001 - €150,000	8%	Nos. 3A/B + 8B/C
Over €150,000	9%	Nos. 3A/B + 8B

* Where a conveyance/lease is exempt from stamp duty, the instrument need only be presented for PD stamping.

Table 3

Certificates for Residential Property Transactions

Transaction Type	First Time Buyer	Owner Occupier	Investor
Secondhand house	Nos. 3A/B + 5 + 6 + 7B + 8A/B ***(reduced rate)***	Nos. 3A/B + 8A/B ***(full rate)***	Nos. 3A/B + 8A/B ***(full rate)***
New House (floor area > 125 sq. m.) - if conveyance/lease gives effect to a site/building contract(s)	Nos. 2C/D + 6 + 7A + 8A/B ***(reduced rate on greater of site value or 25% of total price)***	Nos. 2C/D + 7A + 8A/B ***(full rate on greater of site value or 25% of total price)***	Nos. 2A/B + 8A/B ***(full rate on entire consideration)***
New House (floor area > 125 sq. m.) - if conveyance/lease gives effect to a contract for a completed house	Nos. 4A/B + 6 + 7A + 8A/B ***(reduced rate on 25% of total price)***	Nos. 4A/B + 7A + 8A/B ***(full rate on 25% of total price)***	Nos. 3A/B + 8A/B ***(full rate on entire consideration)***
New House (floor area < 125 sq. m. and > 38 sq. m) - if conveyance/lease gives effect to a site/building contract(s)	Nos. 1 + 2A/B ***(*exempt from stamp duty)***	Nos. 1 + 2A/B ***(*exempt from stamp duty)***	Nos. 2A/B + 8A/B ***(full rate on entire consideration)***
New House (floor area < 125 sq. m. and > 38 sq. m.) - if conveyance/lease gives effect to a contract for a completed house	Nos. 1 + 3A/B ***(*exempt from stamp duty)***	Nos. 1 + 3A/B ***(*exempt from stamp duty)***	Nos. 3A/B + 8A/B ***(full rate on entire consideration)***

***Where a conveyance/lease is exempt from stamp duty, the instrument need only be presented for PD stamping.**

Table 4

Wording of Certificates in Conveyances/Leases

Cert. No.	**Wording of Certificates** (delete as appropriate) Note: Knowingly furnishing an incorrect certificate is a Revenue Offence
1	"It is hereby certified that (a) this instrument gives effect to the purchase of a dwellinghouse/apartment on the erection of that dwellinghouse/apartment, (b) on the date of execution of this instrument, there exists a valid floor area compliance certificate (within the meaning of section 91A(1)(a) of the Stamp Duties Consolidation Act 1999) in respect of the said dwellinghouse/ apartment, and (c) the purchaser/one or more of the purchasers/a person or persons in right of the purchaser/a person or persons in right of one or more of the purchasers will occupy the dwellinghouse/apartment as his/her/their only or principal place of residence for the period specified in section 91A(4)(b) (new dwellinghouse/ apartment with floor area compliance certificate) of the Stamp Duties Consolidation Act 1999, and that no person (other than a person who, while in such occupation, derives rent or payment in the nature of rent in consideration for the provision, on or after 1 April 2004, of furnished residential accommodation in part of the dwellinghouse/apartment concerned or other than by virtue of a title prior to that of the purchaser) will derive any rent or payment in the nature of rent for the use of the dwellinghouse/apartment or any part of it during that period."
2A	"It is hereby certified that section 29 (conveyance on sale combined with building agreement for dwellinghouse/apartment) of the Stamp Duties Consolidation Act 1999 applies to this instrument."
2B	"It is hereby certified that section 53 (lease combined with building agreement for dwellinghouse/apartment) of the Stamp Duties Consolidation Act 1999 applies to this instrument."
2C	"It is hereby certified that— (a) section 29 (conveyance on sale combined with building agreement for dwellinghouse/apartment) of the Stamp Duties Consolidation Act 1999 applies to this instrument, and (b) on the date of execution of this instrument there exists a certificate which complies with section 92(1)(b)(ia) (new dwellinghouse/apartment with no floor area certificate) of the Stamp Duties Consolidation Act 1999."
2D	"It is hereby certified that— (a) section 53 (lease combined with building agreement for dwellinghouse/apartment) of the Stamp Duties Consolidation Act 1999 applies to this instrument, and (b) on the date of execution of this instrument there exists a certificate which complies with section 92(1)(b)(ia) (new dwellinghouse/apartment with no floor area certificate) of the Stamp Duties Consolidation Act 1999."
3A	"It is hereby certified that section 29 (conveyance on sale combined with building agreement for dwellinghouse/apartment) of the Stamp Duties Consolidation Act 1999 does not apply to this instrument."
3B	"It is hereby certified that section 53 (lease combined with building agreement for dwellinghouse/apartment) of the Stamp Duties Consolidation Act 1999 does not apply to this instrument."

4A	"It is hereby certified that— (a) this instrument gives effect to the purchase of a dwellinghouse/apartment on the erection of that dwellinghouse/apartment, (b) section 29 (conveyance on sale combined with building agreement for dwellinghouse/apartment) of the Stamp Duties Consolidation Act 1999 does not apply to this instrument, and (c) on the date of execution of this instrument there exists a certificate which complies with section 92(1)(b)(ia) (new dwellinghouse/apartment with no floor area certificate) of the Stamp Duties Consolidation Act 1999."
4B	"It is hereby certified that— (a) this instrument gives effect to the purchase of a dwellinghouse/apartment on the erection of that dwellinghouse/apartment, (b) section 53 (lease combined with building agreement for dwellinghouse/apartment) of the Stamp Duties Consolidation Act 1999 does not apply to this instrument, and (c) on the date of execution of this instrument there exists a certificate which complies with section 92(1)(b)(ia) (new dwellinghouse/apartment with no floor area certificate) of the Stamp Duties Consolidation Act 1999."
5	"It is hereby certified that this instrument gives effect to the purchase of a dwellinghouse/apartment and that section 92B(3A) (residential property first time purchaser relief) of the Stamp Duties Consolidation Act 1999 does not apply to this instrument ."
6	"It is hereby certified that the purchaser/each of the purchasers is a first time purchaser as defined in section 92B(1) (residential property first time purchaser relief) of the Stamp Duties Consolidation Act 1999."
7A	"It is hereby certified that the purchaser/one or more of the purchasers/a person or persons in right of the purchaser/a person or persons in right of one or more of the purchasers will occupy the dwellinghouse/ apartment as his/her/their only or principal place of residence for the period specified in section 92(1)(b)(ii) (new dwellinghouse/apartment with no floor area certificate) of the Stamp Duties Consolidation Act 1999, and that no person (other than a person who, while in such occupation, derives rent or payment in the nature of rent in consideration for the provision, on or after 6 April 2001, of furnished residential accommodation in part of the dwellinghouse/apartment concerned or other than by virtue of a title prior to that of the purchaser) will derive any rent or payment in the nature of rent for the use of the dwellinghouse/apartment or any part of it during that period."
7B	"It is hereby certified that the purchaser/one or more of the purchasers/a person or persons in right of the purchaser/a person or persons in right of one or more of the purchasers will occupy the dwellinghouse/ apartment as his/her/their only or principal place of residence for the period specified in section 92B(3)(b)(ii) (residential property first time purchaser relief) of the Stamp Duties Consolidation Act 1999, and that no person (other than a person who, while in such occupation, derives rent or payment in the nature of rent in consideration for the provision, on or after 6 April 2001, of furnished residential accommodation in part of the dwellinghouse/apartment concerned or other than by virtue of a title prior to that of the purchaser) will derive any rent or payment in the nature of rent for the use of the dwellinghouse/apartment or any part of it during that period."
8A	"It is hereby certified that the consideration (other than rent) for the sale/lease is wholly attributable to residential property and that the transaction effected by this instrument does not form part of a larger transaction or of a series of transactions in respect of which the amount or value, or the aggregate amount or value, of the consideration (other than rent) which is attributable to residential property, or which would be so attributable if the contents of residential property were considered to be residential property, exceeds €127,000 / €190,500 / €254,000 / €317,500 / €381,000 / €635,000."
8B	"It is hereby certified (a) that the consideration (other than rent) for the sale/lease is partly attributable to residential property, and (b) that the transaction effected by this instrument does not form part of a larger transaction or of a series of transactions in respect of which the amount or value, or the aggregate amount or

	value, of the consideration (other than rent) which is attributable to residential property, or which would be so attributable if the contents of residential property were considered to be residential property exceeds €127,000 / €190,500 / €254,000 / €317,500 / €381,000 / €635,000, and (c) that the transaction effected by this instrument does not form part of a larger transaction or of a series of transactions in respect of which the amount or value, or the aggregate amount or value, of the consideration (other than rent) which is attributable to property which is not residential property exceeds €10,000 / €20,000 / €30,000 / €40,000 / €70,000 / €80,000 / €100,000 / €120,000 / €150,000."
8C	"It is hereby certified that the consideration (other than rent) for the sale/lease is wholly attributable to property which is not residential property and that the transaction effected by this instrument does not form part of a larger transaction or of a series of transactions in respect of which the amount or value, or the aggregate amount or value, of the consideration (other than rent) which is attributable to property which is not residential property exceeds €10,000 / €20,000 / €30,000 / €40,000 / €70,000 / €80,000 / €100,000 / €120,000 / €150,000."
9	"It is hereby certified that — (a) the instrument gives effect to the transfer/conveyance/lease of a site as defined in section 83A (transfer of site to child) of the Stamp Duties Consolidation Act 1999, (b) the person becoming entitled to the entire beneficial interest in the site is a child of the person (or of each of the persons) immediately heretofore entitled to the entire beneficial interest in the site, (c) at the date of this instrument, the value of the site does not exceed €254,000 and that the transaction hereby effected does not form part of a larger transaction or of a series of transactions whereby property with a value in excess of €254,000 is conveyed/transferred/leased to that child, (d) the purpose of the conveyance/transfer/lease is to enable that child to construct a dwellinghouse thereon which will be occupied by that child as his/her only or main residence, and (e) the transaction hereby effected is the first and only conveyance/transfer/lease of a site for the benefit of that child which contains this certificate."
10	"It is hereby certified by the party (or parties) becoming entitled to the entire beneficial interest in the property that the person (or each of the persons) becoming entitled to the entire beneficial interest in the property is related to the person (or each of the persons) immediately theretofore entitled to the entire beneficial interest in the property as a (state relationship(s))."
11	"It is hereby certified that section 81A (young trained farmers) of the Stamp Duties Consolidation Act 1999 applies to this instrument."
11B	"It is hereby certified that section 81B (farm consolidation relief) of the Stamp Duties Consolidation Act 1999 applies to this instrument."
12	"It is hereby certified for the purposes of section 95 (commercial woodlands) of the Stamp Duties Consolidation Act 1999 that trees (within the meaning of that section) are growing on a substantial part of the land the subject of this instrument."
13A	"It is hereby certified that this instrument is a conveyance or transfer on any occasion, not being a sale or mortgage."
13B	"It is hereby certified that this instrument is an instrument effecting an exchange which is not an exchange which is specified in section 37 (exchanges) of the Stamp Duties Consolidation Act 1999."
13C	"It is hereby certified that this instrument is a release or renunciation of property, or of a right or interest in property, which is not a release or renunciation on a sale."
13D	"It is hereby certified that this instrument is a surrender of property, or of a right or interest in property, which is not a surrender on a sale."

Form ST21: Particulars Delivered From (effective from 31 August 1995)

PARTICULARS DELIVERED
FORM ST.21

Please type if possible or complete in block capitals and read notes overleaf when completing this form

A. DATES

Date of Instrument ______ Date of related Contract/ Agreement *if any* ______ Commencement date if Lease ______

B. CLASS OF INSTRUMENT

Tick (✓) if appropriate ☐ Transfer of fee simple ☐ Lease ☐ Assignment

If lease/assignment Term *(years)* ______ Rent review period *(years)* ______

C. DETAILS OF TRANSFEROR / LESSOR

Name 1 ______
Address ______
Tax No. ______
Name 2 ______
Address *(if different from above)* ______
Tax No. ______

D. DETAILS OF TRANSFEREE / LESSEE

Name 1 ______
Address ______
Tax No. ______
Name 2 ______
Address *(if different from above)* ______
Tax No. ______

E. LOCATION AND DESCRIPTION OF PROPERTY

Address ______

Townland ______ Folio No. ______

Tick (✓) and enter details, as appropriate Land Area

☐ Private House/Apartment . . . . . ☐ New . . . . ______
☐ Agricultural Land . . . . ☐ With Dwelling . . . . ______
☐ Non-Agricultural Land . . . . ______
☐ Commercial/Industrial Premises . Description* ______ ______
☐ Other . . . . Description* ______ ______

** A broad description will suffice e.g. Public House, Factory, etc.*

F. CONSIDERATION

TRANSFER / ASSIGNMENT (include liabilities assumed) € ______ *Tick (✓) if appropriate* ☐ Voluntary Disposition

LEASE Annual rent € ______ Premium € ______

G. DECLARATION

(By Transferor/Lessor or Solicitor for Transferor/Lessor)

I/We hereby declare that the particulars in section C are correct to the best of my/our knowledge.

Signed: ______

Name of Firm: ______
in type or block capitals

A tax number has been omitted from section C because (✓)

☐ the party involved is non-resident ☐ other *(specify below)*

______

______

H. DECLARATION

(By Transferee/Lessee or Solicitor for Transferee/Lessee)

I/We hereby declare that the foregoing particulars (apart from section C) are correct to the best of my/our knowledge.

Signed: ______

Name of Firm: ______
in type or block capitals

A tax number has been omitted from section D because (✓)

☐ the party involved is non-resident ☐ other *(specify below)*

______

______

Notes on Completion of Form ST.21

This form should be completed in duplicate and submitted by the transferee or lessee or solicitor for the transferee or lessee. [A word-processed facsimile may be used provided it contains all of the details requested in broadly the same order and layout.]

DATE	Complete the date in numerals. For example, 10 March, 2004 would be written as: **10/03/04.** Date of related contract/agreement need only be completed if one exists. In the case of a lease (or an assignment of a lease) enter the date on which the term of the (original) lease commenced/will commence.
CLASS OF INSTRUMENT	Enter term of the lease and rent review period (where appropriate) in numerals.
DETAILS OF TRANSFEROR / LESSOR AND TRANSFEREE / LESSEE	If there are more than two parties to the instrument, the information required should be provided on a separate sheet to be attached to this form.
TAX (REFERENCE) NUMBER	The following information should be furnished: • In the case of an individual his or her Personal Public Service (PPS) number; • In any other case (e.g. a company, partnership, trust) the reference number stated on any return form or notice of assessment issued to the person concerned by an officer of the Revenue Commissioners. If a Tax Number is not included for one or more of the parties named in sections C or D, complete the appropriate part of the declaration in section G or H. Where a tax number is not included a substantive reason for its omission must be furnished — it will not be acceptable simply to state that a number is not available.
LOCATION AND DESCRIPTION OF PROPERTY	Insert the townland and county if the property is a rural one. If urban, insert street (including number), town and county. Insert Folio No. if the property is registered. Insert Land Area only where an area in excess of 1 acre is being transferred or leased. Location map/plan should be provided.
CONSIDERATION	In the case of the ***transfer of the fee simple*** of any land or any interest in land, whether on sale or as a voluntary disposition, the amount of the consideration (including any liabilities assumed) is to be inserted. In the case of the ***grant of any lease*** of any land the amount of the annual rent payable at the commencement of the term of the lease and the amount of any premium are to be inserted. In the case of an ***assignment of the lease*** the amount of the annual rent payable at the date of commencement of the assignment and any premium payable are to be inserted. The box marked "Voluntary Disposition" should be ticked if there is ***no consideration or*** if the ***consideration is less than the open market value*** of the property being transferred, assigned or leased.
DECLARATIONS	Where the parties to the instrument are not signing, the declarations should be signed by the solicitor for the transferor/lessor or transferee/lessee, as the case may be.

Revenue

Warrant for Adjudication

STAMPS OFFICE

Dublin Castle Dublin 2

Phone: (01) 6792777 Fax: (01) 6748145

Public Office Hours:
10.00 a.m. to 4.30 p.m.

Sullivan's Quay Cork

Phone: (021) 968783 Fax: (021) 968010

Public Office Hours:
9.00 a.m. to 12.45 p.m.
2.00 p.m. to 4.00 p.m.

SELF ASSESSMENT OF STAMP DUTY

WARRANT FOR ADJUDICATION

(UNDER SECTION 20 OF THE STAMP DUTIES CONSOLIDATED ACT, 1999)

STAMPS. REF.
(Official use only)

Solicitor/Applicant

Name ____________________

Address ____________________

____

____

Description of instrument

____

Date of first execution ______ day ______ month ______ year

Names of parties ____________________

to instrument ____________________

____

IMPORTANT: Unless all relevant parts of the warrant are complied with and any duty payable is remitted, adjudication will be delayed.

FOR OFFICIAL USE ONLY	
This instrument is chargeable with Stamp Duty as follows: *and is so stamped.*	*The Adjudication Stamp may be impressed.* *Date Stamp*

Revenue

SELF ASSESSMENT OF STAMP DUTY

Please compute any duty payable on the instrument(s) submitted and enclose the appropriate amount of duty. **Unless the stamp duty is enclosed, adjudication will be delayed.**

INSTRUMENTS TO BE STAMPED

Description of each instrument	Names of parties to each instrument	P.D. Stamp *(tick if required)*	Duty to be impressed	Penalty *	For official use
No. of instruments	TOTAL PAYMENT ENCLOSED		€		

* *for penalty rates, (see Section 14 of the Stamp Duties Consolidation Act, 1999). Instruments are generally subject to penalty if not presented within* ***30 days*** *of execution.*

HAVE YOU

(✓)

- calculated the duty correctly? ☐
- enclosed a completed P.D. form if a P.D. stamp is required on the document? ☐
- enclosed the total payment due (including any penalty)? ☐

: P.D. form required if —

1. Transfer of fee simple
2. Lease exceeding 30 yrs.

STAMPS. REF: *(Official use only)*
YOUR REF: *(Please complete)*

ESSENTIAL INFORMATION REQUIRED WHEN ADJUDICATION IS SOUGHT

Unless sections 1, 2 and 3 below are complied with, adjudication cannot proceed

SECTION 1: PURPOSE OF ADJUDICATION

For official use only (requirements complied with) ☐

PLEASE INDICATE (✓) THE REASON WHY ADJUDICATION IS SOUGHT:

☐ The instrument operates as a **voluntary disposition** or the parties are **related/associated**

or

☐ An **exemption/relief** is sought under *(state the relevant provisions)*

....

or

☐ The instrument(s) effect(s) an **exchange** of properties

or

☐ **Other reasons** *(please state)* ....

....

***Note (i) Spouses Exemption** — transfers between spouses are exempt and **do not require** to be adjudicated (See Section 96 of the Stamp Duties Consolidation Act, 1999)*

***(ii) Penalty** — adjudication is **not required** merely because late stamping penalty is chargeable*

SECTION 2: REQUIREMENTS FOR ADJUDICATION

Official use only

A. Please provide a **photocopy** of the instrument for retention on the adjudication file. ☐

B. Please provide copies of any **memoranda of agreement** relating to the instrument. ☐

C. Please provide any other **information** which is **relevant** and would facilitate an early decision. ☐

D. **CERTIFICATES IN INSTRUMENTS** ☐
Ensure the following certificates are included in the instrument, where appropriate.

(i) **Transaction Certificate**

(ii) **Relationship Certificate** (*Note: Each transferee must be related to the transferor(s) in the required degree — see paragraph 15 of Conveyance on Sale head in Schedule 1 to the Stamp Duties Consolidation Act, 1999)*

(iii) **Building Land Certificate** *(in all conveyances, transfers, assignments or leases of lands — see Sections 29 and 53 Stamp Duties Consolidation Act, 1999)*

CAUTION

Significant penalties exist for omission or misstatement of relevant facts — see Section 8 of the Stamp Duties Consolidation Act, 1999)

SECTION 3: LANDS AND BUILDINGS — Official use only

ONLY COMPLETE IF

- the instrument operates as a **conveyance/transfer/assignment/lease/exchange*** of lands or buildings
- **adjudication is necessary** *(see Section 1 of warrant)*, and
- **exemption** or **nominal duty** is **not claimed**
  (for exchanges, provide the particulars for both properties)*

CAUTION
Significant surcharges exist for understatements of value (see S. 15 Stamp Duties Consolidation Act, 1999)

1. Furnish a **statement of market value** of the property, inclusive of milk or other quotas, as at the date of the instrument. State value: € ☐

   If the instrument is a lease state the **market rent** € ☐ and the **capital value** of any **interest passing,** having regard to the conditions and term of the lease € ☐

2. Indicate *(tick as appropriate)* the **type of property** which is passing: ☐

LANDS	☐ Agricultural	BUILDINGS	☐ Dwellinghouse
	☐ Non-agricultural		☐ Dwellinghouse-cum business premises
	☐ Site only		☐ Business premises
			☐ Farm outhouses

3. Provide **details** of the property under the **following headings**, as appropriate ☐

	REPLIES
Lands	
(a) Rateable valuation	
(b) Area	
(c) Agricultural quality	
(d) Commercial use	
(e) Proposed development	
(f) Milk or other quotas	
Buildings	
(g) Rateable valuation	
(h) Age	
(i) Condition	
(j) Living accommodation	
(k) Area of business premises	
(l) Type of business carried on	
Building Sites	
(m) Area	
(n) Proximity to services and nearest town	
(o) Development potential	
(p) Planning permission applied for or intended to be applied for	

4. Furnish a **map** of the property and a **rate demand note** or **certificate of rateable valuation.** ☐

MUST BE SIGNED AND DATED

SIGNED: ______________________________

DATE: ______________________________

Application Form for Refund/Blockout/Transfer of Stamp Duty

For Official Use Only
Reference No. /SCB
Date application received /199

APPLICATION FORM FOR REFUND/ BLOCKOUT/TRANSFER OF STAMP DUTY

Complete form in BLOCK CAPITALS
Illegible/incomplete forms will not be accepted
See notes on this page when completing this form

GENERAL INFORMATION

1. Full name of applicant ____________________
   Applicant's address ____________________
   ____
   Telephone number ____________________
2. Application completed by ____________________ Solicitor/Agent
3. Applicant's reference number ____________________
4. Address to which a refund is to issue (if different from above) ____________________
   ____
5. Please enter/tick (✓) in appropriate box to identify type of document(s) and enter number of documents submitted.
   - ❑ Conveyance — Number submitted ________
   - ❑ Mortgage — Number submitted ________
   - ❑ Memorial — Number submitted ________

   Other (Specify) ____________________
   ____
6. Identify application requirement (✓)
   - ❑ Full duty transfer — Specify amount € ________
   - ❑ Full refund — Specify amount € ________
   - ❑ Partial blockout, transfer and refund — Transfer amount € ________ Refund amount € ________
7. Indicate (✓) preference for return of documents ❑ Collection ❑ Post
8. Specify reasons for application ____________________
   ____
   ____

NOTES ON COMPLETION

Application will only be considered under the provisions of Sections 151 and 152 of the Stamp Duties Consolidation Act, 1999. The appropriate instrument(s) should accompany the completed application form. Claim(s) for refund of Memorial duty should be accompanied by original Memorial, certified fit for refund by the Registry of Deeds.

2. The identity of the town agent who completed the form often assists with subsequent enquiries.
3. To avoid any ambiguity with the issue of the refund payment, solicitor's reference number is essential.
4. Completion of this entry is necessary where applicant has a preference for issue of the payment to a sub-office.
5. In order to avoid any confusion with processing of application, it is important to specify the type and number of documents.
6. It is essential that the applicant specify which transaction is preferred.
8. The reasoning for the application is required in order to give full consideration under the statutory provisions. Where necessary, the applicant should attach supporting documentation/letter.

9-14. To be completed by Applicant.

Revenue

Form ST RFND 1

RECEIPT FOR APPLICATION FORM FOR REFUND/BLOCKOUT/TRANSFER OF STAMP DUTY

9. Applicant ______________________ 10. Applicant's Ref. No. ______________________

11. Number and type of documents ______________________

12. Refund amount requested € ______________________ 13. Transfer amount requested € ______________________

14. Instrument(s) to be returned by post/or for collection *(see No. 7 overleaf)*

Stamp Office Ref. No. Date of receipt ______________________

Form for the Clawback of Stamp Duty Exemption/Relief granted under Section 91/92 of the Stamp Duties Consolidation Act 1999

Advice of Receipt of Rent or Payment in the Nature of Rent

Clawback of Stamp Duty Exemption/Relief granted under Section 91; 91A: 92; 92A and 92B of the Stamp Duties Consolidation Act, 1999

This notification should be accompanied by (i) copy of the deed of conveyance/lease, including related contracts, in respect of which exemption/relief was granted, and (ii) payment of penalty.

Part 1 – Notification of Payment

(To be completed by person who receives the rent or payment in the nature of rent other than rent in consideration for the provision, on or after 6th April 2001, (on or after 1 April 2004 in respect of section 91A), of furnished residential accommodation in part of the house/apartment)

Stamp Duty Ref. No. (if any): ____________________
Name of recipient (in block capitals): ____________________
Address of recipient: ____________________
____
____
____

Status of recipient (delete as appropriate) **Owner/Agent**

If "Agent" for another name and address of owner: ____________________
____
____
____
: ____________________

Signature of Recipient ____________________
Date: ____________________

Part 2: Calculation of Penalty

(The penalty comprises the amount of stamp duty to be clawed back and any interest due*)

Calculation of clawback

(a) Total purchase price: _€____________________
(b) *Less* any Value-Added Tax: _€____________________
(c) Net purchase price [(a) – (b)]: _€____________________
(d) Amount of duty payable on net purchase price
Had exemption/relief not been granted_€____________________
(e) *Less* any stamp duty already paid: _€____________________
(f) Amount of clawback [(d) – (e)]: _€____________________
(g) Date of commencement of renting ____________________

Calculation of Interest due

(h) From: / / to / / __€____________________

Total amount due (amount of clawback plus interest [(f) + h)]: __€____________________

*Interest is chargeable at the rate of 0.0273% per day from 1st April 2005 (0.0322% per day from 1st September 2002 until 31 March 2005 and 1% per month or part of a month prior to 1st September 2002) from the date the payment (i.e. rent or payment in the nature of rent)is received to the date the amount of clawback is remitted.

Destination Table (Stamp Duty)

This table may be used to trace the present location of older legislation as re-enacted in the Stamp Duties Consolidation Act, 1999.

Former Enactment		*Destination in SDCA 1999*
Stamp Duties Management Act 1891		
s 1		ss 136, 137
2	FA 1924 s 38(1) provides for new recovery provisions consequent on the establishment of Saorstát Éireann. In SDMA 1891 s 2(2) the words "England or" and ", or of the Court of Session sitting as the Court of Exchequer in Scotland, as the case may require," repealed by FA 1999 s 197 and Sch 6. The functions of the High Court existing on the foundation of the Saorstát Éireann were transferred to the High Court established under CJA 1924 s 17. The Constitution of Ireland Art 58 provides for the continuity of the High Court established under the 1924 Act until such time as a High Court was established under the Constitution of Ireland Art 34. This happened in 1961. The High Court established by C(EC)A 1961 s 2 exercises the same jurisdiction as was exercised by the High Court established under the 1924 Act - C(SP)A 1961 s 8 refers.	s 138
3		s 146
4		s 147
5		s 148
6		s 149
7	Repealed by PTSA 1983 s 7 and Sch 3 Pt 1.	
8	The words "Minister for Finance" substituted for the words "Treasury" by RCO No 2 of 1923 para 17.	s 150
9	In para (a) the word "abroad" replaced by the words "outside the State". para (c) to proviso to s 9 unnecessary (obsolete).	s 151
10		s 152
11		s 153
12		s 154
12A	(s 12A inserted by FA 1999 s 185)	s 155
13 (1), (2)	Repealed by FYA 1913 s 20 and Sch.	

Former Enactment		*Destination in SDCA 1999*
Stamp Duties Management Act 1891 (contd)		
s 13 (3)-(9)	In SDMA 1891 s 13(8) the words "any forged stamp or" and in SDMA 1891 s 13(9) the words "any forged die or stamp or" repealed by FYA 1913 s 20 and Sch.	s 139
14	Repealed by FYA 1913 s 20 and Sch.	
15	Repealed by FYA 1913 s 20 and Sch.	
16		s 140
17		s 141
18		s 142
19		s 143
20		s 144
21		s 145
22	The words "Iris Oifigiúil" substituted for the words "the London, Edinburgh and Dublin Gazettes" by IR(Adap)O 1923 para 16(2). The words "Saorstát Éireann" substituted for the words "United Kingdom" by IR(Adap)O 1923 para 9(1) and the words "Ireland" substituted for the words "Saorstát Éireann" by C(CP)A 1937 s 2(1). "Ireland" is referred to as the "State".	s 156(1), (3)
23	Repealed by FA 1999 s 197 and Sch 6.	
24	The words "Saorstát Éireann" substituted for the words "United Kingdom" by IR(Adap)O 1923 para 9(1) and the word "Ireland" substituted for the words "Saorstát Éireann" by C(CP)A 1937 s 2(1). "Ireland" is referred to as the "State". Powers of district justices in relation to administering oaths and taking declarations transferred to peace commissioners by CJA 1924 s 88(3).	s 157
25		s 158
26		s 159
27	(definition of "impressed" inserted by FA 1989 s 67.) Definitions of "chief office", "head offices" and "justice" unnecessary (duplication). In the definition of "Commissioners" "Revenue Commissioners" substituted for "Commissioners of Inland Revenue" by RCO No 2 of 1923 para 11. FA 1934 s 35 confirmed that all the jurisdictions, powers and duties which were vested in, exercisable by, or incumbent on the Commissioners of Inland Revenue in relation to stamp duties became and were, on 21 February, 1923, vested in, exercisable by, or incumbent on the Revenue Commissioners. In the definition of "justice" "district justice" substituted for "justice of the peace" by AE 1922 s 6.	ss 1, 135

Former Enactment		*Destination in SDCA 1999*
Stamp Duties Management Act 1891 (contd)		
s 28	s 28 to "Provided that" repealed by SLRA 1908 s 1 and Sch. Unnecessary (transitional)	
29	Repealed by SLRA 1908 s 1 and Sch.	
30	Unnecessary (short title).	
Sch	Repealed by SLRA 1908 s 1 and Sch.	
Stamp Act 1891		
Part I		
s 1 (1)-(4)		s 2
(5)		s 134
2		s 4
3		s 6
4	(s 4(c) inserted by F(No 2)A 1998 s 8)	s 7
5		s 8
6	Repealed by FA 1998 s 125 and Sch 8.	
7	The words "of an amount not exceeding 7p" and "not appropriated by any word or words on the face of them to any particular description of instrument" repealed by FA 1998 s 125 and Sch 8.	s 10(1)
8	In s 8(1) the words ", or for any postal purpose," repealed by FA 1998 s 125 and Sch 8.	s 10(2)-(4)
9 (1)	In s 9(1)(a) the words "or used for any postal purpose" repealed by FA 1998 s 125 and Sch 8.	s 10(5)
(2)	Repealed by RA 1898 s 7(4).	
10	Repealed by FA 1998 s 125 and Sch 8.	
11		s 11
12		s 20
13		s 21
14	In SA 1891 s 14(1) and (4) the words "Saorstát Éireann" substituted for the words "United Kingdom" by IR(Adap)O 1923 para 9(1) and the word "Ireland" substituted for the words "Saorstát Éireann" by C(CP)A 1937 s 2(1). "Ireland" is referred to as the "State". In s 14(1) the words "and of further sum of one pound," repealed by FA 1999 s 197 and Sch 6.	s 127
15 (1)-(5)		s 14
(6)	Unnecessary (commencement).	
16		s 128
17		s 129(1)
Part II		
s 18	Repealed by FA 1970 s 60 and Sch 2.	
19	Repealed by FA 1970 s 60 and Sch 2.	
20	Repealed by FA 1970 s 60 and Sch 2.	
21	Repealed by FA 1970 s 60 and Sch 2.	
22	Repealed by FA 1970 s 60 and Sch 2.	

Former Enactment		*Destination in SDCA 1999*
Stamp Act 1891 (contd)		
s 23 (1), (2)	The words "or colonial" in s 23(1) omitted as they do not apply to the State.	s 107
(3)	Repealed by FA 1998 s 125 and Sch 8.	
24	Repealed by FA 1970 s 60 and Sch 2.	
25	Repealed by FA 1970 s 60 and Sch 2.	
26	Unnecessary (does not apply to the State).	
27	Repealed by FA 1970 s 60 and Sch 2.	
28	Repealed by FA 1970 s 60 and Sch 2.	
29	Repealed by CA 1927 s 3 and Sch 1.	
30	Repealed by CA 1927 s 3 and Sch 1.	
31	Repealed by CA 1927 s 3 and Sch 1.	
32	The words from "; and the expression 'bill of exchange payable on demand' includes - "to end of section repealed by FA 1998 s 125 and Sch 8.	s 1
33 (1)		s 1
(2)		s 28
34	Repealed by FA 1961 s 39 and Sch 3 Pt III	
35	Repealed by FA 1970 s 41(7)	
36	The words "determining the mode in which" and the words "is to be denoted" repealed by FA 1961 s 39 and Sch 3 Pt III. The words "Saorstát Éireann" substituted for the words "United Kingdom" by IR(Adap)O 1923 para 9(1) and the word "Ireland" substituted for the words "Saorstát Éireann" by C(CP)A 1937 s 2(1). "Ireland" is referred to as the "State". The word "abroad" replaced by the words "outside the State".	s 22
37 (1)	Repealed by FA 1961 s 39 and Sch 3.	
(2)	The words "Except as aforesaid" repealed by FA 1961 s 39 and Sch 3 Pt III.	s 23
38	Repealed by FA 1970 s 41(7).	
39		s 24
40	Repealed by FA 1963 s 104 and Sch 6 Pt IV.	
41		s 129(2)
42	Repealed by FA 1970 s 60 and Sch 2.	
43	Repealed by FA 1955 s 19 and Sch 3.	
44	Repealed by SOLA 1954 s 7 and Sch 1.	
45	Repealed by FA 1955 s 19 and Sch 3.	
46	Repealed by FA 1996 s 119 and Sch 4.	
47	Repealed by FA 1955 s 19 and Sch 3.	
48	Repealed by FA 1955 s 19 and Sch 3.	
49	Repealed by FA 1970 s 60 and Sch 2.	
50	Repealed by FA 1970 s 60 and Sch 2.	
51	Repealed by FA 1970 s 60 and Sch 2.	

Former Enactment		*Destination in SDCA 1999*
Stamp Act 1891 (contd)		
s 52	Repealed by F(1909-10)A 1910 s 96 and Sch 6.	
53	Repealed by F(1909-10)A 1910 s 96 and Sch 6.	
54		s 1
55		s 40
56	The words "or in perpetuity, or for any indefinite period not terminable with life" in SA 1891 s 56(2), (3) repealed by FA 1998 s 125 and Sch 8.	s 42
57		s 41
58 (1)-(3)	(s 58(1A) as inserted by FA 1997 s 119 substituted by F(No 2)A 1998 s 9).	s 45
(4)-(9)	(s 58(7)-(9) inserted by FA 1981 s 47.) In s 58(7) the words "or (3)" repealed by FA 1999 s 197 and Sch 6.	s 46
59 (1)	The words "Saorstát Éireann" substituted for the words "United Kingdom" by IR(Adap)O 1923 para 9(1) and the word "Ireland" substituted for the words "Saorstát Éireann" by C(CP)A 1937 s 2(1). "Ireland" is referred to as the "State". The words "made in England or Ireland under seal, or under hand only, or made in Scotland, with or without any clause of registration" repealed by RA 1909 s 12 and Sch.	s 31(1)
(2), (3)	In s 59(2) the words "except (where appropriate) with the fixed duty of £10" repealed by FA 1999 s 197 and Sch 6.	s 31(2), (3)
(4)	Repealed by FA 1970 s 60 and Sch 2.	
(5)	Repealed by FA 1999 s 197 and Sch 6.	
(6)		s 31(4)
(7)	(s 59(7) inserted by FA 1998 s 119)	s 31(1)
60		s 32
61 (1)	Repealed by FA 1970 s 60 and Sch 2.	
(2)	The words "In any other case" repealed by FA 1970 s 60 and Sch 2.	s 47
62	The proviso repealed by FA 1999 s 197 and Sch 6	s 49
63	Repealed by FA 1970 s 60 and Sch 2.	
64	Repealed by FA 1954 s 29 and Sch 3.	
65	Repealed by FA 1970 s 60 and Sch 2.	
66	Repealed by FA 1970 s 60 and Sch 2.	
67	Repealed by FA 1970 s 60 and Sch 2.	
68	Repealed by FA 1970 s 60 and Sch 2.	
69	Repealed by FA 1905 s 8 and Sch.	
70	Repealed by FA 1905 s 8 and Sch.	
71	Repealed by FA 1905 s 8 and Sch.	
72		s 13
73	The words "in any such case" unnecessary.	s 38
74	Unnecessary (does not apply to the State).	

Former Enactment		*Destination in SDCA 1999*
Stamp Act 1891 (contd)		
s 75 (1)	The words "or tack" wherever they occur omitte as they do not apply to the State.	s 50
(2)	Repealed by FA 1970 s 60 and Sch 2.	
76	The words " or tack" wherever they occur and "tack," omitted as they do not apply to the State.	s 51
77 (1)	The words " or tack" wherever they occur and "tack," omitted as they do not apply to the State.	s 52(1)
(2)		s 52(2)
(3), (4)	Repealed by FA 1998 s 125 and Sch 8.	
(5)	The words " or tack" wherever they occur omitted as they do not apply to the State.	s 52(4)
(6)	(s 77(6) as inserted by FA 1997 s 120 substituted by F(No 2)A 1998 s 10	s 52(5)
78	Repealed by FA 19991 s 91.	
79	Repealed by FA 1964 s 33 and Sch 5 Pt IV.	
80	Repealed by FA 1964 s 33 and Sch 5 Pt IV.	
81	Repealed by FA 1917 s 30(2).	
82	Repealed by FA 1970 s 60 and Sch 2.	
83	Repealed by FA 1998 s 125 and Sch 8.	
84	Repealed by FA 1998 s 125 and Sch 8.	
85	Repealed by CIRA 1893 s 4(2).	
86 (1)	The words "Conditional surrender by way of mortgage" in s 86(1)(a) repealed by FA 1970 s 60 and Sch 2. The words "wadset," in s 86(1)(a) and (e), "and eik to a reversion" in s 86(1)(a) and "back bond" and "or tack" in s 86(1)(d) and s 86(1)(b) and (f) omitted as they do not apply to the State.	s 1
(2)		s 1
87 (1)	The words ", and a reconveyance, release, discharge, surrender, re-surrender, warrant to vacate, or renunciation of any such security," repealed by FA 1998 s 125 and Sch 8.	s 57(1)
(2), (3)		s 57(2), (3)
(4), (5)	Repealed by FA 1970 s 60 and Sch 2.	
(6)		s 57(4)
88		s 58
89	Repealed by FA 1970 s 60 and Sch 2.	
90	Repealed by FA 1964 s 33 and Sch 5 Pt IV.	
91		s 1
92	Repealed by FA 1959 s 80 and Sch 4 Pt II.	
93	Repealed by FA 1959 s 80 and Sch 4 Pt II.	
94	Repealed by FA 1959 s 80 and Sch 4 Pt II.	
95	Repealed by FA 1959 s 80 and Sch 4 Pt II.	
96	Repealed by FA 1959 s 80 and Sch 4 Pt II.	
97	Repealed by FA 1959 s 80 and Sch 4 Pt II.	

Former Enactment		*Destination in SDCA 1999*
Stamp Act 1891 (contd)		
s 98 (1)	The words from "against accident; and" to "a policy of insurance" and from "or as compensation" to the end of that subsection repeald by FA 1959 s 80 and Sch 4 Pt II.	s 1
(2)	Repealed by FA 1959 s 80 and Sch 4 Pt II.	
99	Repealed by FA 1970 s 60 and Sch 2.	
100(1)	The words "other than a sea insurance" repealed by FA 1959 s 80 and Sch 4 Pt II.	s 59(1)
(2)	The words "other than a policy of sea insurance" repealed by FA 1959 s 80 and Sch 4 Pt II.	s 59(1)
101	Repealed by FA 1996 s 119 and Sch 4.	
102	Repealed by FA 1970 s 60 and Sch 2.	
103	Repealed by FA 1970 s 60 and Sch 2	
104	Repealed by FA 1999 s 197 and Sch 6.	
105	Repealed by FA 1999 s 197 and Sch 6.	
106	Repealed by FA 1999 s 197 and Sch 6.	
107		s 65
108	Reference to "Local Autorities Loans Act, 1875" omitted as that Act does not apply to the State.	s 1
109		s 66
110	Repealed by FA 1996 s 119 and Sch 4.	
111	Repealed by FA 1970 s 60 and Sch 2.	
Part III		
s 112	Repealed by FA 1973 s 96 and Sch 11.	
113	Repealed by FA 1973 s 96 and Sch 11.	
114	Unnecessary (does not apply to the State).	
115	Repealed by FA 1998 s 125 and Sch 8.	
116	Repealed by FA 1970 s 60 and Sch 2.	
117		s 131
118	FA 1924 s 38(1) provides for new recovery provisions consequent on the establishment of Saorstát Éireann.	s 130
119	Unnecessary (does not apply to the State).	
120	Repealed by FA 1970 s 60 and Sch 2.	
121	Repealed by FA 1999 s 197 and Sch 6.	
122(1)	(definition of "accountable person" inserted by FA 1991 s 96, definition of "die" inserted by FA 1989 s 68 and definition of "residential property" inserted by FA 1997 s 118. In the Table to the definition of "accountable person" the words "BOND, COVENANT or INSTRUMENT of any kind whatsoever." in column (1) and the words "The obligee, covenantee, or other person taking the security," in column (2) repealed by FA 1996 s 119 and Sch 4 and the words "SETTLEMENT" in column (1) and the words "The settlor" in column (2) repealed by FA 1999 s 197 and Sch 6.	s 1

Former Enactment		*Destination in SDCA 1999*
Stamp Act 1891 (contd)		
s 122(contd)	The words "or colonial" in the definitions of "money" and "stock" and the definition of "steward" in SA 1891 s 122(1) omitted as they do not apply to the State. In the definition of "money" "British" replaced by "currency of the State". In the definitions of "marketable security" and "stock" the words "Saorstát Éireann" substitued for the words "United Kingdom" by IR(Adap)O 1923 para 9(1) and the word "Ireland" substituted for the words "Saorstát Éireann" by C(CP)A 1937 s 2: "Ireland" is referred to as the "State". In the definition of "stock" the words "India promissory notes," repealed by FA 1999 s 197 and Sch 6. Definitions of "Commissioners", "die", "executed", "execution", "impressed", "instrument", "material", "stamp" and "stamped" unnecessary (duplication).	
(2)	Unnecessary (does not apply to the State).	
123	Repealed by SLRA 1908 s 1 and Sch.	
124	Unneccessary (commencement).	
125	Unneccessary (short title).	
First Sch	First Sch as substituted by FA 1970 s 40(1) was substituted by FA 1999 s 176 and Sch 5.	Sch 1, s 113
Second Sch	Repealed by FA 1998 s 125 and Sch 8.	
Third Sch	Repealed by SLRA 1908 s 1 and Sch.	
Customs and Inland Revenue Act 1893		
s 3	Repealed by F(1909-10)A 1910 s 96 and Sch 6.	
4	Repealed by SLRA 1908 s 1 and Sch.	
Finance Act 1894		
s 39	Unnecessary (extension of SA 1891 s 114).	
40	Repealed by FA 1999 s 197 and Sch 6.	
Finance Act 1895		
s 9	Repealed by FA 1970 s 60 and Sch 2.	
10	Repealed by SLRA 1908 s 1 and Sch.	
11	Repealed by FA 1917 s 30(2).	
12	Repealed by FA 1998 s 125 and Sch 8.	
13	Repealed by FA 1959 s 80 and Sch 4 Pt II.	
14	Repealed by FA 1970 s 60 and Sch 2.	
15	Repealed by SLRA 1908 s 1 and Sch.	
16	Unnecessary (does not apply to the State).	
Finance Act 1896		
s 12	Repealed by FA 1973 s 96 and Sch 11.	
13	Repealed by FA 1959 s 80 and Sch 4 Pt II.	

Former Enactment		*Destination in SDCA 1999*
Finance Act 1897		
s 8		s 26
Finance Act 1898		
s 5	Unnecessary (extension of SA 1891 s 114).	
6	Clarification of SA 1891 ss 54 and 57.	ss 1, 39
Revenue Act 1898		
s 7 (1)	Repealed by F(1909-10)A 1910 s 96 and Sch 6.	
(2)	Unnecessary (interpretation).	
(3)	Repealed by SLRA 1908 s 1 and Sch.	
(4)	Repealed by FA 1998 s 125 and Sch 8.	
(5)	Repealed by FA 1999 s 197 and Sch 6.	
(6)	Application of SDMA 1891 s 24 to affidavits and oaths as well as to statutory declarations.	s 157
8	Repealed by FA 1970 s 60 and Sch 2.	
9	Provision relating to Public Offices Fees Act 1879.	
10 (1), (2)	The words "Revenue Commissioners" substituted for the words "Commissioners of Inland Revenue" by RCO No 2 of 1923 para 11. The words "Iris Oifiguil" in s 10(1) substituted for the words "Dublin Gazette" by IR(Adap)O 1923 para 16(2).	s 156(2), (3)
(3)	Repealed by FA 1998 s 125 and Sch 8.	
11	Repealed by FA 1999 s 197 and Sch 6.	
12	Repealed by FA 1999 s 197 and Sch 6.	
13	Amendment of SDMA 1891 ss 9, 10, and 12.	
Finance Act 1899		
s 4	Repealed by FA 1970 s 60 and Sch 2.	
5 (1)	The words "Saorstát Éireann" substituted for the words "United Kingdom" by IR(Adap)O 1923 para 9(1) and the word "Ireland" substituted for the words "Saorstát Éireann" by C(CP)A 1937 s 2(1). "Ireland" is referred to as the "State".	Sch 1
(2)		ss 65, 66
6	The words "marketable security", "a marketable security transferable by delivery, or" and ", as the case may be," repealed by FA 1999 s 197 and Sch 6.	s 64
7	Repealed by FA 1996 s 119 and Sch 4.	
8	Repealed by FA 1973 s 96 and Sch 11.	
9	Repealed by FA 1964 s 33 and Sch 5 Pt IV.	
10	Repealed by FA 1961 s 39 and Sch 3 Pt III.	
11	Repealed by FA 1959 s 80 and Sch 4 Pt II.	
12	Repealed by FA 1925 s 49 and Sch 3.	
13	Repealed by F(1909-10)A 1910 s 96 and Sch 6.	
14	Unnecessary (construction).	
Finance Act 1900		
s 10		s 43

Former Enactment		*Destination in SDCA 1999*
Finance Act 1901		
s 11	Repealed by FA 1959 s 80 and Sch 4 Pt II.	
Finance Act 1902		
s 9	Repealed by FA 1999 s 197 and Sch 6.	
Revenue Act 1903		
s 5	Repealed by FA 1973 s 96 and Sch 11.	
6	Repealed by FA 1905 s 8 and Sch.	
7	Repealed by FA 1970 s 60 and Sch 2.	
8	Repealed by FA 1959 s 80 and Sch 4 Pt II.	
9	Unnecessary (obsolete).	
Finance Act 1905		
s 5	Repealed by FA 1970 s 60 and Sch 2.	
Revenue Act 1906		
s 9	Repealed by FA 1970 s 60 and Sch 2.	
Finance Act 1907		
s 6	Repealed by FA 1970 s 60 and Sch 2.	
7	Repealed by FA 1999 s 197 and Sch 6.	
8	Repealed by FA 1959 s 80 and Sch 4 Pt II.	
9	Repealed by FA 1964 s 33 and Sch 5 Pt IV.	
10	Repealed by FA 1973 s 96 and Sch 11.	
11	Repealed by FA 1970 s 60 and Sch 2.	
Finance Act 1908		
s 5	Repealed by FA 1970 s 60 and Sch 2.	
Revenue Act 1909		
s 7	Unnecessary (cesser of limitation of SA 1891 s 59 in respect of certain contracts).	
8	Limitation of application of SA 1891 s 77(2).	s 52(3)
9	Repealed by FA 1964 s 33 and Sch 5 Pt IV.	
10	Repealed by FA 1961 s 39 and Sch 3 Pt III.	
Finance (1909-10) Act 1910		
s 4	Ceased by FA 1994 s 107(5) for instruments executed before 1 September 1995.	
73	Repealed by FA 1970 s 60 and Sch 2.	
74 (1), (2)	The words "the Revenue Commissioners" substituted for the words "the Commissioners" by RCO No 2 of 1923 para 11.	s 30(1)-(3)
(3)	Repealed by FA 1991 s 103(5).	
(4)	Repealed by FA 1999 s 197 and Sch 6.	
(5)		s 30(4)
(6)		s 30(5)
75	Repealed by FA 1970 s 60 and Sch 2.	
76	Repealed by FA 1970 s 60 and Sch 2.	
77	Repealed by FA 1970 s 60 and Sch 2.	
78	Repealed by FA 1970 s 60 and Sch 2.	
79	Repealed by FA 1970 s 60 and Sch 2.	

Former Enactment *Destination in SDCA 1999*

Revenue Act 1911

s 15 .... Repealed by FA 1970 s 60 and Sch 2.

Finance Act 1911

s 13 .... Repealed by FA 1970 s 60 and Sch 2.

Finance Act 1917

s 30 .... Repealed by FA 1970 s 60 and Sch 2.

Finance Act 1918

s 36 .... Repealed by FA 1961 s 39 and Sch 3 Pt III.

Finance Act 1920

s 34 .... Repealed by FA 1970 s 60 and Sch 2.
35 .... Repealed by FA 1964 s 33 and Sch 5 Pt IV.
36 .... Repealed by FA 1970 s 60 and Sch 2.
37 (1)............ Unnecessary (extension fo SA 1891 s 114).
(2), (3) ...... Unnecessary (obsolete).
38 .... Repealed by FA 1970 s 60 and Sch 2.
39 .... Repealed by FA 1996 s 119 and Sch 4.
40 .... Repealed by FA 1970 s 60 and Sch 2.
41 .... Repealed by FA 1959 s 80 and Sch 4 Pt II.
42 .... Repealed by FA 1996 s 107(5).
43 .... Unnecessary (intepretation and commencement).
46 .... Unnecessary (extension of 1891 s 114).
47 .... Unnecessary (obsolete).

Inland Revenue (Adaptation of Taxing Acts) Order 1923

para 16(1).......... Amendment of SDMA 1891.
(2).......... Amendment of SDMA 1891 s 22.
17.............. Unnecessary (redundant).

Finance Act 1923

s 19 .... Repealed by FA 1999 s 197 and Sch 6.

Finance Act 1924

s 38 (1)............ s 38(1) provided that all stamp duties and also every fine, penalty or forfeiture incurred in connection with any stamp duties would be a debt due to the Minister for Finance, for the benefit of the Central Fund of Saorstát Éireann. It also set out how stamp duties, etc, were to be recovered. C(CP)A 1937 s 7(3) provides that all moneys owed to any Minister for the benefit of the Cental Fund of Saorstát Éireann immediately before th coming into operation of the Constitution of Ireland shall be payable and recoverable, in the same manner as set out in FA 1924 s 38(1), for the benefit of the Central Fund of Ireland which was established by that Constitution. Constitution of Ireland Art 59 provided for the continuance of the Attorney General of Saorstát Éireann. ....ss 130, 138
(2)............ Repealed by FA 1999 s 197 and Sch 6.

Former Enactment		*Destination in SDCA 1999*
Finance Act 1925		
s 46	Repealed by FA 1933 s 46.	
47	Repealed by FA 1998 s 125 and Sch 8.	
48	Repealed by FA 1999 s 197 and Sch 6.	
Finance Act 1926		
s 37	Repealed by FA 1996 s 119 and Sch 4.	
38	Repealed by FA 1970 s 60 and Sch 2.	
39		s 134
Finance (Customs and Stamp Duties) Act 1929		
s 5	Ceased by FA 1990 s 118.	
Finance Act 1929		
s 35	Repealed by FA 1970 s 60 and Sch 2.	
36	Amendment of F(CSD)A 1929 s 5(1).	
Finance Act 1930		
s 15	Repealed by FA 1996 s 119 and Sch 4.	
16	Repealed by FA 1999 s 197 and Sch 6.	
Finance Act 1931		
s 31	Repealed by FA 1970 s 60 and Sch 2.	
32	Amendment of FA 1920 s 39(1).	
Finance Act 1932		
s 49	Repealed by CBA 1942 s 4 and Sch 1 Pt II.	
50	Unnecessary (obsolete).	
Finance Act 1933		
s 40	The word "Ireland" substituted for the words "Saorstát Éireann" by C(CP)A 1937 s 2(1). "Ireland" is referred to as the "State".	s 9
41	Unnecessary (obsolete).	
42	Repealed by FA 1970 s 60 and Sch 2.	
43	Unnecessary (obsolete).	
Finance Act 1934		
s 34	Amendment of F(CSD)A 1929 s 5(1).	
Finance (Miscellaneous Provisions) Act 1935		
s 6(3)	Cesser of certain exemptions from stamp duty.	
Finance Act 1935		
s 35	Repealed by FA 1996 s 107(5).	
36	Repealed by FA 1953 s 13(2).	
Finance Act 1936		
s 25	The word "Ireland" substituted for the words "Saorstát Éireann" by C(CP)A 1937 s 2(1). "Ireland" is referred to as the "State".	s 27
Finance Act 1937		
s 15	Repealed by CBA 1942 s 4 and Sch 1 Pt II.	

Former Enactment		*Destination in SDCA 1999*
Finance Act 1941		
s 47	Repealed by FA 1996 s 119 and Sch 4.	
48	Repealed by FA 1996 s 119 and Sch 4.	
Finance Act 1942		
s 21	Unnecessary (obsolete).	
Finance Act 1943		
s 14	Substitution of F(1909-10)A 1910 s 74(6).	
15	The words ", and no certificate of indebtedness and no such instrument as aforesaid embodied or contained in a certificate of indebtedness shall be prevented from being given in evidence or being made available for any purpose merely by reason of the fact that no stamp duty had been paid in respect thereof" repealed by FA 1999 s 197 and Sch 6.	s 112
16	Unnecessary (construction and obsolete).	
Finance Act 1947		
s 18	Repealed by FA 1970 s 60 and Sch 2.	
19	Repealed by FA 1996 s 119 and Sch 4.	
Finance (No 2) Act 1947		
s 13	Repealed by FA 1970 s 60 and Sch 2.	
Finance Act 1948		
s 11	Repealed by FA 1999 s 197 and Sch 6.	
12	Repealed by FA 1970 s 60 and Sch 2.	
Finance Act 1949		
s 24	The words "shall be deemed never to have applied or had effect" unnecessary (redundant)	s 54
25	Repealed by FA 1970 s 60 and Sch 2.	
26	Repealed by FA 1965 s 66 and Sch 3 Pt VIII.	
27	Repealed by FA 1970 s 60 and Sch 2.	
Finance Act 1950		
s 16	Repealed by FA 1969 s 49(6).	
17	Repealed by FA 1970 s 60 and Sch 2.	
18	Repealed by FA 1970 s 60 and Sch 2.	
19	Repealed by FA 1990 s 113(5)(a)(i).	
Finance Act 1951		
s 17	Repealed by FA 1970 s 60 and Sch 2.	
18	Repealed by FA 1970 s 60 and Sch 2.	
19	Repealed by FA 1970 s 60 and Sch 2.	
20	Repealed by FA 1970 s 60 and Sch 2.	

Former Enactment *Destination in SDCA 1999*

Finance Act 1952

s 18 .... Repealed by FA 1965 s 66 and Sch 3 Pt VIII.
19 .... (s 19(2A) inserted by FA 1990 s 116)................................s 79
20 .... Repealed by FA 1970 s 60 and Sch 2.
21 .... Repealed by FA 1970 s 60 and Sch 2.
22 .... Repealed by FA 1965 s 66 and Sch 3 Pt VIII.

Finance Act 1953

s 12 .... Repealed by FA 1993 s 104(5).
13 .... Repealed by FA 1970 s 60 and Sch 2.
14 .... Repealed by FA 1970 s 60 and Sch 2.

Finance Act 1954

s 23 .... Unnecessary (obsolete).
24 .... Repealed by FA 1970 s 60 and Sch 2.
25 .... Repealed by FA 1970 s 60 and Sch 2.
26 .... Repealed by FA 1970 s 60 and Sch 2.
27 .... Repealed by FA 1970 s 60 and Sch 2.

Solicitors Act 1954

s 72 .... Unnecessary (obsolete).

Finance Act 1955

s 16 .... Unnecessary (obsolete).
17 .... Repealed by FA 1999 s 197 and Sch 6.

Finance Act 1956

s 29 .... Repealed by FA 1970 s 60 and Sch 2.
30 .... Repealed by FA 1961 s 39 and Sch 3 Pt II.
31 .... Repealed by FA 1961 s 39 and Sch 3 Pt II.

Finance (Miscellaneous Provisions) Act 1956

s 24 .... Repealed by FA 1999 s 197 and Sch 6.

Finance Act 1957

s 24 .... Repealed by FA 1970 s 60 and Sch 2.

Finance Act 1958

s 57 .... Repealed by FA 1990 s 113(5)(a)(ii).
58 .... Repealed by FA 1970 s 60 and Sch 2.
59 ....s 111
60 .... Unnecessary (obsolete).

Finance Act 1959

s 75 (1)-(3),
(4)(c)......... Repealed by FA 1970 s 60 and Sch 2.
(4)............ para (a) and (b) unnecessary ....s 59(2)
(cesser of certain provisions).
76 .... Amendment of FA 1952 s 19.

Finance Act 1960

s 35 .... Repealed by FA 1970 s 60 and Sch 2.
36 .... Unnecessary (obsolete).
37 .... Repealed by FA 1970 s 60 and Sch 2.

Former Enactment		*Destination in SDCA 1999*
Finance Act 1961		
s 29	Unnecessary (obsolete).	
30		s 83
31	Repealed by FA 1970 s 41(7).	
32	Repealed by FA 1996 s 107(5).	
33	Repealed by FA 1965 s 66 and Sch 3 Pt VIII.	
34	Repealed by FA 1965 s 66 and Sch 3 Pt VIII.	
35	Repealed by FA 1965 s 66 and Sch 3 Pt VIII.	
Finance Act 1962		
s 15	Repealed by FA 1965 s 66 and Sch 3 Pt VIII.	
16	Repealed by FA 1965 s 66 and Sch 3 Pt VIII.	
17	Unnecessary (obsolete).	
18	Amendment of FA 1961 s 32(2).	
Finance Act 1963		
s 40	Unnecessary (obsolete).	
41	Amendment of SA 1891 First Sch.	
42	Repealed by FA 1965 s 66 and Sch 3 Pt VIII.	
43	Extension of FA 1950 s 19.	
44	Repealed by FA 1970 s 60 and Sch 2.	
45	Repealed by FA 1964 s 33 and Sch 5 Pt III.	
Finance Act 1964		
s 23	Repealed by FA 1999 s 197 and Sch 6.	
24	Repealed by FA 1990 s 113(5)(a)(iii).	
Finance Act 1965		
s 31(1)-(3)	(s 31(1A) inserted by FA 1995 s 144(1)(a).) s 31(1)(A) repealed by FA 1973 s 96 and Sch 11. The words ", nor shall any such duty be chargeable under section 12 of the Finance Act, 1895 on a copy of any Act of the Oireachtas, or on any instrument vesting, or relating to the vesting of, the undertaking or shares in the transferee company" in s 31(1)(B) repealed by FA 1999 s 197 and Sch 6. s 31(1)(proviso)(c) unnecessary (redundant).	s 80(2)-(6)
(4)	Repealed by FA 1973 s 96 and Sch 11.	
(5)		s 80(7)
(6)		s 80(8)
(7)		s 80(9)
(7A), (8)	(s 31(7A) inserted by FA 1995 s 144(1)(b).)	s 80(1).
Finance Act 1966		
s 20	Repealed by FA 1998 s 125 and Sch 8.	
Finance Act 1967		
s 20		s 94.

Former Enactment		*Destination in SDCA 1999*
Finance (Miscellaneous Provisions) Act 1968		
s 10	Repealed by FA 1970 s 60 and Sch 2.	
11	Repealed by FA 1996 s 119 and Sch 4.	
12	Repealed by FA 1999 s 197 and Sch 6.	
Finance Act 1969		
s 47	Repealed by FA 1970 s 60 and Sch 2.	
48	Repealed by FA 1970 s 60 and Sch 2.	
49 (1)		s 91(1)
(2), (2A)	Repealed by FA 1998 s 125 and Sch 8. (s 49(2A) inserted by FA 1981 s 48.)	
(2B)	(s 49(2B) as inserted by FA 1984 s 100 was substituted by FA 1996 s 113(1). The words "Notwithstanding subsections (2) and (2A) of this section," and the words "(apart from the said subsections (2) and (2A))" repealed by FA 1998 s 125 and Sch 8.	s 91(2)
(3)	The words "a conveyance, transfer or lease of a house by a local authority under the provisions of the Housing Act, 1966, or of "repealed by FA 1999 s 197 and Sch 6.	s 93
(4), (5)	Repealed by FA 1999 s 197 and Sch 6.	
(6)	Unnecessary (repeals).	
(7)	Unnecessary (commencement).	
50	Ceased by FA 1978 s 35.	
Finance Act 1970		
s 40 (1)	Substitution of SA 1891 First Sch.	
(2)	Unnecessary (commencement).	
41 (1)	Unnecessary (duplication).	
(2), (3)		s 25
(4)	Unnecessary (obsolete).	
(5)	Unnecessary (commencment).	
(6)	Unnecessary (cesser of duty on certain bills of exchange).	
(7)	Unnecessary (repeals).	
42 (1)	Amendment of FA 1899 s 8(2).	
(2)	Amendment of FA 1907 s 10(1)	
(3)	Unnecessary (commencement).	
43 (1), (2)		s 60
(3)	Unnecessary (commencement).	
44 (1), (2)		s 86
(3)	Unnecessary (cesser of composition agreement under SA 1891 s 115).	
(4)	Unnecessary (commencement).	
45	Amendment of FA 1969 s 50.	
46 (1)(a)	Amendment of SA 1891 s 7.	
(b)	Amendment of SA 1891 s 23(1) and (2).	
(c)	Amendment of SA 1891 s 59(2).	
(d)	Amendment of SA 1891 s 59(5).	

Former Enactment		*Destination in SDCA 1999*
Finance Act 1970		
s 46 (2)	Unnecessary (Commencement).	
47 (1)	Amendment of FA 1907 s 7.	
(2)	Unnecessary (commencement).	
48	Repealed by FA 1996 s 119 and Sch 4.	
Finance Act 1971		
s 43 (1)(a)	Amendment of SA 1891 s 59(1).	
(b)	Amendment of SA 1891 First Sch.	
(2)	Unnecessary (commencement).	
44 (1)	Amendment of SA 1891 First Sch.	
(2)	Unnecessary (commencement).	
Finance Act 1972		
s 34	Repealed by FA 1996 s 119 and Sch 4.	
35 (1)	Amendment of FA 1950 s 19(1).	
(2)	Unnecessary (commencement).	
36	Repealed by FA 1994 s 109(3).	
Value-Added Tax Act 1972		
s 38 (4)	Amendment of SA 1891 First Sch.	
Finance Act 1973		
s 62	Unnecessary (commencement).	
63	Substitution of SA 1891 s 88(2).	
64 (1),(2)(a), (3),(4)	Amendment of SA 1891 First Sch.	
(2)(b)	Unnecessary (interpretation).	
(5)	Repealed by FA 1999 s 197 and Sch 6.	
65	Amendment of FA 1969 s 50(2). (proviso inserted by FA 1974 s 81.)	
66	Unnecessary (revocation).	
67	Definition of "operative date" omitted as unnecessary (redundant).	s 114
67A	(s 67A inserted by FA 1990 s 115.)	s 115
67B	(s 67B inserted by FA 1991 s 110.)	s 115
67C	(s 67C inserted by FA 1995 s 145.)	s 115
68		s 116
69	The words ", without deduction of income tax," in s 69(2) repealed by FA 1999 s 197 and Sch 6.	s 117
70		s 118
71	Unnecessary (transitional).	
72	(s 72(60 inserted by FA 1979 s 52.)	s 119
73	Proviso repealed by FA 1999 s 197 and Sch 6.	s 120
74	para (a) repealed by FA 1994 s 109(3). (para (c) inserted by FA 1999 s 174.)	s 121
75		s 122
92 (6)	Amendment of SA 1891 First Sch.	

Former Enactment		*Destination in SDCA 1999*
Finance Act 1974		
s 81 (1)	Insertion of proviso into FA 1973 s 65.	
(2)	Unnecessary (commencement).	
82	Unnecessary (revocation).	
83	Ceased by FA 1986 s 97(1).	
Finance Act 1975		
s 48 (1)(a),(2)	Amendment of SA 1891 First Sch.	
(b)	Unnecessary (interpretation).	
48 (3)	Unnecessary (commencement).	
49	Unnecessary (revocation).	
Finance Act 1976		
s 47 (1)	Substitution of RA 1898 s 13.	
(2)	Amendment of FA 1969 s 49(5) and s 50(4)(proviso).	
48	Substitution of FA 1969 s 49(2), (3).	
Finance Act 1977		
s 47	Provisions relating to FA 1969 s 50.	
48		s 102
Finance Act 1978		
s 31 (1), (1A)	(s 31(1A) inserted by FA 1999 s 181.)	s 36
(2)	Unnecessary (commencement).	
32 (1)	Amendment of F(1909-10)A 1910 s 74.	
(2)	Unnecessary (commencment).	
33	Unnecessary (revocation).	
34 (1)-(4)		s 33
(5)		s 18
35	Unnecessary (cesser of FA 1969 s 50)	
Finance Act 1979		
s 50		82
51	Amendment of FA 1973 s 70.	
52	Insertion of FA 1973 s 72(6).	
53	Substitution of FA 1973 s 69(2).	
54	Repealed by FA 1999 s 197 and Sch 6.	
55	Repealed by FA 1990 s 113(5)(a)(iv).	
56	Unnecessary (revocation).	
Finance Act 1980		
s 85 (1)	Substitution of FA 1952 s 19.	
(2)	Unnecessary (commencement).	
86	Ceased by FA 1985 s 56(2).	
87	Unnecessary (revocation).	
Finance Act 1981		
s 47	Insertion of SA 1891 s 58(7)-(9).	
48	Insertion of FA 1969 s 49(2A).	
49 (1)	Amendment of FA 1970 s 41(1) and (3).	
(2)	Unnecessary (commencement).	
50	Unnecessary (revocations).	

Former Enactment		*Destination in SDCA 1999*
Finance (No 2) Act 1981		
s 16	Unnecessary (spent).	
17	(s 17(2)(d) inserted by FA 1983 s 91.)	s 124
Finance Act 1982		
s 91	Unnecessary (spent).	
92 (1)-(7)	(s 92(1) definition of "excluded amount" para (d) inserted by FA 1995 s 146 and s 92(8) inserted by FA 1984 s 98.)	s 125
(8)	Repealed by FA 1998 s 121(2).	
93	Unnecessary (spent).	
94 (1)	Unnecessary (definition).	
(2)	Amendment of SA 1891 s 56, 59, 62 and 106 and First Sch, FA 1902 s 9, FA 1920 s 42 and FA 1961 s 30.	
(3),(4)(a),(5)	Amendment of SA 1891 First Sch.	
(4)(b)(i)		s 109
(4)(b)(ii)		s 62
(6)	Unnecessary (commencement).	
95 (1)	Amendment of FA 1970 s 41.	
(2), (3)	Unnecessary (revocation and commencement).	
96 (1)	Substitution of FA 1952 s 19(1).	
(2), (3)	Unnecessary (revocation and commencement).	
Finance Act 1983		
s 90	Unnecessary (spent).	
91	Insertion of F(No 2)A 1981 s 17(2)(d).	
92 (1)	Substitution of F(1909-10)A 1910 s 74(5).	
(2)	Unnecessary (commencement).	
93 (1)	Amendment of FA 1982 s 92.	
(2)	Unnecessary (commencement).	
Finance Act 1984		
s 97	Unnecessary (spent).	
98	Insertion of FA 1982 s 92(8).	
99	Amendment of FA 1982 s 93(5).	
100(1)	Insertion of FA 1969 s 49(2B).	
(2), (3)	Unnecessary (revocation and commencement).	
101(1)	Substitution of SA 1891 s 7.	
(2)	Amendment of FA 1970 s 41.	
(3)	Unnecessary (commencement).	
102	Amendment of F(No 2)A 1981 s 17(1) and (2).	
103	Unnecessary (revocation).	
Finance Act 1985		
s 55	Unnecessary (spent).	
56	Unnecessary (revocation, cesser of FA 1980 s 86 and definition).	
57	Amendment of FA 1982 s 93(5).	

Former Enactment		*Destination in SDCA 1999*
Finance Act 1986		
s 92	Unnecessary (spent).	
93	Unnecessary (spent).	
94 (1)–(8)		s 126
95 (1), (2)	The words "Notwithstanding the provisions of section 23 of the Finance Act, 1964," repealed by FA 1999 s 197 and Sch 6.	s 63
(3), (4)	Unnecessary (revocation and commencement).	
96 (1)		s 34
(2), (3)		s 35
(4)	Unnecessary (commencment).	
97 (1)	Unnecessary (cesser of FA 1974 s 83).	
(2), (3)	Unnecessary (revocation and commencement).	
98	para (a) unnecessary (definitions).	s 84
99 (1)	Amendment of SA 1891 First Sch	
(2)		s 67
(3), (4)	Unnecessary (revocation and commencement).	
100	Amendment of Provisional Collection of Taxes Act, 1927 s 1.	
101	Substitution of FA 1982 s 93(5).	
Finance Act 1987		
s 48	Unnecessary (spent).	
49 (1)	Amendment of FA 1982 s 92(8).	
(2)	Unnecessary (revocation).	
Finance Act 1988		
s 64	Unnecessary (spent).	
65 (1)	Amendment of SA 1891 First Sch.	
(2)	Unnecessary (revocation).	
Finance Act 1989		
s 64	Unnecessary (spent).	
65	Repealed by FA 1997 s 128(3).	
66 (1),(2)		s 106
(3)	Unnecessary (commencement).	
67	Substitution of SDMA 1891 s 27 definitions of "die" and "stamp" and insertion of definition of "impressed".	
68	Substitution of SDMA 1891 s 122 definition of "stamp" and insertion of definitions of "die" and "impressed".	
69	Amendment of FYA 1913 s 8(2)(b) and insertion of FYA 1913 s 18(1A).	
70	Repealed by FA 1995 s 144(3).	
71 (1)	Substitution of FA 1970 s 44(1).	
(2)	Unnecessary (commencement).	
72	Amendment of SA 1891 First Sch.	

Former Enactment		*Destination in SDCA 1999*
Finance Act 1990		
s 108	Unnecessary (spent).	
109	Unnecessary (spent).	
110(1)	Unnecessary (definition).	
(2)-(11)	Amendment of SA 1891 First Sch.	
(12)	Unnecessary (commencement).	
111	Amendment of SA 1891 s 58(8).	
112(1)-(8)		ss 29, 53
(9)	Unnecessary (commencement).	
113(1)-(4)		s 5
(5)	Unnecessary (repeals).	
114	s 114 substituted by FA 1999 s 141.	s 96
115	Insertion of FA 1973 s 67A.	
116(a)	Insertion of FA 1952 s 19(2A).	
(b)	Substitution of FA 1952 s 19(3)(c).	
117	Repealed by FA 1995 s 144(3).	
118	Unnecessary (cesser of, inter alia, F(CSD)A 1929 s 5).	
119	Amendment of Companies Act 1963 s 64(4).	
120	The words "(within the meaning of this section)" in s 120(2) unnecessary (superfluous).	s 95
Finance Act 1991		
s 88	Unnecessary (definitions).	
89	Unnecessary (spent).	
90 (1)	Unnecessary (definition).	
(2)-(4)	Amendment of SA 1891 First Sch.	
91	Unnecessary (repeal).	
92	Amendment of SA 1891 s 88(2).	
93		s 104
94	Substitution of SA 1891 s 1.	
95		s 3
96	Insertion of SA 1891 s 122 definition of "accountable person".	
97	Substitution of SA 1891 s 5.	
98	Amendment of SA 1891 s 12.	
99	Amendment of SA 1891 s 14(4).	
100	Substitution of SA 1891 s 15.	
101(1)	Substitution of SA 1891 s 16.	
(2)	Unnecessary (commencement).	
102	Substitution of FA 1949 s 24.	
103(1)-(3)		s 15
(4)	Repealed by FA 1994 s 103(2).	
(5)	Unnecessary (repeal).	
(6)	Unnecessary (commencement).	
Finance Act 1991		
s 104	s 104(3)(a) repealed by FA 1998 s 125 and Sch 8.	ss 44,55
105(1)		s 19
(2)	Unnecessary (commencement).	

Former Enactment		*Destination in SDCA 1999*
Finance Act 1991 (contd)		
s 106(1)	Amendment of SA 1891 ss 8(3), 9, 17, 83, 100, 107, 109(2), SDMA 1891 ss 20, 21, F(1909-10)A 1910 s 4(2) and FA 1970 s 41(3).	
(2)	Unnecessary (commencement).	
107	Amendment of Stock Transfer Act 1963 s 4(1).	
108(1)		s 132
(2)	Unnecessary (commencement).	
109(1)		s 133
(2)	Unnecessary (commencement).	
110	Insertion of FA 1973 s 67B.	
111	Amendment of FA 1982 s 92(8)	
Finance Act 1992		
s 199	Unnecessary (definitions).	
200	Unnecessary (spent).	
201	Unnecessary (transitional).	
202	Amendment of F(No 2)A 1981 s 17(1) and (2).	
203	(s 203(10) inserted by FA 1993 s 102.) Definition of "date of publication" unnecessary (commencement).	s 123
204(a)	Amendment of SA 1891 First Sch.	
(b)	Amendment of SA 1891 ss 56, 59, 62 and 106.	
(c)	Amendment of FA 1902 s 9.	
(d)	Amendment of FA 1920 s 42.	
(e)	Amendment of FA 1961 s 30.	
205(1)-(9)	Amendment of SA 1891 First Sch.	
(10)	Repealed by FA 1999 s 197 and Sch 6.	
206		s 88
207		s 90
208	(s 208(2) inserted by FA 1999 s 196.)	s 61
209	The words "Notwithstanding the provisions of section 1 of the Act of 1891 and the provisions of the First Schedule," unnecessary (superfluous).	s 98
210		s 108
211	Unnecessary (revocation).	
212	Repealed by FA 1999 s 141(2).	
213	Substitution of FA 1991 s 104.	
214	Amendment of FA 1972 s 45(1).	
215	Unnecessary (repeals and commencement).	
216(1)-(3)		s 100
(4)	Unnecessary (repeal).	
(5)	Unnecessary (commencement).	
217	Amendment of FA 1970 s 44.	
Finance (No 2) Act 1992		
s 28	Unnecessary (provison for cesser of certain levies).	

Former Enactment		*Destination in SDCA 1999*
Finance Act 1993		
s 100	Substitution of FA 1990 s 112(1)(a) and (b) and amendment of FA 1990 s 112(3)(a).	
101(1),(2)(b),(3)		s 103
(2)(a)	Repealed by FA 1999 s 197 and Sch 6.	
(4)	Unnecessary (commencement).	
102(a)	Substitution of FA 1992 s 203(1) definition of "bank".	
(b)	Insertion of FA 1992 s 203(10).	
103(1)	Amendment of FA 1982 s 92(3).	
(2)	Unnecessary (commencement).	
104(1)	Unnecessary (definition).	
(2)	Amendment of FA 1953 s 12 in so far as s 12 covers "exchanges".	s 37
(3)	Amendment of SA 1891 First Sch.	
(4)	Non-application of SA 1891 s 73 to exchanges.	
(5)	Unnecessary (repeal).	
105	Substitution of FA 1978 s 34(5)(b).	
106		s 85.
Finance Act 1994		
s 102	Unnecessary (definitions).	
103(1)	Amendment of FA 1991 s 103(1).	
(2), (3)	Unnecessary (repeal and commencement).	
104(1)	Amendment of FA 1991 s 105(1).	
(2)	Unnecessary (commencement).	
105	Amendment of FA 1992 s 206.	
106	Amendment of FA 1993 s 106.	
107(1)-(3)		s 12(2)-(4)
(4), (5)	Unnecessary (commencement and cesser of F(1909-10)A 1910 s 4).	
(6)		s 12(1)
108(1)		ss 48, 56
(2)	Unnecessary (relates to instruments stamped prior to 11 April, 1994).	
109(1)	Substitution of SA 1891 s 13.	
(2)	Repealed by FA 1999 s 197 and Sch 6.	
(3)	Unnecessary (repeals).	
(4)	Unnecessary (commencement).	
110	Repealed by FA 1999 s 197 and Sch 6.	
111		s 89
112		s 81
161(4)	Amendment of SA 1891 First Sch.	
Sixth Sch.		Sch 2
Finance Act 1995		
s 142	Unnecessary (spent).	
143(1)	Amendment of FA 1952 s 19.	
(2)	Unnecessary (commencement).	

Former Enactment		*Destination in SDCA 1999*
Finance Act 1995 (contd)		
s 144(1)(a)	Insertion of FA 1965 s 31(1A).	
(b)	Insertion of FA 1965 s 31(7A).	
(2)		s 80(10)
(3)	Unnecessary (repeals).	
145(1)	Insertion of FA 1973 s 67(C).	
(2)	Unnecessary (commencement).	
146	Amendment of FA 1982 s 92(1) and insertion of FA 1982 s 92(1) definition of "excluded amount" para (d).	
147	Substitution of FA 1992 s 208(d).	
148	Amendment of FA 1993 s 106(2).	
149	Amendment of FA 1994 s 107(1), (3) and (6).	
150		s 87
Finance Act 1996		
s 101(1)	Definitions of "the Act of 1891", "Commissioners" and "the Stamp Acts" unnecessary (duplication).	s 68
(2)	Unnecessary (commencement).	
102		s 69
103		s 70
104		s 71
105		s 72
106(1), (2)	s 106(1)(a)(ii) and (iii) repealed by FA 1999 s 197 and Sch 6.	s 73
(3)		s 74
107(1)-(4)		s 75
(5)	Unnecessary (repeals).	
108		s 76
109		s 77
110		s 78
111	Amendment of FA 1995 s 150(1) and (2).	
112	Amendment of Companies Act 1963 ss 7 and 14.	
113(1)	Substitution of FA 1969 s 49(2B).	
(2)	Unnecessary (commencement).	
114	Amendment of FA 1992 s 203.	
115	Amendment of FA 1992 s 207(1).	
116	Substitution of FA 1995 s 144(2).	
117(1), (2)		s 105
(3)	Unnecessary (repeal).	
118		s 101
119	Unnecessary (repeals).	

Former Enactment — *Destination in SDCA 1999*

Disclosure of Certain Information for Taxation and Other Purposes Act 1996

s 7	Amendment of SA 1891 s 12(1A) and insertion of SA 1891 s 12(6)(d).	

Criminal Assets Bureau Act 1996

s 24(3)	Unnecessary (deletion of SA 1891 s 12(6)(d) as inserted by Disclosure of Certain Information for Taxation and Other Purposes Act 1996 s 7).	

Finance Act 1997

s 115	Definitions of "the Act of 1891", "the Act of 1978", "the Commissioners" and "the First Schedule" unnecessary (interpretation and duplication).	s 1
116	Unnecessary (commencement).	
117	Amendment of SA 1891 First Sch.	
118	Insertion of SA 1891 s 122(1) definition of "residential property".	s 1
119	Insertion of SA 1891 s 58(1A).	
120	Insertion of SA 1891 s 77(6).	
121	FA 1997 s 121(1)(a)-(d) unnecessary (duplication)	s 16
122		s 17
123		s 92(1)(a)(i)(II), (ii)(II)
124	Declaratory words unnecessary.	s 92(1)(a)(i)(II), (ii)(II)
125	Amendment of FA 1992 s 207(1), (2).	
126	Amendment of FA 1994 s 112(7).	
127(1)-(3)		s 97
(4)	Unnecessary (repeals).	
128(1)		s 99
(2), (3)	Unnecessary (commencement and repeal).	
129(1)		s 110
(2)	Unnecessary (commencement).	
130	Unnecessary (repeal and commencement).	

Taxes Consolidation Act 1997

Sch 31	Amendment of SA 1891 ss 13(1) and (4), FA 1952 s 19(2), FA 1969 s 49(2B)(c), FA 1986 s 94(1)(a), FA 1990 s 112(5), FA 1991 ss 108(1) and 109(1), FA 1992 ss 206(a), (aa) and (c)(ii) and 207(2), FA 1993 s 106(2)(b) and FA 1996 s 108(4).	

Finance Act 1998

s 118	Amendment of SA 1891 s 54.	
119(1)	Insertion of SA 1891 s 59(7).	
(2)	Unnecessary (commencement).	
120	Amendment of SA 1891 First Sch.	
121(1)	Amendment of FA 1982 s 92(1).	
(2)	Unnecessary (repeal).	
122	Amendment of FA 1992 s 203(2).	
123(1)	Amendment of FA 1996 s 107.	
(2)	Unnecessary (commencement).	

Former Enactment		*Destination in SDCA 1999*
Finance Act 1998 (contd)		
s 124	Amendment of SA 1891 s 15(1), FA 1973 s 69(1) second proviso para ii and s 69(2), F(No 2)A 1981 ss 16(6) and 17(5)(b), FA 1982 ss 91(6) and 92(6), FA 1983 s 90(6); FA 1984 s 97(6); FA 1985 s 55(6), FA 1986 ss 92(6) and 93(6), FA 1987 s 48(6); FA 1988 s 64(6), FA 1989 s 64(6), FA 1990 ss 108(6), 109(5), 112(3)(b), 112(6) and 113(4), FA 1991 s 89(6), FA 1992 ss 200(6) and 203(6); FA 1994 s 112(6), FA 1995 ss 142(6) and 150(3), FA 1996 s 107(2).	
125	Unnecessary (repeals).	
Finance (No 2) Act 1998		
s 5	Unnecessary (interpretation).	
6	Unnecessary (commencement).	
7	Amendment of SA 1891 First Sch.	
8	Insertion of SA 1891 s 4(c).	
9	Substitution of SA 1891 s 58(1A).	
10	Substitution of SA 1891 s 77(6).	
11	Amendment of FA 1969 s 49.	
12	Amendment of FA 1990 s 112.	
13	Amendment of FA 1997 s 121(2)	
14		s 92
Finance Act 1999		
s 140	Provision relating to SA 1891 First Sch.	
141	Substitution of FA 1990 s 114.	
142	Amendment of FA 1992 s 207(1).	
143	Amendment of FA 1993 s 106(3).	
144	Amendment of FA 1995 s 150(1).	
145	Amendment of FA 1997 s 121.	
146	Amendment of F(No 2)A 1998 s 6(2).	
147	Unnecessary (interpretation).	
148	Unnecessary (application).	
149	Amendment of SDMA 1891 s 3(3) and (5).	
150	Amendment of SDMA 1891 s 4.	
151	Amendment of SDMA 1891 s 6(1) and (2).	
152	Amendment of SDMA 1891 s 13.	
153	Amendment of SDMA 1891 s 18(4).	
154	Amendment of SDMA 1891 s 20.	
155	Amendment of SDMA 1891 s 21.	
156	Amendment of SA 1891 s 5(3) and (6).	
157	Amendment of SA 1891 s 8(3).	
158	Amendment of SA 1891 s 9.	
159	Amendment of SA 1891 s 16(1).	
160	Amendment of SA 1891 s 17.	
161	Amendment of SA 1891 s 100.	
162	Amendment of SA 1891 s 107.	
163	Amendment of SA 1891 s 109(2).	

Former Enactment | *Destination in SDCA 1999*

Finance Act 1999 (contd)

s 164 .... Amendment of FA 1969 s 49(2B).
165 .... Amendment of FA 1970 s 41(3).
166 .... Amendment of FA 1991 s 109(1).
167 .... Amendment of FA 1994 s 107(2) and (3).
168 .... Amendment of FA 1994 s 112(6).
169 .... Amendment of FA 1996 s 107(4).
170 .... Amendment of FA 1996 s 108(2) and (3).
171 .... Amendment of F(No 2)A 1998 s 14(2).
172 .... Amendment of SDMA 1891 s 26.
173 .... Amendment of SA 1891 s 13.
174 .... Amendment of FA 1973 s 74.
175 .... Amendment of FA 1991 s 103(1).
176 .... Amendment of SA 1891 First Sch.
177 .... Amendment of SA 1891 s 23(2).
178 .... Amendment of SA 1891 s 41.
179 .... Amendment of SA 1891 s 118(1).
180 .... Amendment of F(1909-10)A 1910 s 74(2).
181 .... Amendment of FA 1978 s 31.
182 .... Amendment of FA 1952 s 19.
183 .... Amendment of FA 1965 s 31(1) and (6).
184 .... Amendment of SDMA 1891 s 9.
185 .... Insertion of SDMA 1891 s 12A.
186 .... Amendment of SA 1891 s 1(3) and (4).
187 .... Amendment of SA 1891 s 12(2).
188 .... Amendment of SA 1891 s 14(4).
189 .... Amendment of SA 1891 s 58(8).
190 .... Amendment of SA 1891 s 77(6).
191 .... Amendment of SA 1891 s 122(1).
192 .... Amendment of FA 1899 s 5(1).
193 .... Amendment of FA 1933 s 40.
194 .... Amendment of FA 1973 s 69.
195 .... Amendment of FA 1982 s 92(1) and (6).
196 .... Amendment of FA 1992 s 208.
197 .... Unnecessary (repeals).

Index

All references are to *paragraph* numbers